About the Authors

Mary Mark Sturm, Director of the Bureau of Home Economics for the Chicago Public Schools from 1945 to 1964 and supervisor in the Bureau prior to that time, has given continued leadership to hundreds of educators in the field of clothing. Mrs. Sturm has taught home economics in elementary, junior high, senior high, and adult evening school and has conducted clothing workshops at the graduate level. She has served as a judge in the largest sewing competitions in the country, has served in an advisory capacity to magazines and companies allied with clothing and home economics, and was a Home Economics Education Consultant from 1964 to 1967. She is co-author of the clothing transparencies LINE AND COLOR IN CLOTHES and DESIGN IN CLOTHES.

Edwina Hefley Grieser, Supervisor in the Bureau of Home Economics for the Chicago Public Schools from 1963 to 1967, was for many years a teacher at Morgan Park High School, Chicago, and at the University of Oklahoma. She has done extensive research and experimental work in the area of clothing construction and in the adaptation of the *Unit Method of Clothing Construction* for use in the classroom. She has taught classes and teacher training courses for the Illinois Institute of Technology, the Chicago Teachers College, and the Chicago Board of Education. She is co-author of the clothing transparencies LINE AND COLOR IN CLOTHES and DESIGN IN CLOTHES; also author of a series of twenty-four CLOTHING CONSTRUCTION FILM LOOPS.

Dorothy Siegert Lyle, Director of Consumer Relations Division, the International Fabricare Institute, is recognized as one of the foremost authorities on fashionable fabrics and their care. Among the many professional groups in which she holds membership is the American Home Economics Association, which she served as president between 1960 and 1962. She served on the board of directors for the National Standards Institute, Inc., and is currently a member of the Institute's Consumer Council. She is also a member of the Industry Advisory Committee on Textiles formed in 1966 in cooperation with the President's Special Assistant on Consumer Affairs. Dr. Lyle is the author of the reference book FOCUS ON FABRICS and of the NEA publications THE CLOTHES WE WEAR and CLOTHING FOR YOUNG MEN.

Jane Ellen Roberts, Associate Professor and Teacher-Educator, Department of Home Economics, Western Washington State College, Bellingham, Washington, is co-ordinator and teacher of preservice and inservice programs in Home Economics Education. She has also taught home economics at the junior and senior high school levels. She has served as Home Economics Curriculum Consultant for the middle and secondary levels. Miss Roberts is author of the filmstrip series and multi-media teaching aids: CREDIT CONCEPTS, FABRIC KEYNOTES, CLOTHING CARE CLUES, UP AND DOWN OF FABRIC, and GRAIN OF FABRIC (a finalist at the American Film Festival — filmstrip division), and is co-author of the clothing transparencies DESIGN IN CLOTHES.

Guide to Modern Clothing

Third Edition

Mary Mark Sturm Formerly Director of the Bureau of Home Economics for the Chicago Public Schools

Edwina Hefley Grieser Formerly Supervisor in the Bureau of Home Economics for the Chicago Public Schools

Dorothy Siegert Lyle Director of Consumer Relations Division, the International Fabricare Institute, Silver Spring, Maryland

Jane Ellen Roberts Associate Professor and Teacher-Educator for the Department of Home Economics, Western Washington State College, Bellingham, Washington

WEBSTER DIVISION, McGRAW-HILL BOOK COMPANY
New York   St. Louis   San Francisco   Dallas
Düsseldorf   London   Mexico   Montreal
Panama   Singapore   Sydney   Toronto

McGraw-Hill Home Economics Publications

Barclay-Champion-Brinkley-Funderburk: TEEN GUIDE TO HOMEMAKING

Carson: HOW YOU LOOK AND DRESS

Carson-Ramee: HOW YOU PLAN AND PREPARE MEALS

Hurlock: CHILD GROWTH AND DEVELOPMENT

Landis: YOUR MARRIAGE AND FAMILY LIVING

Morton-Geuther-Guthrie: THE HOME — ITS FURNISHINGS AND EQUIPMENT

Paolucci-Faiola-Thompson: PERSONAL PERSPECTIVES

Peck-Sickler-Washington-Moragne: FOOD: ACCENT ON HEALTH

Shank-Fitch-Chapman-Sickler: GUIDE TO MODERN MEALS

Grieser: CLOTHING CONSTRUCTION FILM LOOPS

Sturm-Grieser-Lyle-Roberts: GUIDE TO MODERN CLOTHING

Sturm-Grieser: LINE AND COLOR IN CLOTHES (Transparencies)

Sturm-Grieser-Roberts: DESIGN IN CLOTHES (Transparencies)

Library of Congress Cataloging in Publication Data
Main entry under title:

GUIDE TO MODERN CLOTHING.

(American home and family series)
SUMMARY: A high school clothing textbook covering basic and advanced sewing techniques as well as tailoring. Includes information on clothing care and management and projecting an image with clothing.
1962 and 1968 editions by M. M. Sturm and E. H. Grieser.
Bibliography: p.
1. Dressmaking. 2. Clothing and dress. 3. Beauty, Personal. [1. Dressmaking. 2. Clothing and dress]. I. Sturm, Mary Mark. Guide to modern clothing.
TT518.G84   1973   646.4   72-6673
ISBN 0-07-062293-0

Preface

Two key interests of the young consumer are his interpersonal relationships and the contributions he can make to society. Understanding that both he and his contributions will often be accepted on the basis of the image he presents, he becomes interested in clothing as a means to identity and self-expression.

Emphasizing the sociological and psychological impact of clothing on the lives of people, the first part of the new GUIDE TO MODERN CLOTHING has been written to encourage students to consider the importance of personal image, creativity in dress, clothing management and care, and consumer needs and responsibilities. Because of the student's keen interest in his own contribution to society, material is incorporated which may direct his thoughts toward one of the many vocations available in the world of fashion. Consideration is given to jobs on the many rungs of the occupational ladder for which a student might have an aptitude or a wish to prepare himself.

All seven chapters in Part 1 of this text may be of interest to both male and female students. End-of-chapter materials provided with these chapters supply ideas for group enrichment activities, for individualized growth opportunities, and for community betterment projects with which the student can become involved.

The last four parts of the book are concerned with the creative and consumer aspects of clothing construction. The contents focus on the presentation of a variety of basic alternatives founded on sound principles. This presentation encourages creative, independent learning.

Each chapter begins with the decision-making process as it relates to consumer and construction problems and ends with a statement of general principles presented in that chapter. With logical, sequential organization from preparatory techniques through basic techniques to advanced techniques, the student can learn to solve problems which move from the simple toward the complex, culminating in a final unit covering basic tailoring. The units are so ordered that each individual user is able to develop through the use of the book to his own optimum level of creativity.

Editor — Margie S. Jennings
Editing and Styling — Mary Lewis Wang
Art Production — Richard O'Leary
Production Supervision — Leo B. Painter

Acknowledgments

The authors of GUIDE TO MODERN CLOTHING, third edition, recognize the following individuals who made significant contributions to this text by providing up-to-date information or ideas, by trying materials in their classrooms, or by evaluating the manuscript:

Dr. Naomi Albanese, Dean and Professor, School of Home Economics, University of North Carolina, Greensboro, North Carolina.

Betty Campbell, Home Economics Education Coordinator, Atlanta City Schools, Atlanta, Georgia.

Dr. Norma H. Compton, Dean, School of Home Economics, Auburn University, Auburn, Alabama.

Dr. James Crews, College of Business Administration, University of Florida, Gainesville, Florida.

Gail Devens, Editor Educational Division, Simplicity Pattern Co., Inc., New York, New York.

Terry Finlayson, Director Consumer Information Services, Sears, Roebuck and Company, Chicago, Illinois.

Bernice Finley, Supervisor Home Economics Education, Topeka Public Schools, Topeka, Kansas.

Francis Gandy, Instructional Supervisor, Memphis City Schools, Memphis, Tennessee.

Dr. Pauline Garrett, Program Officer Vocational Education, HEW OE AVTE, Denver, Colorado.

Bertha Gold, White Consolidated Industries, Inc., Cleveland, Ohio.

Helen Gray, C. M. Offray & Son, Inc., New York, New York.

Janice M. Hamilton, Director Consumer Information and Education, Vogue Butterick Pattern Service, New York, New York.

Louise Harmon, Supervisor of Home Economics, Montgomery County Public School System, Rockville, Maryland.

Hazel Huffman, Director Home Economics and Safety Education, Fulton County Schools, Atlanta, Georgia.

Marian McGinnis, Home Economics Teacher, Ridgewood High School, Ridgewood, New Jersey.

Mary Bushee Murphy, Editor Fashions and Grooming, WHAT'S NEW IN HOME ECONOMICS, New York, New York.

George K. Payne, Head Display Department, Woodward and Lathrop, Washington, D.C.

Elaine R. Pitts, Director of Consumer Affairs, The Sperry and Hutchinson Company, New York, New York.

Frances R. Quinn, Extension Clothing Specialist, University of California.

Betty Saneholtz, Director Consumer Service Bureau, PARENTS' MAGAZINE.

Satenig St. Marie, Manager Education and Consumer Relations, J. C. Penney Company, Inc., New York, New York.

Ruth Stovall, State Supervisor of Home Economics, Montgomery, Alabama.

Cecelia Toth, Fashion Co-ordinator, New York, New York.

Barbara Tucker, Manager Home Economics, General Electric Housewares Division, Bridgeport, Connecticut.

Jean Vizgirda, Educational Director, Talon Educational Service, New York, New York.

Ann Wareham, Director of Publicity, Simplicity Pattern Co., Inc., New York, New York.

Ethel Washington, Supervisor Home Economics Education, Detroit Public Schools, Detroit, Michigan.

Frankie Welch, Owner, Frankie Welch of Alexandria, Virginia.

Ruth Wheeler, Chairman, Department of Home Economics, Evanston Township High School, Evanston, Illinois.

Rose White, Director Consumer Affairs, American National Standards Institute, New York, New York.

Dr. Gaylor P. Whitlock, Director Family and Consumer Sciences, Extension Service, University of California.

Special acknowledgment is also made to the following groups, individuals, and commercial companies:

The many students in Chicago high schools who helped with the development of clothing construction techniques by trying them in their classes.

Present and former teachers and supervisors in the Chicago Public Schools who made garments which served as models and who tested instructions in their classes to determine clarity, adequacy, and correctness: Norma B. Berg, Mary Birmingham, Lillian Exum Bray, Virginia Clancy, Janet Craig, Genevieve Fahey, Estelle Gibson, Esther Handwerk, Dorothy Jones, M. Ruth Krause, Lorraine Kriewitz, Sadie Lussenhop, Amy W. Paula, Mary B. Sims, Rita Sisko, Winifred M. Wagner, Lempi Joan Underwood, and Ruth E. Whalen.

The Simplicity Pattern Co., Inc., the Singer Company, and the Butterick Fashion Marketing Company, Inc. for technical drawings reproduced or adapted.

The numerous commercial companies and magazines that provided illustrative materials for which they are credited throughout the text.

CPC, Inc., for art adapted and used on the cover; Simplicity Pattern Co., Inc., CPC, Inc., the Celanese Fibers Marketing Co., and Armour-Dial., Inc., for art adapted and used as part openers.

Gilbert B. Seehausen, who photographed most of the illustrations of specific construction techniques.

John Ferguson, Mary Gibson, and Marge Mills, who rendered original art for the third edition of GUIDE TO MODERN CLOTHING.

Contents

Part 1

You and the World of Fashion

Building Your Own Image

Each person builds an image which represents him in the eyes of others. It is an expression of his inner self projected through his outer appearance. A large percentage of his outer appearance, and thus of his total image, can be attributed to the clothes he wears. His clothing expresses his values and his feelings about himself.

How important is clothing in your life?

How does your clothing speak for you?

Why do people get their first and sometimes lasting impression of you when they first meet you?

Why does your appearance affect your behavior and your behavior affect your appearance?

What is your definition of good taste in clothing?

What are your likes and dislikes in regard to clothing?

Why do you feel confident when you feel comfortable about your appearance?

How do you feel about fashion?

How does fashion reflect the mood of the time?

How might your appearance help you to secure and hold a job?

How does clothing help you to understand yourself and your place in society?

Projecting Your Image with Clothing

Clothes serve various functions. Fundamentally they provide a protective cover against the elements. In addition, they help a person present an image by identifying the various roles he plays and forming bonds of association with his own group. Together these factors have a broad impact upon his effectiveness as an individual and suggest that clothing will continue to play an important part in modern life.

In relation to the image which clothes help people project, consider your own self-image. Your outer appearance, represented by your clothes, manners, and general grooming, is obvious to those with whom you associate. It is often difficult for a person to reveal his true inner self simply because his outer self can obscure it. People in general tend to draw broad conclusions about other people from the way they look. Unfortunately, if the first impression happens to be negative, the tendency is not to delve beneath the surface. People tend to take others at face value. As a young person, what do you stand to gain by presenting a positive image? What do you risk when you are willing to dress in a way which projects a negative image?

Probably one of the most important roles an adult plays is the one connected with his job. He usually dresses especially for this role. An increasing number of businesses and industries are setting up dress standards to create a desired image for their organization. As a result, you become accustomed to a

A person's ability to project an image helps determine his effectiveness as an individual or as a member of a group.

certain type of dress, or appearance, connected with specific jobs.

Dress standards are by no means limited to the world of work. Teen-agers also dress for the roles they play. In the morning you may dress for school: a student role. After school you may change clothes to do some work: a job role. Perhaps in the evening you plan to put on a special dress for a date: a social role.

Most young people dress the way they do essentially because they want to feel like one of their group. A particular group presents a role, or an image, to others. Clothes help

students fit into their group much as a nurse's white uniform helps identify her in the hospital. In what ways do the clothes you choose help you fit into a group within your school or social sphere?

The trend toward identical clothing for boys and girls, called the *unisex* look, is but another example of group association. In this case the group may be composed of only two people. Togetherness becomes a look as well as an attitude. The unisex concept recurs from time to time. The latest upsurge started when girls began buying pants in men's departments. This encouraged designers and manufacturers to design and produce pants, blouses, and jackets that could be worn by both sexes. Stores, shops, and boutiques then set up Unisex Departments. The extent to which the unisex look will make lasting inroads into the world of fashion remains to be seen. Enjoy it if you like by choosing items which help you identify with your group while presenting your own personal image.

Developing a Value System

Values are ideas so important that they direct the thoughts and actions of a person or a group. They become the basic reason for behavior. For instance, a teen-ager might go on a family outing which is personally distasteful simply because he values family togetherness. As a broader illustration, citizens of a country might value individual rights and educational opportunities. Because these two ideas are values, they shape the actions of all those to whom they are important. Laws are made and moneys appropriated which will guarantee that such values are incorporated into the life of a city, state, or nation. When a number of values such as truth, honor, justice, and freedom become generally important to a group, they become a system of values by which the group can chart its course of living. In the same way values direct the course of an individual life.

Your Personal Value System

Values are influenced by the environment. In the case of a young person, his parents, friends, school, community, and country all interact to help him form his set of values. Each person develops his own personal value system. It is usually more personal than, but often influenced by, a national or community value system. It may include personal happiness, love of family, and meaningful living. It may also include the broader values accepted by those who have influenced him.

In relation to dress and appearance, each individual develops clothing values. Basically these values divide into those which affect his relationships with others and those which give him personal satisfaction. Thus his *psychological-sociological* clothing values relate to the effect his clothing has on his relationships with others. His *taste* and *aesthetic* values in clothing relate to his personal likes and dislikes. Both outwardly show his inner feelings.

Growing up is an experience which often leaves young people temporarily overwhelmed with feelings of insecurity. Are such feelings unavoidable? Most young people find that, at least to a degree, they are. They can, however, be minimized. By developing a sound personal value system and projecting it into your actions and your dress, you can gain rapidly in self-assurance. In the process you will develop an understanding of the psychological-sociological role clothing plays in your life, as well as a taste for clothes which are aesthetically pleasing.

Psychological and Sociological Values

Values are expressed by the clothes you choose and wear. Healthy teen-agers want to grow toward independence. Yet there remains a strong desire on the part of most to conform to group dress codes. There may also be a strong desire to dress to receive recognition from members of the opposite sex. The importance you attach to each of these psychological-sociological values influences your choice of clothing and the appearance you create.

Your choice of clothing, in turn, can help you implement your values. A recent research project carried out in schools across the country brought the following set of facts to light:

1. Students have a better feeling about themselves when they are physically clean.

2. Students who are dressed in appropriate school clothes participate more readily in all phases of school work than do those who are not.

Dress can be used to project a company or a school image as well as a personal one.

3. A pattern of sloppy appearance or extremes in dress is frequently found among those students who are disciplinary problems.

4. Study habits generally improve when appearance and dress are improved.

Your first reaction to this research may be to decide that a person cannot dress to be a successful student and reach his own social goals at the same time. After serious consideration, however, you may decide that your own goals and those set by your school are very similar. Both you and those most interested in your progress hope that you will achieve the following goals:

That you will be liked.

That you will feel wanted.

That you will be accepted.

That you will achieve a measure of success.

That you will feel important to your family, friends, teachers, and employer.

Clothing choices can affect each of these goals. Almost without exception, young people need only intelligent practice in order to learn to make effective clothing choices.

There is a fine line between individuality, which is admirable, and improper dress, which is not. Knowledge and experience will help you find this line of distinction. As you develop your clothing values, it is very important that you build values which will allow you to have successful personal relationships.

Taste as a Personal Value

When any idea becomes important enough to give direction to your life, it becomes a part of your value system. Taste becomes a part of this system when you know what you like and why. Thus, as you develop taste, in clothes, you develop clothing values. These values are formed out of your needs as an individual or as a member of a group. Your taste may be toward the exotic or the simple or toward the colorful or the subdued. Your decision as to what constitutes good taste is probably not as important as the fact that you know what you consider acceptable. The person who knows what he likes and who can decide which clothing choices he can live with happily will be an effective consumer of clothing.

What is often defined as rebellion on the part of young people is frequently an honest search for a real set of values. As values are developed, they can be used in determining taste in clothing. The concepts of good and bad taste vary to some degree with times and fashions. Important, therefore, are independent ideas through which independent taste can develop. Each person develops clothing tastes which are attuned to his personally worked-out value system.

Aesthetic Sense as a Personal Value

Your aesthetic values deal with your ability to appreciate beauty. What makes you feel that something you see or hear is beautiful? Philosophers have long pondered the true nature of aesthetics. Whether it is a song, a poem, a picture, or clothing, your aesthetic feelings toward a certain object depend upon a great number of complex stimuli.

Order · Beauty · Expressiveness · Interest · Variety · Complexity · Disunity · Incompleteness · Disorder · Ugliness · Unmeaningfulness · Triviality · Monotony · Simplicity · Unity · Completeness — arranged around a circle with High Aesthetic Value (top) and Low Aesthetic Value (bottom).

Charts on pages 5 through 7 have been adapted and are reproduced with permission of the *Textile Research Journal* from a paper, "Measuring the Aesthetic Appeal of Textiles," by R. M. Hoffman, *Text. Res. Jrnl.*, Vol. 35, No. 5, May 1965.

At one time it was assumed that the way people felt could not be measured. But today the scientist combines psychology, mathematics, and electronic computations with old-fashioned ingenuity to effectively measure certain feelings or thoughts. This study through which aesthetic values can be measured is called the science of *psychometrics.*

An object appears to you to have high or low aesthetic value according to your reactions to its stimuli. You like or dislike an object to a measurable degree. Consider the three accompanying charts. Try to determine how they can help you measure your feelings toward a certain garment or fabric.

In the chart on this page pairs of stimuli are arranged opposite each other, with high values opposite corresponding low values: order—disorder; completeness—incompleteness; variety—monotony. For example, raw silk fabric has many slubs and nubs that may be called defects, but it is not monotonous. The charm and natural richness of raw silk depend upon the irregularities or imperfections present in the fiber. It will therefore fall in the high-value category of variety. Fabrics with high aesthetic value are pleasing to both the hand and the eye.

The chart on page 6 shows how you can describe your feelings about the sensation to your hand, or the feel, of a fabric. It enables you to both describe and rate this impression to your sense of touch.

The chart on page 7 will help you describe the way a garment looks to you. Emotional reactions to garments influence their desirability. This chart illustrates how you may react to the appearance of clothing you are considering buying. For garments with high aesthetic value, four frequently mentioned terms are attractive, smart, pleasing, and beautiful. Four terms frequently associated with garments rated low in aesthetic value are unpleasant, ordinary, annoying, and boring.

Your Values Affect Your Image
Since values cause you to think as you do and finally to act as you do, they affect your way of life, your personality, and your appearance. The way you see yourself, the way

AESTHETIC CHARACTERISTICS OF FABRICS

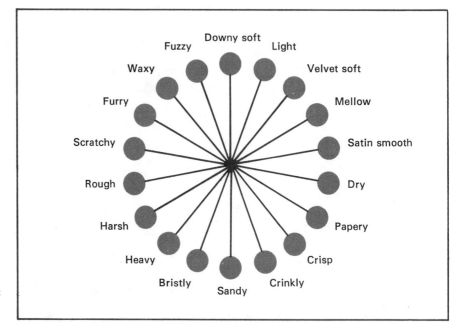

Fuzzy, Downy soft, Light, Waxy, Velvet soft, Furry, Mellow, Scratchy, Satin smooth, Rough, Dry, Harsh, Papery, Heavy, Crisp, Bristly, Crinkly, Sandy

1. Choose one or more to indicate how a given fabric feels.

2. Rate the aesthetic value:

Good   Fair   Poor

others see you, and the way you present yourself all become results of your values.

Can You See Yourself?

Mirror, mirror on the wall,
Am I the fairest of them all?

It is seldom easy to be objective about your own appearance. For many people, it is actually difficult to look into a mirror and admit that they are attractive. It is difficult for others to admit that their hair is stringy or lifeless, that their posture is bad, or that they need to lose or gain weight. Whatever your image, you are not unique in wanting to avoid seeing it. People are universally a great deal alike. They tend to stand tall before a mirror and show their best smile. Somehow they seem to hope the mirror will present an image better than the real one. It won't. A mirror only reflects the image placed before it.

"How can I improve my image?" you may be wondering. It is important that you try different dress styles. Experiment with cosmetics, hair styles, wigs, and wiglets. You may need to exercise for muscle tone

and posture improvement. When you have achieved a good image, your mirror will reflect it.

How Do You Look to Others?

Sometimes you look different to other people than you look to yourself. You can more or less sense how others feel you look. This affects your emotions in regard to the way you feel about yourself. The reactions of others to you become a part of your total image as you see it. Your self-image, then, is rather complex, composed of your own impressions and what you believe to be the impressions of others.

The effect of your image on others is vitally important to you as a person. If positive, it can help you reach many of your goals of being liked, being wanted, being accepted, and achieving success.

What Is Fashion?

Although it is a mixed set of ideas, fashion is the trend, or the prevailing style of dress at any given time. Fashion to very young adults

AESTHETIC CHARACTERISTICS OF GARMENTS

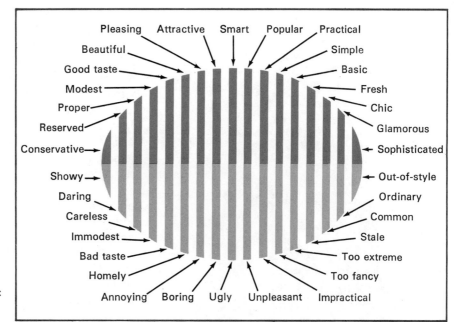

Pleasing Attractive Smart Popular Practical
Beautiful Simple
Good taste Basic
Modest Fresh
Proper Chic
Reserved Glamorous
Conservative Sophisticated
Showy Out-of-style
Daring Ordinary
Careless Common
Immodest Stale
Bad taste Too extreme
Homely Too fancy
Annoying Boring Ugly Unpleasant Impractical

1. Choose one or more descriptions that fit a given garment.

2. Rate the aesthetic value:

Good   Fair   Poor

may mean something quite different from what it means to older people. Moreover, fashion is fickle. It is constantly changing, even when you and others like the styles of clothing you recently purchased.

Fashion is a mirror of a given point in time. It may express freedom or restraint, prosperity or depression. Anatole France once said, "If I were allowed to choose one book from the pile which will be published one hundred years after my death, do you know which one I would take? I would simply take a fashion magazine . . . and its rags would tell me more about the humanity of the future than could all the philosophers, novelists, prophets, and scholars of the time."

Is it possible that this famous French author understood humanity well enough to analyze progress, communication, and even personal relationships just by looking at the clothes people wear? Is it true that thoughts and behavior are expressed in fashion? What prevailing feelings can you see expressed in the clothing your classmates are wearing today?

What Is Acceptable Dress?

Every generation has an influence on dress and appearance. Your generation is no exception. Perhaps history will show that this generation has contributed a sense of freedom to the total fashion picture. You are unique in the freedom with which you can dress for social occasions. Many young people are also free to choose the types of clothes they will wear to school. But as you prepare to go out into the work world you probably will sense a need to adapt to the accepted clothing pattern of the job you select.

Haven't you asked a friend, "What are you going to wear to the football game? To the party?" You were trying to find what your group thinks and feels about clothing for a particular occasion. This same principle applies when you determine the clothes required for a particular job.

Certain basic fashion guidelines apply when you are determining suitable dress, regardless of skirt length or particular style in vogue. During the past century various fashion authorities have developed point systems

Courtesy Rohm and Haas

Whether an outfit is gaudy or gorgeous depends largely on the occasion for which it is worn.

by which a person can tell whether or not she is suitably dressed for a given occasion. Although styles change, the guidelines remain uniquely current. With such a system, success is attained by making sure that you dress within the allotted number of points. One such system allows only 10 points for daytime dress if you are 5 feet 5 inches tall or less, 12 points if you are taller. The shorter person can use 12 points for evening wear, the taller one 15.

Check your appearance against the rating system shown on page 9. If the total adds up to more than your allowance, begin subtracting. Jewelry is a good place to start.

Clothes that make you feel comfortable, poised, and confident are those which are likely to help you project a positive image. If you do not have these positive feelings about your clothes, they are not acceptable for you.

How can you determine whether a person is mature for his age?

How do people sometimes hide their immaturity or their personality problems in the clothing they choose?

How do mental and physical health correlate in the image a person projects?

Why are nutrition and rest essential to attractiveness?

What are the bases for determining the choice of makeup and its application?

What are the considerations in determining whether to buy electric grooming aids?

What are the safety factors to be considered in using electric grooming aids?

Understanding Yourself

High school years are generally happy years in the lives of most people. And they should be. Time is allotted for pleasure, and there is a certain degree of freedom from responsibility. But there is a serious element in these years. Mature teen-agers make marked progress toward understanding themselves during this period. Often they decide what they are

8

Dress or suit	Solid-colored	1 point
	Print or of two colors	2 points
	Two-piece	2 points
	Contrasting collar or belt	1 point extra
	Trimming, such as bows or flowers	1 point each
	Contrasting buttons	1 point extra
	Scarf	1 point extra
Blouse	Of different color from ensemble	1 point
Jewelry	Necklace	1 point
	Bracelet	1 point each
	Pin	1 point
	Earrings	1 point
	Glasses	1 point
	Watch	1 point
	Rings	2 points each
Hat or cap	Plain	1 point
	Trimmed	2 points
Shoes	Plain	1 point
	Sandals	2 points
	With heels or toes out	2 points
	With bow, buckle, strap, etc.	2 points
	With decorative or contrasting heels	2 points
	Boots	2 points
Hose	Plain	1 point
	Colored	2 points
	Textured	2 points
Gloves	Plain	1 point
	With contrasting stitching	2 points
Handbag	Plain	1 point
	Elaborate	2 points
Handkerchief	Colorful	1 point
Hair	Very blond, very red, or black	1 point
Hairdo	Elaborate	1 point

going to do in the years ahead. As you plan for the future, set attainable goals and work toward achieving them.

You will experience conflicts while you are striving to find yourself. Although you may want to conform to the crowd so you can feel comfortable, you may also want to be different, a real individual. But how different can you afford to be without risking the rejection of your group? It is certainly important to your growth toward maturity to learn to live up to your own highest ideals. Also important is the sense of belonging attained by a certain degree of conformity to the group's code of dress. If conflicting values at times pose a dilemma, perhaps it is reassuring to know that, as values become more stabilized with maturity, the problem tends to evaporate.

Courtesy Wrangler Jeans and Sportswear

The way others react to you can give you a positive or a negative feeling about the clothes you are wearing.

Hiding the Real Self

Life sometimes seems to be made up of problems. Some people feel that it is easier to make excuses than to face up to these problems. Excuses are sometimes revealed in their dress and appearance. It is easy to use dress as a disguise for covering up the real person.

The person who is on the defensive usually does not see himself as you see him. This person may have many conflicts. He may feel friendless; he may feel unwanted; he may have other feelings of insecurity.

Not all defenses are bad, particularly if they are used only for a short period of time. Sometimes they help you get through an uneasy stage of life. But successful people eventually face realities. It is the only way to find yourself and your place in life. Note in the accompanying chart a number of the roles

ROLES OF THE COVER-UP

The copier   cannot make individual choices because of insecurity. May be a status seeker wanting to be like everyone else in the crowd.

The flirt   depends upon clothes for sexual attraction rather than on personality and intelligence.

The excuser   finds excuses to buy clothes, not because of needs but because others have bought similar ones.

The rejector   is uninterested in clothes, probably owing to bad experiences or embarrassing situations which happened earlier in life.

The regressor   is sloppy in appearance and dress often due to immaturity or the inability to face realities of the adult world.

The loner   does not want anyone to notice. Consequently may dress in clothes that are nondescript.

The inadequate   dresses in showy and expensive clothes because of insecurity.

The ugly duckling   does not want to be beautiful because it is safe to be ugly. Wants to ignore life.

which people play to disguise themselves. Try to decide whether or not you are playing any of these roles and why.

Revealing the Best You

In general, people are not born attractive. But there are many things which can be done which will improve most any physical appearance. When these are combined with the things you can do to improve your emotional appearance, you can become truly attractive.

The old saying is frequently quoted, "Beauty is only skin deep." This statement is only partially true. Real beauty is a delightful combination of outer appearance and inner self. Since the inner self is quite obvious to those who know you, it is very important that you learn to respect yourself. Your love for living and your consideration and compassion for others also help make you attractive.

Many times you will find that the traits necessary for making yourself attractive require self-discipline. You must *want* to be attractive in order to pay the necessary price. Personal attractiveness requires effort.

Emotions affect your appearance. Perhaps you will find that you need to work hard to control them. Physiological and mental changes take place by either the release or the control of your emotions. In general, it is quite important for you to keep your emotions under control. If you fail to do so, the results may be reflected in such outward physical indicators as oily skin and acne, excessive perspiration, and nail biting. Your failure to control your emotions can also make you feel tired or tense and can cause sleeplessness or such physical discomforts as indigestion, constipation, or diarrhea. Sometimes more serious results can follow.

Everyone needs a time and place for emotional release. This is necessary if you are to maintain the mental health necessary for attractiveness. When you are able to keep your emotions under control, allowing for acceptable periods of release, you can create the appearance of self-confidence, good posture, and poise necessary for attractiveness.

Developing Good Health Habits

Your health is one of your most important assets. It is therefore never too early to begin the practice of good health habits. Since health affects the way you look as well as the

It is important that each girl learns how to express her own individuality.

way you feel, vibrant personal attractiveness is practically unattainable without it. Your state of health is reflected in your skin, eyes, hair, teeth, nails, figure, and posture.

Good nutrition is basic to good health. Realizing the importance of nutrition, the Federal government has established suggested guidelines for adequate nutrition. The guidelines have been incorporated into the *Daily Food Guide.* This guide suggests that you eat each day two servings of meat or a substitute, and four servings each of milk, cereal products, and fruits and vegetables. When you are careful to follow this eating guide, you contribute to both your health and your attractiveness.

Weight Control

Much emphasis is being placed on weight control. If you are underweight, you are taking in too few calories; if you are overweight, you are taking in too many. Your correct weight is related to your height and bone structure.

If your weight is not ideal, you can definitely do something about it. Whether you are overweight or underweight, you usually need to go on a diet and change your eating habits. You may wish to consult someone in a health clinic or your personal physician. He can advise you as to what to eat and how much to eat to supply adequate nutritional needs. Perhaps he will encourage you to join a weight-control club in your school or community. Such clubs tend to give their members regular motivation which will encourage changed eating patterns.

Decide exactly when you are going to start your special diet. Perhaps you should give yourself a weekend to get into the proper frame of mind. Once your diet is started, avoid breaking it. Check your weight on a scale once a week. More frequent weighings may cause you to be discouraged. Keep with your diet until you reach the weight range advised by your doctor.

If you are trying to lose weight, avoid diet pills and crash diets. They are only temporary crutches. Once they are removed, the excess poundage usually returns. Try to develop a sensible eating plan which can be continued after your desired weight is attained. Such a plan will encourage health and prevent the need for future strenuous dieting.

Figure Control

Exercise encourages both posture and weight control, as well as good health. It burns up calories and improves the operation of the circulatory, digestive, and elimination systems.

Your physical education classes provide a good opportunity for group exercise. If you have special posture problems, perhaps your instructor can teach you specific exercises to help you correct your individual faults.

TECHNIQUES OF GOOD POSTURE

To stand   Hold head erect, reaching toward the ceiling, and lift chest. Keep back straight, shoulder blades flat, shoulders relaxed and easy. Tuck hips under, pull abdomen up and in, and keep knees relaxed and almost brushing. Stand with heel of one foot at instep of the other, toes pointing out slightly, knees flexed, and weight on either foot or on both. Keep arms relaxed at sides and gracefully close to body.

To walk   To walk correctly, lift one foot slightly from the floor, move it forward, and place it on the floor again. Transfer body weight to forward foot. As weight rolls forward from outer part of heel to ball of foot and onto the big toe, let back leg swing freely from thigh, knees bent slightly. Take even steps, keeping feet parallel, and move directly ahead.

When walking upstairs, incline entire body forward, but let the thigh do the work. Lift one knee at a slight slant, place foot securely on step, and push upward with back foot. Transfer weight to front leg, and straighten front knee. When walking downstairs, bend knees deeply, advancing one foot in front of the other and crossing legs slightly. Bend back knee until forward foot touches step.

To sit   Press calf of leg nearest chair against chair. Using that leg as a lever and keeping the other foot flat on the floor, lower body into chair seat. Then slide back into place.

While seated, keep back straight with hips and small of back against the back of the chair. Keep head, shoulders, and chest directly over hips in good body balance. When leaning forward, keep back straight and bend from hips. Keeps hands quiet and relaxed when not in use. Avoid wringing or fluttering the hands, tapping the fingers, or masking the mouth with them. Keep legs in good alignment, thighs parallel, lower legs close together. Place both feet slightly to one side with outer foot a trifle ahead.

To rise from a chair   Place one foot behind the other. Then pushing on the back foot and keeping the forward foot flat on the floor, stand erect. Avoid bending at the waist as you rise or using your hands to lift yourself from the chair.

To pick up an object   Bend knees deeply, one foot slightly behind the other, keeping head up and back straight. As you reach for the object, straighten the spine, push lightly with the back foot, and lift the body to an erect position. To take objects from low drawers or shelves, sit back on heels with toes on floor and back straight.

To carry a large package   Use first one arm, then the other. When carrying two packages, carry one in each arm high enough so that they do not pull the body down.

Posture, weight control, and good health are promoted by active physical exercise.

Does your community provide some type of public gym program? If so, investigate its physical exercise programs such as swimming, skating, dancing, tennis, basketball or hand ball, fencing, or judo. If you cannot attend such a program, borrow from your library or buy an exercise book or record and exercise at home.

Rest and Relaxation

Sleep is important to your health, your appearance, and your beauty. With sufficient sleep, a healthy person has energy to do most of the things he needs to do. If you do not get enough sleep, you will often feel tired and drowsy. You may even become irritable, depressed, or discouraged.

The amount of sleep you get affects the appearance of your eyes. Healthy eyes are clear and attractive when you have enough sleep. If you do not sleep well, your eyes become bloodshot and dark circles often develop around them. Sleep also promotes healthy hair, strong nails, and clear skin.

How much sleep do you need? This differs with individuals. Most young people need to sleep 8 to 10 hours out of every 24-hour period.

Oral Hygiene

Perhaps you have heard the phrase, "Even your best friend won't tell you." Good habits of oral hygiene are very important if you wish to be accepted socially or to be successful on the job. Follow these simple steps to good oral hygiene:

1. Brush your teeth twice and preferably three times a day: morning, evening, and before bedtime.

2. Use a deodorizing mouthwash after you clean your teeth. If a bad breath persists, consult your dentist.

3. See your dentist twice a year. Have him professionally clean your teeth, check on teeth that require filling, and advise you if your gums need special care or if your teeth need straightening.

Courtesy FORECAST for Home Economics

Beauty is a delightful combination of outer appearance and inner self.

Personal Hygiene

Most young people live very active lives. Such activity calls for a constant check on personal cleanliness. Unfortunately, your own body odor may not be especially obvious to you while it may be very evident to other people. This makes a daily shower or bath almost essential for effective group living.

Deodorants are helpful in deactivating bacteria after perspiration forms. Antiperspirants help to stop the flow of perspiration. Use your own personal choice of some form of underarm deodorant or antiperspirant. Follow the manufacturers' directions for using these preparations. Shave frequently for the sake of appearance and for cleanliness.

Although there are several ways for removing excess leg and underarm hair, such as

Courtesy Sperry Rand

A favorable image can be created with the minimum of grooming aids.

Frequent shampoos must be worked into the schedule of a busy, active young person.

Courtesy Cannon Mills Inc.

depilatories, abrasives, and electrolysis, shaving is usually preferred. If possible, use a razor designed for women. After shaving, you may want to apply a good dry-skin moisturizer or cream to leave your skin smooth and soft.

The menstrual period can be a critical time for maintaining acceptable personal hygiene. Menstrual blood has a very strong odor. Frequent changing of pads or tubes, frequent changing of underwear, and regular bathing can minimize this problem.

Clean clothes are an important part of effective personal hygiene. Although pants and dresses frequently can be pressed and worn again, underwear needs to be washed after each wearing. Use a good detergent and plenty of water. The directions for hand washing of clothing are given on page 134.

Many products are available to help keep your body fragrant. They range from light colognes to heavy perfumes. None, however, can effectively substitute for daily baths, deodorants, and clean clothes. Use these products sparingly.

Your Eyes

Your eyesight is precious. Keep your eyes healthy, bright, clear, and shiny. The following simple rules will help you do so:

1. Read in acceptably lighted areas to prevent eyestrain.

2. Observe general rules for good health.

3. Use an eye wash when necessary.

4. Go to a doctor who specializes in eye care for corrective procedures if necessary. He will advise you as to the need for glasses, contact lenses, or other special care.

5. Protect your eyes from direct sunlight with sunglasses. If you need prescription sunglasses, get them. They are worth the investment.

Your Hair

Your hair is frequently exposed to steam, heat, cold, wind, sun, humidity, water, and air conditioning. Add to this the soot, grime, and smog of an industrial area, and you can see

Armpits   Apply a deodorant each time underarm area is bathed. Apply an antiperspirant as often as needed.

A deodorant neutralizes the odor of perspiration where it is applied. It comes in numerous forms: cream, powder, liquid, spray, and stick. An antiperspirant reduces the flow of perspiration where it is applied and diverts it to other parts of the body. Antiperspirants come in liquid, stick, and cream forms.

For best results, apply a deodorant or an antiperspirant at least half an hour before strenuous activity. Some brands lose their effect if they are used regularly for a length of time, so it may be well to change brands from time to time. Neither a deodorant nor an antiperspirant should be applied directly after shaving if your skin is sensitive.

Palms of hands   Rub palms of hands with a stick cologne, a stick deodorant, or a stick antiperspirant. If they perspire too freely, dust them with talcum or bath powder.

Feet   Bathe feet frequently with a germicidal soap to destroy the bacteria that give rise to odors. For further prevention of odor and reduction of chafing, use an antiseptic deodorant foot powder between the toes, change socks or stockings frequently, and shake a deodorant powder into your shoes. Should your feet continue to perspire, it may be that you are misusing them or subjecting them to strain. Your shoes may be too heavy. Nonabsorbent socks and nylon stockings may also be a cause.

that environment affects the appearance of every individual, particularly his hair.

Sun is a natural enemy of the hair. Sunlight can make the hair dull or brassy and can even change its color. Overexposure to sunlight dries the hair, causing it to break or split.

Humidity causes curly hair to become curlier and straight hair to become straighter. A new hair set can be lost readily in moist air.

Heat seems to bring out the oil in oily hair and causes dry hair to become drier and more brittle. Heat also causes you to perspire. The bacteria of the perspiration couple with particles which stick to the dampened hair, causing the hair to become dirty.

Air pollutants such as soot, grime, and smog settle on oily hair or hair that has been sprayed with hair spray. Research indicates that the sulphur dioxide in polluted air has a bleaching effect on natural hair, as well as on hair that has been dyed, tinted, or treated with permanent-waving solutions. It may seem that all the elements of nature are working against your hair. However, it is quite simple to follow the steps listed here for clean, gleaming hair:

1. Brush daily. Start at the scalp. Work out with an upward motion on a few strands at a time. Brush at least five minutes.

2. Shampoo your hair as often as dirt, oil, and perspiration build up.

3. Select and use a satisfactory shampoo for your type of hair.

4. Use a hair conditioner if one is needed.

Most hair preparations can be used successfully by anyone who has naturally straight hair. However, those who have naturally curly hair are often encouraged by style trends to

Oval   To retain an oval shape, wear a simple hair style. If the hairline is neat, draw the hair back from the forehead. Wear a center part if you wish.

Round   To create an illusion of length, style the hair to add either height or length.

To add height, pile curls high at the crown, wear high-rolled bangs that start 2 inches above the hairline, or slant curls or waves up and away from the forehead and sides. Brush the hair up and back from the temples with forward and reverse curls at the forehead or a wave at one side of the forehead.

To add length, try a straight bob, either tapered down below the jawline in back or with fullness below the face. Longer hair can be worn severely sleek and knotted low on the back of the neck.

A side part or a part which starts at the crown and comes forward diagonally is good, but a center part overemphasizes the regularity of a round face.

Bangs generally shorten rather than lengthen the face.

Oblong   To create an illusion of width at the cheekbones, wear a fluff of curls at the temples, some waves at the sides of the cheeks, or soft curls either over the ears or behind them. Keep the hair flat on top.

Medium-length hair is attractive. A diagonal part which starts at the center or near the center of the hairline is good. A center part is becoming only if the hair is built out at the sides. Wear soft bangs or waves across the forehead.

Square   To minimize the sharp angle of the jaw, fluff the hair up and out softly at the temples, or wear soft curls and waves slightly up and away from the forehead, with more height at one side.

A side or diagonal part, starting at the crown, is good, but a center part overemphasizes the regularity of a square face. A dipping half bang may be worn.

Heart-shaped   Minimize the width at the forehead by creating an illusion of width at the lower part of the face. Keep the hair smooth on top and at the temples, with either forward-turning curls around the jaw and a soft fluff of curls below and behind the ears or fullness on the sides above and back of the ears with greatest fullness where the jaw starts to narrow.

A side part or a diagonal side part slanting toward the crown is best, but wear a center part only when the hair is pulled up and back on the sides.

Emphasize a widow's peak by keeping the forehead bare, or try a half bang, a soft dip, a fluff, a curl, or a lock of hair on one side of the forehead.

18

PURPOSES OF VARIOUS SHAMPOO TYPES

To build body   A concentrated protein shampoo which gives body and sheen to fine hair.

To heighten color   Nonpermanent color shampoo which increases highlights and intensifies hair color.

To eliminate dandruff   A specifically formulated shampoo which contains medication for control of flaking skin.

To control oiliness or dryness   A shampoo formulated for oily, normal, dry, or tinted and bleached hair. Buy for your particular need.

SOLVING HAIR AND SCALP PROBLEMS

Dry hair   Dry hair should have an oil treatment before each shampoo. To give yourself an oil treatment, loosen any scalp scale, and brush it out. Then part the hair at 1-inch intervals, rub the scalp with cotton that has been dipped in warm olive oil or vegetable oil, and massage the entire head. Wrap the head in a towel which has been wrung out of hot water. If possible, leave the oil on overnight. Shampoo as usual.

Unruly hair   Hair that is very thick and curly or very thin and straight requires special attention. Shampoo and set the hair regularly. If your hair is thick and curly, have it thinned and shaped frequently, brush it often, and use cream rinses. If excessively curly, have it straightened, wear it short, or set it with large rollers. If your hair is thin and straight, wear it straight in a becoming style; or if it is fine, you might want a type of permanent wave recommended by a beautician.

Dry scalp   The cause of dry scalp may be improper washing, washing in hard water, using an excessively alkaline shampoo, or insufficient rinsing of the hair and scalp. It may also be the result of hairbrush irritation, permanents, steam heat, and overexposure to sun, wind, or salt water. To counteract dry scalp, make 1-inch parts and apply a good scalp lotion before and between shampoos. Wash the hair every four or five days with a shampoo designed to combat dry scalp, and avoid permanents until the scalp is in healthy condition.

Dandruff   To prevent dandruff, brush the hair daily, shampoo the hair and the scalp frequently, and use preparations with antiseptic qualities. Dandruff may require medical help, if it is an infectious type.

straighten their hair. Two methods available for effective hair straightening are metal combs and chemical straighteners.

If you decide to straighten your hair with metal combs, proceed with caution. They require great care to avoid burning the scalp or damaging the hair.

Several chemical straighteners are available which are fairly effective for home use, but professional application is recommended. It takes skill and time to do an effective job. Since chemical treatment of hair often makes it brittle, use a hair conditioner to help prevent splitting and breaking it.

TREATING UNWANTED HAIR

Bleaching (for arms, legs, and upper lip)   Mix 1 part ammonia to 3 parts 20-volume hydrogen peroxide. Add enough soap flakes to make a thin paste. Soak pieces of cotton in the mixture, and apply to the area which you want to lighten. Let the mixture dry on the skin; then wash it off with warm water. If one application does not lighten the hair sufficiently, repeat the process.

Tweezing (for the eyebrows)   Hold a hot cloth over the brows just before plucking them. Pull the skin tight with your fingers, and tweeze one hair at a time in the direction in which the hair grows, working fast.

1. Follow the natural brow line.
2. Shape from below the brow.
3. Clear the bridge of the nose of hair for about 1 inch.

Shaving (for legs and armpits; not recommended for arms)   The first time you shave, you may need to clip the hair with scissors; then shave, with a safety or electric razor. Dab any scratch or nick with antiseptic.

Depilatories (for arms and legs; for upper lip and chin—provided skin is clear, unbroken, and not irritated)   There are some good creams for removing hair from arms and legs; others are made especially for removing hair from the sensitive area of the upper lip and chin when it is not too heavy. In using any depilatory, be sure to follow the directions carefully.

Electrolysis (for hair on the face)   Consult a physician, a hospital, or a medical society for the name of a competent operator if you have heavy, dark hair which you wish to have removed by electrolysis—destroying the hair roots by electric current.

Hairpieces, wigs, and wiglets are available to match a variety of hair types. You may decide on one or several to change your appearance for different occasions. Some of them are made of genuine hair; others are composed of man-made fibers. Prices range from inexpensive to very expensive. Care and upkeep differ for genuine and imitation hairpieces. Consider the cost of upkeep if you plan to buy one.

Your Skin

Adequate diet, rest, exercise, digestion, elimination, and cleanliness are all necessary for general good health. They are especially necessary for healthy, attractive skin. Wash your skin at least once daily. A warm bath will loosen the dirt and oil that allow bacteria to breed. The bath will also open pores, remove dead cells, dilate the blood vessels, and relax the body tissue.

Perhaps at times it will be inconvenient to wash carefully every day. However, extra effort pays dividends in the form of attractive skin. If other facilities are not available, you can wash in a pan or bucket instead of the usual sink, tub, or shower. All you need is water, soap, washcloth, and towel. You will feel better if you can lightly dust your body with bath or talcum powder following your

TYPES OF SKIN

Normal skin   This type of skin has fine texture with clean, un-clogged pores. It is clear, soft, smooth, and glowing.

Dry skin   This type of skin is finely textured, sensitive, and often transparent. It chaps easily, roughens in cold winds, and may even crack, with broken veins as a result.

Oily skin   This type of skin tends to be thick and coarse-grained with enlarged pores which are sometimes clogged. It becomes infected easily, so requires thorough cleansing several times each day.

Combination skin   This type of skin appears dry in some places and oily in others. The skin may be dry around the eyes, on the cheeks, and around the throat but oily on the forehead, nose, and chin.

STEPS IN APPLYING MAKEUP TO DARK SKIN

1. Clean your face daily with a deep-pore facial cleanser to remove makeup and soil. Steam the face with hot towels to dry up excessive oil. Follow with the application of an astringent.

2. If you decide to use foundation makeup, select a water-base makeup foundation. Apply foundation on the forehead, cheeks, and nose. Blend evenly. Be sure to cover the inner corners of your eyes and nostrils, and smooth the foundation down to the base of the throat.

3. Select a powder created to blend with dark skin tones. Brush or dust it onto your face and neck lightly.

4. Select lip color in pink shades with beige, brown, or coral tones. A yellow lipstick can be used for corrective purposes. Apply the corrective lipstick underneath the shade you choose. This will help to balance uneven tones and is especially desirable for dark lips. Powder the lips before and after applying color to help keep the color from changing or wearing off. Outline the upper lip first, from the center out to each corner, and then the lower lip from one corner to the other. Fill in with color.

5. Shape the eyebrows to a natural arch by tweezing from the under-side. Pencil in lightly with a brown or charcoal-gray pencil.

6. If you decide to use eye makeup, choose shadow in a muted color that matches or contrasts with the color of your costume. White and beige are frequently used with a dark brown eyeliner. Stroke the color onto the upper lid near the lashes. Blend it to the outer corners of the brow.

7. Eyeliner and mascara are worn together. Select them in identical shades of dull black, dark brown, gray, or navy blue. Stroke the eyeliner along the roots of the upper lid lashes, beginning about ½ inch from the inner corner and extending to the outer corner. Finish with a slight uplift. Stroke mascara from the roots to the tips of the lashes. Dry. Separate the lashes with an eye brush.

Courtesy Johnson and Johnson

Cleanliness is essential for the projection of a positive image.

1. Applying a suitable cleansing agent to remove makeup, to cleanse the skin, and to stimulate circulation.

2. Rinsing oily areas of the face with a freshener or astringent to remove traces of oil and cleansing agent.

3. Washing with a glycerine soap and water. If your skin is dry you may require only one washing a day. If your skin is oily, three washings may be necessary.

4. Rinsing thoroughly with water to remove all traces of soap solution.

5. Applying a moisturizer to the skin.

If you have any skin problems, such as acne, skin irritation, pimples, blackheads, or whiteheads, your doctor may refer you to a dermatologist.

Your Hands and Feet

Your hands tell others a great deal about you because they are generally in sight and often express your feelings. Because they are seen so frequently, try at all times to keep them free from stains. Keep the cuticle around the nails pushed back and the nails themselves clean and smoothly filed.

Nail creams are effective when used regularly on nails which tend to break or split easily. To use this type of preparation, massage it around and under the bare nails at least once a week. Avoid using frosted polishes unless your nails are in good condition. They tend to be destructive to fingernail tissues and aggravate chipping and splitting.

Your feet serve as your foundation. They deserve the best of care. When your feet hurt, you feel as if you hurt all over. This affects your posture, physical comfort, efficiency, and even your disposition.

If you have problems such as arch trouble, foot cramps, athlete's foot, calluses, corns, bunions, or ingrown toenails, consult your family physician. He may refer you to a specialist who deals with these types of ailments.

Enhancing Your Natural Beauty

Makeup can enhance beauty if skillfully used to shift the emphasis to naturally beautiful

daily bath, especially in hot weather. Apply a deodorant or antiperspirant in the underarm areas before putting on clean clothes.

If they are available, you can use such bathing extras as a back brush, a nail brush, bath scents, water softeners, and bath oils. Perhaps you will want to use a pumice stone for rubbing away the dead skin from your heels and elbows.

Your face requires special care in cleaning. First you should determine your skin type. Is it normal, dry, or oily? Recommended daily care for all types of skin includes:

STEPS IN APPLYING MAKEUP TO LIGHT SKIN

1. *Clean your face thoroughly using soap and water or your favorite cleansing agent. Apply a thin layer of skin moisturizer.*

2. *If needed, select a light, sheer, liquid makeup foundation that matches as closely as possible your natural skin tones. Apply foundation on the forehead, cheeks, chin, and nose. Blend it evenly. Be sure to cover the inner corners of your eyes and nostrils, and smooth the foundation down to the base of the throat.*

3. *Choose a shade of powder or cake powder which blends with your skin color, and brush or dust it onto your face and neck lightly. Apply rouge, or blusher, to your cheeks, chin, and forehead, if desired. It may precede or follow the application of powder, depending on the type of coloring agent chosen.*

4. *Select a lip color that harmonizes with your overall makeup and costume. Some lipsticks can be applied from the stick; other coloring agents are best applied with a lipstick brush or your finger. Outline the upper lip first, from center out to each corner, then the lower lip from one corner to the other. Fill in with color. Blot with tissue.*

5. *Shape the eyebrows following the natural curve of the bone over the eye, tweezing from the underside. Apply eyebrow pencil in short, even strokes.*

6. *If you decide to use eye makeup, choose a shade of eye shadow to match your eyes. Use a brush to stroke color onto the upper lid near the lashes. Blend it toward the outer corner of the eyebrow.*

7. *Eyeliner and mascara are worn together. Color fashions vary from year to year. Select colors that look well with your eyes and skin. Stroke eyeliner along the roots of the upper lid lashes, beginning about ½ inch from the inner corner and extending to the outer corner. Finish with a slight uplift. Stroke mascara from the roots to the tips of the lashes. Dry. Make a second application. Separate the lashes with an eye brush.*

features. Its misuse can be distractive. Study yourself, your features, and your coloring in order to decide which colors and types of makeup are best for you. Makeup styles change from year to year. Many girls prefer to use very little makeup, particularly for school. Perhaps they apply more makeup when dressing for dates and parties.

The basic consideration in the successful use of makeup is your natural assets. Makeup can effectively show them off while hiding your facial flaws. There are some general rules to guide you in selecting and applying makeup. If you decide to build a makeup inventory, such a collection might include appropriate cleansing agents, skin moisturizer, foundation, some form of powder and rouge, lip color, and eye makeup. After deciding which, if any, makeup you will wear for a particular occasion, follow the directives given for your personal skin color in order to apply each type of makeup effectively.

SOLVING NAIL PROBLEMS

White spots　　The cause of white spots is an injury to the nail cells by a blow, undue strain, or pressure months earlier while the nail was being formed. White spots last only until the nail plate grows out, and they can be concealed by covering the entire nail plate with a polish.

Nails that split, crack, or break　　These problems may be caused by injuries, poor health, a dietary deficiency, filing the nails in too pointed a shape or too close to the corners, wearing them too long, or giving them hard wear. Massage such nails frequently with warm oil. Solve the problem by remedying the cause.

Nails that curl up or down, separate, peel, or tear easily　　Such nails need strengthening. File them correctly, wear them short, apply colorless iodine to the cuticle once a day for a month, and eat a well-balanced diet, including milk.

Harsh cuticle　　Soften with cuticle oil or warm olive oil.

Hangnails　　These loose strips of skin at the base of the nail may be the result of a lack of proper hand care or of filing the nails too far down in the corners. Remove hangnails with nippers or sharp manicure scissors. Disinfect, and apply cuticle oil or cuticle cream.

STEPS IN GIVING A MANICURE

1. Remove polish with an oily-base remover. Clean the fingernails.
2. Shape the fingernails with a nail file. Smooth the edges.
3. Wash the hands with warm water and soap. Dry them thoroughly.
4. Apply cuticle remover with a cotton-tipped orangewood stick. Push the cuticle back gently.
5. Remove hangnails with manicure scissors or a nipper.
6. Rinse the hands and dry them thoroughly. Either buff the nails or apply liquid polish as follows:
    a. Apply a base coat. Allow it to dry thoroughly.
    b. Apply polish. Allow it to dry thoroughly.
    c. Apply top coat. Allow it to dry thoroughly.

STEPS IN GIVING A PEDICURE

1. Scrub your feet thoroughly with soap and water.
2. Dry them carefully, especially between the toes.
3. Shape your toenails straight across the nail edge and file them smoothly.
4. Apply cuticle remover with a cotton-tipped orangewood stick. Push the cuticle back gently. Rinse the feet and dry them thoroughly.
5. If you wish to polish the nails, use the same procedures as used in polishing the fingernails.
6. Apply foot cream or powder before putting on shoes and stockings.

Choosing Personal-care Equipment

A person can be attractive with the very minimum of supplies and equipment. However, the tasks of grooming can be performed more effectively and easily if you have some grooming aids. Most girls have the common beauty aids such as combs, hand mirrors, hair rollers and pins, tweezers, and some type of razor. Such aids as hair dryers, electric rollers, make-up mirrors, electric manicure sets, electric shavers and toothbrushes, and small miscellaneous electric equipment are time saving and often more efficient than conventional methods of beauty care. You may want to consider these items. Before investing in any of them, however, consider the cost, the amount of convenience it will provide, and the possible self-improvement you can expect to acquire by using it.

Hair Dryers

Hair care is essential for good looks. A hair dryer is an asset in caring for the hair because it ensures fast, even heat for thoroughly drying the hair after a shampoo and set. Hair dryers come in a variety of models, from the small, compact soft-bonnet dryer to the portable-bonnet and the rigid-helmet salon types. Some compact models permit you to move about in a room while your hair is drying.

Shop and compare the various types of dryers available before you buy. Desirable qualities include a variety of heat settings, a bonnet large enough to cover the curlers, and a motor which runs quietly.

Electric Roller Sets

Electric hair rollers are a relatively new appliance. They can eliminate nightly hair setting by providing a quick touch-up for drooping

PRECAUTIONS IN USING ELECTRIC PERSONAL-CARE APPLIANCES

1. Make sure the appliance is turned off before it is plugged into an outlet.
2. Keep electric appliances and outlets dry. Water can carry an electric current which will give you an electric shock.
3. Dry your hands before connecting or operating any electric appliance.
4. Be certain the electric appliance is standing on a dry surface.
5. Never use an electric appliance while you are in the bathtub.
6. Disconnect an appliance at the outlet when you are not using it. Grasp the plug firmly but pull gently.
7. Store the electric cord with the appliance or in a drawer. Protect cords from sharp edges of knives or scissors.
8. Replace frayed cords. Exposed wires are dangerous. So are ineffective home repairs. They can cause shock and fires.
9. Avoid hanging a cord over a nail, bedpost, or pipe which might cut or melt away the insulation from the cord.
10. Avoid running extension cords from one room to another or across traffic areas where people might step or trip on them.
11. Be certain the screws and bolts of a plug are tight. If they are loose, remove the plug from the outlet and tighten loose sections.
12. Keep cords untwisted and unkinked. When they are not in use, keep them off the floor.

Hairdos can be set at home and dried naturally or with the aid of an electric hair dryer.

A tight, crisp curl can be obtained with dry-heated rollers by spraying a fine mist of water on the hair before the hair is rolled.

The length of time the roller is left in the hair regulates the tightness of the curl. The time required to curl the hair as tightly as desired depends on the type and length of the hair, the size of the rollers, and the amount of moisture present.

Do some comparison shopping before buying electric rollers. Sets come in various shapes and with various sizes and quantities of rollers. Check to be certain the unit is thermostatically controlled. Some sets have several temperature settings. A signal light is a desirable feature because it lets you know when the rollers are ready to use. The prongs that grip the hair and secure it to the roller should be cool to the touch, even after the rollers are heated.

Makeup Mirrors

A lighted makeup mirror is an aid to makeup application or hair styling. It is not essential if adequate lighting is provided by other means. Most makeup mirrors are specially lighted so that light rays are focused on your face and hair. The use of such a mirror allows you to see effectively during either daylight or darkness. There are a wide variety of such mirrors from which to choose. Some simulate the lighting under which makeup will be seen: day, office, evening, home. A choice of light settings helps the user apply makeup so that it is properly toned to suit a particular lighting situation. Select one that includes both a regular and a magnifying mirror and that is brightly lighted with fluorescent or incandescent light. Be certain the mirror is contained in a stand that allows it to be adjusted to different angles. A plus value is a carrying case for easy mobility.

Electric Manicure Sets

An electric manicure set is generally considered a nonessential luxury item. Many people agree, however, that such a set is a con-

hair or by relaxing the curl of naturally curly hair. Electric rollers work on the same principle as the old-fashioned curling iron: Hair contains moisture, even though it feels dry. When hair is wound around the heated roller, the heat evaporates the moisture from the hair and sets the hair in its curled position around the roller. With naturally curly hair the heat relaxes the hair, loosening the natural curl, as it sets the hair in the new position.

Several types of electric roller sets are available: rollers which are heated dry, rollers which are heated by a steam mist, and rollers which can be heated either dry or with steam. A combination of heat and moisture produces a tighter curl than does dry heat alone.

venience item which allows for easy and effective manicuring of the nails. Electric manicure sets come with a variety of attachments. Most effective sets contain: a nail filer to give nails smooth, even edges; a buffer to make nails glossy; a callus smoother to keep both hands and feet smooth; a cuticle pusher to push cuticles back; and a cuticle brush to thoroughly clean the nails. When buying, choose a set designed so that attachments can be put in place and used easily. Be certain to check whether the attachments are sturdy and designed for safety and efficiency. Also check to see that replacement parts are readily available.

Electric Shavers

Most girls consider it helpful to own their own shavers rather than to depend on borrowing from other family members. There are a variety of brands and styles of electric shavers. If you are buying one, select a dual-purpose shaver which can be adjusted for both underarms and legs. The case should provide storage for both the razor and the cord. If you travel or camp out frequently, you may want to consider purchasing a cordless model.

Electric Toothbrushes

Teeth are generally cleaner when brushed with an electrically powered toothbrush rather than with a manual one. Although an electric toothbrush is to most people a luxury item, you may decide to buy one. There are several types, categorized according to brushing motion: up-and-down; side-to-side; and orbital, which combines side-to-side with up-and-down. The American Dental Association recognizes brushes with each of these motions. When buying an electric-powered toothbrush, choose one which is classed either as *acceptable* or as *provisionally acceptable* by the ADA.

Dental Irrigators

The dental irrigator is a device used in addition to a toothbrush. It flushes away food particles lodged between the teeth, cleans crev-

Courtesy Clairol Inc.

Makeup mirrors are available which provide suitable lighting for the expert application of makeup.

ices which may be beyond the reach of toothbrush bristles, and cleans and flushes the gum line. The dental irrigator is an excellent cleansing aid for persons who have braces on their teeth. When purchasing an irrigator choose one that has an ADA acceptance rating.

Miscellaneous Electric Equipment

There are many other electric personal-care appliances. Among them are electric combs, clothesbrushes, shoe polishers, nail-polish dryers, and complexion-care kits. Your particular situation will determine whether such appliances will provide convenience which compensates for their cost.

1. Identify experiences you have had when you felt people did not treat you properly because of your appearance or dress. Consider why they reacted to you as they did.

2. Recall experiences you have had when you were acceptably dressed. Discuss the kinds of reactions you received from members of your group.

3. Evaluate a song or a picture and an item of clothing in terms of the aesthetic value chart on page 5.

4. Select a group of fabric swatches, and number each. Describe the fabrics acording to the chart on page 6. Compare the results of the ratings given each fabric by various class members.

5. Assemble pictures of assorted items of clothing. Number each picture. Describe each item according to the chart on page 7. Compare the values given to each item by various class members.

6. Use the point system discussed on page 9 to score pictures of girls dressed in various outfits. Then let each class member select secretly someone in the class to score. Use no names, but tally results as to how many are overdressed and how many are well-dressed according to the 10-point scale. Note that this scale only identifies overdress; it does not consider color, appropriateness, or grooming.

7. Identify youth groups who have adopted conformity in dress and hair style to express their involvement with social changes.

8. Make a survey of what the students in your school are wearing. Record the time, place, and occasion at which you make your survey. List such points of consideration as hair style, type of garment, and length of garment. Summarize your findings and report to the class.

9. Determine the appropriate dress for a student, teacher, sales trainee, beautician, nurse's aide, and secretary-receptionist. List the responsibilities and activities that determine appropriate dress for each specific role. Decide what each should avoid in dress.

10. Ask a professional model to come to the classroom to demonstrate techniques of good posture while standing, walking, sitting, and rising from a chair.

11. Invite a hair stylist to demonstrate hair styles appropriate for faces of various shapes and the use of wigs and wiglets to give a different look. Determine the difference in cost and care of wigs and wiglets made of man-made fibers and genuine hair.

12. Try to secure an eye specialist to speak to your class concerning symptoms of visual problems, the pros and cons of contact lenses, flattering frames for different faces shapes, and the selection of sunglasses.

HELPING OTHERS TO LEARN

1. Some trade groups sponsor an annual *Good Grooming Week.* Ask local businesses to cooperate with your school in promoting grooming during this time. Consult your local newspapers for participating agencies. They may help in the following ways.

As consultants for class discussions

As suppliers of resource materials

By sponsoring field trips

By granting student interviews

2. Many student councils and school clubs are interested in improving the appearance of the student body. Work with such groups on one or more of the following projects.

Promote *Good Grooming Week* positively.

Solicit the help of **the school** paper, inviting English or journalism classes to write articles on good grooming.

Initiate bulletin-board projects on the subject.

Enlist cooperation of local merchants to display in their windows merchandise for the well-dressed student.

Combine the skills of the drama and music departments with those of the home economics department to produce a musical on dress, using popular songs as themes. Invite the public to your performance.

3. Form an exercise class or weight-control class in your community. Invite the public to participate.

4. Talk with authorities in your community to determine if there is any way you can boost the morale of patients in mental hospitals through helping them improve their grooming and dress. Carry through with workable ideas.

INDEPENDENT LEARNING EXPERIENCES

1. Make a grooming plan, daily and weekly. It can be made in the form of a chart to hang on your bedroom or bathroom wall or in the form of notes written in a notebook to lie on your dresser.

2. Build a grooming corner in your room or clothes closet in which to store your grooming supplies. Some possibilities include a portable carrier such as a tackle box, a lunch or sewing box, or a cart on wheels.

3. When dieting, clip photos from magazines of several persons whose figures you admire. Place the photos for easy viewing in your bedroom or bath to remind you of the results you hope to achieve.

4. List ten of the most popular students in your school. Analyze their dress and appearance. Decide which aspects of their image you would wish to imitate.

5. Try on different clothes and analyze why they do or do not fit your self-image.

6. Assemble pictures of people from various walks of life. Judge from appearance what role, or job, you think each represents.

7. Prepare a chart on *Dressing to Suit the Occasion.* List acceptable clothes for school, home, play, job, party, church, and dates.

8. Consult a nutritionist in your community to help you plan daily and weekly meals for maintenance of optimum health.

9. Describe your ideal woman; your ideal man. Emphasize their appearance and clothing.

10. If your values regarding dress and appearance differ from those of your parents, analyze how and why.

Developing Creativity in Dress

What is creativity? It can be defined in various ways. Stated in absolute terms, it means making something from nothing. It is also defined as a process. To most teen-agers, a modified definition might be useful. Creativity might be described as the ability to do something in a way which appears new to them.

How does the asking of penetrating questions demonstrate a person's creative ability?

How do unusual approaches to problem solving demonstrate creativity?

How can nonconformity be used in creativity?

Why is flexibility necessary in the creative process?

Why is a certain amount of daydreaming, or preoccupation with ideas, necessary for active creativty?

Why do creative people often perform beyond assigned limits?

Why do creative people tend to continue to work on a project after other people have given up?

What advantages can be derived through the ability to rearrange ideas and find new relationships?

Why is open-mindedness necessary for creativity?

Expanding Personal Creativity

Personal creativity can be defined in terms of individuality, aptitudes, or environmental conditions. You might say, "She is a creative person," "He has creative abilities," or "She has a creative family background." All of these are correct usages of the word *creative.* Regardless of how creativity is defined, all definitions have one thing in common: the concept of newness, or originality, is included.

Creativity is an attribute almost everyone possesses to some degree. It is a mental process. Whether you are writing a story, making an unusual outfit, or creating a new hairdo, mental activity is involved. As is true of all your inborn abilities, the extent to which you develop your creativity depends largely on your desire to develop it.

How can you become a creative person? When faced with situations which seem to require a creative response, try applying these four steps in the process of creative thinking:

1. Discover problems or unfilled needs.
2. Form ideas as to how the needs might be met.
3. Test and modify your ideas.
4. Communicate the results.

This four-step thinking process, applied consciously or unconsciously, may lead toward creating a wide variety of end products. If you are dealing in verbal areas, perhaps the end product will be a poem, a story, or a song. If you are working in nonverbal areas, perhaps creative thought will bring a change in the way you dress, the way you stand, or the way

CREATIVE LEARNING TECHNIQUES

Brainstorming	*Problem solving*	*Manipulating*
Exploring	*Contemplating*	*Modifying*
Experimenting	*Think tanks*	*Risking*
Testing	*Questioning*	*Researching*

you communicate through body gestures. Dealing with tangible forms of expression, you may create a painting, a gadget, clothing, or accessories. Applying creative thought to the realm of the abstract, perhaps you will develop new ideas or new theories or perceive new relationships.

Research indicates that creative imagination reaches its peak in children between the ages of four and four and one-half years. The capacity for creative thinking, however, increases throughout the grade school and high school years. If you have creative ability but cannot clearly identify it, begin with questioning. Think through questions such as these: How can I use this ability? What do I care about it? How much do I care about it? Do I have a strong sensitivity for what I am doing? How do I respond to my experiences? What are my energies and which way should I direct them? How and when can I accomplish the most? When do I get my best ideas? What excites my curiosity? What is pleasing and meaningful to me?

Creativity begins within the mind of a person, and, if effective, requires the utilization of his various powers. First, a project must be defined. Then a person must possess or acquire the knowledge and ability to translate thought into action. Many times it is necessary to take risks, to dare to be different, and to have the courage to do the new or the unusual. To be creative, a person must be open-minded, flexible, and positive.

If you want to strengthen your creative abilities, it is necessary to meet certain specific demands. Develop your senses of sight, hearing, touch, taste, and smell. Allow your mind to be active and responsive to everything and everyone around you.

It is not easy to develop creative thinking or creative skills in a society composed largely of conformists. Many people will offer words of discouragement. Be ready for such expressions as these: "It can't be done." "It won't work." "It costs too much." "It should be done another way." "It might work for you, but it wouldn't for me." In order to overcome the negativism which surrounds him, a creative person needs a strongly positive attitude.

It is also important to recognize that creative ideas often occur when you least expect them. Write them down immediately. Otherwise, they may not return when you need them.

Ideas are useful only if you are able to develop them successfully. Evaluate them. If you feel, upon evaluation, that an idea is a good one, develop it fully by reapplying the four-step process of creative thinking: (1) discover problems in the idea, (2) form supporting ideas accordingly, (3) test and modify the ideas as may be needed, and (4) communicate the results. Through this process you can produce well-thought-out original ideas or their products.

Creative Learning

Many educators believe that students learn in two ways: from authorities and from creative experiments. Expressed differently, you learn by absorbing the knowledge of others or by creatively discovering it on your own. Both methods are necessary for successful living.

Authoritative learning is basically a submissive method. Through authoritative learn-

Courtesy Best Foods, a Division of CPC International Inc.

Creativity allows you to make choices which show others that you are distinctively yourself.

ing, you accept something as true if authorities say it is true and their claims appear sound. The authorities may be your parents, teachers, newspapers, magazines, or textbooks. Sometimes you may regard your peers as authorities, wisely or otherwise, when they reach a group decision on a particular subject.

Creative learning, by contrast, involves looking at a problem from a fresh point of view. It is based on inquiry, research, problem solving, and usually some preliminary authoritative learning. Answers are determined through the process of reasoning. While this kind of learning often is slow, it is effective in many areas. A problem once solved by this method can be used as a basis for future learning. In the long run creative learning is often a more thorough learning method.

Courtesy Dwight and Church

Discarded ornaments can often be reclaimed and recycled as useful accessory items.

While authoritative learning is essential, particularly where facts are concerned, an overdependence on it can result in acceptance of the status quo beyond reason. The person who most frequently moves ahead in society constantly asks himself, "How can I do things better?" This approach results in creative learning.

Creative learning often develops best under varied and informal conditions. One of its outstanding features is the freedom which it allows. People who in conforming situations have been labeled as slow learners often make rapid strides when allowed the freedom associated with creative learning techniques.

Creativity by Accident

Many times the opportunity for creativity comes along by accident. In such a situation it takes an alert person to recognize the creative implications of the accident. Perhaps you have heard the story of the young laboratory assistant who discovered artificial sweetener. One day at lunch he discovered that the food he touched was sweeter than anything he had ever tasted. A substance he had been mixing in a vat had not washed off his hands properly. Instead of shrugging off the incident, he became intrigued. He coupled practical intelligence with creativity to produce the product now called saccharine.

In a similar way an Italian textile technician accidentally turned cotton into imitation leather. In experimenting with various protective coatings for cotton fabric, the technician was told to apply a silicone resin to the smooth side of a cotton flannel. Instead he applied the resin to the napped side of the fabric, and the silicone finish produced a grained effect.

An aid to the technician took a few yards of the rejected fabric home to his wife, who was a clever seamstress. She designed and made herself a garment. Everyone who saw it thought it was made of leather. It looked like leather; it felt like leather. It was easier to sew than leather. Finally her husband persuaded her to wear the garment to the laboratory, where the technician and the managers of the plant could see it. She did. The fabric was favorably received and was given the trade name *Aerpel*. The name was derived from two Italian words for air and leather. The fabric is said to breathe air through its natural pores.

Creative Recycling

Creative learning can be applied in many areas of creative experience. One such area is that of recycling. Billions of bottles, jars, and cans and millions of tons of plastic and waste paper are thrown away every year. Ways have been found to melt bottles and cans for reuse. Cans and old cars are compacted and stored in abandoned mines against the time when the natural supply of iron may be used up. Paper is being recycled. Although city-planning specialists are trying to find places to dump nearly 4 million tons of solid waste each year, there are individuals who prefer to save certain used items. They therefore use materials that are no longer suitable for their original purpose for creating objects of art. For instance, they might use scraps of wire, wood, paper, cardboard, glass, metal, plastic, or seashells to make articles of beauty such as jewelry and fashion trimmings.

Such recycling is a type of creativity. Can you think of ways to creatively recycle your clothing or waste materials which are routinely thrown away? Perhaps you can think of interesting clothing accessories which can be made from objects scheduled for disposal in your home. The creative recycling of clothing is discussed on page 216.

What are the five elements of design as they relate to clothing?
What are the three primary colors?
What are four color plans commonly used in attractive clothing combinations?
How can you determine if a color is suitable for you?
How do the lines in an outfit affect the apparent size of a figure?
What are the five principles of design?
How can your exact figure proportions be used in choosing an attractive wardrobe?

Using Creativity in Clothing Design

Design as it relates to clothing deals with the attractive combination of the elements of design according to design principles. Clothing which is pleasing to the eye conforms to these principles. Attractive clothing has high artistic values as does a beautiful painting or an elegant building. Each garment can be unique, expressing creativity, while conforming to the high standards of quality design.

Elements of Design

The elements of design as they relate to clothing include color, line, shape, texture, and fabric design. As in any form of art, the degree to which the application of these design elements adheres to the design principles determines the success of a design. The inter-relationships of these design elements can be controlled in such a way as to produce garments which hide figure flaws while highlighting the best features of a particular figure.

Color

Consider how drab the world would seem if everything were the same color. How would the warmth and personality of your home be changed if everything inside and out was pure white? Think of your own appearance. What would be left of your total image if everything including your clothes, shoes, hair, skin, and eyes were all the same shade of blue? What would such a color change do to your personality?

Think of the many colors you can see in nature. Haven't you thrilled to see the variations of color in a rainbow or an especially brilliant sunset? Perhaps you have felt sud-

The color wheel is a circular arrangement of the three primary colors in their full intensities separated by the secondary and intermediate colors.

Courtesy PPG Industries

35

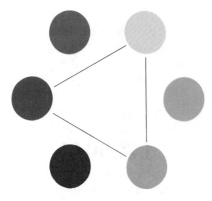

Equal parts of any two of the primary colors—yellow, red, and blue—can be mixed to form the secondary color positioned between the two on the color wheel.

White, black, and the range of grays are known as neutral colors.

Value is the degree of lightness or darkness of a given color.

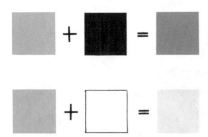

A shade of a particular color is made by adding black to the color, while a tint is made by adding white.

denly alive when the sun came from behind a cloud to brighten the many shades of green within a city park. Color is a very real and meaningful part of life. Through color you can adapt to your environment while creatively projecting your own personality.

Look at the six circles at the left. They are of six different colors, or *hues.* You see hues of yellow, green, blue, violet, red, and orange.

Yellow, blue, and red are called *primary colors.* If you mix equal parts of two primary colors, you make a *secondary color:* Yellow + blue = green; yellow + red = orange; red + blue = violet. You can mix equal parts of a primary and secondary color and make an *intermediate color:* Yellow + green = yellow-green; blue + green = blue-green; blue + violet = blue-violet; red + violet = red-violet; red + orange = red-orange; yellow + orange = yellow-orange. These twelve colors comprise the *standard color wheel* (see illustration on page 35). Innumerable color variations can be made by mixing together differing proportions of the twelve different hues of the color wheel.

Colors located directly opposite each other on the color wheel are known as *complementary colors.* When complementary colors are mixed in equal proportion, they produce gray; when placed side by side, they intensify each other.

White, which has no hue, is caused by the reflection of the rays of all colors, while black is caused by the absorption of all colors. Between black and white, are the grays. You can make gray which is light or dark by mixing unequal parts of black and white. White, black, and the grays are called *neutral colors.*

Value is the lightness or darkness of a given color. The selection of attractive clothing depends as much upon the effective use of value as upon the correct use of color. You will find through experimentation that most colors can be combined successfully if you carefully choose the values of the colors. While it is usually monotonous to combine in a costume equal parts of light and dark values, a light outfit with a dash of a dark accent color can be very attractive. Conversely, a dark outfit brightened by a touch of white or pastel can also be a pleasing combination.

Shade describes the darkness of a hue. A shade is produced when black is mixed with a given color. *Tint* describes the lightness of a hue. A tint is produced when white is mixed with a given color. Shades and tints can generally be used for large areas of garment design. Black and darker shades cause the figure to appear smaller, while white and light tints of color make the figure appear larger.

Intensity describes the brightness or dullness of a color. For example, pure red is an intense color. Its intensity can be lessened by adding black, white, or green, which is a complement of red. The addition of any of these colors will change the intensity of red. The original color is softened or dulled in relation to the amount of neutralizing color added.

The intensity and value of a color interrelate to make the color appear *warm* or *cool.* Though white and black are not colors on the color wheel, they are included when warmth and coolness are considered. White is usually described as cool; black as hot. The reds, yellows, and red-violets appear to be warm colors; the blues, blue-greens, and blue-violets appear to be cool colors. Some hues may appear either warm or cool. For example, blue-greens appear cool, yellow-greens warm. Cool colors seem to recede in relation to the amount of blue they contain. Warm colors seem to advance in proportion to the amount of yellow or red present.

Bright or dull light can make a difference in the way colors look. The bright, strong light of sunshine can make reds, yellows, or greens appear intense, while a man-made light can cause them to appear either intense or softened. Have you ever noticed how colors change when the bright lights of an auditorium are dimmed? As the lights are lowered, colors change from bright to dark. The appearance of the person wearing them also changes. Incan-

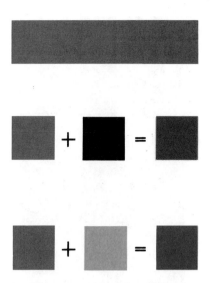

Intensity, the brightness of a particular color, can be lowered by mixing the color with black or by mixing it with its complement.

Colors in the red and yellow range give a feeling of warmth, while the blue and green hues give a cool feeling.

37

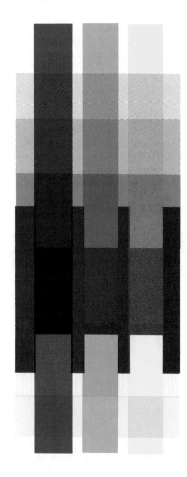

Light affects the appearance of color. Glancing from top to bottom of the color illustration above, notice how the same color may look entirely different when exposed to sunlight, varying degrees of outdoor and indoor shade, ultraviolet (black) light, total darkness, incandescent light, and fluorescent light.

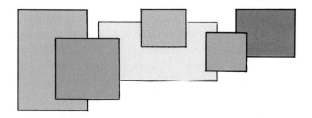

In a monochromatic color plan, several values and intensities of one color may be combined.

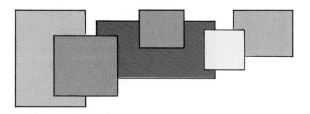

In an analogous color plan, varying tints and shades of colors positioned next to each other on the color wheel may be combined.

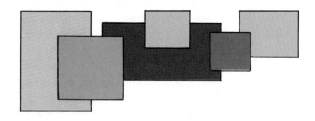

In a complementary color plan, varying tints, shades, and intensities of colors opposite each other on the color wheel may be combined.

descent lights can make a dress seem to be a different color than it was in the store where you saw it under fluorescent light. Black light, or ultraviolet light, can cause colors to look still different. Try to choose colors which look well on you when exposed to the type of light under which you plan to wear them.

You can make colors work to your advantage when you plan your wardrobe. Learn the basic color plans, and study your personal coloring: the color of your hair, eyes, and skin.

Then key the colors of your clothing to your personal coloring.

Basic Color Plans   There are various plans by which colors can be combined in a costume. Four basic plans are: a one-color plan, a related color plan, a complementary color plan, and a triadic plan.

A one-color, or *monochromatic*, plan is based on a single color but with variations in value and intensity. Some areas may be bright, while others are dull.

A related, or *analogous*, color plan includes two or three colors that are next to each other on the color wheel.

A *complementary* color plan makes use of colors opposite each other on the color wheel. In general, such a plan incorporates larger amounts of the cool colors and smaller amounts of warm colors. But you may prefer having these proportions reversed in outfits for special seasons or special events.

A *triadic* color scheme consists of any three colors on the color wheel that are an equal distance from each other. In a triadic color harmony use a tint or shade of one color as a dominant for the large areas, the second color as a bright accent, and the third color for secondary accents and small subordinate areas. If three colors are used in their full intensity and in equal quantity, the final effect will be gaudy and loud. However, with the skillful handling of these colors, a subtle effect may be achieved.

All colors are beautiful if they are used or combined properly. Used improperly, they can appear gaudy or drab. Combined improperly, they may seem to fight with each other. Further, the appearance of color is relative. Color changes with color. An intense color will make its grayed complement appear more neutral than it actually is. While a bright color placed against a large area of white loses some of its intensity, a bright color placed on a large dark area appears more intense. Try to strive for harmony and variety in color schemes.

You can achieve distinction and individuality in dress with the use of color. Color can be used to coordinate separate items of clothing and to give unity to an entire costume. You can use color to create a center of interest or to emphasize an attractive physical feature. You may even use color to disguise a figure fault or to create an illusion of added or decreased height or width.

In choosing clothing, color should be considered in relation to your figure. For example, a pure, bright color will call attention

How do the surrounding colors affect the apparent intensity of the identical red squares of color?

to your figure. The girl with an attractive figure may wish to wear bright colors, while the girl with figure faults may look better in soft colors highlighted with accents of pure color. Experiment with colors in order to know which look best on you.

Hue   The name of a color, such as red, blue, or green.

Value   The lightness or darkness of a color. Light, high values are tints. Dark, low values are shades.

Shade   Color produced when black is added to a hue.

Tint   Color produced when white is added to a hue.

Intensity, or chroma   The strength or weakness of a color. Colors of strong intensity are bright. Colors of weak intensity are dull and muted.

Pure colors   Bright, clear colors of full intensity. Bright, light colors are pure tints. Bright, dark colors are pure shades.

Cool colors   Colors that appear to recede because of the predominance of blue contained in them.

Warm colors   Colors that appear to advance because of the predominance of yellow contained in them.

Full-intensity color wheel   A circle arrangement of all the pure primary, secondary, and intermediate colors.

Value scale   The gradations of a color from its darkest shade to its lightest tint.

Middle-value gray   The combination of equal amounts of white and black, located in the middle of the value scale.

Neutralized color   A pure color that has been dulled by its complement. A neutralized tint is a pure, light color that has been dulled by its complement. A neutralized shade is a bright, dark color that has been dulled by its complement.

Neutrals   Black, white, and gray.

Color plans   Color combinations mechanically devised on the color wheel.

Related harmonies   Color plans made up of one color or of colors close to each other on the color wheel.

Monochromatic harmony   A color plan made up of various values and intensities of one color.

Analogous harmony   A color plan made up of tints and shades of neighboring colors.

Contrasting harmonies   Color plans made up of two or more contrasting colors on opposite sides of the color wheel.

Complementary harmony   A color plan made up of two colors on opposite sides of the color wheel. Variations of a complementary harmony are split complementary and double complementary.

Triadic harmony   A color plan made up of three colors which are an equal distance from each other on the color wheel.

Balanced color schemes   Color plans in which the dark and light values of full-intensity colors and grayed colors are combined in harmonious variety.

For every girl, regardless of face shape or hair or skin color, there are renditions of current fashions, shades and intensities of colors, and adaptations of current hair styles which can be combined to enhance her physical features.

Personal Coloring   Nearly three-fourths of the world's population is composed of dark-skinned people. Skin colors vary, however, from the fairest white to ebony black. The color of your skin depends on the amount of pigment present.

People in general can be grouped into five distinct types. They are considered either black, red-brown, yellow-brown, yellow, or white. There are many variations within each type. There are shades of most colors which look well on each skin-color type. Experiment to find the tints and shades which harmonize with your personal skin coloring.

Line

Line is another of the basic elements of design. Since lines define the shape of a garment, they become an intricate part of the total design. They may be vertical, horizontal, diag-

EFFECT OF CLOTHING COLORS ON PERSONAL COLORING

On skin   Colors near to skin tone flatter. Neutralized shades and tints are generally becoming.

For light skins, the less strength in the person's skin color, the softer should be clothing colors. Delicate clear tints and soft shades are best.

For medium skins, a wide range of both cool and warm colors is possible. Neutralized tints and shades, such as subtle blue-green, are becoming. Off-white, cream, or ivory is better than bone white. Soft yellows are good, but intense colors with yellow in them make skin appear sallow. Brunettes look best in rich, warm colors; redheads look best in blues, soft greens, or warm browns.

For dark skins, related warm hues or contrasting hues in rich, slightly grayed tones, flatter. Warm middle tones of reds, greens, blues, and neutrals are good. Cool colors, slightly grayed, lessen harsh contrast with skin tone. Tans should be darker or lighter than skin tone. Brown, beige, creamy white, and dull gold harmonize with skin tone. Avoid light, clear tints and intense, hard blues, greens, and violets.

On hair   Hues strikingly lighter or darker than the hair emphasize hair color.

On eyes   Colors that repeat eye color make eyes predominate. Intense colors dim eye color.

GUIDELINES FOR SELECTING CLOTHING COLORS

1. Choose colors that suit your personality. In other words, select the colors that make you feel good.
2. Choose colors that are becoming to you. Experiment to determine which colors flatter your eyes, skin, and hair.
3. Choose colors that harmonize. Choose a basic color first. Add variety through contrasting colors.

onal, or curved. In some cases, they may be imaginary rather than real lines. In general, horizontal lines, whether real or illusionary, add width to a shape, while vertical lines add height.

There are two types of lines in clothing: structural and decorative. Structural lines are those created in making the garment. They include seams, hemlines, edges, and folds. Decorative lines are the applied lines such as trim, decorative stitching, ruffles, and accessories.

Shape

Garment shape results from the structural lines of the completed garment. The designer of clothes views the human form, not just from the front, but as a three-dimensional figure. The lines of a high-quality dress design continue from the front around the side to the back, achieving a linear unity, or shape.

Shape determines silhouette. If a strong light is cast upon a figure, the shadow will clearly define its silhouette. Your silhouette reveals whether your clothing is in fashion.

Most garment silhouettes can be reduced to a few basic geometric shapes, such as a rectangle, a triangle, a semicircle, and a square. From time to time, each of these geometric shapes comes into style only to fade from the fashion scene a short time later.

Texture

Texture is the character of a fabric created by the yarn, the weave, and the mechanical and chemical finishes. It includes such structural aspects as firmness, flatness, looseness, and coarseness. It includes such surface characteristics as smoothness, silkiness, glossiness, and roughness. Textures may also be classified by weight. For example, organdy is lightweight, linen is medium-weight, and worsted is heavy. The weight will partially determine the function of a given fabric.

Subtle textural effects in novelty fabrics may change the apparent heaviness or lightness of the fabric. The unevenness of the yarn in tweed may make it appear bulky. The sheerness of organdy makes it seem less stiff than it is. The rib in gabardine and the cord in a worsted modify the textural character of these fabrics. Such effects require consideration in choosing fabric for a given design.

The way a fabric feels and drapes is called the *hand* of the fabric. The hand of a fabric indicates (1) the behavior of the cloth in use and (2) the effect of the cloth in the garment and on the appearance of the figure. Clinging fabrics such as chiffon will reveal the contours of the body. Jersey will cling, but the graceful folds may be used effectively to camouflage figure problems or lead the attention away from them. Taffeta and glossy chintzes will stand away from the body, emphasizing the silhouette. Loosely woven fabrics usually drape well, while firmly woven ones can be easily tailored and molded to your figure. The hand is an especially important texture consideration in choosing fabric for a specific design or figure type.

Different fabrics absorb dye differently and, according to the closeness or looseness of their weave, absorb and reflect light differently. As a result, colors appear brighter or duller according to the texture of the fabric. The rough surface of woolens dulls a color, while the smoothness of satins and velvets intensifies it. Generally, the rougher the texture, the duller the color; the smoother the texture, the more intense the color. Texture may contribute to or detract from the becomingness of a color. When placed near your face, two fabrics of the same color, but of different textures, will produce different effects. Consider texture in order to choose colors which are attractive for you.

When you select fabrics for yourself, consider also the effect of texture on your size and type of figure. Dull-surfaced textures in medium-weight fabrics appear to have a slenderizing effect because they do not have highlights. Pile and fuzzy textures generally tend to add bulkiness, depending on their depth and on the amount of area they cover. Heavy textures are bulky in appearance, adding to the apparent figure size. Crisp textures seem to increase size because they tend to hang away from the natural contours of the body. Shiny or glossy textures also appear to increase size because they reflect light. With practice you can choose fabric textures which drape effectively for your figure type and which reflect color attractively for both your figure and your personal coloring. For further information on fabrics, see Chapter 3.

Fabric Design

With so many fabrics available today, it is wise to know something about fabric design so that both the size and pattern of the designs you choose will be attractive, appropriate, and satisfying.

Designs in fabrics may be small, medium, large, or bold. Regardless of the size, any given design may be realistic, stylized, decorative, or abstract. Each of these types is described here. When selecting fabrics with design, consider the design in relation to the style of the garment, your personality, its effect on

Study the outfits worn by each model. Find positive examples of color *chosen for skin type, garment* line *chosen for figure type, garment* shape *which is becoming to the individual,* texture *which adds individuality to clothing selections, and* fabric design *which adds to the attractiveness of garments.*

your figure, and the occasions for which the garment will be worn. It may then be chosen on the basis of the principles of design as discussed in the next section. For cutting designed fabrics effectively, see Chapter 21.

Realistic Designs   Realistic designs have their basis in fact. Actual photographs or paintings are translated into the design of the fabric. Since such illustrations often lose impact in this type of reproduction, they are not used extensively in fabrics for fashion clothing.

Stylized Designs   Stylized designs are those in which realistic details are eliminated Forms and shapes are merely characterized and simplified to conform to acceptable design and color.

Decorative Designs   Decorative designs usually display themes, subjects, and colors that are derived from primitive or peasant art sources. They tend to show motifs which are not imitations of real objects but merely symbols of them. They usually are simple and employ typical colors.

Courtesy Miss America Division, Brown Shoe Company

Abstract Designs Abstract designs may be geometric or nonrepresentational. Geometric designs include straight lines, directional and crossed bars, circles, dots, triangles, rectangles, squares, or other geometric shapes, or combinations of such shapes. Nonrepresentational designs are characterized by free-flowing lines and shapes.

Principles of Design
The principles of design include balance, rhythm, emphasis, proportion, and harmony.

Whereas the elements of design tell you *what* is included in design, the principles of design tell you *how* the elements are combined. For example, lines, shapes, textures, fabric designs, and colors can be combined in a single outfit. When the design principles are applied effectively, balance, rhythm, emphasis, and proportion result. When each principle is matched against all other principles, harmony is achieved. Each of the outfits featured in the picture above employs some combination of the design principles.

Balance

Balance is the aspect of design which produces equality among its various parts. There are several types of balance. They include:

1. Formal balance, in which one side is like the other.

2. Radial balance, in which all parts are an equal distance from a center point.

3. Informal balance, in which unequal units suggest movement.

When all sides of an object are equal in weight or power of attraction, the article is said to be in balance. In garment design, balance may be achieved through the distribution of structural or decorative lines. A well-designed garment will display pleasing balance, not only from side to side and top to bottom, but also from front to back. For example, the draped neckline of a bodice front may be balanced with softly gathered folds in the skirt back. Balance allows for the distribution of trim and accessories from front to back.

Rhythm

Rhythm is a facet of design that encourages your eye to move from one part of the design to another. Rhythm may be created by:

1. Repeating a color, design, line, or shape.

2. Varying the size of objects, shapes, or lines in a sequence.

3. Using a progression of tints or shades of a color.

4. Shifting progressively from color to adjoining color in the color wheel.

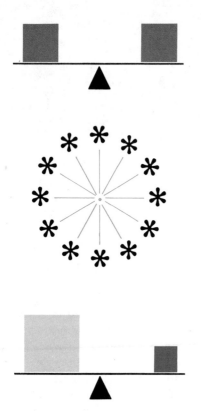

Examples of formal, radial, and informal balance are shown in the drawings above.

Rhythm in design may be created as shown above by repetition, variation, or progression through a single color range or several color ranges.

Whether an outfit is dressy or casual, when the design principles of balance, rhythm, emphasis, and proportion are achieved, the outfit is harmonious in appearance.

TALL, SLIM GIRL

Experiment with high-fashion fabrics.

Select bulky fabrics, bold prints, plaids, checks.

Wear two-piece dresses, tunics, three-quarter-length coats, horizontal and diagonal lines, two-tone color schemes.

Wear full sleeves, full and flared skirts.

TALL, HEAVY GIRL

Select easy-fitting styles that do not fit the body tightly.

Wear slightly flared skirts and two- and three-piece ensembles such as dresses with jackets.

Select smooth-surfaced, dull fabrics.

SHORT, SLIM GIRL

Select vertical lines to create the illusion of height.

Wear slim or gently flared skirts.

Select smooth fabrics and small prints.

SHORT, HEAVY GIRL

Select vertical lines.

Choose V and U necklines and collarless necklines.

Select one-color outfits.

Emphasis

Emphasis in design is the central theme, or singleness of effect, to which the other parts of the design are subordinated. This design principle is sometimes called *dominance*. In dress design, the *center of interest* is the point of emphasis. Without emphasis a dress design looks unplanned or monotonous. Fashion trends often dictate specially designed sleeves, necklines, or hemlines as the center of interest in a costume. This area of emphasis is designated by what the eye sees as the most important focal point. It is reasonable that, when possible, the *primary*, or chief, center of interest

LARGE BUST

Choose garments with details in other areas, such as patch pockets or drape, to detract from too much fullness in bust.

Select vivid colors and nonclinging styles.

Choose vertical lines in bodice and slim sleeves.

Avoid fussy necklines or bodices.

PROTRUDING ABDOMEN

Choose a broad shoulder line and flared skirt.

Select dresses with detail that directs attention away from center front, such as side-draped skirts.

Avoid trim or buttons down center front, sloping shoulder lines, or tight-fitting skirts.

WIDE HIPS

Choose styles that emphasize the upper half of the body such as a dull-surfaced skirt fabric with shiny blouse fabric or vertical lines in skirt.

Avoid horizontal lines or tight skirts that tend to draw attention to the hip area.

SWAYBACK FIGURE

Choose garments with fullness in back.

Experiment with straight-hanging overblouses and dresses and suits with boxy jackets that cover the sway-back area.

Avoid snug-fitting styles such as dresses with princess lines.

in a garment be located near the face, because the face is the most interesting and individual feature of a person

In effective costume design, there is also a point of *secondary* emphasis. For example, if a frilly blouse is the point of primary emphasis with a tailored dark suit, consider carrying a small, bright-colored purse as a point of secondary emphasis.

Proportion

Proportion is the comparative relationship of one part to another and of all parts to the whole with respect to size or quantity. Effective placement results in good design proportions. In clothing design the lines in a fabric design or the design lines in a garment may be positioned effectively on the figure so as to relate a certain measure of width to a certain measure of height, or vice-versa. Few people are endowed with perfect body proportions, but design lines can be utilized to improve the appearance of natural proportions, as shown in the section "Charting Your Figure for Creative Use of Design."

Harmony

Harmony is the pleasing relationship among all parts within a whole. When an outfit is harmonious, the lines in the fabric design, the structural and decorative lines, and the accessories are consistent with each other. They relate to each other, to the total design, and to the person wearing the garment. Harmony in dress requires also that (1) your hairdo and neckline are related to the shape of your face and the shape of your garment; (2) the fabric design and the style of your garment are in keeping with its purpose; (3) the accessories are in keeping with, but subordinated to, your outfit; (4) fundamental design principles are used in the selection and combination of all items of the ensemble; and (5) there is unity in the color scheme.

Complete harmony means a unified oneness. The selection of each part of a well-harmonized costume is made in relation to the other parts with regard to design, color, shape, and size.

Charting Your Figure for Creative Use of Design

It is possible to chart your figure in a way that shows your physical proportions. By comparing your proportions to standard body proportions, you can determine whether parts of your figure are longer or shorter or wider or narrower than the standard.

An understanding of your own figure proportions allows you to improve the appearance of your silhouette. Once you understand your own figure weaknesses, you can hide them in a number of ways. You can choose clothes that *exaggerate or build out* areas of your silhouette to compensate for figure faults, you can select clothes that *cover up* deviations from the standard figure, or you can *direct attention away* from one part of your figure to another.

A chart of your actual figure is very helpful in evaluating your figure. To make such a chart, you will need someone to help you. You will also need the following list of supplies: a piece of shelf or wrapping paper large enough to accommodate a full-size diagram of your figure, a 6-inch-by-12-inch right triangle cut from cardboard, a pencil, masking tape, and a ruler.

The chart may be made as follows:

1. Mark the center of the paper by folding it in half lengthwise.

2. With masking tape, attach the top edge of the paper to a wall or door at a height slightly above that of your head. Crease the paper at the floor level.

STANDARD BODY PROPORTIONS

Standard lengths   The hipline divides the figure in half. A line at the underarm level divides the upper half of the figure equally, and the knees divide the legs equally.

Standard widths   The front view of today's ideal silhouette is a slender figure with shoulders as wide as hips, or slightly wider, and with a narrow waistline.

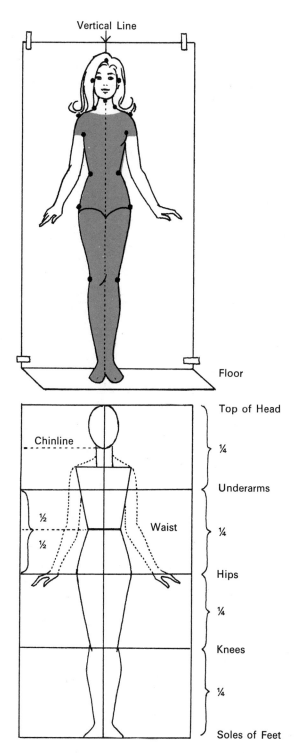

Vertical Line

Floor

Top of Head

Chinline

¼

Underarms

½

½   Waist

¼

Hips

¼

Knees

¼

Soles of Feet

The ideally proportioned figure divides into quarters at the underarms, hips, and knees.

3. Stand, without shoes, with your back against the paper and with your figure centered on the center-fold line.

4. Ask your assistant to mark the points indicated in the figure on the left. For accuracy, use the triangle as a level by holding it with the 6-inch edge against the wall and the 12-inch edge touching the figure at the point to be recorded. Make a pencil dot where the right angle touches the paper. To determine your head length, turn your cheek to the wall so that your assistant can mark a dot at the chin level on the center line.

5. Draw lines to connect the dots. This will produce a basic diagram of the lengths and widths of your figure. Draw the contour of the head as shown in the figure on the left.

6. To find how your figure differs from the standard lengths for a figure of your height, divide your paper figure into fourths horizontally. To do this, fold your figure diagram in half crosswise and then fold it in half crosswise again. The standard lengths indicated by these fold lines can be compared to your own figure length which is indicated on the chart by the horizontal lines. If your body proportions are standard, the crease lines will fall exactly at your underarm, hip, and knee.

Lines and Shapes
for Length Proportions
Most young girls have some variations from ideal length proportions. Most of these variations can be concealed by adjusting the length of the bodice, skirt, jacket, sweater, or sleeves. To conceal figure faults, choose design lines that appear to shorten the garment area where your figure is proportionately long. Choose design lines that appear to lengthen the garment area where your figure is proportionately short.

The drawings on the following pages give ideas for adjustments in lines and shapes of garments which will produce the illusion of an ideal silhouette. Study the drawings in relation to your figure faults and possible choices which will hide them.

51

A line at the knee of the center figure in drawing A is at a height one-fourth the total height of the figure. Use this standard proportion as a guide for adjusting your hemline to best accommodate your own length proportions. For all three of the figures below to appear to be wearing knee-length skirts, the hemlines are adjusted by this standard rather than by leg length or location of knee.

A. ADJUSTING SKIRT LENGTH

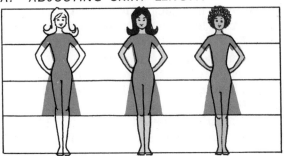

The length of the jacket on the center figure in drawing B produces a pleasing relationship between skirt and jacket. The longer jacket at the left adds the illusion of length to a relatively short body and makes the long legs appear shorter by revealing a shorter expanse of skirt. The shorter jacket at the right breaks the long line of the body and makes the short legs seem longer by disclosing a longer expanse of skirt.

Evaluate your own body proportions. If your body is short in comparison to the average figure, choose long jackets and sweaters. If your legs are short, choose short jackets and sweaters to make them appear longer.

B. ADJUSTING JACKET LENGTH

If, like the center figure in C below, you have standard proportions, probably you can wear all sleeve lengths equally well. The longer sleeves at the left add apparent length to a short body. The shorter sleeves at the right break the length of the long body.

For general good proportion, choose short sleeves if your body is long and long sleeves if your body is short.

C. ADJUSTING LENGTH OF SLEEVE

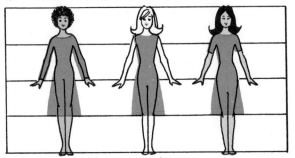

Horizontal lines, made by belts, yokes, or accessories in D below, can be placed to divide your figure lengths pleasingly. On the center figure, the yoke and accessory direct attention toward the face and emphasize the height of the figure. The low waistline lengthens the shorter body line and breaks up the long leg length of the figure at the left. The high, Empire-line bodice at the right is well chosen for concealing the long line of the body and making the legs appear longer. While longer-waisted garments and overblouses make the body appear longer, high-waisted garments or those without waistlines make a long body appear to have better proportion.

D. EFFECTS OF HORIZONTAL LINES

Lines and Shapes
for Width Proportions

The width proportions are as important to the ideal silhouette as the lengths. Two width deviations common to many are a wide waistline and a wider-than-standard hipline.

By exaggerating, or building out, the silhouette at the shoulders, a triangular silhouette is formed. This silhouette directs attention away from the wide waist of the figure below left and the wide hipline of the figure at the right. This silhouette, less exaggerated, can bring the width proportions of both of these figures into better balance.

E. CONCEALING WIDTH WITH INVERTED TRIANGLES

A triangular silhouette made by widening the hemline can be used to balance width proportions. This silhouette minimizes the wider waist of the left figure below. The wider hemline at the right extends from an easy fit over the hips, camouflaging the hip width. Flared skirts are flattering to those who have both a broad waist and broad hips.

F. CONCEALING WIDTH WITH BROAD-BASE TRIANGLES

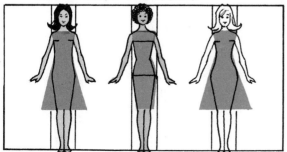

The hourglass silhouette below (left) adds width at both shoulders and hem. This silhouette can minimize either waist or hip width or both. The diamond shape at the right leads the eye away from both hips and waist.

G. CONCEALING WIDTH WITH COMBINATION TRIANGLES

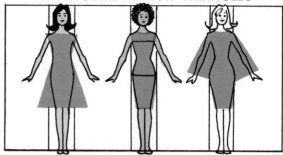

Straight-hanging coats, rectangular in silhouette, conceal both the wide waist below (left) and the wide hips (right).

H. CONCEALING WIDTH WITH RECTANGLES

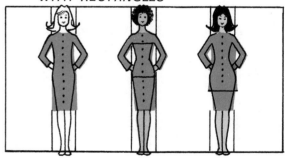

Inner design lines (below) can be chosen to break up plain expanses into smaller areas.

I. EFFECTS OF VERTICAL LINES

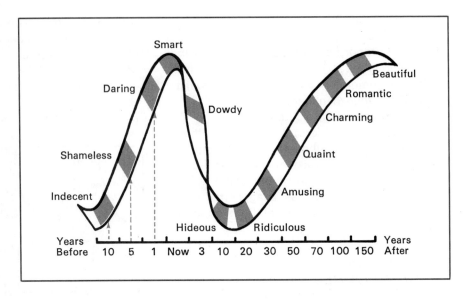

What is fashion?

In what ways do young consumers help determine the fashions which are available for purchase?

How can it be shown that fashion is an aspect of our culture which revolves in a type of cycle?

How are current fashions influenced by other cultures?

What are the advantages and disadvantages to be found in creating fashions in miniature?

Using Creativity in Youthful Fashion

Each of the more than 12 million young people in this country is a potential buyer of clothing. Business firms are searching for creative people who are sensitive to the young consumer's needs and who can satisfy youth by creating fashionable clothing. Such people are able to predetermine, at least to a degree, the kinds of clothing youth will demand. They can design, produce, and display such clothing so that fashions are accepted by large numbers of young people. If you have a high degree of interest in fashion consider it as a potential career as you study the rest of this chapter and Chapter 7.

The Cycle of Fashion

Fashion is a projection through clothing of the attitudes and feelings of a group of people at a given point in time. Many styles are considered indecent ten years before their time, daring one year before their time, and chic when in vogue. Then they become dowdy as they pass out of fashion.

Perhaps in the area of fashion more than in any other area, the need for a generation gap is unnecessary. Since fashion moves in cycles, repeating itself from time to time, fashion of 50 or 100 years ago may become high fashion again today. As a result fashion becomes a natural vehicle for communication between youth and their parents and grandparents.

Cultural and Historical Influences on Fashion

Designers travel far and wide to receive inspiration for today's fashions. They study the costumes of various cultures and different periods of time. They travel to every country in the world looking for customs and dress which can inspire their new creations.

Look at the fashions being worn by members of your class. What cultural influences do you see in current fashion? Many fads and fashions can be related to source countries or specific periods of time.

Creative Design Studios

Fiber and fabric companies are continually developing creative ways for marketing fashion. For example, one large fiber company has a design studio housing a revolving team of relatively unknown designers whose work is featured nationwide. Such an arrangement offers young designers opportunities to express themselves freely, presenting their individual creativity.

If you become interested in creative design, be certain your ideas are workable. Whether you are creating for reproduction on a limited scale or for a mass market, it is necessary to formulate ideas which can be translated into real products.

Successful Young Designers

There are a number of young people who have made history because of their creativity. Every year you can read about people in their teens or early twenties who have made scientific inventions or discoveries, written plays, or composed original music. Others are making inroads into the field of creative clothing design.

Courtesy The Palm Beach Company

Fashion is often inspired by cultural or historical influences.

A number of young women have become famous for design in the area of costume accessories. One such young woman explains that she may get an idea for designing a pair of earrings from the shape of a curtain blown by the wind. She is the chief designer for a major jewelry manufacturer which sells to 8,000 jewelry and department stores. She admits that the long hours of practice which were necessary for developing her first ambition to become a ballerina gave her good work habits which have helped her to succeed as a designer.

The inventor of the electronic dress is another type of young fashion designer. She studied mechanical engineering and design. Putting this training to use, she decided to combine art and technology to create unusual garments. For example, into one of the dresses she designed, she sewed strips of electroluminescent lamps. A small battery-driven power pack was fitted onto the belt. By turning the knob of the power pack, she was able to turn the lamps on and off in a programmed rhythm.

Creative Clothing Selection

There are a number of ways to creatively choose clothing. Effectively chosen clothing expresses the creativity of its owner. It accentuates the strong points of the figure while minimizing the deficiencies. To creatively choose clothing, you need to be aware of the effects of color and the other design elements on your total image and to use the principles of design to your advantage. Often when looking in a mirror, the temptation to look at your own facial features prevents you from looking at your figure objectively. If so, consider asking a friend to take some simple snapshots of you. By looking at such pictures, you will be able to pick out flaws in the clothing you have chosen and worn. Such pictures will also call attention to your figure faults.

Unimaginative clothing choices may soon be largely eliminated through the use of the *fashion mirror*. The fashion mirror is a creative-clothing-selection tool which cuts down on the necessary number of fittings when clothing is being chosen. It helps a shopper immediately see her own image in a particular outfit. Some stores feature the use of the fashion mirror only in their bridal salons. However, this complicated piece of machinery is moving into other areas of large department stores because of the time and effort it saves.

The fashion mirror might be used in the following manner. A shopper who wishes to select a new outfit might sit before a specially designed mirror in a room in the fashion salon. A figure similar to a dressmaker's form is adjusted to her size. The figure disappears, and in its place the young woman sees an image of herself standing, in color, in an outfit she has never seen, touched, or tried on. She can determine whether or not she likes it. She can reject those outfits she does not like, reexamine the ones she likes best, and narrow down her selection to the one or two she really wants to try on for a final choice.

Creating Fashions in Miniature

Many fashion designers feel that industry is paying a premium by producing models of fashions at full size. They feel that size has caused creativity to become expensive and thus almost extinct. To offset this expense, mini-machines, mini-plants, and mini-facilities are coming into prominence. Thus the fashion industry is beginning to develop techniques for trying the new fibers, the new weaves, the new styles, and the new processes speedily and at a fraction of the cost of working on full-sized models.

As fashion in miniature grows in popularity, teaching tools are being developed to teach various phases of the fashion industry. Design and draping, selecting and handling new fabrics and design, fashion illustration and display, and reproduction of historic costumes are being considered in terms of effective tools for teaching in miniature. These miniature tools take different forms. Some find the quarter-sized dress forms a good experimental tool. Others like a fashion minikin proportioned to the size of the young figure. Still others use wood, cardboard, or foam figures for experimentation.

Each tool has its advantages and disadvantages. Regardless of the form of miniature chosen, fashion in miniature enables a designer to think more creatively because it frees the mind from consideration of personal figure and fitting problems. Since only a small amount of fabric is required, the designers can work with beautiful, luxurious fabrics at greatly reduced costs. This allows for wider experience with color, texture, line, and handling and reduces the amount of time required to create a particular fashion. Thus outstanding creations can be copied in full size and poor designs discarded.

Color artwork for Chapter 2 provided by Consumer Relations Department of Sperry Hutchinson Company
Proportion artwork for Chapter 2 adapted from material provided by Frances Quinn and the University of California Extension Service

GROUP LEARNING EXPERIENCES

1. Plan a trip to an art museum. Study the paintings and sculpture regarding their use of color and the other elements of design.

2. Hold a *Design-in.* Agree on a basic fabric. Then let each student design and create an item different from the uses for which the fabric was designed.

3. Plan a History of Costume party. Allow each class member to choose a costume to wear to the party. See whether class members can guess the period of history in which each costume was popular and the person who made the costume famous.

4. Assemble illustrations for one of the following: clothing, a symbol; clothing, a mirror of the time. Discuss the illustrations in class.

5. Find examples of each principle of design in the outfits worn by class members or shown in fashion magazines.

6. Plan a trip to the fabric counter of a department store to observe the current trends in designed fabrics. Describe the scale and size of the designs in the fabrics, the season's color trends, and the types of designs currently featured.

7. Working in teams, experiment with lines to demonstrate their effect on the figure of each member of the team. Let each team member wear a plain dark outfit. Pin white tape to it to mark off the body with lines, both horizontally and vertically. Then try diagonals and curves. Shift the lines to different positions, and study not only the lines but also the geometric shapes they form. Determine which lines and shapes flatter each person and which do not. Cut collars and necklines from fabric or paper. Try them on to find out which shapes are most becoming.

HELPING OTHERS TO LEARN

1. Obtain permission from school authorities to plan an accessory boutique. Merchandise, promote, and sell the items you can purchase from manufacturing sources. Select items that are not in competition with those in your local stores. Plan how you will use your profits.

2. Plan a display showing how historic fashions influence current fashions.

3. Prepare a bulletin-board display to illustrate style, fad, and fashion.

1. If you have made the chart of your proportions discussed on pages 50 through 51, draw a 12-inch-high miniature of your figure chart on graph paper. Using tracing paper over the chart, experiment with necklines, hemlines, jacket lengths, and sleeve lengths. Which ones are best for you?

2. Determine the hue, value, and intensity of your skin, hair, and eyes. What illusion do you want to create? Try on a wide variety of colors. Make a chart to show which colors are becoming, which are wearable, and which do nothing for you.

3. Make a head and hair analysis. With the help of a partner, determine your head shape by using a light to project the front view of your head onto drawing paper. Tie your hair back and pencil in the silhouette of your head. Study your features in a mirror, and determine how your hair shapes your face. Decide which features to emphasize and to de-emphasize.

4. Cut from the center of a 12-inch-high card the shape of a garment. Place the card over pieces of fabric of various tints and shades of warm and cool colors. From a distance, observe the effect of various colors on the apparent size of the silhouette. How does this information affect your choice of colors for clothing?

5. Find illustrations in pattern books or magazines of costumes with formal and informal balance, vertical and horizontal balance, and balance from front to back.

6. Collect swatches of designed fabrics which would be good choices for various garments in your wardrobe.

7. Find examples of rhythm in nature. Find illustrations of garments that use dominance, rhythm, proportion, harmony, and balance in design. Indicate the details that illustrate each principle.

8. Find pictures of garments that illustrate formal, radial, and informal balance.

9. Experiment with different accessories, determining whether each creates a good or poor effect in relation to the outfit you are wearing.

10. Explore the small, unusual shops and boutiques in your community. Talk with the owners to determine how they got started in business. Share your experience with your classmates.

11. Investigate the various programs that are sponsored by businesses in your community that offer an opportunity for you to explore the degree of your creativity in the areas of grooming, modeling, design, and clothing construction.

12. Design and make your dress or wardrobe in miniature before you make it full size. Analyze whether the experience helped you in handling the fabric and creating your design.

Understanding Modern Fabrics

How much does today's consumer need to know about modern fabrics? Research and development in this field move forward so rapidly that even the specialist must limit himself to a specific fabric or apparel area. However, the consumer, to be effective as a buyer and user of modern fabrics and clothing, must know enough about them to buy and care for a wide variety wisely.

What are the two broad groups of fibers used in the making of fabrics?

What are the natural protein fibers which are commonly used in modern clothing construction? The natural cellulosic fibers? The man-made cellulosic fibers? The man-made noncellulosic fibers?

What characteristics of a fabric affect its performance?

What are the advantages of man-made fibers which look like silk over natural silk?

What are some general limitations of most of the man-made fibers?

How do spun and filament yarns differ?

Factors Affecting Fabric Performance

The average young person living at home spends more for clothing than for any other budgeted item. Since most clothes are made either entirely or partially of fabric, perhaps it is wise to study fabrics, particularly from a viewpoint of *performance.* Some are beautiful but are poor choices for garment fabrics because they cannot be made into clothing which looks stylish in current silhouettes. Some are beautiful but the cost of care makes them impractical for everyday wear. A wide range of fabrics, however, can fit into a stylish, serviceable wardrobe if selected wisely and cared for properly.

Learn to study fabrics analytically. Learn to carefully analyze the care instructions provided on their labels. Prejudge how they will perform in action. When you are able to evaluate fabrics, you can buy clothing with increased effectiveness.

Actually, there are seven factors of fabric performance to be considered before purchasing a garment. Learn to consider each of them regardless of the garment you are choosing. These factors are: *fiber content, yarn construction, fabric construction, colorfastness, applied surface design, finishes,* and *compatibility of garment components.*

Fiber Content

Fiber content, probably more than any other single factor, affects the performance of a fabric. Sometimes, however, it is fiber in the trimming rather than in the actual garment which reduces the performance qualities of a garment. Whether for the garment or the trim, only quality fiber can be made into fabric that will look and wear well. Fiber also largely determines the type of care a garment requires.

Fibers may be generally divided into two classifications: *natural* and *man-made.* In the

NATURAL FIBERS

Fiber	Advantages	Limitations
Protein Fibers Silk	Luxurious, strong, wrinkle resistant, absorbent. Dries quickly, resists soiling. Dyes and prints readily and holds color.	Weakened by perspiration and sunlight. Damaged by acids and alkalies. Can be attacked by insects. Yellows with age.
Wool	Warm, comfortable. Absorbs moisture readily. Holds shape and creases well. Naturally water and flame resistant. Resistant to acids.	Can be damaged by alkalies. Susceptible to moth and carpet beetle damage.
Hair Fibers Camel Vicuna Alpaca Llama Angora Cashmere	Soft, beautiful, luxurious.	Expensive. Pill readily. Fibers wear off. Shrink, mat, and felt readily if not properly cared for.
Cellulosic Fibers Cotton	Strong, durable. Dyes and prints readily. Adaptable to many finishing treatments, surface treatments, and fabric constructions. Comfortable. Absorbs moisture readily.	Creases and wrinkles readily unless treated. Susceptible to attack by mildew, rot, and silverfish. Weakened by acids such as found in perspiration. Weakened by permanent-press finishes. Shrinkage is high.
Linen	Strong. Absorbs moisture readily. Dries quickly. Dyes well except for dark colors.	More expensive than cotton. Wrinkles readily unless treated. Finishes decrease comfort and strength. Susceptible to mildew, rot, and color loss.
Jute (Burlap)	Special design effects.	Low fabric strength. Damaged by light. Scratchy, stiff, brittle; breaks on folds. Wrinkles easily; snags readily; lints badly. Difficult to dye. Sometimes develops odor.

charts on pages 60-65 they are subdivided into *natural proteins* and *natural cellulosics,* *man-made cellulosics,* and *man-made non-cellulosic.* The word *cellulosic* comes from the word *cellulose,* of which the cell walls of most plants are composed. The generic fiber groups described in the charts represent those most widely used in consumer goods. Silk, wool, cotton, and linen are called natural fibers because they are used in their natural forms in fabrics. Acetate, triacetate, and rayon are termed man-made cellulosic fibers because they are made from plants. The remaining fibers are made completely in the laboratory and are called noncellulosic because they are made from chemicals rather than cellulose.

Today's trend is toward an increased use of the noncellulosics. Most popular among this group according to volume produced are the

Recommended Cleaning Procedure	Heat Setting for Ironing or Pressing
Hand-wash in slightly warm water or dry clean. Avoid detergents.	Low setting.
Special care required in laundering or drycleaning.	Low setting.
Dryclean only.	Low setting.
Can be laundered or drycleaned. White and colorfast cottons can be washed in hot water. Resistant to alkalies.	High setting.
Launder in warm water or dryclean. Resistant to alkalies.	High setting.
Dryclean unless manufacturer recommends laundering.	Low setting.

Courtesy Celanese Fibers Marketing Co.

Modern fabrics undergo extensive research in which their performance and attractiveness under normal wear and care conditions are tested.

nylons, the acrylics, and the polyesters. Nylon is used extensively in hosiery and undergarments. The acrylics are used widely in sweaters. The polyesters are used in blends with cotton for blouses and shirts and in double-knit fashion garments. The popularity of the noncellulosic group is based primarily on their ease of care.

Some trademark names are listed in the charts for easy identification. These charts list some of the advantages, limitations, and care suggestions for fabrics of 100 percent fiber composition. Blends must be treated as the most delicate fiber in the blend.

Yarn Construction
Yarn construction is a very important consideration in analyzing fabrics. It helps determine the appearance, durability, serviceability, care, and performance of a fabric.

MAN-MADE CELLULOSIC FIBERS

Fiber	Advantages	Limitations
Rayon Avril Bemberg Fibro Nupron	Absorbent, comfortable, resistant to alkalies and moths. Takes dyes and finishes readily. Holds color.	Low strength unless treated. Shrinks unless stabilized. Wrinkles badly unless treated. Damaged by acids and permanent-press finishes. Susceptible to mildew.
Acetate Avisco Acele Celara knits Estron	Resists wrinkling. Resistant to acids, alkalies, mildew, and moths. Excellent colorfastness in solution-dyed fibers.	Loses strength when wet. Affected by light. Heat sensitive; glazes at 300° F. Dissolves in common spotting agents such as acetone. Some dyes affected by conditions in atmosphere.
Triacetate Arnel	Better abrasion resistance than acetate. Can be heat-set for shrinkage control. Takes dye readily. Quick drying; resistant to glazing. Resists moths and mildew. Not affected by weak acids and alkalies. Excellent pleating capabilities.	Will shrink or stretch if not heat-set. Some dyes affected by gases in the atmosphere.

Yarns may be classified as single, plied, or blended. They may be made from staples, or short cuts of fibers, or they may be smooth, long continuous filaments many yards in length. A *single* yarn is made from a single filament or from a group of filaments or staples twisted into a single yarn, whereas a *plied* yarn is made when two or more yarns are twisted together. *Blends* of two different man-made fibers or a man-made fiber and a natural fiber are probably the most common of all yarns. With blended yarns, fabrics can be made with desirable hand, strength, and wrinkle resistance. The variations in yarn construction which may be made to produce unusual appearances and textures are almost limitless. Examples include bouclé, nub, slub, snarl, and spiral or corkscrew yarns.

Many yarns are textured during the spinning process. Because most of the man-made fibers are softened by heat, they may be crimped or twisted during spinning. This texturing adds to the varieties in appearance and uses available in each of the fiber categories.

What are five processes by which fabric can be constructed?

What is a fabric made by interlocking fibers?

How do the processes of weaving and knitting differ?

How is weft insertion similar to and different from both weaving and knitting?

What are some advantages and disadvantages to be found in bonded fabrics?

What factors commonly affect the colorfastness of a fabric?

How can a finish which is applied to a fabric be evaluated?

Why is it important that all components of a garment be compatible with one another?

Fabric Construction

Fabric construction works together with fiber content and yarn construction to determine such qualities as the appearance, hand, strength, absorbency, warmth, and beauty of a fabric. These qualities in turn affect the performance of a fabric in wear and care.

Recommended Cleaning Procedure	Heat Setting for Ironing or Pressing
Launder in warm water or dryclean.	Medium to low setting.
Hand-launder in cool water or dryclean.	Low setting.
Launder in warm water or dryclean.	Medium setting.

Whether buying ready-made garments or fabrics, consider the performance a fabric can be expected to give before the purchase is made.

There are many varieties of fabric construction. They include the interlocking of fibers, braiding, lace making, weaving, and knitting. Various of the fabrics so constructed may be laminated, bonded, coated, quilted, or molded. Mali fabrics and deep-pile fabrics are still other variations.

Interlocking of Fibers

The two major methods of making fabrics by the interlocking of fibers are felting and bonding. *Felting* is the oldest known method of fabric construction. Felted fibers are compressed together by the application of heat, moisture, agitation, and pressure. Chemical action may also be used to make felt fabrics. Originally, felt was made of 100 percent wool. But modern felts are also made of wool combined with rayon, hair, or man-made fibers.

Bonding of fibers to make a nonwoven fabric is a relatively new process. Fibers are usually bonded by heat which melts one or more man-made fiber ingredients, causing the fibers to bond together when compressed.

MAN-MADE NONCELLULOSIC FIBERS[1]

Fiber	Advantages	Limitations

Acrylic
  Orlon
  Acrilan
  Creslan
  Zefran
	Shrink and stretch resistant if heat-set. Good crease and pleat retention when heat-set. Good resistance to sun and weather. Resists acid and alkaline substances. Good abrasion resistance.	Low absorption. Melts easily; pills readily. Generates static unless treated. Wrinkles can become heat-set during extraction and drying cycles.

Anidex Anim/8	Good recovery. Can be dyed, printed, and finished by traditional processes. Retains whiteness.	Useful mainly for stretch garments such as girdles and swimwear.

Metallic
  Lurex
  Lamé
  Metlon
  Mylar
	Adds shiny appearance to garments.	Some tarnish.

Modacrylic
  Dynel
  Verel
	Resistant to moths, mildew, insect damage. Also alkaline and acid resistant. Good pleat and crease retention if heat-set.	Melts. Generates static unless specially treated. Poor absorption and dyeability.

Nylon
  Antron
  Qiana
  Caprolan Touch
  Cantrece
  Many others
	Strong. Quick drying. Resists mildew and insect damage. Resists alkalines.	Melts. Low moisture absorption. Poor color resistance to light. Generates static unless specially treated. Affected by acids. Subject to pilling.

Olefin
  Marvess
  Herculon
	Resistant to acids, alkalines, micro-organisms, insects. High strength; abrasion and weather resistant. Dries quickly. Good for outdoor carpets and upholstery.	Low absorption. Very heat sensitive. Poor dyeability.

Polyester
  Dacron
  Fortrel
  Kodel
  Quintess
  Trevira
	Strong. Wrinkle resistant. Stable to shrinking and stretching if heat-set. Good crease and pleat retention if heat-set. Resistant to moths and mildew.	Low absorption. Holds oily-type soil and stains tenaciously. Some fabrics pill readily.

Rubber Lastex	High strength and holding power.	Discolors with perspiration and age. Loses elasticity and breaks with laundering and wear. Affected adversely by drycleaning solvents.

Spandex
  Lycra
  Vyrene
	High elasticity and strength. Resists perspiration, cosmetic oils, and lotions.	Discoloration of some fabrics in wear.

[1] Glass and saran are omitted because they are not used in wearing apparel. Azlon, lastrile, vinal, and vinyon are omitted because they are not currently manufactured in the United States.

Recommended Cleaning Procedure	Heat Setting for Ironing or Pressing
Launder in warm water or dryclean.	Medium setting.
Launder in warm water or dryclean.	Low setting.
Some are drycleanable only; others are washable in warm water.	Low setting.
Launder in warm water or dryclean.	Low setting.
Launder in warm water or dryclean.	Low setting.
Launder or dryclean.	Do not iron or press.
Launder in warm water or dryclean.	Medium to low setting.
Launder in warm water. Do not dryclean.	Do not iron.
Launder in warm water or dryclean. Do *not* use chlorine bleach.	Low setting.

Blended single yarns can be made by spinning together two or more fibers such as spun polyester and cotton.

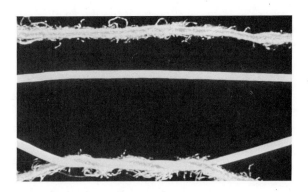

Plied yarns can be made by spinning together two separate yarns such as wool and monofilament nylon.

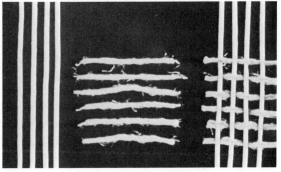

Photos courtesy Eastman Chemical Products, Inc.

Blended fabrics can be made as shown above by interweaving yarns composed of one fiber with yarns composed of another or by weaving together blended yarns such as those shown in the upper photographs.

YARNS CLASSIFIED AS TO RAW MATERIALS

Staple and spun yarns

Cotton	*Carded:* Made from fibers of varying lengths.
	Combed: The short cotton fibers are removed. Only the long cotton fibers are laid parallel and twisted. Quality is generally better than in carded.
	Mercerized: A chemical treatment to make the yarns stronger and more lustrous. The yarns also shrink less than other cotton yarns.
	Pima: Long, fine staple Peruvian cotton.
	Supima: American-grown long staple cotton.
Wool	*Woolen:* Short wool fibers twisted to make a soft, hairy yarn.
	Worsted: Wool fibers laid parallel to make a smooth, highly twisted yarn.
Man-made	*Staple:* Man-made filament fibers cut into lengths that can be spun on cotton or wool spinning systems.

Filament yarns

Silk	*Cultivated:* Continuous long, fine strands.
	Douppioni: A silk filament that comes from two or more cocoons that have grown together. This results in an uneven double yarn.
	Tussah or wild: Made from coarse, uneven silk filaments of uncultivated silk worms.
Man-made	*Filaments:* Very small, individual, long, smooth, round or shaped threads twisted together. Can be made of any man-made fiber.

Predictions call for a growth in the nonwoven fabric market to 1.1 billion dollars by 1980. The greatest market for these specialty fabrics seems to be in the industrial and institutional markets in such forms as disposable surgical gowns and sheets. But some people predict they will also find their way into the clothing market. In fact, they have been in this market for some time in the form of nonwoven interfacings (see page 450).

Braiding

Three or more yarns may be interlaced lengthwise and diagonally to form a fabric. This fabric construction is used most widely for trimmings, accessories, mats, and rugs.

Lace Making

The making of lace fabrics, which includes nets, is an art. It is a very complex method of fabric manufacture using three or more sets of yarns. Laces are classified as to method of construction. These methods include the lever, bobbinet, Nottingham, and Schiffli methods of lace making.

When you buy lace fabric, ask whether it has been stabilized for shrinkage control. Lace fabrics are under tension in manufacture. Drycleaning and the steaming in finishing often release the fibers, causing shrinkage if the lace has not been stabilized. Some laces are heavily sized, and if the sizing is disturbed, they may shrink. Studies show that some laces may

Wool, the most widely used of the natural protein fibers, is used in stylish knits as well as in tailored woven garments.

Cotton, the most widely used of the natural cellulosic fibers, is frequently used in children's school and play clothes.

Rayon and acetate, the common man-made cellulosic fibers, are often used in fairly high-priced garments chosen more for vivid color and style than for everyday hard wear.

Modern man-made noncellulosic fibers are used in all types of garments in which style, beauty, wear, and ease of care are essential.

shrink as much as 10 percent. If you think there is a potential problem, preshrink the lace before using it, as you would shrink a woven fabric (see pages 265-266).

When you buy lace clothing, note the underarm and side seams. Are they ample in width and well finished? Shallow seams pull out with strain in wear. Observe buttonholes. Unfinished or machine-stitched buttonholes fray readily.

Bonded laces, in general, wear and clean well. Some do not, however, as they may separate from the layer of backing or may shrink. The textile industry is continually trying to improve the performance of the various types of laces.

In vinyl-coated laces, observe the manufacturer's recommendations on proper care. The majority require wetcleaning. Many bear labels stating, *Do Not Dryclean.* If so, treat them as delicate washable fabrics.

Examine reembroidered laces. The braid, ribbon, yarn, or cellophane may be stitched to the background with a chain stitch. Once the stitching is broken, damage occurs and the trim falls away. This is also true of beading and sequins which are attached to lace or other fabrics.

Weaving

Woven fabrics are made by the interlacing of two or more sets of yarns at right angles to produce a fabric. The lengthwise yarns are called *warp;* the crosswise yarns, *filling.* While the types of weaves are numerous, the common ones include the plain weave, the twill weave, the satin weave, and the pile weave.

The *plain weave* is the simplest of all weaves. Each filling yarn passes alternately over and under each warp yarn. Examples of plain-weave fabrics include broadcloth and muslin.

The *twill weave* is characterized by diagonal ridges formed by yarns which are exposed on the surface. These may vary in angle from a low slope to a very steep slope, depending upon the design by which heavy yarns pass

over fine yarns. Twill weaves are closer in texture, heavier, and sturdier than plain weaves. They can be produced in many fancy designs. Common variations of the twill weave include herringbone, gabardine, covert, calvary twill, serge, and whipcord.

The *satin weave* is characterized by floating yarns used to produce a high luster on one side of the fabric. Slightly twisted warp yarns float, or pass, over four or more filling yarns. The low twist and the floating of the warp yarns produce a high degree of light reflection, which gives a lustrous appearance. High-twist yarns may be used for the filling. There are many weights of satin fabrics, varying from very lightweight chiffon satin to heavy Duchesse satin. Sateen is a variation of the satin weave. It is made of cotton rather than silk or·man-made fibers.

Pile-weave fabrics are made with three sets of yarns. One set is perpendicular to the other two. The back of the fabric may be plain, twill, or satin weave into which an extra set of warp or filling yarns is woven to form the pile surface. Velvet, velveteen, plush, and corduroy are fabrics made with a pile weave.

Sometimes a pile fabric is made with two pieces of cloth woven at the same time, face to face. A knife on the loom cuts the binding yarn, thus producing fabrics with a short pile surface. When a fabric is not cut apart, it is called a *double cloth weave.* Double-faced ribbons and double-faced coating and jacket fabrics are examples of fabrics made by the double-cloth weaving process.

Knitting

Knitting is a process of fabric making which is carried out by bending, or curving, yarns into a series of interlocking loops. While knitting has been produced by hand as a single yarn process for centuries, most of today's knits are made on machines which can knit with many threads in a simultaneous operation.

Authorities predict that knits will dominate the fashion scene during the decade

Plain Weave

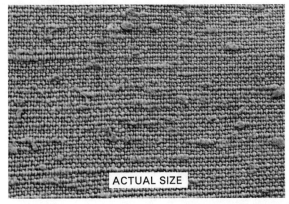

ACTUAL SIZE

Courtesy Talon Educational Services

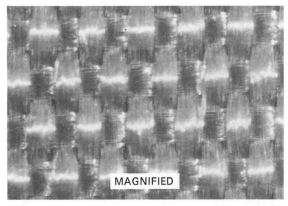

MAGNIFIED

USDA Photo

Twill Weave

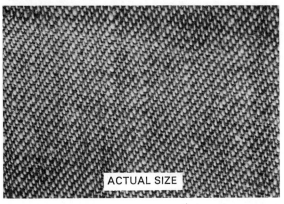

ACTUAL SIZE

Courtesy Talon Educational Services

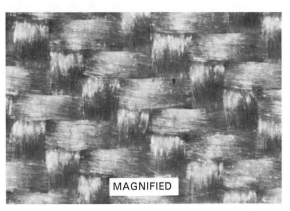

MAGNIFIED

USDA Photo

Satin Weave

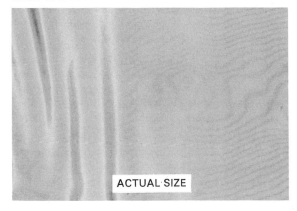

ACTUAL SIZE

MAGNIFIED

USDA Photo

Of all the fabric weaves available today, the plain, twill, and satin weaves remain most popular.

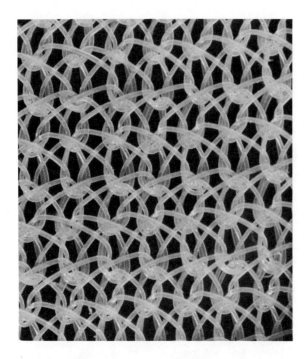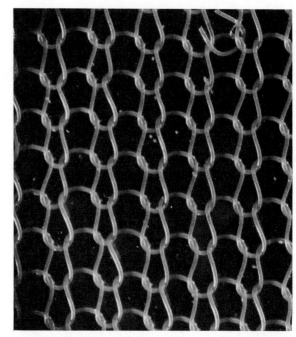

Warp knits (left), such as tricot and raschel fabrics, tend to stretch most in a crosswise direction, while weft knits (right), such as jersey and double knits, tend to stretch a limited amount in both directions.

ahead. During the 1980s, well over half of all the clothing worn in this country may be made of knitted fabrics.

What reasons might account for this big growth in the knitted-fashion industry? The reasons seem to be numerous and varied. People like to wear comfortable, easily-cared-for clothing, and knits fit into this category. The machinery used for making knits can be more easily manipulated to allow for more creativity, or inventiveness, than do traditional weaving looms. Fiber manufacturers have been able to produce yarns of content and texture which can be used for knitting beautiful, luxurious fabrics. Knits can be manufactured more speedily than can most traditional woven fabrics. All these reasons combine to indicate that knits may dominate the fabric market of the future.

Knitting terminology is sometimes difficult to understand simply because it may be unfamiliar. Specific key words are associated with knitted fabrics just as others are used to describe woven ones.

Courses are crosswise rows of loops in knitted fabrics which correspond to filling yarns in woven fabrics. Similarly, *wales,* which are lengthwise rows of loops in knitted fabric, are comparable to warp yarns in woven fabrics. As the fineness of a woven fabric is determined by its thread count, the wales and courses, or the number of loops per inch, determine the fineness of a knitted fabric. Finely knitted fabrics such as women's hosiery are knitted on machinery with a high number of needles per inch, while loosely knitted sports apparel is usually knitted on machinery with fewer needles per inch.

With the variety of knits available on today's market each has been named for identification. These knits are divided into two basic groups known as *warp* knits and weft knits. Warp knits are made by the interlocking of loops in the lengthwise direction of the fabric, while weft knits are made by the interlocking of loops in the crosswise direction of the fabric.

Raschel and *tricot* are popular warp-knitted fabrics. Raschel knits are used in shirts, slacks, and sports jackets, while tricot knits are very commonly used in women's lingerie. *Double knits,* popular for both women's and men's fashions, are fabrics made on knitting machines with double sets of needles. *Single knits,* lighter in weight than double knits, are used in shirts and T-shirts. *Flat knits,* which can be shaped in the knitting process, are used in underwear and sport shirts.

Weft-insertion Knitting

This method of fabric construction consists of a plain knitted base reinforced by filling yarns that are held to the knitted fabric by passing them through selected loops. The filling inlay yarns are held in the fabric in a manner similar to those in woven constructions. Thus, weft insertion on warp knitting combines knitting and weaving.

The major advantage of weft insertion is its fashion flexibility. Other advantages include stability, resistance to abrasion, and the ability to stay flat while being cut. Weft-insertion knitting is said to have the potential for becoming the third major textile-fabrication method, behind only weaving and regular knitting.

Mali Constructions

Mali is such a new form of fabric construction that little is proven about the wearability of mali fabrics under standard conditions. It is known, however, to be a method for forming fabric at speeds and economies exceeding either weaving or knitting. The three mali fabrics available today include the following:

1. Malimo, a fabric structure consisting of an overlapping filling and a superimposed straight warp yarn which are stitched together with interlocking chain or tricot stitches.

2. Malipol, which comprises a pile facing stitched to a backing fabric. It differs from tufting in that the stitching yarn is knitted onto the back of the fabric.

3. Maliwatt, a fortified nonwoven fabric in which a fiber batt or web is interlaced with stitching yarn.

Lamination and Bonding

Fabrics can be given a new dimension by a process of lamination, or bonding to foam. Urethane foam is widely used in coats, rainwear, housecoats, jackets, and ski wear. It is a popular interlining material. The foam itself looks like a cellular sponge. It is often sealed to a fabric, which is then called *urethane foam laminate.*

Fabrics made with foam fall into four groups:

1. Knitted or woven fabrics fused, or laminated, to both sides of a sheet of foam to produce a sandwiched construction.

2. Knitted or woven fabrics fused, or laminated, to one side of a sheet of foam.

3. Fabric machine-stitched, or quilted, to a sheet of foam.

4. Fabric chemically quilted to a sheet of foam.

Fabrics made with foam give warmth with very little added weight. Usually they dry-clean satisfactorily. Performance of foam-bonded fabrics depends on several factors: (1) construction and stability of the face fabric; (2) construction and stability of the backing fabric; (3) the adhesive used for bonding; and (4) control of conditions during bonding. If there is a variance in one of the four conditions, the following may occur: partial or complete separation of the backing from the face fabric, shrinkage of the face fabric, or shrinkage of the backing fabric. When shrinkage occurs in either the face or backing fabric, it is impossible to press or finish the garment to a satisfactorily smooth appearance.

The thickness of the foam affects the laminated fabric. The thinner it is, the better

Bonded fabrics are often good selections for quick-to-make garments because they drape well without additional lining.

its drape. Thick foam is effective as an insulator, and it gives more body to a fabric.

Fabric-to-fabric bonding is another field of fabric manufacture. This permanent bonding of an outer, or face, fabric to a knitted tricot backing fabric so that the two are inseparable imparts certain benefits. It eliminates separate linings, simplifies alterations, imparts wrinkle resistance, protects against skin irritation, helps control shape and fit, and prevents cold clamminess in winter and humid heaviness in summer.

Many fabric-to-fabric bonds dryclean satisfactorily. Bonded fabrics which give satisfactory performance withstand drycleaning or wetcleaning, maintain drapability and original hand, retain color, retain the bond during use

and cleaning, and do not shrink. Most of today's bonded fabrics are acceptable from a consumer point of view. This is because both the surface and backing fabrics are preshrunk and neither is overstretched during the bonding process.

Drycleaning problems that may occur are: shrinkage; separation of the face fabric from the backing fabric, partially or completely; stiffening due to the quality of the adhesive; and staining, or mark-through, of the adhesive to the face fabric. For a discussion of wetcleaning, see page 140.

Coated Fabrics

Coated fabrics range from very luxurious fabrics, such as metallic-plated nylon, to those made by the electrostatic application of flock to foam or fabric to create velvetlike fabrics or simulated leathers. Certain metallic-plated fabrics have limited serviceability in wear and cleaning. Folding of the fabric in either wear or cleaning causes loss of metallic particles from the surface of the fabric. Too, the metallic particles may change color from perspiration or an attempt to remove a spot or stain.

On the other hand, many coated simulated leathers look like genuine suede or grain leather and wear rather well for their intended purpose. There are several kinds of simulated-suede-leather fabrics. They include flocked suede, cotton suede, and suede vinyl. Both flocked and cotton suede can be recognized by their woven backing combined with a napped outer appearance. These fabrics require drycleaning. Suede vinyl can be recognized by the flocked suede coating which is attached to a knit backing. Suede vinyl requires wetcleaning processes such as home laundry or wetcleaning, as do the majority of vinyl-coated fabrics. However, it is expected that drycleanable vinyl fabrics will be perfected and marketed in the future.

Deep-pile or Furlike Fabrics

Deep-pile or furlike fabrics are sometimes called simulated furs, fake furs, or fun-fur

Simulated leathers, because of the applied finishes, can be fashioned into comfortable garments which are distinctively stylish.

Courtesy Crompton-Richmond Company, Inc.

Garments made of regular pile fabrics such as ribless corduroy are often trimmed or lined with furlike fabrics for additional warmth.

fabrics. The majority of deep-pile fabrics may be classified as woven or knitted. They are used extensively in coats and coat linings.

Deep-pile fabrics have a luxurious appearance and feel. They are light in weight and warm to wear. They wear well. They cost less than genuine fur. They are resistant to moth damage. However, since cleaning costs can be sizable, they need to be considered before purchase of a furlike garment.

Some deep-pile fabrics have a tendency to mat in wear and cleaning. Matting is the bunching together of fibers. The problem of matting is related to the fiber content of the fabric, fabric construction, and the finish that is given to both the face and back of the fabric.

While a few deep-pile fabrics can be washed and most of them dryclean satisfactorily, some require special care. This is why you may pay a higher price for drycleaning a deep-pile coat than a regular cloth coat. Some manufacturers recommend that their deep-pile fur fabrics be cleaned by the *furrier* method. Many drycleaners are not equipped to clean by this method. Discuss the problem with your drycleaner before leaving an expensive deep-pile coat for cleaning, making sure that he is equipped to clean it in a satisfactory manner.

In addition to the deep-pile or furlike fabrics, there are many woven and knitted fabrics that have pile. Some are printed or embossed to look like their genuine fur counterpart. Examples are knit pony, leopard,

Quilted fabrics can be used very effectively in warm house coats and lounging wear.

The colorfastness of a fabric to the environment to which it will be subjected can be scientifically pretested in the textile laboratory.

and mole. Velour can be printed to resemble zebra, leopard, tiger, and python.

Deep-pile imitation-Persian-lamb fabrics are made in three ways. In one method the center, or core, of the curl is made of a two-ply cotton yarn. These yarns are twisted to hold synthetic fibers that are curled very tightly around the center. The curls are held to a plain-weave cotton fabric with an adhesive. This fabric cannot be cleaned satisfactorily.

The second method of imitation-lamb-fabric manufacture also employs the curled yarns described above, but in this case they are stitched to the plain-weave fabric by means of Schiffli embroidery machinery. This fabric drycleans satisfactorily.

A third type of imitation lamb is knitted by the sliver method. This pile is finished to

resemble the curled surface of the genuine Persian lamb. It also wears and cleans satisfactorily.

Quilted Fabrics

Quilting is the stitching together of two or more layers of fabric with a layer of padding between them. Quilted fabrics are very popular because they give warmth without undue weight. The type and length of the stitching thread contribute to the quality of fabric serviceability. If the stitches are long and floating, they catch readily in wear and cleaning, causing loss of the quilted design. Be certain you know the kind of fiber batt that is used in the quilted fabric you purchase. Try to choose white fiber batt, which will not stain the outer fabric. Consider also whether

DYEING PROCESS

Solution dye   *Coloring materials are placed into the solution before it is spun into a filament.*

Fiber dye   *Fibers are dyed before they are spun into yarn.*

Yarn dye   *Yarns are dyed before they are woven into a fabric.*

Piece dye   *Solid or plain: A fabric is dyed one color.*

         Cross dye: Yarns of two or more fibers are woven into a fabric. The fabric is placed in a dye bath containing two or more different dyes. Each fiber will select the dye specifically made to dye it a given color. Cross dyeing may also be done at the yarn stage.

the batt will bunch or pack on cleaning. It is important, too, that the outer fabrics have been preshrunk or stabilized for even shrinkage during cleaning, whether the prescribed cleaning method is washing or drycleaning. In particular, choose housecoats and sleeping bags with strong, closely stitched quilted patterns.

Molded Fabrics

Acrylic, modacrylic, polyester, nylon, and olefin fibers can be molded. These heat-sensitive man-made fibers and some blends of them can be given new shapes and dimensional stability when heat and force are applied. Molded fabrics such as those in which heat-printed designs appear to be quilted, or padded, have a great potential for use in garment design.

Colorfastness

Fabrics receive their color from dyeing or printing. Exciting textile developments have provided a great variety of choice in color. Yet, when you go into a store to buy, there may be little information as to what you can expect in terms of colorfastness in dyed and printed fabrics.

  Colorfastness of a reasonable degree is necessary if a garment is to be a good consumer choice. The type of fabric you select and the purpose for which it will be used determine the colorfastness you need in a fabric.

Try to obtain satisfactory answers to the following questions before buying a fabric:

  Is it colorfast to *light?*

  Is it colorfast to *perspiration?*

  Is it colorfast to *gases in the atmosphere?*

  Is it colorfast to *drycleaning* or *laundering at the temperature likely to be used?*

  Is it colorfast to *crocking,* or *rubbing?*

  Is it colorfast to *stain* and *spot removal?*

  You may find that it is very difficult or impossible to obtain the answers to all these questions. Color and dye application to the many kinds of modern fabrics is very complex. However, if you are able to determine the dye process used, you will have at least a clue to the colorfastness of a particular garment. In general, the earlier in the fabric-construction process color is introduced to fabric, the more likely are the chances of colorfastness in the product. Thus an acetate fabric made from fiber which was colored while the acetate was in liquid form will retain color better than an acetate fabric that was printed after it was woven or knitted into fabric. A yarn-dyed fabric generally has better color-retention qualities than does the same fabric which was dyed as piece goods.

Atmospheric-gas Fading

Atmospheric-gas fading, sometimes called fume fading, is a color change caused by exposing fabrics to the gases in the atmosphere.

MODERN PRINTED DESIGNS

Burn-out   Chemicals dissolve one of the fibers in a fabric, leaving a lacy sheer-and-heavy design.

Direct   Sometimes called application printing. Fabric passes between a large cylinder and engraved rollers. Colors are transferred directly from roller to fabric.

Discharge   Dye is chemically destroyed to create a white design on a colored fabric. A colored design may be imprinted at the same time the dye is removed.

Duplex   The same design is printed on the face and back of fabric, registered perfectly to give the effect of a woven fabric design.

Lacquer   Insoluble pigments are mixed with lacquer and roller-printed onto the fabric. The overall design does not stand in relief on the surface of the fabric.

Lacquer stencil   Insoluble pigments are mixed with lacquer and applied to the fabric in designs that stand in relief on the surface of the fabric.

Metallic overprint   Gold and metallic pigments are applied to either a plain or a printed fabric. The design stands in relief on the surface of the fabric.

Pigment-resin   Insoluble pigment is mixed with resin binder and screen- or roller-printed onto fabric and cured at high temperatures.

Plissé   Fabric passes between engraved rollers that permit a chemical solution to contact certain areas of the fabric to make a puckered design.

Resist   Chemicals are applied to the fabric in a desired design. The fabric is dyed and washed. The treated area does not take the dye.

Roller   Pigments or dyes are transferred onto fabric by means of engraved rollers.

Screen   Silk, nylon, or metal screens are treated to resist dye. The color is forced through the untreated part of the screen onto the fabric.

Sublistatic   Pigment designs are made on special paper which is fed through a press and transferred to fabric by heat and pressure.

Warp   The warp yarns on the beam are printed with a design before the plain-colored filling yarns are woven into the warp to make the fabric.

These gases usually come from the burning of coal, oil, or gas. This fading occurs most frequently in fabrics containing acetate. A blue may turn to pink, a brown to red, a purple to pink, a green to yellow, or a gray to pink. Or, there may be a change in intensity, a dark blue turning to a light blue, or a dark green to a light green.

Articles do not always fade evenly. Garments fade most noticeably over the shoulders, down the length of the sleeves, or in lengthwise streaks along the sides of the skirt because of the way they hang in the closet. Sometimes the color change occurs when a garment is drycleaned. There is nothing in drycleaning or finishing, however, that causes

APPLIED SURFACE DESIGNS OTHER THAN PRINTING

Embossed An engraved set of rollers apply heat or chemicals to make raised designs on the surface of the fabric.

Flocked The fabric is printed with an adhesive in the desired design. Short fibers or metallic particles are dusted or drawn electrostatically to the surface of the fabric. They adhere where the adhesive has been applied to the surface of the fabric.

Hand-painted Textile paints are applied by hand to create designs on the fabric surface.

Moiré A roller machine or chemical process is applied to the fabric to produce a wavy watered appearance, or design, on the fabric surface.

Glued-on trim Glues or adhesives hold designs of felt, chenille, sequins, glass, or plastic to the fabric surface.

atmospheric-gas fading. A color change that has already started but has not yet become visible may be developed by heat when the fabric is pressed.

Fluorescent Dyes and Tints

Fibers can be made whiter or brighter by either bleaching, or using fluorescent dyes and tints, or both. Textile manufacturers often use fluorescent compounds to make white fabrics whiter and pastel colors brighter. The whitening agents are sometimes called brighteners. Some surface brighteners change colors when a garment is worn. They can be affected by sunlight, alkaline substances, laundry detergents containing optical bleaches, chlorine bleaches, or the heat of laundry water. Sometimes a chemical reaction takes place between the brightener and the fabric or finish. When a fabric loses its brightness, the color tends to yellow or gray.

The change in brightness of fluorescent-dyed fabrics is not limited to any specific fiber. It may occur in cotton, silk, wool, or any of the man-made fibers.

The brightness in most washable articles may be restored; in some it cannot. There are no suitable brighteners that can be applied with drycleaning solvents. However, a drycleaner may be able to improve an item that will withstand a water treatment. In home laundering, you will be able to successfully use one of the presoaks or brighteners available in most supermarkets.

Applied Surface Designs

A wide variety of surface designs are found on today's fashion garments. When seriously determining whether or not to buy garments featuring these designs, consider how the design will affect the wear life and care of the garment. Sometimes applied designs are little more than fads which will become dated during the season. Others are stylish designs which remain current season after season.

The most common of applied surface designs include printing, embossing, flocking, hand painting, and moiré. Glued-on trims such as felt, sequins, and plastic designs might also be considered applied designs.

Finishes

Finishes applied to fabrics serve several purposes. Probably the two most important functions of finishes are to improve fabric performance and to enhance aesthetic appeal. You cannot see or feel many finishes that are applied to fabrics. Yet they are there, and it is important for you to know that they are there and what they will do for you.

FUNCTIONAL TEXTILE FINISHES

Antiseptic or bacteriostatic   Chemical treatment used to make a fabric bacteria resistant.

Antistatic   Chemical treatment that reduces electric charges in a fabric such as fabrics used in slips and half slips.

Chlorine-resistant   Chemical treatment that prevents yellowing and loss of fabric strength when cotton fabrics are bleached with chlorine-type bleaches whether liquid or powder form.

Crease- and wrinkle-resistant   Chemical or mechanical finish which aids fabric recovery from wrinkles during wear.

Crisp   Chemical finish which adds hand and body to a fabric. It may be permanent or temporary.

Crush-resistant   Resin finish applied to pile fabrics to keep fibers perpendicular, or upright, from the face fabric. When applied to woven fabrics this finish reduces wrinkling.

Flame-resistant   Chemical treatment that prevents a fabric from supporting a flame. This finish is widely used in children's pajamas.

Fume-fading–resistant   Chemical inhibitors that prevent color changes due to gases in the atmosphere.

Mildew-resistant   Chemical treatment which prevents the formation and growth of mildew and mold.

Moth-resistant   Chemical treatment which makes fabric resistant to moth and carpet beetles.

Reflective   Metallic finish applied to the back of a fabric.

Shrink-resistant   A mechanical or chemical finish which stabilizes a fabric so it will not shrink or stretch.

Slip-resistant   Chemical treatment which stabilizes yarns, keeping them from shifting in fabric.

Stain- and spot-resistant   Chemical treatment which makes fabrics resist spots and stains. Such finishes may or may not be permanent.

Wash-and-wear   Chemical or mechanical treatment of fiber or fabric which improves the recovery from wrinkling as garments are dried.

Water-repellent   Chemical treatment to make a fabric resistant to wetting but not waterproof.

Waterproof   Chemical finish that closes the pores of a fabric so that it sheds water.

How can you evaluate finishes applied to fabrics you buy? Perhaps the best way is to ask questions such as these:

1. Does the finish provide the required property I want? For example, will the spot- and stain-resistant finish really give me added protection?

2. Does the finish dictate special care? For example, can I wash and bleach the garment, or will it turn yellow with bleaching because of the finish?

3. Is the finish permanent or temporary? For example, after my raincoat is laundered or drycleaned, will the water-repellent finish

GENERAL TEXTILE FINISHES

Beetling   Mechanical treatment applied to cotton and linen fabrics to give a smooth, flat effect.

Bleaching   Chemical treatment used to whiten fabrics.

Brushing   Abrasive treatment given to raise fibers or nap to the surface of the fabric.

Calendering   Process of passing fabric through rollers to make it smooth and glossy.

Carbonizing   A chemical process to remove vegetable matter from wool.

Crabbing   A wool-shrinking process to stabilize the fabric.

Decating   A steaming process to improve the hand and luster of the fabric.

Degumming   A hot soaping treatment which is used to remove the natural gum from silk.

Delusterizing   Introduction of pigment into a solution which reduces the natural luster of the fiber made from the solution.

Fulling   Application of heat, moisture, friction, and pressure to wool fabrics to increase their density.

Lustering   Application of heat and pressure to give luster to fabric.

Sizing   Addition of coating materials which act as a film around fibers or yarns to prevent their damage during processing.

Weighting   Addition of filling material which increases the weight of the fabric.

AESTHETIC TEXTILE FINISHES

Ciré   A shiny finish obtained by applying waxes or resins, or by mechanically polishing a fabric to produce a luster.

Glazed   A mechanical or chemical treatment to give gloss to the surface of a fabric. The finish may or may not be permanent.

Perspiration-resistant   Chemical finish applied to reduce formation of odor and perspiration damage in a fabric.

Wet-look   High-gloss finish obtained by coating a fabric with vinyl or urethane resin. Sometimes clear film is used alone; sometimes it is laminated to woven or knit fabrics.

still give me protection from the rain, or will I need to have the fabric retreated?

4. Is the finish water- or solvent-soluble? For example, is the finish that gives this fabric the degree of stiffness I want permanent, or will it be removed by laundering or drycleaning, leaving the garment limp and shapeless?

5. Has the manufacturer provided whatever care instructions the finish may require? For example, does the label tell me whether a wet-look finish is a urethane resin, which necessitates drycleaning the fabric, or vinyl, which indicates wetcleaning? Does it indicate the water temperature for washable fabrics?

When choosing a garment, strive to choose one in which the outer fabric, lining, fasteners, and trim can be cleaned effectively by a single method.

Compatibility of Garment Components

If a garment is to perform in a satisfactory manner, each component must be compatible to the wear and care all other parts must receive. In other words, all parts of a garment must be similar in durability and must be cleanable by the same method, whether it is drycleaning, wetcleaning, or laundering. Some components which require particular consideration are buttons and other closures, belts, linings, interlinings, underlinings, interfacings, and padding. Even decorative trim should be given consideration if you want satisfaction from the garments you buy or make.

Buttons and Other Closures

Buttons, zippers, hook-and-loop tape, hooks and eyes, and snaps are among the most commonly used fasteners. Two types of buttons are used. Functional buttons are used simply as closures. They are simple in shape and design and usually are very serviceable. Many functional buttons are subjected to tests in order to determine their serviceability and durability.

Decorative buttons are made for fashion appeal. Some do carry approvals, which guarantee replacement or refund of money. However, if you doubt their ability to withstand laundering or drycleaning, it is better to remove them beforehand than to destroy them.

Metal zippers have been in use for many years and will continue to be used. But recently manufacturers have been turning a large share of their production to the manufacture of a monofilament-coil-type zipper made of nylon or polyester. Manufacturers are also making molded zippers from a product called Delrin.

Coil-type zippers are used in skirts, blouses, dresses, and slacks. They are considered the most important advance in zipper technology in half a century. The new closure replaces individual metal teeth mounted on both sides of the fabric tape with monofilament interlocking elements. The new zippers tend to be more pliable and therefore more comfortable for wear than metal zippers, and they are more likely to last through the wear life of a garment unless high temperatures are used in ironing over them.

Modern zippers are practically foolproof in use and care. Occasionally you may buy a garment in which the zipper tape shrinks more or less than the garment in cleaning. Such a garment should be returned to the place of purchase for replacement.

Hook-and-loop tape is used in place of buttons or conventional slide fasteners on many items of sportswear. The fastener is different in appearance from conventional fasteners. It is made of nylon and consists of two strips of material about ¾ inch wide. One strip is sewn onto one side of the garment, and the other strip is sewn onto the opposite side. When the two strips are merely pressed together, they adhere tightly. They can be separated by being pulled apart with a peeling action. They resist sideways pulling. Thus the fastener does not open accidentally in use.

Belts

When purchasing a belted garment, look for a label stamped on the back of the belt which indicates the manufacturer's name and specifies whether the belt is washable or drycleanable. Many belts will not withstand cleaning because of cardboard, artificial-leather, or paper backings which disintegrate in drycleaning solvents. Some have rubberized interlinings which dissolve in solvent and stain the outer belt covering. Others contain buckram, facings, and linings dyed with fugitive dyes. Still others have backs or buckles fastened with an adhesive which is soluble in water or drycleaning solvents. Choose a garment with a belt which will withstand the type of cleaning recommended for the garment itself.

Built-in Linings

Many dresses are made with built-in linings. These linings serve to give and retain the shape of the garment. In many cases sections of a dress fabric and identical sections of the lining fabric are seamed together. This may sometimes cause a problem. Any difference in the shrinkage or stretch of the two fabrics would result in unsightly puckering of the garment. The only way such puckering can be prevented is by selecting or making garments with compatible fabrics.

Built-in Padding

Padding has been used for years in bathing suits, patio dresses, and play clothes. Built-in bras are sometimes used in dressy tops which are worn with pants and in afternoon, cocktail, and evening dresses.

A built-in bra allows the garment designer freedom to design and shape a garment effectively. It may provide comfort and improved appearance for the wearer. Currently the problem involved with padding is with the choice of material used. In buying padded clothing, try to buy from reputable firms. Their buyers are usually aware that washable clothing requires washable padding and drycleanable clothing requires padding which will not deteriorate in drycleaning solvents. Return garments which do not give satisfactory results in use. A strong consumer-retailer relationship encourages improved choices of fabric combinations by clothing manufacturers.

Decorative Trim

Trims of many types are used to add decoration to a garment. Many dryclean satisfactorily, and most can be laundered. Others simply will not withstand any type of cleaning and render an otherwise wearable garment useless.

Before you buy a garment, determine whether the trim is cleanable. Some trims that can cause trouble are beads, sequins, paillettes, and plastic filaments. Buy trimmed garments from a reputable dealer. Such stores try to buy only garments which will withstand normal wear and cleaning. Faulty garments are usually replaced without question and returned to the manufacturer whose choices of trim were less than standard.

What improvements in the methods of fabric cutting are predicted? What are likely to be the results of these improvements?

What are three methods of heat-fusion sewing?

Why might a man-made fiber be more successfully used in heat-fusion sewing than cotton or wool?

What technical difficulties must be overcome before heat-fusion sewing can be as effective as conventional sewing?

How does ultrasonic sewing differ from heat-fusion sewing?

Trends in Garment Manufacture

Sweeping changes are predicted in the production of wearing apparel. For example, continuous fabric cutting is replacing the electric cutting knives of the past. Small-diameter high-speed fluid-jet machinery cuts fabrics and plastic with precision. Heat-fusion and ultrasonic sewing are other trends in apparel manufacture which may help keep the cost of garment manufacture in line with the consumer's buying power. As alteration of garments made by these methods can be perfected, this type of garment manufacture will probably move to the forefront in the garment industry. Watch for the results as it comes into acceptance.

Heat-fusion Sewing

Stitchless sewing, or joining by heat fusion, is a technique used to bond fabric to fabric by heat sealing. Sometimes heat sealing is used in conjunction with an adhesive or heat-sensitive web. Stitchless sewing has been used successfully to make coat fronts, collar linings, facings, flap and bust darts, side seams, zipper insertions, welts, hems, appliqués, and trim. It is even used for mending. Recently it has been used in men's and boys' suits, rainwear, and a limited number of women's garments.

Different techniques have been developed by the manufacturers who have pioneered stitchless sewing to production reality. They include:

1. Joining heat-sensitive fabrics with heat along seam lines.

2. Inserting a hot-melt adhesive strip between two layers of fabric. The fabrics join at the seam line as the adhesive melts.

3. Joining two layers of non-heat-sensitive fabric with a web which may or may not be attached to carrying paper. The web is attached to one layer of fabric with heat. The carrier peels off, leaving a layer of web which joins the two fabrics when heat is applied.

The manufacturers who have converted to fusing cite several advantages of this type of production. One firm states that the heat-fusion process has helped to eliminate twelve of seventeen traditional stitching and basting operations in the production of men's and boys' sport coats and suits. However, manufacturers are quick to explain that this sewing process requires rigid quality control. Since the fusing operation can tolerate only the barest margin of error, special consideration must be given to accuracy in cutting, careful alignment of seams, control of machinery, and cooperation between designers and engineers. Each of these aspects of production requires utmost attention if garments are to be produced which will please the consuming public.

Stitchless, or heat-fusion, clothing construction is a definite part of tomorrow's wearing apparel manufacture. Eventually it will become a part of the home-sewing picture. As the process improves, fused garments will improve in the following areas.

1. Garments will become more drapable. As less rigid construction techniques are perfected, garments will improve both in appearance and in comfort.

2. Variations in shrinkage of the various layers of a garment will be overcome. This will allow for successful laundering or dry-cleaning of heat-fused garments.

3. The techniques enabling the strength now present in large fused areas will be refined so that fine lines of heat fusion will have equal strength. This will allow for making

Computerized laser-beam cutting, shown here, as well as power-jet-liquid cutting are now perfected for commercial garment production.

The ultrasonic sewing machine is used to join seams in man-made-fiber garments by means of high-frequency vibrations rather than with traditional needles and thread.

heat-fused seams which will withstand wear and strain.

It is obvious that research is needed to improve fusible products to a standard which is satisfactory to the consumer. But stitchless sewing seems destined to become a part of the fashion scene rather rapidly.

Ultrasonic Sewing

An ultrasonic sewing machine has been developed that sews fabrics together without needle or thread. The machine can seam, hem, tack, baste, pleat, and slit and make buttonholes. Ultrasonic sewing, which welds man-made materials by using high-frequency vibrations, can be used on woven and nonwoven fabrics made of virtually any man-made fiber with up to 35 percent natural-fiber content.

The ultrasonic machine operates on standard 110-volt electric current. It operates at a speed of about 50 feet per minute with a hand feed, but it can be stepped up to 150 feet per minute with an automated feed.

Although the ultrasonic sewing machine has been built for clothing manufacturers, it may eventually become available for home sewing. While ultrasonic seams have been perfected to equal in strength those of ordinary thread-stitched seams, the chief values of this type of garment construction are its speed and the possibility of stitching without needles or thread. This speed will tend to reduce the cost of clothing manufacture.

GROUP LEARNING EXPERIENCES

1. Obtain the booklet *Man-made Fiber Fact Book* (50 cents) from the Man-made Fiber Producers Association, Inc., 1000 Connecticut Avenue, Washington, D.C., 20036. Study the material and give a report to your class on man-made fibers.

2. Investigate the impact of knitted fabrics on the woven-fabric market. Report on your findings.

3. Make a research project of determining the consumption patterns of natural versus man-made fibers. Report on your findings.

4. Bring to class a garment in which the fabric has failed to give you satisfaction. Analyze the cause of failure.

5. Compare sweaters of man-made fibers with those of natural fibers as to cost, service qualities, and care required.

HELPING OTHERS TO LEARN

1. Make a display in the library showcase, or some other suitable display area of your school, of bundles of natural and man-made fibers and of fabrics made from each fiber. Complete the display by mounting pictures of attractive clothing made from each of the fibers.

2. Assemble a collection of good used clothing which does not contain care labels. Type on labels or tape the appropriate directions for the care of each garment. Sew the labels in the garments. Repair and package the garments attractively for distribution in an area where they can be used.

INDEPENDENT LEARNING EXPERIENCES

1. Select a fabric and analyze it according to the seven basic factors of fabric performance.

2. Assemble and analyze several fabrics made by weaving and knitting. List their advantages, limitations, and care requirements.

3. Gather hang tags that give information on the finish that is applied to a fabric. Analyze the information regarding the properties of the finish, whether the finish is temporary or permanent, and whether the finish requires special care in wear and cleaning.

4. Assemble fabrics of various design, and classify them according to whether the design was woven, printed, or applied to the surface by some method other than printing.

5. Assemble and mount fabrics that have received their color by fiber dyeing, yarn dyeing, and piece dyeing.

Managing Your Clothing Selections

Management is the ability to make a decision on the basis of a given set of facts and to act on that decision. Each fact involved may have emotional and material overtones. Both are to be considered. Good management will help you build a wardrobe which, while acceptable in itself, will also contribute toward successful relationships with the people with whom you associate.

Why is it necessary that managers be decision makers?

Which values are important to you when you decide upon the type of clothing that you will purchase?

What steps do you take in making a decision about the clothing you purchase?

What information do you need in order to select items of clothing that will adequately meet your needs?

How do business and industry predetermine the types of clothing consumers will demand?

How does advertising affect your clothing choices?

What are the positive and negative effects of modern merchandising?

Decision Making

Decision making permeates all phases of life: personal, home, school, and business. Successful decisions will allow you to use material resources for human needs. The person who can relate resources to needs and make decisions which are conducive to meaningful living is a good manager, whatever the field of consideration.

There are two common patterns in decision making. They are the *centers-of-influence* pattern and the *straight-line* pattern. Centers of influence are those people who influence your thinking. An only child's clothing choices may be influenced largely by the opinion of his parents or their financial resources. In a large family, a young person's decisions may be affected more by brothers and sisters than by the opinions of parents. A person may also be swayed by his friends. Whatever his centers of influence, one's decisions are usually influenced by the same person or group repeatedly. This influence becomes a continuing force in all decision making.

Straight-line decisions are those with which this text principally deals. They are the decisions you make which affect subsequent decisions. For example, you may go to a pattern department and make a selection. Once you decide on a pattern, you need to consider the type of fabric that is suitable for the pattern you selected. The fabric you choose will guide your decision as to what construction techniques to use in making your garment. Thus each decision affects the decision which succeeds it.

In making any decision wisely, a person must know his own goals and values. He must consider the alternative methods of reaching the goal and make choices. His choices will be affected by his centers of influence as well as

Coats and ensembles are major clothing purchases. Before you make such a purchase, consider its purpose in your wardrobe, the climate in which you live, your activities, your coloring and body build, the fabric content, the cost of upkeep, and your financial resources.

by his goals and values. Once the decisions have been made and acted upon, each choice requires evaluation, if the benefits of experience are to be utilized.

The decision-making process can be an aid to the effective selection and buying of clothes. In each case you need to select a goal, relate it to your values, and decide upon the necessary steps to achieve your goal.

Consider the example of buying a coat. Suppose on the basis of your needs and values you have established this goal: *To select a coat that has a good appearance and will keep me warm.* The following series of questions and straight-line decisions might help you implement this goal.

Question 1: Shall I buy a dress coat, a sport coat, or an all-purpose coat?

Decision: If you need a single coat which will look well on a wide variety of occasions, you might decide on an all-purpose coat.

Question 2: What length coat should I buy? A three-quarter length, a full length, or a long coat?

Decision: If you live in a cold climate and are required to wear dresses to school, you might decide on a full length.

Question 3: Shall I buy a woven fabric, a simulated leather, a leather, a simulated-fur-pile fabric, or a genuine fur coat?

Decision: If cost coupled with the need for a coat which will last through several seasons are the considerations, you might decide on a woven-fabric coat.

Question 4: Which of the following types of garments shall I select?

a. A fabric shell with a fiberfill interlining and lining fabric.

b. A fabric shell that is quilted to a fiber batt and lining.

c. A fabric laminated to foam and lined.

d. A fabric chemically quilted to foam and lined.

e. A fabric laminated to a fiber batt, quilted with a stretch yarn, and lined.

Decision: If the climate and your activities suggest that your coat will require frequent cleaning, you might decide on a fabric shell with a fiberfill interlining and lining fabric.

Question 5: What color is most becoming?

Decision: If you have a clear olive complexion and dark hair and eyes, you might select a gold-colored coat.

Question 6: What design is most appropriate for me?

Decision: If you have a stout frame which looks well in slenderizing designs, you might choose a wrap-around style.

Question 7: How much will the coat cost including cleaning or laundering expenses?

Effective buying usually results from careful planning prior to shopping expeditions.

Decision: If your parents have suggested that you try to buy a coat in the $45 to $60 range, you might decide on a coat that costs $50 and requires drycleaning.

Question 8: Where shall I purchase the coat?

Decision: The alternatives here are numerous: discount stores, mail-order houses, department stores, specialty shops, and boutiques. If your parents have a charge account at the department store where you find an attractive coat in your price range, you might decide to purchase your coat there.

Question 9: How shall I pay for the coat? Shall I pay cash, charge it, use the lay-away plan involving monthly payments, or borrow the money and repay the lending agency the principle plus interest?

Decision: If your parents have agreed to let you charge the coat to their account and repay only one-half of the cost from money you will earn, you might decide to charge the coat to your parents' account.

These are not all the decisions you need to make when you purchase clothing. But the example shows there is much a person needs to know if he is to be an intelligent consumer of goods or services. His centers of influence and his own goals and values affect all his decisions.

In later evaluation of his decision, he might ask himself these questions: "In retro-

The purpose of attractive displays is to cause you to feel that through buying specific articles you will be a successful member of society.

spect, were all of my decisions good ones? How could I have improved my buying plan?" Evaluation is the final step of the decision-making process.

Analyzing Sales Information and Promotion

Through research studies, business and industry are making a concentrated effort to understand the thoughts and events which affect young buying. Many firms across the nation establish teen boards. Many work with young adults directly by employing young sales personnel who help other young people when they come into the store to buy. They employ another special group to observe young peo-

ple as they attend a broad range of activities, such as art exhibits, music festivals, movies, and sports events. These specialists talk to designers and manufacturers of young clothes. Their studies help them predetermine what a given store will need to order or reorder so they can fill young people's clothing requests.

Business and industry not only use many techniques to determine what you like but also endeavor to develop within you a desire to purchase it. You are well aware of the influence of advertising on young buyers. The fashion editor of your local paper or your favorite magazine may help you form fashion desires. Such people recognize that young people are frequently fashion leaders. Trends are set by youth, and often adults follow. Examples of young fashion leadership in recent years include the *London Look*, the *American Indian Fashion*, the *Madras Look*, and the *Peasant Look*. Your opinions influence colors, fabrics, silhouettes, and accessories. Business promotes your ideas through editorials, research, merchandising, and advertising.

Modern Advertising

In addition to the radio, television, and magazine advertising to which you have become accustomed, new advertising techniques are developing. These are being used to inform buyers as new products become available. The types of information conveyed help you shop with increased efficiency for goods and services. For example, a network of radio stations called Autonet is emerging throughout the United States, Canada, and Mexico. The radio messages are beamed to approximately 100 million motorists. This network gives local merchants an opportunity to attract motorists into stores with special events and offers.

Many companies are using national advertising campaigns. Some find it to their advantage to use spot or local television messages to back up their magazine or catalogue schedules. This promotional technique is intended to utilize TV as a link between national and local retail advertising.

ADVERTISING CODE OF AMERICAN BUSINESS

1. *Truth*   Advertising shall tell the truth, and shall reveal significant facts the concealment of which would mislead the public.
2. *Responsibility*   Advertising agencies and advertisers shall be willing to provide substantiation of claims made.
3. *Taste and decency*   Advertising shall be free of statements, illustrations, or implications which are offensive to good taste or public decency.
4. *Disparagement*   Advertising shall offer merchandise or service on its merits, and refrain from attacking competitors unfairly or disparaging their products, services, or methods of doing business.
5. *Bait advertising*   Advertising shall offer only merchandise or services which are readily available for purchase at the advertised price.
6. *Guarantees and warranties*   Advertising of guarantees and warranties shall be explicit. Advertising of any guarantee or warranty shall clearly and conspicuously disclose its nature and extent, the manner in which the guarantor or warrantor will perform, and the identity of the guarantor or warrantor.
7. *Price claims*   Advertising shall avoid price or savings claims which are false or misleading, or which do not offer provable bargains or savings.
8. *Unprovable claims*   Advertising shall avoid the use of exaggerated or unprovable claims.
9. *Testimonials*   Advertising containing testimonials shall be limited to those of competent witnesses who are reflecting a real and honest choice.

Point-of-Sale Information

Reliable point-of-sale information is a key consideration if consumer buying is to be satisfactory. It is very difficult to know exactly what you are buying unless information is provided on a hang tag or sewn-in label. Ideally this information is supplemented with reliable information from the sales personnel. A salesperson who can converse intelligently on the fiber content, construction, and wearability of a garment is a far greater asset to the informed buyer than is one who tells you that each garment looks extremely well on you.

Guarantees and warranties are a seller's or manufacturer's written promise to stand behind his product or service. Guarantees are not always easy to understand. Some promises are generous; others are written in beautiful language which says nothing. So that guarantees and warranties will be useful, follow this five-step procedure when buying items:

1. Study the guarantee *before* you purchase the product.

2. Determine whether the guarantee covers the entire item. For example, does it cover both fabric and decorative trim?

3. Check to determine how long the guarantee remains in effect.

4. Determine who is going to stand behind an item if it fails: the retail store or the manufacturer?

5. Keep your sales slip and your guarantee on file in case you need to return the merchandise.

Research studies help the clothing industry predetermine the demands of consumers for all types of garments, high-fashion as well as classic models.

Current Trends in Merchandising

There must be a close tie between the kinds of merchandise a successful store carries and its customers' desires. To further attract customers, many stores try to provide an environmental experience. Retail stores are increasingly using shops and boutiques for dramatic presentations of their merchandise. The trend in merchandising is toward informality.

It is predicted that the imaginative department store of the future will occupy an entire closed mall. It will break out of its four walls and become a series of shops. The old image of boutiques as an outlet for far-out merchandise is disappearing. Already boutiques are relating to consumer demands.

Stores are using data-processing systems to accurately profile their customers. This aids them in reaching the right customer through the right advertising technique.

Customer demands frequently dictate modern merchandising trends. For example, there was a day when textile companies restricted their sale of stylish fabrics to the ready-to-wear trade. The beautiful fabrics found in ready-to-wear garments could not be purchased in the form of yard goods for home sewing until several years later. But more and more textile companies are now selling to both markets at the same time. This trend has developed because of the great increase in home sewing.

Large mail-order houses are adapting their methods of merchandising to appeal to young people. Boutique-concept catalogue stores and the *magalog,* a type of magazine catalogue, are aimed at young people. Merchandise from the magalog is on display in a boutique. Items ordered before a specified time on one day may be picked up at the boutique at a specified time on the following day.

You may expect to see an increase in the current practice of prepackaging wearing apparel. The packaging, usually in see-through bags of merchandise which can be bought without fitting, prevents the wear and tear caused by customer handling.

Merchandising Techniques
of the Future

Business changes with the times, changing technology, and changing consumer needs. Some interesting merchandising changes are taking place, and there are predictions of still other such changes to come.

It is predicted that there will be telephones and television screens in automobiles that will permit you to shop while traveling from one point to another. There will be drive-in stores comparable to drive-in banks.

Cable television is unknown to many city viewers, but the industry has been serving rural areas for many years. It is on the verge of huge expansion. With the use of microwave transmission, TV signals can be bounced from horizon to horizon, extending the range of cable reception indefinitely. It is predicted that this improved transmission system will become the medium whereby you sit at home and look at TV images of merchandise for sale. As this system becomes practical, you can conduct your buying from your living-room chair.

Some stores are now using picturephone service to acquaint their customers with products which are available. The picturephone was featured nationally at the 1963-64 New York World's Fair. Merchandisers foresee the possibility that its use may save time and money. The installation of picturephones will be expensive for some time. However, it is predicted that their usefulness as a merchandising tool will speed their acceptance as one of the mechanical devices in the modern home.

It appears that a portion of the shopping of the future will be an experience in movement. There will be moving aisles to transport you within a store. There will be moving belts that will bring and display merchandise to you.

It is predicted that you will participate in automated shopping in unattended retail stores. Devices will process orders electronically, compute costs, make itemized invoices, and control inventories.

Shopping complexes will increasingly become a part of large skyscrapers, including shops, banks, parking, entertainment, and hotel-motel facilities. Low-cost computerized film commercials will be used to a greater degree to reach you with a sales message. Air freight will be as cheap as surface transportation. This will bring to you rapidly goods and services from all parts of the world.

The retailing and banking community is expected to play an even more important role in your life. Bank credit cards will be used to a greater degree than charge accounts. Your credit will be checked increasingly by a system of point-of-sale authorization. The clerk, by dialing your assigned number into a computer system, can know immediately whether or not you are a good credit risk. Experts predict that the society of the near future will operate by electric fund transfer. There will be an automatic and immediate transfer of money from the customer's cash resources in the bank to the account of a retail store or other business where he makes a purchase.

How can one resource be substituted for another to produce an effective wardrobe?

What are the identifying marks of a successful wardrobe?

How can you determine when it is time to discard a specific garment?

What are the advantages of having a clothing budget, or spending plan, which extends over a season or a year?

What are the advantages and disadvantages of impulse buying?

What are the added costs, both economical and psychological, of spending beyond your means?

Managing Your Clothing Resources

"I don't have a thing to wear." Have you ever made this statement? If so, it may be that you have made some bad decisions while managing your clothing dollars. Perhaps you bought clothes that are unbecoming or of poor quality. Perhaps you purchased piecemeal or spasmodically. Perhaps you spent too much for some items, leaving no resources for completing your wardrobe. Or perhaps you neglected to keep your clothes in wearable condition. Most of these situations can be avoided when you *plan* for the purchase and upkeep of your total wardrobe.

In simplest language, your resources include your money, time, and energy. Other resources are your talents and skills in a given

Courtesy Bobbie Brooks, Inc.

Clothing management means that you have a clean, wearable garment suitable for wear to each event you decide to attend.

who feels a lack of money may compensate for this lack by using extra time and energy to make a gift for a special occasion. His busy father may rush to a store and spend an excessive amount of money on a gift for the same occasion simply because he has neither the time nor the energy to shop efficiently. As long as a person can effectively juggle the resources at his disposal to reach his goals, he is at least to a degree managing his resources.

Clothing management includes both buying clothes and caring for them. Since buying, including the preliminary planning, covers a broad range of subjects and activities, the remainder of the chapter is devoted to this subject. Clothing care is covered in Chapter 5. Chapter 6 deals with the consumer's rights and responsibilities as related to the clothes he buys.

Your Wardrobe Plan

A wardrobe is a collection of clothing that you wear during a given season of the year. It is based on your needs and the money you have to spend. The characteristics of a well-planned wardrobe are:

1. Sufficient variety of garments for day-to-day requirements.

2. Accessories required to make use of or extend the use of basic garments.

3. A basic color scheme on which many combinations can be built.

4. Garments that are attractive, becoming, appropriate, and comfortable.

The wardrobe you build will be influenced by many factors such as your family, your friends, your community, the climate, the season of the year, and your varied activities. Since even a well-planned wardrobe is expensive, most people build their seasonal wardrobes around clothing items they already own.

Your Clothing Inventory

Many teen-agers find that, when they are told to list the contents of their wardrobe, they scarcely know what they own. They know there are many items in their closets, some of

area. Perhaps gifts should also be considered as resources. Still another resource is your *psychic income.* This is the pleasure and satisfaction you derive from wisely combining your talents and skills with your basic resources to reach your goals.

It is possible for a person to have plenty of time, money, and energy. More commonly, however, he has a short supply of one or another of these, or even of two or all three of them. Usually he feels that he has less of one resource than of the other two.

Management of resources for most people is a type of juggling act. The teen-ager

GUIDELINES FOR THE DISCARDING OF CLOTHING

Outdated party clothes   They may be perfectly good, but if they will never be worn again, discard them.

Clothes damaged by moths or silverfish   Although a garment may be in good condition except for a small damaged area, if it is not worth the cost of having the damaged area rewoven, it should be discarded. Consider home mending or remodeling of garments damaged in areas which do not show.

Clothes damaged by poor care techniques   A garment may still be good except for a spot where you removed the dye, scorched it, or shined or glazed the fabric. If you know you will probably never wear it again, discard it.

Clothes that have lost their shape   Garments may become over-stretched with wear at such points of strain as the elbows, knees, or seat. Some may elongate at the sleeve and hemline. Others may shrink in washing. Or they may appear smaller because you have gained weight. When a garment cannot be correctly shaped, even with professional blocking, discard it.

Clothes that need repairs   The fabric and style of a garment may be good. But you may know you will not take the time to let out the seams, replace the buttons, tack the lining, shorten the skirt, turn the collar or cuffs, replace the broken zipper, or sew on the hook, the thread eye, or belt loop. If you know you will never repair it, discard it.

Dead clothes   There is nothing especially wrong with dead clothes. It may be that you just don't like them and so won't wear them. They may be uncomfortable—too hot or too scratchy—or of a color or style no longer appealing to you. If you won't wear them, discard them.

Worn-out clothes   If you know you will never wear these items again because of visible effects of wear such as abrasion, shine, or pilling, then discard them.

which they wish would simply vanish. Guidelines can be set for discarding worn clothing so that space is made available for necessary garments. Often space is of more value than is unused clothing.

Retain those items of clothing that you can wear with confidence because they make you feel and look well groomed. In other words, save clothes that are in good condition and those that can be put into wearable condition by you or a professional. Steps in mending clothes are given on page 117. For suggestions on the recycling of out-of-fashion or slightly worn clothing, see page 216.

Now you have a basis on which to build. List the clothes you have for spring, summer, fall, and winter. The next two decisions to make are: "What do I need?" and "How much money do I have to spend?"

Make a wardrobe chart. Organize your clothes. Decide when you will wear them and the type of garment you will wear for a particular occasion. List those garments that you wear at home; the clothes you wear for school or school-related activities; and the garments you will wear for dates, parties, or church. Do you require formal or semiformal clothes for special parties? You may find that some gar-

A girl needs a few garments in which she can feel uniquely herself.

ments serve double-duty. You can wear them for several types of occasions. When you are able to list each item of wearable clothing and the types of activity to which it can be worn, you have a wardrobe inventory.

Next plan appropriate and becoming ensembles for each of your activities, making as full use as possible of the garments and accessories you already have on hand. List the items you would like to have to complete your ensembles. You are then ready to make a decision as to how you may obtain these items.

Your Spending Plan

A spending plan, often called a budget, requires decisions as to the priorities of the needed items of clothing, the time to make your purchases, and the estimated cost of each item. Consider the cost of upkeep at the time of purchase. The amount of money needed to keep a garment in wearable condition is sometimes a determining factor. You may find that it will be necessary to omit or postpone a specific purchase.

A spending plan serves only as a guide. You may find that even the best plan does not always work out to your advantage. But even a poor clothing budget is better than no clothing budget. Making a written plan will help you to organize your thinking. It will help you to shop intelligently to meet your personal needs. Keeping records of what, when, and where you buy and how much you pay for clothing can furnish guidelines for future shopping and spending. By checking back over your own records you can recall the results of a certain type of purchase. Such records can be an aid to effective buying in the future.

Shopping Skills

Shopping is a very important function in satisfying your needs and wants. Developing shopping skills and techniques requires many managerial resources. They are worth developing if you want to be well dressed without overspending. Prepare for shopping by being fresh and rested. Wear comfortable shoes and

CLOTHING BUDGET FOR THE YEAR

Needs	Estimated Reserves and Expenditures					
	January	February	March	April	Etc.	Total
Outer garments	*skirt 6.00 (make)*			*spring coat 35.00*		
Shoes and hose	*panty hose 2.00*		*shoes 11.00*	*panty hose 2.00*		
Undergarments		*2 bras 4.00 (on sale)*				
Accessories		*navy purse 3.00*				
Clothing care			*dress cleaned 2.50*	*load of dry cleaning 2.50*		
Grooming	*shampoo 1.00*		*hair cut 2.50*	*lipstick 1.00*		
Monthly expenses	$9.00	$7.00	$16.00	$40.50		
Balance brought forward	.00	11.00	24.00	28.00		
Estimated income for clothing	20.00	20.00	20.00	20.00		
Total funds available	20.00	31.00	44.00	48.00		
Balance at end of month	11.00	24.00	28.00	7.50		

the undergarments you expect to wear with the anticipated purchase.

Impulse Buying

When you go shopping, you often find many, many choices of clothing and accessories. You may make a purchase on the spur of the moment, one you really did not plan to make. This is called *impulse buying*. It is usually based on whim rather than sound economics. Impulse buying often results in the purchase of garments which are not really needed. Satisfaction seldom results since resources are used improperly.

Not all impulse buying is erroneous, however. If you buy impulsively, you may be satisfying an unclarified or subjective need. In the back of your mind, you may have temporarily stored away your known need or desire for an item for later consideration. Upon seeing the item, you may be mentally stimulated into action that results in a purchase. For example, suppose you have purchased a pair of gold slacks but have been unable to find a harmonizing color in a sweater. The slacks can be worn only with your brown blouse, which is too frilly to look well with them. Months later, while wearing the slacks, you spot a gold

CHECK LIST OF SHOPPING MANNERS

1. Do you state clearly what you are looking for, giving some indication of price, style, color, and size?
2. Do you avoid taking advantage of the salesperson's time, freeing her to help someone else if you are slow in reaching a decision?
3. When you are not sure what you want, do you shop around and find out what is available before deciding to buy?
4. Do you refrain from interrupting a salesperson who is helping someone else?
5. Do you refrain from chatting with friends about unrelated matters while a salesperson is waiting on you?
6. Are you aware of other shoppers in the same area, giving them an opportunity to look at the merchandise too?
7. Do you handle merchandise only when you are intending to buy?
8. Are you careful with merchandise—hands clean, no lipstick smears, no rough fingernails?
9. Do you avoid going shopping when you have a cold or some other infection?
10. Do you shop with no more than one or two others?

GUIDELINES FOR SHOPPING

1. Determine how much money you have to spend.
2. Make and follow your shopping plan designed to meet your specific needs.
3. Learn to know the reliable stores in your community where you can shop with assurance.
4. Compare the good, better, and best qualities. Purchase the quality that suits your needs.
5. Examine the workmanship. Well-constructed clothing usually fits well, looks well, and wears well.
6. Try on clothing to be certain of proper fit while standing, sitting, and walking.
7. Consider care requirements before you buy. Upkeep costs are an important item in your clothing budget.
8. Learn to know the people with whom you do business. Let them know you rely on them for needed information to make an intelligent choice.
9. Take your time. Avoid rushing. Control impulse buying.
10. Determine whether or not you can save money by purchasing clothing offered on special or closeout sales.
11. If you are disappointed in your purchase because of poor performance, complain fairly and effectively.

PERSONAL CHECK LIST FOR THOUGHTFUL SHOPPERS

1. Wear clothes which are easy to take off and put on again.
2. Wear undergarments that are clean and in good repair.
3. Use an antiperspirant under your arms.
4. Wear a girdle if you are going to try on clothes with which you will ordinarily wear one.
5. Take along a clean comb for combing your hair.
6. Wear socks or stockings if you are going to try on shoes.
7. Keep in mind special circumstances. For example, wear a sweater when you are going to look for a topcoat which you expect to wear over a sweater.

acrylic sweater in the window of a variety store. You purchase it on the spot. The result of this impulse purchase is a beautifully co-ordinated outfit.

Comparison Shopping

When you compare prices and qualities in several stores, you are doing comparison shopping. This type of shopping is usually more effective if you read newspaper and magazine advertisements, watch television commercials, listen to radio advertising, and study mail-order catalogues beforehand. Such preshopping information gives you a general idea of goods available and their current prices.

Comparison shopping is not always possible or wise. Occasionally time is a more valuable item than the best of all buys found by visiting a number of stores. Give careful consideration to the real cost of comparison shopping. Time spent looking in papers and particularly in going from store to store has a certain real value. The expense of travel from store to store is also a valid consideration.

Comparison shopping requires both skill and patience. If it is to be effective, you must be able to compare and interpret labels as well as prices. You must be able to choose suitable design, fit, and color. Yet comparison shopping can give you the satisfaction of knowing you are paying the right price for the goods you want or need.

Paying for Your Clothes

Before making a purchase, a wise buyer decides how to pay for the purchase. Some stores require that you pay cash. Others extend the courtesy of charge accounts. Such charge accounts are a convenience, but they are also an invitation to buy more than you really need. Stores offset the cost of charge accounts by increasing the prices of their merchandise and in some cases by making direct charges for the privilege of using extended credit terms. Beware of credit. By paying the 18 percent annual interest allowable in many states over a period of time, a person can spend almost one fifth of his clothing budget on interest.

All stores which extend credit expect payment at a certain stated time. If you do not pay at that time, a service charge will be added to your account. It is required by law that stores disclose their method of calculating service charges.

Some stores offer lay-away plans, budget plans, or installment buying plans when you make large purchases of clothing. These plans differ in the length of time required for payment, the percentage of service charge, and the percentage of interest or carrying charges. It is important to understand clearly the terms of a contract for a particular purchase, because such charges add substantially to the cost of clothing. Only you can make the decision as to which plans fit your needs, wants, and ability to pay.

Try to make your largest clothing investments in garments which will be
worn many times.

What are frequent causes of dissatisfaction with goods purchased? How does the complexity of the production and marketing system sometimes contribute to a sense of frustration on the part of the consumer?

What help is available for making correct buying decisions?

Why is it important to know your figure type when buying ready-to-wear fashions?

What are the considerations in successfully buying dresses? Coats and suits? Skirts? Sweaters? Blouses? Slacks, pants, and shorts? Swimsuits? Lounging and sleeping apparel? Lingerie? Shoes?

Buying Clothes

Buying clothes can be an exciting adventure or it can be a frustrating experience. When shopping, know what you expect to buy. Try to learn something about the store, shop, or boutique where you plan to buy your clothes. Buy, if possible, in a store which has a wide selection of the type of garment you are considering. Most large department stores and specialty shops group clothing not only according to types of clothes but also according to figure types. It therefore becomes vitally important for you to know what size you really are.

FIGURE TYPES FOR WHICH
READY-TO-WEAR IS FASHIONED

Subteen (7-14 years)   *Trim neat figure. For short waist: sizes 3-15.
For long waist: sizes 6-16.*
Teen (14-18 years)   *Trim neat figure. For short waist: sizes 3-15.
For long waist: sizes 6-16.*
Junior (14-18 years)   *For late teens who are 5'4" to 5'7" and have
a shorter than average waist: sizes 3-15.*
Junior Petite (14-18 years)   *Same as junior sizes 3-15 but applies
only to girls 5'1" or under.*
Misses (all ages)   *For slim or medium figure 5'5" to 5'9": sizes
6-20. Tall girls, choose sizes 8-20.*

You need also to know your figure problems. Is your figure shorter, taller, heavier, or thinner than the average figure? Find the silhouette and proportions best for you. Study again the discussion of proportions in Chapter 2 (see pages 49-53).

Checking for Accurate Fit
When you try on a garment, use a mirror and look at your silhouette from various angles. In addition to the appearance produced when you stand, look at yourself sitting, bending, reaching, and walking. For discussions of the fit of specific garments, see pages 100-112.

Checking the Quality of Clothing
Many people feel that the two chief considerations in successful buying are proper fit and the appropriateness of a garment for the occasion. But today's fashion-wise young people demand more than appropriateness and fit from their garments. They demand fashions which are right for them, fabrics which will serve each specific fashion effectively throughout the wear life of the garment, and adequate workmanship.

Quality is the backbone of fashion, fabrics, and garment construction. But what is this intangible force called *quality?* Quality is in a way like electricity: You can best define what it *is* by effectively stating what it *does.* Quality, then, in terms of clothing construction, might be defined as *the characteristics of a garment which cause it to perform its given function in an acceptable manner.*

Many products and services are manufactured at more than one quality level. A manufacturer may indicate quality levels with such terms as *Good, Better,* and *Best.* This differentiation allows you to choose the quality which best fits your purpose.

You live in a world of fabrics and fashions. Yet, it is extremely difficult to keep up with the new developments in fiber production, fabric styling, sewing techniques, and fabric care. Ninety percent of all the garments made in this country, as well as of those which are imported, give good satisfaction in wear and in care. Consumer problems are likely to occur in a maximum of only 10 percent of total production. Most of these problems can be avoided if, before purchase, garments are carefully checked for quality of fabric, workmanship, and design, for cleanability, and for shrinkability in order to ensure maintenance of fashion and fit. For a discussion of the most common reasons for the misbehavior of textile products, see pages 151-154.

The long route from fiber producer to consumer is complex. There are many opportunities for a breakdown in communications between the different segments of production, distribution, and you, the consumer. Any breakdown results in your feeling that either

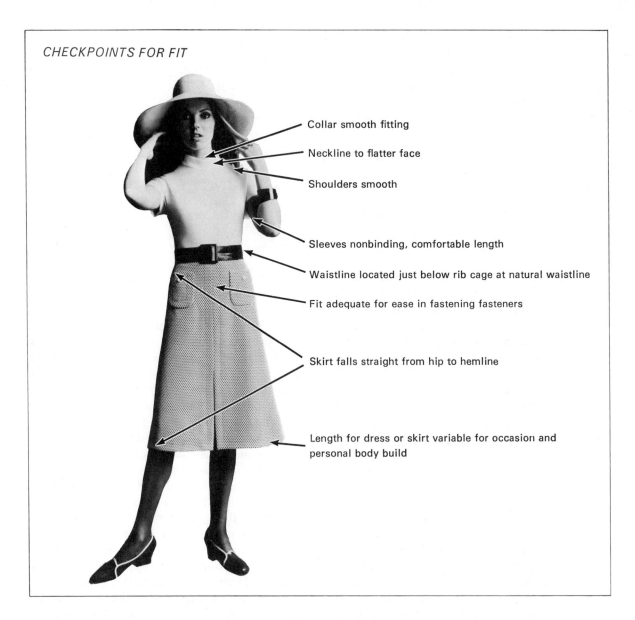

CHECKPOINTS FOR FIT

Collar smooth fitting

Neckline to flatter face

Shoulders smooth

Sleeves nonbinding, comfortable length

Waistline located just below rib cage at natural waistline

Fit adequate for ease in fastening fasteners

Skirt falls straight from hip to hemline

Length for dress or skirt variable for occasion and personal body build

quality, fashion, or both are inferior. Good communication leads toward production of high-quality, fashionable merchandise.

Buying Specific Garments

When buying any garment a person should consider the activities for which it will be worn, the fit of the garment, the fashion and quality of the garment, and the performance which may be expected. Since the fabric grain of ready-made garments is vital to their appearance, study the key grain lines on pages 339-341 before buying ready-made garments. Over a period of time most people are likely to buy at least one dress, coat, suit, skirt, sweater, blouse, pair of pants, swimsuit, sleepwear, lingerie, and pair of shoes. For this reason, guidelines for buying each of these types of apparel are given on the following pages.

CONSIDERATIONS WHEN BUYING

1. *What do I really want: Function? Service? Fashion? All three?*
2. *Does the garment improve my appearance? My self-concept?*
3. *Will it wrinkle badly during wear? Can it be cared for easily?*
4. *Does it match my coat? Do my shoes, scarves, and other accessories go with this new item?*
5. *Do I have a blouse or sweater or skirt, or perhaps two, that I can wear with this new purchase?*
6. *How versatile is this garment? Can I wear it for many occasions?*
7. *Does the garment fit well or will it need to be altered? Is it worth the cost?*
8. *Am I having difficulty in making up my mind? If so, why? Should I shop another day?*

CHECK LIST FOR BUYING A DRESS

1. *Does this dress fulfill a definite need in your wardrobe?*
2. *If a winter dress, can it be worn with your coat? Will it give the service that you need for the length of time you will want to wear it?*
3. *Can it be dressed up? Dressed down?*
4. *Will it go with the accessories you have or are planning to buy?*
5. *Has the dress been cut so that the grain lines of the fabric fall correctly on your figure?*
6. *Does the dress fit? If alterations are necessary, can you make them yourself? Or what will it cost to have them made for you?*
7. *Is the trimming of good quality and well applied?*
8. *Have the hem, closures, and pockets all been attached or finished securely and neatly?*
9. *What care will be required? Is the dress worth its maintenance cost in money, time, and energy?*
10. *Is the total price within the amount you allowed in your budget, or can the difference be justified?*

Dresses

The buying of a dress can be a major expenditure and thus one to which much time and thought should be given. Your selection of a dress, as ot other garments, will be made on the basis of your wardrobe plan and the attractiveness of the dress on you. The dress you choose for frequent wear will differ from one you might buy for a formal party. Durable, easy-to-care-for fabrics will be most service-able for everyday wear. Such dresses receive the hardest wear and should be the best you can afford. On the other hand, a party dress may be satisfactory even though inexpensive. Because a party dress receives less wear, it does not require frequent cleaning and may be made of a fabric which requires drycleaning. If you need a dress to wear for several different types of occasions, you might consider a basic dress and a variety of accessories.

Party dresses, while colorful and beautiful, need not be expensive since they are usually worn only a few times.

IMPROVING MY SHOPPING I.Q.

Rate yourself, allowing 4 points for *Always*, 2 for *Sometimes*, 0 for *Never*
Do not write in this book.

	Always	Sometimes	Never
1. Do I know the difference between my needs and my wants?			
2. Do I make a shopping list to be sure I get the things I need and want?			
3. Do I avoid buying on impulse?			
4. Do I decide on the approximate price I want to pay for specific items before shopping?			
5. Do I balance my spending?			
6. Do I evaluate suitability, value, and quality, as well as price reductions, when I buy at a sale?			
7. Do I buy on the basis of use?			
8. Do I compare values?			
9. Do I read labels, hang tags, and seals?			
10. Do I understand the information found on labels and hang tags? If not, do I ask for help?			
11. Do I inspect the construction of merchandise carefully?			
12. Do I know the different types of stores in my area and the variety of selections and services they provide?			
13. Do I know what can be bought in my shopping area?			
14. Do I state clearly what I want and how I can be helped? If I am just looking, do I explain this to the salesperson?			
15. Do I make necessary exchanges, returns, and complaints promptly and courteously?			
Total			

Moderation in style will prevent your wardrobe from becoming outdated by rapid changes in fashion. High-fashion garments are likely to be extreme in style and may be expensive for the value you will receive from them. If the fashion is short skirts, select a length which is in keeping with the trend, but not the very shortest. If fashion defines the silhouette of the body, choose dresses which fit you smoothly but not too tightly. Do not let attractiveness of style tempt you to overlook correctness of fit. Find your correct size according to the chart on page 99, and carefully check each prospective purchase for fit as shown on page 100.

Some types of dresses do not require lining, while others are fully or partially lined. Lining may add to the cost of the dress, but it will ensure longer wear and better appearance throughout the lifetime of the garment. No matter what the type of dress you are selecting, consider carefully the check list on page 101 before deciding to purchase a particular garment.

Coats and Suits

The sizes of coats and suits are coded similarly to dress sizes (see the chart on page 99). A correctly fitted coat may be a size larger or smaller than your dress size, depending on its cut. Frequently coats cut with raglan sleeves and flowing lines fit best if bought in a size smaller than your dress. Tailored coats may fit better if bought in a larger size.

Select your coat or suit jacket to fit comfortably over the garments you plan to wear underneath it. Avoid choosing a fit so loose that it looks sloppy or one so tight that

CHECK LIST FOR BUYING A COAT OR JACKET

1. *Do the style and fabric suit your activities and the climate?*
2. *Will the coat or jacket be comfortable to wear?*
3. *Do the armholes and shoulders fit smoothly with no wrinkles?*
4. *Are the sleeves roomy enough for whatever you plan to wear underneath the garment?*
5. *Is the grain of the fabric straight on the key grain lines?*
6. *Does the collar lie close to the neck or stand away from the neck comfortably so that it will not be necessary to rearrange the garment when it is worn?*
7. *If the garment has long sleeves, do they come to your wrists when your arms are bent?*
8. *Does the garment fasten smoothly without strain or pull?*
9. *What care will be required?*

CHECK LIST FOR BUYING A SKIRT

1. *Does your wardrobe plan show a need for this skirt?*
2. *Can it be worn with shirts or sweaters you already own? Will extras be needed?*
3. *Is the skirt cut correctly on grain?*
4. *Is the fit right for the type of skirt?*
5. *Does the waistband fasten snugly and comfortably around your waist, and if not, can it be adjusted so that it will?*
6. *Is the length right for you, or can it be corrected?*
7. *Is the skirt well made—the stitching firm and close, the placket smooth and of even width, the edges of the seams suitably finished?*
8. *Can it be cared for easily? What are the care requirements of the fabric and the design?*

strain occurs across the shoulder and in the armholes. The garment should fasten smoothly and evenly with sufficient overlap in front. Test the fit of the shoulders and armholes by folding your arms across your chest and by reaching upward. These movements will cause undue strain to become obvious. If sleeves are a full-length style, choose a sleeve length that reaches the large bone of your wrist when you bend your arm.

Correctly fitted coats fall smoothly from the shoulder. A full-length style is long enough to cover the hemline of the garments which are to be worn underneath it.

A raincoat or everyday jacket may be more economical if washable. A warm winter coat should be drycleanable. Check the trim. Sometimes trims are not cleanable. Double check to be sure all parts of the coat can be cleaned and by the same method.

Skirts
Skirts are sold by dress size or waist measurement. Choose a skirt which fits smoothly, hangs straight without cupping in the seat area, and has enough ease to avoid crosswise wrinkles in front. Check a bias-cut skirt before purchase to see that it hangs evenly around

the bottom. Check pleated skirts for pleats which hang closed and perpendicular to the floor. If the pleats part in the hip or thigh areas, the skirt is not full enough and usually cannot be adjusted. Wrap-around skirts require sufficient overlap to remain closed when you walk or sit. In all types of skirts the waistband should be loose enough not to roll but snug enough for a smooth, comfortable fit.

Sweaters

Select a sweater one or two sizes larger than your blouse size. There are two basic methods of manufacturing sweaters: knitting the pieces to shape, and sewing them together, which produces *full-fashioned* sweaters; and cutting the pieces from knitted fabric and sewing them together at the seam lines. Full-fashioned sweaters usually cost more and hold their shape better than do *cut-and-sew* sweaters. Both types can be purchased in slip-on and cardigan styles.

When you purchase a sweater, check the bustline. Choose a sweater which is comfortable without being snug. If you select a cardigan sweater, make sure that it buttons smoothly without gaps. Check the neck size of a slip-on sweater. Choose one which slips over the head easily to avoid fabric damage. Check the shoulder line for fit. Properly fitted, the shoulder seam line of a garment follows a straight line which extends from the bone behind the ear to a point centered directly over the outer edge of the shoulder. Determine that the sweater is adequately broad across the shoulders without appearing baggy. Check the ribbing of the neck, cuff, and waistline for firmness of construction and smoothness of fit. Check care requirements, as sweaters require frequent washing or cleaning.

Blouses

Select a blouse or shirt that fits comfortably at the neck, bust, and shoulder lines and permits your arms to move freely. Avoid sleeves that bind at the armhole or across the upper arm. Check long sleeves to see that they just

Photos Courtesy Bobbie Brooks, Inc.

Separates prove to be most versatile if bought for their mix-and-match characteristics.

105

CHECK LIST FOR BUYING A BLOUSE

1. Does the blouse or shirt coordinate with your skirts or pants in color, texture, and style?
2. Is it large enough that fastenings do not strain?
3. Is there ample room across the front, back, and shoulders and at the armholes?
4. Is it long enough for adequate tuck-in?
5. Will it fit correctly under the jacket or sweater which you plan to wear over it?
6. Is the fabric colorfast to laundering, perspiration, and other expected wear and care conditions?
7. What care will be required: drycleaning, wash-and-wear, ironing or merely touching up?
8. Will seams, fastenings, and trimmings give satisfactory wear?

CHECK LIST FOR
BUYING SLACKS, PANTS, AND SHORTS

1. Is the fit comfortable when sitting, walking, and bending, as well as when standing?
2. Is the fabric sturdy enough for the intended use?
3. Is the fabric washable for frequently worn garments and in all cases either washable or drycleanable?
4. Does the fabric possess stretch qualities adequate for the activities for which the garment will be worn?
5. Is the grain of the fabric straight on key grain lines?
6. Is the garment length stylish and suitable for your purposes?
7. Are seams, particularly in the crotch area, sturdy and well finished?
8. Are the fasteners, particularly the zipper, of high quality?

touch the wristbone when you bend your elbows. When buying tuck-in blouses, buy those with tails long enough to stay tucked into your skirt, slacks, or shorts or buy body blouses that snap together at the crotch. Since blouses require cleaning after each wearing, check before buying to see that blouses bought for general use are colorfast and can be laundered.

Slacks, Pants, and Shorts
Most pants come in dress sizes, but lengths and styles may vary. Take into consideration your proportions, and find pants that are flattering in length, style, and fit. While the longer style of shorts is often more becoming to heavy thighs and hips, thin figures look well in most pants styles. Regardless of your figure type, check front, side, and rear views for attractiveness. Check the fit while sitting. If it is difficult for you to find pants which are becoming, consider wearing a panty girdle while buying and wearing them.

Swimsuits
Bathing suits may come in dress sizes, or they may be marked according to bust measure. Certain two-piece suits come as separates so that individual garments can be bought for fit

in the bust and hip areas. Be certain that the suit you choose fits comfortably in the under-arm and leg areas. Allow for a little stretching when the suit is wet. Laws require that you try bathing suits on over panties. Be certain you are well satisfied with a suit before you buy it, as swimsuits are not returnable.

Lounging and Sleeping Apparel

Try to choose sleepwear and robes made of washable, minimum-care fabrics which are attractive and help you feel free and comfortable while you are awake or asleep. Sleepwear can be practical and moderately priced, or it can run the gamut of luxury at medium to high prices. Your primary need may be to look beautiful, or it may be to stay warm. Buy to fill your need while staying within your budget.

Sleepwear can be purchased in coordinate sets or separates. In fact, you can buy separates and have the fun of coordinating sleepwear and robes. You may prefer a short or long nightshirt, short or long shift, short or long pajamas, short-sleeved pajamas with boxer-short panties, or a long T-shirt that doubles for both sleeping and lounging. You might also wish to choose one of the many available kimonos, quilted robes, peignoirs, bathrobes, or negligees. Whatever type of cover-up you choose, buy one which is long enough to cover the sleepwear beneath it.

Courtesy Eastman Chemical Products, Inc.

Lounging and sleepwear can be attractive as well as serviceable.

Lingerie

Choose your lingerie so that the various layers will fit smoothly together, and more important-ly, fit smoothly under your outer garments. Fashion changes influence underfashions, but basic concepts remain intact. Buy garments of easily washable, long-lasting fibers.

Slips   Different kinds of slips serve differ-ent purposes. White and beige slips are gen-erally considered all-purpose. Under dark-colored clothes, however, a dark slip is preferable. Slips of many colors are available. To the extent that your spending plan will allow, coordinate your slips with the garments with which you will wear them. Knitted and

permanent-press, or no-iron, fabrics are easy to care for. Stretch fabrics improve fit and comfort. Consider slips made of static-free fabrics or of taffeta particularly for wear under knits or other fabrics which tend to cling. Full-length slips are usually bought according to bust size. Half slips are sold by waist measure or in small, medium, and large sizes. Some are available in proportioned lengths. All should be tried on for a check of the length and fit.

Briefs and Panties   Briefs and panties are generally sized by number according to hip measurement. Briefs and bikinis are available in a variety of colors and may be tailored or

107

Hip Measurement	Size Required
33-34 inches	4
35-36 inches	5
37-38 inches	6
39-40 inches	7
41-42 inches	8
43-44 inches	9
45-48 inches	10

Waist Measurement	Size Required
23-24 inches	Extra small
25-26 inches	Small
27-28 inches	Medium
29-30 inches	Large
31-32 inches	Extra large

lace-trimmed. Important design and quality features include:

1. High-quality elastic attached with zig-zag stitching or enclosed in a hem.
2. Smooth, neatly finished seams.
3. Double-fabric crotch.
4. Soft, smooth fabric.

Bras To determine your correct bra size, put a tape measure around your rib cage, under the bust. Take a snug, but not tight, measurement. Then add 5 inches to this measurement to determine the size to buy.

To determine your correct cup size, measure around the body where the bust is fullest. If this measurement is identical to your bra size, you will require a size A cup. If the measurement is one inch more than the bra size, choose a size B cup. Two additional inches suggest the need for a size C cup, and three additional inches designate a D cup size. Since various companies cut bras to slightly different shapes, and since body size may change from time to time, always try on a bra for exact fit before buying.

A bra with proper fit stays close to your body, has no gaps between the cups, and has cups large enough to allow the breasts to lift naturally and straight forward. If flesh overflows, a larger cup or a style with more coverage is indicated. If the cup is not filled out, a smaller or padded cup may be needed. In choosing padded cups, consider those lined with fiberfill since they withstand wear and care better than do foam-lined cups. Check the underbust band. It should fit snugly but not tightly. If it rides up, it is too tight. If you can run your finger easily under the band, the fit is correct. Check the back. If it rides up, the fit around your body is too tight.

Girdles The size of a girdle is determined mainly by waist measurement. Other determining factors are hip ratio and total height. The hip ratio is the difference between the waist and hip measurement. You can calculate your hip ratio in the following way:

1. Measure your waist.
2. Measure around the fullest part of your hips.
3. Subtract your waist measurement from your hip measurement to obtain your hip ratio.

Your girdle size may then be determined from the accompanying size guide according to the following rules. If your hip ratio is between 9 and 12 inches, try the girdle size your waist measurement indicates. If your hip ratio is less than 9 inches, try a girdle size smaller than your waist measurement indicates. If your ratio is more than 12, try a size larger than your waist measurement indicates. Correct size depends somewhat on your height, as well. With so many factors involved, it is important to try on a girdle before buying. Be certain the one you buy is comfortable when

CHECK LIST FOR BUYING FOUNDATION GARMENTS

A Bra
1. Is the style appropriate for your figure and for the garments you plan to wear over it?
2. Is the fabric durable and easy to care for?
3. Are the inside seams smoothly finished and firmly tacked at both ends?
4. Are the stays and rib bands covered?
5. Is the fastening adjustable, with at least two fastening positions?
6. Are there elasticized sections for comfort and smooth fit?
7. Are the straps adjustable and made partly or entirely of elasticized fabric?
8. Does the bra fit smoothly all around without gaps or bulges?
9. Is the desired support provided without pressure anywhere?
10. Are instructions for care attached?

A Girdle
1. Is the fabric an open-mesh type to provide for ventilation?
2. Are the inside seams flat, with stitching generous enough to permit full elastic expansion without strain?
3. Are the upper and lower edges lined with soft material?
4. Do the garters, if included, have adequate elasticity? Are they secured firmly?
5. Is the desired control provided without pinching, bulging, or riding up?
6. Is the waistband shaped to your figure, fitting snugly without cutting or binding?
7. Do the leg bands permit freedom of movement and comfort without binding?
8. If the garment is a panty girdle, is the crotch seamless?
9. Is the length from waist to crotch sufficient to prevent binding?
10. Are instructions for care attached?

both standing and sitting. Girdles, like swimsuits, are nonreturnable items.

Hosiery   Hosiery is the general term often applied to long stockings, panty hose, and socks. Through the years hosiery has been sold by foot size. For instance, if your foot were 9½ inches long, you would wear a size 9½ sock or stocking. In buying panty hose, however, the total leg length and the figure size, as well as the foot length, are considered in determining correct size. Panty hose can be purchased in short, average, tall, and extra tall, as well as in one stretch size which fits all.

In the hosiery departments of many stores, charts are available that relate the sizes of socks and stockings to the sizes of shoes. Instructions for determining the correct size of panty hose are usually provided on the package. When the foot length is correct, the hosiery has sufficient reserve elasticity to be pulled out at least ½ inch in any direction. Choose hosiery of any type long enough in the foot so that it does not bind your toes but short enough so that it does not wrinkle. Hosiery that is too short may cause your feet to burn. Many people like stretch

Manufacturers currently offer underwear which emphasizes the natural look for girls who prefer comfort rather than restriction.

hosiery because it adjusts to the proper size, giving a smooth, neat fit.

Panty hose combines panties and stockings in one complete garment. The panty section is reinforced, and the leg section is either sheer or opaque for fashion as might be a pair of conventional stockings. It is usually available in a variety of colors. This garment is a leg fashion asset, and it is comfortable to wear because it frees you from the necessity of wearing a garter belt or girdle simply for holding up stockings. You can get the most wear per pair if you choose the correct size and put them on and remove them carefully.

Socks are available in both ankle and knee lengths. They are made from cotton, nylon, wool, and acrylic fibers. Socks are available in many colors and in a variety of knitted patterns. Choose those that will be comfortable in your climate and that suit your costume and the occasions for which they will be worn. Socks are more economical, particularly for sport and casual wear, than are sheer stockings.

Shoes

Shoe sizes include both length and width measurements. Length is indicated by number: 5, 5½, 6, 6½, etc., up to 12. Width is indicated by letter: AAA, AA, A, B, C, D, and E. AAA is usually the narrowest size and E the widest. AAAA, AAAAA, and EE shoes are generally stocked by specialty shoe stores or can be specially ordered for feet which are extremely hard to fit. Novelty and play shoes are often sized in Narrow, Medium, and Wide widths, rather than in the finer gradations. Narrow is usually the equivalent of AA width in regular shoe sizes, Medium of B width, and Wide of C width. Those persons with extremely narrow or extremely wide feet can seldom find novelty shoes which fit their feet properly.

It is sound economy to pay a price sufficient to ensure good fit and quality in the shoes you will be wearing most. Conservative styling might also be considered. Buy less expensive shoes for rare occasions. Party and casual shoes are types which might be

Shirts, pants, and shoes comprise a major portion of the young person's wardrobe. Choose these types of clothing for comfort, fit, style, and ease of care.

Photos Courtesy Celanese Fibers Marketing Co.

Choose boots and shoes to complete the look of a fashion picture as well as to fit your individual foot.

bought in bold colors, if desired, and relatively poor qualities for the sake of economy.

Everyday shoes especially require good fit to give proper support to your feet. Correct fit provides comfort and prevents the development of poor habits of standing and walking, which may lead to foot difficulties. Consider smooth leather or high-quality imitation leather shoes for this purpose. Shop in a store where the salesperson begins by measuring your foot for the proper size. Because no two feet are identical, try on both shoes. Both must be long enough and wide enough so that your feet fill them comfortably without crowding, but not so large that they slip and rub

your feet as you wear them. A shoe which presses on the foot because it is too tight or rubs the foot because it is too loose may cause corns, calluses, bunions, or blisters. If your foot fills the shoe to the tip before you step down in it, the shoe will be too short as you walk, because the foot lengthens somewhat when it bears your weight. The widest part of the shoe should fit the widest part of your foot. The shape of the shoe should conform to your foot at the arch, which it should support. In trying on new shoes, consider these aspects of fit as you walk around in them to determine whether they are comfortable. Comfort, more than style, is absolutely essential.

1. Discuss how poor management of a clothing budget can cause psychological and emotional problems.

2. Analyze reasons why a person may not have appropriate clothing. Prepare a bulletin-board display showing a well-planned wardrobe.

3. Explore how the choice of accessories affects a wardrobe plan. Relate accessories to the wearer, occasions, use, and cost. Analyze how the total cost of an outfit is a sum of its parts.

4. Discuss how the clothing allowance of an individual must relate to the clothing budget for the entire family. Figure the total cost of a $50 coat bought on the various terms provided by stores in your community.

5. Analyze the money needs of a clothing budget. Relate money needs to the human resources which can be used to meet clothing needs.

6. Discuss shopping experiences that resulted in satisfaction and dissatisfaction with purchases. Analyze reasons that led to both situations.

7. Discuss what you should wear when you go shopping and why.

8. Bring to class mail-order catalogues and pattern books to study today's fashions suitable for your activities.

9. Ask a buyer of underfashions to discuss with you the importance of correct size and fit of slips, bras, panties, girdles, and stockings or panty hose.

10. Invite a person in charge of advertising in a local store or an advertising manager of a newspaper or a radio or television station to discuss the code of ethics his organization uses in developing an advertising message.

11. Study newspaper, magazine, radio, television, and direct-mail advertising for discounts, free prizes, or introductory offers.

12. Inquire whether Autonet has reached your community. If possible, study and evaluate an Autonet broadcast.

13. Ask your science teacher to explain to the class how cable television and picturephones work.

14. Analyze shops and boutiques in your community. Observe their point-of-sale and window displays. Observe how they create in you a desire to buy.

15. Invite a buyer of shoes to visit your class to discuss materials used, proper fit, and the influence of fashion on the style of shoes and boots.

1. List and illustrate the characteristics of a well-planned wardrobe. Give a demonstration showing a well-planned wardrobe to a group such as Girl Scouts, a 4-H group, or a YWCA group that meets in your area.

2. Help a family to plan a wardrobe. Determine the difference between clothing needs and wants and discuss your findings with each member of the family.

3. Determine the clothing needs of a family in relation to the total needs of the family.

4. Plan how you can work with a junior high school group in your community to help them manage their clothing expenditures to better advantage.

INDEPENDENT LEARNING EXPERIENCES

1. Plan your next clothing purchase. State your goal. What decisions will you need to make to achieve your goal?

2. Determine how a successful spending plan must be flexible and designed to fit your needs according to changing conditions within your family.

3. Identify the factors that influence your clothing requirements.

4. Keep records of (a) income received including gifts received, with approximate value, and (b) expenses for which you are responsible, such as amusements, clothing, transportation, beauty aids, drycleaning services, shoe repair, medical care, and dental care. Determine good and poor expenditures of money.

5. List the clothing you would like to buy. Decide how advertising has stimulated your interest.

6. Assemble articles written by fashion editors of newspapers and magazines. Analyze how they influence your thinking either positively or negatively.

7. Make a study of national television advertising that is tied into the local advertising programs of your clothing stores.

8. Collect guarantees or warranties that apply to wearing apparel. Determine what they really guarantee.

9. Read catalogue descriptions pertaining to clothing. List the quality levels available, size information, garment design, and workmanship described. Determine which information is useful and why.

10. Shop the clothing stores in your community. Examine the zippers, buttons, and other closures on the garments for general appearance and their likelihood of lasting the lifetime of the garment.

5 Caring for Your Clothing

Probably the most sweeping of the many recent changes in the world of clothing is the move to permanently label all clothing and all fabric bought for clothing as to the care required for effective appearance in wear. This care labeling combined with effective clothing management and laundry and drycleaning techniques can provide for each person the best of possible wardrobes allowable within a given clothing budget.

How can permanent labels which specify acceptable care for a garment increase the effectiveness of the garment as a part of your wardrobe?

When permanent care labels are attached to garments, who is responsible for the proper care of the garment?

How can preventive care decrease the cost of an effective wardrobe?

Why is storage important to the appearance of clothing?

How can drawers, hangers, and covers be effective aids in the care and storage of clothing?

Managing the Care of Your Clothing

A well-groomed appearance depends on a combination of neat, clean, becoming garments and impeccable personal grooming. Giving your clothes the proper care will keep them neat and clean and will increase their wear life as well as your savings in time and money.

The total amount of money you have available to spend on your wardrobe is determined by your spending plan. It is folly to spend all of this clothing budget on the purchase of clothing, failing to consider the cost of upkeep. This cost includes the price in money, time, and energy required for the maintenance of the good appearance of your garments throughout their lifetime. In the long run, adequate care is less expensive than replacement of clothing which has been improperly handled. Sometimes the best management practice is simply not to buy a garment that would be too costly to maintain in terms of time, energy, or money.

The major consideration in determining the maintenance cost of a garment is whether the garment needs to be laundered or drycleaned. The information is readily available on the permanent care label attached to the garment. Many of the problems of clothing management can be prevented if you carefully note and follow the recommended care procedure for each garment. Permanent care labeling is further discussed on pages 120-122.

Preventive Care

A large part of clothing maintenance is *preventive.* This term indicates the care which prevents damage or soiling from occurring. All garments require a certain amount of cleaning and upkeep. But preventive care can cut repair and cleaning costs to the minimum. Work out a simple plan, or schedule, which allows for the daily, weekly, and seasonal preventive care your clothing requires. The upgrading of poorly constructed ready-made garments before wearing is discussed on pages 214-215.

To give your clothes preventive care as you wear them, be aware of the pockets. Do not fill them to the bulging stage. Take care that your pen does not leak or your lipstick smear and stain the fabric. Choose your jewelry carefully. Decorative pins can damage your clothes, and some costume pieces, such as certain types of necklaces and metal pins, can cause fabric discoloration.

Be on the lookout for dusty, dirty seats, tables, and food counters. Because the print rubs off easily, wash your hands immediately after reading a newspaper or pulp magazine. Printer's ink can stain your clothes.

Be careful around cars and buses. Grease will stain, and battery acid will literally eat clothing. Avoid snagging and tearing your clothing as you get in and out of buses, subways, or cars.

Use particular care in protecting your clothes from cosmetics. Allow deodorants to dry before dressing. Use a makeup cap to cover your head when putting on or removing a garment that slips over the head. Do not apply lipstick until after you are dressed, and do not apply perfume or cologne directly to a garment. If you must put on fingernail polish after you are dressed, protect your clothing with a towel.

If you are caught in the rain or snow, remove wet garments and place them on hangers to dry in a cool location. When they are dry, brush them thoroughly and press them, if necessary.

When you get home from school, remove your school clothing and put on more casual clothes. To protect your clothes after you wear them, select suitable hangers, and immediately hang up garments that require hanging unless it is time to launder or dry-clean them. Close side or back zippers, and secure at least the top fastener of front openings so that the garments will keep their shape. Use clothespins or straight pins, if necessary, to secure the garments to the hangers. To remove body odors and wrinkles, air the garments that you plan to hang in a closet by first hanging them in a well-ventilated area. Air garments to be stored in a box or drawer by spreading them over the back of a chair.

Many fabrics need brushing to remove the dust and lint that accumulate in a day's wearing. Select the proper brush: soft bristles for delicate fabrics and hard bristles for firmly woven fabrics. Brush with the nap or grain of the fabric. Lint rollers are useful for removing lint. Nylon combs for use on fabrics are excellent for removing the hard balls of fiber, called *pills*, from sweaters.

Inspect your clothes to determine whether they need to be mended or repaired. Separate those that do from those that are ready to be put away. Set aside some time each week to do necessary mending, spotting, laundering, and pressing.

Space Management

The adage *a place for everything and everything in its place* can be applied very effectively to the care of clothing. When special places are provided and used for each type of clothing, much of the work of clothing care is simply avoided. Many wrinkles fall out of clothes that are cared for properly.

Drawer Space

Drawer space can be considered a necessary part of a teen-ager's clothing-care equipment. Adequate drawer space allows for storage of lingerie, hose, and sweaters in an area which is free of dust and other types of soil. Since hanging causes loosely knitted garments to stretch out of shape, fold them gently and place them in a drawer.

Shelf paper or liner makes a better lining for drawers than does newspaper. Treated shelf paper absorbs grease, repels moisture, and eliminates the risk of stain from printer's ink.

CARING FOR WET CLOTHING

Coats, suits, and skirts   Place on hangers and hang to dry in a cool, well-ventilated area away from direct heat. Hot air will make some garments steam and possibly shrink. When garments are completely dry, brush thoroughly, and press if necessary. Treat wet fur the same way, brushing and fluffing when completely dry rather than pressing.

Shoes   Stuff toes with paper and allow shoes to dry away from heat. Shoe trees inserted into wet shoes may change the shape of the shoes. If leather hardens as it dries, rub a little oil on both the soles and the uppers. Polish in the usual way when completely dry.

STEPS IN MENDING CLOTHES

Secure buttons, snaps, hooks, and eyes   Directions for sewing these on are given in Chapter 18. If belt carriers or thread loops are broken, remove and replace them.

Reinforce torn buttonholes   Place a piece of tape or strong fabric between the garment and the facing. Sew over the torn end of the buttonhole through all thicknesses, using the buttonhole stitch.

Restitch ripped seams or zippers   Resew any sections of the hem that have come loose or any seams that have ripped, and resew shoulder straps to slips and bras as needed.

Renew worn tape   Apply new tape to hems, and restitch hem with an invisible hemming stitch.

Repair girdles   Zigzag-stitch or stretch-stitch over seams that have pulled out, reinforcing by stitching over a patch of elastic lace. Resew lace or other trimming that has come loose.

Apply patches   For three-cornered tears or worn spots use a piece of fabric which corresponds in color, weight, and weave to the fabric in the garment. The patch may be applied with hand stitching or machine stitching, depending upon the location and the fabric. Instead of stitching a patch over a tear or worn spot, a press-on patch or tape may be applied.

When placing garments in a drawer, arrange them loosely to retain proper shapes and minimize wrinkling. Place white or light colored garments on one side of the drawer, dark-colored garments on the other. Protect the light-colored garments with tissue paper or polyethylene drycleaning bags. This is a precaution against crocking, which is the rubbing off of color. It also prevents sublimation, which is the process by which a dye changes to a gas and then redeposits itself as a solid on other garments.

Closet Space

Your clothes closet can be both attractive and functional. Ideally it is large enough to

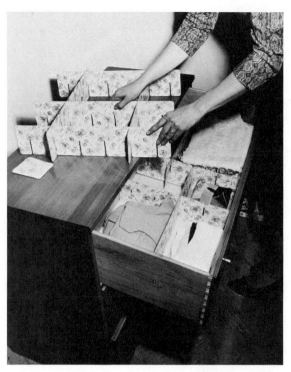

Drawer space can be used to best advantage if adjustable dividers are used to partition off sections of drawers for specific purposes.

A closet which is furnished with shelves, drawers, and poles provides storage space for a wide variety of clothing items.

accommodate your season's wardrobe. Space between the garments will prevent the formation of wrinkles.

Poles　　If a closet is as deep as the width of a hanger, the pole can be attached from end to end of the closet. Plan to have one pole high enough to accommodate long items. For extra space, use a second pole, halfway down and extending only a partial length of the closet, to divide the hanging space on one end of the closet for blouses, suit coats, skirts, and slacks. If your closet is shallow, attach ready-made pull-out fixtures to the back wall or underside of a shelf. Position the fixtures so that shoulders of garments do not rub against each other.

Shelves　　Effective closets have shelves where items can be stored in an organized manner. If shelves are covered with a wash-able, self-adhering material, they tend to be attractive, free of splinters, and easy to keep clean. In organizing closet shelves, select boxes of the shapes required for the various items to be stored, such as hats, purses, and shoes. These boxes can be covered with matching or contrasting self-adhering materials. A window may be cut into each box and a clear polyethylene insert attached across the opening, or a label stating the contents may be placed on the outside of the box.

Hooks　　It is convenient to have several hooks in a closet for hanging belts, scarves, and nightclothes. Hooks are generally of a type which can be screwed into wooden frame areas. Adhesive-backed plastic hooks are also available for closets which lack suitable locations for the attachment of screw-type hooks.

AIDS FOR CLOTHING CARE WHEN TRAVELING

1. Travel-size packages of detergents. Each capsule or envelope contains enough to wash a few articles of clothing in a bathroom washbowl.
2. Plastic hangers on which to hang drip-dry garments.
3. A plastic, stretch clothesline. Sometimes these are packaged with a few clothespins. A braided type permits tucking the ends of garments between the strands of the line, thereby eliminating the need for clothespins.
4. A lightweight travel iron — 110-220 volts, AC-DC current. Also, for foreign travel, assorted plugs.
5. A good clothesbrush.
6. A small shoe-cleaning kit with a special brush for suede shoes, if needed.
7. A small bottle of cleaning solvent.
8. A towel for pressing and wrapping moist lingerie.
9. Plastic zipper bags to carry some of the above items or to hold clothing that may be damp or soiled when you are ready to pack.

Hangers If possible, choose wooden or plastic hangers which are broad enough and strong enough to adequately support the garments in your wardrobe. The hangers with extra-thick ends shaped like a duck's bill are especially effective for tailored garments. They will help keep even rain-soaked coats in shape.

Insofar as possible, avoid using the thin wire hangers on which your garments are returned from the drycleaners. These hangers were designed only to transport garments from store to home. If misused for long-term storage in clothes closets, they may cause garments to lose their shape, they may leave crease marks, and some of them may cause rust marks.

Press-type or clothespin-type hangers are useful for skirts, and pants holders are convenient for slacks. If closet space is limited, you might want to try heavy metal multiple blouse and skirt hangers and shoe racks.

Garment Covers Many people do not use garment bags to protect their clothing from lint and dust because they do not want to invest money in this protection or because they

have limited or shallow closet space that does not lend itself to the size of the bags.

Dark garments especially need protection, and dress clothing which is worn infrequently needs shielding from lint and dust. If you do not want to spend money on garment bags, try using shoulder covers. You may even prefer them to garment bags because they allow clothes to air while in the clothes closet.

Several types of shoulder covers are available commercially, although you can easily make your own. Choose heavy plastic covers to avoid the clinging caused by static electricity. Select the correct cover size for the garment to be protected. If your garments are getting dusty or linty, even though protected with shoulder covers, take stock of your wardrobe. Maybe you are not wearing all of your garments frequently enough to keep them fresh. If so, store the infrequently used garments elsewhere. This will allow more space for the clothes you are currently wearing.

Seasonal Storage of Clothes

Careless storage can be a real hazard to clothing. The most important thing to remember is,

119

Courtesy Portex Products Company

Garment bags and boxes, while relatively expensive, can be bought from time to time as your clothing budget allows. Once purchased, they can be used immediately to protect your wardrobe from the damages of the environment.

never store clothing that is dirty. Dirt and food stains are an invitation to textile-eating insects. Larvae hatched from eggs deposited on garments can eat many times their weight daily, and your clothing is their favorite meal. They eat many types of fabrics.

Wash or dryclean all garments before storing them. Also, make necessary minor repairs, or ask your drycleaner to make them, before putting the clothing in storage. Many cleaners do not charge for this service.

Before storing garments, remove belts from their loops and hang them from a hanger. This helps prevent the belt backings from cracking and the garments from sagging.

Close all fastenings so that garments will not hang out of shape. Then hang the clothes carefully, or pack them into boxes.

Sweaters and other loosely knitted garments should be stored flat. To prevent fold marks, stuff them with tissue paper.

Make sure all stored garments are well mothproofed. Sprinkle a reliable moth preventive into the clothes containers or closets, or have your drycleaner mothproof your garments after cleaning them.

Once garments are cleaned and mothproofed, they must be sealed from air and moisture to be completely safe. Storage areas should be kept cool and dry and should be out of the sunlight to discourage the hatching of insects. After removing dust which gathers in cracks or crevices, spray storage closets with a fumigant.

Cedar chests and cedar-lined closets are satisfactory for seasonal storage if there are no moth eggs in the garments stored in them. While the cedar will not kill moths or silverfish, insects avoid garments surrounded by cedar.

Leave plenty of air space in storage compartments. If you do not have ample storage space, you might wish to note that many drycleaners provide sealed storage vaults with controlled humidity and temperature where your garments can hang safe and insect-free after drycleaning. The charge made for such storage is usually small, and garments are insured. Garments are returned at the end of the season cleaned, pressed, and ready to wear.

Using Permanent Care Labels

The need for permanent care labeling has not always been a valid one. Early in the history of mankind only a few fibers were available from which to make clothing. Still fewer cleaning methods were available. It was only with the technological progress of the twentieth century that a multiplicity of fibers and

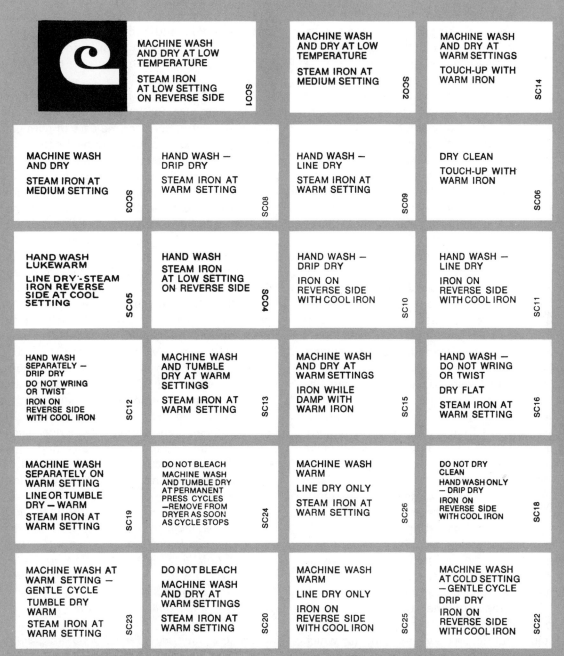

MACHINE WASH AND DRY AT LOW TEMPERATURE / **STEAM IRON AT LOW SETTING ON REVERSE SIDE** — SC01

MACHINE WASH AND DRY AT LOW TEMPERATURE / **STEAM IRON AT MEDIUM SETTING** — SC02

MACHINE WASH AND DRY AT WARM SETTINGS / **TOUCH-UP WITH WARM IRON** — SC14

MACHINE WASH AND DRY / **STEAM IRON AT MEDIUM SETTING** — SC03

HAND WASH — DRIP DRY / **STEAM IRON AT WARM SETTING** — SC08

HAND WASH — LINE DRY / **STEAM IRON AT WARM SETTING** — SC09

DRY CLEAN / **TOUCH-UP WITH WARM IRON** — SC06

HAND WASH LUKEWARM / **LINE DRY - STEAM IRON REVERSE SIDE AT COOL SETTING** — SC05

HAND WASH / **STEAM IRON AT LOW SETTING ON REVERSE SIDE** — SC04

HAND WASH — DRIP DRY / **IRON ON REVERSE SIDE WITH COOL IRON** — SC10

HAND WASH — LINE DRY / **IRON ON REVERSE SIDE WITH COOL IRON** — SC11

HAND WASH SEPARATELY — DRIP DRY / **DO NOT WRING OR TWIST** / **IRON ON REVERSE SIDE WITH COOL IRON** — SC12

MACHINE WASH AND TUMBLE DRY AT WARM SETTINGS / **STEAM IRON AT WARM SETTING** — SC13

MACHINE WASH AND DRY AT WARM SETTINGS / **IRON WHILE DAMP WITH WARM IRON** — SC15

HAND WASH — DO NOT WRING OR TWIST / **DRY FLAT** / **STEAM IRON AT WARM SETTING** — SC16

MACHINE WASH SEPARATELY ON WARM SETTING / **LINE OR TUMBLE DRY — WARM** / **STEAM IRON AT WARM SETTING** — SC19

DO NOT BLEACH / **MACHINE WASH AND TUMBLE DRY AT PERMANENT PRESS CYCLES —REMOVE FROM DRYER AS SOON AS CYCLE STOPS** — SC24

MACHINE WASH WARM / **LINE DRY ONLY** / **STEAM IRON AT WARM SETTING** — SC26

DO NOT DRY CLEAN / **HAND WASH ONLY — DRIP DRY** / **IRON ON REVERSE SIDE WITH COOL IRON** — SC18

MACHINE WASH AT WARM SETTING — GENTLE CYCLE / **TUMBLE DRY WARM** / **STEAM IRON AT WARM SETTING** — SC23

DO NOT BLEACH / **MACHINE WASH AND DRY AT WARM SETTINGS** / **STEAM IRON AT WARM SETTING** — SC20

MACHINE WASH WARM / **LINE DRY ONLY** / **IRON ON REVERSE SIDE WITH COOL IRON** — SC25

MACHINE WASH AT COLD SETTING — GENTLE CYCLE / **DRIP DRY** / **IRON ON REVERSE SIDE WITH COOL IRON** — SC22

Courtesy Celanese Fibers Marketing Co.

Government regulations require that every garment available on today's market be provided with a permanent label similar to those shown here which gives clear instructions as to correct care procedures.

cleaning alternatives made care labeling a necessary part of modern living.

The care of clothing has developed along with civilization. Early Egyptian women were said to have washed their clothes in the Nile River and laid them on the grassy river banks to dry. Both the grass and the sunshine provided bleaching action so that the clothing could be attractively bright or white.

Pioneer American women made soap from animal fat cooked together with lye, a product extracted from the ashes of their wood fires. This lye soap lowered the surface tension of the water and held dirt in suspension so that it could be flushed from their clothes in the wash and rinse waters. When possible, the laundered wash was dried in the sunshine.

As the petroleum industry flourished in this country, drycleaning solvents were developed which were inexpensively available for home and commercial use. It was found that many fabrics such as woolens and silks could be more effectively cleaned in these solvents than in water-soap solutions.

Detergents were developed during the first third of this century. Because of their gentleness and because they had the ability to dislodge dirt from garments without curding in hard water, they largely replaced soap as a cleaning agent.

When only natural fibers were available for clothing production, clothing care methods were relatively easy to determine. Cottons and linens could be washed in hot water with either soap or detergent. Silks or woolens, depending on their construction and value, could be washed gently in cool water or cleaned in a drycleaning solvent.

Technology of the twentieth century, while developing a wide range of beautiful, adaptable fabrics, ended the era in which clothing could be cared for on a "look and decide" basis. With the introduction of natural cellulosics, such as rayon and acetate, as well as a broad range of noncellulosic fabrics, even highly trained professional launderers and drycleaners had some difficulty identifying specific fibers and blends of fibers. Consequently many garments were damaged both in home and professional care simply because there were no clear guidelines as to the preferable solvent or cleaning temperature for a given garment.

Consumer groups became effectively verbal in their plea for labels which would give adequate instructions for the care of garments. Through the joint efforts of the Federal government, fiber producers, textile and garment manufacturers, the clothing care industry, and these consumer groups, permanent care labeling became required by law in 1972. Consequently all garments and all fabrics bought for garments must be adequately labeled as to necessary care in cleaning and pressing. For further details regarding the Permanent Care Labeling Rule, see pages 148-150.

Clothing care labeling has evolved to a point where it is now effective. Each garment must by law be labeled in a manner which allows the person who is cleaning it to do so in a suitable manner. It is now the responsibility of each individual to read care labels and see that his clothing is laundered or cleaned in the recommended manner. The choice of care procedures is no longer guesswork for the person who reads and heeds care labels. Consequently, clothing losses due to improper handling can be greatly reduced.

Why is it important to be informed about available laundry equipment?

Why is it important to read current articles regarding laundry and cleaning products in relation to water pollution and other environmental problems?

Why is it important to know the content of a stain?

What are the advantages of home laundry systems? Coin-operated systems? Professional laundries?

What can be done to increase the effectiveness of hard water as a laundering solvent?

What are the differences between ironing and pressing?

Most modern home laundry equipment provides for preselection of soaking time, washing action, and temperature control of both wash and rinse water. Some makes are provided with additional small baskets for small loads.

Laundering

A generation or so ago families set aside a day known as *wash day.* This was a day of hard work which often included heating and carrying water, hand-scrubbing and rinsing the clothes, hanging them out to dry, and finally folding them away for ironing on another day. Times have changed. With the new laundering equipment and laundering aids available, home laundering is no longer a drudgery. It can be done easily at any time during the week.

Figuring Laundry Costs

If you use a professional laundry service, your dollars-and-cents expense is obvious. The bill represents your costs. If you do your laundry at home or at a coin-operated laundry, the following considerations might help you estimate the cost of your choice of laundry service:

1. How much of the initial investment and installation charges on your home laundry equipment do you charge off with each load of washing you do?

2. Do you add the cost of repairs, replacement of parts, and service?

3. How much water do you use? What does it cost? How much does it cost to heat it?

4. What is the cost of the gas and electricity you use to run your home washing machine, dryer, and iron?

Courtesy Frigidaire Division, General Motors Corporation

Washers and dryers designed to be installed in a stack arrangement provide washing and drying facilities in a minimum of space.

5. How much do laundry aids such as water softener, detergent or soap, bleach, and fabric conditioner cost per load?

6. What is the value of your time spent laundering clothes at home? At the coin-operated laundry?

7. What is the cost of transportation to and from the coin-operated laundry?

8. What is the value of the convenience of a home laundry service you can use at any hour of the day or night?

9. What additional costs must be included in the laundry method of your choice?

In comparing the costs of the various laundry methods, estimates of the clothing depreciation resulting from each available method are also factors to consider. The real cost of laundry, however, is hard to determine. Some authorities feel that the coin-operated laundry is most economical for families who need to wash six or less loads of clothes per week. For the family with heavy laundry needs, home equipment is usually both economical and convenient.

The choice of laundry procedures is a management decision. When you choose the form of laundry service which requires the resources of which you have the greatest supply, you have chosen the laundry method most effective for you.

Washing Equipment

Home equipment is available for the washing and drying of clothes. Similar equipment is also available in modern coin-operated laundries. While most drying equipment is at least to some degree automatic, washers are sold in various conventional and automatic models. Because there is such a wide variation in the capabilities and costs of the various models of washers and dryers, each should be considered by a potential purchaser in terms of personal laundry needs. If your family is considering laundry equipment, each of the following factors should be considered in relation to the equipment available:

1. Size and frequency of wash loads.

2. Types of garments to be laundered.

3. Flexibility and degree of automatic control needed.

4. Special features desired or needed.

5. Installation and servicing requirements necessary.

6. Space available.

7. Warranty responsibility of the manufacturer.

Conventional Washers

Two types of conventional washers are sold. One washes the clothes until they are removed by hand from the wash water and rolled through motor-driven rollers which wring out the wash and rinse water. The other has a separate spinning basket to extract

COMMON WATER PROBLEMS

Problem	Cause	Cure
Grayed laundry ring in tub.	Hardness from calcium and magnesium.	Increased detergent, packaged water conditioner, or water-conditioning equipment.*
Brown to black stains on fabrics and porcelain.	Iron and manganese.	Water-conditioning equipment with special filter.*
Cloudy water.	Sand, silt, or clay in suspension.	Filter*
Rotten egg odor.	Hydrogen sulfide.	Chlorination and filtration.* For laundry, a *very* small amount of chlorine bleach.
Yellow, red, or brown stains on fabrics and porcelain.	Organic matter or mineral.	Consult water-equipment dealer for remedy.
Red stains from iron or galvanized pipes.	Corrosion of pipes.	Neutralizing filter.*
Blue stains from copper piping.	Corrosion of pipes.	Neutralizing filter.*

*Consult water-equipment dealer for proper equipment.

water. Choices are available as to agitation speeds, timers, and automatic pumps for draining.

Automatic Washers

Automatic washers come in several types. The top-loading agitator washer cleans by means of a central agitator that keeps fabrics and water in motion, gently forcing water through the fabrics. Front-loading machines clean by tumbling the clothes and water together in a vertical orbit or by spraying the wash water through the revolving clothes.

Varying water temperatures are available on most automatic washers. The deluxe models usually have several extra features and settings. They often feature three agitation speeds, two spin speeds, five combinations of wash-rinse temperatures, and many washing cycles. For some families all such features perform a useful function. For other families they are an unnecessary expense.

Determining Load Size

The collection of items laundered together in a machine is called a *load.* The load size permissible for a given machine is often stated in weight alone. However, consider also the *bulk* of fabrics for effective laundering. If the fabrics are light and fluffy, the load can weigh up to the maximum poundage indicated on the machine or in the instruction booklet. If the fabrics are bulky and heavy, fewer items will fill the washer to the maximum load level. Be sure the items are loose in the machine so that water and detergent can penetrate them easily.

Water

Water is the solvent used to wash fabrics. Water supplies vary from community to community because of the amount and type of minerals present. Most large cities treat the water supply so that it is effective for laundry purposes when combined with common laundry aids such as detergents and softeners.

Water hardness is measured in grains per gallon. Water in the home usually falls between 3 and 30 grains per gallon. When hardness exceeds a 10-grain concentration, it is beneficial to install a water-conditioning unit, which may be available on a rental basis.

Another way of expressing water hardness is *parts per million* (ppm). One-grain hardness equals 17 parts per million; 10-grain hardness equals 170 parts per million.

If your water comes from a municipal water supply, the water department can tell you how hard the water is. If you have a private water supply, you may wish to test it with a simple testing kit available at chemical supply houses.

One of the most important factors in washing clothes is the temperature of the water. Hot water, 140 degrees Fahrenheit, is best for removing soil from fabric that can withstand the high temperature. Detergents and bleach are most effective at this temperature. The water heater can be adjusted, if necessary, to deliver hot water to the washing machine. Hot water is generally used for all white and colorfast fabrics except delicate fabrics. The latter include silk, wool, rayon, acetate, and certain man-made fibers. Most man-made fibers, wash-and-wear, and permanent-press fabrics can be washed in relatively warm water. It is best to give them a final cold-water rinse, however, to avoid permanent creasing or wrinkling.

Warm water, 100 degrees Fahrenheit, is not entirely effective in removing soil but it must be used on delicate fabrics and for colors that may fade or bleed. Most wool and silk fabrics which are safely washable should be washed in warm or cool water.

Cold water is generally ineffective in removing heavy, greasy soil and some germs. It can be used with special cold-water detergents for washing delicate woolen garments and dainty lingerie. Moreover, some people prefer to use cold water with cold-water detergents for general laundry to reduce the possibility of shrinkage and color loss, as well as the cost of heating water.

For each specific garment, note and follow the laundry directions given on the permanent care label. It is important that hot water be used only for white or colorfast fabrics. You may find it helpful to refer to the list of recommended water temperatures for washing specific fabrics on pages 60-65.

Laundry Aids
An ever-increasing number of laundry aids appear on the shelves of supermarkets and other stores. They include a variety of detergents, soaps, water conditioners, softeners, bleaches, whiteners, starches, and finishers. It is sometimes confusing to decide what products will serve you best. When you see a new laundry product which might help solve your laundry problems, you might want to consider buying a small package for trial use. More can be purchased later if it proves to be worthwhile.

Synthetic Detergents
Synthetic detergents are chemical compounds which, when mixed with water, hold dirt and grease in suspension, permitting them to be floated out of clothes. There are two general types of detergent: normal-sudsing and low-sudsing detergents.

The first synthetic detergents, developed in the 1930s, were light-duty products, mild enough for delicate hand-washables. They had only limited cleaning abilities and were not considered suitable for the family wash. They produced billows of suds. In some products, special *foam boosters* were added. Similar products are popular today, usually in liquid form. These mild detergents contain few or no *builders* to increase the detergents' cleaning ability.

Many of today's all-purpose detergents have had chemical builders added for effective cleaning. They are available in both liquid and powder forms. Although they are *heavy-duty* in their ability to clean, they are generally still safe for anything which can be safely machine-washed. Foam boosters are added to some of these products to please the laundress who likes to see suds.

Low-suds detergents produce only a controlled amount of suds. They do not foam as do other detergents, but they generally

AMOUNT OF DETERGENT FOR AVERAGE SIZE LOAD

Type of Detergent	Average Soil			Heavy Soil		
	Soft Water	Normal Water	Hard Water	Soft Water	Normal Water	Hard Water
Low Sudsing	½ c	¾-1 c or more	1-1⅓ c or more	¾ c	1 c or more	1¾-2 c or more
Normal Sudsing	¾ c	1-1½ c or more	1½-2 c	1 c	1¼-1¾ c or more	2-2½ c or more

clean more effectively. Synthetic detergents have at least some water conditioner added.

Directions on detergent packages are based on the minimum amount of detergent needed for a normal size load, average soiling, and average water hardness. For smaller than normal loads, decrease the amount of detergent somewhat. With practice, you can learn to adjust the amounts of detergent needed according to the individual size and type load and water conditions. A normal-sudsing detergent should maintain thick suds during washing. A low-sudsing detergent must be judged on its effectiveness in cleaning, since practically no suds are formed. Use only a low-suds detergent in a front-loading automatic or in a combination washer-dryer.

In recent years there has been concern over water pollution caused by the ingredients in detergents. Read current material on the subject frequently so that you will be able to co-operate wisely in reducing the water-pollution problem.

Soaps
Soap is a cleaning agent made by combining a strong alkali such as lye with fat. Although it is no longer used to any great degree in laundering fabrics, it is an excellent cleansing agent when used with soft water. Soap, as a laundry aid, has been almost totally replaced by synthetic detergents. This is due to the fact that soap mixed with hard water creates curds which adhere to the fabric. These curds cause the graying and stiffening of fabrics. Soap may be used increasingly in the laundry process, however, because of the water pollution caused by some detergents.

Water Conditioners
Water conditioners help detergent or soap to clean clothes effectively. Two types of packaged water conditioners are available. Each works on one of the following principles:

Type 1: Removes the hard-water minerals from the water through the process of settling.

Type 2: Inactivates the hard-water minerals so that they remain inert during washing.

Either type can be used satisfactorily in washing clothes.

Bleaches
Bleaches are chemical products designed to remove stains and make fabrics whiter. Some bleaches destroy bacteria. There are three types of laundry bleach: liquid chlorine, which is strong; powdered chlorine, which is mild; and all-fabric, or oxygon, bleach, which is very mild. All bleaches should be used with caution according to directions on the package. Misuse can be harmful to fabrics and colors. Avoid bleaching those garments which are labeled *Do Not Bleach*.

Because a number of machines can be rented simultaneously, coin-operated washers and dryers provide for the maximum amount of washing and drying in the minimum amount of time.

Liquid chlorine bleach, which is very effective for stain removal, is harmless if used according to directions. However, it cannot be used without damaging results on silk, spandex, wool, or fabrics that contain even the smallest percentage of these fibers. Avoid pouring liquid chlorine bleach directly onto any kind of fabric. It will burn holes in most garments. This damage may not be apparent until later. Instead, dilute this form of bleach according to label directions before adding it to the wash water. Some washing machines are equipped with bleach dispensers. Such equipment adds bleach at the right time and in the right way. Follow the directions on the bleach bottle, never using more than the manufacturer recommends.

Powdered chlorine bleach offers the same general type of bleaching as the liquid, but it is gentler in action since it releases bleaching ingredients more slowly as it dissolves. Never sprinkle powdered chlorine bleach directly on clothes. Add it to the wash water after the washer has filled with water and agitation has started. Avoid using this type of bleach also on fabrics which contain silk, wool, or spandex.

Oxygen bleaches are generally safe for all washable fabrics and colors, producing little if any fabric damage even with overuse. They are harmless to most colors and do not yellow chlorine-retentive finishes and fibers. Used regularly, they help to maintain the brightness of white and colored items.

Perborate-based oxygen bleaches do not become effective until quite high temperatures are reached, which means they must be used in very hot water to perform. Many fabrics and colors cannot withstand the hot water required for the effective use of this type of bleach.

Potassium monopersulfate-based oxygen bleach contains an active bleaching agent which is effective in mildly warm water. This bleach is especially useful for whitening and brightening spandex underwear, lingerie, and delicate blouses.

Softeners

Softeners are products added to the final rinse water. They are popular because the addition of a measured amount to the last rinse water leaves fabrics feeling soft. They are also effective for controlling static electric charges in fabrics of man-made fibers. This reduces the tendency of such fabrics to cling. Avoid using too much softener in towels, however, as this practice reduces the absorbency.

Optical Brighteners

Optical brighteners are incorporated into most modern laundry detergents. They are colorless dyes that make whites or colors appear brighter when exposed to light. They create the optical illusion that the clothes are white or bright.

Starches

Starch is a stiffening product sometimes used in the final step of the washing process or just before ironing certain garments. Its use prevents fabrics from soiling readily and aids in soil removal when the fabric is washed again. Starch is used less extensively today than in previous times because of the wide use of permanently finished fabrics.

Starches may be classed as vegetable starch or synthetic starch. Vegetable starches have been on the market for many years in both dry and liquid forms. They are diluted with either hot or cold water, and garments are dipped into the solution. They are also available in aerosol cans.

Synthetic starches may be classified as soluble plastics or durable plastics. Most plastic starches are sold in spray cans. They are sprayed onto garments before or during the ironing process. The soluble starches must be renewed after each washing.

Spot and Stain Removal

Spots and stains on clothing are caused by many types of foods and other materials with which you come in contact. When stains are spilled, rubbed, or splattered onto your clothes, give them quick attention before they have time to set. Depending on the fabric, use water or a cleaning solvent, which can be purchased at a drug or food market. Take difficult stains on drycleanable fabrics immediately to a reputable drycleaner.

Types of Stains

Soluble spots and stains in general fit into two groups: those which will dissolve in water and those which will dissolve in cleaning solvents. Some stains are *dual* stains. They must be treated with one solvent and dried before they are treated with the other solvent. Heavy collar soil is an example of a dual stain. Since cleaning solvents and water *do not* mix, treat a dual stain with a cleaning solvent and let the garment dry before water is applied. Treat any unidentified stain on a washable garment by this process.

In addition to soluble stains there are three other types of removable stains. These are stains which can be removed by lubrication, stains which can be removed with chemicals, and stains which can be removed by digestion.

Lubrication is the removal of a stain by the application of mineral oil. For example, hardened peanut butter or paint saturated with mineral oil can be dislodged by the oil, though not dissolved. The oil itself can be removed with a cleaning solvent after the staining agent has been removed.

Courtesy Celanese Fibers Marketing Co.

*Ideally, a wide range of laundry aids are located
conveniently near the laundry area to provide specific
treatments for the variety of laundry problems common
in family laundry situations.*

Chemical action is necessary for the removal of some stains. In such instances a chemical spot remover reacts with the stain to produce a new compound. The new compound is often colorless and easily removed. An iodine stain is an example of one which can be treated by chemical action. The iodine can be treated with ammonia. This will result in the formation of ammonium iodide, which is a colorless water-soluble substance that can be easily flushed from the fabric. Iron rust is another stain which can be chemically treated. However, it is important that rust-removing chemicals *never* be used on fabric containing metallic threads.

Digestion is the process by which enzymes convert complex, insoluble substances into simpler substances that are soluble and readily removed from fabrics. Enzyme presoaks which attack blood and food stains are examples of stain removers which work by the digestive process. Read current publications on pollution in order to choose those which are least harmful to the environment.

The Removal Processes

Most stains can be removed by processes which are labeled *wet* and *dry.* If the garment is washable, the *wet* procedure simply entails soaking it in warm, sudsy water, scrubbing the stain specifically, and rinsing the garment thoroughly. Garments which are drycleanable but which have been stained by foods or chemicals which require wet removal should be taken to a drycleaner. He can remove the stains by spotting with water and detergent before drycleaning the garment.

Certain stains must be removed by *dry* procedures. If the garment is to be washed at home, use the dry procedure to remove the specific stain before laundering it. If the stained garment requires professional drycleaning, identify the stain if possible for the spotter. He will remove it before the garment is drycleaned.

The dry spot-removal process can be accomplished in the following manner:

1. Place an absorbent pad under the stained area. A white pad is preferable as it more readily reveals the transfer of staining material from the stained fabric to the pad.

2. Apply the solvent to the stain. Saturate the area.

3. Rub the stain lightly with your fingertips. Let the fluid loosen the staining substance and rinse it through the fabric into the pad. Continue rubbing with the fingers until the staining material is gone.

4. Remove the pad.

5. Moisten a piece of cheese cloth with the cleaning fluid and wipe lightly around the outside edges of the spotted area. Wipe to-

STAINS REMOVED BY THE WET PROCESS

Catsup
Coffee and tea*
Cream
Food stains
Fruit juices
Grass*

Household glue†
Ice cream
Leather dyes
Library paste†
Mercurochrome*
Merthiolate

Milk
Mustard*
Soft drinks
Urine
Washable inks (not ballpoint)
Wine and berry stains

*These stains are often very difficult to remove, especially if they are not attacked when fresh. To avoid risk of failure and even damage to the fabric, it may be wise to entrust them to a professional drycleaner.
†There are many glues and adhesives which cause very stubborn stains. It is wise to entrust these to a professional drycleaner and not attempt home spot removal. Those listed here are normally responsive to home methods.

STAINS REMOVED BY THE DRY PROCESS

Ballpoint and marking ink
Candle wax*
Carbon and tracing paper
Cooking oils and greases
Foundation makeup
Lipstick*
Paints

Printing inks
Road oil and tar
Rouge and mascara
Rubber base adhesives
Salad oil and dressing
Typewriter ribbon
Wax shoe polish*

*These items consist of a wax and a dye. The wax is removed with *dry* procedures. The dye will remain, requiring treatment with *wet* procedures. Use the dry procedures first. Be sure the wax is removed completely before using *wet* procedures.

ward the center. This is to prevent formation of a ring.

6. Allow the garment to dry.

In using the dry procedure, work the stain slowly. Patience is necessary. Check frequently to see whether the staining substance has transferred to the pad. Change the position of the pad to keep a clean portion of it next to the stained area.

Stain-removal Precautions

Some spots and stains cannot be removed by any home or professional process. Sometimes you must decide whether you prefer a stained garment or no garment at all. However, there are a few remedies to try when both *wet* and *dry* spotting attempts fail.

Bleaching can be considered as a last resort. Ordinary medicinal 3 percent hydrogen peroxide bleach, available at the drugstore, is the easiest bleach to use. But test the bleach first on an unexposed seam or a sample of the fabric. Pour some bleach on the sample piece of fabric. Wait 5 minutes for a reaction. Many white fabrics contain an optical brightener which will turn yellow when bleached. Very bright-colored fabrics may contain these optical brightening agents, too, and a bleach can cause these colors to become dull.

Some stains and some fabrics do not lend themselves to home spot-removal methods. It is best to take these to the professional drycleaner whose skill and equipment will be needed to get the spots out. Among those you should avoid working on at home are dark-colored marks from tracing paper, spots of paint and fingernail polish, and most medicine, glue, and adhesive stains. It is wise *not* to

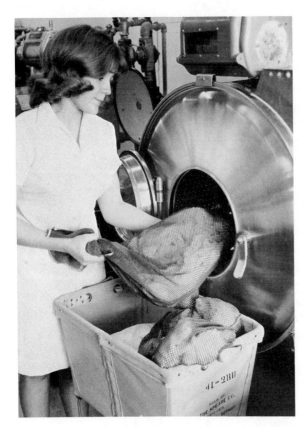

Courtesy International Fabricare Institute

In commercial laundries, clothes are separated into individual bags, washed under sanitary conditions, ironed, and packaged for return to the owner.

attempt home spot removal on leather, suede, furs, vinyl, or fabrics that are heavily sized such as silk, certain taffetas, nets, and satins, or fabrics that have colors which run.

Invisible Stains

It may seem strange, but some stains are invisible before the clothing is cleaned. Many fruit juices disappear into the fabric without visibly staining, though the sugars are deposited there. Drycleaning fluid does not dissolve the sugars. Later, however, heat may brown them, causing a stain which does not come out. When you spill fruit juice on a fabric, flush it out promptly with clear water, even though the stain is invisible.

Machine-washing Procedures

The total laundry process includes preparing the items for washing and putting them away afterwards, as well as the laundering itself. Care and time spent in preparing items for washing saves both time and effort during the actual washing. Consider how the following steps will help you launder clothes effectively whether you are working at home or at the coin-operated laundry.

1. Sort the items as follows:

a. According to soil. Heavily soiled or greasy clothes should be washed separately.

b. According to color. Whites and very light fast colors may be washed together, dark clothes separately.

c. According to fiber content. For best results, nylons and delicate washables should not be mixed with sturdy, heavy items. Separate silk, wool, spandex, and chlorine-sensitive fabrics from loads that are to be bleached with a chlorine product.

2. Empty pockets, close zippers, hook hooks, and remove any trimmings or buttons which might be damaged or lost.

3. Mend rips and tears and sew on loose buttons. Pretreat any deeply embedded spots or stains.

4. Follow washing instructions provided by the garment manufacturer or those provided on the washing machine.

5. Wash white nylon with white items *only.* Nylon picks up color easily from other clothes.

6. When in doubt as to what bleach can be used, use an all-fabric bleach.

7. Wash separately any napped and quilted items, such as chenille robes and fleecy coats. These fabrics produce lint, which is easily picked up by many other fabrics, such as corduroy and some man-made fibers.

8. Do not mix light and dark colors. Dark colors that tend to fade may bleed onto lighter-colored fabrics.

9. Use the delicate, or gentle, cycle, if the machine has one, for sheer, lace-trimmed, and delicately made garments of all types.

10. Give heavily soiled clothes, other than wool, a prewash or soaking. Such preliminary treatment aids greatly in stain removal. Use warm or cold water with a detergent added to give best results when prewashing or soaking.

11. Keep items heavily stained with grease and oil separate from other loads. Grease travels from one garment to another.

12. Wash each load with the water temperature, machine agitation, and laundry aids suitable for the particular garments in the load.

Agitation and Spin Speeds

Most automatic washers are designed to offer a choice of agitation and spin speeds. While agitation speed describes the movement of the fabric in the wash and rinse water, spin speed describes the speed with which fabrics are whirled to remove moisture after the water has been drained. Many models offer programmed cycles that are preset for correct agitation and spin speeds and water temperatures.

Agitation speeds are described as follows: *Normal agitation* speed can be used for all sturdy fabrics and most well-made items. *Medium agitation* is usually best for loosely woven fabrics, all silks, and man-made fibers and well-made garments with delicate construction. *Slow agitation* is designed for any garments that, because of fiber, fabric, or construction, require the gentlest of care.

Normal spin speeds are used on most wash loads. *Slow spin* is designed for such fabrics as permanent press and wash-and-wear, which become wrinkled by excess spinning, and garments of very delicate fabrics and construction.

If your automatic washer has cycles marked for various kinds of fabrics and loads, use them. These cycles provide the proper water temperature and agitation and spin speeds for the loads indicated.

Rinsing

Most automatic washers give you a choice of warm or cold rinse temperature. *Warm* is used

Courtesy The Maytag Company

Heavily soiled items often require pretreatment with specific laundry aids before washing and drying with other items in the wash load.

for the bulk of the wash, while *cold* is used to minimize wrinkling of permanent press and wash-and-wear fabrics. Extra rinsing may be necessary after an extra-sudsy wash. An extra rinse cycle can be achieved in most home automatic washers by manipulating the control knob for additional rinses after the cycle is completed.

Water Level

Many automatic washers allow you to vary the water level to fit the size of the load. When choosing the amount of water, be sure you provide enough water to let the clothes tumble or slosh freely in the washer. Overloading can be as much of a problem at low water levels as at high levels.

When washing permanent-press and wash-and-wear fabrics, it is best to fill the washer with water.

Wash Period

The length of the wash period varies with the amount of soil and the type of load washed. Generally, lightly soiled garments can be washed for a shorter time than heavily soiled ones. Use a short wash time for delicate fabrics.

Hand-washing Procedures

Certain items of clothing are washed by hand even though hand washing is not as thorough as machine washing.

In hand washing, use water of the temperature the fabric and color will allow. Use water conditioner if you are washing with soap or if the water is hard. Add the detergent or soap to the water, and soak the garments for 20 to 30 minutes. At the end of the soaking period, you can add cool water if necessary to handle the items comfortably. Repeat the sudsing process if necessary.

Rinse the garments through several waters until the rinse water is clear, using warm or cool water. Add fabric softener to the final rinse, if desired.

Drying Procedures

Before the introduction of automatic dryers, people dried their freshly laundered clothing either by hanging it on a line or by spreading it out on a flat surface. The latter method is still desirable for clothing such as woolen sweaters that must be dried to shape. Line drying is still widely used, particularly in areas of the country where the humidity is low and the weather mild.

Automatic dryers are available for public use at most coin-operated washing centers. Also many homes have automatic drying equipment. The chief advantages of automatic dryers are that they are convenient, they reduce drudgery and drying time, and they can be used in any kind of weather.

Most dryers have some means of controlling the drying temperature and time. Many machines also have an air setting for drying items that cannot be dried with heat and for automatically airing items such as pillows and draperies.

Most modern dryer models offer flexibility, with programmed cycles to ensure the proper drying temperature and time for each specific load. Many are quite versatile, providing automatic temperature control plus a variety of user-selected dryness levels. Some offer a choice of drying speeds and include dampening devices to prepare items for ironing.

Deluxe dryers approach complete automation, incorporating a sensing system that shuts them off when the clothes are dry. Some models can be set to shut off when a chosen degree of dryness is reached in the items being dried.

Ironing Procedures

The process of ironing is used for removing wrinkles from clothing. As the use of permanent-press items increases, ironing decreases in importance. Some ironing, however, is necessary in most homes. It is usually done with an electric iron which depends more on heat than weight to smooth fabrics. Controls maintain proper heat for the type of fabric. Most irons have dials that can be set correctly for various man-made and natural fibers.

Steam irons and steam-and-spray irons combined with easy-iron fabrics have practically eliminated the need to sprinkle garments. However, some people feel ironing is faster if clothes have been dampened. All irons come with operating instructions that should be followed for best results.

Ironing boards are large, flat, well-padded wood or metal surfaces usually raised to a convenient height by supportive legs. They hold the garments which are spread upon them for ironing. Many boards are adjustable for varying individual heights. Many are made with open-metal-work surfaces which scatter

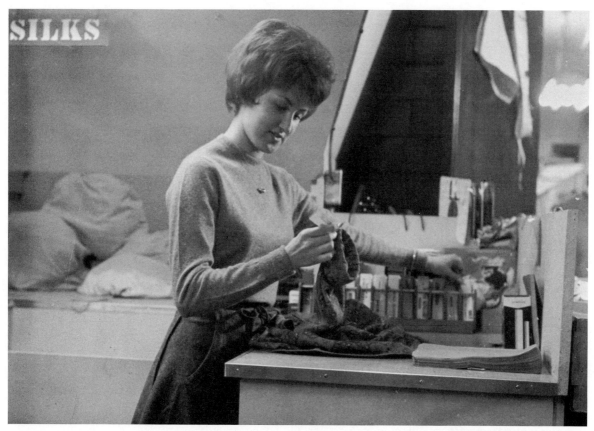

SILKS

Courtesy International Fabricare Institute

If at all possible, identify stains when leaving garments at the drycleaning plant so that they can be removed by the most effective method available.

and throw off the heat and moisture. Treated covers which will not scorch are available. For smoothest ironing results, be sure the board is padded adequately. Sleeve boards and various padded pressing shapes help ease ironing chores and are almost a necessity for effective clothing construction. (For further discussion of pressing tools see Chapter 9.)

Home Pressing Procedures

Pressing is a process of removing wrinkles from or restoring shape to garments. It is most frequently required by garments after hanging, packing, wearing, or, in the case of wash-and-wear garments, after washing. Garments not specially treated to minimize wrinkling may need more thorough ironing after washing (see preceding section). Press garments on the underside whenever possible. When this is not possible, use a pressing cloth if necessary to prevent shine or scorch marks on the outside garment surface. Create steam by using a steam iron, a steam-and-spray iron, or a damp cloth, rather than by sprinkling the garment. Press with an up-and-down motion rather than a gliding motion whenever possible.

Each fiber has a danger temperature. Be sure to use the temperature setting on the iron labeled expressly for your fabric. Test the temperature on a hidden area of the fabric. A thermostat is a sensitive instrument. A heavy jolt can cause it to malfunction, and frequent

135

STEPS IN IRONING A GARMENT

1. Be sure the ironing board is well padded and has a clean cover.
2. Check the iron to see that it is free from particles of starch or other material.
3. Set the iron at the correct temperature for the particular fabric, noting any ironing instructions provided on the garment label.
4. Iron collars, cuffs, belts, bows, and inset pockets first; then bodice; and, last, skirt.
5. Always iron with the grain of the fabric.
6. Press all seams open on the inside of the garment except those which should lie flat.
7. Press facings on the inside as well as on the outside of the garment.
8. Iron around buttons carefully, being sure not to touch the buttons with the iron, because, if plastic, the buttons are likely to melt.
9. Smooth tucks and pleats lengthwise, and hold them taut while ironing.

STEPS IN PRESSING A GARMENT

1. Make sure the ironing board is well padded and has a clean cover.
2. Empty pockets, remove belts, pins, bows, and other removable trim.
3. Brush garment thoroughly, especially inside the pockets and under the collar, cuffs, facings, and seams.
4. Surface-clean woolens by rubbing lightly with a cloth of the same color saturated with a cleaning solvent or by sponging with very dilute ammonia water.
5. Determine the fabric type, and note any pressing instructions provided on the label.
6. Press with an iron heated to a temperature suitable for the fabric. Avoid excessive heat, extreme pressure, or excessive moisture, each of which can damage fabric.
7. Hang the freshly pressed garment on a hanger in an airy place. Allow it to dry thoroughly before wearing.

use over a long period of time can impair its accuracy.

If the thermostat and iron are working properly, the iron will glide easily over fabrics of various fiber contents. In general, man-made fibers are pressed at low temperatures, silks at a slightly warmer temperature, wool at a moderate temperature, and cotton and linen at high temperatures. Excess heat can cause an iron to stick or move haltingly. If this occurs, stop before you damage the fabric. Allow the iron to cool to the proper temperature if it was set too high. Discontinue use of the iron until it has been repaired if it is not functioning properly. Excessive temperatures scorch fabrics made of the natural fibers and may melt some man-made fibers.

If your iron fails to move smoothly, clean the soleplate with a damp cloth. If the iron still fails to glide smoothly over the fabric, run it over waxed paper several times. Substances adhering to the soleplate might be removed by gently rubbing the spots with a paste made of scouring powder and water. Further information on the care of irons and other pressing tools is given on page 237.

What is the basic difference between laundering and drycleaning?

What are the advantages of taking clothing to a professional drycleaner? To a self-service drycleaning establishment?

What responsibilities must the user of a self-service drycleaning machine accept if his clothing is to look well?

Why are leather garments generally considered to be luxury garments?

In what types of instances are garments taken to a professional drycleaning establishment for wetcleaning?

Drycleaning

Drycleaning is the process of cleaning garments in solvents other than water. Drycleaning is especially effective for removing soil which does not dissolve in water, for killing bacteria, for cleaning garments containing fabrics, dyes, or finishes which might be damaged by water, for minimizing shrinkage, and for preserving tailoring details. Although the permanent care label will indicate whether drycleaning is the correct care procedure for a specific garment, you may also find it helpful to refer to the charts on pages 60-65. If wetcleaning seems indicated, you might wish to discuss the possibility of using this method with a drycleaner (see page 140).

Drycleaning as a process is divided into two types usually called professional drycleaning and self-service drycleaning. Professional drycleaning is rendered when you take or send garments to a drycleaning establishment. This process usually entails the spotting and minor mending of garments, as well as the finishing and pressing of garments after they have been cleaned.

Self-service drycleaning has come into widely accepted use during recent years. The person using a self-service drycleaning machine accepts the responsibility for spotting, mending, pressing, and finishing his own garments.

Professional Drycleaning

Garments taken to a professional drycleaner are separated by color and fabric type. The garments and any removable parts, such as belts and ornaments, are tagged for identification. They are inspected for spots, stains, and soil that must be removed before drycleaning.

Garments of similar color and fabric are placed in the cylinder of a drycleaning machine. Perforations in the cylinder allow a measured amount of solvent to flow through it. Mechanical action provides the agitation necessary to remove the soil or dirt from the fabrics. After a detergent and rinse cycle, the solvent is extracted. The garments are either tumble-dried or air-dried in a cabinet.

The garments are hung and passed to the spotting department. It is the responsibility of a trained spotter to remove spots or stains without damaging the fabric. The spotter may have twenty different chemicals, or reagents, from which he chooses the right chemical for a particular stain on a particular fabric. He uses specialized equipment along with steam and compressed air to remove spots and stains remaining after the general cleaning process.

The garments then move on to the finishing department. Special steam and air equipment, along with the conventional hand and steam iron, are used to remove wrinkles and restore fabric shape, texture, and luster.

From the finishing department, the garments move to the sewing department, where minor repairs are made and buttons, shoulder pads, and trim are replaced. The inspector gives the garments a final check to see that they have been thoroughly cleaned, that spots and stains have been removed, that repairs are made, and that details have been finished properly.

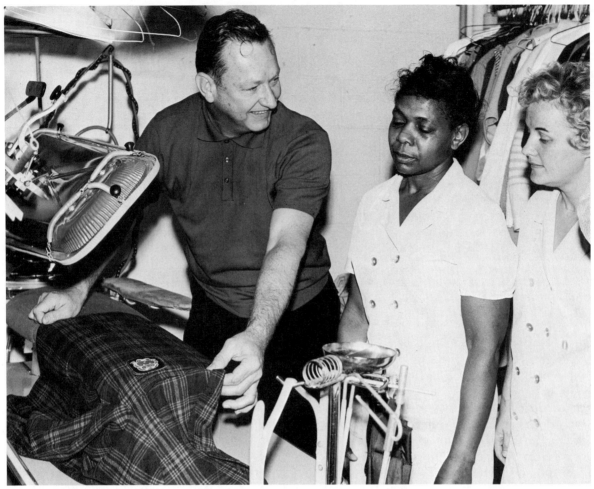

In a professional drycleaning establishment, each garment is finished with special steam and air equipment after it has been cleaned and spotted.

The complete order is then assembled, a final inspection is made, and the garments are bagged to protect them until they reach the home. Should you be dissatisfied with the results of drycleaning, return your garment to the drycleaner. Reliable establishments are glad to correct the quality point which has been overlooked.

Self-service Drycleaning

Self-service coin-operated drycleaning machines are available in most parts of the coun-try. Their chief value lies in the low cost of the service they provide as compared to the cost of professional drycleaning.

Most self-service machines are automatically set so that all articles are cleaned for the same length of time and by the same process. Further, delicate garments are tumbled as rigorously as are sturdy sport-type garments. It is important, therefore, to consider all component parts of a garment before cleaning it by this method. It is wise also to discuss the possibility of damage with the

STEPS IN SELF-SERVICE DRYCLEANING

1. Check and follow the cleaning instructions on garment labels.
2. Clean light-colored fabrics separately from dark fabrics and fragile garments separately from heavy clothing.
3. Brush out lint-catching areas, such as trouser cuffs and inside pockets, and remove trimmings, fancy buttons, and belts which are not suitable for cleaning.
4. Remove loose articles from pockets.
5. Make necessary repairs.
6. Get help with difficult stains from the person in charge of the cleaning operation.
7. Follow the instructions for using the machine, particularly those which warn against overloading it.
8. Remove the garments immediately after the cleaning and drying cycles are completed, and place them on hangers to prevent wrinkling.
9. If a cleaning-solvent odor persists, hang the garments in the open air or a well-ventilated room until they are thoroughly dry and odor-free.

LEATHER CARE

1. Protect the neckline of a leather garment from cosmetics and hair preparations by wearing a scarf.
2. Allow leather garments to hang between wearings in an area where air circulates freely.
3. Protect leather garments from long exposure to light, since light fades certain dyes used on leather.
4. Allow a damp or wet leather garment to dry slowly, avoiding exposure to excess heat.
5. Leave stain removal to the professional leather-cleaning specialist.
6. Do not allow leather garments to become heavily soiled before having them cleaned.

person in charge before subjecting delicate articles to this cleaning process.

The amount of pressing needed after self-service drycleaning depends on the type of fabric and the garment's style. Some apparel needs little or no touching up after drycleaning by this method. Most, however, require some pressing.

Leather Care

Because leather is a product of nature, it often has irregularities which no one, including the tanners and leather garment manufacturers, can overcome. Dyeing suede and leather garments to a different color from the original is seldom satisfactory. This is due to the variation within the skins and the difficulty with which leathers take on colorfast dyes.

Coordinated or matching leather garments should be cleaned at the same time to avoid color variations. The dyes used to achieve fashion colors on leather are partially or completely removed in cleaning. Therefore, each garment must be redyed and finished to shade.

*Modern fabrics tend to require little or no ironing.
Wrinkles caused from wear usually fall out
if a garment is hung in a steamy bathroom
or touched up with a steam iron or a portable
hand steamer.*

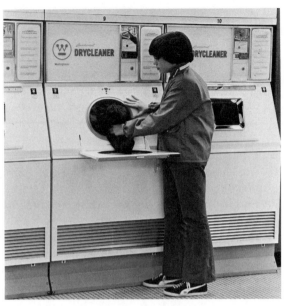

*Self-service drycleaning allows you to inexpensively
and rapidly return soiled clothes to a useful
place in your wardrobe.*

Leather-trimmed garments, beaded leather garments, and fringed leather must be considered luxury items. Since it is almost impossible to predict how they will perform in wear and cleaning, it is poor planning to depend on them as a basic part of your season's wardrobe.

Some suede and leather garments are treated by the tanner to make them water and stain resistant. Such garments can also be retreated after drycleaning, but they cannot be made so water resistant as to be capable of serving as rainwear. If leather is not properly cared for when it becomes wet, it may waterspot or mildew. Avoid wearing leather garments on wet days.

Wetcleaning

Wetcleaning is a special process available at professional drycleaning establishments. It is not washing in the manner in which garments are washed at home. It is a hand-brushing operation which is used when garments have been so badly soiled that drycleaning solvents do not clean them. In the wetcleaning process, equipment for quick drying is used along with dye-setting agents and sizings.

Exceptional skill is required on the part of the wetcleaner to produce good results. Some garments may require bleaching. Some types of albuminous stains, such as blood, must be digested. Some stained garments are placed in a water bath with enzymes which react with the stain so it may be removed.

The wetcleaning process is a necessary method of cleaning fabrics of certain types, such as vinyls and those made of glass, and fabrics marred by deep soiling, such as heavy perspiration or blood staining. It is sometimes the only method of making a garment wearable again.

GROUP LEARNING EXPERIENCES

1. Discuss the factors that influence wardrobe care. Make a personal daily, weekly, and seasonal plan for the care of your wardrobe.

2. Visit appliance centers in your area. List the features available on modern home laundry equipment and the costs of such features.

3. Invite a drycleaner to come to the classroom to answer your questions and discuss drycleaning services such as mothproofing, water-repellency treatments, sizing, and flameproofing.

4. Plan a tour through a modern laundry or drycleaning plant including the storage area.

5. Plan and give a demonstration to show the differences between drycleaning, wetcleaning, and laundering.

6. Visit the notions department of a nearby department store, and list the variety of products available for home care of clothing.

7. Give a demonstration showing the features of laundry equipment available in your home economics department and how to correctly use each piece of equipment.

8. Visit a coin-operated laundry and a self-service drycleaning establishment. Evaluate the services available in relation to cost of service.

9. Ask your chemistry teacher to give your class a demonstration on testing water hardness. Have him demonstrate how precipitating and nonprecipitating water conditioners react with the minerals in the water.

HELPING OTHERS TO LEARN

1. Help a younger brother or sister with his clothing care for one week. Report to the class the problems you encountered and how you solved them.

2. Inquire of your local Chamber of Commerce or Better Business Bureau whether they sponsor consumer-education programs. Offer to gather hang tags with useful information and to mount them in a display that would be helpful to groups being served.

3. Bring good but used clothing to class. Clean it according to accepted methods and mend the clothing as a class project. Distribute the clothing among people who can use it or deliver it to an organization which specializes in this type of distribution.

4. Arrange a bulletin-board display of copies of labels which give understandable, concise garment-care instructions.

5. Give a demonstration for a Girl Scout, 4-H, or other, similar group showing proper procedures for removing spots and stains of various types from drycleanable and washable fabrics.

1. Estimate the costs of laundering clothing at home in terms of time, energy, and money. Compare this with the costs of laundering it in self-service machines and of having it laundered by a professional laundry service.

2. Evaluate labels that give instructions on clothes care. Analyze different sets of instructions as to effectiveness.

3. Make a plan which you can use to remodel your clothes-storage area.

4. Make a check of all the clothing you are wearing this season, and jot down all the items needing attention and what attention they need. For example: loose strap on slip needs sewing; black shoes need polishing; brown shoes need repairing; gray skirt needs zipper repaired or replaced; blue dress needs stitching of armhole seams. After you have made the list, consider how much your wardrobe is limited in versatility because of the many items that are not wearable. Set a time to put these items into wearable condition.

5. Examine the garments in your wardrobe which were purchased most recently. Study the chart on page 214, and do whatever is necessary to improve their condition.

Accepting Consumer Responsibilities

One of the country's leading textile producers predicts that this nation will increase its consumption of textile products over the next ten years by at least 50 percent. If this prediction proves to be true, such rapid growth in the textile and clothing industries places a great responsibility on manufacturers, retailers, and consumers alike. Each group needs to be informed, to be heard, and to be protected during this rapid growth period.

What complexities have been added over the past century to the buyer-seller relationship?

What product information is necessary in order to make sound buying decisions which relate to your values, goals, and needs?

What are the implications of today's consumer interest in the field of textiles?

What are the types and purposes of textile-product labeling?

What labeling of clothing and fabrics is required by law?

How does modern permanent care labeling of fabrics and clothing help a consumer to buy clothing more effectively than was previously possible?

What is the consumer's responsibility in making informative labeling work?

How can you obtain help and guidance from a salesperson regarding expected garment performance? From the buyer for a store?

National Concerns
Related to Consumer Needs

As early as 1962 it was determined by the Federal government that in the area of goods and services the consumer had four basic rights: (1) the right to *be informed,* (2) the right to *choose,* (3) the right to *be heard,* and (4) the right to *safety.* Later it was decided that the consumer had a fifth right, the right to *be protected.*

It is good that the consumer's needs and rights have been recognized at a national level. Even better will be the time when all people understand that the producer, seller, and consumer all have rights and problems. When the needs of all three groups are understood and provided for, the position of each will improve.

The recognition of consumers' rights suggests that the whole scope of business has changed during the course of history. A hundred years ago consumer protection was largely unnecessary. This was a rural nation then, a nation of farms and small towns. Even in the growing cities, neighborhoods were closely knit. Most products were locally produced, and there was a personal relationship between the seller and the buyer. If the buyer had a complaint, he went straight to the miller, the blacksmith, the tailor, or the corner grocer. Products were less complicated. It was easy to tell the excellent from the inferior.

Today all this is changed. A manufacturer may be thousands of miles away from

1. *How to obtain product information.*
2. *How advertisements help the consumer become informed.*
3. *What seals of approval and warranty claims mean.*
4. *How care labeling can help a person become a better consumer.*
5. *How to keep informed on new product development.*
6. *The responsibilities of consumers in regard to handling merchandise in retail stores.*

his customer. He is even further removed by a merchandising route that includes distributors, wholesalers, and retailers. His products may be so complicated that only an expert can pass judgment on their quality.

This country is able to sustain a vast and impersonal system of commerce because of the ingenuity of our technology and the honesty of most of our businessmen. But this same vast network of commerce, this same complexity, also presents opportunities for the unscrupulous and the negligent.

The government has accepted the role of protector of the consumer and the honest businessman alike against fraud and indifference. One goal of government has become the assurance of every American business and individual consumer of a fair and honest exchange for his goods or dollar.

The Right to Be Informed

The consumer has a right to be informed about the clothing and fabric he buys. Probably the most popular means of conveying this information from the manufacturer to the consumer is an attached label. Such labels are useful in many ways. They serve to:

1. Identify the product.

2. Aid the businessman in selling his product.

3. Aid the consumer in making an intelligent selection.

4. Help the consumer and the drycleaner or the laundryman in properly caring for the item.

Labels may take various forms. They may consist of printed identification on the bolt, roller, spool, garment, or wrapper; identification woven or printed on the selvage; printed labels pasted to the merchandise; hang tags; woven or printed labels permanently attached; or woven or printed labels attached to a bolt end so that with each purchase of yardage the customer may be given a label which he may permanently attach to the finished article. Some fabrics can be purchased as yard goods to which instructions for care and sewing are attached in the form of an inserted tape.

It is an ideal situation when garments are labeled by both of the following methods: (1) A temporary cardboard tag hanging from the garment carries factual or promotional material or both. (2) Information as to how to care for the garment is given on a permanent label attached in a seam or on a facing or is permanently stamped inside. The permanent care labeling is required by law.

Types of Labels

In addition to a printed or woven label which provides care instructions, informative, brand, certification, or union labels may also be attached to a garment. Frequently these labels include promotional information. (See illustrations on pages 145-147.)

Informative Labels

An informative label attempts to help the consumer make a wise choice and to care for the item correctly. It may state fabric construction, special finishes, and serviceability

Both the consumer and the merchandiser have a right to expect proper handling of clothing during display and purchase.

or performance properties. It may give special instructions or precautions for care. The factual information may be based on laboratory tests. It may include the size of the item and the manufacturer's name.

Informative labeling may also include information required by Federal legislation such as the fiber content or a statement that the article has met standards such as those of L-22 of the American National Standards Institute.

Brand Labels

This type of label is a distinctive mark, design, symbol, word, or combination of designations serving to identify the goods of a particular seller or manufacturer. Trademarks fall into this category. While a brand name alone does not necessarily indicate quality, it may come to mean high quality to the con-

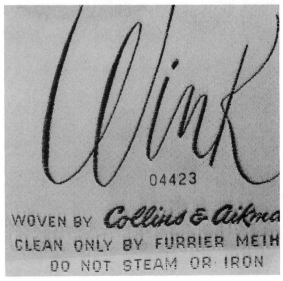

An informative label may include a certain amount of advertising along with specific information.

145

Eye-catching brand labels help you choose again a brand of garment you have learned to trust.

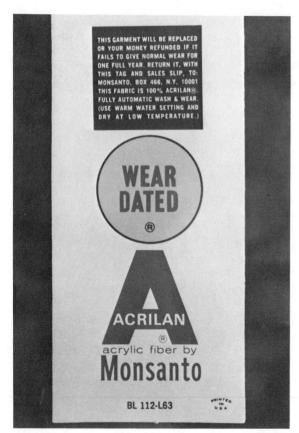

THIS GARMENT WILL BE REPLACED OR YOUR MONEY REFUNDED IF IT FAILS TO GIVE NORMAL WEAR FOR ONE FULL YEAR. RETURN IT, WITH THIS TAG AND SALES SLIP, TO: MONSANTO, BOX 466, N.Y. 10001 THIS FABRIC IS 100% ACRILAN®. FULLY AUTOMATIC WASH & WEAR. (USE WARM WATER SETTING AND DRY AT LOW TEMPERATURE.)

WEAR DATED ®

A

ACRILAN ® acrylic fiber by Monsanto

BL 112-L63

Certification labels usually imply a money-back guarantee if goods are handled by the recommended procedure.

sumer who finds goods of a certain brand dependable.

Certification Labels

A label of certification indicates that an item has been tested by a laboratory, often one independent of the manufacturer of the product. Each laboratory may establish its own fixed standards of quality. The labels it issues to approved products are often referred to as *seals of approval.* Examples include the Wear Dated seal provided by the textile division of the Monsanto Company and the seal of washability issued by the International Fabricare Institute. Frequently no information is given on the label except that the article has been approved or guaranteed by the laboratory or agency.

Union Labels

In addition to an informative, brand, or certification label, you may find a union label in ready-to-wear clothing. This label assures you that the garment was made under fair working conditions. Unions operating in the clothing area are the Amalgamated Clothing Workers of America, the International Ladies Garment Workers' Union, and the United Garment Workers of America.

Textile Labeling Laws

The Wool Products Labeling Act was one of the earliest fabric identification aids to American consumers. As man-made fibers were introduced into clothing manufacture, the actual fiber content of nonwoolen clothing became increasingly indistinguishable. To clear up this confusion, the Textile Fiber Products Identification Act was introduced. By understanding and applying information provided through these laws, the alert consumer is able to identify the fibers from which a particular garment is made.

The Wool Products Labeling Act

The Wool Products Labeling Act, which became a Federal law in 1939, requires that all articles containing wool shall be so labeled. If the wool fiber is mixed with other fibers, the percentage of wool must be stated on the label. The type of wool fiber must also be indicated. There is no provision in the law, however, requiring disclosure of the quality of the fiber. The act indicates the types of wool fibers according to a specified system of classification.

Wool   The label *Wool* signifies new wool fiber that has not been previously manufactured into cloth. The terms *Virgin Wool* and *New Wool* are also used by some manufacturers to label products made from new wool. These terms usually appear on fabrics of good quality, but they do not guarantee quality, because less desirable parts of the fleece and pulled, or dead, wool may have been used.

Reprocessed Wool   The label *Reprocessed Wool* indicates wool fiber that has been reclaimed and remanufactured from wool materials never before used, such as combings, clippings, and scraps salvaged during the manufacturing of wool products.

Reused Wool   The label *Reused Wool* refers to wool fiber that has been salvaged from wool materials previously used, such as rags, old clothing, and other worn products. These fibers are usually blended with new fibers in order to make fabrics which are usable but in which appearance and durability are less important than low cost.

The Textile Fiber Products Identification Act

The Textile Fiber Products Identification Act, which became effective in 1960, requires that each fiber be identified by its generic name on the hang tag or label. The Federal Trade Commission divides fibers into eighteen generic groups. However, only eleven of these are found in clothing; the other seven are used in other textile products. (See the charts on pages 62-65.)

One purpose of the law is to protect producers and consumers against misbranding and false advertising of the fiber content

Courtesy International Ladies Garment Workers Union

Union labels, often sewn in the seam of garments, indicate that a garment has been made in this country under conditions which the union feels are fair.

PURE WOOL

WOOLBLEND MARK

Courtesy The Wool Bureau, Inc.

An insignia indicating that a garment is made of wool or a blend of wool and other fibers is frequently stamped on garment hang tags. Federal regulations require that the tag also describe the type and percentage of wool contained in the fabric.

of textile products. Manufacturers are required to stamp, tag, label, or otherwise provide the following information. Additional information which does not violate the act is permissible.

1. The fiber or combination of fibers used in the item. Fibers must be designated with equal prominence whether they are natural or man-made. Fibers must be identified by their generic name in order of predominance by weight, if the weight is 5 percent or more of the total fiber weight.

2. The percentage, by weight, of each fiber present in relation to the total fiber content must be given. This is exclusive of ornamentation. If the ornamentation comprises 5 percent or less of the total fiber weight, it may be called *other fiber* or *other fibers.*

3. The tag, label, or stamp must carry the name, or other identification, of the manufacturer of the product or of one or more persons subject to the act.

4. If the item is imported, the name of the country where the product was made or processed must also appear on the label.

Practically all fabrics, including clothing, accessories such as scarves and handkerchiefs, and narrow fabrics except packaged ribbons are covered by the act. Those that are excluded include certain stiffenings, trimmings, and facings. Linings or interlinings are exempt if used only for structural purposes but must be included if used for warmth. Any fabrics mentioned in advertising or labels must be specified on the label as to fiber content.

The Permanent Care Labeling Rule
Probably the labeling law which helped the consumer most was the Federal Trade Commission's Permanent Care Labeling Rule made effective in 1972. This rule was instigated after years of cooperative research by textile and garment manufacturers, merchandisers, the clothing-care industry, and interested consumer groups.

In 1966 an Industry Advisory Committee on Textile Information was appointed at the national level by the Presidential Assistant for Consumer Affairs. This committee approved and adopted a Voluntary Guide for Improved and Permanent Care Labeling of Consumer Textile Products.

Still later the Federal Trade Commission gave notice that it intended to establish rules relating to care labeling of textile products. As a result, consumers, consumer groups, professional associations, every segment of the textile industry, and laundering and cleaning associations testified before the Federal Trade Commission early in 1970.

On December 9, 1971, the Federal Trade Commission announced a trade regulation requiring that textile products in the form of finished articles of wearing apparel bear permanent labels clearly disclosing instructions for their care and maintenance. The regulation also requires that piece goods sold to consumers for the purpose of making wearing apparel must be accompanied by care labels which the consumer can affix permanently to clothing. The rule went into effect on July 3, 1972. It applies to imports as well as to domestic items.

The FTC states that the items of wearing apparel that are exempted include nontextile products, footwear, handwear, headwear, and articles which do not require maintenance such as disposable items. Eligible to be considered for exemption are those sold at retail for $3.00 or less and which are washable under all normal conditions. Household textiles are not subject to the labeling rule.

Under the rule, the care-labeling instructions must:

1. Fully inform the purchaser how to effect such regular care and maintenance as is necessary to the ordinary use and enjoyment of the article; that is, washing, drying, ironing, bleaching, drycleaning, and any other procedures regularly used to maintain or care for a particular article.

2. Warn the purchaser as to any regular care and maintenance procedures which may usually be considered as applying to such an

Permanent care labeling of garments became necessary because the variety of fibers and blends of fibers could often be determined only through laboratory analysis.

article but which, in fact, if applied, would substantially diminish the ordinary use and enjoyment of the particular article concerned.

3. Be provided in such a manner that they will remain legible for the useful life of the article.

4. Be made readily accessible to the user.

The responsibility for a label and its care information lies with the person or organization that directed or controlled the manufacture of the finished article or piece goods.

Effective labeling has come from the co-operation of many groups. Fiber manufacturers, converters, and fabric suppliers now supply specific and clear instructions concerning the content, use, and care of their fibers and fabrics. Garment manufacturers use substantial labels and attach them in a permanent way to the articles they produce. Retailers by law now give specific attention to retaining the labels on articles so the consumer can read and use the information. Consumers, too, need to do their part. A responsible consumer follows these procedures:

1. Asks for and uses informative labels and hang tags.

2. Patronizes retailers and mail-order firms that label their merchandise accurately.

3. Tells the salesperson, buyer, or store manager that helpful labels influence him to buy their products.

4. Asks, when necessary, for better and more information.

5. Reads and heeds the information provided.

Who pays for permanent care labeling? It is no secret that the ultimate cost of labeling is borne by the consumer. Is it worth the cost?

One leading mail-order company calculated the total cost of the simplest, smallest, permanently attached label that conforms to the rules for labeling textile products as 0.028 cents per label. Such labels cost this single company over 200 million dollars annually. However, the cost of a permanent labeling system pays for itself many times over. When you consider that the destruction of one $30 garment due to lack of care information offsets the cost of over a thousand labels, the cost becomes relatively meaningless. Permanent care labeling has become a part of garment manufacture because business and the consuming public realized it was necessary.

Other Trade Practice Rules

The Federal Trade Commission has, from time to time, set up other trade practice rules in regard to textile fibers. Many of these rules have no longer been necessary since the Textile Fiber Products Identification Act and permanent care labeling became effective. There are still several other areas, however, where the Federal Trade Commission maintains control. For example, since the weighting of silk was not covered by the act of 1960, the Federal Trade Commission still requires the public disclosure of any metallic weighting or adulterating of silk other than dyeing and finishing necessary to produce the desired color or finish.

The Federal Trade Commission also regulates the use of terms to describe shrinkage. It specifies that fabric labeling regarding shrinkage must be accurate. For example, if a label states that shrinkage is less than 2 percent and a fabric shrinks to a greater degree, the fabric is mislabeled. Its producer is subject to Federal penalty.

How can the consumer be heard? When should he be heard?

Why does the quality of performance vary in clothing?

What is your responsibility if the clothing or fabric you buy does not perform acceptably?

Where and how may you complain effectively if you are not satisfied?

What is the National Fair Claims Guide for Textile Products?

How often do you make suggestions as to how a product or item might be improved by the manufacturer? How can you get these ideas relayed to the manufacturer?

The Right to Be Heard

Sometimes things go wrong with the clothes or fabrics you buy. Many times there is no relationship between the price you pay and the performance you receive. Adjustments are in order. Winning a satisfactory adjustment may take a long, hard fight which is costly in time, effort, and money. Yet consumers have a right to be heard. In order to preserve this right, it should be used as frequently as is reasonably necessary.

Manufacturers may say that the customer is at fault because he has not read the care labels and followed instructions. The manufacturer may claim that he has produced millions of these garments or yards and yards of this fabric and has received no previous complaint. He is often unwilling to accept the fact that only a few unsatisfied consumers are vocal.

The customer, on the other hand, may feel that the manufacturer is at fault, or perhaps that the professional drycleaner or launderer is responsible for the destruction of his clothing. In any event, the customer generally is the one with the most to lose and the one least likely to win in the battle for satisfactory adjustments. It is this feeling of consumer futility which has been brought to the attention of the press and the government. Now, more than ever before in history, consumers as a group are being heard.

Reasons Textile Products Misbehave

When things go wrong with a garment or fabric, there is usually an explainable reason. The problem lies somewhere between the producer and the consumer. Tracking down the cause of a product's misbehavior may result in self-blame or blame for which the manufacturer is responsible.

Often the consumer truly contributes to fabric and garment failure. He may be unconscious that he has spilled something on a garment, only to find later that the color is damaged. Occasionally he may take a chance and wash an item marked *Dryclean Only.*

Sometimes the manufacturer is at fault. When a new fiber, fabric, finish, or decorative design is made, reputable manufacturers go through a period of experimentation. Yet they are pressured to develop a new product which will quickly meet consumer demands. Sometimes the result can be the marketing of an unsatisfactory product. These products are frequently marketed with a money-back guarantee. Under such an arrangement, the consumer does not stand to lose if he takes the time to return ineffective merchandise.

In satisfactory garment production, ideas for new products often come from consumers. Once the idea is born, an experimental fabric or garment is made. It is tested by a limited number of people to get consumer reaction. If there are no major complaints, the product is manufactured and put into a limited number of stores and sold. These are called *test areas.* Complaints that are received from consumers are studied; then the manufacturer changes the product to improve it. Finally, it is sold to consumers all over the country.

During the testing procedure, washing or cleaning procedures are determined. Garments may then be accurately labeled so that homemakers and cleaners alike can know how to care for a new kind of fiber or fabric. When a manufacturer skips one or more of the testing procedures to beat the competition to the marketplace, his goods often cause consumer dissatisfaction.

Courtesy Celanese Fibers Marketing Co.

When a garment fails to give expected service, it is the consumer's responsibility to return it to the point of purchase. It is the responsibility of the store to return the garment to its source, where most problems can be solved through research.

There are also several other reasons why fabrics and garments misbehave. Those most often cited are:

1. Tough price competition. Makers try to reduce production costs as much as possible in order to reduce the selling price below that of the competition. As a result quality often suffers.

2. Lack of quality control and the lack of standards in testing of fabrics. Many firms do not maintain testing laboratories. Some do not even employ methods of setting and meeting quality levels for satisfactory performance.

IMPLIED-SERVICEABILITY DESIGNATIONS AND LIFE-EXPECTANCY RATES

Item		Renovation Method	Rate (yrs.)
BLOUSES (Dress & sports)	White cotton	Hot wash; dryclean	1
	White synthetics & colored	Med. wash; dryclean	2
COATS & JACKETS	Cloth, dress	Dryclean	4
	Cloth, sport	Dryclean	
	Pile (imitation fur)	Dryclean; cold tumble only; no steam	
	Fur	Fur-clean	10
DRESSES	House & sports	Med. wash; dryclean	1
	Afternoon	Dryclean	3
	Street	Dryclean	2
	Evening or cocktail	Dryclean; special handling of delicate & decorated styles	3
	Basic	Dryclean	5
GLOVES	Fabric	Med. wash separate; dryclean	1
	Leather	Leather-clean	2
HATS	Felt	Clean by special hat-renovation methods	1
	Straw	Same unless trim detail	2
	Fur	Fur-clean	5
LEATHER JACKETS & COATS	Suede & grain leather products	Special care. Colors normally subject to fading & some loss in cleaning. Most restorable by application of color & finishing products.	3
RAINWEAR	Film & plastic-coated fabrics	Hand-wash; no press	2
	Unlined fabric	Med wash; dryclean	3
	Lined quilted fabric	Dryclean	
	Rubber	Wipe down with damp cloth; no press	3
ROBES	Silk or wool	Dryclean	3
	Other: Unlined, lined	Med. wash; dryclean	2
SHOES	Dress & walking		2
	Work		1
	Evening, formal		5
SKIRTS	Winter & fall	Dryclean-wetclean	2
	Resort & summer	Med. wash; dryclean	

CALCULATION OF CLAIMS ADJUSTMENT VALUES

Life-Expectancy Rating of Article	1	2	3	4	5
Age of Article in Months and Years	0 to 4	0 to 4	0 to 4	0 to 4	0 to 4
	4 to 7	4 to 7	4 to 10	4 to 13	4 to 16
	7 to 9	7 to 13	10 to 19	13 to 25	16 to 31
	9 to 11	13 to 19	19 to 28	25 to 37	31 to 46
	11 to 13	19 to 25	28 to 37	37 to 49	46 to 61
	13 mos. & older	25 mos. & older	37 mos. & older	49 mos. & older	61 mos. & older

IMPLIED-SERVICEABILITY DESIGNATIONS AND LIFE-EXPECTANCY RATES *(continued)*

Item		Renovation Method	Rate (yrs.)
SLACKS & SHORTS	Lounging & tailored	Dryclean	2
	Active sport	Hand-wash; dryclean	2
	Dress	Dryclean	3
SLEEPWEAR	White goods	Hot wash	2
	Colored goods	Med. wash	
SNEAKERS		Med. wash; bleach; air or tumble-dry	0
SOCKS	Wool	Hand-wash	1
	Other	Med. wash	
SUITS	Basic	Dryclean	4
	High-fashion	Dryclean; special handling of delicate & decorated styles	3
SWEATERS	Wool & synthetics	Hand-wash; dry flat only; dryclean; wetclean	3
SWIM WEAR		Hand-wash	2
UNDERWEAR	Slips	Mild wash; bleach white cottons	2
	Foundation garments	Med. wash	1
	Panties	Med. wash; bleach white cottons	1
UNIFORMS	Unlined & work types	Med. wash; dryclean	1
	Lined & dressy	Dryclean	
WEDDING GOWNS		Dryclean	*
WORK CLOTHING	Customarily shows noticeable signs of wear, depending on amount of use.	Withstands strains of use & laundering at 160° F. with heavy-duty soap	2

*Indefinite life expectancy.
Adapted from Table I, Implied Serviceability Designations and Life Expectancy Rates; National Fair Claims Guide for Textile Products; National Institute of Drycleaning.

	Adjustment Values: % of Replacement Cost		
10	Excellent	Average	Poor
Less than 1 year	100%	100%	100%
2 to 4 years	75%	75%	60%
4 to 6 years	70%	60%	45%
6 to 8 years	50%	40%	30%
8 to 11 years	30%	20%	15%
11 years & older	20%	15%	10%

STEP-BY-STEP USE OF CHARTS

1. Determine the cost of replacing the article. This is called Replacement Cost.
2. Determine the Age of the Article.
3. Determine the condition of the article as Excellent, Average, or Poor.
4. Select from the upper chart the Life Expectancy rating of the article.
5. Refer to the column in the lower chart at the top of which is shown the Life Expectancy rating selected in step 4. Read down to the Age of Article and across to the Adjustment Value.
6. Select the line under "Adjustment Values" which applies according to condition of the article.
7. Multiply the percentage figure given by the Replacement Cost figure determined in step 1. This will be the Adjustment Value.

153

3. Lack of understanding on the part of the manufacturer as to what is involved in consumer wear and care of clothing.

Increasingly it becomes apparent that there is a need for better communication between the manufacturer and the retail outlets as well as between the manufacturer and the laundering and drycleaning industries. As the consumer is heard, improvement in all of these channels of communication results.

A Guide for Arbitrating Complaints

In 1961 a National Fair Claims Guide for Textile Products was agreed upon by the following organizations: the American Home Economics Association, the National Institute of Drycleaning, the Better Business Bureau, the National Retail Merchants Association, the Menswear Retailers of America, the Association of Home Appliance Manufacturers, and adjusters from a number of major insurance companies. This guide provides a means of determining who is responsible and to what extent when a textile product falls short of reasonable expectations.

Suppose that a garment falls apart in wear or home laundry, that it shrinks out of shape, or that it develops objectionable odors. In such cases the garment should be returned to the store where it was purchased for a settlement of claims. You deal directly, if possible, with the retailer from whom it was purchased.

Suppose that a garment returned to you by the drycleaner appears to be damaged. You might assume that the drycleaner is at fault and feel that he should pay for the damages. He may disagree. He may tell you to take the garment back to the store where you bought it and ask for your money back. The store may then tell you the drycleaner is at fault. What can you do?

When you buy a garment, you have a general idea of how long it should last, how it should behave during wear, and how it should look after it is laundered or drycleaned. All these ideas make up your per-

sonal concept of *implied serviceability.* The National Retail Merchants Association defines implied serviceability in this way: "In the sale of merchandise, there is an implied warranty that goods will afford reasonable service in use and unless otherwise specified they can be cleaned and refreshed by customary methods."

The National Fair Claims Guide, which is available in many drycleaning establishments and some department stores, also introduces the concept of life expectancy for textile products. It provides estimates of how long garments can be worn. Since wear, care, and fashion changes all influence the life expectancy of clothing, you will note that the fair claims table bases the value for an adjustment on a percentage of replacement cost rather than on the price paid. This percentage of replacement cost depends on both the percentage of the *life expectancy* of the item which has been used and the *condition* of the garment at the time you make a claim. These factors have been worked out and set in tables which are used for figuring a reasonable estimate of the amount of loss. (See pages 152-153.)

Suppose your best dress is returned from the cleaners in a spotty condition. Perhaps the lining is in shreds and the dress unwearable. How can you and the drycleaner work out an adjustment with which both of you can be happy? Try applying the following seven steps, substituting your own calculations for those used for illustrative purposes here.

1. Estimate the purchase cost of a similar dress: $50.00.

2. Note the age of your dress: 1 year and 4 months, or 16 months old.

3. Note the condition of your dress: Excellent.

4. Estimate the expectancy rate of your dress: 2 years.

5. In the lower table on pages 152-153, put your pencil on *2* under the heading *Life-Expectancy Rating of Article.* Move it down the column under *2* to the pertinent figures

indicating the age of the article in months. (16 falls within *13 to 19.*)

6. Move your pencil across the line to the *Excellent* replacement column. The adjustment value is 50%.

7. 50% of $50 = $25.00. This is your adjustment value.

Sources of Help

If you are disappointed with your garment when it is returned from the drycleaner, ask to talk with the person in charge of customer service. The reputable cleaner who is at fault, and knows he is at fault, will make fair adjustment immediately.

If the drycleaner feels he is not at fault, and if he is a member of the International Fabricare Institute, he can send the garment to their Textile Analysis Laboratory to determine whether he, the consumer, or the manufacturer is responsible for the unsatisfactory results. If he is at fault, he makes the necessary adjustment. If not, he receives a report, which he can give you, stating whether you or the manufacturer is at fault. If the report designates the manufacturer as the source of the difficulty, you can take the report and the garment to the store where you made your purchase and ask the store to make an adjustment. Stores cooperating in this type of consumer-business arbitration faithfully return unacceptable goods to the manufacturer for adjustment. This three-way cooperative venture quickly puts an end to the display and the sale of shoddy, untested merchandise.

It seldom happens that both the drycleaning and retail stores are unwilling to cooperate when a consumer is unhappy. They realize that profits come from dealing with happy customers. However, occasionally you may find both uncooperative.

In such a situation you still have avenues for arbitration. You might complain to your local Better Business Bureau. Some bureaus have an arbitration committee to settle complaints. Such a committee is made up of representatives of the area's consumers, re-tail stores, and drycleaning and laundering firms, and a member of the bureau. It reviews complaints and places responsibility either on the drycleaner, store, or consumer. Sometimes such a committee exists with the local Chamber of Commerce serving as an arbitrator.

You might take your complaint to the department of your local or state office which handles consumer affairs. If this fails, enlist help from the Office of Consumer Affairs, Executive Office of the President, Washington, D.C., 20506. This office forwards the complaints to the industries involved. Complaints on apparel are channeled through the American Apparel Manufacturers Association.

As a last resort you can go to the Small Claims Court. Legal action can be costly. Therefore, be certain you are right in making your claim before you take court action.

Complaining Effectively

Few people enjoy complaining. But in some cases you have a right to complain. You have, in fact, a *responsibility* to complain if there are just reasons. If you do not, businesses profit while offering inferior goods and poor services. Retailers, manufacturers, launderers, and drycleaners are discovering that complaints really help them in the long run to increase their sales and profits. They learn from the nature of the complaints what changes must be made in their management, the quality of their merchandise and service, and the attitudes and actions of personnel.

Experts agree there are certain simple, basic rules to follow in making a complaint. These include the following:

1. Indicate your complaint in a letter and keep a carbon copy. A letter puts your complaint on record and helps you to clarify it.

2. For prompt service, address your letter to the Customer-Relations Department of the firm concerned.

3. Type your letter. Complaint department heads state that a typed letter gets faster action than a handwritten one.

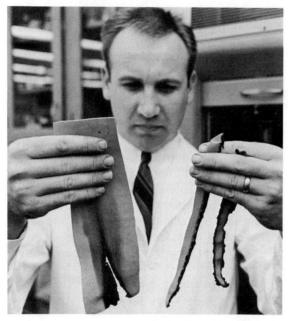

Courtesy Celanese Fibers Marketing Co.

Fiber and fabric manufacturers work diligently to produce fabrics and garments which will conform to government specifications.

4. State the facts clearly. Curb your emotions, and avoid sarcasm and profanity.

5. Return the article in clean condition.

6. Include copies of the sales ticket and labels if possible. Keep the originals.

7. Be honest in your reporting. False statements are easily recognized.

8. Be good natured. You will get results.

What are the consumer's responsibilities in the area of clothing safety?

How can you determine whether merchandise is safe to wear?

What laws specify that your clothing must be safe to wear?

Why is it important that you follow the warning instructions the manufacturer provides on hang tags and labels?

How can consumers encourage the production of fire-resistant garments?

How can skin irritation from certain fabrics be minimized?

The Right to Safety

You have a right to be informed about the safety of the clothing you buy. You also have a responsibility to protect yourself by following care instructions provided on labels. This practice will preserve safety features built into your clothing.

Fabric Flammability

Many accidents are reported annually in which people of all ages are killed or badly injured because the clothes they wear or their bedclothing is flammable. Many of those who survive undergo physical suffering and long and costly medical treatment. Some are disfigured for life; others suffer emotionally. Though flammability laws cannot overcome consumer carelessness, they may in many instances reduce the damage of fire-connected accidents.

In 1969 the Secretary of Commerce created the Office of Flammable Fabrics and appointed an advisory committee to this office. In December 1970 a flammability standard was published covering carpets, rugs, and bath mats. A standard for blankets and household textiles such as curtains and draperies has not yet been proposed.

A standard for children's sleepwear was published in November 1970 and became effective in July 1972. Flammable sleepwear in sizes 0 to 6X marketed in the interim period between July 1972 and June 1973 is to be marked with permanent warning labels. All sleepwear in this size range sold after 1973 is required to be nonflammable. Flammability standards for children's dresses are expected to be established to cover sizes 0-12.

Consumer Indifference

Unfortunately flame-retardant finishes have found relatively little acceptance by consumers. The reasons consumers give for their lack of interest in fire-retardant finishes are substantially higher costs, the reduced aesthetic appeal of some fabrics, and, in some cases, downgraded physical properties.

Probably the real reason for lack of consumer interest in fire retardants is general lack of information or lack of direct experience with serious accidental burns which could have been prevented by retardant fibers or finishes. Often, as is the case with fire retardants, the government and industry work together for consumer protection before the general public understands the seriousness of the situation. Laws cannot create safety, however. The consumer must practice rules of safety in order to protect himself and his family. He must be willing to accept fabrics less pleasing in order to avoid tragedy.

Research in the Field
of Fabric Flammability

The textile industry is hard at work trying to solve complex problems of flammability. Some manufacturers are modifying their fibers or putting flame-resistant chemicals into the solution before it is made into fiber. Others are blending fibers to achieve fire-resistant fabrics. Still others are developing new finishes to apply to the surface of the fabric.

Consumer demands will encourage producers to market only garments which are properly described as to flammability. *Flameproof, Flame-resistant after washing*, and *Flameproof finish effective for at least three washings* are examples of the designations which are helpful to consumers.

Health Irritants
Connected with Fabrics

The trend in modern garments is toward easy-to-handle, easy-to-wear, and easy-to-care-for fabrics. These *easy* features are often difficult to produce in fabrics. They can be obtained, but the chemicals required to produce them are sometimes harmful to those who wear them. Irritants most commonly reported are those affecting the skin and eyes. Probably less damaging, but nonetheless objectionable, are odors which render garments unpleasing to those who must wear them and to those who must be near them.

Skin Irritants

Testing laboratories have received complaints of skin irritation from durable-press garments. The irritation has been traced almost exclusively to formaldehyde-type resin compounds present in durable-press garments. The irritation can be prevented by laundering or wet-cleaning the garment to remove excess chemicals which remain in the fabric after the finishing is completed.

Some individuals are sensitive to other finishing compounds, fibers, and dyes present in fabrics. They may become sensitized the first time they wear a certain garment, but the effect may not be immediately noticeable. Later the sensitivity may become apparent when they wear the garment in a different season of the year or when there is a change in their body chemistry.

Cases are on record in which fiberglass curtains, bedspreads, and tablecloths have been washed in the washing machine along with clothing with unfortunate results. Microscopic particles of glass deposited on clothing have sometimes caused itching and other skin irritation. To prevent this type of difficulty, wash glass fabrics separately. Rinse the machine thoroughly before using it to wash clothing. Inform the manager of a coin-operated laundry whenever you use public washing equipment to wash fiberglass products.

If your skin becomes irritated and you suspect the problem was caused by a certain garment fabric, avoid wearing the garment. If the condition persists, consult an allergist. He can usually determine the source of irritation and prescribe a remedy.

Objectionable Odors

Although an objectionable odor does not harm a person physically, it can affect him psychologically. His distaste for an article, strictly because of unpleasant odor, often makes him unwilling to buy it. This buyer resistance makes it worth a manufacturer's time to destroy the odor if he can do so without damaging the article.

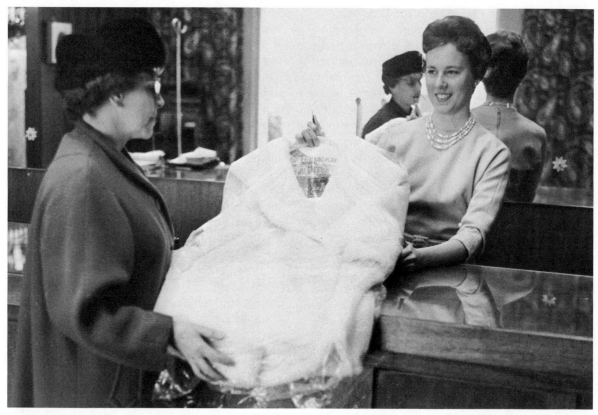

Courtesy International Fabricare Institute

Destroy or be particularly careful with plastic film bags as these bags may be the agent by which a young child is suffocated.

Textile producers use many types of resin finishes to impart crease resistance and shrinkage control to fabrics. Some resins, when improperly cured in textile finishing, may break down. Their objectionable odor may not become noticeable until after wear, storage, or drycleaning of a particular garment. Some resins give off a fishlike odor. This problem may occur if a textile finisher fails to wash out the excess chemicals after the curing or heat-setting operation. It can also occur if the fabric is cured for too long a time or at too high a temperature. Another cause of the problem is fabric finishing with a previously used resin solution that has been stored for too long. These improperly cured resins may break down and produce odor-forming compounds at any time after manufacture.

Proper curing of the resin finish by the textile finisher is the only sure method of odor control. There have been cases where objectionable odors have been removed by wetcleaning in an alkaline solution of water and detergent, but there is no guarantee that this treatment will always be effective. Frequently fabric combinations and garment design do not lend themselves to such a treatment. A consumer is within his rights to return a garment of objectionable odor to the store that sold it. When a sufficient number of such garments are returned to the manufacturers, more care will be given to producing non-odor-forming finishes.

Hazards of Plastic Films and Bags

Plastic film is a popular packaging material and covering. It is desirable because of its transparency and protective qualities. Its danger is related not to its use but rather to its misuse after it has served its purpose. Small children have been smothered under the bags made of this material.

The Surgeon General of the United States says the principal danger of plastic bags involves their use as a protective covering for crib mattresses, pillows, or blankets. Rarely does death result from older children playfully pulling plastic bags over their heads.

Realizing the danger involved with the misuse of this very useful film, the drycleaning industry warns through posters and by printing on the bags information concerning potential danger. In many states and several large cities it is now illegal to use plastic film which has not been stamped in some way warning about the possibility of suffocation of young children and babies.

How do government, business, science, and industry work for you so that you have better satisfaction with the fabrics and clothing you buy?

Which departments, bureaus, or commissions of the Federal government have programs that help to improve the fabrics and clothing you buy?

How can the Better Business Bureau or the Chamber of Commerce improve their methods of helping consumers of clothing?

What scientific associations are working to improve the performance of fabrics and clothing?

What kinds of programs do apparel manufacturers undertake that are beneficial to the customer?

Where do buyers for retail stores get help in making selections when they go into the market to buy?

How do retail stores, mail-order houses, and some magazines help to improve fabric and clothing performance?

The Right to Be Protected

Although the rights of the consumer were not spelled out clearly until recent years, agencies have long worked separately or in groups to satisfy consumers' needs. National and local agencies, scientific and professional groups, trade associations, manufacturer's associations, and research laboratories have each contributed to the upgrading of the textile industry. Each has contributed in a general or specific way.

National Agencies
Protecting the Consumer

Attempts are being made to develop a more effective industry complaint-handling system. If the existing system can be improved or a new one devised, consumers can expect manufacturers to become more attentive to their complaints.

As people in high government positions recognized the fact that consumer complaints often fail to reach the proper person, or area, of a company, the President of the United States formed a special presidential committee on consumer interests. He also appointed a special assistant for consumer affairs. At present, nearly every state has some form of office specifically designated for the protection of the consumer. In addition, there are many departments, bureaus, commissions, and offices of the Federal government that work for you. Included in this group are the U.S. Patent Office, the U.S. Business and Defense Services Administration, the Federal Trade Commission, the National Bureau of Standards, the U.S. Bureau of Census, and the U.S. Bureau of Labor Statistics.

The U.S. Patent Office

The U.S. Patent Office, within the U.S. Department of Commerce, plays a key role in invention and innovation. This office administers the patent laws enacted by Congress. It also examines applications and grants patents, publishes and distributes patent information, maintains search files of United

States and foreign patents and a Patent Search Center for public use. In addition, trademarks are issued by this office.

The Textile Group of the Patent Office is divided into three segments, known as Art Units. These units are concerned with the fields of textiles, sewing and apparel, and winding and reeling.

The U.S. Business and Defense Services Administration

The U.S. Business and Defense Services Administration, of which the Office of Textiles is a part, is concerned with promoting and fostering the development of domestic business and industry. Its objectives are to provide information, services, and assistance essential to business growth and technical development within the framework of the free enterprise system.

Many of the activities of the Office of Textiles are involved with international trade. They include the promotion of exports and the regulation of imports. The office is also involved with the National Bureau of Standards in implementing regulations dealing with flammability of clothing and other textile goods.

The Federal Trade Commission

The Federal Trade Commission is often called the *watch dog* of the government. It administers and enforces laws in the fields of antitrust and trade regulations, thus protecting competition in private enterprise. It also issues numerous Trade Practice Rules, or codes of ethics, for the textile and apparel industries. Thus it protects these industries from unlawful practices such as misrepresentation, deceptive price representation, and commercial bribery. It is responsible for the enforcement, through its Bureau of Consumer Protection and its Textile and Fur Division, of the Wool Products Labeling Act, the Textile Fiber Products Identification Act, the Permanent Care Labeling Rule, and other rules and laws involving the textile industry.

The Federal Trade Commission is equipped to find realistic, workable solutions to consumer problems. It is responsibly staffed both to regulate business conduct and to protect the consumer.

The National Bureau of Standards

The National Bureau of Standards works with the Federal Trade Commission in establishing and defining the generic names of textile fibers required for the labeling of textile products. It also conducts tests and testifies in court on the performance of specific textiles when textile acts are violated. Through the activities of its Office of Engineering Standards and Services, the NBS assists the textile and apparel industries in developing voluntary trade standards for the quality criteria of materials. The sizes of boxes, tubes, and cones used by the textile industry and the sizing of apparel, body measurements, and model forms for use by the apparel industry are also developed under the guidance of NBS. It has the responsibility for the development of flammability standards.

The U.S. Bureau of Census

The U.S. Bureau of Census is responsible for giving timely information to manufacturers. It issues reports for industry groups, for individual industries, and for geographic divisions such as states and large standard metropolitan areas. Such reports include information on employment, man-hours, payrolls, value added by manufacture, expenditure for new plants and equipment, cost of materials, year-end inventories, and value of products shipped.

The U.S. Bureau of Labor Statistics

The U.S. Bureau of Labor Statistics acts as the chief economic fact finder for the U.S. Department of Labor. It collects, analyzes, and distributes information on prices, as well as on employment, unemployment, wages, jobs, and conditions of work. For example, the bureau employs people to determine the price asked for apparel in various stores. These employees look at clothing of all sizes and varieties. They visit hundreds of stores throughout the nation. They talk to buyers, merchandise managers, and owners of stores. They repeat the shopping trips for several months. Their primary interest is the price tag. Their findings contribute to the monthly *Consumer Price Index*, which charts the rise and fall of the purchasing power of the consumer's dollar.

The bureau looks also for changes in the types of stores where clothing is sold and for shifts in the amount of money spent on clothing in comparison with that spent on food and shelter. The list of clothing checked for price is geared to middle-income earners. High-fashion clothing is not included.

The bureau's specifications for each item of apparel on the pricer's lists are quite specific. Item 32-644, for instance, is a girl's skirt. But it is not just any girl's skirt. Item 32-644 must be an A-line skirt or hip-hugger of a soft-finished fabric such as flannel or tweed, and it may be bonded with acetate tricot. The yarn must be either all new woolen or flannel with a 15-20 percent blend of nylon or acrylic. Its hem may be up to 2 inches wide, and it may have a tape finish. The seams must be plain, with pinked or plain edges. The waistband must have a double layer of fabric, it may be elasticized, and it must have a zipper closure. In addition, it may have a self-belt or plastic belt and other minor trim or detail. Similar details of requirements are set for every item.

Each bureau pricer must follow four basic rules in selecting items for price research:

1. The item must meet specifications.

2. It must be available in salable quantities; that is, it must cover a specified size range.

3. It must be in good condition. No *seconds* or *irregulars* are included.

4. It must be the volume seller among items meeting specifications.

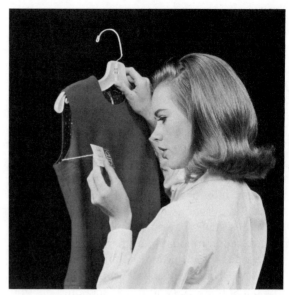

Courtesy American Cynamid Corporation

Employees of the U. S. Bureau of Labor Statistics visit hundreds of stores to determine the actual price being charged for garments of exact specifications.

If the pricer sees four coats in one store that meet the requirements, the buyer is asked which is the best seller. That is the one that is priced. Through this exhaustive system of research, the Consumer Price Index is established.

Local Agencies
Protecting the Consumer

Various business groups work together with consumers and with the Federal government for a better national business climate. They realize that satisfied customers increase the general profitability of their business. Probably best known among such business groups are the Better Business Bureau and the Chamber of Commerce.

The Better Business Bureau

The Better Business Bureau is a nonprofit, independent agency of business located in principal cities throughout the country. Each bureau is financed by membership, dues, or subscriptions paid to it by business and professional firms in a given city. Each bureau is governed by an elected Board of Directors or Trustees and independently financed by its own community. However, all bureaus cooperate with each other through their affiliation with the Council of Better Business Bureaus.

Although the purposes of the Better Business Bureau are pure in intent, the consumer is wise to understand something of business relations in dealing with the bureau. Since the bureau is supported by dues or subscriptions, dues-paying members often receive higher recommendations than equally stable businesses which do not belong to the bureau. While the Better Business Bureau is a help to the consumer, it cannot be accepted as the final word in all matters of consumer-business relations. Nevertheless, it continues to try to improve its influence and usefulness in the community. For example, some bureaus have recently established Consumer Affairs Councils. The council is a forum through which consumer needs and problems can be heard and acted upon. These types of efforts tend to help the general consuming public.

The Chamber of Commerce

The local Chambers of Commerce are loosely organized groups of businesses in various communities. Members pay dues. Often a paid secretary or executive secretary carries out the promotional work of the group. At the local level the Chamber functions to promote good will between member businesses and consumers. At the national level, the Chamber of Commerce of the United States, located in Washington, D.C., has also taken steps to bridge the gap between consumers and business. It has appointed a Consumer Affairs Council to study trends and long-range plans regarding national issues to be faced by consumers and the business community of the future. Members of this council were chosen from business, education, and the professions.

Scientific and Professional Groups Working for the Consumer

Various scientific and professional groups work to improve textile products. As a result consumer goods are improved by the knowledge of individual members in their personal field of specialty. Prominent among these groups aiding in the research are the American National Standards Institute, the American Association of Textile Chemists and Colorists, the American Society for Testing and Materials, and the American Home Economics Association.

The American National Standards Institute

The American National Standards Institute (ANSI) is a federation of trade, technical, labor, and consumer organizations, companies, and government agencies. The ANSI's Consumer Council was established in 1967. Its purpose is to determine and satisfy the consumer's need for standards and to represent and protect the consumer's interests in national standardization programs.

What is a standard in relation to clothing and fabrics? A standard may be a unit of measure such as an inch, foot, or yard. It may be a measure of the safety of a fabric from melting, flaming, or charring. A quality standard is one that specifies exactly the required content of a product such as 100 percent wool or 50 percent wool and 50 percent acrylic.

The ANSI group is working toward a number of improved standards in fabrics. Eventually it hopes to have specific requirements as to colorfastness, fabric strength, retention of finish, and maximum presence of foreign odor. Its work has served to upgrade many textile products, even though the standards it has achieved are not indicated on labels and hang tags.

It is assumed that in the near future our system of measurement will be changed to comply with the international metric system. The ANSI group will help to standardize measurements when this system is accepted.

162

The American Association
of Textile Chemists and Colorists

The American Association of Textile Chemists and Colorists is a professional technical society that has promoted the development of standardized tests for measuring color in fabrics during consumer use. This group works to determine characteristics of fabrics such as colorfastness to light, to crocking, to gases in the atmosphere, to washing, to drycleaning, and to perspiration. It also designs tests to measure shrinking, stretching, wrinkle resistance, and the effectiveness of finishes such as durable press, water repellency, and flammability. Many dyes and finishes are checked and controlled by the association's testing methods. Through this association, nearly 75 National Research Committees, composed of representatives from 300 major textile and chemical companies, are presently developing new standard test methods.

The American Society
for Testing and Materials

The American Society for Testing and Materials establishes many standards for consumer textiles. This organization is made up of members of more than 2,600 companies. The organization aids the consumer by publishing the standards by which many textile products can be measured.

The American Home Economics
Association

The American Home Economics Association works for and with consumers. The Textile and Clothing Section of AHEA publishes research findings and educational literature. Its membership participates in the work of scientific organizations in developing test methods and standards of performance of fabrics and clothing. Its members also testify before Congressional committees in the interest of the consumer. When the metric system of measurement becomes meaningful in this country, this group will figure largely in the general education of the people.

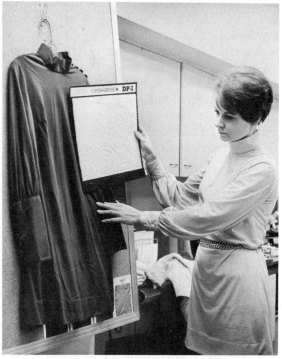

Courtesy Celanese Fibers Marketing Co.

Commercial, private, and government research groups test the various aspects of a fabric both before and after its sale.

Trade Associations
Aiding the Consumer

Trade associations, actually established to help members of a specific association, are an indirect, but very obvious, aid to the consumer. By keeping their members informed on current textile trends and methods for handling them, associations perform important services to the consumer. These associations include the International Fabricare Institute and the Association of Home Appliance Manufacturers, as well as various groups of textile trade associations and retail merchants.

The International Fabricare Institute

The Drycleaning Division of the International Fabricare Institute comprises some 9,000 drycleaners. More than 30,000 fabric and garment problems are forwarded each year to its Textile Analysis Laboratory in Silver Spring, Maryland, and its Western Laboratory in Glendale, California. The problems they analyze are those due to faulty drycleaning plant practices, those that occur through wear or misuse by the consumer, and those that can be attributed to the manufacturer. Most textile weakness attributed to the manufacturer can be corrected somewhere along the line between fiber production and garment manufacturing.

The division also engages in education and research that indirectly benefit the consumer. It maintains a trade and management school to educate anyone who wants to take advantage of its educational program. It carries on research on drycleaning processes and fabric research that results in educational bulletins used by drycleaners, retailers, and textile manufacturers. It publishes and distributes educational literature based on its research.

The Laundry Division includes more than 3,000 professional laundrymen. Its functions are rather similar to those of the Drycleaning Division in that it serves consumers through its members. Its technical staff, laboratories, and other facilities are available to its members. Through research they recommend procedures for the continual improvement of laundry services. Their testing laboratories are also used to help manufacturers produce garments, fabrics, and other products that are fully washable during a long wear life.

The Association of Home Appliance Manufacturers

The Association of Home Appliance Manufacturers (AHAM) is a nonprofit association of the manufacturers of over 90 percent of the major appliances produced in this country. These appliances include home water heaters, washers, and dryers, as well as appliances not closely associated with the care of clothing.

This association functions to acquaint consumers with products produced by the industry and to acquaint the industry with the needs of consumers. It develops standards for products by working closely with Underwriters' Laboratories, American Gas Association, American National Standards Institute, and others. These standards serve as a quality guide for AHAM members.

The Association of Home Appliance Manufacturers produces educational materials and teaching aids which are available for student and adult classes. Through their association manufacturers inform the public about available advances in home appliance manufacture and answer questions pertaining to new products.

Textile Trade Associations

There are many textile trade associations that publish information about their products. The information is written to help the consumer understand the properties of specific fibers and what can be expected of them in wear and care. Some of the groups are: the National Cotton Council of America, the Linen Trade Association, the Man-made Fiber Producers Association, the International Silk Association of America, and the Wool Bureau.

The National Retail Merchants Association

The National Retail Merchants Association is a trade association of department, chain, and specialty stores. It conducts conferences and workshops and provides extensive groups of manuals and bulletins on various phases of retail merchandising. Through working to inform its members, this association benefits the consumer.

Manufacturers' Associations

Manufacturers' associations are organizations for member companies. Their research, however, much like that of trade associations, is indirectly of value to the consumer. The manufacturers act as middlemen by implementing for consumer benefit the research performed by their own laboratories.

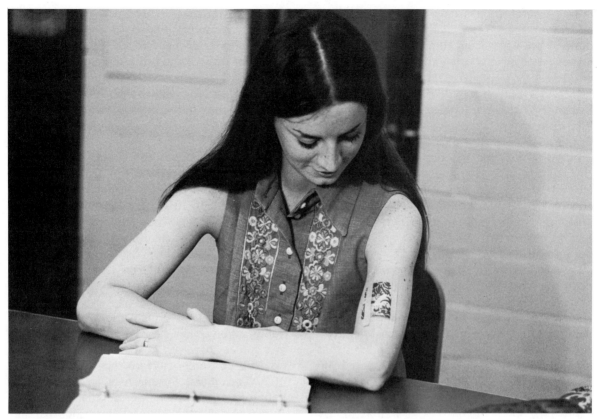

Finishes which appear to be very effective may prove to be irritating to a wide range of consumers. Therefore they must be tested and perhaps adapted to avoid unpleasant side effects.

The American Apparel Manufacturers Association

The American Apparel Manufacturers Association is the largest and most representative trade association of this country's apparel industry. Its members produce every major item of wearing apparel for men, women, and children, as well as uniforms for personnel of the military and space programs.

The association has a Consumer Affairs Committee. The function of this committee is to cooperate with industry, consumers, and governmental representatives in the development and implementation of programs designed to meet demonstrated consumer needs involving the apparel industry.

The National Association of Manufacturers

The National Association of Manufacturers is an association to serve its business and industry members. Indirectly, however, it serves the consumer through some of its publications, such as *The Tips Handbook,* a manual of information on consumer products and services.

Research Groups
Helping the Consumer

Consumer interest in goods of stable quality makes guarantees or warranties mandatory. So that these guarantees can be substantiated on a profitable basis, the establishment of research laboratories was necessary. Most of these research groups have been organized to test for a specific producer or manufacturer. Some work for many companies, while still others work strictly from the consumer point of view.

Research Within the Fiber Industry

The leading fiber producers, such as Celanese Corporation, E.I. DuPont, Eastman Chemical Products, American Viscose Division of FMC Corporation, and others maintain large quality-control laboratories that indirectly benefit the consumer. Many engage in licensed trademark programs covering all phases of protection from fiber to fabric. These programs set up standards that a specific fiber or fabric must meet before it can be labeled with the company's trademark. This kind of program assures the consumer of a specific quality and gives technical guidance and control to the manufacturer. Some of these companies have extensive consumer education programs that help the consumer learn more about the products he buys. They also publish for school use pertinent current information which explains new fibers and finishes as well as trends in fashion which affect fiber choices.

Research for Retail Stores and Mail-order Firms

The consumer's demand for product performance calls for accurately described pretested merchandise which has correct care instructions attached. Such demands have caused the large chain stores and mail-order catalogue companies to expand their testing laboratories. Retail-store buyers look to these laboratories as a resource to back up manufacturers' claims. The consumer can increase the speed at which effective testing becomes mandatory by returning goods which perform poorly to the store where they were bought.

Commercial Research Laboratories.

Some manufacturing firms are not large enough to support their own research and development or quality-control laboratories. They must rely on independent commercial testing laboratories. The Better Fabrics Testing Bureau and the United States Testing Company are perhaps the best known of the independent testing laboratories.

Nonprofit Research Organizations

Probably the most active nonprofit research organization in the country is *Consumers' Union*. Its special publication, called *Consumer Report*, is distributed to millions of consumers. Its testing reports include information on textiles, electronics, and chemicals. With the Federal government now setting standards in a variety of industries, Consumers' Union, as an organization, hopes to become involved in new consumer legislation and to see that both government and industry develop consumer performance standards.

Consumers' Research is an educational, nonprofit organization that serves consumers. It makes scientific and engineering tests of many of the products which consumers buy and use. Its findings are reported in monthly issues of *Consumer Bulletin* and in the *Consumer Bulletin Annual*. Products are rated by brand name as *Recommended, Intermediate*, and *Not Recommended*. Considerable work is also done in developing test methods and devices. Many of this organization's methods have been made available for the use of government agencies, research institutions, commercial testing laboratories, and manufacturers.

An important aspect of the work of Consumers' Research is its service to schools, colleges, and universities. *Consumer Bulletin* is used as an educational aid.

GROUP LEARNING EXPERIENCE

1. Invite your mathematics teacher to explain the metric system. Discuss how, if used, it would affect the fabric and garment measurements in use in this country today.

2. Tour an industrial plant in your area. Try to determine ways by which industry shows that it cares about the needs of the consumer.

3. Investigate to determine which local, state, and Federal government agencies function in your community to protect the consumer of clothing and fabrics.

4. Invite the manager of a drycleaning establishment to come to your class to explain how the National Fair Claims Guide for Textile Products is used to help consumers.

5. Determine whether there is a department, bureau, or office of consumer protection in your community. Invite a member of the staff to talk to you about consumer complaints and how they are handled.

6. Invite a fabric buyer or a buyer of teen clothing to come to the classroom and explain how he goes into the market to buy for the individuals who live in your community.

HELPING OTHERS TO LEARN

1. Make a bulletin-board display to show the different labeling systems used to help the consumer in his selection of textile products.

2. Ask your librarian to help you plan a consumer information center. Assemble pamphlets, booklets, and books that will help people learn more about selecting suitable fabrics for specific clothing.

3. Determine whether you can be of assistance in organizing and preparing a consumer information center in your community on the selection and care of fabrics.

4. Invite a member of your local fire department to the classroom to talk about fire hazards of clothing. Determine how you can develop a community program to help people learn how to protect themselves from such hazards.

1. Assemble a collection of labels and hang tags. Read, study, and evaluate the information. Divide them into the following groups: informative, brand, certification, and union.

2. Write the U.S. Patent Office, U.S. Department of Commerce, Washington, D.C. 20231, for its publication *Questions and Answers about Trademarks.* Give a report to your class on your findings.

3. Write to the U.S. Department of Labor, Washington, D.C. 20210, and request its pamphlet *Department of Labor* or to the U.S. Government Printing Office, Washington, D.C. 20402, for its publication GPO 937-617, which describes the U.S. Department of Labor. Give a class report on what bureaus within the Department of Labor may be of service or interest to members of your class.

4. Write to the Federal Trade Commission, Washington, D.C. 20580, regarding information on the *Permanent Care Labeling Rule.* Report your findings to the class.

5. Write to the U.S. Department of Commerce, Office of Public Affairs, Washington, D.C. 20230, and ask for a copy of *Do You Know Your Economic ABC's? Patents, Spur to American Progress.* Report your findings to the class.

6. Read *Tailors Progress* by Benjamin Stolberg, published by Doubleday, Doran and Company, Garden City, New York, 1944. It will give you an insight into the International Ladies Garment Workers' Union and those who made it. Give a report to your class.

7. Write to the Federal Trade Commission, Washington, D.C. 20580, for a copy of *Here is Your Federal Trade Commission* (0-749-639). Give an oral report to your class.

7 Wage Earning in the World of Fashion

Your career decision is one of the most important decisions you will ever make. This decision is important for a number of reasons. Your choice directs the course of your adult life. It determines to a degree how much money you will earn. It has an effect on what others think of you. It can influence your personal feeling of well being. You can perform best if you choose a job in which you can find satisfaction.

What are useful considerations for a person entering the work world?

Why is choosing a career goal one of the most important decisions you will make in your life?

How does the amount of education and training you receive help to determine your advancement in the work world?

How can your occupation influence your chances of steady employment, your role in the community, the friends you make, and the person you marry?

How can you evaluate your interests, abilities, aptitudes, and personality to determine whether you are suited for a job?

How will the courses you take in school aid in your preparation for the job you choose? .

Which agencies in your school or in your community offer help in selecting the job best suited to you?

How do you feel about work experience on Saturdays? After school? During the summer?

Steps Toward Successful Employment

Your parents, teachers, principal, and superintendent want you to attain career goals through which you can contribute to society. You are their product, and they want to be proud of you. So do your friends. They all want you to feel secure and happy. Business and industry frequently set up training programs and create job opportunities for young people. They, too, are interested and concerned about the future achievement of those they train and hire. The government is also interested in your success. A successful wage earner contributes to, rather than detracts from, the general prosperity of the country.

As you consider job choices and the steps you must take in finding employment, keep in mind that people really care. Your home and school, as well as industry and government, all have valid reasons for their interest in your successful entrance into the world of work.

WHICH OF THE FOLLOWING DESIRABLE PERSONALITY TRAITS CAN BE ACQUIRED?

Sociability	Sound judgment	Enthusiasm
Initiative	Effective speech	Orderliness
Cooperativeness	Empathy	Loyalty
Tactfulness	Poise	Adaptability
Honesty	Dependability	Persistence
Consideration	Patience	Emotional control
Self-confidence	Courtesy	Alertness
Intelligence	Ambition	Stamina

Preparation for a Job

Successful preparation for a role in the work world includes careful planning and study. Courses can be chosen at school which are geared toward a future job role. Many school courses and self-teaching courses are available which help students prepare for meaningful work. Any person who considers working needs to give special attention to personality development and maintenance of health practices.

The first important step in choosing a career or job is to learn to know yourself. What kind of work do you like to do? What special skills do you now have, and which ones can you acquire? What further education do you need? When you have made a self-analysis, consult a guidance counselor who can help you make a choice if you are not certain.

Adequate Education

It is important that you look at the total curriculum offered by your school. Then select the courses that will help you build toward a successful future. Formal education alone is not the key to job success. It is desirable that you acquire a good balance between formal education and practical application. Practical use of knowledge comes most frequently through work experience. School programs which provide for work experience are valuable, even though they may seem unrelated to your job goals. Such an experience will often widen your view. Work experiences may cause you to see new opportunities and new challenges. Work-study programs carried on in many high schools and colleges allow students to study part of the time. During the remainder of each day or semester, they learn through actual work experiences. Through such programs students frequently find full-time employment when their formal education is completed.

Personality Development

Much of the preparation needed for future employment can be classified as personality development. In job preparation, as in other phases of living, the ideas of desirable and undesirable personality become submerged in the real meaning of personality: *the characteristics which distinguish a person.* It becomes important, however, that you develop characteristics, or personality traits, which will be needed in your work.

Most personality traits necessary for success in a vocation are qualities that are acquired rather than inborn. Those who try can become successful at some kind of work. Since working is a lifetime undertaking, it is important to begin early to cultivate those traits which will be needed throughout the rest of your life.

Sound Health Habits

If you plan to be an effective worker, you need to develop good health habits or to continue to practice those already developed. Your energy is generated in relation to good health. Your body supplies energy reserves for both the expected and the unexpected demands of a job. Develop good health habits, as described on pages 11-22.

Avoid allowing your job or other activities to drain your energy reserve completely. A certain reserve is necessary if you are to maintain sound mental and physical health. A sound mental attitude combined with adequate food and adequate rest will keep most people strong enough to meet the rigors of wage-earning occupations.

Job Hunting

When you are ready to join the work force, go to your school counselor. Many schools have regular job-training or job-placement departments to which counselors can direct interested students. In some schools the guidance counselors themselves have business-industry contacts within the community. Knowing recruits are available from time to time, those businesses needing employees may send regular requests to schools. In schools where such arrangements are provided, counselors are often able to refer students to specific job openings.

In addition, counselors can help students look in various advertising media for suitable jobs. They also know of the various employment agencies which effectively help young people in the search for jobs.

School and College Placement Offices

Some high schools and most trade schools, colleges, and universities have placement offices which try to help their students and alumni find jobs. Where such services are available, the student is expected to take the initiative in preparing and filing a résumé.

Advertised Positions

The daily newspaper may lead you to the job you want. Read the help-wanted ads, both in the classified section and in the section where companies advertise positions for experienced personnel. Professional and technical magazines also carry want ads for people with special training.

Blind ads are often listed among the general help-wanted ads. They are used by employers who do not want to be bothered with unqualified applicants. If you answer a blind ad, be sure to include all the information requested.

You may want to consider placing a situation-wanted ad in a local paper or a magazine. If you do this, be certain to describe the job you want and your qualifications for the position.

Sometimes you may get a lead for a job by reading general news stories or the business and financial pages of the newspaper. For instance, you may see a report of the opening of a new business. It may offer just the job you would like to have. Often the owner of such a new business does not know he needs you. In such a case you must sell him the idea that he needs your services, indicating what your specific abilities are and how they could be of help to him.

Public Employment Agencies

State and Federal government employment offices are tax-supported. Such offices are located in major cities in most sections of the country. These offices are usually staffed with persons well qualified to help you find satisfactory employment. There is no charge for their services.

Private Employment Agencies

In some seasons and in some years jobs are very hard to find. It is at such a time that you might want to consult a private employment agency. Deal with a reputable agency. You may find it to your advantage to deal with several agencies. Fees are paid either by you or by your employer. Sometimes the fees are shared. You are liable for a fee only if you agree to pay it and if you accept a position

When jobs are difficult to find, consider consulting an employment agency.
Make an appointment by telephone and take your résumé with you to the
appointment.

obtained through the agency. If you do not
want to pay an employment fee, be certain
to tell the agency in advance, so that you will
be referred only to jobs for which employers
are willing to pay the finder's fee. Read the
contract carefully. Be certain you understand
it completely before signing it. Fees may vary
from 5 to 15 percent of the first year's salary.

Other Placement Services
Professional and technical societies and
unions and other trade associations often
maintain a job clearing house for their members. While these placement services are very
effective for members, the beginning employee usually does not qualify as a member
of the society or association until he pays the
dues or fees required.

Your Own Independent Business
If you are creative and have business sense,
you may want to go into business for yourself. There are many cases on record in
which young people just out of high school or

RÉSUMÉ

Name: Mary Ann Matthews
Address: 612 Virginia Avenue, St. Louis, Missouri 63187
Telephone: 966-8557

What I Can Do for You:

Meet people pleasantly and help them decide which stylish clothing looks best on them. Determine which styles are likely to be favorites of the buying public.

Education:

Date	School	Degree	Major
1970-1974	Central High School	College preparatory	Liberal arts
1962-1970	Adams Grade School	Diploma	General

Work Experience:

Date	Job	Type of work
6/73-9/73	High school fashion board in local department store	Informal modeling and helping students choose their fall wardrobes
6/72-9/72	Counselor in summer camp	Assistant to instructor in clothing construction and in crafts classes

Extracurricular Activities and Achievements:

Attended Fashion School in local department store
President of High School FHA Chapter
Member of Junior Achievement Group

Interests and Skills:

Hobbies: Sports. Spoken French and Spanish
Skills: Typing and clothing construction

Personal Data:

Age: 18   Height: 5 ft. 6 in.   Weight: 125 lbs.
Health: Good   Marital Status: Single

Sample form for a beginning position in the clothing and fashion industry.

List schools in reverse chronological order, beginning with the school most recently attended.

List jobs in reverse chronological order, beginning with the job most recently held.

---

college have become very successful in establishing businesses of their own. The National Federation of Independent Business and the Small Business Administration are interested in helping young people who would like to find new jobs or start their own businesses.

Your Résumé

Before you approach anyone for a job, you have some homework to do. Prepare your job résumé, or the summary of your qualifications for the job you seek. Write it yourself and then ask someone to check and perfect the presentation. You will find if you prepare your own résumé that you feel more at ease during interviews, because you will be well acquainted with the information and its organization.

The form shown here is a typical résumé. It gives personal and educational information. It indicates work experience and extracurricular activities and achievements. Hobbies and special skills are also listed. References should be omitted from the résumé. Have

Courtesy Celanese Fibers Marketing Co.

When dressing for a job interview, choose clothing that gives you self-confidence while showing your potential employer that you are seriously interested in fitting into the world of work.

When your résumé is completed, ask yourself, "Does the information support my objective of being invited for an interview?" It sometimes pays to have your presentation finalized by a person who specializes in such work. Usually help is available at both public and private employment agencies. In any case, be certain the résumé is neatly typed and well spaced with several blank spaces between areas of type. Use only one side of heavy white bond paper. If you need several copies, have the résumé reproduced by offset printing or photocopying. If you have it mimeographed, see that the work is first rate. Avoid sending carbon copies to potential employers.

If you apply for a job in an area some distance from your home, it will be necessary to include a personal letter along with your résumé. Be certain it is clear, specific, and neatly typed.

Do not waste your time, effort, and money in sending your résumé to random employers. Select the organizations which especially interest you. Then mail your résumé to the person within each of these organizations who deals with job requests.

Applying for a Job

Most modern employers are looking for the type of person who is quietly assured that he can do the job which needs to be done. Most are not greatly impressed by loud self-applause or by gaudy or expensive clothing. They do notice whether you are clean and appear to have pride in your appearance. While they do not expect an interviewee to be dressed exactly as he would dress for work, they look for some indication that he could fit easily into the group with whom he might work as an employee.

Employers like to feel that you want to work for them. They are more interested in what you can do for their company than in your need for work. It is important, of course, that you find a job which pays enough for your needs. It is also important that you understand which, if any, fringe benefits exist. How-

them available, however, in case they are needed during a personal interview. Be courteous in obtaining such references, asking the persons you choose if you can use their names as references. Avoid including relatives. Your teachers, your minister, and local business people whom you know will generally be happy to act in this capacity.

ever, job applicants who become employees are usually those who want to fit in and help do a job, rather than those who are planning mainly for their own benefit.

Avoid limiting yourself if you have the education, training, or skill to fit more than one type of job. This sometimes results if you list a single job title on a résumé or application.

Try to be positive in your speaking or writing. When reacting positively, you will avoid such statements as, "I never have done this kind of work, but maybe I could try it." The same idea stated positively might be expressed, "I feel certain I could do the work, given the opportunity." Employers react positively to people who think positively.

It is advisable to omit reference to salary until you can talk face-to-face with your prospective employer. If asked in an application to name the amount for which you would work, rather than specifying the exact amount it is better to state that the salary is open for discussion. This will help you avoid pricing yourself over the market for a particular job. Too, it will prevent your selling yourself short. You deserve to be paid the amount your services are worth.

It is also advisable to omit your photograph when applying for a job. Sometimes photographs are deceiving. Some interviews never materialize because the interviewer did not react favorably to a photograph, even though the interviewee had good qualifications for the job.

The Successful Interview

Suppose that a certain company needs to fill a position. Suppose, also, that you fit the qualifications and send the company an effective résumé. In all probability, you will be granted an interview.

Your goal is to make the interviewer feel that you are the right person for the job. In job hunting, first impressions count. Your appearance and behavior are two of the three points on which the interviewer can judge you.

He must decide for himself whether he feels you can do the job. Prepare to sell yourself effectively.

Preparing for the Interview   Try to learn ahead of time the policies of the company and the products or services it sells. Review your qualifications and experiences that you feel fit you for the job.

Get your clothes ready, and get yourself ready physically and mentally. Select clothes that are neat and appropriate. Get a good night's sleep; this will help you feel well and act with confidence. Take the required time needed to groom and dress yourself properly.

Along with a copy of your résumé, assemble everything else you might need. Include a pencil and note paper, your work permit, your social-security card, and references, including their telephone numbers and addresses.

Manners During the Interview   Be on time. If possible, allow yourself enough time to arrive a little early. If you cannot be punctual, phone to explain the delay. Make sure you know where to go and whom to see.

Once inside the office, wait until the interviewer has invited you to be seated. Stand tall when standing, and sit straight but relaxed when sitting. Avoid smoking unless your interviewer invites you to join him. If you do not smoke, remark casually, "Thank you, no."

If you are asked to wait, be understanding and agreeable. You may be asked to fill out a company application. Do this willingly, referring if necessary to a copy of your résumé and to your references. If the company wants you to take tests, be ready to comply on request.

Answer questions honestly and directly. Stress your qualifications for the job. Indicate that you are flexible, that you are willing to learn, and that you will accept guidance. You may want to ask questions about the background and functions of the company. Maybe you will want the interviewer to clarify the duties of the position.

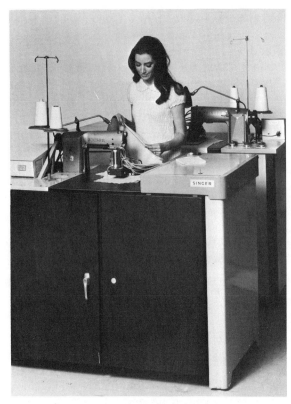

Courtesy American Apparel Manufacturing Association

Students can frequently move directly from technical training into jobs in the garment manufacturing industry.

Choosing a Job

Suppose you are offered a job. How will you decide whether to take it or to wait for a better one? The decision is perhaps most often made by determining how badly money is needed and how quickly. Important as a pay check and fringe benefits may seem, however, there is more to a job than money. Your job or career development affects your psychological and social development, as well as your potential for achievement. To progress effectively, you must feel good about the work you do. You must be satisfied and feel you are successful in what you are doing. Every job has its advantages and disadvantages. You will be expected to do some things from time to time that you may not like to do.

Successful employees take such tasks in stride, realizing they are part of the job.

Salary

Numerous factors determine your salary. The company's need for the services you can provide, your education, and your work experience are usually the factors which affect it most.

Salary to most people includes the total amount they are paid including taxes which are withheld. Most large companies provide an employees' manual that explains the method by which employees' pay is determined. Such a manual also spells out important salary items such as frequency of pay days and necessary deductions.

When you and your employer agree on a salary figure, he is usually willing to help you determine your take-home pay. You might inquire about the amount of your salary which will be withheld for Federal income taxes, local taxes, social security, and other purposes. You might also inquire as to whether you are covered by workmen's compensation and unemployment compensation.

Fringe Benefits

Fringe benefits vary from company to company. You may inquire whether you are covered by medical, disability, or life insurance. If they are available, your employer will also explain pension plans offered by the company. He may explain profit-sharing plans or annual bonus plans if they exist within the company. Some firms offer discount privileges to their employees.

Most companies provide some plan for sick leave, and there is usually some provision for vacations either with or without pay. Fringe benefits often include convenience factors, such as rest and recreational facilities, parking areas, cafeterias or dining rooms, and a medical department on the premises.

Fringe benefits are exactly that. They are benefits in addition to your salary. You are not required to pay income taxes on fringe

GUIDES TO SELF-MOTIVATION ON THE JOB

1. *Develop your plan on paper. Determine your goals and the way to reach them.*
2. *Put your plan into practice.*
3. *Break a big job down into logical segments.*
4. *Establish check points by which to measure progress.*
5. *Determine the benefits you expect to receive when the job is done.*
6. *Start early.*
7. *Put first things first and get started.*
8. *Stay on the track.*
9. *Recognize your limitations.*
10. *Take advantage of your energy peaks during the day.*
11. *Try new methods.*
12. *Set up a time-control budget for the job to be done.*
13. *Set deadlines and hold to them.*
14. *Remain aware of the consequences if you do not finish assigned tasks.*
15. *Learn to know when you are reasoning and when you are rationalizing. Make a distinction between* I can't *and* I don't want to.
16. *Be optimistic, increasing your chances for success.*
17. *Read on subjects that relate to your problem.*
18. *Use notes, reminders, and other self-signaling devices.*
19. *Promise yourself rewards for work well done.*
20. *Avoid self-pity when there is extra work to be done.*
21. *Recognize conflicts and make the necessary decisions.*
22. *Avoid self-punishment when you make mistakes.*
23. *Keep your sense of humor.*

benefits. While important to the modern employee, it is also important that you never allow them to replace the joy of choosing a job you like and of doing it well.

Protection

Private and governmental agencies work to protect you as an employee. There are Federal laws such as the Fair Labor Standards Act and the Equal Employment Opportunity Act designed to protect the worker. Special Federal and state laws have been passed to protect women in particular. Unions and other associations concern themselves with protection of employees' rights. It is important that you study how and why these agencies and laws serve to protect you.

How can you determine whether you are performing acceptably in a job?

How can a person motivate himself to be a good employee?

What can be gained by beginning at the bottom and working your way to the top in a job situation?

What are the characteristics of a person of high vocational achievement?

Why is the field of fashion a natural vehicle through which women can express creativity in the world of work?

What careers are available for young women in the field of clothing manufacture? In commercial pattern making? In fashion projection? In merchandising? In the textile industry? In the textile care services?

Your First Job

It is one thing to get a job and quite another to keep it. Suppose you are appearing for your first day on a new job. How do you dress? To create self-confidence and a favorable impression, arrive at your job well groomed and dressed neatly and appropriately for the work at hand. How do you act? There are many demands to be met. If you want to be a success on the job, it is necessary to follow instructions carefully, especially in the beginning. Be cheerfully cooperative in meeting the job requirements, and keep an eye out for additional ways in which you can be helpful. Do you have some useful skill such as typing

Courtesy Simplicity Pattern Co., Inc.

Persons who have art training and special abilities in sketching may consider jobs in pattern designing or fashion cataloguing.

or filing? Offer your skills willingly. Then your effectiveness on the job can become realistic.

As your work progresses, make a self-appraisal now and then. How are you doing on the job? Are you getting along with other people? What are you doing to improve yourself both mentally and physically? Are you trying to develop qualities of leadership? Not everyone needs to be a leader. Perhaps you can improve your work habits and become a better follower. Get involved with your work. It is generally quite easy to attain some degree of success. Only involved employees can maintain it.

In giving your best to your first job, you may well find that your rewards exceed your giving. Even if your first job is menial, it can broaden your vision. It can also offer an opportunity to earn money while you are gaining even more valuable experience. Once you have work experience to your credit, it is easier to get a job which to you is more interesting or desirable. Everyone must start somewhere and sometime. Avoid feeling discouraged if your starting position is located near the bottom of the career ladder.

If your first job happens to be summer employment, it will help you see at first hand many aspects of the world of work. The work experience will help you develop self-respect, competence, and responsibility. It can give you an insight into specific types of careers. For example, a job in a retail store, hospital, restaurant, laundry or drycleaning plant will help you decide if you might like permanent employment in that field of service. Such rewards are greatest if you are fortunate enough to have a job that relates to courses you are studying or planning to study in school.

The experience you gain on the job and the people you meet and work with are often more important than actual money received for summer employment. Experienced employees you work with may be of great help to you in opening doors for future employment. They may even serve as your inspira-

EIGHT TRAITS COMMON TO
HIGH VOCATIONAL ACHIEVEMENT

Self-esteem   A deep conviction of your own worth.
Sense of responsibility   A willingness to account for your own be-
havior and your own decisions.
Optimism   A positive expectation of success.
Dedication   A devotion of your time and energy to your goal.
Awareness   A knowledge of what is happening.
Creativity   A constant searching for ways to do things better.
Effectiveness in communication   The ability to transmit information
between the various groups concerned.
Positive response to pressure   The ability to give high performance
under undesirable circumstances.

tion because you can see how they work and live. You can observe at close range the satisfactions, the problems, and the fruits of their labors.

Modern Trends in
the Feminine World of Work

For many years most young women planned only for marriage. Even though they often were well-educated scholastically, they usually planned to be full-time mothers and homemakers rather than wage earners. This pattern continues to change. Most girls today realize they must prepare themselves to enter the world of work. The U.S. Bureau of Labor Statistics states that almost 90 percent of all women join the labor force at some time during their lives. While many women work through choice, others find it is necessary to combine work and marriage.

There are many social and economic changes which influence women to work outside the home. Women live longer today than previously. They have increased educational opportunitities and freedom. And the world of work needs them. If women work for no other reason, a job can fill many of their psychological and emotional needs, helping them to feel like useful, interesting people.

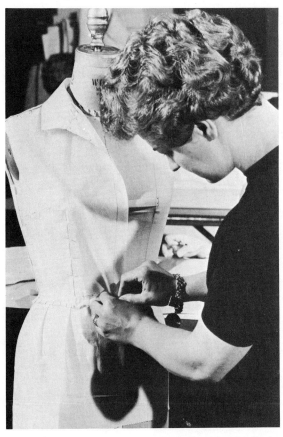

Courtesy Simplicity Pattern Co., Inc.

A person who works in a pattern draping department usually has a college education and years of experience in the field of fashion design.

179

It is probably much easier for modern women to work than it was for women of previous generations. Technology has made it possible to accomplish the chores of homemaking more easily. Communities, industry, and government, recognizing their need for women in the work force, are providing day-care centers, nursery schools, and youth centers for the young. This willingness on the part of the community to free a few hours of a mother's time each day allows for expanding the size of the work force to accommodate an expanding economy.

Careers in
the Apparel Industry

Social and economic changes have broadened the range of job opportunities for women. For many years careers for working women focused mainly on the fields of teaching and nursing. Today they include the whole gamut of occupations, including the increasingly varied opportunities involved in the design, production, and maintenance of clothing.

There is a wide range of career opportunities within the apparel industry. Choosing

Courtesy Students of Massey Junior College, Atlanta

Designers are trained to envision fabrics as finished products which suit the tastes of others.

BEGINNING CAREER OPPORTUNITIES IN CLOTHING MANUFACTURING

Position	Job Description	Job Requirements
Sewer	Performs hand sewing not readily done by machine.	
Trimmer	Applies decorative stitching to garments.	High school education preferred.
Inspector	Checks that finished garments or portions of garments meet specifications. May repair small defects.	Vocational training in special skill area helpful. A few weeks to several months of on-the-job training necessary, depending on difficulty of job.
Presser	Presses garments upon completion to smooth the surface, flatten seams, and provide needed shaping.	Cutters may be required to serve apprenticeship.
Cutter	Cuts out pieces of garments from fabric according to pattern.	

180

Quality control exists in each phase of clothing manufacture from fiber production to the completion of fashion garments.

one of them might help you reach your ultimate career goal. You might find the apparel industry exciting in that it sets styles for people of all ages.

Among the industrial giants, the apparel industry is the second largest manufacturing industry, the third largest consumer industry, and the fourth largest employer. It offers careers connected with production, art, journalism, and fashion. It provides jobs for people with a wide variety of interests and skills. It covers the fields of clothing construction, pattern making and distribution, fashion projection, merchandising, and the entire field of textile research, production, distribution, and care. There are, in addition, a broad range of special opportunities in textile- and clothing-related fields for the well qualified.

Careers in Clothing Manufacturing

The person who has clothing-construction skills is usually among the first selected for employment by the apparel manufacturing industry. This industry can be the source of a good-paying job for the person who chooses to enter the work force directly out of high school. Beginning jobs can lead to promotions within the industry, or they can provide a background of experience for the person who plans to serve business as a manager or an owner.

Most supervisors, section leaders, technicians, fashion designers, pattern makers, engineering aides, and job instructors in the apparel industry begin their careers in the area of clothing construction with such jobs as those described in the chart on page 180.

CAREER OPPORTUNITIES IN COMMERCIAL PATTERN MAKING

Position	Job Description	Job Requirements
Art Graphic artists Fashion illustrators Fashion photographers	Provides art work for commercial patterns, ranging from simple line drawings to graphic designs and layouts. Illustrates or photographs garments constructed from the patterns.	Post–high school training in graphic design, fashion art, or photography. Courses in typography required of artists.
Cataloguing Editors Editorial assistants Copywriters	Selects and compiles styles for consumer market. Prepares catalogue copy, proofreads, keeps records and files.	Post–high school fashion training. Ability in writing, copy editing, and typing. Understanding of fashion. Editorial, merchandising, or retail experience helpful.
Fashion promotion Promotion director Promotion assistants Training stylists	Promotes fashions directed mainly toward retail market. Works with buyer, directs style shows, may supervise making of dresses for style shows.	Post–high school training in textiles, fashion, retailing, and garment construction. Ability to plan and execute details of promotion. Advertising or publishing experience useful.
Pattern grading Drafters Stampers Graders	Handles precision work involved in drafting, stamping, and grading of patterns.	Graduate of fashion school or completion of apprenticeship training. Precision skill. Thorough knowledge of clothing construction. Experience in garment industry or trade school training also helpful.
Instruction writing	Provides copy for instruction sheets accompanying patterns.	Post–high school training in technical writing preferred. Ability to write simple, intelligible directions at a speed sufficient for meeting deadlines. Knowledge of clothing construction details necessary.
Computation Specialists in measuring and photography	Determines amount of each width of fabric required for each pattern size. Makes, photographs, and rechecks paste-ups of pattern layouts.	Expert dressmaking ability or skill in photography combined with knowledge of pattern layouts.
General promotion Copywriters Stylists Advertising employees	Handles promotion for pattern company. Works with magazines, fabric manufacturing and advertising agencies, as well as other departments in own company.	Post–high school training in fashion journalism helpful. Supervisory positions require home economics or liberal arts education with some work in journalism, art, retailing, and designing.
Pattern designing	Designs patterns, determining future style trends and creating designs which can be reproduced in home sewing situation.	Post–high school art training with sketching and drawing ability. Thorough knowledge of clothing construction. Foresight and good judgment.
Dressmaking	Translates test patterns into test garments.	Expert dressmaking ability.

Position	Job Description	Job Requirements
Draping	Provides special draping effects in patterns.	Thorough training in fashion designing, usually including college degree with major in fashion design.
Education Educational director Educational assistants Copywriters Correspondents Traveling representatives	Prepares educational materials suitable for wide range of uses.	Home economics degree. Experience in the field of teaching or extension service also required of traveling representatives. Thorough knowledge of clothing construction, design, and color. Journalism, public speaking, typing, and office procedure helpful.
Fabric research Fabric editor Fabric assistants	Recommends fabrics suitable for specific patterns. Works closely with other departments and maintains fabric library.	Post—high school training in art and textiles. Thorough knowledge of fabric resources, trends, and colors.
Journalism	Handles all phases of publication of fashion magazines published by the pattern company. Writes, edits, proofreads, coordinates art work, and supervises fashion styling and dressmaking.	Post—high school training in journalism or publishing suggested.

Thus, sewing opens the door to many opportunities in the bigger world of fashion.

Careers in
Commercial Pattern Making

Career opportunities vary slightly from one pattern company to another. In general, pattern companies offer jobs for qualified applicants in the fields of art, cataloguing, fashion promotion, pattern grading, writing, computation, general promotion, design, dressmaking, draping, education, fabric research, and journalism. If you have skills and interests in one or more of these areas, consider talking with a specialist from one of the pattern companies. Perhaps such a person can help you plan preparation for a career in the area of commercial pattern making.

Careers in Fashion Projection

If you are a creative person who enjoys serious work, consider a job in the field of fashion projection. Many young people have worked their way up the ladder to very important positions within the fashion industry. Among the careers offered by fashion are jobs in the areas of art, design, modeling, journalism, and promotion. Charts describing the positions available, the description of various jobs, and necessary training and abilities are shown on pages 185, 186, 189, and 190.

Careers in Merchandising

Merchandising is the buying and selling of goods. It offers a wide opportunity for jobs and careers in retail stores, shops, and boutiques. Job opportunities, job descriptions, and job requirements are listed in the chart on pages 187-188. Relatively simple, easy-to-find jobs are listed first, with more complex ones following. In large cities, similar jobs are available in wholesale markets, as well as in stores which provide materials for fashion manufacturing.

Courtesy Students of Massey Junior College, Atlanta

Fashion coordinators are able to demonstrate to consumers how a wide range of fashion items can be combined.

Specialists in merchandise control are able to tell by the rate of flow how well a certain item is selling in a general locality.

CAREER OPPORTUNITIES IN FASHION MODELING

Position	Job Description	Job Requirements
Fashion modeling in general	Shows clothes in a way to sell them.	
Fashion modeling in retail stores and manufacturers' showrooms	Shows fashions to customers and buyers.	
Fashion modeling for catalogues	Models fashions for photographers so that customers can make a choice from the illustrations.	High school education. Course in modeling usually required. Good appearance. Ability to project personality and uniqueness. Good health and physical stamina. Patience. Physical measurements for junior, misses, or high-fashion model sizes.
Fashion modeling for fashion magazines, trade publications, direct-mail flyers, display advertising, or billboards	Models fashions for photographers to illustrate fashion or create a demand for products or services.	
Fashion modeling for television	Models clothes and accessories for advertising and retail-store promotions on television.	

CAREER OPPORTUNITIES IN FASHION PROMOTION

Position	Job Description	Job Requirements
General fashion promotion	Selects clothes, props, accessories, and models. Arranges them to dramatize a specific fashion idea.	High school education necessary. College degree preferred. Apprenticeship training. Knowledge of wholesale and retail market. Good health and physical stamina.
Advertising agency promotion	Makes appropriate displays to project the client's product to its best advantage.	
Product promotion	Works with manufacturer to develop his product. Gives suggestions on packaging and marketing. Recommends change in color, style, or shape for greater market appeal.	
Television promotion	Understands color, lighting, and arrangement. Coordinates details and timing of a specific promotion.	

CAREER OPPORTUNITIES IN FASHION ART

Position	Job Description	Job Requirements
Art director	Responsible for layout and artwork of advertisements or fashion stories. Assigns illustrators and photographers to specific jobs. Works with editorial and merchandising personnel. Coordinates staff and free-lance artists.	Graduate of art school. Organizational and administrative ability. Ability to deal with creative people.
Illustrator	Presents merchandise in a unique manner to sell fashion.	Post—high school training in wide variety of art media and studio equipment. Knowledge of fine arts, design, and layout. Ability to present a visual approach to advertising and merchandising. One to three years apprenticeship.
Photographer	Photographs still and action shots of models. Takes motion pictures of fashions for television advertising, promotion, or education. May travel extensively. May develop a free-lance business.	Post—high school training in technical aspects of photography and fashion styling. Ability to work with assistants, apprentices, and clerical staff.
Assistant photographer	Takes test shots. Prepares sets and backgrounds. Tests lighting. Develops pictures.	Apprenticeship or post—high school education in photography and fashion styling.

From purchase to checkout counter, the aim of each member of a merchandising team is to help consumers make useful selections with which they will continue to be happy.

CAREER OPPORTUNITIES IN MERCHANDISING

Position	Job Description	Job Requirements
Stock girl	Unpacks, counts, and tickets merchandise to prepare it for sale.	High school education preferred.
Head of stock	Keeps departments fully stocked with merchandise. Fills special orders. Keeps records of incoming, outgoing, and returned merchandise. Works closely with the buyer.	High school education preferred.
Unit control clerk	Keeps track of merchandise, the rate it moves, and the number and reasons for returns.	High school education. Computer training.
Salesperson	Effects the transfer of the merchandise from the store into the hands of the customer.	High school education preferred. Salesmanship training helpful. Knowledge of the product or service very important.
Assistant buyer	Supervises sales staff; keeps records and places orders for merchandise. Observes rate of movement of merchandise from store to customers.	High school diploma necessary. College degree preferred. Business training. Ability to work with others.

Continued on page 188

Position	Job Description	Job Requirements
Buyer	Selects from the market the merchandise customers want and need. Responsible for major buying decisions involving large expenditures of money. Travels to major fashion centers. Works closely with merchandise manager, unit control clerk, and fashion coordinator. Displays and advertises merchandise.	High school education necessary. College degree preferred, plus training in merchandising, advertising, and display. Business training helpful. Ability to withstand pressure to meet budget and sales figures.
Merchandise manager, divisional	Oversees the budget of each buyer in the division. Supervises the plans and activities of the buyer. Coordinates activities with store policies and goals. Works with advertising and sales promotion departments. Reports to general merchandise manager or to the store president.	Training as described for buyer but with the addition of years of experience.
Comparison shopper	Makes comparisons between prices and qualities of the store's merchandising and those of its competitors. Compares advertising and displays. Reports on findings. Is able to collect facts necessary for a price adjustment if a customer questions price of a product sold less expensively elsewhere.	High school education preferred. Selling experience. Knowledge of fabrics, styling, workmanship, and manufacturer's claims. Ability to assemble facts, make decisions, and write reports.
Display director Display manager Supervisor of window displays Supervisor of interior displays Trimmers, junior trimmers Helpers, stockkeepers, porters, maids Supervisor of art Artists Carpenters, painters	Ability to sell merchandise by appealing to the customer's senses of sight and touch. Displays, window and point-of-sale, are sometimes keyed to special promotions, special events, holidays, or community events. Store-connected fashion shows are often the job of the display manager and his assistants.	High school education necessary. Apprenticeship often required. Training in aspects of art and display. Skills to accommodate the specific display job assigned. On-the-job training.
Fashion coordinator	Promotes sale of merchandise by developing a fashion image for the store. Visits and interviews designers and textile and ready-to-wear manufacturers. Prepares seasonal forecasts of color, styles, and fashion concepts for store buyers. Sometimes presents fashion shows in the store and at special community events.	Usually a college education required. Specialized training in modeling, styling, and merchandising. Ability to project fashion dramatically, to communicate effectively, to write fashion commentary, and to work well with people.

CAREER OPPORTUNITIES IN FASHION DESIGN

Position	Job Description	Job Requirements
Designers in general	Creatively translates ideas into salable merchandise.	Two to four years of special training in a technical school or college. Knowledge of art and literature. Skills in sketching, designing, and sewing. Marked creative talent. Awareness of psychology of dress and how social changes affect dress.
Ready-to-wear designer	Works with garment manufacturers who produce fashion merchandise in quantity within a given price range.	Post—high school training. College degree usually required. Ability to make patterns, sketch, sew, and drape. Knowledge of fabrics, trim, and total clothing manufacturing process. Color sense.
Custom designer	Works with individual customers in designing garments to order.	Post—high school training. Internship or college degree preferred. Ability to sketch, drape, make patterns, and sew. High proficiency in design techniques. Ability to adapt designs to the customer's physical, emotional, and aesthetic requirements.
Designer of theatrical costumes	Designs costumes for the theater, television, opera, and ballet.	Post—high school training or apprenticeship necessary. Wide range of skills. Ability to sketch, make patterns, drape, and sew. Broad knowledge of costuming, lighting, photography, television, and color. Membership in United Service Artists of America.
Designer of accessories	Varies according to the accessory. May design jewelry, belts, gloves, shoes, handbags, or other such items.	Apprenticeship usually necessary. Ability to make patterns, sketch, sew, and drape. Skills highly specialized in the area of acessory designs.
Textile designer	Styles woven or knitted fabrics.	Post—high school training necessary. Varies widely, depending on specific career chosen. Includes knowledge of fibers, yarns, constructions, colors, finishes, and surface design, and applications.

CAREER OPPORTUNITIES IN FASHION WRITING

Position	Job Description	Job Requirements
General fashion reporter	Interviews textile and garment industry leaders, attends meetings, fashion shows, and fabric exhibits. Listens and records information for reports, articles, or news stories.	High school education plus training in journalism. Ability to write and spell; knowledge of grammar and punctuation; good vocabulary. Typing and shorthand are assets.
Newspaper fashion reporter	Collects facts by interviews, phone calls, or research. Writes stories on a daily or weekly basis.	Post—high school training in journalism. Ability to meet and talk with people. Ability to write with speed and clarity. Typing and shorthand assets.
Fashion editor on newspaper	Writes copy adequate for scope of newspaper. May supervise fashion reports. Communicates with key people in fashion industry.	College degree preferred. Professional training and experience in retailing and merchandising helpful. Strong fashion sense. Ability to work with people; knowledge of the audience to be reached. Thorough knowledge of market, manufacturers, and retailers.
Magazine fashion writer	Prepares copy that relates to photographs selected by fashion editor. Preselects themes for given issues and presents them for consideration of fashion editor.	Post—high school training in journalism. Ability to write quickly, clearly, and interestingly.
Trade writer	Responsible for a specific area of fashion, working as a reporter. Brings news of trends to the manufacturer, supplier, distributor, or retailer.	Post—high school training in journalism preferred. Ability to write clearly and speedily.
Public relations representative	Prepares and tells story of her employer's products or services through various media or in person. May be employed by a public relations firm, manufacturer, retail store, or trade association.	Post—high school training required. Ability to write quickly and clearly. Poise in meeting and talking with people. Ability to persuade newspapers, magazines, radio, and TV personnel to report on company's products or services.

Careers in the Textile Industry

This country's textile industry is the largest in the world, producing 17 billion square yards of fabric per year. While you may think of textiles in terms of apparel and home furnishings, 25 percent of the annual volume is used for industrial purposes, such as automobile upholstery. Textiles are also used in the space program. Such space materials as flight suits and parachutes are products of the textile industry. Today's textiles, in turn, are the product of the combined efforts of industry, art, and science. The field of textiles provides a rapidly expanding job market.

CAREER OPPORTUNITIES IN THE TEXTILE INDUSTRY

Industry	Science	Art
Marketing	Research and Development	Fabric Styling and Design
Market research	Research in chemistry, physics,	Art direction
Merchandising	and biology	Color dynamics
Sales		Color selection
Sales management		Designing fabrics
Technical sales		Drawing and drafting
Writing		Fashion selection
		Sketching
		Styling fabric lines
Manufacturing	Engineering	Fashion Coordination
Inventory	Chemical, electrical, industrial,	Contacts with clothing designers,
Machine operation	and mechanical engineering	apparel manufacturers, accessory
Maintenance and repair	Fiber and fabric testing	manufacturers, and retailers
Mill management	Optimum scheduling	Fashion study and style
Production scheduling	Quality control	forecasting
Transportation	Time study	Planning and counseling
Warehousing		
Administration	Data Processing	Advertising
Accounting	Analysis	Art and layout
Auditing	Estimating	Campaign planning
Community relations	Forecasting	Liaison
Credit	Inventory control	Media selection
Economics	Programming	Product publicity
Electronic data processing	Production control	
Industrial relations	Sales and administrative	
Insurance	recording	
Management		
Personnel		
Public relations		
Purchasing		
Research and development		

Is there a career for you in the textile industry? Opportunities are available for all types of workers. There are jobs for those marketing textiles. Other jobs are available for those who enjoy developing through research new textiles, textile finishes, and colors. There are jobs, too, for those who are interested in the creative coordination of colors and fabrics in new fashions. Whether your interests lie in the areas of industry, science, or art, there are jobs available in the textile industry. General fields in which jobs are almost certain to be found are listed in the chart shown above.

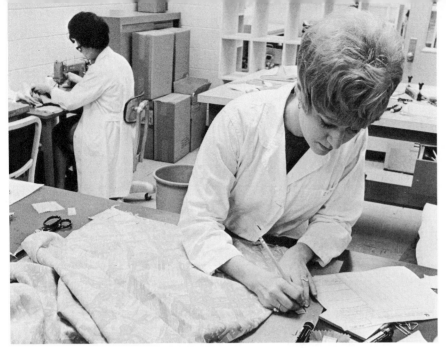

In the field of textile research there is a place for those who can carefully check and record findings as to the effectiveness of specific fabrics fashioned in today's styles.

There are a wide variety of jobs available in the textile manufacturing industry for those who can concentrate and act quickly when problems arise.

CAREER OPPORTUNITIES IN TEXTILE CARE SERVICES

Position	Job Description	Job Requirements
Store sales personnel, telephone operators, customer service, home counselor	Serves as contact between the business and its customers. Sells laundry or drycleaning service directly or indirectly. Serves customers, answers questions about services and prices, takes orders, and handles complaints and adjustments. Home counselors may engage in consumer educational programs.	High school diploma preferred. Courses in distributive education, business methods, commercial arithmetic, public speaking, textiles helpful. Good appearance, pleasing voice, friendliness, sales ability, tact in handling people, even temper, courtesy, and patience.
Marker or laundry-marker	Opens bundles of garments brought into the department by routemen and from stores. Inspects garments for unusual stains, rips, tears, and damaged areas and marks them for spotting and repair; removes buttons and trimming as necessary; classifies articles according to basic composition and color; and sets aside items that require special handling. Marks items and makes out sales invoices.	Limited formal education acceptable. Ability to work with arithmetic, general understanding of textiles and clothing construction necessary. Ability to concentrate, accuracy in counting and writing, good eyesight, alertness, physical strength.
Drycleaner, drycleaner's helper	Sorts garments into proper classifications. Weighs and records poundage of each load. Determines if items need to be prespotted. Drycleans garments in specialized automated equipment. Determines which items should be tumble-dried and which should be cabinet-dried. Periodically tests condition of drycleaning solvent. Operates distillation equipment and pressure filtration equipment to keep solvent pure.	Limited formal education acceptable. Ability to concentrate and make decisions. Mechanical dexterity and physical strength. Technical training. A general understanding of chemistry, physics, mathematics, and textiles is helpful.
Owner or manager of coin-operated laundry or drycleaning establishment	Supervises operations, makes change, and weighs garments to maintain permissible load size. May package cleaned garments, and may advise on difficult stains.	Post–high school business courses helpful. Ability to supervise operations, get along with people, and determine when machine repairs are needed. Some knowledge of fibers and fabric care desirable.
Wool or silk spotter	Inspects articles to determine fiber content and dyes used in the garment and the types of spots and stains. Selects removal agents accordingly. Determines which articles require wetcleaning and which articles must be given a second drycleaning treatment.	Post–high school technical training or apprenticeship necessary. A general understanding of chemistry, physics, and textiles. Basic knowledge of drycleaning and wetcleaning. Ability to solve technical problems. Ability to plan ahead and make color distinctions.

Continued on page 194

Position	Job Description	Job Requirements
Laundry collector, laundry foreman, laundry operator, washing-machine operator, washing-and-ironing supervisor, laundryman, laundress	Collects and tickets laundry either in homes or at the laundry. Checks incoming laundry against tickets. Classifies soiled articles for washing. Irons, machine-presses, and hand-presses articles. Mends damaged items. Wraps bundles and readies them for distribution.	Distributive education courses or on-the-job training preferred. Ability to work with arithmetic. Understanding of textile handling techniques.
Seamstress for laundry or drycleaner	Makes simple hand or machine repairs, such as sewing broken seams, reattaching loosened linings, rehemming skirts, replacing shoulder pads, replacing buttons and trimming. In some plants makes major alterations of garments and performs intricate reweaving and repair work.	Limited formal education acceptable. Skill in clothing construction. Fashion awareness. Ability to make decisions and to concentrate.
Silk finisher, wool finisher, lining finisher	Restores drycleaned and wetcleaned garments to their original appearance on various types of finishing equipment. Softens fabrics, removes wrinkles, and restores original garment shape and style by using presses of various types in combination with electric and hand steam irons.	Vocational training or apprenticeship necessary. An understanding of textiles, clothing construction, and fashion design. Style consciousness, ability to make decisions, ability to concentrate, good physical health, good eyesight, and manual dexterity.
Inspector	Examines all garments for standards of cleaning, spotting, finishing, alterations, and repair. When the quality of the work does not meet plant standards, returns it to the proper department for correction. Attaches special memos to customer regarding specific garments.	High school education preferred. Apprenticeship desirable. An understanding of textiles, clothing construction, and fashion design. Knowledge of drycleaning plant operation and quality standards. Initiative, accuracy, ability to make decisions, alertness, ability to concentrate, good judgment, tact, fashion consciousness, and good physical health.
Assembler	Examines and matches invoice descriptions and garment tags to ensure correct identification of garments. Assembles garments into individual customer orders.	Limited formal education acceptable. Ability to work with arithmetic. Knowledge of plant marking system and lot system. Accuracy, ability to make decisions, visual alertness.

The commercial laundry provides a wide variety of jobs for those with discerning eyes and physical dexterity.

Careers in the Field of Textile Care

Numerous jobs are available in the area of textile care. Most of these jobs are found in commercial laundries and drycleaning establishments, including both the professional and the coin-operated types. They are also available with laundry appliance manufacturers, iron manufacturers, textile manufacturers, and laundry detergent manufacturers. Frequently such jobs can be found in areas near your home. If you are interested in a career in this field, the following steps may help you determine the seriousness of your interest:

1. Visit local laundry and drycleaning plants. Make an appointment to talk with a progressive plant owner or plant manager about the various job opportunities available.

2. Determine whether a vocational school in your community offers training in the field of textile care.

3. Read the trade journals and other literature published about the industry.

Regardless of the exact job you choose in the field of textile care, it will be necessary for you to go through a training period to master the procedures, skills, or techniques required to do the job well. In general, the time required for training is determined by the difficulty of the job. Job opportunities, descriptions, and requirements are listed in the chart on pages 193-194.

A wide variety of jobs including those as a seamstress and as an inspector are available in the drycleaning industry to the young person who is adept in clothing-care skills.

Careers for
the Graduate Home Economist

A broad range of careers related to the textile and clothing industries is available to college graduates who study home economics. More than 400 colleges and universities in the United States offer degrees in home economics. A typical four-year course of study includes a broad basic education with courses in social sciences, physical sciences, and the humanities, as well as specialized courses in the major field of home economics. The specialized courses cover the areas of art, family economics, home management, family relations, child development, food and nutrition, housing, furnishings and equipment, and textiles and clothing. With a degree in home economics you are prepared to look for a job in fashion, business, teaching, extension service, research, communications, or health or welfare. Those who are interested in jobs which offer service to others might well consider this area.

Courtesy Celanese Fibers Marketing Co.

The fields of consumer research and consumer education in the textile industry are usually filled by graduate home economists.

TEXTILE- AND CLOTHING-RELATED CAREERS FOR THE GRADUATE HOME ECONOMIST

Advertising account executive for textile or clothing business
Clothing consultant
College, trade, vocational, or general secondary high school home economics teacher
Color coordinator
Consumer education specialist
Costume designer
Department-store clothing or fabric buyer
Dress pattern designer
Exhibit designer
Extension clothing specialist
Fashion coordinator
Fashion designer
Fashion editor
Fashion illustrator
Home equipment specialist
Laundry products specialist
Museum curator of clothing or textile artifacts
Retail-store training specialist
Sewing center director
Teacher of clothing and textiles
Textile or clothing manufacturer's representative
Textile designer
Textile lab technician
Textile product developer
Textile product publicity director
Textile research specialist

1. Visit a textile mill, pattern company, laundry equipment manufacturer, iron manufacturer, retail store, drycleaning establishment, detergent manufacturer, or other textile- or clothing-related industry which operates in your vicinity.

2. Give oral reports on women who have made an outstanding success in the careers of store management and manufacturing.

3. Discuss whether it is more difficult for women than men to climb the ladder of success. Decide what the concepts are that women must accept if they are to succeed on the job.

4. Investigate what career opportunities are available for those persons interested in curbing the growing problem of shoplifting.

5. Invite outstanding business and professional people to your classroom to discuss *Holding a Position.*

6. Ask members of professional associations, such as the American Personnel and Guidance Association, American Vocational Association, National Education Association, and the American Home Economics Association, to discuss how their organizations can give vocational guidance.

7. Discuss the issue *Why Summer Employment Is Desirable.* Investigate the opportunities available for summer employment in your community.

8. Invite a person from the Office of Social Security to discuss *How the Social Security Act Affects You.*

9. Discuss the goals and values one should consider in selecting a job or career.

10. Ask a personnel or training director of one of your leading stores to discuss the relation of good grooming and appearance to your first interview.

11. Invite the manager of a private or public employment agency located in your community to speak to the class on *Using an Employment Agency Effectively.*

12. Read and report to the class the provisions of the Fair Labor Standards Act, the Equal Pay Act, and the Equal Employment Opportunity Act.

13. Invite your guidance counselor to meet with your class to discuss personality traits important for vocational achievement.

14. Let each class member investigate a specific vocation and give an oral report to the class on the educational preparation which it requires.

15. Let each member of your class prepare his own résumé. Working in groups, improve each of the résumés in your group. Have the final versions typed into usable form so that class members can actually use them in their job interviews.

HELPING OTHERS TO LEARN

1. Obtain and show the film *Careers in Retailing and Marketing,* Fairchild Visuals, 7 East 12th Street, New York, New York 10008.

2. Plan a Career Day. Invite leaders of business and industry to come to the school and explain the job opportunities available in the community.

3. Prepare a bulletin-board display entitled *Climb the Stairway to Good Grooming.*

4. Prepare a bulletin-board display to acquaint students in the high school with meaningful careers related to home economics.

INDEPENDENT LEARNING EXPERIENCES

1. Explore the possibility of summer employment through Federal aid.

2. Make a list of on-the-job benefits you feel are important. Use this as a check list when you plan your career.

3. Prepare a résumé you can use when you apply for a position or job.

4. Find out what on-the-job training programs, vocational scholarship programs, and work-study programs are available in your community.

5. Study the help-wanted ads in your daily and Sunday papers. What jobs are available? Consider for which of these you would qualify.

6. Investigate whether there is a job training center in your community. Find out what kinds of programs are available.

Part 2

Preparing for Your
Sewing Project

The Process of Creative Sewing

Technology's *fabric explosion* produces new fabrics each season. New sewing techniques and styles are developed and the new fabrics are incorporated into the world of fashion. Then, quite suddenly, huge supplies of very similar clothing appear on the market. Women, particularly young women who need many types of clothing, are faced with the problem of look-alike monotony unless they can adapt ready-made clothes for individuality or can creatively make their own.

What factors make sewing a creative process?

How does the decision-making process lend itself to creative sewing?

How may your ability to sew increase the individuality of your wardrobe?

What factors should be considered when deciding whether to make or to buy a specific garment?

What are the principles of the Unit Method of Construction?

Major Components of Creative Sewing

Creative sewing can help you to have an individualized wardrobe. Like painting or sculpting, it also provides a means of expressing your talent and personality. It can help you increase the size of your wardrobe, provide attractive gifts, modify and upgrade ready-to-wear clothing, judge the quality of merchandise, and recycle out-of-date outfits. In some instances it may even lead to a part-time or full-time sewing career.

There are three major components of creative sewing. Decision making is the *planning* component that provides the framework for your action. The Unit Method of Construction is the *procedure* component that helps you reach your goal efficiently. The third important element is your own *imagination.* It places *you* in the center of the sewing process and puts a stamp of individuality on your projects. These three components—decision-making, the Unit Method, and imagination—are intertwined like fibers in a woven fabric. Each affects the other, and together they turn an idea into a garment.

Decision Making in Creative Sewing

The decisions made in planning a sewing project determine the subsequent steps. They involve thinking the project through, determining what needs to be done, and deciding how to do it. When handled systematically through the decision-making process, they re-

Creative clothing construction is a means by which you can express both your personality and your talent.

sult in a specific plan for spending your time, energy, and money.

As discussed in Chapter 4, the steps in the decision-making process include identifying the goal, exploring alternative methods of reaching the goal, making choices, putting the chosen plan into effect, and evaluating the choices. Consider how the steps are followed in creative sewing.

Suppose you need a new outfit. You have determined that you have a certain number of dollars to spend. Your desire, then, is to obtain the necessary outfit within your allotted budget. This conclusion identifies your goal.

The first decision you will face is how to acquire the outfit—whether to buy it ready-made or to make it. To explore these alternatives you would consider first all the known facts involved in each. These might be as follows: the decision to buy a ready-made garment would give you the new outfit immediately, it would guarantee one that is wear-

TO MAKE OR TO BUY

Make new garments when:
1. *You have the ability and experience to assure success.*
2. *You find great enjoyment in sewing; it is a creative hobby for you.*
3. *Sewing equipment and a satisfactory place to sew are available.*
4. *You cannot find what you want in ready-to-wear at the price you can pay, but you can find the fabric for that price or less.*
5. *The fabric is already available, for example, as a gift.*
6. *You have a special fitting problem which makes the altering of ready-made garments impossible or impractical.*
7. *You want individuality of style or fabric.*

Buy new garments when:
1. *Time for sewing is limited.*
2. *No sewing machine is available, and the expense of buying or renting one is too great.*
3. *An exceptionally good buy in a ready-made garment is available.*
4. *The difficulties of handling the fabric or of making a garment of complicated design are beyond your sewing ability.*
5. *The cost and value of a ready-made garment and of a similar garment you would make are about the same.*

able, and it would require less of your free time. Sewing, on the other hand, is an activity you enjoy and the less expensive solution. The larger balance it would leave in your clothing budget would enable you to acquire other clothes. Your time, however, is limited.

To collect the additional facts needed for a sound decision, you further investigate both the alternatives of buying and of sewing the garment. Upon exploring the dress shops, it appears that you cannot find exactly the outfit you had in mind. The ready-mades you try on do not fit well. Major alterations would be needed. Moreover, the price of the outfits is several dollars more than you have planned to spend.

Next you explore the fabric and pattern possibilities. You find at least two fabrics and several patterns that you like. The patterns, however, are more difficult than any you have previously tried.

With these facts known, you are now able to weigh the alternatives intelligently. You ask yourself, is time or money more important to me at this point? How would the actual cost of a ready-made affect my budget? Would a difficult pattern mean a sewing project that might be too time consuming or that might yield unsatisfactory results?

Seldom is an alternative in the decision-making process a perfect one. Each has some advantages and some disadvantages. There is not always a *right* answer. Besides, the best decision for you today may not be the best one tomorrow.

Suppose you choose the alternative of buying the outfit. Other decisions will then be required of you in the chain-reaction effect of decision making. For example, where can you get the additional money to pay for the ready-made outfit? If there is no source of additional money, what planned purchase can you do without? Will you have to pay extra for the alterations? If so, how much? Who will make the alterations?

On the other hand, suppose you chose the alternative of making the outfit. As a result of this major decision, a series of smaller

The ability to make sound decisions permits you to choose the best of possible combinations from a wide range of patterns, fabrics, and notions.

decisions must be made. The first of these is the choice of a fabric. Will it be the drycleanable fabric which costs $4 per yard, or will it be your second choice, the fabric which costs $3 per yard and has easy-care features? The two patterns you like best are a pattern priced at $2.50 and a standard design costing 75 cents. Which is the better choice for this situation?

Interfacing and trimmings will be needed, involving more decisions. One interfacing is inexpensive and crease resistant but drycleanable only. Another costs more per yard, is wider, somewhat stiffer, and crease resistant, but is both washable and drycleanable. The

trim you like best costs $1.75 per yard and is drycleanable only. Another trimming lacks individuality, but it is washable and costs 98 cents per yard.

You will need to weigh all of these alternatives as you consider your wants and your budget. Consider also the cost of maintenance of the outfit in terms of your time, energy, and money. You are a unique individual and will make all your sewing decisions according to your values, based on your specific needs and wants. Seldom will two people make the same series of decisions. One person may prefer putting money into high-quality fabric, another may value quantity in a

A well-planned sewing corner can provide maximum sewing convenience in minimum space.

wardrobe, while still another may feel that the most important factor is ease of maintenance.

Through these steps, the decision-making process helps you to think through the implications of each decision before taking action. After you have done so, make your decisions and carry your project through to the production of the garment.

As the last step, evaluate your satisfaction with the total results. Determining the wisdom of past choices helps you learn from the experience and thus aids future decision making. For example, suppose you chose to sew the outfit using a *designer* pattern, but the sewing process took much more time than

you had planned. While you are satisfied with the product, you might conclude that a less complicated pattern should be chosen next time. The time and money spent, the satisfaction derived from the project, and the end product obtained are all to be considered in the evaluation process.

The Unit Method of Construction

The second component, the Unit Method of Construction, is the efficiency factor in the process of creative sewing. It is an organized way of making a garment, unit by unit. The

UNITS IN BASIC CONSTRUCTION PROJECTS

UNITS IN A BASIC BLOUSE

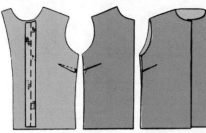

Unit 1—Front interfaced. Darts completed. **Unit 2**—Back stitched to front.

Unit 3—Collar interfaced, attached to blouse.

Unit 4—Sleeves.

Unit 5—Cuffs interfaced, stitched to sleeves. Sleeves stitched to blouse. Hem and finishing details added.

UNITS IN A BASIC SKIRT

Unit 1—Front: darts completed.

Unit 2—Back: zipper attached, stitched to front.

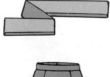

Unit 3—Waistband, hem, and finishing details added.

UNITS IN A BASIC DRESS

Unit 1—Front: darts completed. **Unit 2**—Back: zipper attached, shoulder seams stitched.

Unit 3—Neck facings made and stitched to dress. Side seams stitched.

Unit 4—Armhole facings made and stitched to dress. Hem and finishing details added.

Unit Method, which is the basis of the sewing principles provided in this book, is not unlike the assembly-line procedure employed in the mass production of cars, refrigerators, stereos, or even ready-made clothes. A unit is one part of a garment, but it may consist of one or more pieces. Small units are completed first. These units are then assembled to make larger units. Finally, efficiently, the larger units are joined into the completed product.

The Unit Method of Construction has many advantages over other methods of sewing. Work is simplified so that the time and effort required are minimized. The confusion of not knowing what to do or how to do it is lessened. Because the learning is gradual, it can be easily understood and retained. In learning to sew by this method, the home seamstress identifies key sewing principles so that she can adapt her sewing techniques to varying situations, including new fibers and fabrics. For example, the principle of fabric grain is equally applicable to woven fabric, stretch fabric, or the rib in solid-color knits. The principles of using the grain as a guide, machine sewing, fitting, and organizing work into units can be applied over and over again. Further, a systematic approach gives you the opportunity to visualize where each part of the garment is located, how the parts are joined, and the relationship of one part to another.

The Unit Method of Construction is based upon learning certain techniques and procedures and using them when applicable to complete each unit of a garment. A progression of learning, planning, completing the units, using the grain line as a guide, emphasis on machine stitching and pressing, minimizing basting, accurate fitting, and continuous evaluation are all integral parts of the Unit Method of Construction.

Progression of Learning

The Unit Method of Construction is based on a progression of learning from the easy to the more difficult. From a first simple project you

Courtesy J. C. Penney Company, Inc.

Evaluation of a successful project allows you to feel proud of your progress while planning for future improvements.

can move to another project which is slightly more difficult. You will use some of the same techniques that were employed on the first project along with some new ones. Because learning to sew is a gradual building process, the Unit Method is easy and satisfying. Making a series of projects, each one progressively more complicated, will enable you to accumulate experience and specific knowledge that will help you to make attractive, well-fitted garments in a minimum of time. You will also be able to apply the principles of sewing embodied in the Unit Method to the making of clothing accessories, items for your home, and various gift items for others.

TERMS IN THE UNIT METHOD OF CONSTRUCTION

Bias   A diagonal across the two grains of a fabric.

Bodice   The upper part of a dress.

Construction stitching   Stitching which holds the pieces of a garment together.

Crosswise grain   Threads that run crosswise through a fabric.

Cutting to fit   Cutting a garment to fit individual measurements.

Directional cutting   Cutting in the direction of the fabric grain.

Directional pinning   Placing pins in the direction of the fabric grain.

Directional pressing   Pressing in the direction of the fabric grain.

Directional stitching   Stitching in the direction of the fabric grain.

Fabric grain   The lengthwise and crosswise threads, or yarns, of a fabric.

Fitting with the grain   Fitting a garment so that the grain lines of the fabric fall correctly on the figure.

Grain perfect   With the lengthwise and crosswise threads at right angles to each other throughout the fabric.

Identical grain   The grain of two pieces of fabric in which the lengthwise and crosswise threads are in exactly the same position.

Lengthwise grain   Threads that run lengthwise through a fabric.

Machine basting   A line of long machine stitches to hold pieces of a garment together temporarily.

Off grain   Not with the grain of a fabric.

On grain   With the grain of a fabric, parallel to the lengthwise or crosswise threads.

Pin basting   Pinning pieces of a garment together temporarily for fitting, stitching, etc.

Staystitching   A directional line of stitching through a single thickness of fabric to hold the grain line.

Staystitch-plus   A line of staystitching in which the threads are crowded together to provide ease.

Straight-grain-of-fabric marking   A straight line on a pattern piece which must be laid exactly on the grain of a fabric.

Unit   One part of a garment; it may consist of one or more pieces.

Unit Method of Construction   A method of making a garment unit by unit.

STEPS IN THE UNIT METHOD OF CONSTRUCTION

1. Complete each unit as far as possible before starting another unit.
2. Join the units when two have been completed.
3. Complete another unit and joint it to the others, continuing the procedure until all the units are joined.
4. Finish all further construction details.
5. Give the garment a final pressing.

Time gained through the efficiency of the Unit Method of Construction will enable you to make a larger proportion of your wardrobe than will more time-consuming construction techniques.

Whenever possible, garment construction is begun with the unit of fewest details. This enables you to gain self-assurance with a new project during the beginning stages of your work with a pattern and fabric. Later, when you feel more at ease, you can move to the units requiring more construction detail.

Throughout the sewing process, learning is made easier and more understandable if you make choices that advance in similar progressions:

From easy-to-handle to difficult fabrics

From easy-to-make to complicated patterns

From easy-to-fit garments to advanced fitting problems

From simple techniques to tailoring procedures

Planning

A well-thought-out plan saves time, lessens mistakes, and gives the best results. Such a sewing plan will include the selections of pattern, fabric, tools, and supplies needed to make the garment; a careful study of the necessary directions that are given in this book and on your pattern guide sheet; and an outline of the procedure you expect to follow. The step-by-step procedure suggested in the illustrations on page 206 and on your pattern guide sheet can clarify steps of procedure.

Completing the Units

In the Unit Method, when the outfit is cut out, each individual piece is considered a unit. For example, the units of a blouse might be the bodice front, the bodice back, the pocket, the

A garment will hang correctly if the fabric from which it is cut is straight, if the pattern is accurately pinned to the fabric, and if each piece is cut and sewn directionally.

collar, the neck facing, and the sleeves. Before the front and back are joined, the darts are formed in both the back and the front, and the pocket is completed and attached to the front. The front and back units are then joined to form a bodice unit. Similarly, the collar, neck facing, and sleeves are completed as far as possible before they are joined to the bodice unit. Finally all parts are assembled into a single unit.

The same general procedure is followed in the making of any type of garment by the Unit Method. The illustrations of the units in a basic blouse, a skirt, and a dress show typical sequences of steps in construction by the Unit Method (see page 206).

A modified unit plan can be used to organize sewing into a logical step-by-step sequence for school sewing projects. This plan helps you plan in such a way that you are doing similar jobs together, thereby reducing the number of trips to the sewing machine. For example, when the sewing machine is out and threaded, this plan allows for machine-stitching on as many units as possible. Hand-sewing jobs, like fastening down facings and hemming, are saved until last, so that a minimum of sewing-machine time is needed for each garment. Such a method encourages good time management and allows for increased progress in a given period of time.

Using the Grain as a Guide

Observance of grain is one of the most important factors in making clothes that have a professional appearance. In the Unit Method of Construction the grain of the fabric is important in every process involved in the making of a garment. In the preparatory steps preceding the actual sewing, the observance of grain is as significant as during construction, because early processes must be performed accurately if construction is to be effective. Specifically, the grain of fabric is the center of emphasis in the following procedures:

1. In preparing the fabric for use. Preparation includes restoring the grain to its correct position so that the fabric is grain perfect.

2. In laying the pattern. A garment can be grain perfect and can hang and fit correctly only if it has been cut with a pattern laid on the correct fabric grain.

3. In pinning. Observance of the grain in pinning a pattern to a fabric or in pinning two fabrics together makes the process easier and more accurate. Directional pinning of the units helps to hold the grain in position for stitching.

4. In cutting. If directional, the cutting is easier and more precise at all stages of construction, including the cutting out of a garment, the trimming of seam allowances, and the pinking of edges.

5. In staystitching. This directional stitching is inserted to maintain the grain of the fabric and the original line of the pattern throughout the entire construction process.

6. In construction stitching. The original fabric grain is preserved in both temporary stitching, such as basting, and permanent stitching, such as seam stitching, if the stitching is inserted directionally.

7. In fitting. The fabric grain is the guide to an accurately fitted garment. It must fall correctly on the figure of the wearer, if the garment is to fit correctly.

8. In pressing. Directional pressing helps maintain the grain perfection of the fabric throughout the making of a garment.

For a general discussion of fabric grain, see pages 260-265.

Emphasis on Machine Sewing

Machine sewing is emphasized and hand sewing is minimized in this streamlined, modern approach to sewing. Considerable time is saved by using the sewing machine whenever possible. Most basting is done by machine. Sewing on fasteners, hemming, the occasional use of hand basting, and possibly the whip or pick stitch for a custom-tailored look are usually all the handwork required.

Emphasis on Pressing

Careful and correct pressing is as important as accurate stitching. Pressing is continual throughout the construction of a garment. Each construction detail of a unit is pressed. The unit as a whole is pressed before it is joined to another unit. A unit may be held, however, until the unit to which it is to be joined is also ready for pressing. Then the two units may be pressed during a single trip to the pressing board. When all the units have been assembled, the finished garment is given a final pressing.

Minimum Basting

Very little basting is required in the Unit Method for two reasons. First, the garment is cut to fit the figure for which it is made. Second, staystitching maintains the original pattern line and prevents stretching of the fabric. If basting is necessary, pin or machine basting is generally preferred to hand basting.

Fitting

Fitting with perfection includes cutting to fit and fitting the garment during construction. If the garment is cut to fit accurately, there will be little need for fitting adjustments during construction. In checking the garment fit, the correct position of the grain lines on the figure is the key to a perfect fit (see pages 340-341).

Continuous Evaluation

Evaluation is an essential part of learning. To be of most benefit, it must be a continuous process—a constant judging of what is being done. In the Unit Method it is also a progressive process, as judgment is developed. This ability will help you make wise decisions on subsequent projects.

How can your imagination aid you in upgrading the quality of your wardrobe?

How can original-looking garments be made from standard patterns?

How can you express your creativity in selecting fabric for a garment?

How can the various features and stitches of a modern sewing machine be used to individualize clothing?

How can inexpensive sale clothing be creatively upgraded after purchase?

How can imagination be used to make worn clothing wearable?

Imagination in the Sewing Process

Imagination is the third important component of the creative sewing process. It enables you to see the possibilities of fabric, patterns, and garments old and new, to visualize unique adaptations or combinations that increase clothing attractiveness or serviceability. It is

Courtesy 1001 Decorating Ideas

A person who learns to express creativity in simple clothing projects usually wants to move rapidly to more complex construction problems.

the factor that makes creative sewing truly creative.

Imaginative thinking can enhance sewing projects in small ways or large. Patterns or fabrics can be combined in unique ways. Decorative monograms, appliqués, or tucks can be added to garments. Chosen appropriately, creative ideas can be used to upgrade ready-to-wear garments, to recycle used clothing, and to make gifts from leftover fabric.

In Adapting Patterns

Suppose that in selecting a pattern, you find one that is exactly what you want except in one detail: Whereas you want a collarless model, it includes a collar for every view.

What can you do? Simply omit the collar and face the neckline. If you should want a detachable collar, this adaptation is made by facing the garment and binding the neck edge of the collar. On the other hand, perhaps you want to add a collar not provided for in the pattern of your choice. This can be done by using the collar from another pattern which has a neckline of similar size and shape. Perhaps the pattern is just what you want except that you feel the neckline is too high, too low, too wide, or too narrow. In most instances a small adjustment can be made. Patterns with low or wide necklines can be built up with tissue or wrapping paper before the garment is cut out. Necklines that are too high or narrow can be trimmed out if caution is used to retain the basic design of the neckline.

Suppose you find the perfect pattern, except that long, cuffed sleeves are provided rather than the short sleeves you prefer. Several alternatives are possible. The pattern for the long sleeve can be tried on and cut off, or marked to be folded back at an appropriate length as the garment is cut out, allowing sufficient length for the hem. However, it may be easier to choose a short sleeve from another pattern. Sleeve patterns are interchangeable if the sleeve caps are of similar shape and size. If you prefer a sleeveless version of a pattern which provides sleeves for all views, finish the raw edges of the armholes with a binding or a bias or fitted facing. A small adjustment is often needed in the bodice when converting from a pattern with sleeves to a sleeveless version. The lower part of the armhole usually needs to be raised about ½ inch so that the bodice fits higher under the arm. This adjustment should be made before the garment pieces are cut, as should all adjustments affecting garment fit (see Chaper 10).

Even more daring creative adjustments can be made by interchanging pieces of two or more patterns. This can result in very interesting garments. Since it is often a difficult procedure which requires some skill and experience in sewing, it should not be attempted by a beginner. It is possible to mix patterns from more than one envelope as long as the areas to be joined fit each other. For example, if the bodice of one pattern is to be joined to the skirt of another, be sure that the waistline seams are of similar contour and size.

In Selecting Fabrics

There is almost unlimited scope for creative imagination as you select a fabric from the variety available today. The choice is uniquely yours. You may decide to apply a creative touch by combining two different fabrics for one outfit. For example, plaids or stripes might be combined with a solid color, textures with plain fabrics, vinyls with washable tweeds, leathers or suedes with knits, and man-made furs with wools or blends. It is essential that your innovative choices require a single cleaning method.

You can increase your creativity by selecting fabric from unusual sources. For example, an Indian bedspread purchased on sale might be used to make a poncho or a long vest with a fringe. Terry toweling in Jacquard designs can be employed effectively for shower robes or beach cover-ups. The striped ticking that often covers mattresses and pillows can also be used to make sturdy, attractive beach bags. Upholstery fabrics are possibilities for purses or vests.

Creativity is often expressed through illusions provided by attractive fabric combinations. For example, a sheer fabric might be used over a print or lace over taffeta of a contrasting color. The results of your creative efforts are bounded only by the limits of your imagination and sewing ability.

In Using the Sewing Machine

A sewing machine is a versatile tool. It not only converts yard goods into garments but also offers wide-ranging possibilities for artistic creativity. By imaginative planning, you can take full advantage of your machine to turn out attractive garments of varied and unique design.

Courtesy Simplicity Pattern Co., Inc.

The variety of stitches provided by many modern sewing machines can be used for creating individualized garments.

A sewing machine can be used to bind edges with a colorful bias plaid, checked, or polka-dot binding. It can be utilized to shape flat fabric in a variety of ways such as inserting tucks, attaching lace inserts, and making gathers and pleats. It can be employed to stitch designs of innumerable shapes and sizes, including decorative trim, monograms, and appliquéd figures. Machine embroidery includes zigzagged, triangular, and rectangular designs stitched in thread of blending or contrasting color. A machine can be used to make seams and seam finishes which are creatively decorative as well as durable. In adapting patterns or creating your own designs, keep in mind the versatility of your machine.

213

Hems   Correct an uneven hemline as when making a hem on a new garment. Repair broken hemming stitches by pulling out enough stitches to permit threading a needle and securing both ends of thread. Then replace missing stitches.

Special problems   Reinforce narrow skirts at hemline to prevent seams from pulling out as you walk. Open hem at seam areas. Stitch about 4 inches of matching tape on inside of turned portion of hem across the seam. Tape should be positioned at right angles to seam line, and its lower edge should be aligned along fold of hemline. Resew hem, and press.

Reinforce pleat ends by (1) machine-stitching lines in form of a triangle on right side, or (2) by hand-sewing a square of tape or other firm fabric to wrong side of skirt.

Pockets   Reinforce corners of patch pockets to prevent their pulling out or tearing. Place a narrow tape on underside of garment in line with upper edge of pocket, and restitch corners, catching tape in stitching.

Openings   Overcast or hem down loose or frayed edges of plackets which might get caught in teeth of zipper. Tack lower ends of zipper tape to waistband if there is strain.

Seams   Restitch poorly made seams. Stitch over original stitching. Make narrow seams wider by stitching a new seam inside original seam line. Remove original stitching, and press seam.

Reinforce weak underarm seams on raglan or cut-on sleeves by over-stitching the seam or by stitching a piece of tape or a ribbon seam binding to the seam line.

Finish seam allowances on fabrics that fray by overcasting by hand or by using a zigzag machine stitch. A second row of regular stitching near the cut edge may be used as a substitute.

Fasteners   Check buttons, snaps, and hooks and eyes. On thin or loosely woven fabrics, add a piece of tape on the underside of the garment beneath the fastener to act as a reinforcement. On coats, use a small flat button on the underside of garment.

Buttonholes may need extra stitches at each end if they seem weak or likely to rip out.

*In Upgrading the Quality
of Ready-to-Wear*

Your creative imagination can be used to upgrade an inexpensive ready-made outfit into one that has an expensive, one-of-a-kind look. Minor additions and subtractions such as replacement of buttons, removal of poor-quality trim, removal or replacement of belts, or hand-stitching the last step of the zipper application are just some of the possible ways to upgrade the appearance of ready-made garments.

For example, you might find a well-styled suit but feel that its unattractive plastic buttons and belt ruin its appearance. Replace them with items more in keeping with the

ALTERING READY-MADE GARMENTS

Altering skirt length   *Rip out hem, remove tape, and press lower part of skirt flat. Mark desired hem length, and rehem as for a new skirt. Garments made from permanent-press fabrics cannot be lengthened or widened.*

Altering skirt band   *Remove band, fit and alter both skirt and band, and reattach band to skirt as when making a new skirt.*

Altering bodice length   *Lengthening is feasible only if there is a sufficient allowance at lower edge. To shorten bodice, rip out zipper and waistline seam. Try on bodice, and mark new location of waistline by tying a string around natural waistline and marking encircled area. Adjust bodice width to size of waistline tape. Attach seam tape and restitch waistline seam. Reset zipper.*

Altering waistline   *Rip bodice and skirt apart, removing zipper. Make major increase or decrease in darts or pleats, rather than at side seam line, to retain fabric grain. Restitch waistline seam and reset zipper.*

Altering hip size   *Rip skirt from bodice or band, and fit and alter as if you were making a new skirt. Keep in mind all standards of a well-fitted skirt. Make identical alterations on each side unless figure is irregular. Corrections can sometimes be made in a seam that does not necessitate removal of zipper.*

Altering darts   *Location, slant, and size of darts may be altered at any place in a garment. A dart may be enlarged without ripping original dart stitching. Stitching must be ripped from a dart being shortened, made narrower, or relocated. Rip also any seam which involves the dart. Reshape the dart as desired. Press to shape. Restitch seams as necessary.*

Resetting zippers   *Follow identical stitching lines of original application. If alterations change stitching lines, press seam flat and apply zipper as when making a new garment.*

quality of the garment. Plain garments, sturdily constructed but rather dull in appearance, can be brightened with a colorful, contrasting belt or the addition of trim or accessories.

Inexpensive, mass-produced garments may have been stitched with large stitches or may have loose buttons, dangling threads, or raveling seams. A few minutes skillfully spent at the sewing machine to reinforce such weak spots or repair the seams can make good buys from poor ones. Give special attention to the edges of pockets, underarm seams, ends of pleats, hems, buttonholes, and fasten-

ers. Reinforcing a garment before it is worn tends to upgrade its quality most effectively.

In Altering Ready-to-Wear

Your inventiveness can be used in making minor alterations in ready-to-wear garments. It can also aid in evaluating whether changes are needed, feasible, or worthwhile. Thus sewing ability is a considerable asset in buying ready-to-wear garments. You can use this ability to quickly identify alterations that could be easily accomplished, such as lengthening or shortening a garment, taking in seams

A worn sheet might be recycled to become a tie-dyed skirt which could be used as a colorful party garment.

Consider minor adjustments, made with touches of creativity, that take very little time and money. Good decisions can help put dead items in your wardrobe back into circulation. The possibilities in recycling clothing are limited only by your imagination and creative effort. Any of the following are workable ideas. You may think of others.

1. Change a tight pullover sweater into an attractive cardigan by cutting down the center front. Add braid or binding to the edges. Perhaps the binding can be made from leftover fabric to match one of your skirts.

2. Upgrade the mix-and-match combinations in your wardrobe. For instance, do you have a good plaid skirt left from an out-of-date suit? If so, combine it with a solid-color sweater in your wardrobe, or purchase fabric in a coordinated color and make a jacket or vest trimmed with plaid binding cut from the outdated jacket.

3. Cover up the tiny moth holes or threadbare areas of a sweater with bold patches of leather or suede or with colorful appliqué or embroidery.

4. Conceal a too-low neckline by adding a wide ruffle, a dickey, or a piece of contrasting fabric.

5. Recycle a suit jacket with shabby buttonholes and outdated collar by cutting it into a smart collarless design. Apply braid edging.

6. Change a dress which has tight, uncomfortable sleeves into a sleeveless dress by removing the sleeves and finishing the armhole edges with bias or shaped facings cut from the sleeves.

In Using Remnants

Creative imagination can be expressed by making small useful items or colorful gifts. Look at the larger scraps of fabric left from previous sewing projects. They might include scraps too big to discard but too small to make into a blouse or vest. Could they be used to make a handy beach bag? Colorful throw pillows? A fashion belt? A cuddly

at the waistline, or leveling an uneven hem. It can also help you foresee the necessity of major alterations that would involve shaping, such as changes in sleeves, the shoulder area, or necklines. Unless ready-made garments requiring major alterations are exceptionally good buys, they are best avoided.

In Recycling Outdated or Seldom-worn Clothing

Your resourcefulness can be used to recycle out-of-fashion or slightly worn clothing. Examine the seldom-worn clothes hanging in your closet. Consider which are valuable and could be adapted with the minimum effort.

Scraps and remnants can often be used to inexpensively make stuffed toys or children's garments.

stuffed animal? A record tote? A patchwork skirt? Colorful placemats?

Even long, narrow strips of leftover fabric can be made into useful scarves by hemming or facing in a contrasting color. When trimmed with fringe, or decorated with hand embroidery or decorative machine stitching, such strips can be used as belts or headbands.

Small squares of assorted leftover scraps can be made into a colorful patchwork apron or skirt. Work out the design on paper first, cut all scraps to an identical size and shape, and sew them together to form a fabric of the required dimensions.

Stuffed toys can be made from scraps. All you need are small pieces of scrap fabric, a pattern, and some old nylon stockings or lingerie. Nylon stockings or lingerie scraps are especially good stuffing material, because they are washable. If button noses and eyes are used, attach them sturdily before stuffing.

A record tote or beach bag can be made from leftover sportswear fabric such as denim, duck, or sailcloth. Edge the bag with braid or binding. Decorate it with an appliqué design or with colorful press-on tape cut in a variety of shapes to express your individuality. In such ways imagination can expand your horizon in the world of creative sewing.

1. To sew creatively and efficiently, plan projects according to the decision-making process, follow the Unit Method of Construction, and employ imagination throughout.

2. The decision-making process includes identifying the goal, exploring alternative methods of reaching the goal, making choices, putting the chosen plan into effect, and evaluating the choices.

3. The Unit Method of Construction is an efficient method for systematizing the sewing process for professional-appearing results.

4. In the Unit Method small parts are completed first and then assembled to make larger units.

5. The Unit Method is based on a gradual progression of learning from the simple to the more complex decisions, procedures, and techniques.

6. Creativity can be expressed by devising imaginative adaptations or combinations of patterns, fabrics, decorations, and garments.

Equipment for Sewing

Like any skilled craftsman, the person who sews creatively needs the right tools to do an effective job. Knowing the kinds of sewing tools available and the function of each makes it easier to choose, use, and take care of the equipment you need. Acquiring tools is a long-term investment. Sewing gives you the opportunity to be creative in everything you do—from the selection of sewing equipment to the finished product.

How does the decision-making process help you in selecting sewing equipment?

What sewing equipment do you need?

In what ways does the quality of tools affect the quality of sewing?

What considerations relate to the selection of a sewing machine? Should you buy, rent, or borrow one?

What sewing-machine attachments do you need?

Decisions About Sewing Equipment

The decision-making process can be applied to the selection of sewing equipment. Each person will feel differently about sewing and will base her decisions on her own value system. The choice that is best for you may be totally unsuited to someone else. Furthermore, your best choice now may not be the best when you enter the world of work and later establish a home and family of your own.

The selection of sewing equipment is an individual matter. But the first step for anyone beginning to collect the needed implements is to become familiar with the wide variety of sewing tools available. As you look at each one in turn, use the decision-making process to help you choose the right ones for your purposes.

The Sewing Machine

The sewing machine is the most expensive piece of sewing equipment. There are many kinds of machines and many ways of acquiring one. If you are thinking of obtaining one for home use, it is worthwhile to consider the alternatives open to you.

Acquiring a Sewing Machine

Depending upon the amount of sewing to be done, you may rent or buy a sewing machine. Both alternatives need to be weighed against the time and money available and the amount and kind of sewing to be done. For example, renting a machine for a few days to sew, alter, or repair garments may be your best solution. However, if you enjoy sewing and would use

When choosing a sewing machine, consider the features of the various machines. Determine whether you need a console type or portable sewing equipment, and relate the costs of the suitable models to your financial resources.

the sewing machine for creative projects of many kinds over a long period of time, you may wish to buy a machine of your own.

If purchasing a machine, consider some of the basic consumer decisions which need to be made. The first one is the selection of a reputable dealer who is selling the kind of machine you prefer. Such a dealer will stand behind the performance of the product he sells. Next there is the decision between a new and a used machine. A sleek, new model may be pleasing to the eye but relatively expensive.

A used machine in good condition may show its age but still offer many years of service for a modest price.

An additional step in your decision-making process is the choice between a portable and a console sewing machine. If you want your machine to serve also as a piece of furniture, perhaps the console is your best choice. On the other hand, if floor space is limited and if you would prefer a machine that could be readily carried from room to room, you might decide upon a portable.

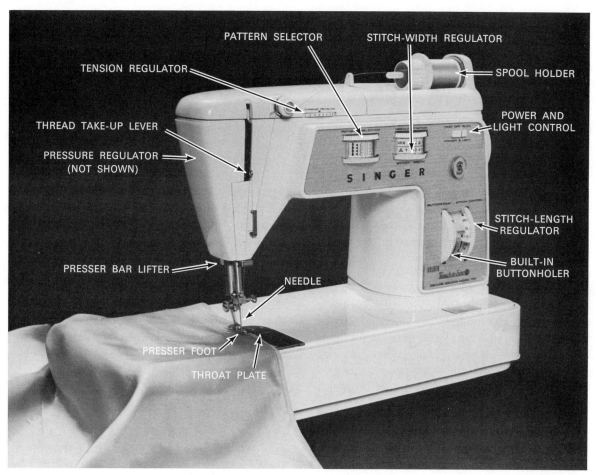

PATTERN SELECTOR STITCH-WIDTH REGULATOR

TENSION REGULATOR SPOOL HOLDER

THREAD TAKE-UP LEVER POWER AND LIGHT CONTROL

PRESSURE REGULATOR (NOT SHOWN)

STITCH-LENGTH REGULATOR

PRESSER BAR LIFTER

NEEDLE BUILT-IN BUTTONHOLER

PRESSER FOOT

THROAT PLATE

Courtesy Singer Sewing Machine Co.

Most modern sewing machines have one or more of the following features: stitch-length and stitch-width regulators, built-in buttonholer, tension and pressure regulators, and mechanisms to produce several types of stitches.

Next you will need to consider the many models from which to choose. There are variations in these models—variations in the types of stitches they make, the type of bobbin, and the system of operation, as well as in the number of attachments included or available separately. All of these factors should be considered with your individual requirements in mind. In general, the price of a model depends upon the number and kinds of special stitching and convenience features offered. For example, a straight-stitch machine, which sews only in a straight line unless attachments are added, may have a low price because the attachments will need to be purchased additionally. An automatic, or zigzag, machine may be higher priced because it performs a wide variety of operations without attachments.

Suppose you decide to rent a sewing machine instead of purchasing one. You will have a choice of type, brand, and model. In fact, each time you rent, you may have the chance to try a different model. It is often possible to try out a machine that you have considered buying. Frequently, if you decide to buy from that dealer, rental charges are applied toward payments on the machine purchased.

Basic Machine Parts

Regardless of the model of sewing machine, the person who sews is the most important part of the sewing process. With practice, you can learn to get the best possible performance from the machine, to keep it operating properly, and to avoid unnecessary service calls. For this reason you will want to read carefully the manual accompanying and explaining your particular machine. Be sure to choose the correct type and size of needle for a given project: regular needles for woven fabrics and ball-point needles for knitted fabrics. For plain weaves choose a regular type needle of size 11 to 14. Small sizes work best with lightweight weaves, whereas larger sizes are used with heavy ones. For the exact needle size and type for other fabrics, see the charts on pages 430-437.

An automatic machine will require understanding of the stitch pattern selections available as well as of the stitch-width regulator. Study the manual which comes with your machine, and practice the various stitches and widths on scrap fabric before attempting to use them on an actual project.

You will also want to become familiar with three machine parts basic to all sewing machines. These include the stitch regulator, the tension regulator, and the pressure regulator.

Stitch-length Regulator

This device controls the stitch length by regulating the distance which the *feed dog* moves the fabric for each stitch. As stitch-length regulators control the size of the stitch, they also determine the number of stitches per inch. On certain machines, the position of the stitch-length regulator may be reversed for back-stitching.

Tension Regulator

The tension regulator is the part of the machine which controls the interlocking of the needle and bobbin threads as they form a stitch. You will find that the tensions on the needle and bobbin threads must balance in order to form a perfectly locked stitch. If properly balanced, the upper tension, which controls the pull on the thread from the needle, and the lower tension, which controls the pull on the bobbin thread, lock the stitch within the fabric.

If the machine tensions are not properly adjusted, the fabric may pucker, loops of thread may be left dangling on one or both sides of the fabric, and the stitch may pull out easily.

Tension adjustments vary with the fabric but are easily made. They are important, as they affect the durability of the stitch and the wearability of the garment. To adjust the tension on the particular machine you are using, follow the instructions in the manual.

Pressure Regulator

The pressure regulator controls the force exerted on the fabric by the presser foot. It may be a thumb screw, located at the top of the needle bar, or, in new machines, it may be built in the form of a dial and positioned on the upper left side or front of the machine head. The pressure is just right when the presser foot holds the fabric firmly yet lets it move smoothly with each stroke of the feed dog. Too much pressure hinders the movement of the fabric, which might then become stretched and disfigured by the feed dog. Too little pressure makes it difficult to control the location of the stitching.

Basic Machine Stitches

There are two basic types of sewing-machine stitches: the chain stitch and the lock stitch. Some machines produce only one type of stitch without special attachments. Other machines have a built-in feature which produces both stitches.

Chain Stitch

The chain stitch is a machine stitch formed with only one thread. Because it pulls out easily, it is not practical for most home sewing. It is sometimes used effectively, however, for machine basting. This stitch is generally produced by children's toy sewing machines and by machines used for novelty and decorative stitching. It is an additional convenience feature on certain models of several brands of machines. Consider its value before investing in this particular feature.

Lock Stitch

The lock stitch, which includes both the straight and the zigzag stitch, is a stitch formed when the upper and lower threads are locked together between two thicknesses of fabric. This type of stitch securely attaches two or more pieces of fabric together and does not pull out easily. It is used for most home sewing.

Straight Stitch This stitch, which is the lock stitch sewn in a straight line, is effective for most basic home sewing and repairs, including speed basting. Because of the mechanics involved in producing this stitch, it is more likely than the zigzag stitch to be perfectly formed. When doing straight stitching on a zigzag machine, it is advisable to use a special throat plate and presser foot, especially for knits, tricots, and clinging fabrics. Such special fittings will help keep the fabric from stretching down the opening of the throat plate and prevent skipped stitches.

Zigzag Stitches These stitches are a form of the lock stitch sewn in a zigzag line. They are popular for sewing knits and stretch fabrics. They are also used extensively for finishing seams in garments made of fabrics which fray easily, for sewing on buttons, for making buttonholes, and for mending.

Reverse-action Stitches Some sewing machines produce reverse-action stitches which join and overlock in one operation. Used for purposes of decoration, strength, or elasticity, these stitches include the feather stitch, the

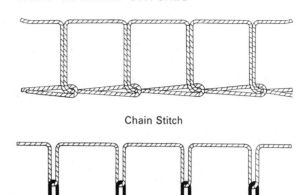

Chain Stitch

Lock Stitch

Courtesy TSM Company

Of the many stitches made by a modern sewing machine, all are variations of the chain or lock stitch. The chain stitch is formed by a single thread, while the lock stitch is made of an upper thread and a lower thread which interlock within the layers of fabric.

decorative reverse-action stitch, the stitch and overlock, and the super stretch. They are particularly useful for making garments of knit and stretch fabrics or for mending broken seams and worn areas in stretch and knit garments.

Machine Attachments

Sewing-machine attachments are tools designed to serve a wide variety of purposes. Most of the attachments are included with the purchase of a deluxe sewing machine. If you decide to buy a machine and attachments separately, at first you might want to get only the attachments you will need for the sewing projects you have actually planned. Others might be added later as needed. In addition to those here described, attachments that sometimes come with the machine include a braiding foot, an overedge foot, twin needles, a blind-stitch foot, a button-sewing foot, a quilting guide, and a ruffler.

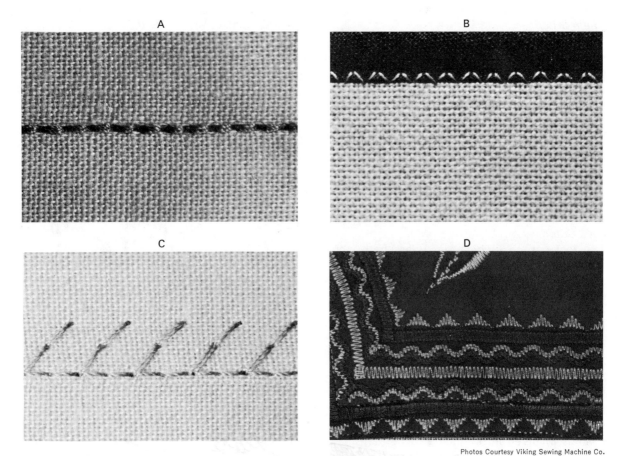

| A | B |
| C | D |

Photos Courtesy Viking Sewing Machine Co.

The straight stitch (A), the zigzag stitch (B), the stretch stitch (C), and a wide range of embroidery stitches can be made on modern sewing machines. Each stitch can be used to advantage on today's fashion fabrics.

Roller Foot The roller foot is a special type of attachment used instead of a presser foot to hold the fabric when machine-stitching knits or laminated fabrics. It has a loose hinge and two rollers which permit it to move over the fabric with ease. The foot creates a top feed to complement the lower feeding mechanism, thus moving the top and bottom layers of fabrics at the same rate. It is useful also in matching plaids and stripes.

Zipper or Cording Foot This attachment is a narrow foot used instead of the presser foot to hold the fabric when applying a zipper or cording. Most models can be moved varying distances either to the right or left side of the needle, allowing for stitching close to the edge of a zipper or cord.

Invisible Zipper Foot This is a special type of zipper foot recommended for use only when inserting an invisible zipper. As the zipper is stitched, the chain of the zipper passes through the groove in the base of the foot.

Seam Guide This device is a metal guide that helps ensure straight seams of even width. It guides the stitching to keep it an accurate distance from the cut edge. It must be readjusted, however, for each different seam width. Substitutes for this metal guide can be made by using varied colors or marked

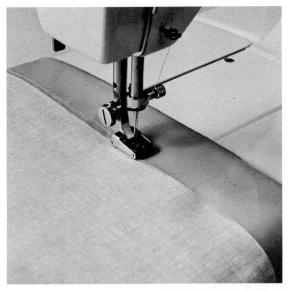

Courtesy Viking Sewing Machine Co.

The roller foot, which allows the sewing machine to glide easily over knitted, bonded, or other thick fabrics, is available for most brands of sewing machines.

Courtesy Viking Sewing Machine Co.

A zipper or cording foot is adjustable to allow for stitching very near both the left and right sides of zippers or cords.

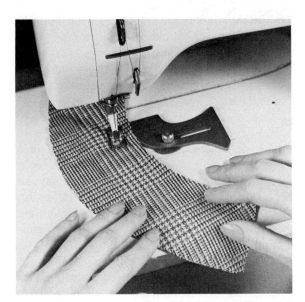

Courtesy Belding Corticelli

An adjustable seam guide which can be fastened to the bed of a sewing machine is a useful aid in stitching curved or otherwise difficult-to-stitch seams.

Courtesy Viking Sewing Machine Co.

The hemmer folds a fabric for hemming as it is fed through the apparatus and stitched by the sewing machine.

strips of adhesive tape. Most new sewing machines have throat plates which are etched to indicate commonly used seam widths.

Bias Binder   The bias binder serves to apply bias tape. It siphons the tape to a position under the needle allowing it to be sewn to both sides of the raw edge of fabric in one operation.

Hemmer   The hemmer turns a narrow hem as the fabric is fed into it, readying the hem for stitching. Where such a hem is desired, it eliminates pinning and basting and permits the turning and stitching to be accomplished in a single operation.

Tucker   The tucker is a type of marker used to position rows of uniform tucks or pleats in widths of $1/8$ to 1 inch or more. Tucks of varying size and spacing can be easily and quickly formed with this attachment.

Blind-stitch Hemmer   This attachment for a straight-stitch machine sews a hem that is practically invisible, similar to hand hemming. It combines the final step of clean-finishing a raw edge with the hemming process in one operation. This attachment is frequently used for blind-hemming dresses, skirts, and draperies.

Zigzagger   This device can be added to a straight-stitch machine to make zigzag stitches. By inserting metal cams which produce varied patterns, zigzag stitches of innumerable designs can be made. The spacing of the stitches can be controlled by the stitch-length regulator. The zigzagger is useful for joining interfacings and for finishing seams.

Buttonholer   The buttonholer is a straight-stitch-machine attachment for making buttonholes. Some automatic machines also include a buttonholer, because this attachment usually permits greater precision in buttonhole construction than does the ordinary zigzag stitch. To use the buttonhole attachment, choose a template, or metal pattern, of a size to fit over the button. Insert the template into the buttonholer, and then attach the buttonholer to the machine. Make a sample buttonhole on a double thickness of scrap fabric to check stitch perfection and size before working on a garment.

How can you obtain the sewing tools that meet both your needs and your budget?

What is the difference between scissors and shears?

What is a tailor's ham? A padded roll? A needle board?

How can you substitute do-it-yourself equipment for manufactured pressing tools?

How do you care for the iron? The shears? The sewing machine?

Other Sewing Tools

In addition to the sewing machine, you will need a number of other tools to make a garment. These include tools for measuring, pinning, cutting, marking, hand sewing, and pressing. If you buy these tools, first consider your basic needs and determine the total amount you have to spend. Then before you buy, comparison-shop in several kinds of stores. Prices and qualities vary.

Select a reliable store which will stand behind the quality of its products. Carefully read any tags or labels attached to the product. They may give you information about the materials from which the product is made, its expected performance, or suggestions for its use and care.

Cutting Tools

When you select shears or scissors, consider their quality and intended use. Although tools may look alike, outward appearance may be deceiving. The quality, and often the price, of shears or scissors depend on the materials they are made of and their method of manufacture.

Consider your sewing needs carefully to determine whether shears, scissors, specialty cutting tools, or a combination of types best meets your needs. Always try out cutting tools before buying them to see that they handle easily and cut evenly to the tips of the blades.

When acquiring cutting tools for your various needs in home sewing, consider buying bent shears (A) for cutting garments of woven fabrics, bent shears with serrated edges (B) for cutting garments from knitted and bonded fabrics and leathers, pinking shears (C) for finishing seams in garments made of sturdy fabrics, short scissors (D) for clipping fabric during construction, and ripping scissors or snips (E) for cutting threads.

Shears

Shears are two-bladed cutting tools at least 6 inches long. One of their two handles has an opening large enough for two or more fingers, permitting good control in cutting fabric. In addition, some shears have a bent-handle design which permits the blade to rest on the table during cutting, allowing the pattern and fabric to remain flat for precision cutting. Called *bent trimmers*, they are recommended for cutting most fabrics.

Each section of a pair of high-quality shears is made of one solid piece of high-carbon steel manufactured by the hot-hammer forged method. Such shears are resilient and durable enough to withstand hard, constant use. There are other clues to quality: Good shears have an adjustable tension screw rather than a rivet, a one-piece-handle-and-blade design, chrome plating to prevent rusting, and a sharp cutting edge.

Shears of poor quality may break easily, lose their cutting precision, or fail to stay sharp with use. They are usually made by one of the following ways: by casting, which produces a hard but brittle blade; by the forged-steel method, which results in a soft, dull blade; or by the inlaid-blade method, which produces sturdy blades but frames that are not durable.

Pinking or *scalloping shears* are a special type used for making ravel-resistant seam finishes or for cutting designs for decorative purposes. They are usually more expensive than other shears. They are also less versatile because they do not permit sufficient precision to cut out a garment effectively. Pinking shears cannot be sharpened easily. When purchasing a pair, check to see whether the manufacturer offers a sharpening service or can supply replacement blades.

Scissors

Scissors are similar to shears but are shorter in length, usually 3 to 6 inches, and have ring handles. Sharp points and slender blades are well suited to delicate cutting jobs, such as ripping or slashing fabrics or snipping threads. Some of the same buying guidelines for selecting shears can be followed for selecting scissors.

Ripping scissors, small scissors which are dull near the tip, are used when stitching errors must be removed from garments. To use ripping scissors, see the discussion and illustrations on page 299.

Specialty Cutting Tools

With the rash of new fabrics on the market, new tools have been developed to cut each type. *Electric scissors* are available both in battery-driven and regular electric-current-driven models. These scissors are especially recommended for reducing the actual physical effort of cutting heavy fabrics or large quantities of fabrics. *Lingerie shears* are rather fine shears with a serrated blade. They are recommended for use with tricot knits and other lingerie fabrics which tend to slip while cutting, causing cutting inaccuracies. *Extra heavy shears* are available which effectively cut the heaviest of leathers, but which would be unsatisfactory for cutting regular fabrics. *Razor-type knives* are useful for intricate cutting of leather and plastic goods.

Also to be considered are *heavy-weight shears with a serrated cutting edge.* Such shears can be used to cut almost any fabric from delicate lingeries to heaviest double knits. They are also useful for cutting most leathers and plastics. In addition to the actual cutting tools, *scissor gauges* are available. This device can be attached to the lower blade of scissors to facilitate accurate cutting of strips of fabric such as bias binding.

Measuring Tools

Clothes look attractive and feel comfortable only when they fit well. For achieving accurate fit, good measuring tools are essential.

Tape Measure

Used chiefly for taking body measurements, tape measures are usually 60 inches long. The most effective tape is clearly marked in $\frac{1}{8}$-inch divisions, with markings starting from each end on opposite sides of the tape. Buy a tape measure with metal ends attached to firmly woven cloth treated to resist shrinking or stretching. Some nonstretch plastic types are also effective in use.

Yardstick or Ruler

The yardstick is a long, flat measuring device used for accurately taking measurements on a flat surface. Choose a smooth wood, metal, or plastic measuring tool that will not catch on the most delicate fabrics. A ruler can be used if short distances are to be measured.

Skirt Marker

Hems can be leveled most easily and accurately by means of a skirt marker. There are several types of skirt markers. They include those with which pins are used, those with which tailor's chalk is used, and those with which chalk powder is used. The pin types are the most accurate, but they require the assistance of another person to insert the pins.

Adjustable Gauge

A short metal gauge with a sliding marker is a convenient tool for measuring small areas or for turning a hem.

Tailor's Square

This L-shaped wood, plastic, or metal rule serves to measure straight lines and right angles, such as straight of fabric positions on pattern layouts.

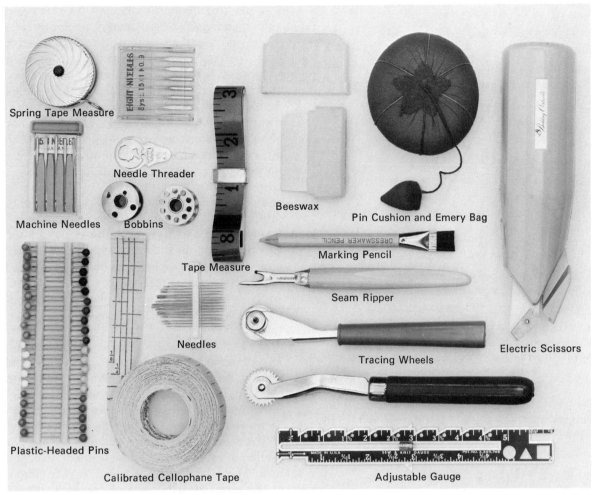

Spring Tape Measure

Needle Threader

Machine Needles

Bobbins

Tape Measure

Needles

Plastic-Headed Pins

Calibrated Cellophane Tape

Beeswax

Pin Cushion and Emery Bag

Marking Pencil

Seam Ripper

Tracing Wheels

Electric Scissors

Adjustable Gauge

A broad range of sewing tools is available in most department stores and five-and-ten-cent stores. Choose those items which will help most in your clothing construction and garment repair.

Hem Marker

A hem marker is a flat metal measuring tool designed to help make hems of even width.

Marking Tools

Marking tools are needed to transfer pattern markings to the fabric and to indicate certain measurement details. They are inexpensive items which can be purchased at the sewing and notions counters in department stores or five-and-ten-cent stores. Marking tools such as tailor's chalk and dressmaker's tracing paper are prepackaged as a unit in a variety of colors. In addition to the tools here described, needles and thread and irons can sometimes serve as marking tools also (see pages 283-284).

Tracing Tools

To transfer construction markings from pattern to fabric with accuracy, tracing paper and the tracing wheel provide the quickest method.

229

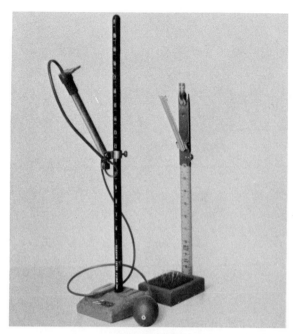

Skirt markers are effective for marking the lower edge of a flared skirt either with chalk or pins.

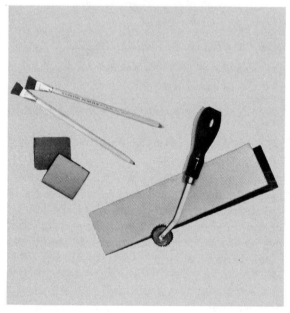

Marking equipment includes the tracing wheel used in combination with tracing paper, marking pencils (top), and both wax and clay chalks.

It is also the method producing the most durable markings. When using tracing tools, always protect the working surface by placing heavy cardboard, beveled plate glass, or other firm material between the working surface and the fabric. It should be noted that traced markings are sometimes hard to remove from the fabric when removal is desired. They should therefore be accurate and made with an inconspicuous color of dressmaker's carbon on the *wrong* side of the fabric.

Dressmaker's Tracing Paper   This paper is coated with colored or white wax. Except with fabrics too light-colored for the white to show, white-coated paper is recommended. Colored wax is likely to show through on the right side of the fabric. When you must use colored paper, choose a shade which can be seen but which is very nearly that of the fabric. Avoid using dark paper on light-colored or sheer fabrics.

Tracing Wheel   Tracing wheels are small, smooth-edged, needle-pointed, or saw-toothed wheels, with a handle attachment. They are used to transfer pattern markings to fabric. The smooth-edged wheel marks effectively on lightweight fabrics. The needle-pointed wheel will mark certain fabrics without the use of tracing paper. The saw-toothed wheel, which is used with tracing paper and makes large, conspicuous dots, is useful for many firmly woven fabrics but is not recommended for knits.

Marking Chalk

Marking chalk, or tailor's chalk, is chalk of various types used in sewing to identify the right and wrong sides of plain fabrics, the right and left side of a garment, the upper and undercollar and cuffs, and the top and bottom of garment fabrics. The fabric will determine which type of chalk to use.

Wax Chalks   These chalks may be white, transparent, or colored. They are recommended for use only on wool, because on other fabrics they are likely to leave a grease spot after pressing.

Clay Chalks Other varieties of chalk are made of clay. They include regular dressmaker's squares in white, black, and colors; powdered chalk; colored marking pencils, or tailor's pencils; and sharpened blackboard chalk.

Pins

Regular *dressmaker's pins* or *ball-point pins* can be used for specific marking requirements. Dressmaker's pins are recommended for use on woven fabrics and ball-point pins for knits. The pins are placed at intervals along the area to be marked. They are then removed as a marking-pencil dot is used to mark the pin's location. Pins are considered the least accurate and least effective marking tool, as they cannot be positioned exactly and frequently slip from the fabric before the marking can be used or permanent marks can be substituted.

Small Sewing Tools

Not to be forgotten in the sewing process are the very small but important tools such as needles, thread, and thimble. Each of these items plays a significant role in the appearance of the finished product. For example, a needle that is too coarse for the fabric will leave tiny holes wherever it has penetrated the fabric, and a blunt needle will snag the fabric threads. The kind of sewing thread you use can determine whether seams will pucker or break when the garment is worn.

Needles

An assorted package of needles is a good choice for hand sewing, because it includes the sizes most commonly used. *Sharps,* used for most sewing, are medium-length round-eyed needles. *Betweens* are similar to sharps but shorter in length. They are especially good for fine sewing and close stitching. Similar to sharps but longer, *milliners* are used for hand basting and running stitches. *Crewels,* used for embroidery, are the same length as sharps but have a special long eye for easy threading. *Ball-point needles* of varying sizes, available

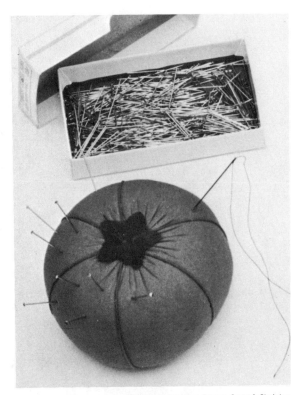

Courtesy Educational Bureau, Coats & Clark Inc.

Ball-point pins are available which are made especially for pinning knit fabrics, in which fibers are often cut by regular pins.

in most knit-fabric shops, are effective for use when hand stitching is necessary on projects made from knit fabrics.

Use large needles for heavy fabrics and small ones for lightweight fabrics. Needles should be a fine-quality steel, neither brittle nor easily bent. A perfectly polished needle will slip in and out of the fabric easily, and the eye will not cut or snarl the thread. To prevent needles from rusting, keep them in the package in which they were bought, rather than in a pin cushion.

Thread

Except when used for decoration or temporary stitching, thread should match the fabric of a garment as closely as possible in color, luster, yarn size, and elasticity. Heavy fabric requires

231

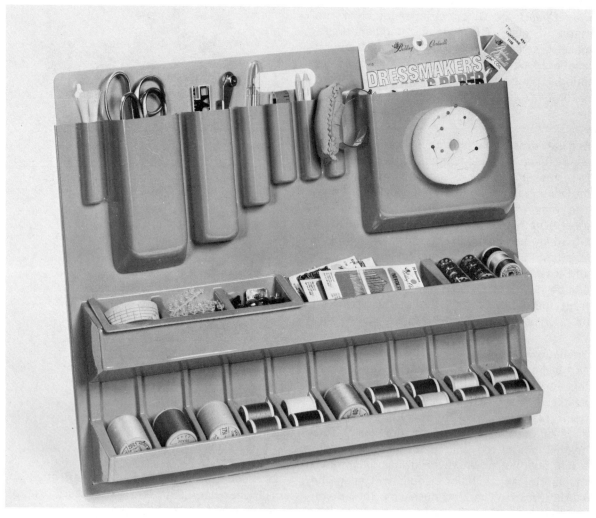

Develop some type of organizing method for keeping your small sewing equipment in usable order.

heavy thread, while lighter fabric requires lighter thread. Threads vary in size from number 8 to 100 in cotton. Mercerized threads are made in size numbers 50 to 60, and silk thread is available in sizes A, B, and C. Nylon, polyester-cotton combinations, and polyester threads are available only in one size for each type. Heavy-duty mercerized cotton thread, buttonhole twist silk, and linen are all heavy threads for use where extra strength is required. Mercerized cotton thread is stronger, has more elasticity, and is available in a greater variety of colors than is plain cotton thread. It is therefore preferable for making many articles of clothing. Silk, nylon, combination, and polyester threads are the most elastic and so are the best suited for wool and stretch fabrics. While silk and mercerized cotton threads work best on woolen fabrics, polyester, combination, and some nylon threads are satisfactory for stitching fabrics of the man-made fibers or blends including knits.

Polyester and combination threads usually do not slip or twist so easily as nylon. However, a soft-textured nylon thread is available that is especially effective for stitching nylon tricot and similar lingerie fabrics.

Thimble

A thimble is used in sewing to protect the end of the middle finger when pushing the needle through the fabric. The depressions over the thimble's surface should be cut deeply and sharply enough to hold the needle in place as it is pushed. Thimbles may be made of either metal or plastic and with either a closed or open top. They come in different sizes.

Pressing Tools

A variety of pressing equipment is available to aid the creative seamstress. Knowing the function of each piece of equipment will help you decide just what pieces you need for the kind of sewing that you plan to do.

Certain equipment, such as the pressing ham, iron, and padded roll, are basic tools for most clothing construction. Other items, such as the needle board, seam board, and clapper, are used mainly for tailoring or working on special fabrics such as corduroy, velvet, and furlike fabrics. As a consumer, decide on the tools you need and then shop for the price and quality you wish. It might be wise to limit your investment to only one or two pieces of basic pressing equipment at first. Other items can be acquired gradually as needed.

Irons

The selection of an iron is important not only for sewing but also for general use. Irons are available in various sizes, weights, and models. Some irons are designed for dry pressing only, some for combination steam-and-dry, some for dry-and-steam-and-spray, and some for steam only. Some people choose a small travel iron to use while sewing because it can be convenient for pressing small, hard-to-reach areas of a garment. For further discussion on irons, see page 237.

Pressing Boards

Boards used for pressing need to be well padded. They may be covered with heavy muslin or other sturdy, washable cloth. An additional cover can be made which is removable for frequent laundering to assure a clean pressing surface. Pressing boards are of various types. For a discussion of the regular ironing board, see pages 134-135.

Sleeve Board

The sleeve board is a miniature ironing board which can be placed on any flat surface. It will enable you to press small areas easily. It is particularly convenient for blocking the caps of sleeves and for pressing short seams and the inside seams of slacks and shorts.

Seam Board

This board, sometimes called a seam-edge presser, or a point presser if it is made with a pointed end, is a small board specially shaped for pressing curves, contours, and pointed edges. It is generally used without a cover. It prevents formation of an imprint of the seam on the right side of a garment when a seam is pressed open on it. The corners of collars and lapels may be pressed on the pointed end.

Needle Board

The needle board, or wire press board, is a strip of canvas covered with fine upright steel wires set close together. It is used for pressing napped and pile fabrics such as corduroy, fleece, velvet, velveteen, and furlike fabrics. Its use in pressing prevents the matting or flattening of such fabrics.

Clapper

The clapper, sometimes called a beater or pounding block, is a shaped, uncovered wooden block used to pound and flatten faced edges and seams when working with thick,

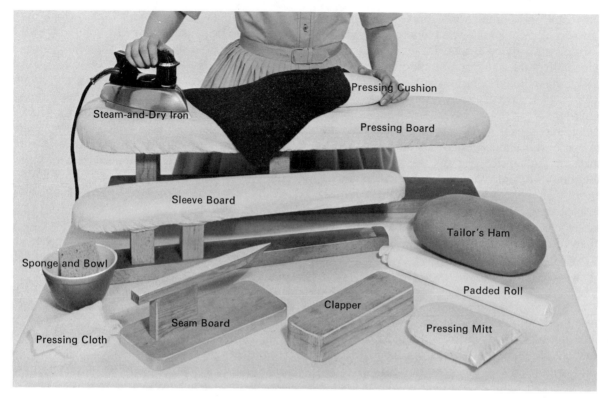

Steam-and-Dry Iron

Pressing Cushion

Pressing Board

Sleeve Board

Tailor's Ham

Sponge and Bowl

Padded Roll

Clapper

Seam Board

Pressing Mitt

Pressing Cloth

High-quality pressing equipment is a contributing factor in the production of high-quality garments.

bulky, fabrics. It makes a thin, flat finish and sharply creased edges without leaving a shine on the fabric.

Pressing Cushions

These pressing aids are cushions of various sizes and shapes used to retain the shape of curved parts of a garment being pressed. They can be filled with sawdust, wool, or strips of nylon.

Tailor's Ham

The tailor's ham is so called because of its hamlike shape. It is usually covered with a lightweight wool fabric, which is ideal for pressing any fabric and resists soil. The ham is used for pressing areas which need shaping,

such as darts, curved seams, and tailored collars.

Padded Roll

The padded roll, or seam roll, is a long, slim, firm, cylindrical cushion used to press seams. It can be used instead of a seam board. It can also be used for molding curved ends of collars or arched lapels.

Pressing Cloths

The pressing cloth is a small piece of fabric used to cover a garment during construction pressing. Most fabrics which are to be pressed on the right side should be pressed under a pressing cloth. With a dry iron, a pressing cloth should be used whether the right or the wrong side of the fabric is pressed. For most home sewing, two or three thicknesses of fine cheesecloth serve very well as a pressing cloth. Because silks and rayons frequently water-spot, it is advisable to use tissue paper alone or under cheesecloth when steam-pressing them.

When pressing wool, it may be desirable to use a piece of wool fabric of a weight similar to that of the garment to avoid flattening the nap. Chemically treated pressing cloths are also practical for woolen garments.

A handy pressing cloth is one that slips over a steam iron and is held in place by elastic or ties. It can be made of heavy cotton canvas or a fabric treated with silicone. It protects the right side of the fabric while leaving it visible for effective pressing.

Dampening Aids

A sponge and bowl of water provide a convenient means of adding extra moisture where needed. The spray feature on certain irons is also effective.

Pressing Equipment Substitutes

The many different pressing tools which may be available in a school sewing laboratory could be a costly investment if you were to acquire them all for home use. However, you may have thought of the possibility of making substitute equipment yourself. A little imagination, a little time, and a few simple resources can easily result in good, workable pressing tools. For example, a padded roll can be made by using a rolling pin or several tightly rolled magazines as a base and then covering it with several thicknesses of cotton or wool fabric. A tailor's ham can be made with sturdy, washable cotton or wool casing which is stitched together securely and filled with sawdust. A temporary substitute can even be made by folding a terry-cloth towel into the desired shape and size. Several clean and sturdy pieces of corduroy or pile fabric, placed right side up on the ironing board, can serve as a temporary needle board.

A small ironing board and a thin, pointed iron, such as a travel iron, are helpful in pressing seams which are difficult to reach. Such equipment is particularly desirable when sewing space is limited.

Your own creative thinking will suggest many other possibilities and will reduce expenses as you explore and discover other ways to substitute for ready-made tools and equipment.

Care of Sewing Equipment

Tools that are given routine care work best. Each piece of sewing equipment requires certain care, and that can best be determined from the instruction book or the hang tag that comes with the product. Even tools identical in function sometimes require very different care. However, certain basic guidelines for general care can be applied to most sewing equipment.

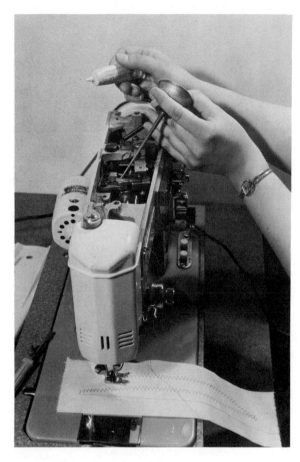

Oil and lubricate your sewing machine on the schedule suggested in your sewing-machine manual.

Protect the machine from dust by keeping it covered when it is not in use.

Lint deposits that accumulate around the feed dog and bobbin as you sew will need to be removed. Clean these areas with a small lint brush regularly so that the machine will operate smoothly. To remove lint and dust, gently rub a lint-free cloth between the upper tension discs which are visible.

A sewing machine needs oiling and lubrication regularly. It takes only a few minutes to do this, once you have become familiar with the oiling locations. A rule of thumb suggests oiling every week if the machine is used daily, and every other month if it is used infrequently. A machine area designated in the manual to receive oil should never be lubricated and vice-versa. In oiling your machine, use only special sewing-machine oil, which is a pure oil with no detergents added, and apply only one drop at each oiling position. Then run the machine slowly with a soft cloth under the presser foot. The cloth will absorb excess oil and prevent the metal parts from rubbing against each other. Running the machine permits the oil to work in between all moving parts and reduces the chance of oil stains on your garment during construction. Follow the sewing-machine manual for frequency, as well as points, of lubrication.

Care of Electric Sewing Equipment

Keep the electric cords for the sewing machine and other sewing equipment in good condition. Repair or replace any cord which becomes noticeably worn, particularly if wires are left exposed at the plug. If this equipment overheats, develops a short circuit, or gives you a shock, your safety is at stake. Have needed repairs made immediately.

The general care given your sewing machine determines how well it will serve you. Study the manual that comes with it to determine its specific care requirements. You will need to know, for instance, the location of the areas to be oiled, lubricated, and cleaned.

Care of Small Sewing Equipment

Store machine attachments and other small sewing equipment in containers for protection. A little creativity and some fabric, wallpaper, or paint can transform an empty carton into a clever sewing supply box. Such a box is particularly useful for storing needles, pins, and other very small sewing aids. It keeps such items together and prevents damage from rust or the settling of lint or dust. Do not store pins or needles in emery bags. Emery bags, small bags of fine mineral powder used for polishing needles, are attached to most pincushions. They tend to hold moisture, which causes pins and needles to rust if left in the bag for any length of time after polishing. Replace any bent or dull needles or pins in your supply box. This will prevent the snagging of fabrics caused by the insertion of blunt points.

Shears and scissors of high quality can last a lifetime if cared for properly. Keep them sharp by using them only to cut fabric. They are dulled, for instance, if used to cut paper or string. Store shears in a dry place with the blades closed and protected. To prevent rust, occasionally wipe the insides of the blades lightly with sewing-machine oil and place a drop or two on the screw between the blades. Be sure to remove any excess oil before using the shears again. When shears need sharpening, return them to the manufacturer or take them to a competent sharpening service. If an electric sharpener is included as a feature of your electric can opener, this, too, can be used effectively for sharpening most shears and scissors.

Care of Pressing Tools

Pressing equipment such as the tailor's hams, padded rolls, and other cloth-covered items can be kept lint-free by occasional brushing. Store padded items in a covered, dry place.

Launder ironing-board covers frequently. They should be kept free particularly of dark-colored lint, which would show if rubbed onto light-colored garments.

Keep the needle board free of threads and lint. Store it in a safe, dry place where no surrounding objects can bend the wires.

To protect the soleplate of your iron from scratches, avoid ironing over pins, zippers, or other metal objects during clothing construction. Keep the soleplate clean by using the correct temperature setting for the fabric you are pressing. Always wait for the iron to cool when changing from a higher to a lower temperature setting.

Steam irons require filling with water. It is usually wise to use distilled water, especially in hard-water areas, to avoid clogging the iron. Water which has been boiled or chemically treated at home can sometimes be substituted for distilled water. After each use, empty the iron of any remaining water while it is still hot. Store the iron in an upright position until it is cool.

To clean an iron, first make sure that it is cool. Then a light wipe with a moistened soft cloth is usually all that is needed, particularly if the soleplate has been coated with Teflon. However, if sizing, starch, or other substances have stuck to a noncoated soleplate, rub the spots gently with a paste made of scouring powder and water.

If melted plastic or man-made fibers should accidentally adhere to the iron, they are hard to remove. Several methods might be tried. First, you might try heating the iron until the residue softens. Then scrape it off as much as possible with a thin piece of wood, such as a wooden tongue depressor. Use scouring powder for removing any remaining residue. Another way to remove residue is to heat the iron until it is slightly warm. Then on the ironing board, over a protective layer of old, clean cloth or newspaper, place a sheet of waxed paper sprinkled with salt. Rub the iron gently over this surface several times. Then wipe it off. Other alternatives are the special cleaning preparations available on the market which are made especially for this purpose.

1. In selecting a sewing machine, decisions are based on the choices available at the given time.

2. The most efficient way to buy sewing tools is first to determine your needs and your budget and then to buy accordingly through comparison shopping.

3. A sewing machine that produces a lock stitch, whether a straight-stitch or a zigzag type, is suitable for most home sewing.

4. To ensure that a sewing machine may be used to best advantage, the accompanying manual should be read carefully and kept with the machine for ready reference.

5. The distinguishing characteristics of high-quality shears include sturdy construction of high-carbon steel, one-piece-handle-and-blade design, an adjustable tension screw, chrome plating, and a sharp cutting edge.

6. A tracing wheel and tracing paper provide a quick and accurate means of transferring pattern markings to sturdy fabric.

7. Ball-point pins and ball-point needles are most suitable for knit fabrics as they do not cut threads in such fabrics.

8. For each project the thread is specially selected to match the fabric as closely as possible in color, luster, yarn size, and elasticity.

9. To prevent the matting of napped and pile fabrics, a needle board, or wire press board, is used in pressing these fabrics.

10. In pressing areas which need shaping, a tailor's ham or a substitute is used.

11. An assortment of pressing equipment can be obtained at minimum expense by making your own substitute equipment.

12. For properly functioning equipment and for your own safety, it is essential to follow the care instructions provided by the manufacturer of the equipment and to have needed repairs made promptly.

13. Small sewing equipment is best maintained by using it according to the manufacturers' directions and storing it in suitable containers.

Pattern Selection and Fit

A pattern is for a seamstress what a blueprint is for a home builder. It provides the specifications of size, shape, and materials needed. It also indicates how to put the various pieces together. A pattern must be selected and fitted with care if a successful end product is to be attained.

What are the factors to consider in pattern selection?

What is your figure-type category?

What is your pattern size?

What are the features of an easy-to-make pattern?

How may the taking of accurate body measurements affect the ease or difficulty with which a clothing project can be completed?

What is the fallacy in buying a pattern which is too small for you?

How may the necessary alterations in a pattern be determined?

Decisions About Patterns

The decision-making process of selecting a pattern is an exciting one. There are many styles from which to choose. You might find one that could be used to make an outfit expressing your personality, an outfit similar to one you have admired in a store window but could not afford, or an outfit in the style currently popular among your friends. A knowledge of patterns will help you to select a style and size that will enhance your figure and reflect your own creative talent and taste.

Decisions will also be needed regarding adjustment of your chosen pattern. Will alterations be needed? What alterations will be needed? How should the alterations be made? How can the grain line in each piece of the garment be correctly retained when major pattern alterations are necessary? When should the alterations be made? A knowledge of figure types, pattern sizes, and pattern alteration methods will help you use your patterns so that well-fitted garments are achieved with minimum effort.

Factors Affecting Pattern Choice

To select a pattern, you will need to know the kind of garment you want to make. You will need to have some idea of the purpose and style of the garment desired, the kind of fabric it is to be made of, your figure type and pattern size, your sewing ability, and the amount of money you wish to spend on the needed materials. If you know that you tend to have serious problems with the fit of clothing, study this chapter together with Chapter 17, "Fitting a Garment."

For each project try to choose both pattern and fabric which will offer new challenges while providing opportunity for completion of a successful project.

Purpose of Garment

The garment you are making should be a part of your general wardrobe plan. It should fulfill a need and be wearable for the occasions and activities in which you will take part. Select a pattern design appropriate for the purpose of the garment. For example, a garment selected for active sports requires sufficiently loose fit to permit freedom of movement, a school outfit might be basic in style, and a party dress might be a little fancier.

Kind of Fabric

Choose a pattern style compatible with the fabric you have in mind. An easy-to-handle fabric is the best choice for a beginning project, as is discussed in Chapter 11. Further help in coordinating pattern styles with specific fabrics is given in Chapters 3, 11, and 21.

Figure Type and Pattern Size

Before selecting a pattern, you will need to know your figure type and your pattern size according to the system of measurement developed by the pattern companies. Only a pattern designed for your figure and for your particular size will provide the proper fit. For help in determining your figure-type category and your pattern size, see pages 244-247.

A pattern can be selected to flatter your figure. Even figure imperfections, common to

1. *Few pattern pieces.*
2. *Few curved seams or details.*
3. *Pattern pieces cut on the straight of the fabric.*
4. *A minimum of construction details.*
5. *Gathers or gores rather than pleats or a yoke.*
6. *Sleeveless or with sleeves that are short, straight, or cut-in-one with the garment.*
7. *A simple neckline rather than a notched or tailored collar.*
8. *A minimum of inset details such as belts, gussets, pockets, or pleats.*
9. *Right and left sides cut by same pattern.*
10. *Simple, straight darts rather than curved darts or those combined with other details.*

most people, can be made less noticeable if the pattern style is correctly chosen to conceal them (see pages 48-53).

Sewing Ability
Patterns range in difficulty from those with a few basic pieces to those which are very complex. Basic, or easy-to-make, patterns are usually located in a special section of a pattern book. (See illustrations on page 240.) The relatively expensive *designer* patterns tend to have many detailed pieces. In general, the fewer the pattern pieces, the simpler the garment is to complete.

A beginning seamstress is wise to select a pattern that is not too difficult for her skill and sewing experience. It should be a style that is easy to sew and to fit so that the learning process and the pleasure of accomplishment will not be hampered at the start by complexities or failures. It is best to begin with a basic pattern requiring few changes.

Taking Body Measurements
A preliminary step to determining figure type and pattern size is the taking of body measurements. These measurements are the actual dimensions of your body taken over a slip or well-fitted garment and the proper foundation garments. Bulky garments, sweaters, jackets, and belts should be removed before taking your measurements, as they tend to distort the accuracy of the measuring process.

For accuracy in measurement, it is best to work with a partner. You can take turns measuring each other and recording the measurements. Each measurement should be taken twice and the two numbers recorded, since the two measurements should be within $\frac{1}{2}$ inch of each other. If they are not, check by measuring a third time.

In addition to height, four basic body measurements are needed for the selection of most patterns. They are the bust, waist, hip, and back-waist-length measurements.

The bust measurement is taken over the fullest part of the bust and the tips of the shoulder blades. Sometimes it is helpful to know the chest, or high-bust, measurement also. If so, this may be taken around the body directly under the arms.

The waist measurement is taken around the natural waistline, which is the smallest part of the midsection, just below the rib cage. If you should find the natural waistline a difficult area to determine precisely, you can tie a string or ribbon around it to provide a visible line to measure.

TAKING BODY MEASUREMENTS

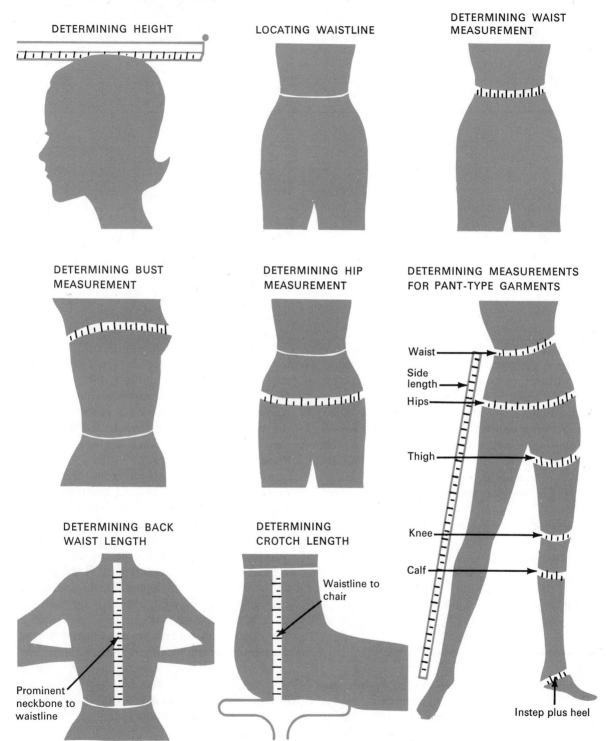

DETERMINING HEIGHT

LOCATING WAISTLINE

DETERMINING WAIST MEASUREMENT

DETERMINING BUST MEASUREMENT

DETERMINING HIP MEASUREMENT

DETERMINING MEASUREMENTS FOR PANT-TYPE GARMENTS

Waist

Side length

Hips

Thigh

Knee

Calf

Instep plus heel

DETERMINING BACK WAIST LENGTH

Prominent neckbone to waistline

DETERMINING CROTCH LENGTH

Waistline to chair

242

COMPARISON OF BODY AND PATTERN MEASUREMENTS

(Do not write in this book.)

Measurement	Body	Pattern	Necessary Ease	Alterations +	−
Bodice:					
Bust—over the fullest part of the bust.					
Shoulder—from base of neck to tip of shoulder (the armhole seam line).					
Length of bodice front—center of shoulder over fullest part of bust:					
1. To crown of bust.					
2. To waistline.					
Width of bodice front—from underarm seam to underarm seam, over fullest part of bust.					
Length of bodice back—center back from base of neck to waistline.					
Width of bodice back:					
1. At shoulder—4 inches below base of neck from armhole to armhole.					
2. At underarm—from underarm seam to underarm seam at armpit.					
Sleeve:					
Width—around upper arm, midway between shoulder and elbow.					
Length—from top of armhole down outside of arm, elbow slightly bent:					
1. To elbow.					
2. To wrist.					
Skirt:					
Waist—at natural waistline.					
Hip—at fullest part, 7 to 10 inches below waistline.					
Length of skirt:					
1. At center front.					
2. At center back.					
3. At right side.					
4. At left side.					

The hip measurement is taken approximately 7 to 9 inches below the waist, over the fullest part of the hips (see illustration on page 242).

The back waist length is an important measurement in determining your figure type. It is taken from the prominent bone at the base of the neck to the normal waistline.

Again, a string around the waist will help, providing a visible line to which to measure.

Record all measurements carefully and note the date on which they were taken. This record will serve as your guide in selecting and adjusting the pattern for proper fit. It may also be useful when purchasing patterns at a later date.

243

GIRLS'

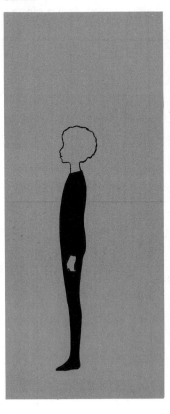

YOUNG JUNIOR/TEEN

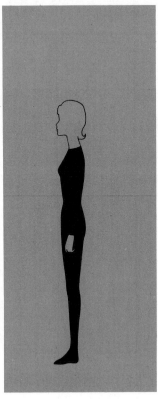

JUNIOR PETITE

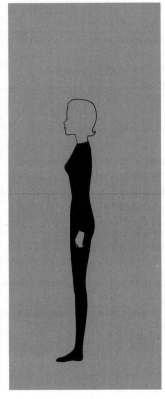

JUNIOR

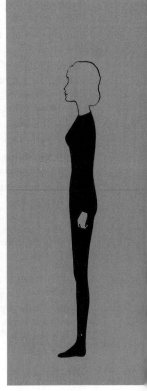

GIRLS'—From 4'2" to 5'1" without shoes. Girls' patterns are designed for the smallest of the eight types. The figure is just beginning to develop, but needs no underarm dart fitting in dress bodices because the bust line is not defined.

YOUNG JUNIOR/TEEN—About 5'1" to 5'3" without shoes. Young Junior/Teen patterns are designed for the developing teen and pre-teen figure. It has a very small, high bust and the waistline is larger in proportion to the bust.

JUNIOR PETITE—About 5' to 5'1" without shoes. Junior Petite patterns are designed for a short, well-developed figure, with small body build. It has a shorter waist length than any other type.

JUNIOR—About 5'4" to 5'5" without shoes. Junior patterns are designed for a figure that is slightly shorter than the Misses'. It is also a well-developed figure. The figure has a shorter waist length than the Misses'.

Size	7	8	10	12	14
Breast	26	27	28½	30	32
Waist	23	23½	24½	25½	26½
Hip	27	28	30	32	34
Back Waist Length	11½	12	12¾	13½	14¼
Approx. Heights	50"	52"	56"	58½"	61"

Size	5/6	7/8	9/10	11/12	13/14	15/16
Bust	28	29	30½	32	33½	35
Waist	22	23	24	25	26	27
Hip	31	32	33½	35	36½	38
BackWaist Length	13½	14	14½	15	15⅜	15¾

Size	3JP	5JP	7JP	9JP	11JP	13JP
Bust	30½	31	32	33	34	35
Waist	22	22½	23½	24½	25½	26½
Hip	31½	32	33	34	35	36
BackWaist Length	14	14¼	14½	14¾	15	15¼

Size	5	7	9	11	13
Bust	30	31	32	33½	35
Waist	21½	22½	23½	24½	26
Hip	32	33	34	35½	37
BackWaist Length	15	15¼	15½	15¾	16

MISS PETITE

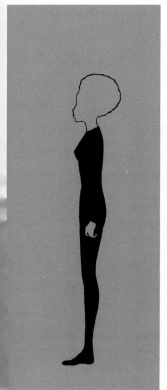

MISSES'

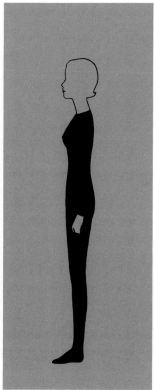

HALF-SIZE

WOMEN'S

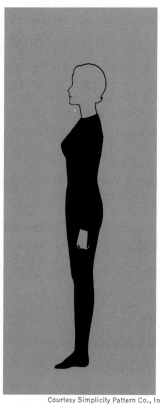

Courtesy Simplicity Pattern Co., Inc.

MISS PETITE—About 5'2" to 5'4" without shoes. Miss Petite patterns are designed for a figure that is as well-proportioned and well-developed as the Misses', but is shorter. The waist length is shorter than the Misses', and the bust and hips are the same as the Misses', with a slightly larger waist.

MISSES'—About 5'5" to 5'6" without shoes. Misses' patterns are designed for a figure that is well-proportioned and well-developed in all body areas. It is the tallest type and could be considered the "average" figure.

HALF-SIZE—About 5'2" to 5'3" without shoes. Half-Size patterns are designed for a fully-developed, but shorter figure. It has narrower shoulders than the Misses' and the waist is larger in proportion to bust than other mature figure types.

WOMEN'S—About 5'5" to 5'6" without shoes. Women's patterns are designed for the larger, more fully mature figure that is about the same height as the Misses'. Because of a fuller back it has a longer back waist length. All measurements are proportionately larger.

Size	6mp	8mp	10mp	12mp	14mp	16mp
Bust	30½	31½	32½	34	36	38
Waist	22½	23½	24½	26	27½	29½
Hip	32½	33½	34½	36	38	40
Back Waist Length	14½	14¾	15	15¼	15½	15¾

Size	6	8	10	12	14	16	18	20
Bust	30½	31½	32½	34	36	38	40	42
Waist	22	23	24	25½	27	29	31	33
Hip	32½	33½	34½	36	38	40	42	44
Back Waist Length	15½	15¾	16	16¼	16½	16¾	17	17¼

Size	10½	12½	14½	16½	18½	20½	22½	24½
Bust	33	35	37	39	41	43	45	47
Waist	26	28	30	32	34	36½	39	41½
Hip	35	37	39	41	43	45½	48	50½
Back Waist Length	15	15¼	15½	15¾	15⅞	16	16⅛	16¼

Size	38	40	42	44	46	48	50
Bust	42	44	46	48	50	52	54
Waist	34	36	38	40½	43	45½	48
Hip	44	46	48	50	52	54	56
Back Waist Length	17¼	17⅜	17½	17⅝	17¾	17⅞	18

New Sizing as approved by the Measurement Standard Committee of the Pattern Fashion Industry, December, 1968.

Determining Your Figure Type

After you have taken your body measurements, you are ready to determine your figure type.

The pattern companies have developed at least seven basic figure categories for teen-aged girls and women: Young Junior/Teen, Junior Petite, Junior, Miss Petite, Misses, Women, and Half Size. These figure categories vary in height, body proportions, slope of the shoulder, shape and height of the bust, and length of the body, arms, and legs. Your age or your ready-made-clothing size is not necessarily an indicator of your figure category. It is possible that a high-school girl and a housewife, both with a height of only 5 feet 1 inch and with approximately the same body measurements and back waist length, will have the same figure type: Junior Petite. On the other hand, two people with the same height and similar body measurements but with different back waist lengths may be two different figure types, such as Misses and Half Size.

The following are guidelines to assist you in determining the pattern figure-type category best for you. You may wish to use one or several of these guidelines when establishing your figure type.

1. Compare your basic body measurements with those of various figure-type categories in the pattern book from which you are selecting your pattern. Of these basic measurements, your height and back waist length are of crucial importance in determining your figure type.

2. Use one of the try-on patterns which have been designed by some pattern companies. These are patterns printed on non-woven fabric which you can cut out, machine-baste, and try on. A try-on pattern for your correct figure type and size can be used over and over again as a standard by which to gauge alterations on other patterns or clothes.

3. Try on a sample garment or shell. A shell is a basic-type garment made from a standard-size pattern. If shells representing various figure types and sizes are available, trying them on will quickly show which figure type and size to buy.

When you have determined your figure type, select your patterns only from that special section of the pattern book. In this way you can ensure proper fit without complicated alterations.

Determining Your Pattern Size

Once you know your figure type, it is easy to determine your pattern size. Pattern sizes, much like figure types, are based on body measurements, not on age or on ready-to-wear sizes. They are designed from specifications set up by the Measurement Standard Committee of the pattern industry. The major pattern companies base their pattern sizes and types on these latest standard measurements for bust, waist, hip, and back waist length. (See pages 244-245.)

Your body measurements, especially the back waist length, help you determine your figure type. They can also help you determine your pattern size. Compare your body measurements with the Standard Body Measurement Chart printed in the pattern book and also on the pattern envelope. Few people have measurements identical to those given in the chart. For this reason some general rules of thumb have been developed as to which body measurements should be the determining factor when yours and the chart's do not agree.

1. Your bust measurement usually determines the pattern size for any garment that requires fit in the bodice, such as blouses, dresses, coats, and suits.

2. Your hip measurement is the most important one for those garments which are not affected by bust measurement and which fit snugly over the hips. Fitted skirts, shorts, and slacks are examples. The reason for giving hip measurement priority over the waist measurement in such garments is that the waist measurement is easier to alter.

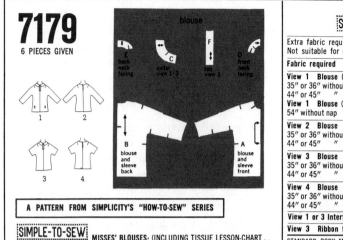

7179
6 PIECES GIVEN

blouse

E back neck facing — C collar view 1-3 — F tab view 2 — D front neck facing

1   2
3   4

B blouse and sleeve back — A blouse and sleeve front

A PATTERN FROM SIMPLICITY'S "HOW-TO-SEW" SERIES

SIMPLE-TO-SEW MISSES' BLOUSES: (INCLUDING TISSUE LESSON-CHART . . "How to make straight darts".) The blouses have high round neckline and kimono-type sleeves. V. 1 & 2 have below elbow-length sleeves. V. 1 & 3 have two-piece collar and back zipper. Button trimmed V. 1 has self fabric carriers and purchased belt. Collarless V. 2 & 4 have back loop and button closing. V. 3 & 4 have short sleeves. V. 2 has tab with button trim. V. 3 has optional ribbon bow.

Suggested fabric types — Cottons and blends; pique, denim, cotton double knits. Linen. Silks, synthetics and blends; crepe, homespun. V. 1 also in lightweight wools and blends; wool double knits, wool crepe, jersey.
*Reg. U. S. Pat. Off.

SIMPLE-TO-SEW MISSES' BLOUSES.

Extra fabric required for matching plaids, stripes, one-way design fabrics. Not suitable for obvious diagonal fabrics.

Fabric required	Sizes	8	10	12	14	16	18	20	
View 1 Blouse (cut crosswise)									
35" or 36" without nap		2	2	2⅛	2⅛	2¼	2¼	2⅜	Yds.
44" or 45" " "		1½	1½	1½	1⅝	1⅝	1¾	1⅞	"
View 1 Blouse (cut lengthwise)									
54" without nap		1¼	1⅜	1⅜	1⅜	1⅜	1⅜	1⅜	"
View 2 Blouse Even lengthwise striped or plain fabric (cut crosswise)									
35" or 36" without nap		2	2	2⅛	2⅛	2¼	2¼	2⅜	"
44" or 45" " "		1½	1½	1½	1⅝	1⅝	1⅝	1⅝	"
View 3 Blouse									
35" or 36" without nap		1⅝	1⅝	1¾	1¾	1¾	1¾	2	"
44" or 45" " "		1⅛	1¼	1¼	1¼	1½	1½	1½	"
View 4 Blouse Even lengthwise striped or plain fabric									
35" or 36" without nap		1½	1½	1½	1½	1½	1½	1⅞	"
44" or 45" " "		1⅛	1⅛	1⅛	1¼	1½	1½	1½	"
View 1 or 3 Interfacing ¼ yd. 18", 25", 32", 35", 36" woven or non-woven fab.									
View 3 Ribbon for bow (optional) — ¾ yard of ½" wide.									

STANDARD BODY MEASUREMENTS

Sizes	8	10	12	14	16	18	20	
Bust	30	31	32	34	36	38	40	Ins.
Waist	23	24	25	26	28	30	32	"
Hip	32	33	34	36	38	40	42	"
Back length — neck base to waist	15½	15¾	16	16¼	16½	16¾	17	"
Finished back length of blouse	22¾	23	23¼	23½	23¾	24	24¼	"

Sewing notions — Thread, bias seam binding. View 1 and 3: 7" neck zipper. View 1: Eight ¾" buttons, 1" belt. View 2: Four ¾" buttons.

Courtesy Simplicity Pattern Co., Inc.

To determine the amount of fabric needed for a project, draw a line downward on the chart on the pattern envelope from the number indicating your pattern size until it intersects one running across from the listing for your fabric width.

3. Your waist measurement usually determines the size for skirts with flare, pleats, or fullness which starts at the waistline.

If you find, when comparing your measurements to those in the pattern book, that you fall between two sizes, there are further guidelines you can follow. First, check your pattern book to see whether it includes patterns that are adjustable in size. There is an *Adjust-for-You* type which provides interchangeable pattern pieces of two consecutive sizes within one pattern envelope. For example, it might include both sizes 12 and 14 dress pieces so that, if necessary, you could use a size 14 bodice pattern and a size 12 skirt pattern which match perfectly at the waistline. Another adjustable type is marked with a series of alteration cutting lines or a built-in tape measure, simplifying size adjustments. A sec-

ond solution might be to select the smaller size if you are small-boned or the larger size if you are full-bodied or have a large bone structure. If the pattern envelope includes more than one type of garment, such as a jacket and skirt, it is sometimes worthwhile to purchase two different pattern sizes: one size for the jacket and another size for the skirt.

Checking the Pattern Fit
Though you buy patterns according to your figure type in the size that is the most nearly correct for you, it is still necessary to check patterns after purchase to determine whether adjustment might be needed. Any alteration should be made on the pattern or during the cutting; only in this manner can fitting problems be effectively solved.

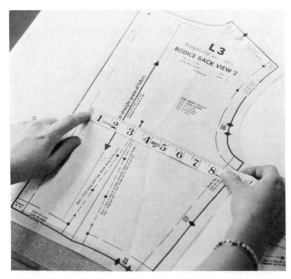

To determine necessary alterations, compare the measurements of your pattern with your body measurements. Allow space in the pattern for ease.

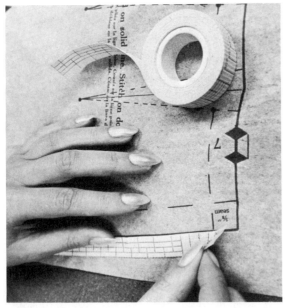

Small adjustments can be made along pattern seam lines and marked with calibrated tape to avoid cutting errors.

There are several good methods of checking the fit of a pattern. The method you choose will be determined by your particular figure problems, the exact garment in question, and the circumstances under which you are working. You may even wish to use more than one method or to combine features of several methods.

Comparing Measurements

One method of checking pattern fit is simply to compare your individual measurements with those of the pattern. Measure the pattern to determine any measurements which are not listed on the pattern envelope. It must be remembered, though, that your body measurements do not allow for the extra room needed in a garment for movement and comfort. Pattern pieces allow a few inches of *ease* to ensure that your garment will be comfortable to wear. In addition to this standard ease, some patterns also include *design ease.* Design ease provides certain fashion effects and will vary seasonally with the fashion trends. The total amount of ease differs with the make of the pattern and the style of the garment, but it must be considered in regard to pattern dimensions.

List the pattern measurements on your "Comparison of Body and Pattern Measurements" form (see page 243). Compare your measurements with those of the pattern, and note the differences. These differences, with ease considered, are the adjustments which must be made in your pattern.

Comparing the Pattern with a Well-fitted Garment

This method of checking involves taking measurements of a garment that fits you well and comparing these measurements with those of the pattern. It is an excellent way to determine the amount of ease needed in the garment you are making. The crotch seam length in slacks or shorts is a detail which can be checked more satisfactorily by this method than in any other way.

Holding Pattern Pieces Against the Body

It is possible to check the location and size of certain style features of a garment by holding pattern pieces against the body, one at a time. Care must be taken to hold the pattern piece in exactly the position in which the corresponding piece of fabric will be located when the garment is made. The location, slant, and length of darts and the placement of pockets and trim are features for which this method of checking is especially well adapted. Fit of the pattern cannot be accurately checked in this way.

Trying on a Shell

If a sample garment or shell is available in your pattern size, you would be wise to try or retry it on after selecting your pattern to observe the location and the amount of change needed to make it fit your figure perfectly. The alterations can then be made in the corresponding pieces of your pattern.

Making a Trial Garment

If you have a particularly difficult figure problem, or are planning a fashion garment of expensive fabric, it is often worthwhile to first make a basic garment of muslin and have it carefully fitted. After it fits perfectly, the changes can be transferred onto the pattern before the actual cutting of the garment. The adjusted pattern may thereafter be used as a master pattern, serving as a guide by which the size and shape of other patterns can be adjusted with only minor differences to accommodate fashion lines.

Why are pattern adjustments necessary?

What are the two methods of making a garment of a size different from the original size of the pattern?

What are the advantages of cutting a garment to fit over trying to adjust a partially completed garment?

What types of alterations may be necessary in darts?

Adjusting Your Pattern

The garment that you make should fit you satisfactorily. The first step in making a well-fitted garment is to have a well-fitted pattern from which to cut it. For perfect fit, any individual variation from the standard should be adjusted. Such adjustments are best accomplished by making the alterations in the pattern before the fabric is cut or by making them during the cutting process, so that the garment pieces will be exactly the right size when cut out. This procedure is known as *cutting to fit.* When a garment is cut to fit, mistakes are avoided, difficulties are decreased, and the success of the garment fit is assured in advance. The reasons for these advantages in cutting to fit are as follows:

1. The lines, spaces, and designs of a pattern that make the style attractive are retained so that the appeal of the original pattern is not affected.

2. All alterations are possible when cutting to fit, whereas in fitting the garment itself some alterations are not possible.

3. The construction of a garment is made easy, saving time and energy and eliminating the frustration of errors that cannot be corrected.

Minor pattern alterations in length and width can sometimes be made along cutting lines by removing or adding a small amount. Generally, an amount totaling 1 inch or less can be added or subtracted without disturbing the original lines of the design. For example, a garment piece may be slightly lengthened or shortened along the lower cutting lines. Width can be slightly increased or decreased by adding to the outer edges of the pattern.

Some corrections in fit may be possible by changing the markings on the pattern. Examples of such changes are: the location, direction, or size of darts; the size of pleats; and the relocation of pockets or trim. If changes in the pattern are needed because of an individual figure problem, follow the specific instructions given on pages 254-255 for making that particular alteration.

Guidelines for Pattern Alterations

Whatever method of pattern alteration you choose, follow these steps for effective changes.

1. Change the pattern measurements without changing the pattern proportions or the lines of the design.

2. Use the simplest method of alteration that will give the desired correction.

3. Change the size of the pattern without changing the grain line.

4. Make any needed pattern adjustments with the pattern pieces laid flat on the table so that measuring, cutting, shifting, or marking will be accurate.

Planning the Alteration

If checking indicates that your pattern needs adjustment, the next step is to plan the alteration. There are three steps in making such a plan:

1. Determine *what* alterations are needed, the amount and extent of the change, and the number of pattern pieces that will be involved. Do not forget that a change in one pattern piece frequently necessitates a change in the adjoining piece, so that the edges of the two pieces may be keyed.

2. Decide *how* the alterations are to be made. To help you decide how the pattern can be changed to make it right for you, refer to the instructions and the illustrations that follow and choose the method of alteration that will give the desired correction.

3. Decide *when* the alterations are to be made. When cutting to fit, the changes will be made either in the pattern pieces before they are laid on the fabric, or as the cutting is done. If the change can be made within the outline of the pattern, make the change on the pattern piece. Minor alterations in garment length and width and certain others for individual figure problems can usually be made in this way. If changes such as a major change in length or width are needed, decide whether you prefer to alter the pattern before cutting or to shift the pattern during cutting.

Many changes can be made easily and accurately as the garment is being cut by moving the pattern piece into a new position and using it as your guide for cutting. In this way the original outline of the pattern is not changed and the cut edges are precise. Another advantage is that the original pattern markings may be traced without change.

Making the Alterations

After you have formulated an alteration plan, you may follow the procedure for the type or types of alterations decided upon. The alternative procedures, changing the pattern and shifting the pattern, are described below, as is also the procedure for altering the darts.

Changing the Pattern

If your pattern is one with built-in adjustment features, your task is simplified. You need only to follow the instructions in the guide sheet. (See page 251.)

The easy-rule guides that are printed on some patterns are another effective aid in alteration. Using the printed ruler for measurement, make a fold equal to the amount the pattern is to be shortened, or cut the dotted lines and spread the pattern apart the amount it is to be lengthened.

If your pattern has no built-in features to aid you, size may be decreased by folding a pleat in the pattern or may be increased by cutting the pattern apart, separating the pieces, and inserting strips of paper between them. Care must be taken that the fold or the cut is exactly on the straight-of-grain.

Shifting the Pattern

In addition to the particular directions for each specific alteration, there are five general steps to follow in making an alteration by shifting the pattern:

1. Lay the pattern piece in the correct position.

2. Partially cut the garment piece along the edges that are not to be changed.

3. Shift the pattern into a new position

PRINCIPLES FOR ALTERING A PATTERN FOR FIT

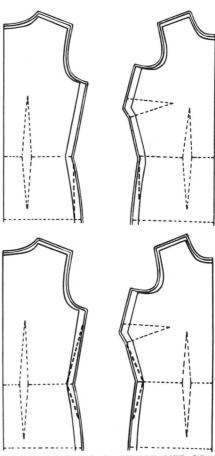

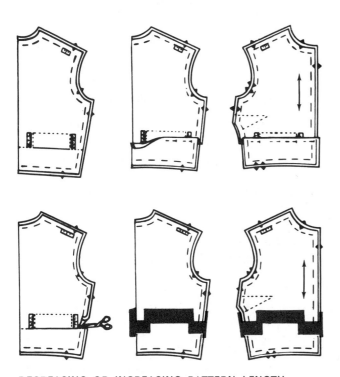

DECREASING OR INCREASING PATTERN LENGTH

DECREASING HIP OR WAIST SIZE OF *ADJUST-FOR-YOU* PATTERNS

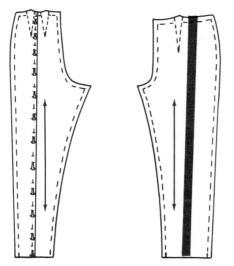

DECREASING OR INCREASING PATTERN WIDTH

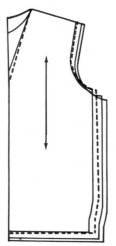

CHOOSING CUTTING LINE TO FIT BODY SIZE

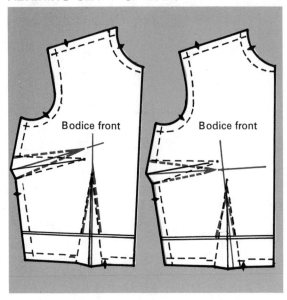

The slant of darts can be raised (left) for a high bust or lowered (right) for a low bust.

to give the desired change, retaining the original grain line.

4. Complete the cutting of the garment piece.

5. Transfer the markings when the pattern is in the original position or after it has been shifted, depending upon which will give the better location for the details marked.

Alteration of Darts

One common type of alteration in patterns is a change in darts. This might be a change in the slant of a dart, in the length or width of a dart, or in the number of darts. Each dart in your pattern should be checked to see whether such adjustments are needed.

Locating the Crown of the Bust   To check the slant and length of an underarm dart, you will first need to check the location of the crown of the bust on the pattern. If your pattern includes an underarm dart, be sure that the narrow end of the dart points toward the fullest part of your bustline. The crown of the

pattern bustline should coincide with the fullest part of your bust. To locate the crown of the bust on the pattern piece, extend the center line of the underarm dart and the center line of either the shoulder dart or the waistline dart, or both, with a ruler until the lines cross. The point where these lines cross is the crown of the bust. If the crown coincides with the fullest part of your bust, the underarm dart is correctly placed.

Altering the Slant of a Dart   If the crown of the bust is not correctly placed, the slant of the underarm dart requires changing. To change the slant of an underarm dart, causing it to point toward the crown of the bust, follow this step-by-step procedure:

1. Locate and mark your own bust crown on the pattern by holding the pattern in place against your body with the center front and neckline in position.

2. Draw a new center line from the point where the center fold line of the original dart crossed the seam line of the garment at the wide end of the dart to your newly established bust crown marked on the pattern.

3. On either side of the new center line draw a straight line which starts where the outer edge of the original dart crossed the pattern seam line and extend it to a point 1½ inches from the new bust crown mark.

Altering the Size of a Dart   The size of a dart may be altered by either of the following procedures.

To alter the *length* of a dart:

1. Locate the new dart point on the dart center line so as to increase or decrease the dart length as desired.

2. Draw new stitching lines from the new dart point to the points at which the original dart intersected the seam line at the edge of the pattern.

To alter the *width* of a dart:

1. Relocate the points at which the dart intersects the seam line at the edge of the pattern.

2. Move the intersection points so that one-half of the necessary change is made on

INCREASING OR DECREASING PATTERN WIDTHS

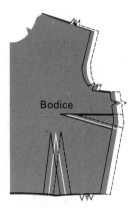

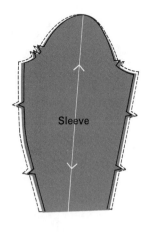

INCREASING OR DECREASING PATTERN LENGTHS

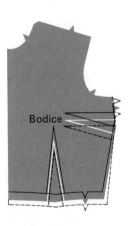

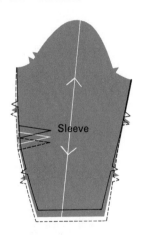

Legend for Pattern-shifting Illustrations

Colored background: Original pattern piece
White lines: Original pattern markings
Broken black lines: Change made by increasing
Solid black lines: Change made by decreasing

each side of the dart. To make a dart *narrower*, move the points toward each other. To make a dart *wider*, move the points away from each other.

3. Draw new stitching lines from the intersection points to the narrow point of the dart.

When an underarm dart is altered in size, it is necessary to increase or decrease the length of the underarm seam accordingly so it will remain of proper size to match the back section of the garment.

Making New Darts   When it becomes necessary to make new darts, as when chang-

253

LARGE BUST

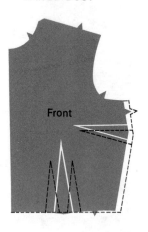

LARGE UPPER ARM

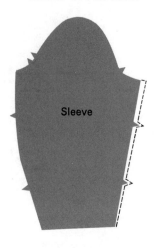

ROUND SHOULDERS

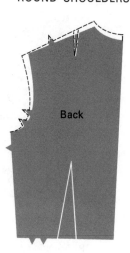

SQUARE SHOULDER

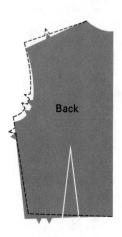

SMALL, FLAT BUST

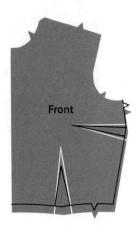

LARGE, LOW BUST

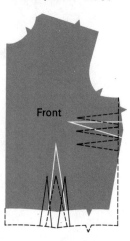

ing a gathering line to darts, complete the following steps:

1. Select the location for the dart point.

2. Draw a center line for the dart on the grain line on the pattern, extending from the dart point to the edge of the pattern.

3. Draw stitching lines on each side of the center line from the point to the edge of the pattern, making the dart the desired width at the wide end.

Making Two Darts from One Sometimes two small darts are more effective than one large one. If converting from one to two darts, follow this procedure:

1. Locate the points of the two new darts, one above and one below, or one to

HIGH OR LOW BUSTLINE

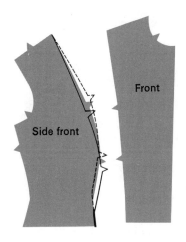

Side front

Front

LARGE OR SMALL BUST

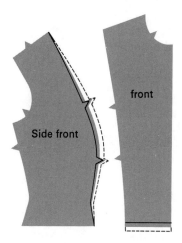

Side front

front

SWAYBACK

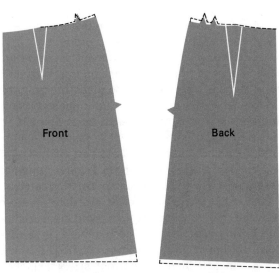

Front

Back

LARGE ACROSS BACK OF HIPS

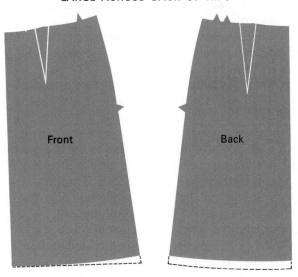

Front

Back

the right and one to the left, of the original dart point. Make them equidistant from the crown of the bust or, in hip adjustments, from the center back of the garment.

2. Draw new dart lines according to the preceding directions, making the total width of the two darts equal to the width of the original dart.

Altering for
Special Figure Problems

Pattern alterations to accommodate special figure problems are generally made by shifting the pattern during the process of cutting, as described on pages 250-253. The alterations required for the most common of the special figure problems are shown here.

255

1. Accurate body measurement requires the prior removal of bulky garments, sweaters, jackets, and belts.

2. The waistline measurement is correctly taken by tying a string or ribbon around the small part of the midsection, just below the rib cage, and measuring with a tape placed directly over the string.

3. Accuracy in taking body measurements is aided by working with a partner and by taking each measurement at least twice.

4. The hip measurement is taken about 7 to 9 inches below the natural waistline, over the fullest part of the hips.

5. The back waist length is determined by measuring from the bone at the base of the neck to the normal waistline.

6. Figure-type categories are determined on the basis of height, bust, waist, hip, and back-waist-length measurements.

7. In selecting the correct size in a dress, blouse, or jacket pattern, the most important measurement is the bust measurement.

8. In selecting the correct size in slacks, shorts, or fitted skirt patterns, the hip measurement is the one to consider.

9. In selecting a pattern for separates, the problem of falling between two pattern sizes may sometimes be solved by buying and combining patterns of both sizes.

10. A pattern alteration is successful if the pattern size or shape is changed to fit the body without changing the proportions or the lines of the design.

11. Pattern alterations may be simplified by the purchase of a pattern with *Adjust-for-You* features or premarked alteration lines.

12. Only minor changes in length or width can be made along cutting lines without affecting the basic shape of the garment.

13. When pattern alterations are major, they can be made either by altering the pattern pieces before they are laid on the fabric or by shifting the pattern in the process of cutting.

14. In making a pattern alteration in the length of slacks, shorts, or pants, a part of the needed amount of alteration is made in the crotch and the other part is made in the leg.

15. The crown of the bust is located on the pattern by extending the center lines of the underarm, shoulder, and waist darts until the lines cross.

16. A dart may be altered in location, direction, or size. A new dart may be created by first locating its point and then drawing the center and stitching lines as desired.

Selecting and Preparing Woven Fabrics

Woven fabrics have for several centuries been the most popular type of fabric. Because you are almost certain to work with woven fabrics when either making or caring for your clothes, it is important that you know something of their construction. An understanding of woven fabrics will enable you to make professional-looking garments which hold their shape and remain smart looking throughout their wear life.

How do you choose the best fabric for your project?

What factors influence the ease with which a given fabric can be handled?

How does fabric width affect yardage needed and project cost?

What is fabric grain and what is its role in clothing construction?

How can a fabric be made thread perfect?

How can an off-grain fabric be made grain perfect?

How can a fabric be preshrunk?

Decisions About Woven Fabrics

The decision-making process is vital to the successful selection of fabric. In choosing fabric for a project, several decisions must be made and placed in proper perspective to one another. To make wise decisions, you will need to know the characteristics of fabrics suitable for your project. You will also want to know the type of preparation that some of these fabrics may require. With this knowledge, you will then be able to apply the decision-making process and to obtain fabrics that prove successful in construction, wear, care, and attractiveness.

Selecting Fabrics

When you select fabric for your sewing project, you will find a wide variety from which to choose: fabrics in bright colors and dull colors, small prints, easy-care cottons, and blends. Without some guidelines to follow, the diversity may be confusing and selection difficult.

Your first guideline is the list on your pattern envelope of fabrics specifically recommended for the pattern you have chosen. Even though you are not obligated to select one of these fabrics, the list is a valuable aid.

A second guideline is that, for a beginning project, an easy-to-handle fabric is a good selection. Such fabrics present fewer

When time is a factor, choose for a sewing project a fabric which is easy to match at the seam lines, easy to straighten, easy to cut, and easy to handle in sewing.

problems than others in preparing the fabric, laying the pattern, cutting, marking, and sewing. By using one of these fabrics your learning of sewing techniques will not be complicated by problems arising from the fabric itself. Examples of easy-to-handle fabrics are percale, gingham, Indian Head, and many of the sturdily woven blends of cotton and man-made fibers. After the basic sewing processes have been learned, you will be ready to work with fabrics which require special handling. Some of the fabrics that are difficult to handle include stretch fabrics, corduroy, velveteen, pile fabrics, stripes, and plaids. They are described along with others in Chapter 21.

Easy-to-Handle Fabrics

Easy-to-handle fabrics are woven and finished to wear well under the stress expected of the intended garment, to be easily cared for, to be grain perfect or easily made so, and to result in an attractive completed garment. In seeking such fabrics, keep in mind both these general characteristics and the more specific

QUALITIES OF EASY-TO-HANDLE FABRICS

Medium-size, firmly twisted yarns   Fabrics made of medium-size yarns that have been firmly twisted are easier to handle than fabrics made of extremely fine or heavy yarns which slip in the cutting and stitching. Fabrics with loosely twisted yarns and slick yarns, unless set in the finishing process, ravel badly and require special seam finishes.

Plain weave   Fabrics that are firmly woven in a plain weave with little or no difference between the right and wrong sides are the simplest to handle. Loosely woven fabrics and fabrics with weaves which form designs that require matching are more difficult. Diagonals and satins present special problems in laying the pattern. Crepes tend to slip when being cut and to stretch when being stitched.

Medium weight   Fabrics that are easiest to handle are medium-weight and not bulky. Heavy fabrics and those that are extremely light-weight, regardless of the fiber from which they are made, are difficult to handle. Bulky fabrics, even though they are lightweight, also present difficulties. For example, terry cloth, though made from medium-weight cotton yarn, would not be a good fabric for a beginner.

Smooth texture   Fabrics that are smooth but not slippery and that have no nap and little irregularity in the yarn are easier to handle than highly glazed or polished fabrics, which show pin or needle holes; stiff fabrics, such as organdy and taffeta; or pressed fabrics, such as felt.

Solid color   Fabrics of one color and no design give the fewest problems in laying the pattern, cutting the fabric, and assembling the units of the garment.

Small allover designs   If a designed rather than a plain fabric is preferred, one with a small allover design which requires no matching is the best choice for a beginner. The design should be one that has no variable lengthwise or crosswise effect, no diagonal effect, and no stripes or plaid. One advantage of fabrics with an allover design is that inaccuracies of stitching are less prominent.

qualities listed in the accompanying chart. Information about available fabrics is usually provided by the fabric and bolt labels and hang tags. Be sure to read these before making a purchase. If the labels do not give all of the facts you want, look for printed signs above the fabric display, or consult the salesperson or buyer. Obtain all the available information regarding fiber content, special fabric finishes, fabric width, and care instructions. This information will be helpful as you buy the fabric and as you cut, sew, wear, and care for your garment. Fiber content provides clues to pressing temperatures required during the construction process. Knowledge about fabric finish is helpful in straightening fabric and selecting construction techniques. You might find it helpful to refer to the charts on pages 60-65 and 78-79.

Fabric Width
It is important to check the width of a fabric you are considering. Fabric width is a major factor in determining the amount of yardage to

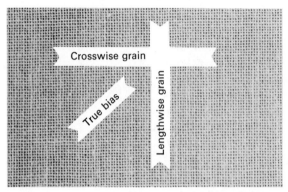

Courtesy Educational Bureau, Coats & Clark Inc.

Particularly when buying fabrics with permanent finishes, be certain before purchase that they have been finished in grain-perfect position.

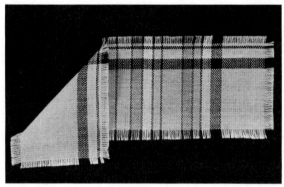

USDA Photo

When buying plaid fabrics, be certain to choose only those in which the design is woven or those which have been printed perfectly on grain.

buy and thus in estimating the total cost of the project.

Fabric width can vary considerably from bolt to bolt. For example, any fabric made of wool, whether woven or knitted, is usually 54 to 60 inches wide, though some are wider. Cotton and linen dress fabrics are usually 36 to 45 inches wide. Fabrics made of man-made fibers, however, may vary in width from 35 to 72 inches. Fabric blends of man-made and natural fibers are usually the same width as the fabrics of the natural fiber in the blend.

That is, a blend of polyester and wool is probably 54 to 60 inches, while a blend of acrylic and cotton is likely to be 36 to 45 inches wide.

Fabric width obviously affects the cost of a sewing project since less yardage is needed with wider fabrics. For example, 4 yards might be required of fabric that is only 36 inches wide, while just 2 yards of 54-inch fabric might be sufficient. Greater width usually permits more pattern pieces to be laid out side by side, thus requiring less yardage. A chart on the back of the pattern envelope indicates the yardage required for various fabric widths. This amount varies when all pattern pieces must be cut in a single direction as in corduroy, velvet, and fabrics printed or woven with a one-way design. (See the illustration on page 247.)

Fabric Grain

In selecting woven fabrics of any kind, it is important to check the fabric grain. Grain exists only in woven fabrics. A woven fabric is made by the interlacing of yarns which cross each other at right angles. These yarns, generally called threads, comprise the grain of the fabric. The lengthwise grain is firmer and less stretchy than the crosswise grain, because the lengthwise threads are stronger and form the foundation of the fabric. When the threads are at right angles to each other, the fabric hangs true and is said to be *grain perfect.*

Sometimes the fabric is pulled off grain during the finishing process. It is therefore worthwhile to evaluate the fabric grain before buying a fabric. This can be done by examining the threads closely. Do they appear to be at right angles to each other, or do they slant or curve? If the fabric is only slightly off grain, you may be able to straighten it as described in the next section. Generally it is better not to buy fabric that is badly off-grain. If the threads are cured in a curved or diagonal position, it is possible that such a fabric cannot be straightened. To determine whether a fabric has been cured, check the hang tag or label. Does the fabric have a permanent finish, such as crease resistance, easy care, or permanent press? If so, the grain has been permanently locked into position. The best solution for seriously distorted grain is not to buy the fabric.

If you are considering a fabric with a printed geometric design, such as checks or a plaid, there is one more detail to check. Has the design been printed on the straight grain? If the design is grain perfect, the same line of the design will repeat at exactly the same position all across the fabric width, that is, along a crosswise thread. Printed fabrics are generally less expensive than woven ones of comparable design. Unfortunately, a design printed off-grain cannot be straightened. Were you to buy such a fabric, you would have a difficult choice confronting you. If you ignored the grain and cut with the design, the result would be a garment off-grain which would not hang or fit correctly. If, on the other hand, you cut with the grain, the design would always appear crooked—a sight unpleasant to the eye. More importantly, sometimes the garment does not fit properly and is uncomfortable. It is best to avoid buying off-grain prints.

Straightening Fabric Grain

The good fit and attractive lines that give garments a professional appearance depend on grain perfection. Grain-perfect fabric must be kept in perfect position throughout the entire construction process in order to result in clothes that fit and hang correctly. An off-grain fabric should therefore be straightened before cutting unless the finish has permanently set the threads and made straightening impossible.

Making a Fabric Thread Perfect

The first step in straightening grain is to make the fabric thread perfect. *Thread perfection* means that the last crosswise thread at the end

A fabric is thread perfect when a single thread can be pulled from each end of the fabric, from selvage to selvage, without breaking.

of the fabric can be pulled all the way across the width of the fabric without breaking. A fabric must be made thread perfect at both ends before it can be made grain perfect. You can make your fabric thread perfect by tearing, pulling a thread and cutting along the crosswise line where the thread was removed, raveling a thread, or cutting along a prominent crosswise thread or line. Choose the method that seems the easiest, remembering that some methods are unsuited to certain fabrics.

Tearing

Tearing is a method that quickly makes a fabric thread perfect, but some fabrics cannot be torn. Check first to see whether your fabric *can* be torn. With some fabrics, tearing would damage the finish or distort the grain. Examples include sheer, pile, ribbed, loosely woven, and a few designed fabrics.

To use the tearing method, first clip through the selvage about ½ inch from the side edge of the fabric. With a quick, firm motion, tear the rest of the way across the fabric to the opposite selvage, which may be clipped. The fabric will tear along one crosswise thread, thereby making it thread perfect.

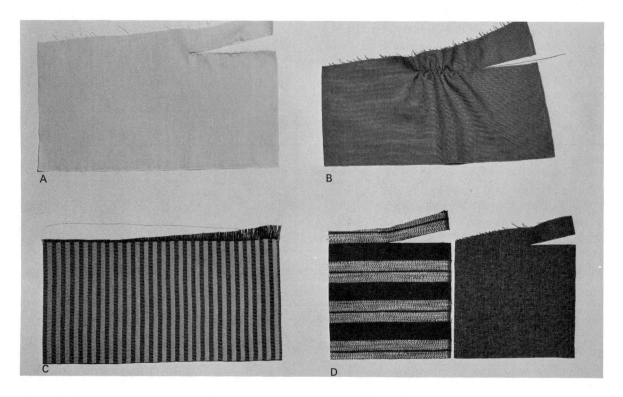

Fabrics may be made thread perfect by (A) tearing, (B) pulling a thread and cutting along the pulled area, (C) raveling, or (D) cutting along a prominent thread.

Pulling a Thread

This method of making a fabric thread perfect can be used safely on any fabric in which a thread can be pulled. It is often the only method that can be used without distorting the grain or finish, but it is time consuming. Pulling a thread requires picking out one or two crosswise threads with a pin, and then pulling the thread gently with one hand while slipping the fabric along the thread with the other hand. Whenever possible, pull the thread across the entire width of the fabric. If the thread breaks, cut the fabric with shears along the *run*, or path, made by the thread up to the point where it broke. Then pick up the loose thread end and resume the pulling and cutting. Threads are more easily pulled from some fabrics than others, depending on fabric construction and finish.

Raveling a Thread

Still another method for making fabric thread perfect can be used for fabrics which ravel easily. Crosswise threads can be unraveled until one crosswise thread can be drawn off the entire width of the fabric from selvage to selvage. When you have accomplished this, you can cut off the uneven fringed edge. The fabric is then thread perfect.

Cutting Along a Prominent Thread

An easy method applicable to certain fabrics is to cut across the end of the fabric along a crosswise thread or line that is distinct enough to be followed precisely. This method can often be used with woven plaid or striped fabrics. It is useful when any type of color differentiation makes the crosswise threads easy to follow.

Woven, untreated fabric can be made grain perfect by pressing across the folded fabric from the selvages toward the center fold. If possible, work on a broad, padded pressing table.

Making a Fabric Grain Perfect

After the fabric has been made thread perfect, the next step in the fabric-straightening process is checking the grain perfection of the fabric itself. To do this, lay the open fabric on a table. A fabric is off grain if the ends are not square, or are not at right angles to the selvage. Its grain perfection can be checked against the ends and edges of a square-cornered table, or a T-square may be laid so that one crosswise and one lengthwise edge of the fabric are aligned with the T-square. If the grain is not perfect, the fabric can be straightened by one or several of the following methods.

Pulling on the Diagonal

This method for straightening fabric can be used on short lengths of fabric other than wool. Determine whether the crosswise ends of the fabric are uneven when the fabric is folded lengthwise. If they are, identify the shortest ends. Then pull along the true bias of the fabric at intervals from one short end to the other until threads are once again at right angles to each other. Press the fabric with steam to set the yarns in grain-perfect position.

Steam Pressing

Fold the fabric in half lengthwise. Then machine-baste or pin the selvages and thread-perfect crosswise ends together. Complete the straightening of the fabric in the following manner:

1. Lay the fabric lengthwise on the ironing board or padded pressing table, with the selvages straight along the front edge of the

263

A fabric is grain perfect when a T-square can be laid to fit simultaneously along the selvage and along a thread-perfect end of the fabric.

board. If possible, the board or table should be wide enough to allow the full half-width of the fabric to lie flat.

2. Steam-press, moving the iron straight back across the folded fabric from the selvage to the fold, as shown in the illustration on page 263, at all times keeping the crosswise threads perpendicular to the selvage. Use a steam iron or a dry iron with a dampened cheesecloth *under* the folded fabric. If the board is not wide enough for the full half-width of the fabric, press the part along the selvage first. Then move the fabric

forward on the board, and press the part along the fold. Avoid pressing a sharp crease on the fold line which will later have to be removed.

3. When one section of the fabric has been pressed, move it along the length of the board, and fold it over so that another section may be laid flat for pressing. Be sure not to stretch either the upper or lower layer of fabric. It may sometimes be necessary to turn the folded fabric over and repeat the steam pressing on the other side.

4. Check for grain perfection, and repeat the pressing if necessary.

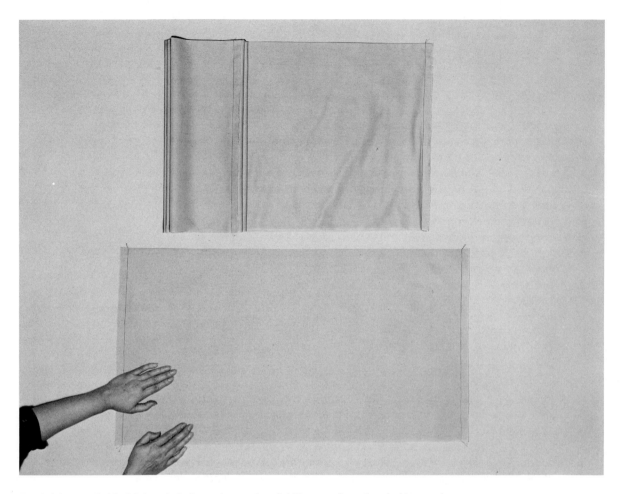

To shrink a washable fabric, stitch the ends together, fold it accordian-pleat fashion, and submerge it in warm water. Smooth the fabric as it dries, and press it crosswise to retain its grain perfection.

Submerging in Water

This fabric-straightening method is applicable to washable fabrics only. Fold the fabric in half lengthwise, and baste the selvages or crosswise ends together. Then place the fabric in warm water and soak it until thoroughly saturated. Press the water from the fabric by flattening it between your hands or by wrapping it in a terry towel. Do not wring it. On a flat surface, smooth the fabric gently with your hands from the selvage to the fold to ensure grain perfection. Smooth it at intervals while it is drying, keeping it on a flat surface.

When the fabric is completely dry, press it with the steam iron on the crosswise grain. Then remove the bastings.

Although washable, some fabrics such as corduroy may crush if this straightening process is applied. In such instances, it might be better to have the straightening done by a professional drycleaner.

Preshrinking Fabrics

Most fabrics today are either man-made, blends, or natural fibers which have been

SHRINKING WOOLEN FABRICS BY THE LONDON METHOD

1. *Prepare the fabric as follows:*
   a. *Make the fabric thread perfect.*
   b. *Fold the fabric lengthwise, wrong side out, with selvages and ends even.*
   c. *Machine-baste the two layers together at both ends.*
   d. *Lay the fabric on the table as smoothly as possible.*
2. *Moisten the fabric in a wet sheet as follows:*
   a. *Spread a wet sheet, folded in half lengthwise and with excess water wrung out, on the dry fabric with the end of the sheet about 8 inches from the end of the fabric.*
   b. *Fold the end of the fabric over the end of the sheet, and continue folding the fabric and sheet together for the entire length.*
   c. *Cover with paper or Turkish towel to prevent the fabric from drying too quickly. Let it stand.*
   d. *After several hours unroll the sheet and fabric, and press the fabric with the hands from the selvages to the fold on the crosswise grain. If the fabric is off grain, force the threads back into their original position.*
   e. *Refold the fabric, and let it stand until the wool has been thoroughly dampened.*
3. *Dry the fabric on a flat surface as follows:*
   a. *After six or eight hours, open the roll and remove the sheet.*
   b. *Check the grain lines to be sure they are straight, and smooth out the fabric.*
   c. *Let the fabric dry while it is flat on the table.*
   d. *Smooth with the hands occasionally, from the selvages to the fold on the crosswise grain, to ensure grain perfection. This will make pressing unnecessary on most fabrics.*

given special stabilizing finishes making them easily cared for and crease resistant. Therefore, they need no preshrinking. Check the label or the hang tag for shrinkage information. If the label indicates a 2 percent or less shrinkage expectancy, the preshrinking of a fabric is relatively unnecessary. If the percentage of shrinkage or finishing process is not indicated, assume that the fabric needs to be preshrunk. This situation most often applies to cotton fabrics in the low price range and to some knitted fabrics. Special problems with knits are discussed in Chapter 21, pages 412 and 414.

Washable Fabrics

You may preshrink an untreated washable fabric by folding it and submerging it in warm water until it is thoroughly wet. Remove the excess water by blotting or by wrapping the fabric in a terry-cloth towel. Avoid wringing the fabric or hanging it to dry, since doing so would distort the grain. With your hands, smooth the fabric gently from selvage to fold to ensure that the grain is in correct position. Allow the fabric to dry on a flat surface, smoothing it occasionally. Steam-press the fabric when it is dry. Check again to determine that it is grain perfect before cutting.

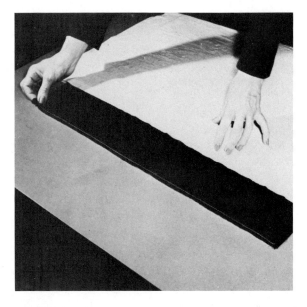

Wool fabric can be shrunk by laying a wet sheet over the fabric (left). The fabric and sheet are rolled together for several hours (right) so that the dampness is absorbed by the wool. The fabric is straightened by smoothing with the hands during the drying process.

Woolen Fabrics

Woolen fabrics are often preshrunk by the manufacturer, as will be indicated on the hang tag or bolt. If you should purchase a woolen fabric that has not been preshrunk, it can be taken to a professional drycleaner. Woolens are most likely to retain their new, finished look through the preshrinking process if the job is handled professionally. If you decide to shrink woolen fabric as a learning experience connected with your project, follow the steps listed on the chart titled "Shrinking Woolen Fabrics by the London Method," page 266. Also see the illustrations above.

Pressing Fabrics

To be assured of having the garment cut accurately, it is usually necessary to press the fabric before laying the pattern. Press out any wrinkles, and press out the center fold unless the fabric has been folded wrong side out and does not need refolding to lay the pattern.

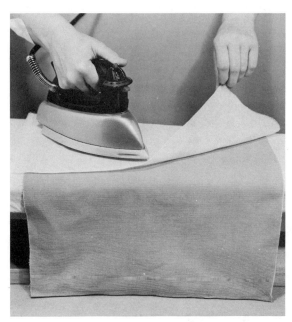

Courtesy Sunbeam Mfg. Co.

As a final step before laying the pattern, press existing wrinkles and folds from the grain-perfect fabric.

267

1. Fabric width is an important factor in determining the required yardage since the wider the fabric, the less yardage necessary for a particular garment.

2. Fabric ready for the pattern to be laid on it is thread perfect, grain perfect, preshrunk, and pressed.

3. Fabric must be made thread perfect before it can be made grain perfect for use in a project.

4. Choices for making a fabric thread perfect include tearing, pulling a crosswise thread before cutting, raveling a thread, and cutting along a prominent thread.

5. A fabric can be considered thread perfect if the last crosswise thread at each end can be pulled all the way across the width of the fabric.

6. In a grain-perfect fabric the lengthwise threads and the crosswise threads are perpendicular to each other.

7. If a fabric label does not in some way indicate a shrinkage expectancy of less than 2 percent, it must be assumed that the fabric requires preshrinking.

12 Pattern Layout, Cutting, and Marking

After a pattern and fabric are selected, the next step in a clothing construction project is to study carefully all the information accompanying the pattern. The pattern envelope, the pattern guide sheet, and the pattern pieces themselves all contain essential information on pattern layout, cutting, and marking.

What are the main considerations in laying out a pattern?

How do you determine which layout to follow?

How can you identify the right side of the fabric?

How can you check the accuracy of a crosswise fold? A lengthwise fold?

What is the solution when the pattern layout calls for both a lengthwise and a crosswise fold?

How do you avoid cutting two sleeves for the same armhole?

What is the correct procedure for pinning the pattern to the fabric?

Decisions About Layout, Cutting, and Marking

Particularly when you are learning to sew, it is helpful to follow closely the pattern directions for layout, cutting, and marking. Even these steps, however, can offer opportunity for creative decisions. As you gain sewing experience, you may on occasion want to adapt a pattern layout or perhaps design your own.

Considerable variation is possible as long as the basic principles of pattern layout are maintained. Other decisions may be required as to the most effective and convenient marking method. A knowledge of the layout, cutting, and marking procedures will help you arrive at good decisions where needed. It will also help you to interpret the pattern directions.

Preparing the Pattern

The pattern envelope contains pattern pieces for various views of your selected pattern as well as a guide sheet. The pattern guide sheet offers a number of diagrams, or pattern layouts, from which you can choose one. Each shows the precise placement of the pattern pieces for one of the views. Like any set of well-planned instructions, the layout will save you considerable time, trouble, and expense if you follow it carefully.

Choosing the Pattern Layout

You must first select the specific diagram to follow. Your pattern size, the view, or style,

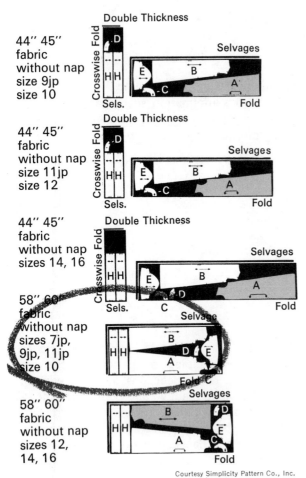

44" 45"
fabric
without nap
size 9jp
size 10

44" 45"
fabric
without nap
size 11jp
size 12

44" 45"
fabric
without nap
sizes 14, 16

58" 60"
fabric
without nap
sizes 7jp,
9jp, 11jp
size 10

58" 60"
fabric
without nap
sizes 12,
14, 16

Courtesy Simplicity Pattern Co., Inc.

For easy reference, encircle the pattern layout for your pattern view and fabric width.

you have chosen, and the type and width of your fabric will determine your specific layout plan. For example, if you have decided upon View B, have purchased a size 10 pattern, and have selected fabric which has no nap and is 58 inches wide, you first will look on your guide sheet under the major heading *View B.* Beneath this heading you will see a variety of layouts for a range of sizes and fabric widths. In this case, select the cutting layout labeled *fabric without nap, size 10,* and *58 inches.*

For quick reference while working, encircle the layout you have chosen. Study it

thoroughly before proceeding. Check whether you can understand all that it tells you to do. For an explanation of how to interpret a pattern, see page 271.

Selecting Pattern Pieces

It is important to become familiar with the pattern itself before attempting to use it. Identify each pattern piece by a comparison with the diagram of that piece on the envelope or the guide sheet. Select the pieces that are required for the view you have chosen. If the small pieces are printed together on one sheet of paper, cut out the ones you will use, leaving a ½-inch margin beyond the cutting line. To avoid confusion, return to the envelope any pieces not needed. If the pattern pieces you will use have become wrinkled in the envelope, press them smooth with a slightly warm iron.

Planning Alterations

Few patterns fit perfectly without some alteration, because patterns are made to standard measurements and most people vary somewhat from those standards. The alterations necessary should be made in the pattern before laying it on the fabric or as the garment is being cut. If the alterations are made with accuracy, cutting to fit will assure a successful fit of the garment.

Chapter 10, "Pattern Selection and Fit," gives detailed instructions for determining necessary alterations and for making them. If the alterations are to be made by shifting the pattern during the cutting procedure, the pattern layout must be planned to provide sufficient fabric space for this procedure (see pages 250-253).

Folding the Fabric

The fabric, having been straightened, preshrunk, and pressed as needed, is ready to be folded according to the guide-sheet instructions. In folding, handle the fabric carefully to prevent unnecessary stretching or distortion

PATTERN SYMBOLS

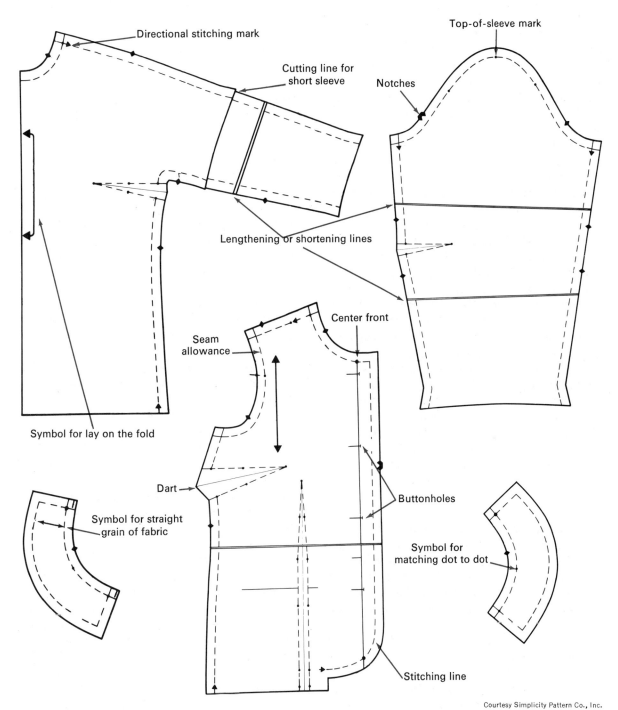

Directional stitching mark

Top-of-sleeve mark

Cutting line for short sleeve

Notches

Lengthening or shortening lines

Symbol for lay on the fold

Seam allowance

Center front

Dart

Symbol for straight grain of fabric

Buttonholes

Symbol for matching dot to dot

Stitching line

Courtesy Simplicity Pattern Co., Inc.

of the fabric grain. It is important to keep the grain line straight throughout the folding and cutting process.

Determining the Right and Wrong Sides

Before you fold the fabric, identify its *right* and *wrong* sides. Some fabrics have a distinct right side easily distinguished by weave, color, design, or texture. Other fabrics are reversible, so that either side can be right and the choice is yours. Still other fabrics have right and wrong sides which are not readily distinguishable. With this last group, it really does not matter which side you select as right as long as you are consistent. You can, however, look for certain clues as to which side of the fabric the manufacturer considered right:

1. Observe which side is out when your fabric is folded on the bolt. Be sure to note, however, that whether the right side is in or out usually depends on the fiber from which it is made. Cotton, linen, man-made fabrics, and many blends and bonded fabrics are displayed with the right sides out. Woolens, silks, and many knits come with the right sides in to protect their surface.

2. Examine the selvage, which is usually smoother on the right side than on the wrong.

3. Examine the weave closely. The right side usually looks more finished than the wrong side, which may contain rough spots, long yarns, and other imperfections.

Kinds of Fabric Folds

After determining which is the right side of the fabric, consult your pattern layout to determine the kinds of fabric folds necessary for the laying of the pattern. The layout will show various pieces of the pattern laid either on a single thickness of the fabric or on a double thickness.

When the fabric is spread out flat, usually with the right side up, in a single thickness, it is called *open fabric.* Because a layout on single thickness requires more cutting than one in which two identical pieces are cut together and because there is always some chance of variation when a process is repeated, this type of layout is used only when others are not practical. For example, a design which is not the same on both sides of the figure, as a right and left front, must be cut on a single thickness.

While a single thickness eliminates folding, a double thickness involves one or more of the following folds: lengthwise fold, crosswise fold, double fold, off-center fold, bias fold, and combination fold. The most common of these folds are considered here. Your layout will indicate which are required for your pattern.

Fold a fabric wrong side out except when the matching of designs is necessary. Doing so will make the wrong side readily available for the pattern markings and will protect the right side from soil and damage. Further, this method of folding provides for easy and immediate stitching of identical garment pieces that are to be joined, such as garment back or front pieces to be joined along a center seam.

All folds must be made exactly on either a lengthwise or a crosswise thread of the fabric so that the garment pieces will be cut on grain. With the exception of center lengthwise and center crosswise folds, each fold should be checked. To check, measure on a perpendicular line from the fold to the selvage or to the thread-perfect end at intervals. If the fold is straight, the distance measured from fold to selvage or end is the same at all points.

Lengthwise Fold

A lengthwise fold is a fold along a lengthwise thread with the thread-perfect ends of the two thicknesses of fabric even. There are two kinds of lengthwise folds: a lengthwise center fold, in which the selvages are even and parallel to the fold, and a fold that is less than half the fabric width, in which one selvage is parallel to the other and the width of the fold is adapted to the pattern pieces.

KINDS OF FABRIC FOLDS

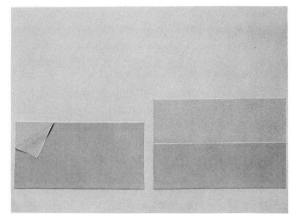

LENGTHWISE FOLDS

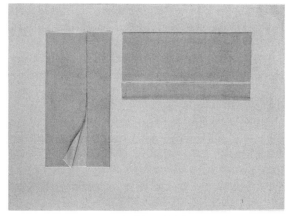

DOUBLE FOLDS

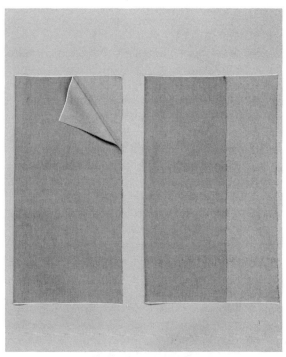

CROSSWISE FOLDS

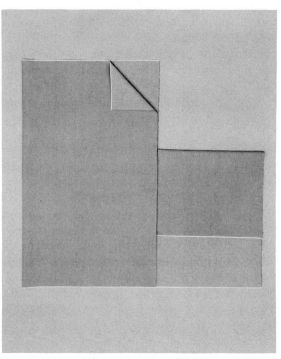

COMBINATION FOLDS

Fabric folds are determined by the pattern layout. In general, folds are made so that the right sides of fabric are together.

Crosswise Fold

A crosswise fold is made along a crosswise thread with perfect alignment of the two selvages. This fold is indicated when the pattern piece is too wide for a lengthwise fold or when it would best accommodate the fabric design. Crosswise folds include: a crosswise center fold, which results in two complete, full-width layers of fabric and even alignment to the thread-perfect ends; and an off-center crosswise fold, less than half the fabric length, in which one thread-perfect end is parallel to the other and the length of the fold is adapted to the pattern piece.

Double Fold

When several pattern pieces are to be cut on a fold, the double fold is often indicated. A double fold is made by opening the fabric out flat and folding in the two ends or the two sides. This fold allows the ends or selvages to meet or lie parallel to each other. The length or width of a double fold is determined by the pattern piece it is to accommodate. The fold line must be parallel to the selvages or straight ends.

If you are making double folds where selvages or fabric ends do not meet, make the folds grain perfect by folding exactly on a lengthwise thread or crosswise thread. Keep the folds parallel along the full length or width of the fabric.

Combination Fold

Sometimes a pattern layout calls for more than one kind of fold as well as an area of fabric of single thickness. Many combinations are possible within a layout. See the illustration at the lower right on page 273.

Pattern Layout

The pattern layout which you encircled shows the most workable arrangement for placing your pattern pieces on the width and type of fabric you have chosen. It is essential that you follow this layout, particularly for beginning projects. Otherwise, you may make serious cutting errors, such as cutting garment pieces in half by accidentally placing them on selvages rather than on folds or cutting two sleeves for a single armhole.

Placing the Pattern on the Fabric

It is helpful to plan the entire layout before actually pinning any pattern pieces to the fabric. To do this, place all the pattern pieces on the fabric tentatively in the position which the layout on your guide sheet indicates. If two thicknesses of fabric are to be cut at one time, lay the pattern pieces on the wrong side of the fabric. If a single thickness of fabric is to be cut, lay the pattern on the right side.

Lay the large pattern pieces first, fitting the smaller ones in afterwards. The wide ends of pattern pieces are usually placed at the cut ends of the fabric. Place the pieces as closely together as you can without having them overlap.

Check the placement of each pattern piece by measuring to determine that the ends of the straight-grain-of-fabric markings are an equal distance from the edge of the fabric.

Make sure you observe the direction of the grain in laying the pattern. You can check the direction of the grain by these standards:

1. The lengthwise lines of the garment are usually placed on the lengthwise grain of the fabric.

2. Facings, yokes, pockets, collars, cuffs, and bands are usually positioned identically with the garment piece to which they will be attached. They may sometimes be placed on the bias or opposite grain for decorative effect.

3. Interfacings and reinforcing strips are usually placed on grain that is identical to the grain of the garment piece to which they will be applied. There are two exceptions: Hem cushioning strips are always cut on a true bias, and reinforcing strips for pocket openings are always cut on the lengthwise grain to prevent stretching.

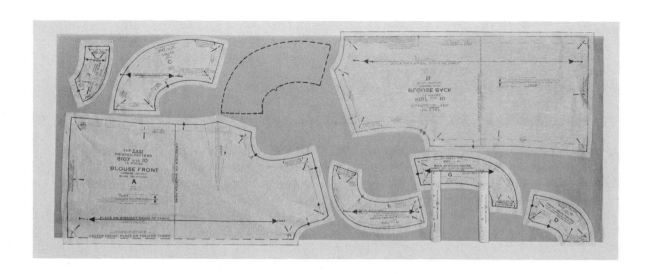

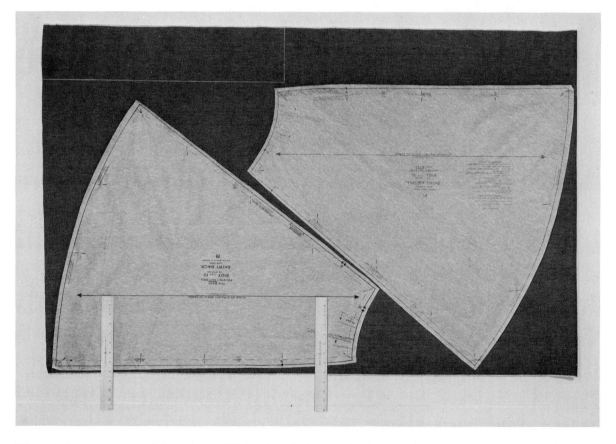

When placing a pattern on plain, unnapped fabric, place the large ends of pattern pieces toward the ends of the fabric, measure each piece to be certain it is on the straight grain of the fabric, and reserve space for pieces which require double cutting.

1. *Planning the entire pattern layout before pinning and cutting any of the pieces ensures a minimum of cutting errors.*
2. *When fabric is folded into double folds, a combination of folds, or a combination of a fold and a single thickness, each fold is correctly made no wider than required for the pattern pieces which will be placed on it.*
3. *A pattern layout in which each pattern piece is placed correctly on the grain of the fabric is essential to a grain-perfect garment. Check each piece for accuracy.*
4. *The pattern pieces can be most easily fitted onto the fabric if the larger pieces are laid first and the smaller pieces fitted in afterwards.*
5. *Cutting duplicate pieces together on a double thickness of fabric whenever possible helps to prevent cutting errors. If duplicate pieces must be cut on a single layer, the pattern piece must be turned over before the duplicate is cut.*
6. *To prevent running out of fabric before the completion of the layout, the pattern pieces should be placed as closely together as possible.*
7. *The wide ends of pattern pieces are generally best positioned at the cut end of the fabric.*
8. *If pattern alterations are to be made by shifting the pattern, allow space in the layout for making the alterations.*

4. Linings are placed on grain that is identical with that of the corresponding piece of outer fabric.

If the pattern pieces do not all seem to fit onto the fabric, check for wasted space between them. Perhaps some pattern pieces could be dovetailed. Margins can be overlapped without affecting the shape of the garment pieces. Usually, after slight adjustments, it is possible to fit the pattern onto the fabric successfully.

If the layout requires some of the pieces to be placed on a single thickness of fabric and some on the fold, position first those pieces which are planned for cutting on a single thickness. Mark the area with pins or chalk and remove the pattern pieces. Then, without cutting, fold the fabric as indicated in the layout and place the remaining pieces on the folded fabric beyond the pin or chalk mark. As you may discover, it is easy to over-estimate the fabric needed for the single thickness and then to run short of fabric for the remaining pieces.

If the layout requires both a lengthwise and a crosswise fold, tentatively lay the pattern pieces on the lengthwise fold first and then refold the fabric to arrange the remaining pieces on the crosswise fold. The extra minutes spent working out the complete layout ahead of any cutting prevent serious cutting errors.

Interpreting the Pattern Layout

Suppose in attempting to follow your pattern layout you see one of the drawings illustrated on page 277. What do these sketches mean? How do you follow them? The pattern guide sheet sometimes does not explain certain sketches or markings. The following drawings and explanations will help you interpret some of the typical layouts you might encounter.

In each case be sure *not to cut the fabric until you are confident that there will be adequate space for every pattern piece.*

Pattern layout 1 (right) requires both lengthwise and crosswise folds. Fold the fabric so there is just enough room for pieces A, C, and F. Mark the area with pins or chalk. After cutting the major pieces, refold the fabric and position the remaining pieces. Note that you will have two large pieces of fabric with which to work.

In layout 2, piece E extends past the fabric, indicating that it is to be cut after a future fold is made in the fabric. This fold can be made and piece E cut after pieces A, B, C, and D have been cut and removed from the cutting area.

If you are cutting two pieces of a kind, such as sleeves, from a *single* thickness of fabric, be sure to turn over the pattern before cutting the second piece, as shown in layout 3 on the right. This will prevent cutting two sleeves for the same armhole.

Notice also that layout 3 indicates how to cut a garment piece which does not lend itself to cutting on a fold. To accomplish this cutting maneuver, first cut pieces A, B, and C. Then open the fabric under pattern piece D to single thickness and cut piece D twice.

A dotted area the same shape as an adjacent pattern piece indicates the pattern piece is used twice so that two identical pieces may be cut on a single thickness. In layout 3 pattern pieces D and G will be used twice. For correct placement the second time, mark the outline with chalk or pins to reserve the space.

For cutting layouts which require a double fold and an area of single thickness, use folds such as those in layout 4. Part of this layout is placed on a lengthwise fold and part on a single thickness. Fold the fabric so that there is just enough room in the folded area for the pattern pieces requiring a double thickness. This will leave one large area of single-thickness fabric rather than a number of relatively useless scraps.

TYPICAL PATTERN LAYOUTS

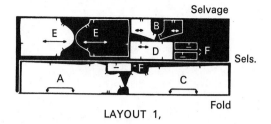

LAYOUT 1,

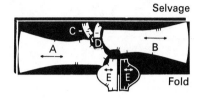

LAYOUT 2,

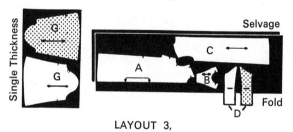

LAYOUT 3,

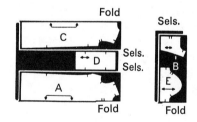

LAYOUT 4

Courtesy Simplicity Pattern Co., Inc.

Designing Your Own Pattern Layout

There may be times when you will want to plan your own pattern layout. Such times may occur when your fabric is much wider than any shown on the guide sheet, when you are combining two different patterns, when you eliminate many optional pattern pieces shown in the layout, or when you make major pattern alterations.

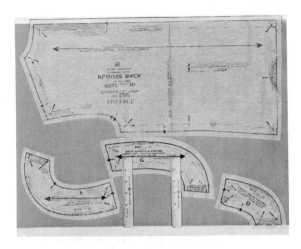

Pin the pattern pieces to the fabric so that each piece is straight with the edge of the fabric or with the fabric grain. Recheck to see that the arrow heads at both ends of each pattern piece are parallel with the fabric edge. Pin the corners of the pattern to the fabric, and insert enough pins to hold the edges of the pattern flat for cutting.

These occasions offer opportunity to experiment. You can use your own creativity to design a layout that is workable while being as economical as possible with the amount of fabric used. Try several folds and layouts until you find the most suitable one for your fabric. Lay your pattern according to the ''Guidelines for Laying a Pattern'' given on page 276. Place on a fold of the fabric all pattern pieces marked for a fold.

Pinning the Pattern

After all the pattern pieces have been arranged on the fabric, you are ready to pin them in place. Make sure that the fabric is on a firm surface so that the pinning process will not stretch the fabric out of shape. Pick up only a few threads with each pin to keep the fabric and the pattern flat and grain perfect. Be certain that all pattern pieces are pinned in place or that space is reserved for them before you start cutting. Completing the pinning first will reduce the chances of cutting errors.

Pin Pattern Pieces Along the Fold

When pinning pattern pieces to the fabric, first smooth the pattern lightly from the fold and place pins along the fold line at 6- to 8-inch intervals.

Pin and Check Grain Line

So that each piece of a garment will be grain perfect, the pattern must be pinned to the fabric with precision. To accomplish a satisfactory degree of accuracy, pin each pattern piece, excluding those laid on a fold, to the fabric at the point of the arrow marked *Straight Grain of Fabric.* This anchors the pattern piece on the grain line. Insert the first pin at the end of the arrow toward the wider end of the pattern piece. Then pivot the pattern on the first pin until the point at the other end of the arrow measures the same distance from the straight edge of the fabric as does the end already pinned. Check the accuracy with a yardstick or ruler. Then pin the point at the narrower end of the fabric.

Pin Corners of Pattern Pieces

Smooth the pattern in all directions from the straight-grain-of-fabric marking. Fasten the pattern to the fabric by inserting pins diagonally into the corners. This will hold the pattern close to the fabric to provide an accurate cutting line.

Pin Edges of Pattern Pieces

Except in the corners, place the pins on the grain of the fabric just inside of, and at right angles to, the cutting line of the pattern piece, with the points of the pins toward the edge of the pattern. Avoid letting the pins extend over the cutting line where they would interfere with the cutting. Pin close enough to hold the pattern firmly to the fabric but not so close as to make the pattern appear bumpy. The number of pins will depend upon the fabric and the shape of the pattern piece. Sheer or slippery fabrics require more closely spaced pinning than firm fabrics; curves require more pinning than straight edges.

1. *Cut directionally with the grain of the fabric whenever possible. This is the same direction in which the seams will be stitched, usually from the wider part of the pattern to the narrower, and is indicated on many patterns by arrows on the seam lines.*

2. *As you cut, hold the fabric down flat with your other hand close to the edge of the pattern. To prevent slipping of the fabric, walk around the table rather than move the fabric and pattern during the cutting process.*

3. *Use long, firm cutting strokes on straight edges to obtain a smooth edge. Use shorter strokes for curves. Avoid closing the shears completely, except when cutting to an exact point.*

4. *Cut the notches away from the pattern rather than into the seam allowances. Cut multiple notches as one. If there is not room to cut the notches out, they may be marked with tracing tools or a pencil, or they may be indicated by a short clip at the edge of the fabric.*

5. *Cut slash and clip lines later, when you are ready to attach an edge which requires slashing or clipping to another section of the garment.*

6. *Indicate center lines, fold lines, and the top of the sleeve by clipping ⅛ inch into the edge of the fabric. A notch may be cut instead of clipping, if preferred.*

7. *If certain pieces are to be altered by shifting the pattern, keep your plans for altering in mind during the cutting and shift the pattern or mark the fabric as may be necessary.*

8. *Avoid cutting into the fabric beyond the pattern corner, because such a cut may spoil an area of the fabric from which another garment piece is to be cut.*

What steps must be completed before you start cutting?

How do you cut and mark the fabric?

What type of shears is best for cutting out a garment?

What are the various methods of transferring the pattern markings to the fabric?

How can you tell which construction-detail marks you need to transfer to the fabric?

Cutting the Garment

When you are ready to cut your garment, there are some basic guidelines to follow. Remember that you are trying to maintain the grain of the fabric as you work with it. Fabric grain can easily be distorted or stretched when it is handled excessively or carelessly. To preserve the grain, handle the fabric as little as possible, particularly before it is stay-stitched.

Cutting lines on a pattern are indicated in different ways. Most printed patterns have a single or double *solid* line to follow for cutting. A perforated pattern which has no cutting lines to follow is cut along the outer edge.

Accurate and easy cutting requires the use of sharp cutting shears with a bent handle. Such shears permit keeping the fabric and pattern flat on the table and allow you to cut accurately. Pinking shears should not be used to cut out a garment because they distort fabric grain, are difficult to handle, and yield inaccurate lines for stitching. Cut your

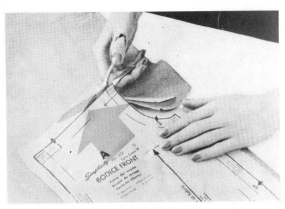

Courtesy Simplicity Pattern Co., Inc.

When cutting the pieces of a garment, use shears with bent handles and follow the arrows on the pattern which direct you to cut with the grain of the fabric.

garment according to the "Guidelines for Cutting a Garment" given on page 279.

Marking the Fabric

Have you ever been lost because a street or road was not well marked? Consider how welcome the following road markers are to a driver under the conditions given: the yellow center line during a dense fog; the hairpin curve symbol along a narrow unfamiliar road; bright reflectors indicating a barricade on a dark night.

To the seamstress the pattern markings are similarly important. They show where and how to place sewing details. The few minutes that it takes to transfer the construction details from pattern to fabric is time well spent. During the construction process, the ease and convenience with which you are able to follow clearly made markings will prevent confusion, guesswork, and sewing errors.

When to Mark

A few of the pattern markings served their purpose as the pattern was laid and the cutting was done. Examples are center front, fold lines, and straight-grain-of-fabric markings. However, most other markings are construction markings and need to be transferred from the pattern onto the fabric. This is done after the garment pieces have been cut and before the pattern is removed from the fabric.

What to Mark

There are three kinds of markings which should be transferred to the fabric: shaping details, construction details, and position details. The shaping details include darts, tucks, pleats, ease, and gathers. The position details which need to be transferred are pockets, buttons and buttonholes, and lines for applied decorations. The construction details which you will need to mark are slash and clip lines, corners, and short curves. Straight seam lines do not need to be marked by hand since a sewing-machine attachment can do the job better. However, sharp curves, sharp corners, or other seam lines which are difficult to stitch with the seam guide require marking.

Methods of Marking

There are a variety of methods from which to choose when transferring the markings. They include tracing paper and tracing wheel, tailor's tacks, pins, marking chalk and pencil, pressing, and machine basting. Each of these methods is described below with the exception of machine basting, which is described on page 297.

Each marking method has its advantages and limitations. There is no one method that works best on all fabrics. The method to select for your fabric depends on the characteristics of the fabric and the fabric finish. For example, the method which gives a distinct, clear line on a plain weave of solid color may be invisible on a bulky tweed. A method that works effectively on velveteen or corduroy may permanently damage a more delicate, sheer fabric.

It is a good idea to experiment on scraps of fabric with several marking techniques which you think might be suitable for the fabric. Then evaluate the results. Do the markings leave permanent imprints or damage the fabric in any way? Does a mark intended only for the wrong side of a fabric show through to the right side of the fabric? Does a method intended to mark two layers of fabric simultaneously produce marks sufficiently visible to follow on both layers? Consideration of these questions will help you choose the type of marks which are best for your garment.

Tracing Paper and Tracing Wheel

Dressmaker's tracing paper and a tracing wheel provide a simple way to transfer pattern markings to most fabrics. The paper, available in packages of assorted colors, has a waxy surface that is transferred to the fabric usually by means of a tracing wheel. A ruler

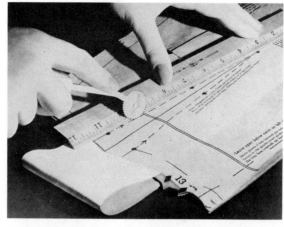

Courtesy Simplicity Pattern Co., Inc.

Tracing wheel and tracing paper are simple, speedy, and accurate marking agents. Before using them on light-colored or sheer fabrics, however, consider whether they will mark the fabric in such a way as to show on the finished garment.

GUIDELINES FOR USING TRACING TOOLS

1. *Place tracing paper on the fabric with the face of the paper on the wrong side of the fabric.*
2. *For simultaneously marking two pieces of fabric with right sides together, fold a strip of tracing paper, right sides together. Slip one end of the folded strip under the fabric and the other end between the top layer of the fabric and the pattern.*
3. *Trace markings with the tracing wheel, going over the lines only once, with firm pressure. Use a ruler as a guide for the tracing of all straight lines. If the center line of the dart is marked first, it will be easier to retain the pattern position while the other two lines of the dart are marked.*
4. *Indicate ends of stitching by termination lines at right angles to the stitching line.*
5. *Mark uncut notches by a line perpendicular to the edge through the point of the notch.*
6. *Retrace markings on hard-to-mark fabrics as follows: Turn back the pattern and top layer of the tracing paper, and retrace the markings on the top layer of fabric. The underlayer of fabric will be marked more distinctly.*
7. *Use a needle-point wheel without paper to mark fabrics that will retain the pricked marks of the wheel. Use a smooth-edged wheel for marking lightweight fragile fabrics.*

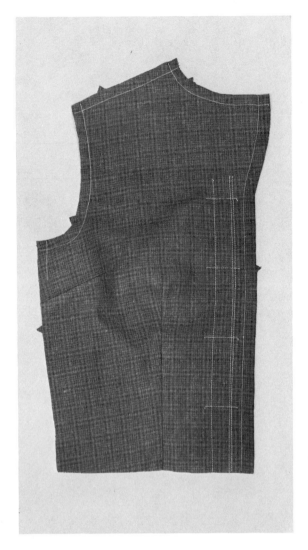

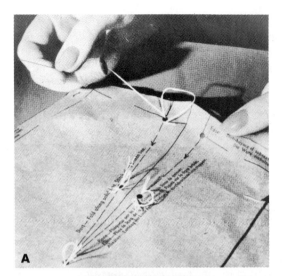

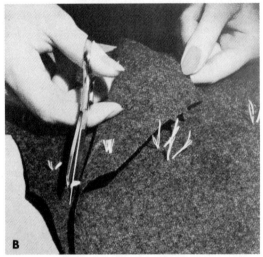

Photos courtesy Simplicity Pattern Co., Inc.

Tracing marks made on the wrong side of the fabric can be machine-basted into the garment, producing visible, but removable, marks on the right side of the garment.

Tailor's tacks, hand-inserted stitches made through the pattern and fabric (A), and clipped apart (B), are an effective means of marking white, sheer, napped, or pile fabrics.

or other straight edge used with the paper and wheel assists in making straight lines.

Before marking your fabric, test the tracing paper on a scrap of the fabric to determine the correct color and amount of pressure for a delicate, visible line. It is important to select a color of tracing paper that is inconspicuous but visible on the fabric. Usually,

this, means only one shade lighter or darker than the fabric to be marked. If, despite your best precautions, you are left with a tracing-paper mark on the right side of the fabric which you cannot remove, it is advisable to seek the help of a professional drycleaner.

Use strips of the tracing paper covering only the area to be marked so that smudges from the waxy surface are not accidentally left on the rest of the fabric. Be sure to place the colored, or waxy, side of the paper against the *wrong* side of the fabric (see the section "Determining the Right and Wrong Sides" on page 272). Work on a firm surface for accurate marking, and protect the table with cardboard, a sheet of heavy plastic, or a magazine.

To mark fabrics successfully by this method, follow the rules in the "Guidelines for Using Tracing Tools" on page 281.

Tailor's Tacks

The method of transferring pattern markings to fabric with loops of thread is called tailor's tacking. Making tailor's tacks is time consuming and for most fabrics less accurate than tracing paper. However, it is sometimes the best marking technique for use on white, sheer, napped, and pile fabrics and other fabrics that might otherwise be hard to mark. The tacks may be made through one or two layers of fabric. Soft cotton thread, such as darning cotton, stays in place better than smoother varieties, such as mercerized or nylon thread.

To make tailor's tacks through two layers of fabric, follow the directions given below and in the illustrations on page 282.

1. Use a double thread about 30 inches long without a knot.

2. Take a small stitch on the marking line through both thicknesses of fabric, letting the end of the thread extend about 1 inch.

3. Draw the thread through, leaving a loop about ¾ inch to 1 inch high. Repeat, making a double or triple loop.

4. Carry the thread along the marking line to the next position to be marked.

5. Repeat steps 2, 3, and 4, making a series of loops at each position to be marked.

6. Clip the threads at the top of the loops and those between the loops.

7. Remove the pattern carefully after all tacks have been made. If it is a printed pattern, it will first need to be slit slightly at

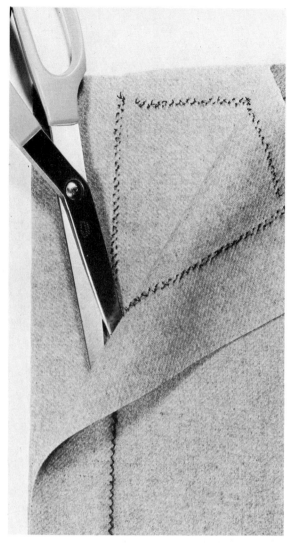

Courtesy Viking Sewing Machine Co.

Machine basting can be used for marking two layers of fabric at once if the machine is set with a loose tension and large stitch.

each loop with the point of a needle or pin to prevent excessive damage from tearing.

8. Gently separate the two thicknesses of fabric, clipping the threads between them as you do so. This will produce thread tufts to serve as markings on each layer of fabric. The tufts can be removed when a specific area of the garment is completed.

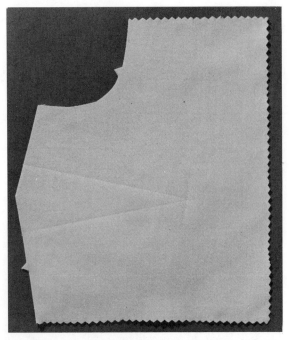

Temporary markings can be pressed with an iron or applied with the tracing wheel alone onto solid-colored fabrics with crisp textures.

Pins

Pins provide a simple method of marking that requires no special marking equipment. However, the marking may not be accurate unless it is carefully done, and the pins drop out easily. Pins should be employed only as a temporary marking.

Marking Chalk or Pencil

Marking chalk or marking pencil can be used to transfer pattern markings onto fabrics. It is recommended for use on fabric from which it can be easily brushed off. Consider chalk for the following marking situations:

1. The right and wrong sides of the fabric.

2. The left and right sides of the garment.

3. The undercollar and undercuffs.

4. The direction of the nap.

5. Extensions of pieces which will be necessitated by pattern alterations made during the cutting process.

If you are using a flat piece of marking chalk, mark with the long, thin edge to obtain sharp, accurate lines. Place the edge of the chalk against a straight edge. Remember that only one layer of fabric can be marked at a time, so each side of a double thickness must be marked separately. For types of chalk available see pages 230-231.

Pressing

Marking with an iron is a method suited only to non-crease-resistant fabrics and those not supersensitive to the heat of an iron. It is a method of transferring pattern markings most often used for center lines, extended facings, fold lines, center lines of darts, and pleats.

To mark with an iron, fold the pattern and fabric as one along the line to be creased. Press the fold at the iron temperature best suited to the fabric. After the pattern is removed, the crease marking will remain in the fabric. The pressing must be done carefully to obtain marking precision.

Use caution in employing the pressing method on thermoplastic or heat-sensitive man-made fibers. For such materials, the creases it produces could permanently disfigure your garment.

PRINCIPLES FOR LAYING A PATTERN, CUTTING, AND MARKING

1. The choice of pattern layout is determined by the style choice, the size of the pattern, the width of the fabric, and the weave or design of the fabric.

2. When pattern alterations are made by shifting the pattern, the layout must provide ample fabric space for the necessary alterations.

3. The folds of a fabric during layout are determined by the size of the pattern pieces.

4. If a garment is to hang correctly, folds of the fabric must be made on a lengthwise or crosswise thread, perpendicular to the selvage or end of the fabric.

5. To conserve fabric in cutting a garment, place the wider sections of pieces toward the cut ends of the fabric.

6. When laying a pattern, position all pieces or reserve space for them before cutting is started.

7. If a garment is to fit and hang properly, each piece of the garment must be pinned and cut on the straight grain of fabric.

8. When pinning a pattern to fabric, use enough pins to secure the pattern adequately, pinning on the grain of the fabric.

9. When cutting a garment, cut directionally from the wide area toward the narrow.

10. When cutting a garment, cut notches away from the garment piece into the extra fabric and cut multiple notches as one.

11. As each fabric has certain unique characteristics and each marking method has its advantages and limitations, the best marking method to choose will vary from fabric to fabric.

12. If the marking method is appropriate to the fabric selected, the mark will be distinct, easy to remove without leaving a trace, or invisible on the right side when the garment is completed.

13. As tracing paper leaves waxy imprints, it should be of a color that makes markings visible but inconspicuous.

14. For marking white, sheer, napped, pile, and other hard-to-mark fabrics, tailor's tacks are often the best choice.

15. If tailor's tacks are made of darning cotton, the threads will not slip out of the fabric easily.

16. If the fabric has no special finish and creases easily, marking with an iron may be a possible choice.

Part 3

Basic Sewing Techniques

13 Principles of Machine Sewing

The sewing machine is a relatively modern invention useful for making almost any stitch you would like to make. However, any stitching, whether practical or creative, can be accomplished only when your ideas and your skills are used to put the sewing machine into operation. *You* are the most important power behind the machine: the one with the ability to produce a unique product. Without you the machine can do nothing.

What is the principle upon which the sewing machine operates?

How can the stitch length be adjusted? The machine tension?

How is the correct machine pressure for a given project determined?

How is even stitching achieved?

What is directional stitching?

Decisions About Sewing-machine Operation

Practically all machines can be used for regular stitching and for reverse stitching. Many modern ones are equipped to perform zigzag and stretch-type stitching. Some can be used for chain stitching. Decisions pertaining to the operation of a machine involve determining which of the various available stitches to use for a given project. Further choices deal with the adjustments of the various parts of the machine to best accommodate a given fabric. The selections of the size and type of needle, the size of stitch, the type and weight of thread, the amount of machine tension, and the amount of machine pressure are decisions which must be made anew for each new project. Your ability to combine the various decisions effectively determines to a marked extent the success of a sewing project.

Operating the Sewing Machine

In order to make a sewing machine operate as you desire, it is important to have some basic knowledge of it before you begin to sew. Worth your study is the manual that comes with the sewing machine. This manual will show you how to operate the machine, make simple adjustments, oil and care for the machine, and keep it in good working order. It is a useful reference whenever there is any doubt about machine parts, function, or operation.

In a few easy steps, and with some practice, you can learn to handle the sewing machine with enough efficiency to produce attractive garments. But before you begin to

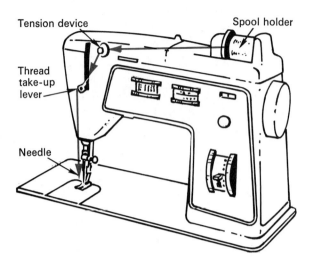

Regardless of the brand or model of sewing machine, the upper part is threaded by a four-step process. The thread moves from the spool holder past a tension device, then through the thread take-up lever, and into the eye of the needle.

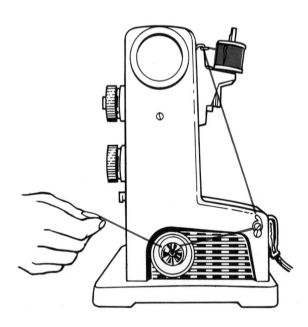

A conventional bobbin is filled on the outside of a sewing machine by setting in motion a system of gears which allows thread to flow from a spool onto the bobbin. The filled bobbin is then placed in position according to the directions for the particular model of machine.

stitch on your first project, you need to know how to thread and operate the machine.

Practice starting and stopping the machine to gain easy control over it. Then, without threading it, run the machine along lined paper or cloth for experience in guiding the stitching. A smooth, steady rhythm and accuracy, not speed, are the secrets to good stitching. Operate the machine slowly at first so that you can readily follow the lines. Soon, with practice, you will be able to sew at a speedier pace.

Threading the Machine

Although lock-stitch sewing machines come in a wide variety of models, they all produce the same kind of basic stitch and operate on many of the same principles. A lock-stitch machine sews by locking two threads, the upper thread and the bobbin thread, into a stitch. Therefore, to make it operate, it is necessary to thread both the upper and lower parts of the machine. Models vary in the position of their threading devices, so follow your manual as you learn to thread your machine.

Threading the Upper Part

Each machine has a series of thread guides which lead the thread along its route from spool to needle. A thread take-up lever controls the amount of thread fed to the needle for each stitch, and a tension device holds the thread taut. Check the manual to see that the thread accurately follows the thread guides. Inaccurate placement of thread will cause incorrect tension, poor stitching, or a thread lock in the machine.

Threading the Lower Part

Wind the bobbin and place it in the machine according to the directions in your machine manual. Make sure to wind it smoothly, so that the thread will unwind properly in the machine. Avoid winding the bobbin too full. An overloaded bobbin is likely to slip in the bobbin case, fail to unwind evenly, and result in poor-quality stitches.

Selecting and Inserting the Needle

Good machine stitching requires a sharp needle of correct size for woven fabrics and a ball-point needle of correct size for knits. A needle too fine for the thread or fabric may break when you sew or it may cause the thread to fray. A needle too large may leave visible holes in the fabric.

Check carefully that the point of the needle is not bent or blunt. A bent needle cannot be centered properly in the machine needle hole and will make an imperfect stitch. Moreover, if continued in use, it may damage the mechanism involved in stitch formation, thus resulting in expensive machine repairs. A blunt needle may snag or pull your fabric.

A machine needle has two sides, one which is flat and one which contains a long groove. When inserting it into the needle clamp, set it so that the long-groove side faces the direction from which the needle will be threaded. Whether this groove is on the right, the left, or the front depends on the model of the machine. Refer to your machine manual for further details on inserting the needle in your machine.

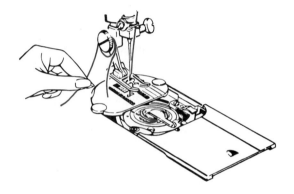

An automatic bobbin is filled while in position within the machine. The filled bobbin is then ready to use in sewing.

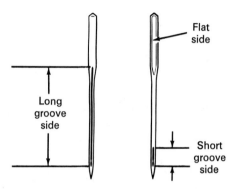

Insert a sewing-machine needle by sliding it in place so that the flat side is turned away from the last thread guide. Tighten the needle-clamp screw.

COMPLETING THE THREADING OF A SEWING MACHINE

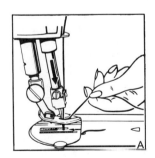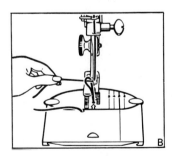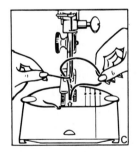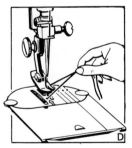

After the top of the machine is threaded and the filled bobbin is in position, complete the threading of the machine by (A) holding the end of the upper thread as the needle is lowered, (B) pulling on the upper thread to bring up a loop of the bobbin thread to the surface, (C) pulling the end of the bobbin thread to the surface, and (D) pulling both the upper and bobbin threads slightly to the side and back so that stitching can begin.

COMMON SEWING-MACHINE DIFFICULTIES

	Problem	Cause	Solution
	Loud, clicking noise, knotted thread on underside of seam line.	Machine improperly threaded, or top tension set too loose.	Remove the fabric and cut away knotted thread. Rethread the machine. If necessary, adjust the upper tension.
	Stitches are skipped in places.	Machine needle of wrong brand or wrong point style, bent needle, or needle set in machine improperly.	Use a straight, sharp needle of same brand as machine and correct point style. Set it high in the needle clamp and tighten the screw.
	Looped stitches or tangled threads on underside of seam line.	Bobbin improperly inserted, or bobbin tension too loose.	Rethread the bobbin. In extreme situations, tighten the bobbin tension.
	Looped stitches or tangled threads on upper portion of seam line.	Machine improperly threaded, or upper tension too loose.	Rethread the machine. If necessary, tighten the upper tension.
	Size of stitches irregular.	Undue pressure placed on fabric during stitching.	Guide, rather than pull, the fabric through the machine.
	Threads within the fabric pull, draw, or break.	Blunt needle caused by stitching over pins, or thread unsuited to size or type of needle.	Replace needle. Stitch on knitted fabrics with a ball-point needle. Avoid stitching over pins.
	Sewing threads break.	Machine threaded incorrectly; thread of wrong weight; wrong needle or needle incorrectly inserted; or tension too tight.	Rethread upper machine and bobbin. Replace needle, following instructions in machine manual. If necessary, adjust tension.

Making Stitch Adjustments

Different fabrics have different requirements as to the length of the stitch, the tension, and the machine pressure needed for perfect stitching. At the start of each new sewing project, therefore, the machine needs to be adjusted accordingly.

Adjusting Stitch Length

Generally, heavier fabrics require longer stitches, and fine fabrics shorter stitches. For most medium-weight cottons, twelve to fifteen stitches per inch is about right for regular stitching. A longer stitch is used for basting and gathering. The stitch length is controlled

BALANCED STITCH

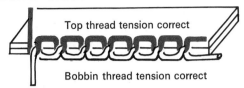

Top thread tension correct

Bobbin thread tension correct

TIGHT UPPER TENSION

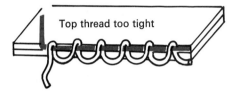

Top thread too tight

TIGHT BOBBIN TENSION

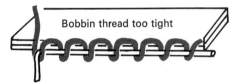

Bobbin thread too tight

Loosens   Tightens

Courtesy Educational Bureau, Coats & Clark Inc.

The upper and lower tensions are balanced when the upper thread and bobbin thread interlock between the layers of fabric.

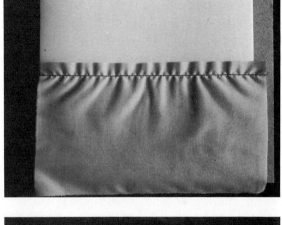

Photos courtesy Educational Bureau, Coats & Clark Inc.

Puckered threads in a line of stitching indicate that one or both tension threads are too tight (above). Strive for a smooth row of stitches (below).

by adjusting the stitch-length regulator, which regulates the distance which the feed dog moves the fabric for each stitch. The stitch-length regulator is located in different positions on different models of machines. Check your manual for further help in adjusting the stitch length for the particular fabric on which you are working.

Adjusting Machine Tension

The tension on a lock-stitch machine is controlled by two tension regulators: an upper one, which controls the pull on the thread in the needle, and a lower one, on the bobbin case, which controls the pull on the lower thread. When the two tensions are balanced, the stitches lock within the fabric and look the same on both sides. If not balanced, the thread tension is too tight on one side and too loose on the other. If the fabric puckers, the tension is usually too tight on both the needle and the bobbin. Before stitching on your project on a lock-stitch machine, check the stitching balance on a scrap of your fabric. If it is faulty, consult your manual for instructions regarding tension adjustment.

291

To determine what change is needed in tension adjustment, fold a 6-inch square of your fabric in half diagonally, forming a triangle. Make a line of regular machine stitching ½ inch from the fold. Then, grasping the stitching line at each end, pull it with a snap to make the threads break. If both threads break at the same time, the tension is well adjusted and you have a balanced stitch. Although the top and bottom threads may break at different places in the stitching line, they are still balanced if they both break on the same snap. If only the top thread breaks, loosen the upper tension and repeat the test. If only the bottom thread breaks, loosen the lower tension and repeat the test. If a perfectly balanced stitch cannot be achieved, consider the stitch acceptable if the bottom thread breaks first. Usually a balanced stitch can be produced by an adjustment of the upper tension only.

Adjusting Machine Pressure

The machine pressure is correct when the presser foot holds the fabric firmly enough so that it does not rise with the needle and yet gently enough so that the fabric moves smoothly with each stroke of the feed dog. Too much pressure creates difficulty in operating the machine and sometimes causes the feed dog to stretch the fabric or to push one layer of the fabric out faster than the other. Too little pressure makes it difficult to control the location of the stitching. Velvets, satins, and other fabrics that are easily marred are stitched with a light pressure. Curved lines, which require constant turning of the fabric, are also stitched with light pressure. Refer to the manual for your particular machine for further suggestions on adjusting the presser foot for best results.

Check the machine pressure on your particular fabric before beginning the actual stitching on your garment. On lengthwise or crosswise grain, cut two strips about 6 to 8 inches long from scraps of your fabric. Pin them together along the lengthwise edges with the pins at a right angle to the edge. Guiding the fabric with your hand in front of the presser foot, stitch a plain seam. If the fabric does not feed smoothly, the pressure on the presser foot is too light. If the fabric ripples, the pressure on the presser foot is too heavy. Make any necessary adjustments, and test the seam again.

Techniques of Machine Stitching

If you start and stop the machine carefully and maintain a smooth, steady rhythm in operating it, you will avoid such time-consuming annoyances as knots or breaks in the thread or a loosened needle. Techniques necessary for adequate control of the machine include starting and stopping the machine, operating the machine, stitching, fastening the stitches, removing the fabric from the machine, and turning square corners.

To Start and Stop the Machine

Raise the take-up lever to its highest point before starting a row of stitching and before removing the fabric from the machine. This will help prevent the thread from breaking or slipping out of the needle. To help maintain control of the machine, place your right hand on the handwheel when starting or stopping operation.

To Operate the Machine

A smooth, steady machine-operating rhythm and even stitching are achieved by controlling the speed of your machine. On an electric machine the speed is regulated by foot or knee pressure on the control. Too much pressure will race the motor beyond a controllable speed. A steady, moderate pressure without speed-ups or slow-downs produces the best stitching results.

To Start the Stitching

Before starting to stitch, place both sewing threads to one side of the presser foot so that the weight of the presser foot will keep them from being pulled into the bobbin case and becoming tangled. Make sure the take-up lever is at its highest position. Place the fabric under the presser foot so that the beginning of the stitching line is just under the point of the needle. Lower the needle at the exact point where you want the stitching to start, and then lower the presser foot. Make sure the fabric has been placed under the needle and the presser foot has been lowered before you start the machine. To set the machine in motion, move the handwheel, and depending on the type of machine, press on the foot or knee control or treadle the machine.

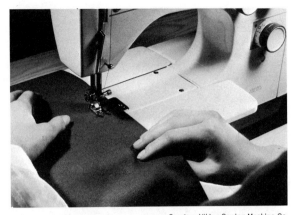

Guide the fabric through the machine, keeping the seam at a preselected width. Avoid pushing or pulling on the fabric.

To Stitch a Seam
While stitching, guide the fabric only in front of the presser foot. This degree of control is usually sufficient for smooth, even stitching. Avoid pulling or pushing the fabric through the machine, as this would result in a bent or broken needle and an irregular stitch length. (See the chart on page 290.)

To End the Stitching
To stop the stitching at the precise point desired, reduce the speed of the machine as the needle approaches the terminal point. Then slow the machine further by placing your right hand on the handwheel. Stop the machine with the take-up lever at its highest point. This will complete the last stitch, prevent the thread from coming out of the needle, and allow both the upper and lower threads to pull freely from the needle and bobbin.

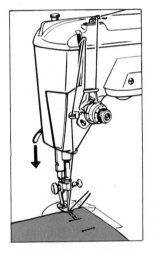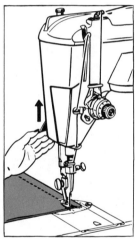

Threads may be secured at the beginning and ending points of seams by backstitching (left) or by lock-stitching (right).

To Secure the Stitching
You may secure the stitching by one of the three following methods:

1. Reverse the stitching by either backstitching or retracing. If your machine will reverse, you may backstitch by moving a lever on the machine to *reverse* position. Otherwise, you may retrace the stitching by pivoting the fabric on the needle with the presser foot raised, lowering the presser foot, and overstitching for about ½ inch.

2. Lock-stitch by raising the presser foot slightly and taking two or three stitches in the same place.

3. Tie the thread ends after removing the fabric from the machine. To do so, first turn the fabric to the wrong side. Pull on the end of one thread, and draw a loop of the

293

To make a square corner, leave the needle in the fabric, raise the presser-bar lifter, and pivot the fabric on the needle.

Directional stitching is stitching with the grain of the fabric. It progresses from the wider to the narrower part of a garment piece.

other thread through the fabric so that the ends of both threads are on the wrong side. Then tie a square knot.

To Remove the Fabric
from the Machine

When a line of stitching has been completed, see that the take-up lever is at the highest point, and raise the presser foot. Push the fabric under the presser foot, and draw it out from the left side, making sure that both threads are under the presser foot. Cut the threads close to the fabric if the stitching has already been secured; otherwise, leave a sufficient length of thread for tying. Always leave several inches of thread extending from the eye of the needle and an equal amount flowing from the bobbin in readiness for the next stitching procedure. (See illustration D on page 289.)

To Turn a Square Corner

Keeping your right hand on the handwheel whenever you start or stop the machine can help you to stitch a sharp, accurate corner. When stitching such a corner, lower the

needle into the fabric at exactly the point of the desired turn. Raise the presser foot, and pivot the fabric on the needle to the correct position for the continuing stitching line. Then lower the presser foot to continue the stitching. Further discussion of the technique for turning square corners is included on pages 400-401.

Directional Stitching

Directional stitching is stitching with the grain of the fabric. If all machine stitching is directional, the fabric is kept on grain and free of distortion. Staystitching is always inserted directionally. Machine basting and construction stitching should be directional unless the edges have already been directionally staystitched.

To determine the proper direction for stitching, run your finger along the cut edge of the fabric to see whether the ends of the threads are smoothed down or roughed up. If the threads are stroked down, or smoothed, your finger is moving in the proper direction for stitching, that is, with the grain.

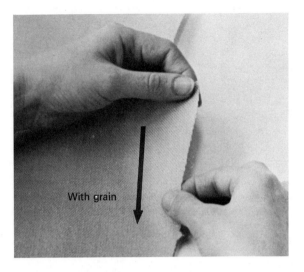
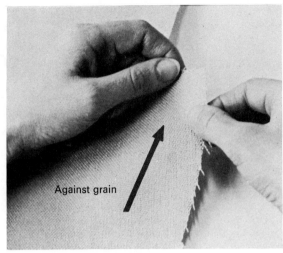

With grain

Against grain

·Photos courtesy Educational Bureau, Coats & Clark Inc.

To determine the direction for stitching, stroke the edge of the fabric. Stroking with the grain smoothes the edge of a fabric, whereas stroking against the grain ruffles it. Stitching direction is indicated on most patterns.

With your pattern pieces still pinned to the fabric, however, you can easily determine the grain just by noting the pattern markings which indicate the direction for stitching each seam. Another guide is the rule of thumb for directional stitching: Stitch from the wide part of the garment piece to the narrow.

Exceptions to the general rule that all machine stitching should be directional are the short sections of curved edges. When the direction of the grain changes for only a short distance, it is not necessary to change the direction of the stitching. It is preferable in such instances to stitch the entire edge continuously in the direction that will be with the grain for the greatest distance. Examples of such areas are armholes and rounded ends of a collar.

Where is staystitching necessary?
What are the purposes and methods of basting?
What are the general rules for stitching seams together?
What is the best way to rip machine stitching?

Staystitching

Staystitching is a line of permanent machine stitching sewn through a *single* thickness of fabric to hold the fabric grain. It is the first stitching done on a garment, preceding the sewing of darts and seams. Its purpose is to prevent fabric edges from becoming stretched out of shape before being joined during the construction process.

Staystitching must be directional to be effective. Before you start, therefore, make sure that you will be stitching in the right direction. (See the preceding section on directional stitching.)

If staystitching is correctly directional, then either the wrong or the right side of the fabric may be up. Staystitch with matching thread, regular tension, and the length of stitch that is suitable for your particular fabric. Do not secure the stitching threads.

Staystitching is usually placed in the seam allowance close to the seam line. The exact location may vary, however, depending on the seam widths and the construction that is to follow. Where a plain seam is to be made, staystitching is placed not more than

Courtesy Viking Sewing Machine Co.

Staystitching, inserted directionally within the seam allowance on all except vertical seams, prevents a garment from stretching out of shape during construction (left). It can be used to insert ease in the process of staystitch-plus (center) or in a combination staystitch and gathering line (right).

⅛ inch outside the seam line. If the edge is to be hemmed or finished, the staystitching is placed ¼ inch from the edge.

Where to Staystitch

Except for long vertical seam lines, staystitching is used on all edges. It is particularly important to staystitch edges that are cut off grain, those that are cut on crosswise grain, and those that are curved or bias. Vertical seams, because of the nature of the fabric grain, usually give slightly with the garment in wear. They are therefore not staystitched since this might cause them to draw or pucker. The only exception is a straight seam over the hips in a garment with a side placket opening; here staystitching is done on both side seams for the length of the opening to keep the grain alike on both hiplines.

Armholes, necklines, waistlines, and shoulder seams are examples of curved or bias edges which are usually staystitched because they are particularly subject to stretching. Small pieces such as armhole and neckline facings are staystitched along the edge that will be attached to the garment. The inner edges of such pieces are also staystitched if they are to be clean-finished.

Staystich-plus

Staystitch-plus is a staystitching technique in which the fabric threads are crowded together during the stitching process to provide extra ease. It is accomplished as follows:

1. Press the index or middle finger of the right hand against the back of the presser foot so that the fabric piles up against the finger while you stitch for several inches. The more ease required, the harder you will need to press against the presser foot.

2. Release the fabric.

3. Repeat steps 1 and 2 until you have completed the section that is to be so stitched.

The fabric should be fed into the machine with the left hand and manipulated according to the amount of ease desired. (See the illustration above center.)

Continuous Staystitch and Gathering Line

Where extra fullness is needed, a continuous line of stitching is placed exactly on the seam line. Regular-size stitches are used for that portion which is not to be eased or gathered, and long stitches for that portion which is to be eased or gathered. Examples of such places are around the top of the sleeve, under

296

Basting stitches are inserted directionally to fasten two sections of a garment together for fitting before final stitching.

Basting stitches are effective for marking construction details such as buttonhole and pocket locations.

the bustline, and below the yoke of a bodice front or back.

Basting

Basting is a temporary means of holding layers of fabric together in preparation for further construction processes or for fitting. In addition, it is sometimes used to mark construction details. True basting, involving stitching with thread, may be done either by hand or by machine. In pin basting, pins are substituted for the thread. In the Unit Method, if basting is necessary, machine or pin basting is preferred. Detailed instructions for hand basting are given on pages 390-391.

Machine Basting

Machine basting is made with a long machine stitch or chain stitch to serve a temporary purpose. It is used both to mark construction details and to hold the units of a garment together for fitting. Machine basting is usually removed as seams are finished.

To Mark Construction Details

Machine basting used for marking construction details is stitched on a previously traced line in order to transfer the marking from the wrong side to the right side of the fabric. Machine basting is often used in this way for such markings as those for buttons, buttonholes, pockets, and trim. Thread of a contrasting color increases their visibility.

To Hold Units Together for Fitting

Machine basting for fitting purposes is stitched very near the seam line but within the seam allowance so that it will not be caught in the permanent stitching. This stitching location facilitates the removal of the basting stitches, which is necessary if seams are pressed open.

Pin Basting

To prepare for seam stitching, the fabric can be held together temporarily by pin basting. This method is most successful on easy-to-handle fabrics with straight seams.

There are three effective methods of pin basting. They include pinning vertically, but away from the seam line; pinning horizontally across the seam line; and pinning vertically along the seam line. The choice of method depends upon the hand and design of the fabric, the location on the garment, and the type of seam.

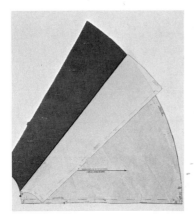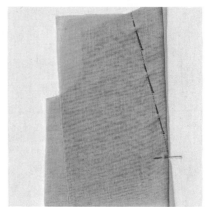

Seams may be pin-basted (left) on the grain at a distance away from the seam line, (center) directionally across the seam line, or (right) vertically along the seam line.

The most commonly used method of pin basting is the first one: placing the pins in the direction of the grain, away from the line of stitching, but close enough to the seam line to hold the two layers of fabric together with the grain identical and the edges even. This method has the advantage of making it unnecessary to remove the pins as the seam is stitched.

In the second pinning method, the pins are inserted directionally across the seam line. This pin-basting method is particularly effective for seams in fabrics which require matching of plaids or stripes. A hinged foot on the sewing machine allows for stitching directly over the pins to retain precision matching. It involves some risk of blunting or bending the machine needle, however, and the stitch made over the pins may be slightly irregular. For more perfect stitching the pins can be removed just in front of the presser foot as the stitching advances.

In the third pin-basting method, sometimes called the vertical-pinning method, the pins are inserted into the fabric at intervals directly along the seam line with the points toward the machine needle. This pinning procedure allows the seamstress to grasp each

pin by the head and remove it immediately before machine-stitching that area of the seam.

Seam Stitching

Seam stitching is a row of regular-size stitches which hold together permanently two or more thicknesses of fabric. This stitching is located exactly on the seam line or, in the case of darts and other details, exactly on the construction line. For seam stitching, select a thread of suitable fiber content that matches your fabric in color or is just a shade darker. After stitching, secure the threads at both the beginning and the end of the seam. Make sure the stitching is inserted directionally unless the fabric edges have already been stay-stitched. Full directions on making seams are given in Chapter 14.

Ripping Machine Stitches

Ripping machine stitches by any method requires careful work to avoid damaging the fabric. Avoid pulling the fabric edges apart, which will distort the shape of the garment, or cutting the stitching with a razor blade, which endangers your own safety as well as

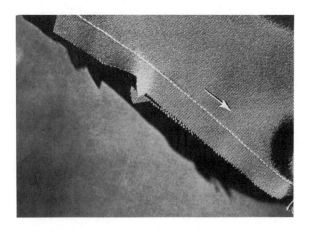

Seam stitches, regular-size stitches located exactly on the seam line, are inserted directionally, with the grain of the fabric.

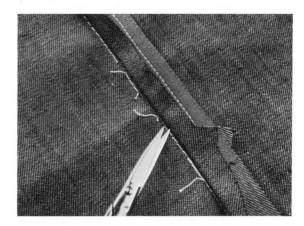

A good way to rip most stitches is to clip them at intervals and then pull the long line of stitches from the opposite side of the seam.

that of the fabric. There are several good methods of ripping machine stitches.

Using Ripping Scissors

The easiest and safest way to rip machine stitches without leaving broken threads in the fabric is to use ripping scissors. These scissors are like any other scissors except that the points of both blades are dulled for a distance of about ¾ inch from the tips. They can be used to remove stitching as follows:

1. Hold the scissors near the tip of the blades, slip the point of a blade under a stitch, and pull until the threads break.

2. Slip the point under adjacent stitches, and pull one end through until you have a single thread and a loop.

3. Grasp the thread end and loop as close to the fabric as possible by closing the blade and twisting the fingers slightly. Keep the blades parallel to the fabric.

4. Pull the closed blades back along the line of stitching toward you in one quick motion. A section of the stitching will pull out before the threads break, leaving the area clean of threads.

5. Repeat steps 1-4, until you have pulled out all of the stitching to be removed.

Pulling Alternate Threads

Another safe method of removing stitching is by pulling alternate threads. You may do this as follows:

1. Grasp one thread with your fingers, a pair of tweezers, or ripping scissors.

2. Pull the thread, sliding the fabric along the thread with the left hand, until the thread breaks.

3. Turn the fabric to the other side, and grasp the long end of the underthread close to the fabric.

4. Pull this thread until it breaks.

5. Repeat steps 1-4, alternating fabric sides each time the thread breaks.

Clipping Threads

When neither of the first two ripping methods is practical because of the smallness or tightness of the stitches, there is still another way to rip machine stitching. You can clip the threads. To do this, clip the stitches with the points of a pair of sharp scissors or with a seam ripper at frequent intervals along the seam line on one side. Then pull out the thread on the other side, and remove any short threads which still remain in the area along the seam line.

1. Effective machine stitching requires adjustment of the stitch length, the tension, and the pressure for the specific fabric to be stitched.

2. If the stitching appears the same on both sides of the fabric, with no loops or puckers visible, the tension is properly adjusted.

3. Thread tangles may be avoided in machine stitching by placing the needle and bobbin threads under the presser foot before starting to stitch.

4. The fabric grain is maintained through the machine-stitching process by stitching directionally, keeping the bulk of the fabric to the left of the needle, and guiding the fabric *in front* of the presser foot only.

5. Preservation of fabric grain is aided by staystitching all curved or bias edges.

6. After markings have been made on the wrong side of the fabric, machine basting stitches which show on both sides can be superimposed for buttons, buttonholes, pockets, and trim.

7. Machine basting may be used to hold garment units together for fitting.

8. To stitch right-angle corners, pivot the fabric on the needle while the presser foot is raised.

9. Machine stitching can be removed by using ripping scissors, by pulling and breaking the thread on alternate sides of the seam, or by clipping threads and pulling them from the fabric.

Seams and Seam Finishes

Since the appearance of a garment can be no better than the quality of its seams, seams and seam finishes play a vital role in the sewing process. Smooth, well-finished seams are essential for both a professional appearance and garment durability.

What factors determine your choice of seam and seam finish?

What types of seams and seam finishes should you select for your garment?

What is a plain seam?

How is a long seam edge joined to a shorter one?

What is an appropriate seam for a sheer fabric? A bulky fabric?

What seam finishes are most effective for a fabric that ravels easily?

How are the edges of outward and inward curved seams treated?

Decisions About Seams and Seam Finishes

The decision as to the type of seam and seam finish is yours to make. It will vary from garment to garment, and there may be several equally satisfactory ways of finishing the seams of a given garment. The edges of the seam allowances in a garment of medium-weight firmly woven fabric, for instance, could be appropriately pinked, zigzagged, edge-stitched, or perhaps turned and stitched. You will be aided in making decisions concerning seams for each project by a knowledge of seams and seam finishes and of the situations for which each type is appropriate.

Factors Affecting Choice of Seams and Finishes

There are many types of seams and seam finishes, and to ensure the success of a project, both seams and finishes must be carefully chosen. For example, French seams can cover the raw edges in a sheer, see-through garment. Seam curl resulting from a poor selection of seam width and finish can be prevented by trimming and clipping seams which tend to curl. If the seams of a fabric that ravels easily are finished effectively, the threads will not ravel nor will seam allowances disintegrate.

In making a choice of seams for any garment, there are four factors to consider. These include the type of fabric, the style and purpose of the garment, the sewing equipment available, and your own time and sewing experience.

Type of Fabric

Fabric is one of the most important factors in determining the type of seam and seam finish for a garment. If the fabric is sheer, the raw edges of the seam allowances will show unless the seams are enclosed. The narrow, enclosed seam finish appropriate for a delicate sheer, however, would not suit a heavy wool fabric. The thick seams of velour or velvet require a

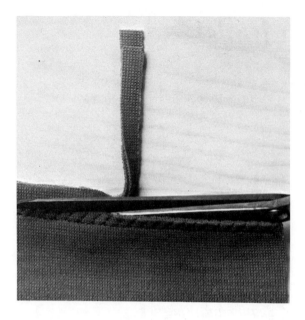

With automatic sewing equipment, garments can be made almost completely with machine-stitched seams and finishes.

seam finish that controls fraying but is not bulky. (For further information on matching seam finishes to specific fabrics, see the chart on page 309.)

Style and Purpose of Garment

The style of the garment you have chosen influences the selection of a seam finish. For example, slacks for active sports wear need a flat, tailored, and very sturdy seam finish to withstand heavy wear. An unlined jacket of a firmly woven material needs a neat seam finish which covers the outer raw edges of the seam allowance and leaves the seam flat and smooth. A child's play outfit needs stronger seams than a woman's street dress.

Sewing Equipment Available

The number of ways in which you can make and finish seams depends to some extent on the sewing equipment available to you. Sewing-machine attachments such as the zigzagger and the binder, which binds seam edges, increase your choice of seam-finishing methods. A sewing machine that can make special stitches in different lengths or widths for knit and stretch fabrics provides other possibilities. Your decision ultimately must be based on choices open to you at the time.

Time and Sewing Experience

Some seam finishes are quick and easy to apply and require only a limited amount of sewing experience, while others require a greater degree of sewing skill but give a more finished appearance. Pinking, for example, is done quickly and easily with the pinking shears. The turned-and-stitched edge finish, on the other hand, involves considerable time, skill, and patience. The overcast seam finish, when done by hand, is easy but time consuming. When accomplished by using the zigzag feature on a sewing machine, however, it is a simple and speedy process.

When you are choosing a seam finish, consider the fact that special enclosed seams, such as the French and flat-fell seams, serve double duty as both a seam and a seam finish.

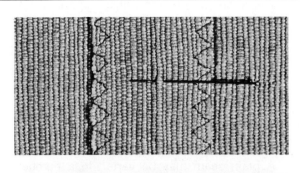

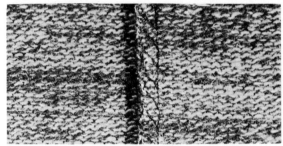

Photos courtesy Viking Sewing Machine Co.

STANDARDS FOR A PLAIN SEAM

1. *Machine stitching secured at each end.*
2. *Even, accurate seam allowances.*
3. *Seam flat and smooth.*
4. *Grain line maintained without distortion.*
5. *Seam pressed flat or open.*

Making a Plain Seam

The plain seam is the most commonly used method of joining one garment section to another. It is the basic seam from which many other seams and seam finishes are derived. A plain seam is a seam on which the edges of the seam allowance are left exposed on the inside of the garment. The edges may be finished in some way to make them more durable or to reduce bulk.

Steps in Making a Plain Seam

To make a good basic seam, the following procedure is suggested:

1. Prepare your sewing machine by selecting the correct tension, pressure, stitch length, type of needle, and needle size.

2. Select thread that matches the fabric or is one shade darker.

3. Place the right sides of the fabric together with notches matched, edges even, and ends of seam lines keyed exactly.

4. If pin-basting, place the pins so that they will not interfere with the stitching and can be easily removed (see "Pin Basting," pages 297-298). Use machine basting only in areas where fitting difficulties are anticipated. If machine-basting, adjust the stitch length accordingly and place the basting stitches a few threads away from the seam line, within the 5/8-inch seam allowance.

5. Stitch directionally, using a seam guide to keep the stitching an even distance from the cut edge.

6. Secure the machine stitching at each end of the seam by backstitching, by tying the threads, or by lock-stitching (see pages 293-294).

7. Remove the basting if basting has been used. Press all seams, when finished, in open or closed position as the seam finish requires (see illustrations on page 313).

8. Understitch any seam which lies along an edge where a sharp turn is desired, as on a facing, a collar, or a cuff (see "Understitching," pages 387-388).

9. Finish the seams with a finish appropriate for the garment and fabric.

Ease is the process of fitting together two edges which are of different lengths to form a smooth, attractive seam.

10. To ensure perfect alignment of intersecting seams, such as bodice and skirt seams, pin them together and check for alignment before stitching.

11. Reduce bulk in corners where seams intersect by cutting off the corners of the seam allowances with sharp shears.

Ease in a Seam

It is sometimes necessary to ease a plain seam. This is the case when one seam edge is longer than the edge to which it will be joined. Such instances occur at the shoulder seam, the elbow seam, and over the bustline in a princess-style dress.

The ease may be handled in either of two ways. One method is to insert machine basting close to the seam line on the longer edge and pull the thread slightly so the two fabrics are equal in length on the seam line.

The alternative method is to ease in the fullness by hand as the two edges are pinned together. With either method, match the seam lines at each end or at strategic notches, and distribute the fullness in between, pinning at frequent intervals. Stitch with the longer edge on top.

Variations of Plain Seams

A plain seam may be varied in a number of ways to serve different purposes or give different effects. Curved and other shaped seams, topstitched seams, lapped seams, welt seams, corded seams, and slot seams are all variations of the basic plain seam.

Curved and Other Shaped Seams

A plain seam on a curved edge needs to be handled in a special way to prevent bulging or puckering. The edge may be curved inward or outward or both. On an inward curved edge, clip the seam allowance to the stayline at intervals to release the fabric. On an outward curved edge, cut wedges from the seam allowance to remove bulk and permit the seam to lie flat. The procedure for handling curved seams is discussed in detail in Chapter 20. (See pages 401-403.)

Square corners are another common feature of seams that require special stitching techniques. These, too, are described in Chapter 20. (See pages 400-401.)

Topstitched Seam

A plain seam with extra stitching added from the right side for decorative effect or for seam reinforcement is called a topstitched seam. To make a topstitched seam, first stitch a plain seam, clip or cut wedges in the seam allowances if it is curved, and press both seam allowances in the same direction. Then stitch, from the right side of the fabric, through one thickness of the garment and both seam allowances. A single line of stitching may be located close to the original seam line, or two lines of stitching may be inserted, one near

A topstitched seam can be used for decorative purposes.

A lapped seam is made by placing a folded edge over another edge and stitching them together.

the seam line and one approximately ¼ inch away to give the appearance of a flat-fell seam.

Lapped Seam

A variation of a topstitched seam, the lapped seam, is useful when joining a plain edge to a gathered or shaped edge. A lapped seam is made in the following series of steps:

1. Staystitch the upper layer to mark the exact turn line and to reinforce the curves and corners which require clipping. On curved edges, clip or remove wedges.

2. Turn the edge under on the stayline, and pin it in exact position, pinning perpendicularly to the edge. Press the folded edge.

3. Mark the seam line on the underlayer with basting.

4. Place the fold of the upper layer along the line of machine basting on the underlayer, and pin it in place.

5. Stitch as close to the folded edge as possible to keep the stitching inconspicuous, or farther from the edge for a decorative effect. A second row of stitching gives a tailored effect.

Welt Seam

A plain seam with the addition of topstitching on one side of the seam line is called a welt seam. It is used for a tailored effect.

To make a welt seam on straight edges, stitch a plain seam, press both seam allowances in the same direction, and topstitch from the right side of the garment through both seam allowances and about ¼ to ½ inch away from the original seam.

To make a welt seam on a curved or intricately shaped edge or when matching plaids, the seam will need to be slip-basted. To do the basting, first staystitch the upper edge, turn under the seam allowance, and

A slot seam is made when a double row of decorative stitching is used to fasten a piece of fabric beneath a gap between the two garment pieces being joined.

A welt seam, which features topstitching on one side of the seam line, produces a tailored effect.

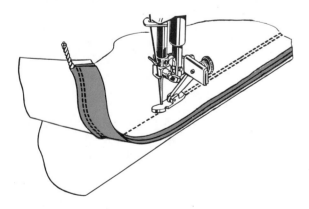

A corded seam contains covered cording, stitched between the layers of fabric at the seam line.

press. Then, place the upper layer on the underlayer, pin, and slip-baste. (See page 391 for specific instructions on how to do slip basting.) Turn the fabric to the wrong side and stitch as for a plain seam. Then topstitch the desired distance from the seam line.

Corded Seam

A plain seam into which a strip of folded bias or covered cord has been inserted between the two thicknesses of fabric is called a corded seam. It is used as a tailoring detail or decorative feature on a garment.

Prepare the cording by inserting cord into folded bias fabric and stitching near the cord, using a zipper or cording foot. Continuing to use the zipper or cording foot, stitch the cording to the right side of one seam allowance about $\frac{5}{8}$ inch from the outside edge and with the corded edge facing toward the garment. Then place the two seam allowances together, and stitch ⅝ inch from the edge through all four thicknesses of fabric.

Slot Seam

A plain seam made with an underlay and top-stitched on both sides of the seam line is called a slot seam. It is used for decoration or to prevent sagging or stretching of a seam. To make a slot seam, baste the seam and press it open. Then, with the underlay centered beneath it, topstitch about ¼ inch on each side of the seam line. Remove the basting.

Enclosed Seams

Enclosed seams are seams in which the seam allowances are concealed. Some are plain seams that have become enclosed during the construction processes. Examples are the seams of collars, cuffs, and facings. With other types of enclosed seams, the enclosure is part of the original seam design, as in the French and flat-fell seams.

Treating the Bulkiness
of Enclosed Seams

When a seam is enclosed during construction, the seam allowance needs to be treated to reduce bulkiness. Generally, the treatment consists of reducing the width and cutting off the corners of the seam allowance. The following are variations of this process:

1. The width of the ⅝-inch seam allowance is reduced by trimming. Both seam allowances are cut away to an even width.

2. If the fabric is thick or bulky, the trimming of the seam needs to be done in steps, or layers. Each layer in the seam allowance is trimmed to a different width. In this way, the thickness is reduced by *grading*, sometimes called beveling or layering. The widest seam allowance is always the one next to the outer fabric of the garment.

3. If the enclosed seam is curved, in addition to trimming or grading, the seam will also need to be slashed or notched (see page 403). This will relieve the seam allowance of outward curves of excess fabric and permit inward curves to be shaped as desired.

Special Enclosed Seams

The French seam and the flat-fell seam are seams specially designed to be enclosed. Their constructions provide for both seam and seam finish simultaneously. Depending on how the mock French seam is made, the seam may or may not be enclosed.

French Seam

A French seam is a narrow seam enclosed within another seam. It is practical for sheer fabrics in which the concealment of raw fabric edges is desirable, and for children's clothes which will receive hard wear and frequent laundering. French seams cannot be used successfully on curved seams such as armholes.

A French seam may be made as follows:

1. Make a plain seam on the *right* side of the fabric, stitching on a line about ¼ inch from the seam line, in the seam allowance. The distance of this stitching from the seam line determines the width of the finished seam.

2. Press the seam open.

3. Trim the seam allowances, holding them together, to slightly less than ¼ inch.

4. Fold the right sides of the fabric together with the stitching exactly on the fold line.

5. Press the seam on the wrong side, and pin or baste it together if necessary.

6. Stitch on the original pattern seam line.

Mock French Seam

A mock French seam is a variation of a plain seam, with the seam allowances given a special treatment. It is especially desirable on curved seams on sheer fabric. A mock French seam may be made as follows:

1. Make a plain seam, stitching on the regular seam line.

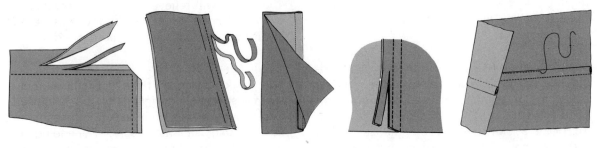

Enclosed corner, graded and clipped

French seam

Mock French seam

Flat-fell seam

2. Complete the seam in one of the following ways, depending on the fabric. (1) Stitch the two seam allowances together, ¼ inch from the seam line, and trim, leaving ⅛ inch of fabric beyond the second line of stitching; or (2) trim the seam allowances if too wide, turn the edges in toward each other, and stitch them together close to the folded edges.

Flat-fell Seam

A flat-fell seam is an enclosed seam which has a tailored appearance. It is very durable. It is most frequently used in women's tailored garments, play clothes, and boys', men's, and children's clothing.

A flat-fell seam may be made in the following series of steps:

1. Make a plain seam on the *right* side of the fabric, stitching on the seam line.

2. Press both seam allowances in the same direction, pressing across the seam to keep the fabric flat and to avoid pressing a pleat in the underside.

3. Trim the lower seam allowance to a scant ¼ inch and the upper seam allowance to ⅜ inch.

4. Open the garment on a table, and lay the seam flat.

5. Turn under the edge of the wider, or upper, seam allowance ⅛ inch, folding it over the narrow, or under, seam allowance.

6. Crease the fold, and place pins perpendicular to the folded edge with heads out for easy removal when stitching.

7. Stitch very close to the folded edge.

Seam Finishes

The purpose of a seam finish is to provide a neat edge and to prevent raveling, distortion, or pulling out of a seam. Some seams such as French and flat-fell seams are so constructed that they include their own seam finish. Some do not require seam finishing, unless noticeable on the outside of a garment, because the fabric weave is sufficiently firm to resist raveling. More frequently, however, the garment fabric has characteristics that make it necessary to finish the raw seam edges.

Some examples of finishes for seams are pinking, pinking and stitching, overcasting, turning the edge under and stitching, binding the edge with tape, and zigzag stitching.

When selecting the appropriate seam finish, consider the factors listed in the section "Factors Affecting Choice of Seams and Finishes" on pages 301-302. Additional points to keep in mind might be the location of the seam, whether the garment is lined or unlined, and whether it will be laundered or drycleaned. For further help in matching seam finishes to specific situations, see the accompanying chart.

FINISHES FOR PLAIN SEAMS

The Finish	Use	How to Make	Advantages	Disadvantages
Pinked	For firmly woven fabric that does not ravel.	Use pinking shears. Pink the seam allowances along the outermost edge.	Fast, easy to do.	May not withstand repeated laundering.
Pinked and Stitched	For fabrics that ravel slightly.	Machine-stitch close to the cut edges; pink the edges.	Easy to do. Gives a flat finish.	May not withstand repeated laundering.
Overcast	For fabrics that ravel.	Press seam open or closed. Overcast by hand.	Does not require a sewing machine.	Time consuming.
Turned and Stitched	For lightweight or medium-weight fabrics used in unlined garments.	Press seam open; turn under the raw edge of each seam allowance (⅛"). Stitch close to the fold.	Neat, prevents raveling.	Time consuming. Can be bulky.
Zigzagged	For fabrics that ravel.	Zigzag-stitch over edge of seam or away from seam edge.	Easy to do. Quick and versatile.	Stitches may be slightly bulky.
Bound (Open or Closed)	For heavy fabrics, for fabrics that ravel easily, and for unlined garments.	Bind the edges of the seam allowances with seam tape or bias binding.	Prevents raveling. Neat appearance in unlined garments.	Time consuming. Difficult to do.

1. An effective plain seam requires sewing with the grain of the fabric and keeping a straight, even seam allowance.

2. Pressing a seam open before it is crossed by another seam ensures a smooth intersection.

3. If joining an eased edge to a straight edge, stitching with the eased side up prevents bulges and puckers.

4. Clipping a curved enclosed seam by slashing or notching releases the fabric, producing smooth seams.

5. A seam is graded by trimming each seam allowance to a different width, keeping the wider one toward the outside of the garment.

6. Decorative variations of the plain seam include the lapped, the corded, and the slot seams.

7. An enclosed seam, such as the French seam, is appropriate for a sheer fabric because it conceals raw edges.

8. The flat-fell seam is durable and particularly suitable for sportswear.

9. The type and weight of the fabric, the tendency of the fabric to fray, and the style of the garment are important considerations in the selection of a seam finish.

15 *Pressing*

One of the keys to a custom-made look in the clothes you make is an art that involves neither sewing machine nor needle. It is the art of working with the iron and other pressing equipment to mold and shape the fabric. You, as the artist, can use these tools to accomplish several purposes. With them you can straighten the fabric grain, shape the fabric, maintain the original texture, and provide a finished look after the garment is completed.

What is pressing? How does it differ from ironing?

At what stages of clothing construction is pressing required?

What are the three pressing variables? How do you adjust them to your fabric?

When is a tailor's ham used? A needle board? A padded roll? A seam board?

What are the techniques for pressing seams? Pleats? Darts?

What is blocking?

Decisions About Pressing

Pressing involves thought as well as action. The selection of the correct equipment and technique for each situation is as important as the actual pressing itself. Equipment for pressing is discussed in Chapter 9. Skillful use of the equipment requires such further knowledge of pressing as when to press and how to press, which are discussed in the following pages.

Uses of Pressing in Clothing Construction

Pressing is essential at strategic times throughout the construction of a garment, from the beginning to the end of the project. Before the pattern is laid, pressing is necessary to smooth out the fabric and sometimes to straighten the fabric grain and preshrink the fabric. During the actual construction, pressing aids in blocking a hem or shaping such details as darts. It is an important part of seam construction. Also, each unit is pressed before it is joined to another unit. A final pressing finishes the completed garment.

Techniques of Pressing

The pressing process used in clothing construction is unique. It differs from the ironing technique used in finishing laundry. Pressing is an *up-and-down* lifting and lowering of the iron that exerts the downward pressure of the iron directly on the fabric. It is usually applied

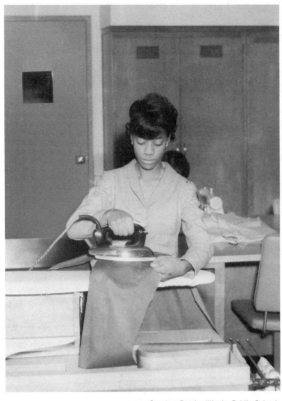

Pressing during construction employs the technique of lifting and lowering a heated iron as sections of a garment are flattened or blocked into shape.

with moisture or steam and a pressing cloth. Ironing, on the other hand, involves a *gliding* motion of the iron as it moves back and forth, directly over a dampened fabric, in long strokes to smooth out wrinkles. As ironing exerts stress against the fabric, it can easily stretch or distort its grain. Home pressing procedures which combine pressing and ironing are generally used to remove slight wrinkling from garments and to smooth easy-care clothing after washing (see pages 135-137).

The amount of heat, moisture, and pressure that should be applied in construction pressing varies with the fabric. The requirement for each of these variables depends upon the fiber content and the construction of the fabric.

Generally, higher iron temperature settings are required for untreated natural fibers than for man-made fibers. For example, 100 percent linen fabric without a special finish requires a hot iron. A man-made fiber that *looks* like linen is correctly pressed at a low temperature setting. A few heat-sensitive fibers cannot be pressed.

Many fabrics require some moisture for pressing. Excessive moisture, however, may

WAYS PRESSING HELPS IN CLOTHING CONSTRUCTION

1. Can remove wrinkles and creases from the fabric, as in the preliminary pressing before cutting.
2. Can aid in straightening the grain of the fabric.
3. Can create shape, as in the blocking of the top of the hem.
4. Can help define shape that has been created with a construction detail, such as a dart or an ease line.
5. Can make the construction processes speedier and more accurate.
6. Can decrease the amount of handling that is necessary and the need for basting.
7. Can help maintain the original texture of the fabric, such as the luster of linen, the glaze of chintz, the soft nap of wool, and the crispness of cotton.
8. Can restore texture that has been destroyed by incorrect pressing or by the garment wear.
9. Can contribute to the finished appearance of the garment.

cause water spotting, give an overpressed look, and destroy the texture. Some fabrics, such as certain silks, may water-spot if any moisture, including steam, is used in top pressing. When working with a silk fabric, test a scrap of it for water spotting before steam pressing the garment. Generally, the pressure on the fabric is light to prevent imprinting of the fabric by the iron.

Special pressing techniques are needed to maintain the beauty of fabrics with textured effects or an unusual surface. Examine your fabric to see whether it has a luster, a soft nap, a raised design, or some other distinguishing feature you want to preserve. Pile fabrics may be pressed over a needle board or a terry-cloth towel to preserve their surface beauty. Napped fabrics are often brushed while moist. Some fabrics need only to be steamed to preserve their distinctive surface.

Certain fabrics, colors, and finishes require the use of a pressing cloth when the fabric is pressed on the right side. Dark colors and dull finishes, for instance, are best pressed in this way.

Check the fabric label or hang tag for information about fiber content or specific instructions. Pretest the heat, moisture, and pressure variables on a scrap of your fabric before starting the actual construction pressing. The specific pressing requirements for various fibers and special fabrics are given later in this chapter.

The following guidelines may help you accomplish construction pressing effectively:

1. Test the iron temperature on a scrap of fabric first.

2. Press on the wrong side as much as possible to prevent shine. Where top pressing is necessary, use a pressing cloth to prevent damage to the fabric.

3. Press directionally, with the grain of the fabric, to prevent stretching or distorting the fabric.

4. Press with an up-and-down motion of the iron, keeping the weight of the iron in your hand.

STEPS IN FINISHING A SEAM

Courtesy Viking Sewing Machine Co.

Fasten the threads at both ends of the seam.

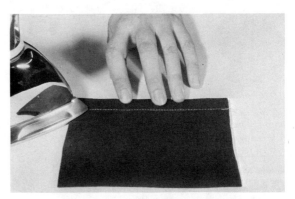

Courtesy Viking Sewing Machine Co.

Press the seam flat with the point of the iron.

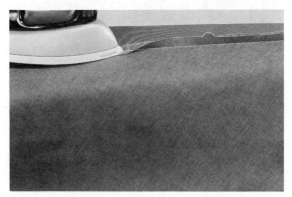

Courtesy Sunbeam Mfg. Co.

Press the seam open directionally from the wider section of the garment to the smaller section.

Paper placed between the seam allowance and the garment prevents the imprint of the seam allowance from showing on the surface of the garment.

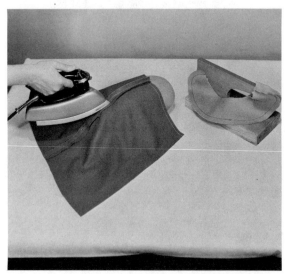

Curved seams can be opened by pressing with the point of the iron as they are shaped over padded equipment such as the tailor's ham or over a seam board.

5. During construction, press each seam before crossing it with another seam.

6. Use the point of the iron for pressing seams open.

7. Press flat areas on a flat surface.

8. Press curved areas over a tailor's ham or another curved surface.

9. Avoid pressing over basting stitches whenever possible.

10. Avoid pressing over pins to prevent marking the fabric or scratching the soleplate of the iron.

11. Avoid excess moisture.

Kinds of Pressing

There are three kinds of pressing: underpressing, blocking, and top pressing. Each serves a unique purpose in garment construction. A particular one or all three kinds may be used during the making of a garment and after it is finished. An understanding of each kind provides background information for decisions as to the best one to use in a given situation.

Underpressing

Underpressing is the pressing of garment details on the wrong side, or underside, of a garment. Individual construction details such as seams, darts, collars, sleeves, and bodice front should be underpressed before they are joined to other portions of the garment. Complete units such as the skirt and bodice are also underpressed before they are joined by pinning or stitching.

Underpressing Seams

Seams are correctly pressed directionally along the line of stitching. There are three ways to avoid having their imprint show on the right side of the garment. Seams can be placed over a seam board and pressed with the point of the iron only, strips of paper can be inserted under the seam allowance, or the garment area under the seam allowance can be re-pressed after the seam is pressed.

Seams may be pressed open or pressed flat, depending on their location in the garment.

Pressing Straight Seams Open . . . . To press a seam open and give an inconspicuous line, follow these steps:

1. Place the seam, wrong side up, on a padded roll, a seam board, or the edge of an ironing board.

2. Smooth the fabric so that the seam lies flat, and open the seam allowance.

3. Press with the *point* of the iron, on the stitching line, in the direction of the grain.

4. When the fabric requires moisture and only a dry iron is available, apply moisture to the seam line with a sponge, a damp cloth, or a small brush, or lay a damp pressing cloth over the opened seam.

Pressing Curved Seams Open   If the area on either side of the seam is to be shaped, as at the hipline, press the seam over a tailor's ham. If the seam is to be opened only, as on the curved edge of a collar, press it on a seam board. (See lower illustration on page 314.)

Pressing Seams Flat   If the seam line is to be emphasized by further stitching or if it is desirable to turn both seam allowances the same way, press the seam flat without opening it. Complete the pressing according to the location of the seam in the garment, using the following guidelines:

1. Turn the waistline seams toward the bodice.

2. Turn the armhole seams for a regular set-in sleeve toward the sleeve in most garments. The direction in which the seam is pressed for various other types of sleeves will depend upon fashion and the type of garment.

3. Press understitched seams only after the understitching has been done, making a fold as nearly on the line of the seam stitching as possible.

4. Press edge seams of pleats flat in the same position as when stitched.

5. Press inside pocket seams flat in the same position as when stitched.

6. Press flat all topstitched seams, such as lapped seams.

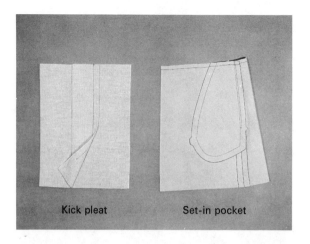

Kick pleat   Set-in pocket

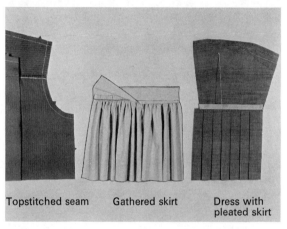

Topstitched seam   Gathered skirt   Dress with pleated skirt

Photos courtesy Sunbeam Mfg. Co.

Kick pleats, set-in pockets, topstitched seams, and waistlines are seams which are pressed flat during garment construction.

7. Press seams flat that join a gathered or pleated edge to a flat edge with both seam allowances turned toward the edge that has no fullness.

Underpressing Darts

First press the dart flat. Smooth the lines of stitching with the point of the iron, and crease the center fold of the dart by pressing in the same direction as the stitching was inserted. Then block the dart as indicated in the section on "Blocking" (see pages 316-317).

Pleats in tailored garments are first basted closed. They are then pressed flat, next pressed flat against the garment, and finally top-pressed with a pressing cloth over the surface of the garment to prevent shine.

Underpressing Pleats

All pleats except those in cotton fabrics and those in fabrics which have been durably pleated should be basted before pressing. Machine-baste the pleat-marking lines together on the wrong side whenever possible. (See the illustration above. Also see the directions for top-pressing pleats in cotton fabrics on page 320.)

Underpress the pleat flat along the line of stitching, in the direction in which the stitching was done, and along the fold to set the crease if the edge of the pleat is on a fold. Turn the pleat in the correct direction with the garment spread flat, wrong side out, and press, taking care to open the fabric all the way to the line of stitching.

Remove the basting, and turn the garment to the right side, Top-press the pleat, with a lifting and lowering motion of the iron, using a pressing cloth if the fabric requires it. If the fabric marks easily, slip a strip of paper under the pleat to prevent the edge from making an imprint. To remove such marks, turn the fabric

again to the wrong side, lift the edge of the pleat, and re-press along the line of marking with the point of the iron.

Blocking

Pressing which shapes the garment as well as smoothes the fabric is called blocking. Blocking is done over a curved surface, usually with steam. It is done in the direction of the grain, from either the right or the wrong side of the garment, and usually with the flat forepart of the iron.

A garment may be blocked to contour the area at the end of the dart. Blocking over a tailor's ham or pressing cushion shapes such curved areas as shoulder, bust, elbow, and hip. Sleeve caps and hems are blocked by shrinking out the fullness at the upper edge to avoid puckers and pleats. A bias strip may be shaped by blocking to fit a curved edge. A tailored collar can be blocked to fit closely around the neckline, and a tailored skirt to fit smoothly around the waistline. Whenever one of these types of shaping is required, the individual units are usually blocked as they are completed, before they are attached to other units.

Blocking a Dart

After a dart has been underpressed to smooth the stitching and to crease the center fold line, shape it in the following way:

1. Place the dart, wrong side up, over a tailor's ham, a pressing cushion, or the small end of a pressing board with the garment opened out and the point of the dart at the end of the ham or board.

2. Turn the dart in the correct direction for its position. Vertical darts, such as waistline or shoulder darts, are usually turned toward the center of the figure: front darts toward the center front, back darts toward the center back. Horizontal darts, such as underarm bust darts, are usually turned toward the lower edge of the garment.

3. Press the dart crosswise, gently pulling the garment fabric away from the line of

stitching so that the fabric is opened completely. This prevents pressing in a crease or pleat on the right side. Avoid making an imprint on the right side of the fabric by slipping a strip of paper under the fold line of the dart.

4. Top-press lightly (see page 320). If the imprint of the dart shows on the right side, turn the fabric back to the wrong side and remove the imprint by pressing beneath the edge of the dart with the point of the iron.

Double-pointed darts require clipping at the widest point to release the fabric before pressing.

Darts made in heavy fabric are slashed on the fold line or trimmed to ½ inch and pressed open before blocking.

Dart tucks are not blocked but are pressed flat only for the length of the stitching.

Blocking the Shoulder Area

The shoulder area of many garments is made to fit the figure by easing the fabric along the back shoulder line. Further shape may be given by blocking the area over a tailor's ham or pressing cushion. To block a shoulder, see the illustration at the lower right and follow these directions:

1. Press the shoulder seam flat, directionally, along the line of stitching.

2. Open the seam by pressing directionally with the point of the iron along the line of stitching.

3. Block the shoulder over a ham or cushion, shrinking in the ease along the seam line to give the back a rounded shape.

4. Top-press lightly on the right side of the fabric to avoid making an imprint of the edges of the seam allowances.

Blocking a Sleeve

The cap of a sleeve in a fabric which is shrinkable requires blocking before it is set in a garment. Since many fabrics of man-made fibers cannot be blocked to fit, try to choose pattern styles which require gathers or the minimum of ease when working with these fabrics. De-

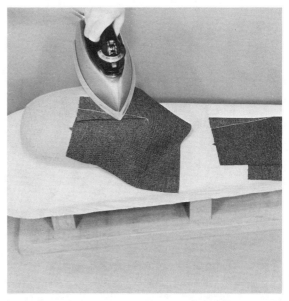

Courtesy Sunbeam Mfg. Co.

To block a dart, first press it to smooth the stitching line. Then with a crosswise lifting and lowering of the iron, shape the dart over a ham or some other curved piece of pressing equipment.

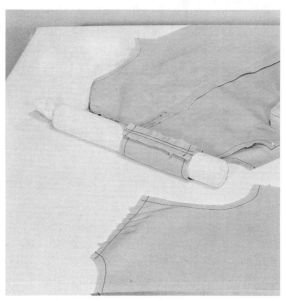

Courtesy Sunbeam Mfg. Co.

To block the shoulder area, first press the shoulder seam along the line of stitching. Then open the seam and press it flat directionally, using the point of the iron.

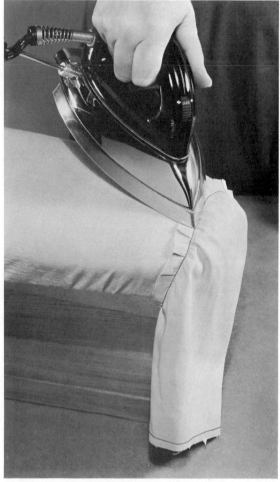

To block the cap of a sleeve, pull a row of gathering stitching so that the sleeve fits the armhole. Using the point of a steam iron, shrink out the fullness in the cap along the seam line. Tucks may be formed if necessary in the seam allowance.

armhole edge of the sleeve. The cap of the sleeve should be left rounded with no pleats at the seam line, although there may be small pleats in the seam allowance itself. The underarm section of the armhole seam, the area between the notches, requires no pressing.

Blocking a Hem

The method used for the turning and blocking of any hem is the same regardless of where it is located on a garment or how it is to be finished. If tape is to be used for finishing the upper edge of a hem or if a bias strip is to be used for cushioning, blocking is required before its application. After a hem has been turned and either pinned or basted along the fold line, it is ready to be blocked. (See pages 376-377 for turning the hem. Also see pages 505-507 for hemming tailored garments.)

The blocking can be accomplished according to the following steps:

1. Spread the turned hem flat on the board, and press it from the wrong side to crease the fold line. If pins have been used to hold the hem in place, crease the fold line between the pins, then remove the pins and press the areas where the pins were located.

2. Shrink out the fullness at the top of the hem by steam pressing in the direction of the grain from the fold line to the cut edge.

3. To shrink hem tape to shape, place the tape in a curved position over a tailor's ham or on the board, and block it so that one edge is slightly longer than the other.

4. To block a cushioning strip to the exact shape of the hem, place the bias strip on top of the garment hem, and shape the cushioning strip to match the garment hem by steam pressing.

Blocking a Tailored Collar

The collar on a tailored coat or jacket is shaped into a curve at the neckline for a close fit. This shape is achieved by blocking the undercollar after the interfacing has been applied. The blocking procedure is as follows:

termine the amount of ease in a fabric which will yield to blocking by pinning the sleeve into the armhole (see pages 472-473). Then lay the cap over the curved edge of a sleeve board with the cap extending no more than ¾ inch over the end of the board. Using the point of the iron, press the seam allowance only. Shrink out the fullness at the seam line, working with the point of the iron toward the

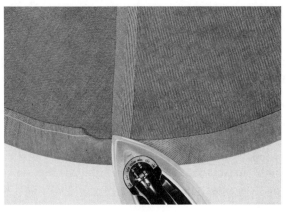

To block a staystitched hem in a lightweight skirt, first block the hem directionally against the garment to reduce bulk. Then turn under and press the seam allowance before pinning the hem to the skirt.

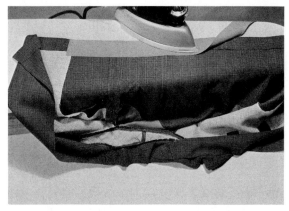

To block a bias cushioning strip, lay the strip over the blocked hem, and shrink it to the exact shape of the area it will cushion.

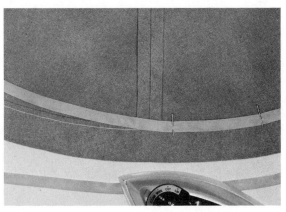

Hem tape can be blocked to fit a flared skirt by shrinking one edge more than the other. Handle the tape gently while pinning it to the upper edge of the hem for machine stitching.

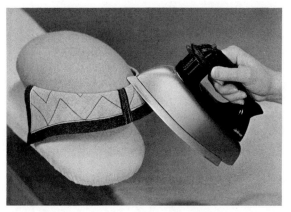

An undersection of a tailored collar is blocked to shape the neckline by using a steam iron, pressing from the outer edge of the collar toward the fold line.

Fold the collar lengthwise with the interfacing side out. Keep the neckline and outer edges even at the center back. Continue the fold to the seam line at the front end of the collar or to the notch on the neckline edge, depending on the collar design.

Shape the collar over a tailor's ham by steam-pressing on the grain, from the outer edge to the fold, forcing the threads together at the fold line and avoiding any stretch at the outer or the neckline edges. Continue pressing until the desired shape is obtained.

Blocking a Tailored Skirt Band

A skirt band will fit better if it is blocked after it has been interfaced. To block the band, see the illustration at the top of page 320 and follow these directions:

Courtesy Sunbeam Mfg. Co.

To fit the curve of the body, a tailored waistband is blocked from the open edges toward the top fold. Use a pressing cloth to prevent shine on the fabric surface.

Courtesy Sunbeam Mfg. Co.

A completed garment is top-pressed for a finished look. Use a pressing cloth to protect the garment from the heated soleplate of the iron.

Fold the band in half lengthwise, wrong sides together, and re-press the fold line to a sharp crease for the top edge of the finished band. Shape the band so that it is curved, with the top folded edge slightly shorter than the open edges. Place the folded band in a slightly curved position on the pressing board or over the end of a tailor's ham. Press it to the desired curved shape from the open edges to the fold in the direction of the crosswise grain.

Top Pressing

Pressing from the right side, or top, of a garment is called top pressing. The principle use of top pressing is for the final pressing of a garment. Top pressing can also be used for completing the blocking of a dart or shoulder line during the construction process. It cannot, however, replace pressing as you sew. In top pressing, it is best to use light pressure to prevent impressions of construction details from showing on the right side of the garment. A pressing cloth will help prevent fabric shine.

Pleats in cotton fabrics are top-pressed during construction. To do so, crease the fabric on one marked line and fold it to the next marked line. Then pin the upper and lower ends of the pleat to the ironing board to hold the pleat taut until the top pressing is completed.

Why do fabrics react differently to pressing?
How might the pressing requirements differ for linen and a man-made fiber that looks like linen?
How is the pressing temperature for fabric blends determined? For fabrics of man-made fibers?
How can wool be pressed effectively?
What are the techniques for pressing fabrics with heat-sensitive finishes?

Pressing Requirements for Particular Fibers

As the reaction of a fabric to pressing depends largely on its fiber content, always check the label or hang tag on your fabric for fiber content or specific instructions. Test the heat of the iron on a scrap of the fabric or on an inside seam before pressing. It will help also if you know the special requirements of the common textile fibers.

Cotton and Linen

Relatively high pressing temperatures and moisture are required to make untreated cot-

Courtesy Simplicity Pattern Co., Inc.

STANDARDS FOR A WELL-PRESSED GARMENT

1. *The original texture of the fabric is maintained.*
2. *No shine or press marks show.*
3. *Seams and darts are smooth along the stitching line.*
4. *Edges of seam allowances and dart folds form no ridges on the right side of the garment.*
5. *Shaped or curved edges are blocked to maintain shape.*
6. *The garment looks professionally finished.*

ton and linen smooth. These fabrics are not damaged by a heated iron placed directly on them, and they may be pressed from either the right or the wrong side. However, if they are textured, dull-surfaced, or dark-colored, they will look better if pressed on the wrong side whenever possible.

Cottons and linens that have been treated for crease resistance or given permanent-press finishes cannot stand the high pressing temperatures acceptable for untreated fabrics. Such finishes are sensitive to heat. Use steam and a moderate pressing temperature. Sometimes you will need to use a pressing cloth or to press on the wrong side.

Blends

Fabric blends include two or more kinds of fibers. It is important to know what these fibers are. A rule of thumb is to select the pressing temperature suited to the most heat-sensitive fiber in the blend.

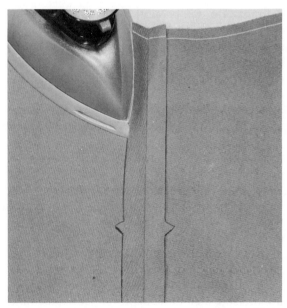

Courtesy Sunbeam Mfg. Co.

Untreated cottons and linens require moisture and a relatively hot iron temperature for effective pressing.

Wool fabrics require an iron heated to a medium temperature, limited moisture, and protection from direct contact with the soleplate of the iron.

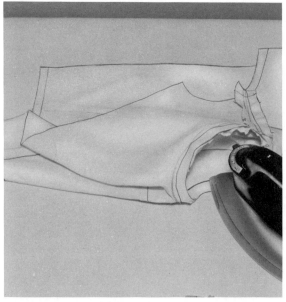

A fabric composed of thermoplastic man-made fiber is pressed with an iron set for low heat.

Wool

A moderate temperature and limited moisture are required for wool because it is sensitive to excesses of pressure, moisture, and heat. Press the fabric with a steam iron on the wrong side, or with a dry iron and a damp pressing cloth on the right or wrong side. Avoid pressing wool entirely dry. Doing so will make the fabric shiny and harsh. If the nap becomes flattened during pressing, re-press and brush the fabric gently while it is damp to restore the nap.

Many times wrinkles can be removed by hanging wool garments in a bathroom in steam produced by running hot water in the shower or tub. When the wrinkles disappear and the pile is raised, remove the garment from the steamy area. Avoid touching the fabric until it is completely dry. The use of such an improvised steam room or a hand steaming device is often effective and less damaging to wool garments than are regular pressing techniques.

Silk

Silk is a delicate fiber and should be pressed at a moderate temperature. A dry pressing cloth over the fabric will help to prevent water spots or a shine. It is sometimes possible to press this fabric on the wrong side with a steam iron.

Man-made Fibers

Many fabrics composed of man-made fibers have been woven or finished to resist wrinkles. They require little or no pressing. Pressing temperatures vary according to the fiber family. Each fiber family has a different heat sensitivity. For example, the rayon family is less heat sensitive than are the acetates. For the pressing requirements of specific man-made fibers, see the charts on pages 62-65.

Pressing Special Fabrics

Many fabrics require special pressing techniques to preserve the beauty of their dis-

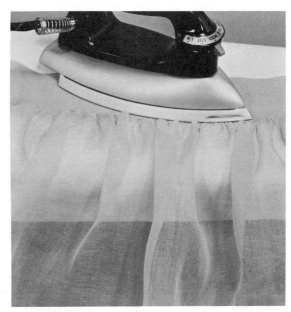

Courtesy Sunbeam Mfg. Co.

Sheer fabrics are best pressed with an iron set at a lower temperature than the fiber indicates. In pressing gathers, move the point of the iron toward the gathered seam line (left). Then press the ungathered section above the gathering line.

tinctive construction and texture. Almost without exception, garments made of such fabrics can be pressed with home techniques during the construction process. However, often they will look far more professional and stylish if pressed by a professional drycleaner upon completion of the project. Information on the pressing requirements of several categories of special fabrics is included here. Details for pressing other, specific special fabrics is given in the extensive charts on pages 430-437.

Heat-sensitive Finishes

Among the variety of fabric finishes, some are sensitive to heat. Before pressing, be sure to make an iron-test on a scrap of your fabric. While a low temperature setting is sometimes recommended for underpressing, a slightly higher setting with steam and pressing cloth is often needed for the final pressing. If the fabric is bonded to a knit tricot, the backing is sometimes more heat-sensitive than the fabric itself and so the wrong side requires a *low* pressing temperature.

Raised-surface Designs

Fabrics with woven, embossed, or embroidered designs are effectively pressed by placing them on a softly padded board and pressing on the wrong side. Plenty of moisture is needed. Light pressure is best on woven or embossed fabrics, but a heavier pressure will emphasize the design of embroidery.

Crepe Fabrics

Press crepe fabrics with great care because their size and shape may be easily distorted. Press with the grain, using no more moisture than necessary. Stretched crepe can usually be returned to its original shape by steaming with little or no pressure.

323

1. Pressing is an up-and-down motion of the iron that exerts heat, moisture, and downward pressure on a fabric.

2. Pressing is a means of straightening fabric grain, shaping fabric, shrinking fabric, maintaining and enhancing fabric texture, and providing a finished look to a completed garment.

3. The correct pressing temperatures and pressing techniques depend upon the fiber content of the fabric and the construction of the fabric.

4. Seams are underpressed with the point of the iron before garment units are joined.

5. To prevent seam imprints, heavy paper may be inserted under the seams and hems of garments before pressing.

6. Steam pressing may be accomplished with a dry iron by using a dampened pressing cloth.

7. A garment piece may be shaped, or blocked, by means of steam pressing over a curved surface with light pressure of the iron.

8. Top pressing is used in clothing construction mainly for the final pressing.

9. Fabric blends are correctly pressed at the temperature setting suited to the most heat-sensitive fiber in the blend.

10. A pile or napped fabric may be pressed over a needle board or a terry-cloth towel to prevent flattening or matting.

11. Special fabrics require special pressing techniques to maintain their original texture and appearance.

16 *Waistline Finishes*

The waistline is an important part of a garment because it contributes
to both appearance and comfort. The waistline finishes found in patterns
vary in style from time to time as fashions come and go. The principles of their
design and construction, however, apply at all times and to all styles.

How do you join a skirt and bodice?
What is a waistline stay?
*How do you determine the length of the waist-
band?*
How do you interface a waistband?
How do you attach a waistband to a skirt?

Decisions About Waistline Finishes

Although the beginning seamstress is generally
wise to follow the pattern guide sheet, a
waistline sometimes offers opportunities for
creativity. If you are making a dress, you
might decide you would prefer a lapped
seam to the specified plain seam. Or perhaps
you would like to substitute decorative cording for a self-belt. Or possibly you would like
to complete the garment with a bias sash, a
rope tie, or a leather belt. With shorts, slacks,
or skirts, you might decide to add a waistband or to omit a band, replacing it with a
facing. With imagination, you can vary such
details and add your own creative touches.

Factors Affecting Choice of Finish

You have the alternatives of following precisely, adapting, or revising the waistline
finish described on your pattern guide sheet.
Whatever your choice, it is important to consider the three factors that determine the appropriateness of a waistline finish: the function of the garment, the type of fabric, and
your time and sewing skills.

Garment Function

The function of a garment determines the
suitability of a particular seam choice. For
example, the treatment of a waistline seam on
a sheer party dress with an Empire waistline
is apt to be different from that of a tailored
wool dress. While the waistline of the tailored
dress may need anchoring to prevent sagging,
the waistline of the sheer dress may need
binding to hide the seam edges. A garment
such as a tennis dress for active sports requires a sturdier waistline treatment than that
of a dressy dress because it must be con-

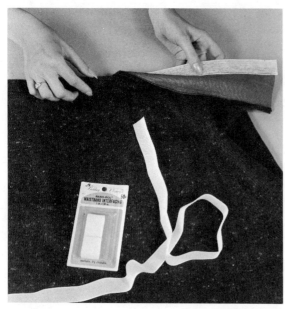

A stiff, but pliable, interfacing can be stitched inside certain bands made of stretchy fabric to provide firmness without added bulk.

structed to withstand vigorous activity and frequent laundering.

For comfort and sturdiness in wear, the waistline finishes of skirts, slacks, and shorts require that their waistline seams be completely enclosed. Each garment must be considered from the standpoint of function before a final choice of waistline seam finish is determined.

Type of Fabric

Different types of fabric usually require different waistline treatments. For example, a waistline finish appropriate for a knit or stretch fabric is not likely to be suitable for a firmly woven cotton fabric. While the stretch fabric requires a seam which will give with the rest of the garment, other fabrics may require a seam which will not stretch. Some fabrics require that a waistband be lined, while others require no lining. A bulky tweed or furlike fabric may be too thick for a waistband and will need to be faced at the waistline with a lighter-weight fabric. A loosely woven fabric that ravels easily often requires binding, while a firmly woven fabric may require only a waistline stay. Suggestions on the pattern guide sheet are often helpful in showing suitable finishes for the fabric recommended for the specific pattern.

Time and Sewing Skills

Some waistline treatments involve more skill and time than others. For example, a waistline which includes scallops, an intricate band, or special stitching would probably not be suggested on an easy-to-make pattern, nor should it be elected by a beginning seamstress. Such treatments, however, can produce attractive results in a garment. The joy of successful accomplishment of intricate sewing details is a reward for the seamstress who has mastered the basic skills. Early in your sewing experiences simple treatments are best. The simple, well-made garments of a beginning seamstress can be dressed up with accessories.

Joining Bodice and Skirt

Regardless of the type of seam made, there are some basic guidelines to follow when attaching a bodice to the skirt. A basic understanding of this procedure can assist you in sewing any waistline.

First, locate *your* natural waistline. This can be done by tying a cord or measuring tape around your waist so that it fits comfortably. Then try on the bodice and the skirt *before* joining them to determine whether the bodice is too long or too short for your figure. Trim away any excess bodice length, that is, any fabric beyond the ⅝-inch seam allowance, before attaching it to the skirt. (See page 242.)

When joining the bodice to the skirt at the waistline, there are key points to be matched. In garments with a side opening, align the center front, center back, and side seams of the bodice and skirt, and pin them together horizontally from the bodice side of the garment. Place the pins at the seam line

Courtesy Simplicity Pattern Co., Inc.

STANDARDS FOR WAISTLINE SEAMS

1. *Seam is located at the normal waistline.*
2. *Waistline fits snugly but not tight.*
3. *Seams are flat and not bulky.*
4. *Darts and seams on bodice and skirt are perfectly aligned.*
5. *The waistline is smooth without wrinkles or bulges.*
6. *Seam does not buckle, stretch, or pucker.*

and perpendicular to it, with heads out for easy removal. If the opening is located at the center back, align and pin the side seams of the bodice and skirt, then the center fronts, and finally the edges of the waistline seam at the center back opening. Align darts in the skirt with corresponding darts in the bodice, and pin them accurately.

You will find in most instances that the waistline of the bodice is larger than that of the skirt. This requires that the bodice be eased to the skirt to avoid obvious puckers or pleats. If the difference between the size of the bodice and skirt waistlines is extreme, recheck the seams and darts to be sure they have been stitched accurately. Check any minor alterations made in the bodice or skirt, because changes in seams or darts made in one unit affect the other. If you find that the bodice and skirt cannot be eased together, make necessary alterations, keeping the key grain lines straight so that the garment will hang accurately (see pages 339-341).

Baste the waistline seam together, making sure that all darts and side seams are accurately aligned. Stitch from the bodice side of the garment to distribute the ease smoothly.

After basting, once again try on the garment to check the fit at the waistline. To determine its fit, ask yourself the following questions: Does the seam fall at my natural waistline? Is it too high or too low? Does it feel too big or too small? Generally, the waistline of a fitted garment should be $\frac{1}{2}$ to 1 inch larger than your actual waist measurement.

If the waistline fits correctly, stitch a permanent seam along the seam line, using regular-size machine stitches. For reinforcement, either insert another row of stitching $\frac{1}{8}$ inch inside the $\frac{5}{8}$-inch seam allowance or topstitch it from the right side of the garment. To topstitch, press both seam allowances toward the bodice and stitch through the garment and both seam allowances $\frac{1}{8}$ inch above the seam line. (For a discussion of topstitching, see pages 388-389.) To keep the seam from stretching when the garment is worn, attach a waistline stay following the directions given below.

Waistline seams are usually pressed upwards toward the bodice, or top, of the garment, rather than pressed open. This helps a waistline seam to fit smoothly against the garment. If the waistline seam, which is smaller than the part of the skirt just below the waistline, were forced in place below the top edge of the skirt, the waistline area would pucker unattractively.

Waistline Stays

A waistline stay is a strip of seam tape or fabric used to stabilize the waistline seam to the dimensions of the body. It might be called an inside, or invisible, waistband. It can help to relieve strain on the zipper and waistline seams and prevent the seam from stretching. It can also be used to ease a skirt and bodice together during garment construction. The stay is often effective in holding the shape of garments which do not have waistline seams.

A waistline stay can be made from pre-shrunk seam, or hem, tape, narrow grosgrain ribbon, or a narrow strip of selvage cut from firmly woven fabric. Cut the strip an inch or two longer than the waistline measurement. One inch is added for ease, and extra length is allowed for fasteners if they are to be used. The stay is usually attached to the skirt before it is joined to the bodice. It can be attached to a completed waistline, or it can be attached to a dress without a waistline seam.

To apply the stay to the skirt during construction of a dress, first position the tape on the front and the back of the skirt, distributing the ease as necessary. Leave one-half of the extra length of the stay at each edge of the placket opening so that hooks and eyes can be attached to it later. Machine-stitch the stay ½ inch from the edge of the waistline seam.

By attaching a stay of the correct length to the skirt first, it is possible to ease the full-

A stay cut to comfortably fit the waistline can be used to ease together a skirt and bodice and to support the waistline seam.

ness of the bodice waistline smoothly as it is attached to the skirt. After the stay has been attached, the bodice waistline can be eased, or adjusted, to fit the measurements of the skirt waistline.

If no waistline adjustment is necessary, the stay can be attached after the waistline seam has been sewn. To do so, stitch the stay to the waistline seam allowance by hand or by machine close to the original stitching line.

If the stay is to be attached to a dress which has no waistline seam, locate your nat-

1. Stitch the stay to the inside seam line of the skirt. This stay will help to hold the shape of the skirt during fitting and stitching to the bodice.

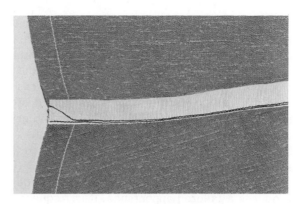

3. Machine-stitch the bodice and skirt together, slanting the stitches in the zipper area to prevent puckering of the zipper seam. Double-stitch or topstitch the waistline seam for added strength.

2. Ease and pin the bodice and skirt together at the waistline seam, keying center fronts, center backs, and side seams, as well as waistline tucks or darts.

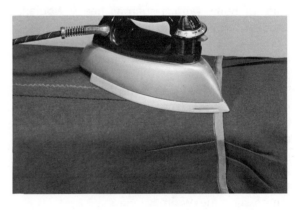

4. Press the completed waistline seam upward into the bodice of a garment.

ural waistline and mark this line on the inside of your garment with chalk, tailor's tacks, or pins. Next, divide the waistline stay into four major sections proportionately similar to the size of the garment sections, and position these at the center front, center back, and the two side seams of the garment. The two front sections of the stay will be longer than the two back sections for proper fit with the garment. Place the ends of the stay at the placket opening. Fasten the stay to the darts and side seams with hand stitches. Hooks and eyes may be sewn on the free ends of the stay so that it can be fastened together in wearing, before the opening is zipped closed or buttoned in the case of buttoned plackets.

Waistbands

For a good fit, waistbands are cut from a straight strip of fabric, usually on the lengthwise grain of the fabric. The fit of the entire garment often depends on accurate construction of the waistband.

There are a variety of waistband applications. Although you may decide to follow the pattern instructions for applying a waistband, at times there is room for creativity if your changes are appropriate. Alternative choices most frequently made include a waistband of self-fabric attached by machine topstitching or invisible machine or hand stitching, a waistband faced with some form of backing, and a faced waistline with no band.

A waistband topstitched on the outside produces a tailored appearance. It is frequently found on washable sportswear such as shorts, slacks, and skirts. A less sturdy and less tailored band is made by fastening the inside of the band to the garment with hand stitching. This type of finish is especially suitable for bulky fabrics such as heavy woolens and corduroy.

Determining the Length and Width of the Waistband

The width of a waistband can vary from narrow to wide, depending on the fabric, the pattern style, and individual preference. Generally, the measurements of a band are predetermined by your pattern and guide sheet. If you decide to make changes, however, there are ways for you to determine both the length and the width.

You may make the band any width that you consider appropriate for the garment and flattering to your figure. For example, a waistband of lightweight, washable cotton, in which one layer serves as an interfacing, might be two or three times wider than a band of wool knit or corduroy. Having decided upon the finished width, you can determine how wide a band to cut by adding together twice the desired width plus two seam allowances of $5/8$ inch each. An exception is the waistband which has a self-interfacing. This type of band is three times the desired width plus two $5/8$-inch seam allowances.

The length of the waistband can be determined as follows: Measure your waist and add 1 inch for ease. Then add an additional 3 inches for the seam allowances at the ends of the band and for the underlap. For example, if your waist measures 25 inches, then the cut length of the waistband is 25 inches (your waist measure) plus 1 inch (ease) plus 3 inches (seam allowances and underlap). The waistband when cut is correctly 29 inches long.

Interfacing and Attaching the Waistband

Most waistbands require interfacing to give added body and firmness. Whether to interface and how to interface depend on the type of fabric used for the waistband, the style and width of the band, the degree of stiffness desired, and the current fashion. If making a

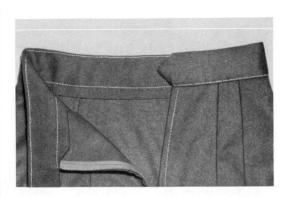

STANDARDS FOR WAISTBANDS

1. *Even in width at all points.*
2. *Firm enough to retain shape.*
3. *Cut on the true lengthwise grain.*
4. *Flat and smooth with no bulges or ripples.*

waistband of stretch fabric you might want to omit interfacing altogether to maintain the stretch quality. On the other hand, the band of a dressy skirt of soft polyester puff might require an interfacing of a stiff fabric such as organdy. Most cotton and cotton-polyester blends can be self-interfaced satisfactorily. In any case choose an interfacing which will add to, rather than detract from, the appearance of the garment and attach it in a manner attractive for the specific fabric.

Interfacing with Interfacing Fabric

When a waistband is interfaced with fabric other than the outer fabric, the following procedure can be used:

1. Cut the interfacing either from a special interfacing pattern provided or from the waistband pattern itself. Usually, the interfacing is cut only half the width of the waistband plus ¼ inch. Transfer the markings from the pattern onto the interfacing.

2. Place the interfacing on the wrong side of the waistband fabric on the half which will be toward the outside when the band is finished. If one edge of the waistband has a selvage, use the selvage portion as the inside of the band. In such a case the interfacing will be placed along the cut or torn edge of the waistband.

3. Stitch the interfacing to the band ½ inch from the outer edge and ⅛ inch beyond the inner edge, or fold line, in the band. Trim the seam allowance of the *interfacing* to ⅛ inch along the outer edge.

4. Fold the band in half lengthwise, wrong sides together, and press it. The stitching of the inner edge of the interfacing will be ⅛ inch beyond the pressed fold line and on the *inside* of the finished waistband.

5. Block the waistband before attaching it to the skirt (see pages 319-320).

6. Attach the band to the right side of the skirt with regular-size machine stitches, leaving a ⅝-inch seam allowance.

7. Close the ends of the waistband with machine stitching, turning the right sides

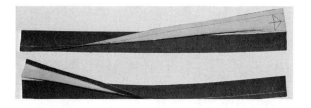

After cutting and marking the interfacing fabric, stitch it to the waistband ½ inch from the outer edge and ⅛ inch beyond the fold line. Block the band before attaching it to the skirt.

With right sides together, pin the interfaced edge of the band to the staystitched upper edge of the garment waistline.

Stitch the band to the garment, leaving sufficient length at one end for shaping and at the other end for an underlap.

Machine-stitch to close the ends of the band along the marked lines. Clip the corners, grade the seams, and press the ends of the band, using a seam board or other pressing equipment (top). Then turn the band right side out for finishing (bottom).

Machine-stitch the band in place from the outside of the garment, or fasten it in place with an appropriate hand-hemming stitch.

of the band together and reversing the lengthwise fold. If shaping markings were transferred onto the interfacing, use them as a guide for shaping the ends of the band, either square or triangular.

8. Grade the seams at the ends of the band and press them carefully into shape.

9. Pin the remaining edge of the band in place against the skirt. Turn under a ⅝-inch seam allowance for a hand-finished band, and pin it on the *inside* of the skirt. Turn under a ½-inch seam allowance for a machine-finished one, and pin it on the *outside* of the skirt. An alternative method is to let the seam allowance of the band extend into the top of the skirt without turning, to serve as a cushioning for the waistline seam.

10. Stitch the band in place with machine topstitching or with an appropriate hand-hemming stitch (see pages 392-395).

Interfacing with Self-fabric
Often waistbands in garments of cotton fabrics and lightweight blends can be interfaced with the fabric of the outer garment. To accomplish this interfacing process easily, complete the following steps:

1. Cut a strip of fabric of accurate length and width, allowing the proper length for your waist measurement plus 1 inch for ease and 3 inches for seam allowances and underlap. Allow a width three times the desired width of the completed band plus 1¼ inches for the seam allowance.

2. Fold the strip in thirds lengthwise, right sides out, and crease the folds by pressing.

3. Lifting the top fold, machine-stitch the inside edge to the fabric beneath it, ⅛ inch from the fold line.

4. Press and block the band-interfacing combination before attaching it to the fitted skirt.

5. With right sides together, attach the single thickness of the band to the fitted skirt with a ⅝-inch seam allowance, using regular-length stitches.

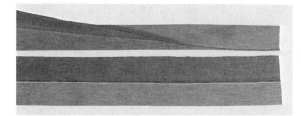

1. Cut a strip of self-fabric 4 inches longer than your waist measurement and three times the desired band width plus 1¼ inches. Fold and press the strip into thirds lengthwise (top). Lift the top edge and machine-stitch the center layer to the underneath layer (bottom).

2. With right sides together, pin the single layer of the band to the upper edge of the garment.

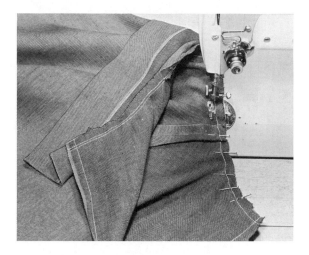

3. Stitch the band to the garment from placket edge to placket edge.

4. Fold the ends of the band wrong sides out and stitch along the seam line (top). Grade the seams, clip the corners, and press the ends of the band, using a seam board or other pressing equipment (center). Turn the band right side out for finishing (bottom).

5. Complete the band by machine-stitching from the outside of the band. Add hooks and eyes or a button and buttonhole.

Well-made waistlines of pant- and skirt-type garments, whether faced or finished with waistbands, are smooth enough to remain inconspicuous under a jacket and are sturdy enough to withstand the pressure of a belt.

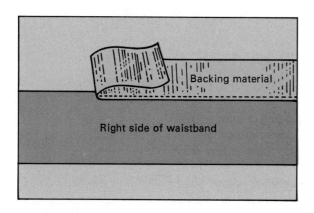

To apply backing to a band, stitch grosgrain ribbon or special backing material to the single layer of fabric which will be used as the outside surface of the band.

6. Finish the ends of the band by turning the right sides together, reversing the fold, and aligning the stitching on the front end of the band with the edge of the placket. Allow length for an underlap beyond the back edge of the placket. Then grade the seams, and press them to shape.

7. Turn the band right side out, and pin the self-interfaced section against the wrong side of the skirt. Be careful to keep the upper fold flat so that the stitching line which is near the top of the band will not show on the right side of the garment. The seam allowance on the band will extend below the waistline seam.

8. Complete the band either by stitching from the right side exactly on the line of stitching which joins the skirt to the band, or by stitching slightly above the original row of stitching to provide decorative topstitching.

Applying Backing

This method of preparing and attaching a waistband differs somewhat from the other two methods in that a special backing serves as both the interfacing and the inside layer of the waistband. It is a method used to reduce bulk when the fabric of a garment is very thick.

The backing can be made of preshrunk grosgrain ribbon or a stiffened, rubberized material available at sewing notions counters in most department stores. Choose the backing in a width suitable for the finished waistband. Buy a length an inch or two longer than that of the waistband pattern and preshrink it (see pages 265-266).

The waistband is cut from the skirt fabric to accurate length but to the width of the finished waistband, plus two seam allowances. To accomplish this cutting procedure, fold the waistband pattern in half lengthwise and add a ⅝-inch seam allowance to the upper edge as the band is cut.

Attach the backing to the waistband in the following manner:

1. Topstitch one edge of the backing to the seam line along the unnotched edge of the waistband as close to the edge of the backing as possible.

2. Fold the upper edge of the band along the stitched edge to prevent the backing from showing on the outside.

3. Attach the lower edge of the band to the garment, right sides together.

4. Press the seam upward into the band.

5. Complete the ends of the waistband by folding and topstitching them together.

6. Pin the backing to a point just below the lower seam line of the band, pins perpendicular to the waistline seam, from the *right* side if the band is to be attached by machine stitching or from the *inside* if the band is to be attached by hand.

7. Stitch the band to the skirt by machine or by hand. Machine stitches may be located exactly on the seam line or a fraction of an inch above it for a decorative effect. If hand stitches are used, choose the pick stitch (see pages 392 and 394).

1. A waistline seam requires alignment of the darts and seams of the bodice with those of the skirt.

2. If seams and darts do not align correctly when the bodice and skirt are joined, adjustments are necessary.

3. A waistline seam may be reinforced by adding a second row of permanent machine stitching $\frac{1}{8}$ inch inside the seam allowance.

4. A waistline stay is added to prevent a waistline seam from stretching when the garment is worn.

5. A waistline stay can be made from preshrunk seam tape, narrow grosgrain ribbon, or the selvage edge of firmly woven fabric.

6. The length of a waistline stay is determined by adding 1 inch to your waist measurement. Extra length may be added on which to attach fasteners in garments without waistlines.

7. If a waistline stay is to be attached to a garment without a waistline seam, it may be hand-tacked to the side seams and darts.

8. The length of your waistband can be determined by adding 4 inches to your waistline measurement.

9. Interfacing applied to a waistband preserves the shape of the waistband.

10. Final stitching of the waistband to the garment can be done with hand stitching or machine stitching.

11. A waistband even in width, smooth, and adequately firm will retain its shape.

Fitting a Garment

Well-fitted clothes always look as if they belong to the person who is wearing them. They make the wearer appear comfortable and poised. They flatter the figure, emphasizing the best features and skillfully hiding imperfections. Poor fit is more likely than poor workmanship to be responsible for the nonprofessional appearance often found in home-sewn apparel. Skill in fitting is insurance against the homemade look.

How is a garment fitted?

Why is it necessary to try on a garment when making fitting changes?

Where are the key grain lines located in a garment and what is their role in the fitting process?

What clues regarding fit can be provided by the position of wrinkles in a garment?

What are the guidelines for determining ease?

What are the standards of fit for a blouse? For skirts and slacks? For a dress?

Decisions About Fitting a Garment

Fitting is the process of adjusting a garment to the shape of the wearer. Personal preference helps determine decisions as to the type, location, and amount of fullness. Fashion also plays a role in fit. In some years it is stylish to have a soft, clinging, drapable look which follows the contour of the body. In other years, a tailored or crisp stand-away silhouette may be popular.

When making decisions about the fit of a garment you are constructing or altering, consider the basic design of the outfit. Then try to maintain the basic garment lines, but be aware that there are several ways of doing so. Do not hesitate to experiment with several approaches to a fitting problem.

Consider your sewing ability in analyzing fitting problems. For example, is the problem a minor one that you can manage on your own with the aid of a mirror and available sewing equipment? Will it require the advice or assistance of a more experienced seamstress? Once you have become acquainted with the basic principles of fitting, you will find you are able to successfully handle a wide variety of garment alterations yourself.

Purposes of Fitting a Garment

There is only one major purpose of fitting a garment which has been cut to fit. That is to check the garment during construction. However, newly purchased ready-made garments frequently require fitting also.

To Check a Garment During Construction

If your pattern has been compared and adjusted to your own measurements, the gar-

BASIC FITTING GUIDELINES

1. *Fit the garment over the undergarments you will be wearing with the outfit.*
2. *Fit the garment with the right side out.*
3. *Fit the garment along the major construction seams, rather than along design seams. Construction seams include the side seams, waistline seam, underarm seams, armhole seams, and basic darts.*
4. *Start the fitting process at the neck and shoulders and work downward to the hemline.*
5. *Make similar adjustments on both sides of a garment, unless allowing for irregularities of your personal body build.*
6. *Maintain the original grain lines and the silhouette of the garment.*
7. *Avoid making drastic changes in any one seam or dart.*
8. *Analyze the horizontal and vertical wrinkles in each area of the garment to determine fitting difficulties.*

ment that you make should fit you satisfactorily. (For instructions on adjusting a pattern, see pages 249-255.) The person with figure irregularities particularly difficult to fit will have first cut her garment in muslin, adjusted it, and shaped her pattern to accommodate her figure (see page 249.) Theoretically a garment made by an altered pattern would fit so perfectly that trying the garment for fit would be an unnecessary step. Omitting it, however, would be a risky sewing procedure. It is far better to take the time to check the fit and alter as you go along rather than to discover upon completing the garment that major alterations are necessary.

In any work plan for the construction of a garment, definite times for fitting should be included. It is usually recommended that a garment be fitted when each major unit is completed and when minor units are attached to major ones. For example, in making a dress, complete the bodice and skirt and fit them. Attach the two units and recheck the fit. When sleeves and collar are attached, further checking of fit is desirable. Finally, the length of the finished garment requires checking. Continual fitting is particularly important if pattern alterations have been made. Then, if the fit is faulty, it can be corrected at the

earliest possible stage. Mark the alterations that are needed with pins or chalk. Make them according to the marking, and try on the garment again for a recheck. If alterations during construction are anticipated, it is best to check the fit after the seams have been machine-basted, rather than waiting until after they have been permanently stitched and finished.

To Adjust a Ready-made Garment

Ability to recognize a well-fitted garment is an art that is as necessary for the successful choice of ready-made clothes as for those that are made at home. The person who makes her own clothes learns to recognize correct fit in all clothes and develops basic skill in the procedures of fitting. This basic skill is a special asset to those who have difficulty in finding ready-to-wear garments that fit properly. The checking of garments for fit before purchase is discussed in detail in Chapter 4.

If a ready-made garment has been purchased which requires adjustment, try it on and check it carefully against the standards of good fit described in this chapter and in Chapter 4. The procedures for adjustment of ready-made garments are discussed on pages 215-216.

Basic Fitting Guidelines

Certain grain lines in every garment are known as *key grain lines* because their position indicates whether a garment has been fitted correctly. They are the key to both judging the fit and correcting it.

Before you try on a garment for a fitting, it is a good idea to mark the key grain lines with large, easily removable hand-basting stitches in a contrasting color. Then, when you are trying on the garment, these grain lines will be readily visible, enabling you to spot quickly any possible trouble spots. The illustrated chart on pages 340-341 indicates the location of these key grain lines.

In checking the fit of a garment, observe whether there is sufficient ease. Watch for bulging, sagging, or wrinkles. Crosswise wrinkles indicate that a garment is too tight. Diagonal wrinkles show that strain is pulling a garment off grain. Note whether the seams hang straight. Other guidelines for fitting a garment are shown in the chart on page 338.

General Standards of Fit

The general standards of a well-fitted garment remain the same from year to year. Fashion may influence some variation in a detail, such as the amount of ease that is desirable, but the basic standards do not change greatly because they are based on the structural lines of the human figure. When you become familiar with these standards and learn how to test the fit of garments by them, you can judge the fit of any garment in any year or season.

The general standards of good fit involve grain line, conformity to body structure, smoothness, ease, and balance. Overall comfort of the garment, or of the combination of garments, is a further fitting consideration.

Key Lines on Grain

For a garment to be well fitted, both the lengthwise and crosswise grain of the fabric must be in proper relation to the structural lines of the body. To check the grain in fitting, watch for the key lines, indicated on pages 340-341.

Conformity of Lines to Body Structure

Garment lines may either flatter or detract from the contours of the figure. The basic silhouette lines of a well-fitted garment follow the general outline of the body. The silhouette seams, underarm bodice seams and the side skirt seams, are perpendicular to the floor and divide the front and back of the body about equally. The curved seam lines follow the natural curves of the body.

Garment Smoothness

The well-fitted garment hangs straight and remains in place on the body. It is free from wrinkles, bulges, sagging, and strain. The basic lines located at the center front, center back, shoulder line, waistline, and side seams fall into normal positions on the figure. After activity, they return to normal position without pulling or tugging. A dress should carry slight fullness on each side of the front of the bodice from the shoulder tip to the waistline and should hang straight down from the hips without cupping in.

Adequate Ease

The well-fitted garment is the right size, neither too tight nor too loose. It is loose enough to be comfortable, to allow for freedom of movement, and to soften body curves, but it is not so loose that it looks baggy or too large. Common sense and caution can be your guidelines for determining ease. There should be enough ease for walking, sitting, bending, raising the arms, and bending the elbows without breaking threads or disrupting the set of the garment or the fashion lines. The amount of ease varies, of course, with such factors as fashion, activity, body build, and type of fabric. For example, the same pattern may require less ease when used for a stretch fabric than for sheer or clinging fabrics.

KEY GRAIN LINES

Bodice Front

The chestline   about 4½ inches below the shoulder line on the crosswise grain.

The bustline   across the crown of the bust on the crosswise grain.

The waistline   about 1½ inches above the waist on the crosswise grain.

The halfway line   halfway between the center front and the side seam, over the crown of the bust, on the lengthwise grain and parallel to the center front marking.

Skirt Front and Back

The hipline   7 inches below the waist, parallel to the floor but not necessarily on grain. On straight, slim skirts, the hipline is on the crosswise grain, perpendicular to the halfway line in the skirt.

The halfway line   halfway between the center front or center back and the side seam. On straight, slim skirts, the halfway line is on the lengthwise grain, perpendicular to the floor and to the hipline.

Sleeve

The sleeve-cap line   about 3 inches below the top of the shoulder, straight across the cap on the crosswise grain and at right angles to the sleeve halfway line.

The halfway line   midway in the sleeve extending from the top of the shoulder to the wrist, perpendicular to the floor on the lengthwise grain.

Bodice Back

The shoulder line   about 4½ inches below the top of the shoulder on the crosswise grain. This line corresponds to the chestline on the bodice front.

The underarm line   about 1½ inches below the armhole, across the shoulder blades, on the crosswise grain. This line corresponds to the bustline on the bodice front.

The waistline   1½ inches above the waist, as on the bodice front, on the crosswise grain.

The halfway line   halfway between the center back and the side seam, from the center of the shoulder to the waist, on the lengthwise grain. This line corresponds to the halfway line on the bodice front.

Pants, Slacks, and Shorts Front and Back

The hipline   7 inches below the waist, parallel to the floor but not necessarily on grain.

The halfway line   halfway between the center front or back and the side seam, on the lengthwise grain, and perpendicular to the floor and to the hipline.

Dart fold lines   on straight grain of fabric.

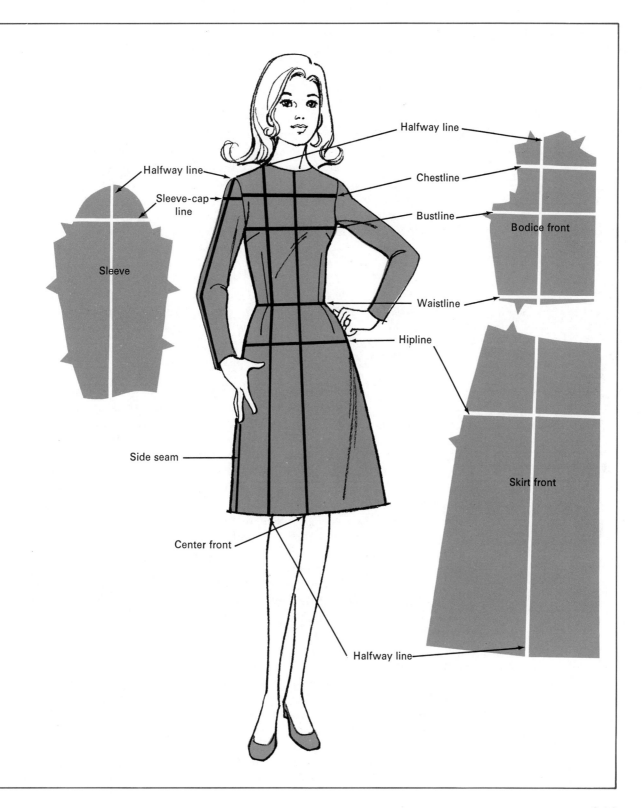

Halfway line

Halfway line

Chestline

Sleeve-cap line

Bustline

Bodice front

Sleeve

Waistline

Hipline

Side seam

Skirt front

Center front

Halfway line

STANDARDS OF FIT IN A BLOUSE OR BODICE

Shoulder seam   This seam lies along the center of the top of the shoulder in a straight line from the highest point at the neck to the tip of the shoulder at the armhole. To check the correct position of the shoulder seam, place a pencil against the bone behind the ear, holding it so that it rests on the shoulder and is perpendicular to it. The shoulder line begins at this point and extends to form a right angle at the armhole. It is not noticeable from either the front or the back on a normal figure. On a round-shouldered figure the seam may be placed slightly back of the center to reduce the length of the back. On a figure with a prominent low bustline the seam may be placed slightly forward to reduce the length from shoulder to bustline. The shoulder area is smooth without pulling, straining, or wrinkling.

Neckline seam   For a garment with a simple fitted neckline, the neckline fits the curve at the base of the neck, crossing the center back on the vertebra that is most prominent when the head is bent forward and crossing the center front at the pit of the neck just above the collarbone. It is as high as the upper point of the shoulder seam at the center back. The neckline fits smoothly and close to the neck at the sides and back—not so tight as to ride up or so large as to pull away or stand out. A slipover neckline is large enough so that the garment will slip on and off easily. A wide or low neckline lies close to the body.

Underarm seam   This seam falls in a vertical line directly beneath the arm, starting from the center of the underarm and dropping perpendicularly to the floor. It is inconspicuous from either front or back. It does not exaggerate the width of either front or back when viewed from the side. The underarm seam of the bodice exactly meets the side seam of the skirt.

Darts   Fabric may be shaped to the curves of the body by darts. A dart removes excess width or length above, below, or to the side of a curved area and gives a rounded shape at the end. Well-positioned darts point toward the fullest part of the figure but end 1 to 2 inches away from that point. It is the correct width to give perfect fit and keep the grain lines straight. The fabric at the end of a dart is smooth.

Tucks, dart tucks, and gathers   These may serve the same purpose as darts but give a softer and easier effect. They need not reach but should direct the fullness toward the largest part of the figure.

Armhole seams   This seam forms a smooth curve over the top of the shoulder bone, appears almost vertical for about halfway down the front and back to where the arm joins the body, and then curves again under the arm to the underarm seam, fitting as closely as is comfortable. The curve on the front armhole line is always deeper than on the back armhole line. The top of the armhole does not droop down onto the arm. The correct placement of the lower half of the armhole is also important for the sake of both appearance and comfort. If the armhole is not right, the garment may be affected in any one of the following ways: The sleeves may pull or bind, the neckline may be drawn down, or the bodice may draw or wrinkle.

Sleeves   It is important that the sleeves be placed so that the grain lines fall in the correct position. A plain sleeve has no gathers but lies loosely on the upper arm, with a rounded look across the cap at the armhole seam line. A gathered sleeve has the fullness evenly distributed around the armhole. The sleeve cap is wide enough to enclose the entire arm with ease. If the sleeve cap is too narrow, it will pull on the bodice. The sleeve cap is long enough to keep the crosswise grain straight but is not droopy.

There must be roominess at the elbow to permit bending the arm without pulling or twisting the sleeve. If elbow ease is provided by darts or gathers, it is located at the point of the elbow. A long sleeve comes well down over the wristbone when the arm hangs down. The underarm seam line extends from the center of the armpit (the end of the side seam line of the bodice) to a point on the lower edge at the center of the palm.

Courtesy Simplicity Pattern Co., Inc.

STANDARDS OF FIT IN A SKIRT OR PANT-TYPE GARMENT

Center lines   In both the front and back sections of skirts and pants, the center lines hang straight down the center of the figure.

Side seams   These seams hang perpendicular to the floor and close to the body, giving the appearance of continuing the underarm seam of the bodice and of dividing the garment evenly front and back.

Hipline   To allow for freedom of movement, the hipline is easy. Above the hipline the garment lies smoothly, and below the hipline it falls straight to the hem.

Darts   The darts in skirts and pants may be judged by the same general standards of fit that were given for the darts in a blouse or bodice. Darts are used to distribute the ease so that the fabric lies smoothly on the figure and the grain lines fall in the correct position.

Pleats   The pleats hang straight, closed, and perpendicular to the floor when the wearer is standing.

Waistband   The waistband fits smoothly around the normal waistline of the body. It is loose enough to be comfortable and to remain flat without wrinkling, but it is tight enough to hold the garment in the correct position on the body. Making the finished waistband 1 inch larger than the body waist measure will usually assure a good fit.

Hem   The hem is level—equidistant from the floor all the way around—except in designs where an uneven hemline is a style feature.

STANDARDS OF FIT IN A DRESS

Bodice and skirt   The bodice and skirt of a dress fit according to the standards for a skirt as given above and for a blouse as given in the charts on pages 342-343.

Dress with waistline seam   This type of dress is really a bodice and skirt joined by a waistline seam. This seam encircles the figure at the normal waistline (the smallest part of the midsection), except when fashion decrees a higher or lower location. It fits snugly to hold the dress in correct position but does not look or feel tight. The skirt lies smoothly below the waistline without drawing, wrinkling, or riding up. Center fronts, center backs, and side seams of bodice and skirt are keyed. Opening edges of a placket or zipper closing lie flat.

Princess dress   This type of dress has no waistline seam and usually has no bust darts. The same general rules of fit apply in the princess dress as in other dresses. Cutting to fit is especially important in the princess dress, because alteration in the garment is very difficult or impossible to make. Before laying the pattern, check these points carefully: the length of the bodice, front and back; the location of the crown of the bust; and the location of the waistline.

Courtesy McCall Pattern Company

Courtesy Simplicity Pattern Co., Inc.

Balance

The silhouette of the well-fitted garment appears to be the same on both sides even though the corresponding parts of the garment are not always identical. For example, in a balanced garment, both sides of the skirt appear to extend the same distance from each leg and the same distance from the floor. If one hip is larger or higher than the other, this balance is attained by cutting one side of the garment longer or wider than the other. If one side of the bust is noticeably larger than the other, balance in fit can be attained by adjusting or adapting the dart size and the side seams of the garment. In the case of protruding hips, balance can be attained by adding length to the back skirt section. In each instance balance is achieved by compensation.

Specific Standards of Fit

In addition to the general standards of good fit, there are specific standards that apply to like garments and to like parts of garments. A separate blouse and the bodice of a dress will have many of the same standards of good fit. Likewise, a separate skirt, the skirt of a dress, slacks, pants, and shorts may be judged by many of the same standards. Other standards apply specifically to dresses, coats, and jackets. The preceding charts specify the standards for ideal fit for specific areas of most garments.

Correcting Fit in a Garment

As discussed in Chapter 10, a pattern can be adjusted to fit your figure. If the adjustment was correctly made in the pattern, the garment was cut to fit. Occasionally, however, even with careful pattern alterations, cutting errors are made. In such cases, minor adjustments can be made during construction to improve the fit of the garment. Study the problems and their solutions shown in the illustrative charts presented on the following pages.

Problem	Solution

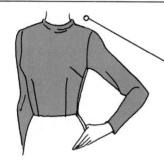

Full Neck
Neckline is tight, resulting in pulling and wrinkling.

Clip neckline carefully as shown until it sets properly. Mark new neckline. Adjust collar and facings to new size.

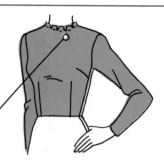

Broad Shoulders
Garment pulls across chest, back, and top of sleeves.

Remove sleeve. Pin new fitting line out to edge at shoulders, increasing shoulder width up to ⅜ inch. (The additional width is taken from seam allowance.) Reset sleeve.

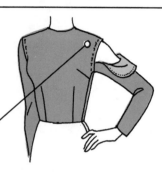

Narrow Shoulders
Sleeve seams fall off shoulders.

Remove sleeve. Make a new fitting line over top of armhole, taking out excess width across shoulders. Reset sleeve.

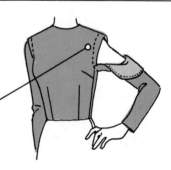

Sloping Shoulders
Fullness shows around the armhole and shoulder.

Pick up and pin excess at shoulder, tapering seam to minimum at neck. Slightly sloping shoulders can be improved by use of shaped shoulder pads.

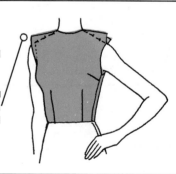

Problem	*Solution*

Square Shoulders

Fullness appears in the area between the bust and neckline or between the back shoulder area and neckline.

Rip shoulder seams. Add to shoulder edges at armhole, tapering seam to neck edges.

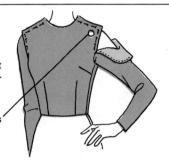

Round Shoulders

Back bodice pulls above waistline, and fullness appears at back armhole.

Rip shoulders, shoulder darts, and waistline seams. Lift excess armhole fabric at back and bring it into shoulder dart, taking up to $3/8$ inch from armhole seam allowance. Repin armhole fitting. Drop back neckline. Add up to $3/8$ inch at waistline for additional length.

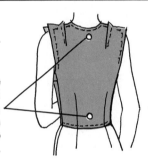

Full Upper Arm

Tightness and drawing across upper arm. Not enough ease to swing arm freely.

Let out underarm seam allowance up to $3/8$ inch from armhole edge, tapering to normal seam allowance at elbow.

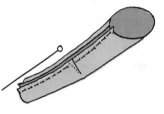

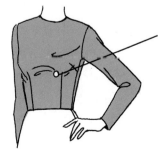

Small Bust

Fullness appears at bustline as a result of darts that are too deep.

Rip side seams, waistline seam, and underarm darts. It may also be necessary to rip waistline darts. Pin smaller darts. Fit side and waistline seams.

347

Problem   *Solution*

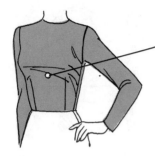

Full Bust
Tightness occurs across bust and back. Waist may rise at sides.

Rip side seams, waistline seam, and underarm darts. It may also be necessary to rip waistline darts. Pin deeper darts. Fit side and waistline seams.

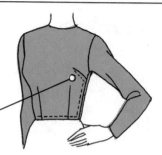

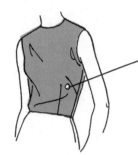

Raising or Lowering the Bust Darts
Bust darts fail to point to crown of bust. They are too low or too high.

Rip side seams and repin dart higher or lower, parallel to original dart.

Large Elbow
Tightness and wrinkles at elbow only.

Remove stitching at elbow. Holding ⅝-inch seam allowance at top and wrist, taper it up to ¼ inch at elbow.

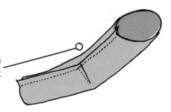

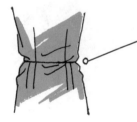

Large Waist
Not enough ease at waistline to fit comfortably. Wrinkles above and below waist.

Decrease size of darts, and let out side seams between bust and hips.

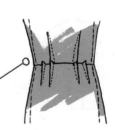

Problem	*Solution*

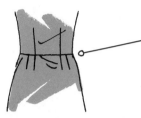

Small Waist

Excess fabric at waistline. Natural waistline is not evident.

Increase size of darts, and take in side seams between bust and hips.

High Hip

Dress appears shorter on one side. Center of skirt shoots off at an angle.

Release waist edges and drop skirt on high-hip side up to ⅜ inch until hem is parallel to floor. Any larger adjustment must be made on the pattern before cutting.

Large Hips

Tightness results in wrinkles around hips.

Add the needed width equally at both side seams. Increase waistline darts to compensate for the adjustment.

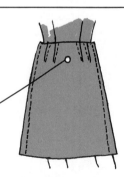

Sway Back

Wrinkles or excess fabric appears between waist and hips at back of skirt.

Rip waist. Repin, taking up excess fabric from bodice and skirt and, if necessary, refitting darts.

PRINCIPLES FOR FITTING A GARMENT

1. Before a garment is fitted, the key grain lines are marked with basting stitches to help identify the location of fitting problems.

2. Garments are fitted with the *right* side out.

3. The key grain lines of a garment fall in a straight crosswise or vertical direction.

4. The fitting process progresses from the neckline to the hemline.

5. A carefully fitted garment is characterized by straight seams and an absence of wrinkles, bulges, and sagging.

6. A simple fitted neckline fits the curve at the base of the neck smoothly and closely.

7. Crosswise wrinkles in a garment indicate that it is too tight.

8. Diagonal wrinkles in a garment indicate that strain is pulling the garment off grain.

9. Adequate ease provides for a comfortable fit and freedom of body movement.

18 *Fasteners*

Fasteners are important to both the appearance and the serviceability of a garment. They serve both functional and decorative purposes. Well-chosen fasteners can increase the convenience with which a garment can be worn and add to the usefulness of an outfit. They can often help you express your individuality, add a center of interest, or complete the fashion look desired.

What are the considerations in choosing a fastener?

Where are zipper plackets used? Bound plackets? Faced plackets? Hemmed plackets?

What factors must be considered in choosing between metal and monofilament-coil zippers?

What are the unique features of invisible zippers?

How do you determine the method of zipper application?

Decisions About Fasteners

Fasteners include zippers, buttons, snaps, hooks and eyes, nylon hook-and-loop tape, and frogs. They can be ornate or simple, conspicuous or concealed, large or small. They offer in their variety a chance for the expression of your creativity.

The pattern envelope often provides specific guidelines as to the selection of fasteners, but you have some choices since you are free to adapt the suggestions given. It is a good idea to shop around to explore the wide variety of fasteners available.

Factors Affecting Choice of Fasteners

There are several points to keep in mind when selecting fasteners. As you shop, consider the function of the fasteners, the purpose of the garment, and the relative costs.

Function of the Fasteners

Different kinds of fasteners are suited to different purposes. If their function is primarily serviceability, base your selection on how well they effect the opening and closing of the specific garment area and how well they fit the requirements of space and convenience. For example, suppose you need a sturdy fastener for a placket concealed beneath a flap of fabric. Hook-and-loop tape may prove too bulky for the particular garment. Buttons and buttonholes may be too thick and

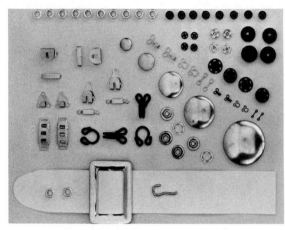

From the wide variety of fasteners available at a sewing notions counter, choose those best suited for your specific project.

cause the garment to gap. Snaps alone would probably provide insufficient sturdiness. A sleek, lightweight zipper may be the best choice. On the other hand, if you need an easy-to-open fastener for a child's garment, hook-and-loop tape or heavy snaps might be your choice.

If a highly ornamental fastener is desired, you will base your choice largely on aesthetic considerations. Decorative fasteners can be chosen to play up style lines and play down figure faults.

Purpose of the Garment

Different kinds of garments require different fasteners. For example, tailored slacks with a closure concealed beneath the fabric requires a type of fastening quite different from the fancy buttons that might decorate a party dress. The ornamental frog, just right for a dressy outfit, is impractical for the stress and strain given to a play outfit.

Suitability of design is another consideration. The bold, geometric lines of a plaid fabric would compete with the delicate floral design of a set of hand-painted buttons. Such buttons, however, might well complement a sheer dress or blouse of solid color. Further,

the same set of hand-painted buttons might look well with a solid-color wool fabric, but fail to serve their purpose because their dressy appearance would not harmonize with the tailored design for which the fabric was chosen. Fasteners must fit the general purpose of the garment and its design as well as their initial function of fastening two edges together.

Cost of the Fasteners

The cost of the fasteners should be considered in relation to the total cost of the garment. If you have put a major investment of time and dollars into fabric, avoid fasteners which may downgrade the entire outfit. On the other hand, if your garment is an inexpensive one to be worn for just a few occasions, the price of expensive fasteners could amount to one-third or more of the total cost of the garment. Careful decision making will help you to avoid unwise spending.

The *designer* fasteners made of high-quality materials are usually more expensive than those that are mass produced. A decorative fastener is apt to cost more than a plain one.

Fasteners prepackaged in quantity may or may not cost more than those sold individually. For example, a card of six buttons might be a good buy at 49 cents, or about 8 cents per button. However, should you need seven buttons, you would be compelled to buy another card at 49 cents in order to get *one* more button. This would bring your total investment for seven buttons to 98 cents, or 14 cents per button. In this instance, it would probably be cheaper to purchase seven buttons individually. On the other hand, if you need twelve buttons, two cards of six might be an economical purchase. Regardless of your decision, extra buttons for replacement of lost ones are a worthwhile consideration.

The maintenance cost of fasteners is also important in terms of both time and money. Are the fasteners you have chosen a delicate type that will require removal each time the garment is cleaned? If the drycleaner sews them back on, is there a charge for this service? Are the fasteners sensitive to the temperatures needed to adequately clean, dry, and press the fabric of the garment? Zippers and hook-and-loop tape made of man-made fibers may become difficult to operate after a few trips to the cleaners, and some buttons may become distorted by proximity to a warm iron. The necessity of replacement could increase the cost of fasteners considerably.

Plackets

A placket is an opening that permits a garment to be put on and taken off easily. Plackets are used in snug-fitting garment areas such as waistlines, necklines, and sleeves. Acceptable plackets are long enough to be functional, easy to fasten, strong, and inconspicuous.

Plackets are most frequently finished with folds of fabric or facings combined with a zipper, snaps, or hooks and eyes. Regardless of how it is made, a placket of quality construction does not interfere with the smooth, flowing lines of the garment design.

There are four basic types of plackets: the zipper placket, the bound placket, the faced placket, and the hemmed placket. Each has its advantages as well as its limitations.

Zipper Placket

Zipper plackets, except where zippers are used as a part of a decorative scheme, are made by inserting a zipper into a seam in such a way that it is covered by fabric. Zippers are very popular because they give an inconspicuous appearance, are easily applied, and are sturdy, functional, and convenient. The length of a zipper placket is determined by adding the length of the zipper coil and the necessary seam allowance.

Selecting a Zipper

Zippers consist of a series of teeth along a track. The teeth lock and unlock as a tab is pulled up and down. Today's zippers have

Courtesy Talon Educational Services

When fabric is loosely woven or frays easily, seam tape sewn to the seam allowance of plackets acts as a reinforcement.

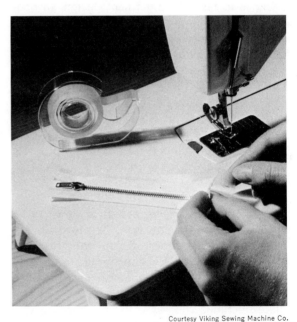

Courtesy Viking Sewing Machine Co.

Cellophane tape attached to the zipper tape and then to the placket will hold a zipper in place during its application.

353

Courtesy Simplicity Pattern Co., Inc.

been streamlined to adapt to contemporary changes in fabric and garment design. In general, they are now flatter, narrower, and less bulky than those made in earlier years. The tabs are now made to lock at any point along the track and are designed not to snag the fabric.

Zippers may be purchased in a wide variety of materials, types, sizes, and colors. Knowledge of the choices available will help you select the right one for the varied projects on which you will be working.

Kinds of Zippers

The composition of the teeth of a zipper is its critical mark of distinction. Today's zippers have teeth made either of man-made material or of metal. They are constructed in a way which makes them suitable for neck or skirt plackets, for dress side plackets, or for complete openings such as those in sport jackets.

Metal Zippers   The metal zipper probably is the most familiar type. It is made with individually pressed, interlocking teeth. It comes in a variety of weights from light to heavy, and it is sturdy and dependable. Metal zippers seldom separate under strain. They are recommended for garments that are washed and ironed at high temperatures. Their limitations are their lack of a self-healing feature and, on occasion, their tendency to lose teeth and eventually break.

Monofilament-coil Zippers   Monofilament-coil zippers are so named because their teeth are formed in a continuous coil. The teeth, usually made of polyester or nylon, are fastened to sturdy tape. Because of their continuous-coil feature, individual teeth do not fall off or come loose. The zippers are flexible enough to follow the line of the garment and the contour of the body. A unique advantage of these zippers is their self-healing feature. If fabric becomes caught in such a zipper, it can be released almost instantly by a simple maneuvering of the zipper tab.

The chief limitation of the coil zipper is similar to that of man-made fiber. It is limited in the degree of heat it can withstand in washing or pressing. Also, coils, especially in the longer lengths, have a tendency to separate under conditions of stress or strain on the seam. While such an occurrence can be highly embarrassing, the zipper can be put in workable order again when the garment is removed.

Invisible Zippers The invisible zipper, also called the zephyr, is a version of the zipper in which the teeth are completely concealed under the zipper tape. Such zippers are available in both metal and plastic versions. The invisible zipper is strong, flexible, light in weight, and particularly suited to knitted garments and heavy-weight fabrics. Because of its unique construction, it will not snag a garment. It can be machine-washed and tumble-dried. At present it is used extensively in long back openings in full-length dresses.

Length of Zippers

Zippers range in length from 4 to 36 inches. Their length is determined by the type of opening, the style of the garment, and the function of the placket. Generally, the length of zipper suggested on the pattern sheet refers to the actual coil, or chain length, portion of the zipper.

While each pattern envelope provides specific guidelines as to the zipper length, you may wish to vary the selection to suit your individual figure type. If you are tall, for example, you may prefer a 9-inch zipper in a skirt rather than a recommended 7-inch length. The added length would permit greater ease in getting into and out of the garment and reduce chances of breaking the zipper. If, on the other hand, you are a short person, a suggested dress zipper length of 22 inches probably would be too long. You must also consider that any pattern alteration affecting the length of the placket would also affect the length of the zipper.

Methods of Zipper Application

There are three basic methods of zipper application: lapped, slot, and invisible. In addi-

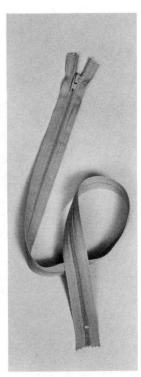

Courtesy Unique Zipper Co.   Courtesy Belding Corticelli

Metal zippers (left) and monofilament-coil zippers (right) are available in a variety of lengths and weights. Both types are also available for invisible applications (left) as well as for lapped and slot applications.

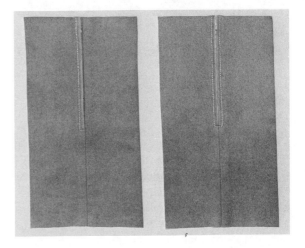

Lapped and slot zippers are the two most frequently used zipper applications.

LAPPED ZIPPER APPLICATION

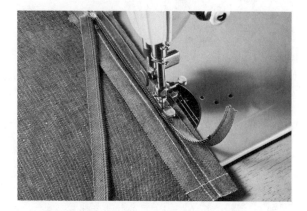

1. Staystitch within the seam allowance. Machine-baste the opening closed. Press the seam open. With the zipper open and face down, stitch one edge against the seam allowance of the back side of the garment.

3. With the zipper closed, open the placket area flat under the machine needle. Stitch across the bottom end of the zipper tape and along the woven guide, fastening the zipper to the front side of the garment.

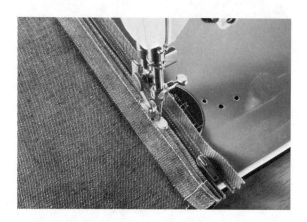

2. Turn the zipper right-side-up and stitch again, this time through a double thickness of the seam allowance.

Photos courtesy Talon Educational Services

4. Rip the bastings and top-press the zipper area carefully before continuing construction of the garment.

tion, zippers are sometimes custom-stitched into specially designed garments to give a hand-tailored effect. Whatever the type of application, it may be made easier by using the adhesive tape provided for attaching the zipper to the garment for stitching. Your choice of application will be influenced by personal preference, sewing experience, the garment design, and the weight of the fabric. For example, the invisible zipper is quick and easy to apply. It is concealed by a seamlike closing with no stitching visible on the right side. It is suited to almost all medium-weight fabrics and is especially good for bulky or pile fabrics. Its application, however, does require the use of a special zipper-foot attachment.

SLOT ZIPPER APPLICATION

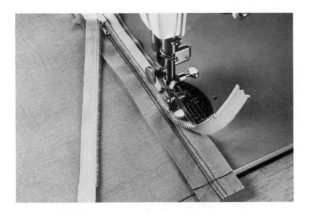

1. With the zipper open and the teeth against the basted seam line, stitch with regular-length machine stitches one side of the zipper, face down, to one of the seam allowances. Backstitch or tie the threads to fasten them.

3. Fold the garment out flat on the bed of the machine and stitch completely around the zipper, pivoting the needle to produce square corners at the lower end of the opening. Adjust the pressure control if necessary to prevent pulling the fabric off grain.

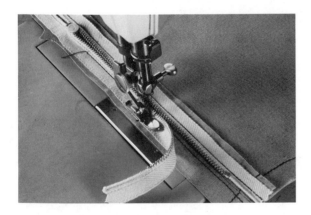

2. Refold the garment and stitch the other side of the opened zipper against the other seam allowance, fastening the threads.

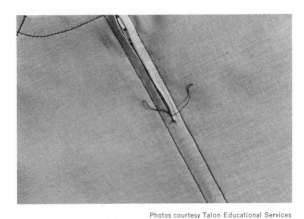

Photos courtesy Talon Educational Services

4. Fasten all permanent stitching. Remove the basting threads and carefully press the completed zipper area.

Lapped and Slot Applications   The lapped and slot zipper applications, which are both traditional applications, result in stitching which is visible on the right side of the garment. The zipper itself is concealed by a fold of fabric.

The lapped method is especially suited to lightweight or medium-weight fabrics. It has a wide, single flap that amply covers the zipper. Only one row of stitching is visible on the right side of the garment.

The slot, or centered, zipper application is preferred for thick, heavy, or pile fabrics to reduce bulk. It has a double flap with visible stitching on both sides of the zipper. Owing to the symmetrical appearance of the stitching, it

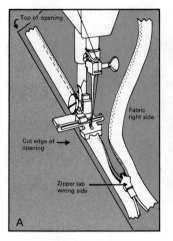
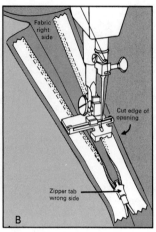
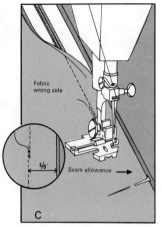
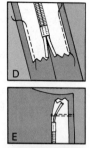

Drawings courtesy Educational Bureau, Coats & Clark Inc.

1. *Shift the zipper foot so the* right *hand groove fits over the zipper coil. With the opened zipper face down against the right side of the garment's right side, stitch from the top to the zipper tab (drawing A).*
2. *Shift the zipper foot so the* left *hand groove fits over the unstitched zipper coil. With the opened zipper face down against the right side of the garment's left side, stitch from the top of the zipper to the tab (drawing B).*
3. *Fold the zipper seam allowance together below the closed zipper. Stitch the seam from the zipper lower edge to the bottom of the garment (drawing C).*
4. *Fasten the lower edge of the zipper tape to the seam allowances. Fasten the top edge to the neck edge. Complete the garment neck facing (drawings D, E, F).*

can be used for front, back, or slash closings, enclosed in a pleat, or featured as part of the garment design.

There are some basic guidelines for making either lapped or slot zipper applications. They are as follows:

1. Stitch directionally at all times.

2. Staystitch the edges of the placket opening before inserting the zipper.

3. Use a zipper foot for stitching all steps of the zipper application. Position the zipper foot on the opposite side of the needle from the zipper teeth or coil.

4. Stitch the zipper only to the seam allowances of the garment in all steps preceding the final stitching operation.

5. Use the woven sewing guide on the zipper tape as a guide in stitching a straight line.

6. Leave a seam allowance between the top of the garment and the end of the teeth or coil of the zipper of neckline, skirt, and pants plackets.

7. For a flatter placket and easier stitching, turn the zipper tab up during stitching procedures.

8. When stitching in a zipper, turn sharp corners by pivoting the fabric on the needle. This may be done by leaving the needle in the fabric, raising the presser foot, turning the fabric, then lowering the presser foot and continuing with the stitching.

9. Perform all steps but the final stitching on the *wrong* side of the garment. Final stitching may be inserted on either the right or wrong side.

Invisible Zipper Application   The application of the invisible, or hidden, zipper has some basic differences from traditional methods. It varies according to the structure of the zipper itself and the desired finished appearance of the placket.

Unlike other zippers, the invisible zipper itself is covered by tape. Its placket has no stitching visible on the right side and, except for a visible pull tab, looks like a plain seam.

To apply an invisible zipper, a special zipper-foot attachment is required. The entire seam in which the zipper is located is left open for the zipper application, and the zipper is applied to the *right* side of the fabric. The remainder of the zippered seam is closed after the zipper is applied to the garment. One of the chief advantages of the invisible zipper is the speed with which it can be applied.

Custom Stitching   An expensive, custom-made look can be achieved through a variation in the final step in the application of a lapped or slot zipper. The variation involves stitching the final step by hand instead of by machine. It is used with certain fabrics such as velvet, corduroy, thick wool, furlike fabric, lace, crepe, and sheer fabrics which have special textures likely to be crushed or marked by machine stitching. With the hand-application method, buttonhole twist or heavy-duty thread is used instead of regular sewing thread. No zipper foot is needed.

You can give a machine-applied zipper a customized look by blind-stitching the last step of the zipper application with a sewing machine. This stitching is done with an automatic machine, with a blind-stitch attachment on a regular machine, or by blind-stitching with a regular machine.

Care of Zippers

The length of its functional life and the quality of the service you receive from a zipper depend to a great extent on the care it is given. Guidelines for zipper use that will increase longevity are as follows:

1. Close the zipper when the garment is stored, washed, or drycleaned to prevent stretching or puckering of the zipper seam.

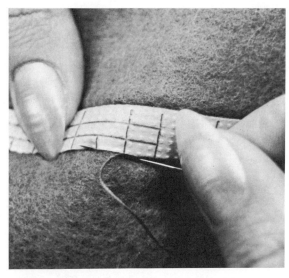

Calibrated tape attached along the seam line produces an accurate marking line to follow when custom-finishing a zipper application.

2. Completely open the zipper before removing or putting on the garment to prevent straining or breaking the zipper.

3. Use a pressing cloth and an iron set at a low temperature setting for pressing over a zipper in which the coils are made of a plastic material.

4. Occasionally after washing or drycleaning the garment, lubricate the coil of the zipper by rubbing it with beeswax or soap.

Replacing a Zipper

Regardless of the care you give a zipper, sometimes a replacement is needed. There are two methods for doing this. In the first method, remove the broken zipper and press open the seam allowances. Then apply the replacement zipper in the same way that an original zipper is installed. (See pages 355-359.)

The second method involves replacement of the zipper in the existing folds of the garment. This method is the only alternative when the original zipper stitching has marred the fabric permanently. To apply a zipper by

A faced placket, commonly used at front and back neckline openings, is usually made by stitching the two sections of the facing together at the center seam line, attaching it to the garment, understitching the seams, and pressing and fastening the placket inconspicuously to the garment.

this method, observe closely how the old zipper was inserted because you will need to follow the original stitching lines. As a result, you may need to adapt the zipper-application method used in making new garments. Most of the stitching of the zipper may need to be done from the right side of the garment, and hand basting may be necessary for accuracy.

Bound Placket

The bound, or continuous-lap, placket is a soft, pliable type of placket used at the lower edge of sleeves, in pajamas, and in certain types of pleated and gathered skirts. It is made with a strip of self-fabric which binds the raw edge. It can be made as a continuation of a seam allowance or applied to a slashed opening.

The steps for making a bound placket are as follows:

1. Cut a strip of the garment fabric on the lengthwise grain about $1\frac{1}{2}$ inches wide and twice the length of the placket opening.

2. Fold and press under a $\frac{1}{4}$-inch allowance on the free edge of the strip.

3. Pin the right side of the strip to the *wrong* side of the placket edge, with the seam lines even. The seam in the binding will be $\frac{1}{4}$ inch; the seam on the garment will taper from $\frac{1}{4}$ inch at the open end to $\frac{1}{8}$ inch at the inner end.

4. Stitch the seam from the garment side.

5. Bring the folded, free edge of the strip over to the right side so that it just covers the first stitching line.

6. Topstitch it close to the folded edge.

7. Press the binding on the top side of the placket under, that is, against the wrong side of the garment. When the stitching lines are brought together to form the placket, no stitching will be visible from the right side of the garment and the placket will be pliable.

8. Use snaps, nylon hook-and-loop tape, or hooks and eyes as a placket fastener.

Faced Placket

A faced placket is often found at a neckline front or back opening, at the bottom of side seams in slacks, shorts, or skirts, and at the wrist opening of long, full-sleeved garments. It is used where a slit is desired. It differs from a bound placket in that the edges of the placket meet but neither edge extends beyond the seam line. Since the finished edges of this placket come together without lapping, frequently a hook and eye, a button and loop, or hanging snaps are used if it is desirable that the edges be held together.

To make this placket, a shaped facing is cut of self-fabric in the same shape but longer than the edge to be faced.

If the opening to be faced is a slashed edge, special care must be taken in stitching the point of the slash. The stitching must taper almost to the point of nonexistence where the slash ends, and yet it must catch the fabric. It can be done successfully by using a very small stitch and pivoting the fabric precisely at the point of the slash. Understitching is necessary for the placket to lie flat in wear.

If a faced placket is inserted on a seam line, the process is somewhat simpler than on slashed edges. To insert such a placket, use the following procedures:

1. Cut the facing in two sections, allowing for a center seam line.

2. Stitch the seam below or above the planned placket.

3. With right sides together, pin accurately and stitch one seam allowance of the placket to one seam line of the opening. Then stitch the opposite edge of the facing to the other edge of the opening.

4. Grade the seams.

5. Understitch the opening so the placket will lie flat in wear. Press the seams first flat, then back against the garment.

6. Hand-fasten the facing against the garment, if necessary, with the slip stitch or another suitable hand-hemming stitch.

Hemmed Placket

It is sometimes simpler to hem a placket than to bind or face it. The hemmed placket is often used in the lower edges of blouse sleeves. Allowance for the hem is made by tucking the sleeve at the upper edge of the placket after the placket edges have been hemmed. The steps in making a hemmed placket are as follows:

1. Slash the placket on the lengthwise grain to the desired length at the location line given on the pattern. Such plackets in sleeves are usually about 3 inches long.

2. Clip a ⅛-inch crosswise slash into the sleeve in both directions at the upper end of the placket.

3. Using the tiny crosswise slash as a guide, crease a ⅛-inch fold on both edges of the placket.

4. Turn a ¼-inch hem to the wrong side of the fabric on the back edge of the placket, and machine-stitch it to the garment. This hem is nearest the lengthwise or, on two-piece sleeves, the underarm sleeve seam line.

A hemmed placket is made by machine-hemming each side of a slash. Space for the hems is provided by a tuck made in the closed end of the placket.

5. Turn a ⅜-inch hem on the front edge of the placket, and machine-stitch it to the garment.

6. Lap the narrow hem over the wide hem so that the fold edge of the narrow hem meets the stitched edge of the wide hem, making a ½-inch pleat in the garment fabric.

7. Stitch the pleat in place with a reinforced straight-across row of stitching or with a right-triangle pattern in which the right angle lies across the top of the opening and along the fold edge of the pleat.

8. Attach the cuff to the sleeve, positioning it to allow for buttons on the front cuff edge. For French cuffs, make four buttonholes, one in the center of each end of each layer of the cuff.

How are buttonholes made and buttons attached?

How are buttons correctly positioned on the front of a garment?

How can buttonholes be spaced or respaced?

How is a machine-worked buttonhole made? A hand-worked buttonhole?

Why is a button shank necessary? How is it constructed? What substitutes are available for thread shanks?

Buttons and Buttonholes

The most commonly used fastener is probably the button and buttonhole. It makes a versatile fastening for garments that open down the front, such as jackets and blouses. It can also be used for cuffs, collars, waistbands, and pockets. Buttons may be made of wood, metal, glass, plastic, or ceramic materials. They may be set with jewels such as rhinestones, or they may be fabric-covered. The variety is almost limitless.

Location and Spacing of Buttonholes

Buttonholes are usually located on the horizontal, or crosswise, grain of the fabric at right angles to the closure. When properly placed, the strain of the button will come at the end of the buttonhole. This placement will prevent the closure from gapping when the garment is buttoned.

Your pattern will indicate the accurate location of the buttonholes in your garment. However, a pattern alteration such as the lengthening of the bodice may require that the size and spacing of buttonholes be adjusted accordingly.

There are some general guidelines to follow if you are determining your own placement of buttonholes:

1. Generally, the larger the button, the wider the spacing between buttonholes. Smaller buttonholes can be spaced close together or in groups.

2. The buttonhole should be positioned far enough from the edge of the opening to prevent the button from extending to the edge.

Courtesy William Prym, Inc.

Choose buttons you can afford which blend with your fabric and garment style.

3. When locating buttonholes in a blouse or bodice front, align one buttonhole with the fullest part of the bust to prevent gapping.

4. In spacing or respacing buttonholes, it is sometimes helpful to experiment with various arrangements. Lay the buttons on the garment, and move them around until you achieve a spacing that is visually pleasing.

Determining the Size of Buttonholes

The diameter and the thickness of the button are the important measurement considerations in computing the length of the buttonhole. To determine this length, measure the distance across the button and add its thickness. The sum is the correct length for the buttonhole. For example, a button ½ inch in diameter and ⅛ inch thick would require a buttonhole length

362

BUTTONS AND BUTTONHOLES

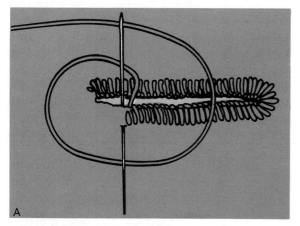

HAND-WORKED BUTTONHOLE

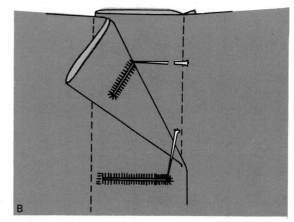

POSITIONING BUTTONS

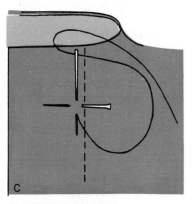

FASTENING THREAD

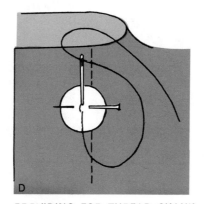

PROVIDING FOR THREAD SHANK

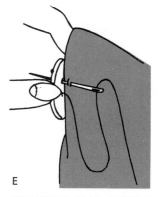

ATTACHING FLAT BUTTON

COMPLETING THREAD SHANK

ATTACHING SHANK-TYPE BUTTONS

Butterick Fashion Marketing Company

363

The location marks for buttons and buttonholes are first traced onto the wrong side of garment pieces and then machine-basted to indicate on the outside of the garment the exact placement of the buttons and buttonholes.

Marking Buttonholes

The pattern markings for buttons and buttonholes are first traced on the wrong side of the garment pieces at the same time other construction markings are made. These must later be transferred to the right side of the fabric by hand or machine basting to indicate the *location* of each buttonhole. These stitches are correctly placed either on the straight grain horizontally or exactly parallel to the folded edge of the fabric.

In addition to the location of the buttonhole, several other positions need to be marked to assure straight and evenly aligned buttonholes. These positions are the fold line of the garment nearest which the buttons and buttonholes are to be positioned and the termination lines indicating the *size,* or the beginning and end, of each buttonhole.

Making Buttonholes

There are two basic types of buttonholes. You have a choice between thread, or *worked,* buttonholes and *fabric* buttonholes. Fabric loops will be considered here. However, since bound and corded buttonholes are difficult sewing techniques usually associated with tailored garments, these fabric buttonholes are considered separately in Chapter 27. The directions given here for both thread loops and fabric loops can be used also for making *belt carriers.* The correct length for a belt carrier is determined similarly to the size of a buttonhole: by adding the width and the thickness of the belt (see pages 362-364).

Machine-worked Buttonholes

Machine-worked buttonholes are made either with a buttonhole attachment or with a zigzag stitch on an automatic machine. They are composed of thread which covers the edge of the opening. Machine-worked buttonholes are sturdy and are suitable for washable garments such as children's clothing, pajamas, blouses, and summer dresses. They can be made in all fabrics, although their construction requires greater care in fabrics that are very thick or

of ⅝ inch. If the button is a ball type or some other unusual shape, however, a variable length may be needed in the buttonhole. A method of checking the calculated buttonhole length for such a button is to wrap a narrow strip of paper around the button and then measure the length of paper required to encircle the button. By dividing the length of the paper strip in half, you can determine the accurate length for the buttonhole. Make a sample buttonhole in a scrap of fabric to try its size for accuracy. This will prevent your making serious errors on the garment itself.

highly textured, that ravel excessively, or that are very loosely woven. Follow the directions given with the machine if you are using an automatic machine.

A *buttonhole attachment* consists of the attachment itself, the metal template that regulates the size of the buttonhole, and the adjustment knob that controls the width of the stitch. The attachment is used as follows:

1. Select the template that will make a buttonhole of the correct size for your button, and insert the template into the attachment.

2. Remove the presser foot, and place the attachment on the machine.

3. Determine the depth of the buttonhole stitch by experimenting on a scrap of fabric. Unless the fabric is unusually thick or bulky, the thickness of the button determines the depth of the stitch. Thick buttons require sturdy buttonholes of considerable depth, while thin buttons call for fine, narrow buttonholes. Numbers along the side of the buttonhole attachment indicate widths from wide to narrow. Turn the adjustment knob to the width required.

4. With each buttonhole, position the attachment carefully on the termination line at the inner end of the buttonhole. This will ensure that the ends of buttonholes will be in perfect alignment and the outer ends will be reinforced with continuous lines of stitching. To make certain of accurate positioning, reset the adjustment knob after the completion of each buttonhole, and place the needle exactly on the mark specified.

5. Stitch around each buttonhole twice for reinforcement. The second time the stitching could be either slightly narrower or slightly wider than the first stitching.

6. Cut the buttonholes after the stitching has been completed.

Hand-worked Buttonholes

Hand-worked buttonholes are made with a variation of the blanket stitch (see drawing A on page 363). They require time, sewing skill, and patience, but the artistic touch they can

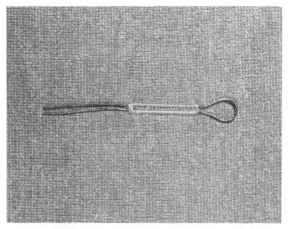

Courtesy Viking Sewing Machine Co.

For emphasis, machine-worked buttonholes can be made over a lightweight cord.

add to your garment may be well worth the effort. Hand-worked buttonholes can be used on delicate fabrics and for buttonholes of a size or shape for which a buttonhole attachment template is not available.

Your choice of thread for hand-worked buttonholes depends on the weight of the fabric. It may be either a special *buttonhole twist* or a regular thread. Use a fine needle that moves through the fabric easily.

A hand-worked buttonhole is slashed open before it is stitched. Before it is cut, however, its edge is reinforced with a row or two of small machine stitches about $1/16$ inch apart. These stitches can serve as a guide in determining the length of the hand stitching.

The stitches for a hand-worked buttonhole are made very close together to completely cover the raw edges. When you reach the end of the buttonhole that is nearest the center or edge of the garment, fan out five to seven of the stitches to circle the end of the opening. Then resume the close stitching until you come to the other end. A *bar tack* is made at this end. To make a bar tack, take several stitches across the end of the buttonhole, and then make buttonhole stitches over the original stitches and at right angles to them.

STANDARDS FOR BUTTONHOLES

1. Accurately and evenly spaced on the garment.
2. Adequately reinforced to retain shape.
3. Positioned to prevent gapping.
4. Positioned so that the top edges and lower edges of the garment are evenly aligned.
5. Positioned to give a desirable background for the button when the opening is closed.
6. Made on the true grain of the fabric.
7. Sized correctly for the buttons chosen.

Thread Loops

Thread loops are usually made from the type of thread called buttonhole twist or, on washable garments, with heavy-duty thread. They are made with a blanket stitch. Thread loops are effective when the use of tiny buttons is necessary or desirable.

A thread loop is made on the finished edge of the garment, directly across from the button. To make a thread loop, take several stitches through the garment edge, leaving even loops of thread extending out far enough to allow the button to pass through. Then make a series of blanket stitches over these strands, from one attached end to the other. Secure the thread on the wrong side.

Fabric Loops

This form of buttonhole is made from narrow strips of bias fabric that extend beyond the

HAND-WORKED THREAD LOOPS

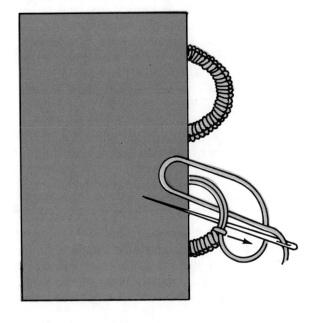

FABRIC LOOPS

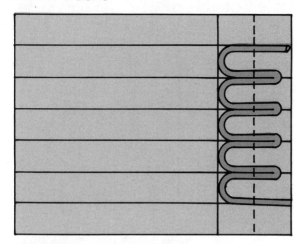

POSITIONING LOOPS ON PAPER

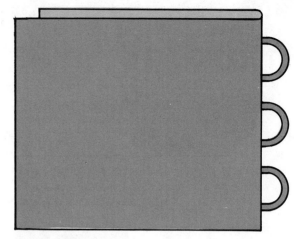

COMPLETED LOOPS

garment edge. Button loops can be used instead of regular buttonholes when a decorative effect is desired or when edges meet but do not overlap. They can be made from bias strips of self-fabric or from ready-made bias tubing.

When making self-fabric loops, cut true bias strips. Generally, bias is cut about 1⅛ inches wide. The type of fabric and the size and spacing of the buttons will determine the precise width. Fold the bias strip in half lengthwise, and stitch it with a small machine stitch about ¼ inch from the fold, stretching it slightly as you stitch. (See "Bias Bindings," pages 403-405.)

Leave a *funnel* on one end of the bias strip so that the stitched strip can be turned right side out upon completion. A needle and thread, safety pin, or bodkin can aid in turning it right side out.

To make loops of uniform size, mark two vertical lines on a sheet of paper. These will indicate the depth of the loops. Horizontal marks made at equal distances along the lines can be used to regulate the spacing between the loops.

Tape or pin the loops in position on the paper, and then machine-stitch them to the paper along the seam line. Move the paper with the loops attached into position on the garment. Securely fasten the loops to the garment, and tear away the paper. Then face the edge to which the loops are attached.

Attaching Buttons

According to construction, buttons are of two types: those with an extended stem, or *shank*, at the bottom and those with holes in the button itself.

To locate the correct position of buttons down the center front of a garment, close the garment and overlap the edges until center front markings are aligned. Insert a pin at the point where the center front mark crosses the buttonhole to indicate that the button placement will be directly underneath this point on the lower layer of fabric.

Sew on buttons with heavy-duty thread, buttonhole twist, or a double thread of the same fiber content as the garment fabric. If cotton thread is used, first draw it through tailor's beeswax to strengthen the thread. The *buttoneer*, a button-attaching instrument, is an especially convenient machine for attaching buttons. By inserting plastic through the shank or eye of the button, it produces a

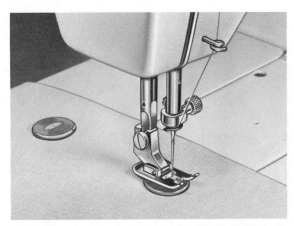

Courtesy Viking Sewing Machine Co.

Courtesy Viking Sewing Machine Co.

Courtesy William Prym, Inc.

Buttons can be used for decoration as well as for utility reasons.

Courtesy Penn Products Company

Buttons can be machine-attached to a garment flat (top) or with a shank (center) by using a button reed. Plastic shanks may be attached below a button (bottom).

quick, permanent attachment for both general and emergency use.

As you gain proficiency in handling the sewing machine, you can learn to use it to attach buttons. Regular buttons and other fasteners can be sewn on with a zigzag stitch.

Buttons used as fasteners on fragile fabrics or those used in places of strain need added reinforcement. This reinforcement can be a small square of fabric, a tape under a series of buttons, or a flat button placed on the wrong side of the garment under the button itself.

368

Each button that is to go through a button-hole needs some kind of shank to prevent breaking the thread that holds it to the fabric, to prevent undue strain on the buttonhole, and to prevent wrinkles and pulling of the fabric around the button. If the button lacks a shank, a thread shank can be made as the button is sewn to the garment. Other alternatives are the shank-type devices available in molded nylon or plastic which can be attached as the button is sewn in place.

To make a thread shank follow these instructions:

1. Take the first stitch downward from the right side of the fabric, bring the needle up through a hole in the button, and then bring it down through another hole.

2. Place a toothpick across the top of the button under the stitch, and sew up and down over the toothpick for about four stitches. Remove the toothpick, and pull the button taut away from the garment.

3. Starting at the base of the button and ending at the fabric, wrap thread tightly around the stitches, forming a shank.

4. Draw the needle to the wrong side of the fabric, and secure the thread.

A rule of thumb is that the correct length of the shank should equal the thickness of the fold of fabric in the accompanying buttonhole area.

What are the specific functions of snaps, hooks and eyes, hook-and-loop tape, and ornamental frogs?

What is an easy way to align the two sides of a snap accurately?

When is hook-and-loop tape recommended? Hooks and eyes? Snaps?

How do you make ornamental frogs?

Snaps

Snaps are small, inconspicuous metal fastenings of a ball-and-socket design. One part of the snap consists of a ball surrounded by a smooth, flat base. The other part contains an

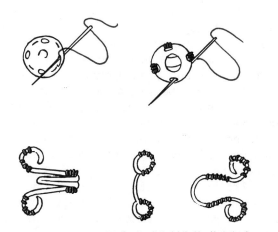

Courtesy Butterick Fashion Marketing Company

Snaps and hooks and eyes are usually attached to a garment by hand with simple whip stitches or buttonhole stitches.

indented socket to clasp the ball. Some snaps contain a centered hole which aids in locating them in correct position.

Snaps are used as fasteners only in garment areas having minimum strain, such as in a continuous lap placket or between buttons and buttonholes to prevent gapping. They are effective in holding overlapped edges flat, but they will not stay fastened under conditions of considerable stress.

The size of snaps varies from size 4/0, the smallest, to size 4, the largest. Black snaps may be used on black and dark-colored garments, and silver or white ones are recommended for use on white and light-colored garments.

In attaching snaps to the garment, usually the ball portion of the snap is sewn to the overlap. Then, with the closing pinned together, the location of the socket can be marked. The location is determined by pressing the outside of the overlay with an iron until the ball makes an imprint on the underlap.

To attach either part of a snap to a garment, make two to five whip or buttonhole stitches in each hole of the snap, working from right to left. Slide the needle through one hole and under the snap to the next hole. Secure the thread when finished.

Hooks and Eyes

The hook and eye, as its name implies, is generally a metal fastener consisting of two parts: a hook and a small round or flat eye. It is designed to be used as an invisible closing at points of strain on the garment. It is commonly used to fasten ends of collars, neck edges, waistbands, and waistlines. In closings on delicate or soft fabrics, a thread eye can be substituted for a metal eye.

The hook is usually attached to the underside of the overlap. To locate it accurately, overlap or match the edges in the correct position for closing, and mark the position of both the hook and the eye. Then place the hook in the exact position desired. To attach the hook, secure the thread with a small stitch on the underside, and then sew several whip or buttonhole stitches through each of its eyelets. The stitches should not show on the outside of the garment. When the eyelets are securely fastened to the garment, slip the needle between the two layers of fabric and bring it out at the end of the hook. Then take three or four stitches, encircling the end of the hook so that it is held down firmly. Secure the thread with several tiny stitches, and clip it close to the fabric.

If the eye is rounded, it is usually placed opposite the hook on the underside of edges that must meet and it extends just slightly beyond the edge of the garment. Straight eyes are usually applied on the underlap when one edge extends over another. To attach either type of eye, secure the thread with a small stitch on the underside of the garment, sew a few whip or buttonhole stitches through each eyelet, and secure the thread.

Hook-and-Loop Tape

A unique and relatively new type of fastener is nylon hook-and-loop tape. It consists of two strips of fabric, one with a stiff, fuzzy, many-hooked surface and the other covered with innumerable tiny loops. When these strips are placed against each other, they adhere. To

Nylon hook-and-loop tape is used to hold one part of a garment fast against another.

open them, the two strips are merely pulled apart.

Hook-and-loop tape is not meant to replace zippers or buttons. It is too bulky for many purposes. It is effective, however, for use in wrap-around skirts, detachable collars and cuffs, and some continuous-bound plackets. It is used extensively in theatrical, military, and industrial clothing and for closures on beach garments and beach bags. Because it can be easily unfastened, it is well suited to children's clothing and to clothing for handicapped persons.

Made of man-made fibers, hook-and-loop strips are sensitive to hot pressing temperatures. When possible, avoid touching the fibers with a hot iron since such may cause them to lose their capacity for adherence.

To attach hook-and-loop to a garment, follow the specific instructions provided by the manufacturer. The general procedure, however, is as follows:

Position the strips at the garment edge. Place one strip on the underpart of the opening, and place the other strip on the underside of the upper part of the opening. Align the strips accurately, and make sure that both will not be visible when the placket is closed. Hand- or machine-stitch the strips along their outer, finished edges. If necessary, hand-stitch the ends of the strips to the garment.

Ornamental Frogs

Ornamental frogs are a type of fastener which can be functional and at the same time add decorative trim to your garment. This type of fastener, while very attractive, is not suited to areas of strain or to a long opening.

Frogs can be hand-made, or they can be purchased ready-made. They may be created from a variety of cording or bias tubing, which can be purchased or cut from self-fabric.

If you wish to make your own frogs, sketch on a sheet of paper the particular size and design you want. Using the sketch as a guide, choose appropriate cording and shape it into a frog. Hand-tack the frog from the underside to hold it firm until it is ready to be attached to the garment.

Courtesy Educational Bureau, Coats & Clark Inc.

Ornamental frogs, made at home or purchased, can be used as decorative fasteners on dressy garments.

Hand-stitch the frog to the garment, securing each loop with small stitches on the underside. Complete the frog by adding fabric-covered buttons or Chinese ball buttons. Generally, the finished ornamental frog extends 2 to 3 inches away from the center front of the garment.

FORMING FROGS ON PAPER BACKING

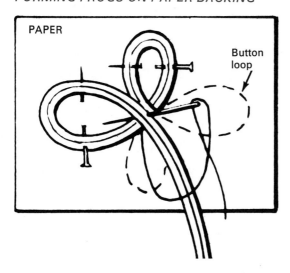

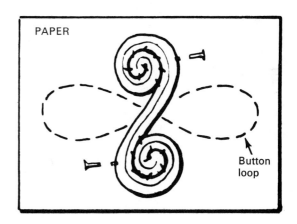

1. Well-chosen fasteners hold the closure flat and smooth without gapping.

2. The alternatives of a zipper, bound, faced, or hemmed placket can be considered when a placket application is necessary.

3. The length of a neckline or skirt-type zipper placket is determined by totaling the length of the zipper coil and the necessary seam allowance.

4. Selection of an appropriate zipper is based on the requirements of the specific garment.

5. A zipper foot correctly positioned for stitching is placed on the opposite side of the needle from the teeth or coil of the zipper.

6. Hand stitching or machine blind stitching can be used to give a custom-made look to the outside stitching of a zipper placket.

7. The correct length for a buttonhole is determined by totaling the diameter and the thickness of the button.

8. Hand-worked buttonholes and thread loops are made with a variation of the blanket stitch.

9. Every button that is to go through a buttonhole requires some type of shank to provide space between the button and garment, thus preventing puckering or gapping.

10. Snaps, hook-and-loop tape, and ornamental frogs are suitable fasteners only in areas of little strain.

19 Hems

Making a hem is one of the most useful aspects of sewing a person can learn. The knowledge gained from completing the hems of your early sewing projects will probably be useful to you throughout your life. Whether or not you make garments later on, you are quite likely to have frequent occasion to adjust hems.

What factors must be considered in planning a hem?

What factors determine garment length? Hem width? Hem finish?

How is the method for measuring and marking hem length selected?

On what basis is the method of ease distribution chosen?

Decisions About Hems

Fashion trends continually shift hemlines from the *mini* to the *midi* to the *maxi* and back again. In planning a hem, you will want to consider currently popular styles as well as garment lengths that are becoming to you and appropriate for the type of garment. The actual making of a hem involves other decisions. You will need to decide upon a hem width, a hem-marking method, a hem edge finish, and a hemming stitch. Knowledge of the basic principles of hemming will enable you to make good choices in hemming projects of all types.

Factors Affecting Choice of Hem Treatment

In planning the construction of a hem, there are several factors to be considered. These include the garment cut, the type of fabric, and the garment style.

Garment Cut

The cut of the garment will influence the hem treatment. For example, the bias cut of a circular or widely flared skirt requires a narrow hem that will not sag out of shape. A fitted skirt of wool calls for a 2- to 3-inch hem to provide the weight needed for proper hang.

Type of Fabric

The type of fabric is an important consideration in planning a hem. A woven fabric acts differently in a hem than does a knitted fabric. A lace garment is best given a hem that is narrow, inconspicuous, and follows the design. Sheer fabric requires either an inconspicuous, narrow hem or a very wide hem that is neatly finished.

Courtesy Simplicity Pattern Co., Inc.

Because of the give of stretch fabrics, garments of such fabrics need hems with body and firmness to prevent irregular stretching or sagging. A bulky fabric that ravels, such as widewale corduroy, requires a hem finish that will reduce bulk as well as cover raw edges.

Garment Style

Each garment style requires a unique hem treatment that carries out the design to best advantage. In choosing a hem for a garment, consider each of the following questions: Do you want the hemline to stand out, as in a full-skirted party dress, or to drape softly? Do you want a smooth, flat, creased hemline or one with a soft, unpressed look? Do you want a hem that is sturdy enough to withstand hard wear and frequent washing and yet is invisible?

Measuring and Marking a Hemline

There are several methods to choose from when marking a hem. They include putting on the garment and having someone else mark the hem, marking the hem yourself with the aid of a table or a chalk marker, and a combination marking and turning process in which a metal hem marker is used to turn and press the hemline. Since this combination process deals with both marking and turning a hem, it is described along with turning hems (see page 377). Each marking method has its advantages and limitations. Whatever the method chosen, determine the desired hem width before marking the hem.

Determining the Hem Width

The first step in making a hem is to determine the hem width for your garment. The width of the hem is important because it relates to the overall appearance of the finished garment. Hems that are too narrow do not hang properly. Hems that are too wide may be bulky. There is a rule of thumb to guide you in deciding on a hem width: The greater the flare of the skirt, the narrower the hem. Skirts cut in a full circle require a narrow hem. Flared or gored skirts that are less than a half circle in diameter are given hems of moderate width. Narrow skirts require 2- to

3-inch hems. (See "Guidelines for Hem Width," page 378.)

Having the Hem Marked by Another Person

After determining the desired hem width, put on the garment, making sure that the side seams, center front, and waistline are in proper position. Wear the same type of shoes and undergarments that you will wear with the outfit. Decide on an attractive length. The hem can be marked either at the garment hemline or at a distance below the hemline equal to the width of the hem. Your assistant can mark the hem with either a yardstick or a skirt marker (see "Measuring Tools," pages 228-229). If the initial marking provides for the width of the hem, representing the upper edge of the finished hem, the later steps in the hemming process will be simplified.

It is important in marking the hem that the garment hang straight. For hems in bias-cut skirts, it is best if the garment is allowed to hang at least 24 hours before pinning. This amount of time will allow most fabrics to stretch to their fullest length for the particular cut of the garment.

During the marking process it is necessary that you stand straight with your arms at your sides, looking straight ahead. If you bend over, even slightly, to observe the pinning process, an uneven hemline may result. Any pulling or tugging on the garment by your aide during the marking process will also distort the line.

This method of marking can be used for all types of skirts. It is particularly effective, however, on circular, flared, and gored skirts which tend to stretch and hang unevenly because of their bias cut. Its chief limitation is its dependence on the availability of another person at the right time.

Using a Table as a Hem-marking Aid

Another, rather unique method of marking a hem is especially handy for marking a bias-cut skirt when no one is around to help you.

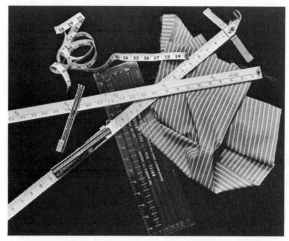

Courtesy John Dritz and Sons

Measuring tools are necessary for measuring and marking hems. An extra-long skirt marker or a yardstick can be used for marking short, circular skirts or skirt-pant combinations.

Although this method is more difficult and time consuming than others, it may sometimes be the only acceptable alternative.

A table or some other flat-topped piece of furniture can serve as your marking aid. When using this method, select a table of the same height from the floor as your hipline. Using the table edge as your marking point, tape to it a piece of marking chalk or a marking pencil. Then stand against the table and turn around slowly, letting the chalk mark the garment at 3- to 4-inch intervals. When the marking is completed, carefully remove the garment so as not to disturb the chalk marks. These marks establish a guideline for the remainder of the marking process.

Next measure the height of the table from the floor. Then determine the distance from the floor you would like the finished hem to be. Subtract this second measurement from the first one to determine the distance the skirt will extend below the hipline.

Lay your garment on a flat surface. With a yardstick, measure down from the chalk line the number of inches arrived at in your computation, and mark the point with chalk or pins. Continue marking the measurement all the way around the garment. This line is your hemline. The skirt will later be trimmed at a distance below the hemline equal to the width of the hem, as described on page 377.

Completing the Marking

Upon completion of the initial marking by the method of your choice, the next step is to spread out the lower part of the garment smoothly on a flat surface and check the accuracy of the marked curve indicated by the pins or chalk. Correct any irregularities.

Whether or not the hem should be trimmed at this point depends upon whether the initial marking was positioned at the hemline or at a distance below the hemline to provide for the hem width.

If the initial marking represents the garment hemline, do not trim the hem at this stage but proceed directly with the final steps in completing a hem.

If the initial marking provides for the width of the hem, representing the upper edge of the finished hem, trim the edge ¼ inch below the marking line. This ¼ inch allows for a first turn of the hem or for a ¼-inch seam allowance in finishing the hem edge. Use the lower edge of the pattern as an accurate guide for cutting. The hem will then be ready for the final steps of completion.

Steps in Completing a Hem

Regardless of which method is used in marking the hemline, the next steps of the hemming process are basically the same for all hems. They include turning the hem, distributing the ease, preparing the hem for finishing, finishing the edge, and attaching the edge to the garment. Sometimes, as in the combination machine hem and finish, the order in which the steps are completed may vary.

Turning the Hem

When turning a hem, keep the lower part of the garment flat on the table and measure

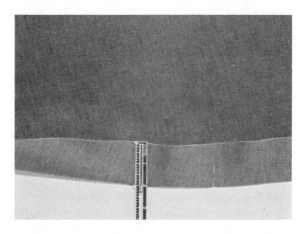

Turn a straightened hem to the underside of the garment, and pin it at regular intervals. If the fabric yields to blocking, block between the pins, rearrange the pins, and complete the blocking process.

After blocking the hem, finish the upper edge with an appropriate finish and pin it against the garment.

the hem width with a gauge for accuracy. You can purchase or make a gauge. A purchased metal gauge can be adjusted to the desired width. If cardboard is used, choose sturdy cardboard. Select a piece that is an inch or more longer than the hem width and about 3 inches wide. Cut a notch in both sides of the cardboard at the exact point which measures the correct hem width.

If the hem edge has been trimmed, proceed as follows:

1. Fold the hem to the wrong side of the garment, providing for a finished hem of the desired width plus the ¼ inch allowed for the first turn or finishing.

2. Pin the hem along the hemline, placing the pins perpendicularly to the fold with heads out for easy removal when pressing. The hem may be hand-basted ¼ inch above the hemline if necessary. The hem is then ready to be blocked for ease distribution.

If the initial marking was on the hemline, proceed as follows to turn and trim the hem:

1. Fold the hem to the wrong side of the garment along the hemline marking.

2. Hand- or pin-baste the hem at a point about ¼ inch above the hemline to keep it even while completing the remainder of the hemming steps. Narrow hems such as those in the lower edges of blouses do not require this treatment. (For hand-basting directions see pages 390-391.)

3. Adjust the hem width by measuring from the hemline toward the raw edge with a gauge and marking the desired width all the way around with marking chalk or a marking pencil.

4. Trim away the excess fabric from the upper edge of the hem. The hem is then ready to be blocked for ease distribution.

Combination Marking and Turning with a Metal Hem Marker

An alternative method for marking and turning a hem is to use a metal hem marker. The metal hem marker is a flat piece of metal on which a series of hem lines have been marked. With this device, the hemline can be pressed directly into the skirt without your having to stand to have it marked. An ironing board, an iron, and a metal marker are all that are needed.

There are, however, limitations to this method. Although it works well on straight, gathered, and pleated skirts that have been cut on-grain, it is not suited to hems in circular or bias-cut skirts or to figure irregularities. The lower cut edge of the skirt must be level, that is, an even distance from the floor, for this method to be satisfactory.

To mark with the metal hem marker, place the portion of the garment to be hemmed on the ironing board, wrong side up. Next place the marker at the predetermined location of the garment hemline. Fold up the lower edge of the garment to the line on the hem marker which corresponds to the predetermined hem width. Press the hemline with the iron, always using an up-and-down motion and observing the fabric grain.

Distributing the Ease in a Hem

After the hem has been marked, the fullness must be eased in, or compacted, to prevent bulkiness in the finished hem. This is especially important in bias-cut skirts.

There are several alternatives for distributing ease. Your choice depends on the amount of curve in the hem and on the fabric of the garment. One method is designed for fabrics that will shrink when steam is applied. The alternative method is used for fabrics which do not easily yield to ordinary shrinking procedures.

In Shrinkable Fabrics

Ease distribution by blocking is best suited to fabrics that can be easily shaped or shrunk. Such fabrics include many cottons, wool, wool-like blends, and knits. After the hem has been turned up the desired width, align the seams of the hem with the seams of the skirt. Then insert a sheet of heavy brown paper or a metal hem marker between the hem and the skirt. Steam-press the hem to shrink out the fullness. (See "Blocking a Hem," page 318.)

In Nonshrinkable Fabrics

To adjust the hem fullness in fabrics that resist shrinking, such as permanent press, blends, and stiff fabrics, or where there is a large amount of fullness, staystitch-plus or an

Skirt Type	Fabric	Width of Hem
Straight, narrow, gathered, or pleated	All fabrics except sheers	2-3 inches
A-line, flared, or gored	All fabrics except sheers	1-2 inches
Circular	Any fabric	⅛-1 inch

ease line may be inserted near the top of the hem.

Staystitch-plus is most successful on off-grain edges, though it can be used to ease in a small amount of fullness on crosswise edges. (See page 296 for instructions on making staystitch-plus.) Always stitch in the direction of the grain, turning the skirt over on alternate gores if necessary. Then match the seams of the hem with the seams of the skirt, place brown paper between hem and skirt, and block the gathered hem as flat as possible against the garment. (See "Blocking a Hem," page 318.)

A hem ease line is inserted by machine-stitching all around the hem, about ¼ inch from the cut edge, using a size 8-10 stitch. After the hem has been turned up the desired width, align the seams of the hem with the seams of the skirt. Draw up the excess ease at intervals in the hem by pulling on the bobbin thread in the machine stitching. Place brown paper between the hem and the skirt, and block the gathered hem as flat as possible.

Preparing the Hem for Finishing

A wide variety of alternative steps must necessarily be considered when preparing a hem for finishing. Generally a hem is blocked during the process of ease distribution. This blocking compacts the filling threads of the fabric so that the grain line of the hem is coordinated with that of the portion of the garment to which it is attached. A line of staystitching, stitched directionally, along the edge of the hem as the fabric is carefully guided through the sewing machine, is used to hold the hem in shape accurately during further finishing processes. On some hems, such as those in which ease is gathered or held in by staystitching-plus, no other staystitching is necessary. On others, such as tailored hems, the edge is finished by staystitching and is then ready to be attached to the garment. The preparation of each hem for finishing presents a series of problems unique to the combination of the fabric, the pattern, and the initial hemming method which was chosen for the project.

Courtesy Viking Sewing Machine Co.

When a hem is full or will not yield to blocking, it can be fitted by zigzag-stitching over a cord and gathering the hem flat against the garment.

What are the characteristics of a well-chosen hem edge finish?

How is hem tape applied? Iron-on tape? Hem facing?

What is the procedure for machine-finishing a hem?

How is the choice of a hand-hemming stitch determined?

Finishing the Edge of a Hem

There are a variety of hem finishes suitable for various fabrics and types of garments. Each finish has unique characteristics which make it appropriate for specific hem types. Again the choice depends on the garment cut, the fabric type, and the garment style. For each individual garment, therefore, a new decision is required regarding the choice of edge finish for the hem.

The chart on pages 380-381 can help you select the best finish for specific garments. For example, suppose you are making a fitted skirt of a firmly woven woolen fabric. A glance at this chart will quickly review the alternatives for a hem edge finish. A taped finish, while not inappropriate, is really unnecessary on a firmly woven fabric. Iron-on tape either might not adhere to the napped surface or might stick so firmly as to make later alterations difficult. A bound hem, suitable but unnecessary, might require more than your allotted time to complete. A clean-finished, or turned-and-stitched, hem would be bulky and cause a ridge on the outer surface of the garment. Rolled and faced finishes are quickly ruled out because a roll is inappropriate and the facing unnecessary. A lace binding would be too fancy and probably not firm enough to withstand wear. The remaining edge-finishing alternatives of the chart appear to be the tailor's, or pinked and stitched, hem and the overcast, or zigzagged, finish. Because the fabric is firmly woven, zigzagging is unnecessary. A tailor's hem probably would be the best choice for this garment.

Hem finishes include pinking, overcasting or zigzagging, clean finishing, and rolling. These processes are quite easily understood by studying the illustrations in the charts on pages 309 and 381.

Since taped and bound finishes and the finish made as the hem is machine-attached to the garment are considered to be more difficult, each of these special finishes is discussed below in more detail.

Tape Finishes

There are a number of kinds of tape that can be used to finish the raw edge of a hem. There are hem tape and lace, both of which may be sewn on, there is iron-on hem tape, and there is a wide hem facing. All are available at notion counters.

Hem Tape or Lace   Hem tape, also called seam tape or seam binding, is especially effective for use along the edge of hems made in heavy fabrics that ravel. Lace can be purchased and used instead of tape when this finish is desirable in lightweight or medium-weight fabrics. When using this finish, select a tape or lace of suitable fiber content in a color which blends with your fabric and make sure that it is preshrunk before application. If

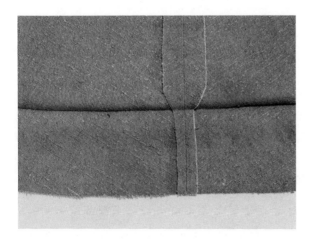

Before finishing the edge of a hem, trim to a ¼-inch width the sections of the skirt seams which are located in the underlayer of the hem. This trimming produces the effect of grading and reduces bulk in the seam areas.

HEM EDGE FINISHES

Finish	Characteristics	Recommended Use	Advantages	Limitations
Taped Hem	Smooth, flat edge.	Fabrics that ravel. Hems with excess ease. Medium-weight and heavy fabrics.	Sturdiness. Raveled edge hidden. Concealment of ease line. Tape adaptable to curved edges.	Tape requires pre-shrinkage and careful fitting to avoid drawing or puckering of hem.
Iron-on Hem Tape	Speedy application. No sewing required.	Any fabric to which it will adhere except sheers. Inside of hems that pucker or resist creasing.	Speed of construction. Ease of construction. No sewing required.	Loss of adherence with wear. Possible puckering if applied incorrectly. Lack of give.
Faced Hem	Reduced hem thickness.	Very bulky fabrics. Garments with no fabric available for hem.	Substitute for self-fabric hem. Bulk reduction. Normal hem appearance.	Impossibility of lengthening garment. Possible stretching or sagging.
Bound Hem	Custom-tailored look. Neat, finished appearance.	Suits and coats.	Sturdiness. Tailored, finished edge.	Bulkiness. Difficulty of construction. Length of construction time.
Combination Machine Hem and Finish	Sturdiness. Nonbulky finish.	Narrow hems. Washable, firmly woven fabric. Knits. Straight, full, gathered, or pleated skirts.	Sturdiness. Ease of construction. Completion of finish and hem in one step.	Experience requirement. Difficulty of removal. Visibility of hem stitches on right side.

Finish	Characteristics	Recommended Uses	Advantages	Limitations
Turned-and-stitched, or Clean-finished, Hem	Raw hem edge hidden and stitched for sturdiness.	Firmly woven, light-weight fabrics. Straight skirts. Washable garments.	Sturdiness. Prevention of raveling. No tape or special supplies needed.	Possible bulkiness. Possible ridge on right side.
Overcast, or Zigzagged, Finish	Flat, smooth finish. Control of raveling.	Knits and stretch fabrics.	Prevention of puckering. Flat, smooth finish.	Possible rippling or stretching of edge.
Tailor's Hem, or Pinked and Stitched Hem	Nonbulky finish. Tailored look.	Firmly woven fabrics. Medium-weight and heavy fabrics. Straight skirts.	Inconspicuous, flat hem. Ease of construction.	Unsuitability to loosely woven fabrics and fabrics that ravel.
Rolled Hem	Narrow, delicate hem. Inconspicuous hem.	Circular skirts. Sheer or delicate fabrics. Party dresses.	Daintiness. Stretch control of hems on circular skirts. Adaptable to hand or machine stitching.	Skill requirements. Length of con-struction time.
Lace Binding	Decorative hem finish. Elegance.	Fabrics that ravel. Hems with excess ease. Medium-weight and heavy fabrics.	Lightness of weight. Flexibility.	Added cost.

381

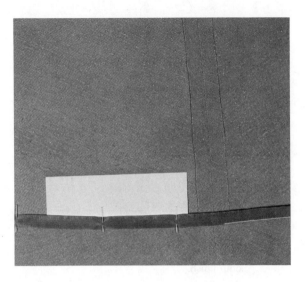

Tape or lace stitched to the upper edge of a hem produces a good edge finish for a wide variety of garments and fabrics.

the garment to which it will be applied is cut on the bias, the tape or lace may be shaped as follows to fit the contour of the hem.

1. Shrink and shape the tape or lace with a steam iron on the ironing board or over a tailor's ham so that one edge is slightly longer than the other.

2. With the hem flat on the worktable, lay the tape or lace over the raw edge of the hem, with the longer edge of the tape along the stayline.

3. Pin-baste the tape or lace to the hem edge, checking to see that it covers the raw edge at all points. A card slipped between the hem and the skirt will prevent pinning through to the right side of the skirt. Let the tape or lace overlap the raw edge for only half the tape width. Be careful not to stretch the shaped edge.

4. Machine-stitch the tape or lace to the hem, stitching very close to the lower edge of the finishing material to prevent ripples in the tape or lace.

Iron-on Hem Tape   Iron-on hem tape requires no stitching. The tape is laid along the upper edge of the hem with the lower edge of the tape along the stayline and the upper edge of the tape lying on the skirt fabric. Then it is pressed onto the hem and the skirt with the iron according to the directions on the package. Because iron-on tape may adhere to different fabrics with varying degrees of firmness, it is wise to test it on a scrap of the fabric first. If you have doubts as to the quality of the adhesion, or if the garment is likely to undergo considerable wear and tear, you may want to take the added precaution of stitching the tape to the garment. This is particularly true of garments which require frequent and heavy washing.

Hem Facing   Hem facing is a wide, bias-cut strip of fabric sometimes used instead of hem tape. Its use is recommended when there is insufficient fabric for an adequate hem or when the fabric is too bulky for a self-hem. The steps of application for hem facing are similar to those used for attaching hem tape. Since bias hem facing stretches easily, it is often more effectively applied by opening out one edge and machine-attaching the strip along the fold line to the right side of the garment. Then the facing strip can be folded to the underside of the garment and blocked before it is attached to the garment with a suitable hemming stitch.

Bound Hem Finishes

The bias-bound hem finish gives a tailored finish to hems made in wool fabrics or wool-like fabrics. It is especially well adapted to heavy coats and suits.

For a bias-bound hem finish, make a bias binding 1 inch wide and of adequate length for the entire hem. Use a lightweight underlining or lining fabric. (See pages 403-405 for a discussion of bias binding.) Stitch the strip to the right side of the hem, with a $\frac{1}{4}$-inch seam allowance. The stitched raw edges may be trimmed to $\frac{1}{8}$ inch. Then fold the bias strip over the raw edges to the wrong side of the hem, and machine-stitch the fold in the ridge made by the first seam line. Press the tape.

Combination Machine Hem and Finish

Machine hemming provides a hem that is usually pleasing and durable. It also finishes the hem edge as it is attached to a garment. The small stitches are relatively inconspicuous on the right side, are sturdy enough to hold up well through wear and repeated washings, and stretch with the fabric. Machine stitching is therefore especially effective for washable garments including knits. Hems which have been finished by pinking, zigzagging, or turning and pressing are suitable for this hemming process.

The machine-made hem can be attached either with an automatic sewing machine or a straight-stitch machine. Invisible hemming with a straight-stitch machine requires either the aid of a special attachment or skillful manipulation of the fabric. The stitching procedure is described on pages 384-385.

Attaching the Hem to the Garment

The upper edge of the hem may be attached to the garment either by hand or by machine. The method to choose for a given project depends upon the type of garment, the location of the hem on the garment, and the type of fabric.

Certain hems, such as the narrow hems in the lower edges of blouses or very full skirts, the hems in some linings, and the hems in children's clothes, may be attached by regular machine stitching. Because this stitching is placed close to the upper edge of the hem and penetrates the garment fabric to the right side, it is visible on the outside of the finished garment.

More frequently an attachment of the hem that will not be visible on the outside of the garment is preferred. This may be accomplished either by hand hemming or by invisible machine hemming.

Hand Hemming

Most quality garments are hemmed with a hand-hemming stitch. Depending on the fabric, the style of the garment, and the type of hem,

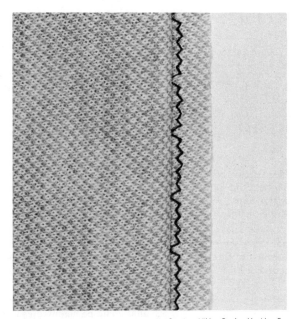

Courtesy Viking Sewing Machine Co.

The combination hem and finish attaches the hem to the garment at the same time the upper edge of the hem is finished with a straight or zigzag stitch.

Hems in blouses may be finished by completing a narrow machine-made hem or by stitching around the garment and pinking the lower edge for a finish.

SPECIAL HEMS

Type of Garment	Problem	Solution
Garment of Sheer Fabric	Making hem inconspicuous but attractive when garment is combined with undergarment.	Make hem very wide (3-8 inches) or very narrow (⅛-½ inch).
Pleated Skirt	Keeping hem flat at bulky seams and intersections of pleats and hemline.	Complete hem before making a kick pleat or before garment is pleated and attached to waistband or bodice.
Garment of Plaid or Horizontally Striped Fabric	Hemline marked an even distance from the floor which does not follow line of plaid or stripe, causing garment to appear uneven around the bottom.	Adjust garment at waistline to accommodate for horizontal design, or fold hem along a specific line for visual accuracy rather than measured accuracy.
Garment of Stretch Fabric or Knit	Ripples around lower hem edge.	Interface hem with bondable interfacing or a bias strip of permanently finished interfacing fabric.
Lined Garment	Should lining be hemmed separately or should lining hem be incorporated into garment hem?	Either method may be used; base selection on fabric. French-tack lining to garment seam if it is otherwise unattached.
Circular or Flared Skirt	Tendency to stretch and hang unevenly.	Let garment hang at least 24 hours before hemming. Keep hem narrow to reduce bulkiness and to prevent further stretching.

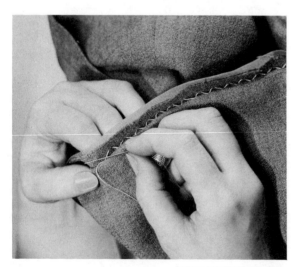

Courtesy John Sheffield Chapman

The pick stitch, one in which the thread is inserted between the layers of the hem, is the most versatile of the popular hemming stitches.

the *pick, catch, blanket, slant, vertical,* or *slip* stitch may be chosen. For details and illustrations relating to these hemming stitches, see pages 392-395.

Invisible Machine Hemming
A hem may be invisibly attached by machine as follows:

1. Prepare the hem as previously described including blocking, staystitching, and finishing the upper edge. If the edge is to be clean-finished as the hem is attached, turn it under on the stayline and press it. To hold the hem accurately throughout the machine stitching, you may find it necessary to hand-baste or pin the hem to the garment about 1 inch from the upper edge of the hem.

2. Fold the hem toward the right side of the garment with the upper edge of the hem

extending about $\frac{1}{8}$ inch beyond the fold of the garment. With the wrong side of the garment up, place the edge of the hem under the presser foot and insert the machine needle in the upper edge of the hem.

3. Attach the hem by one of the following methods. (a) To attach the hem with straight stitching, take five to seven machine stitches on the extended edge of the hem and then nip one stitch into the garment, picking up only one or two threads. Allow a distance of $\frac{1}{4}$ to $\frac{1}{2}$ inch between stitches on the garment side, depending upon the fabric and the location of the hem. (b) To attach the hem with a hemming attachment or the hemming stitch on an automatic machine, follow the directions which come with the hemming attachment or those in the machine manual. Stitch all the way around the garment.

4. Press the completed hem.

Hems in Lined Garments

If a lining is attached to a garment only at the waistline, it may be hemmed separately from the garment. The type of hem is selected on the basis of fabric, the goal being a flat, inconspicuous hem unmarred by a visible ridge. This type of hem is also appropriate for many linings which hang from the shoulders.

If the lining is sewn into the side seams of the garment, it is treated as one with the garment. The hemming procedure is generally the same as for any other hem. It is necessary, however, to accurately pin the garment and the lining together at intervals and to baste the lower edges together to hold both layers in correct position for hemming. Otherwise, the lining may draw and cause the hem to pucker. The upper edge of the hem may be attached only to the lining on some fabrics; on others it may be necessary to insert the hand-hemming stitches through the lining to the outer fabric.

If the skirt fabric is medium-weight or heavy, it may be desirable to remove the bulk produced by a double layer of lining. To do so, trim the lining so that it is $\frac{1}{4}$ inch shorter than the completed garment. Pin the garment and lining together smoothly. Then fold the hem in place over the lining, and proceed with the hemming process.

1. Well-made hems are flat, smooth, even, of uniform width, and inconspicuously stitched.

2. To have a hem accurately marked by an assistant, it is necessary to stand up straight with your head upright and your arms at your sides.

3. A metal hem marker can be used to mark the hem of a straight-cut skirt if the lower edge of the skirt is an even distance from the floor.

4. Letting bias-cut skirts hang for at least 24 hours before the hem is marked will accommodate for the stretching which occurs.

5. The more curved the hemline, the narrower the hem.

6. A-line, flared, and gored skirts can be expected to hang smoothly and evenly if hems are no more than 2 inches wide.

7. Circular skirts can be expected to hang smoothly and evenly if hems are no more than 1 inch wide.

8. Selection of an appropriate hem finish is based on the type of fabric, the garment style, and the garment cut.

9. Hem tape requires preshrinking and shaping with steam before application to the garment hem.

10. A hem facing may be applied if there is inadequate fabric for a hem.

11. Selection of appropriate hand-hemming stitches depends upon the fabric, the garment style, and the type of hem.

20 Specific Construction Techniques

In making a garment, you may encounter features that require special sewing techniques. Even a relatively simple project may call for special types of stitches and varied sewing procedures. Because the particular features vary from pattern to pattern, descriptions of many of the techniques they involve have been assembled in this chapter for quick reference.

What is the function of understitching?
How do topstitching and overstitching differ?
What are the uses of short machine stitches?
In what situations is the even basting stitch particularly useful? Uneven basting stitch? Diagonal basting? Slip basting?
What type of hem might you sew with a pick stitch? A slip stitch? A catch stitch?
What are French tacks?

Decisions About Specific Techniques

In adapting a pattern or creating original garments, and sometimes in interpreting pattern directions, you may have to make decisions as to the best techniques to use for certain details. You may have occasion to choose a hand stitch for hemming a garment or joining seams. Perhaps you may want to select a simple but appropriate style of pocket. Or perhaps you may wonder whether to include darts, gussets, gathers, shirring, or pleats in a particular garment. Understanding the purpose and application of such techniques

will help you to reach good decisions in specific situations.

Special Machine-stitching Techniques

With special types of machine stitching, the clothing you make can be enhanced by its quality of construction, beauty of detail, and variety of style. Included in this discussion are understitching, topstitching, overstitching, quilting, stiffening, and the use of short machine stitches. Other basic machine-stitching techniques, including clean finishing, are described in the chapters on seams (see pages 301-310) and hems (see pages 373-386).

Understitching

Understitching is a row of permanent machine stitching applied to facings to prevent them from rolling over and showing on the right side of the garment. It provides a smooth, flat, professional-looking edge. It is used on neckline, armhole, and front facings, as well as on facings of sleeves and of slacks.

Underststitching, applied through several thicknesses of fabric, does not show on the outside of a garment. It is used to produce a sharp turn in areas which may roll.

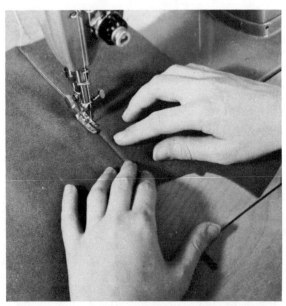

Topstitching, visible on the right side of a garment, can be used either for reinforcement or for decoration.

Facings are understitched after they have been attached to the garment but before they have been tacked down. They are stitched on the right side close to the original seam line. So placed, the stitching is invisible on the right side of the garment.

To understitch a facing, first trim and clip the seam where appropriate. Then turn both seam allowances toward the facing. On the right side of the facing, machine-stitch through the facing and the two seam allowances not more than $\frac{1}{8}$ inch from the original seam line. Press the facing after stitching.

Topstitching

Topstitching is permanent machine stitching applied to show on the right side of a garment. It is a construction technique which can also be a decorative feature. Topstitching can reinforce a seam, accent style lines, and provide an attractive trim especially appropriate to tailored outfits. It can be sewn with matching or contrasting thread.

Because topstitching is conspicuous and affects the overall appearance of a garment, it must be straight and accurate. It may be applied close to a seam line or a folded edge or an even distance away or both.

Several types of guides are available as aids for even topstitching. They include premarked lines on the machine, a strip of adhesive tape, a seam guide attached to the throat plate of the machine, and the edge of the presser foot. If you are topstitching along areas other than outside edges, either hand basting or a quilting attachment makes an effective stitching guide.

Choice of thread varies with the weight of the fabric and the effect desired. For example, buttonhole twist gives a prominent saddle-stitch effect suited to medium-weight and heavy fabrics. When using silk twist and other large threads, wind the thread onto the bobbin and sew with the top of the garment facing the bobbin. With the machine tension adjusted accurately, this method will produce a smooth, decorative line on the top of the garment.

REGULAR MACHINE STITCHES

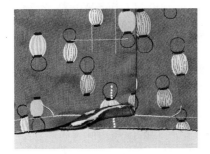 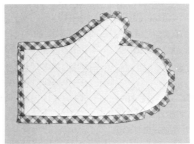 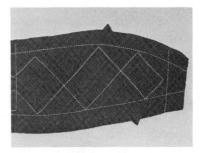

FOR OVERSTITCHING   FOR QUILTING   FOR STIFFENING

SHORT MACHINE STITCHES

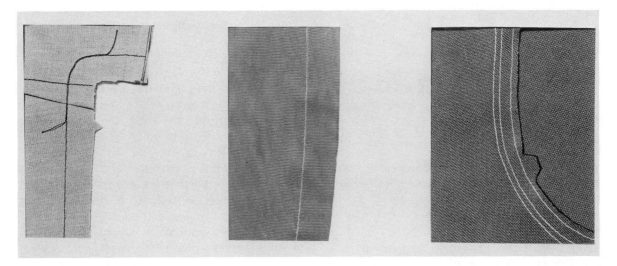

FOR REINFORCEMENT   FOR ELASTICITY   FOR AN EDGE FINISH

It is wise to pretest the topstitching on a scrap of fabric for the best stitch size and correct tension for the particular project. Generally, some adjustment of the machine is necessary. (See page 222.)

Overstitching

Overstitching is a form of restitching over a line previously stitched. It serves to reinforce curved seams, such as the armhole of a bodice, or to join two sections of a garment which must meet precisely, such as two sections of a divided collar.

Quilting

Multiple lines of stitching, usually forming a design, that hold together several thicknesses of fabric or of fabric and padding are known as quilting. The lines of stitching may or may not intersect. Quilting is a decorative technique which adds strength and body.

Stiffening

Rows of regular machine stitching may be placed close together to impart stiffness to a fabric. The closer the rows are placed, the greater the degree of stiffening.

Short Machine Stitches

Short machine stitches are used for stitching lightweight fabrics, as mentioned on page 290. In addition, they are used for reinforcement, elasticity, or as a finish for certain raw edges.

For Reinforcement

At corners, curves, and at points of strain, short stitches provide reinforcement. This stitching is added directly on the seam line before a slash is cut or before the seam is clipped. Underarm seams of a cut-on sleeve always require reinforcement with small stitches. Additional strength is provided when seam tape is applied along the seam line as the stitching is done.

For Elasticity

A short stitch is used on stretch and sheer fabrics and on bias seams in any fabric to ensure elasticity in the line of stitching. This prevents the seam stitching from breaking during wear and care.

For Raw Edges

A line of short stitches may be used to finish the cut edges of fabrics which ravel badly.

Basic Hand Stitches

Hand stitching is important in garment construction. It is most commonly used to temporarily hold pieces of the garment together or to permanently stitch areas that would be less satisfactorily sewn by machine. Temporary stitches are long, usually of a contrasting color, and easy to remove. Permanent stitches are small, inconspicuous, and firm.

The instructions given here are for right-handed persons. If you are left-handed, always use the opposite of the hand and horizontal direction indicated. You will also find it helpful to place a mirror beside each diagram and next to your teacher's hands as she demonstrates any hand sewing. The reflection gives the exact position for the work and the hands of a left-handed person.

Temporary Hand Stitches

Basting is a row of long stitches which serves to hold fabric together during stitching or as a guide during the construction of a garment. Temporary hand stitches provide one method of basting. These temporary stitches are removed when the permanent stitching has been completed. Machine basting is discussed on page 297.

There are four types of hand basting: even basting, uneven basting, diagonal basting, and slip basting. Each has a specific function in clothing construction. Hand basting is time consuming but accurate and easily removed. It is often chosen over machine basting for matching intricate designs at seam lines or for working with extremely delicate fabrics.

A long, slender needle is best for hand basting. Generally a thread of contrasting color is used for easy visibility. White thread is preferable for use on white and light-colored fabrics, however, to avoid the conspicuous traces of colored lint which frequently adhere to such fabrics.

Hand-baste close to, but not on, the stitching line, so that the temporary stitching will not later be caught in the permanent stitching. Use a single thread with a knot at the end. Upon completion, secure the stitching with a couple of stitches positioned one on top of the other or arranged to make a cross stitch.

Hand bastings are removed as soon as they have served their purpose. If left in, they prevent proper opening and pressing of seams. Avoid pressing over bastings, as it might leave an imprint on the fabric which is difficult to remove. When removing bastings, cut the knot at the end of the thread, and clip every third or fourth stitch. Tweezers are an aid in removing these short lengths of thread.

Even Basting

Even basting is the most commonly used temporary stitch for holding parts of a garment together for fitting. It is also used in stitching curves and areas where easing is required. In even basting the stitches are the same size on both sides of the fabric.

Uneven Basting

This stitch is used to make guidelines, to hold a hem in position, to mark center lines, and to indicate the location of pockets and trimmings. Uneven basting is usually sewn one stitch at a time: a long stitch on the upper side of the fabric and a short stitch on the underside. It is stitched from right to left.

Diagonal Basting

This type of hand basting is used to hold two pieces of fabric together so that neither of them can shift its position. Diagonal basting is most frequently used in making tailored garments. In making this stitch, hand-baste from right to left, inserting long, slanting stitches from $\frac{1}{4}$ inch to 1 inch apart. This produces a long, slanting stitch on the upper side and a short, straight stitch on the underside.

Slip Basting

Slip basting is used when it is necessary to baste from the garment's right side, as when matching plaids or designs or joining an intricately shaped seam. It is applied as follows:

1. Press under the $\frac{5}{8}$-inch seam allowance on one side of the seam.

2. Overlap the pressed edge to the seam line of the adjoining section. Pin it with the pins at right angles to the seam line.

3. Slide the needle inside the fold, taking a $\frac{1}{4}$- to $\frac{1}{2}$-inch stitch. Push the needle down through the underlayer of fabric for a second stitch of about the same size.

4. Return the needle to the upper layer, pushing it through the fold. Continue the stitching to the end of the basting line. The needle is never brought through the upper surface of the top layer. The resultant basting is almost invisible on the right side of the garment, but it looks like even basting on the wrong side.

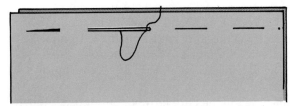

EVEN BASTING

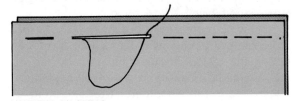

UNEVEN BASTING

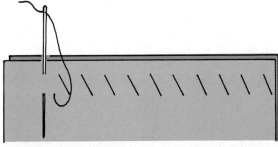

DIAGONAL BASTING

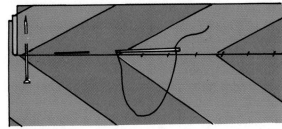

SLIP BASTING

Permanent Hand Stitches

Stitches that remain in the fabric after the garment is completed are referred to as permanent stitches. Those that are hand-sewn are generally used for attaching hems or for finishing details. Hand stitching can be time consuming, but the custom-made look it can give to a garment may be well worth the while. It is inconspicuous and particularly useful in areas where machine stitching would be unsatisfactory.

Permanent hand stitching is applied with a fine needle and with thread of a color that matches the fabric. The stitches are small and spaced closely enough to hold the fabric. A certain amount of care is necessary to ensure that the stitches are firm but still loose enough to prevent drawing or puckering on the right side of the fabric.

In sewing permanent hand stitches, hold the area to be stitched with the wrong side up, letting the rest of the garment remain flat on the worktable. Sew with the needle slanted toward your left shoulder. After stitching a few inches, it is helpful to pin the finished portion to a cushion or anchor it with a weight to hold the fabric taut. This makes the rest of the stitching proceed more easily. Fasten the thread at the beginning of the stitching line with two or three tiny stitches placed one on top of another. Secure the stitching upon completion with several similar stitches.

Hand-hemming Stitches

Hand hemming is a very useful skill for persons wishing to present a good image through the clothing they wear. In addition to helping you effectively complete new garments, mastery of this skill will prove invaluable when you need to take up or let down hems in other garments in your wardrobe.

There are a variety of hand-hemming stitches from which to choose. Some stitches have a great amount of flexibility, making them appropriate for use on knits, stretch fabrics, and fabrics with loose weaves. Other hand stitches are sturdy but less flexible. Some, such as the slip stitch, are hidden between the hem and the garment. Others, such as the catch stitch, form a decorative pattern on the wrong side of the hem.

There may be several kinds of hemming stitches appropriate for a specific hem. Your choice will depend upon your sewing experience, the garment style, the fabric used, and the type of hem you have chosen.

For hand hemming it is best to use a thread of matching color and of a fiber content which is compatible with the garment fabric.

Pick Stitch   Pick stitches are the least conspicuous of the hemming stitches because they are flexibly positioned between the hem and the garment. The pick stitch is a running stitch between two layers of fabric. After some practice, it can be more quickly accomplished than any of the other hemming stitches. It may be used on hems that are clean-finished, those bound or finished with tape, or those finished by zigzagging or pinking. In tailored garments the stitches may be long and loose; in general, the looser the stitches, the more nearly invisible they are.

Pick stitches are made as follows:

1. Hold the garment with the wrong side toward you and the lower edge of the hem up.

2. Turn the hem back toward the outside of the garment, making a fold of the garment at the top of the hem. Pin the hem in this position for ease and accuracy of stitching.

3. Using a short piece of matching thread and fine needle, fasten the thread to the edge of the hem. In the fold of the garment, catch a thread or two of the garment with the needle, and about $\frac{1}{4}$ inch away pick up a stitch near the top edge of the hem.

4. Continue the stitching, taking a stitch first in the garment and then in the hem edge, until the hem is finished. Secure the thread by taking several small stitches and clipping the thread.

Slip Stitch   The slip stitch consists of invisible stitches hidden in the fold of the hem. It is used effectively when both the right and the wrong side of a garment are likely to show, when two folded edges such as the edges of a fabric belt need to be fastened together, or when a garment hem requires invisible stitching. Slip stitches are made as follows:

1. Secure the thread and hide the knot by inserting the needle into the hem fold. Then bring the needle out at the edge of the fold.

2. Take a tiny stitch in the garment op-

posite the point where the thread leaves the hem fold, keeping it parallel and close to the hem.

3. Insert the needle in the fold of the hem exactly opposite the point where the thread emerges from the garment stitch, and slip it along the fold. Bring it out about $\frac{1}{4}$ inch away, unless a longer or shorter stitch is desirable.

4. Repeat steps 2 and 3 until the row of stitches is complete, being careful not to draw the thread too tight. Secure the thread inside the hem fold, and clip it close to the garment.

Catch Stitch   This stitch is particularly well suited to stretch fabrics because it allows for give between the two layers of the fabric. It can also be used when the hem is a single thickness, whether pinked, taped, or raw-edged. In making the catch stitch, hemming progresses from left to right. Catch stitches are made as follows:

1. Secure the thread in the hem, and then bring it out through the hem close to the upper edge.

2. Take a tiny backstitch in the garment. Pick up only a few threads keeping the stitch parallel to and close to the edge of the hem. For each stitch, move forward about $\frac{1}{4}$ inch to the right of the point where the thread is attached to the fabric.

3. Take a second stitch in the hem edge, progressing to the right, and forming a slanting thread from hem edge to garment.

4. Continue the stitching in this zigzag fashion around the hem. Fasten the thread securely to the edge of the hem, and clip it close to the garment.

Blanket Stitch   This stitch is useful in hand-working belt carriers and thread loops and in making certain types of hems. Blanket stitches are made as follows:

1. Secure the thread in the hem, and then bring it out through the hem close to the edge.

2. Holding the thread under your left thumb, take a tiny vertical stitch in the garment, picking up only a few threads and keep-

ing the stitch perpendicular and close to the edge of the hem. Pull the needle out over the thread, forming a thread loop at the hem edge.

3. Repeating step 2, continue the stitching to the end of the row, positioning the stitches $\frac{1}{2}$ inch apart. Secure the thread at the end, and clip it close to the garment.

Vertical Hemming   Vertical hemming is used on firm edges which have been turned in or finished with seam binding, but not on raw or pinked edges. The stitches which are visible are short vertical stitches, perpendicular to the edge of the hem. Long stitches which carry the work forward are almost entirely concealed under the edge of the hem. To do vertical hemming:

1. Secure the thread beneath the hem, bringing the thread up through the edge of the hem.

2. Take a tiny stitch in the garment, parallel to the hem and directly opposite the point where the thread comes up. Bring the needle up through, and very close to, the edge of the hem about $\frac{3}{8}$ inch away, slanting the needle toward your left shoulder.

3. Repeat until the hem is finished, and secure the thread by taking several small stitches under the hem.

Slant Hemming   One of the most durable of hemming stitches when the stitches are placed close together, the slant hemming stitch succumbs quickly to wear when long threads are exposed, as such threads can be easily broken when caught or pulled. For this reason slant hemming desirably consists of closely spaced stitches that are quite visible from the right side. Therefore, slant hemming is best suited to areas where the stitches can be concealed. Examples are the edge of a band, bindings, collars, and cuffs, where there are several thicknesses of fabric along the line of stitches that fasten the edge down. To do slant hemming:

1. Secure the thread in the hem, bringing it through the folded edge of the hem.

2. Take a stitch, catching a few threads of the garment, close to the folded edge of the

PERMANENT HAND STITCHES

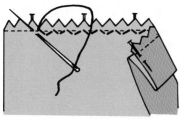

PICK STITCH

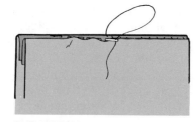

SLIP STITCH

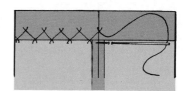

CATCH STITCH

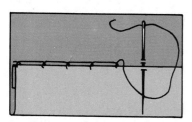

BLANKET STITCH

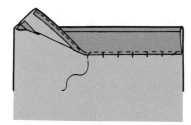

VERTICAL HEMMING STITCH

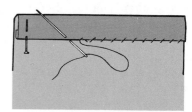

SLANT HEMMING STITCH

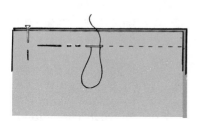

RUNNING STITCH

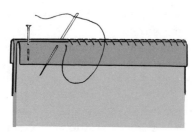

WHIP STITCH

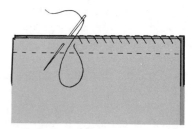

OVERCAST STITCH

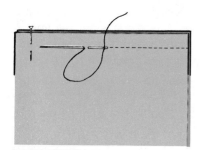

BACK STITCH

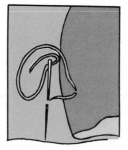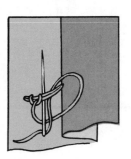

FRENCH TACK

hem and slightly in front of the point where the thread came out. Slant the needle forward and to the left just enough to catch the hem edge.

3. Repeat, keeping the stitches ⅛ to ¼ inch apart, depending upon the fabric and the location of the hem. Keep the stitches tiny, and avoid making them more than ¼ inch apart. Secure the last stitch by making several stitches, one on top of another.

Other Permanent Hand Stitches

In addition to hemming stitches, there are numerous other types of permanent hand stitches. Most of these are used for finishing details.

Running Stitch   The small, even stitch known as the running stitch, is used for handmade seams. The stitch is made by working from right to left through the following series of steps:

1. Take a small stitch in the fabric, leaving the needle in the fabric.

2. Hold the fabric taut between the thumb and first finger of each hand. Leave about an inch of fabric between the two hands.

3. Insert the needle in the cloth, holding it close to the point, and weave it in and out quickly as you push with the thimble finger.

4. Progress to the left, shifting your hands and allowing the stitches to push off the eye end of the needle so that the thread need not be drawn through until the line of stitching is complete.

5. Secure the stitching with several stitches positioned one on top of another.

Whip Stitch   The whip stitch is a permanent hand stitch used to join two finished edges together. It is frequently used to attach a lining to a tailored garment. To make whip stitches, insert the needle from the back of the fabric, pointing it toward your left shoulder. Bring the needle through the fabric each time a stitch is taken. Make short, closely spaced stitches, sewing from right to left.

Overcast Stitch   This stitch is a variation of the whip stitch used to prevent raveling of the seam allowance. Overcast stitches are longer than whip stitches and are more widely spaced. They may be inserted through one or more thicknesses of fabric. Though made similarly to whip stitches, overcast stitches may be placed on the needle several at a time by winding the needle around the edge of the seam allowance. The thread is then drawn up loosely, so that the cut edge will flatten out.

Back Stitch   This stitch is useful whenever hand stitching of extra strength is needed. To back-stitch, take a ⅛-inch stitch, sewing from right to left. Then insert the needle back at the start of the first stitch and bring it out about ⅛ inch beyond the end of the first stitch. Reinsert the needle at the end of the first stitch, and continue the procedure.

French Tacks   French tacks are used to join two units of a garment when a certain amount of flexibility is desired, such as in joining the hem of a lining to the hem of a full-length coat. French tacks are made similarly to thread loops (see page 366) except that each end is secured in a different piece of the garment.

How do darts, gathers, and pleats differ in their methods of controlling fabric fullness?

What is the relationship between the shape and the function of a dart?

How is a gathered edge attached to a straight edge?

Why do patterns for all-around-pleated skirts often have two sets of markings?

Why should a kick pleat extend the full length of the skirt?

Making Darts

Darts are the means whereby flat pieces of fabric can be shaped to fit the human figure. Darts are folds in the fabric which widen where garment fullness is to be reduced and which taper to a sharp point where fullness is to be increased. They are widely used in clothing construction, particularly in shaping bustlines, waistlines, shoulders, and hiplines.

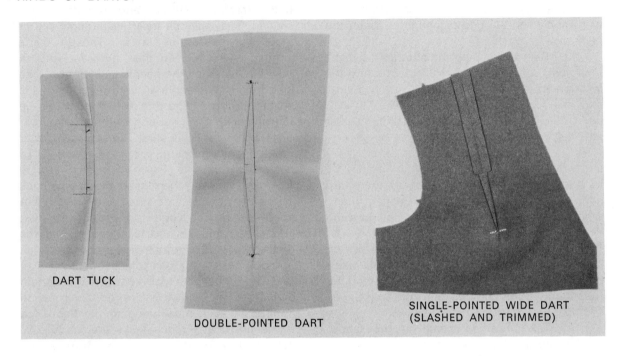

DART TUCK

DOUBLE-POINTED DART

SINGLE-POINTED WIDE DART
(SLASHED AND TRIMMED)

Darts vary in size and shape. They can be long, as in a one-piece dress, or very short, as in the elbow of a sleeve. They can be straight or curved to conform to the contour of the body. They may be pointed at only one end or at both ends. Regardless of their size or shape, all darts serve the same purpose: They shape straight fabric to fit curved areas of the figure.

Folding and Pinning Darts

Darts are constructed on the wrong side of the fabric. Fold each dart along its center fold line, matching its stitching lines carefully. Then pin the dart together on the side from which the stitching is to be done. The pins may be placed on the stitching line with points toward the wide end of the dart or at right angles to the stitching line.

Sometimes only a single line serves as the marking for a tiny, narrow dart. Such a dart may be folded along the single line indicated and pinned for ease in stitching.

Stitching Darts

When stitching a dart, position the bulk of the fabric to the left of the presser foot. In this way, you can stitch directionally with ease. Stitch single-pointed darts from the wide end to the point, keeping the fabric flat and smooth. Remove the pins as you go to prevent distortion of the stitching line.

A straight edge, such as a piece of light-weight cardboard held along the marked stitching line, aids in stitching a straight dart. Stitch the last three stitches precisely on the fold to eliminate a bulge in the garment at the dart point. End all dart stitching precisely at the marked termination line at the narrow end of the dart by running the last stitch off the fold. Such precision will ensure that paired darts will be even in length. Secure the stitching by tying the ends of the threads.

For a very small dart marked only by a single line, begin each stitching line $\frac{1}{8}$ to $\frac{1}{4}$ inch from the fold line at the dart's wide end. Then angle the stitching line to end at the other end of the fold line, forming the dart point.

A double-pointed dart is stitched similarly to a single-pointed dart. However, the stitching lines must start at the center, with overstitching at the wide center section, and must taper to a point at each end as if it were the point of a separate dart. A double-pointed dart should be slashed at the widest point to avoid puckering.

Wide darts need to be slashed open or trimmed to reduce bulkiness. To slash, cut along the fold line, stopping about one inch from the point of the dart.

Pressing Darts

Darts require special pressing techniques, depending upon their position in the garment. The procedures are described in Chapter 15 (see pages 315-317).

Handling Fabric Fullness

When a wide garment piece is joined to a narrower one, the difference in widths must be compensated in some way. One method, that of easing the excess fullness, was discussed in the chapters on seams (see page 304) and on hems (see pages 377-378).

Other methods of handling this situation which are, at the same time, noteworthy for their beauty of design include gathering, shirring, and pleating.

Gathering and Shirring

Gathering is a commonly employed method of handling fullness in skirts, blouses, and dresses. It consists of one or more lines of long stitches which are used to draw up the excess fullness of the fabric. It can be applied by hand or machine. Several rows of gathers that are left visible on the outside of the garment to create a decorative effect are called *shirring.*

With some machines a special gathering attachment is provided. To make gathers without an attachment, use a basting stitch, or

GATHERING

SHIRRING

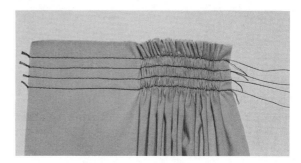

the longest stitch on your machine. The more rows of stitching inserted, the greater is the degree of control of the fullness. Two evenly spaced rows of stitching are recommended for most gathering.

To gather, place the first row of stitching on the seam line. The other rows, stitched within the seam allowance, can be placed about ¼ inch apart. A seam guide can be used to keep the rows straight and even. Secure one end of each row of stitching by wrapping both the upper and lower threads around an inserted pin. Manipulate the fullness from the other end of the rows of stitches.

To draw the gathers, gently grasp the loose ends of all the bobbin threads, one from each row of stitching. Pull gently on those threads all at one time, sliding the fabric along with your fingers.

When you have gathered the fabric to the approximate width desired, anchor the threads at this position by winding them around a pin in a figure 8. This will tem-

STEPS IN MAKING A PLEAT

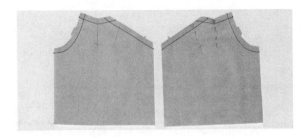

Mark and pin the pleat.

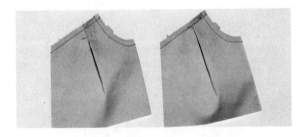

Fold and press on the pin line and overstitch along the seam line.

porarily hold them while you check the width of the gathered area. If an adjustment of the gathers needs to be made, the pin can be removed and the threads easily manipulated into another position. Leave the pin in the end of the gathered area until the area is stitched to an adjoining part of the garment.

To gather a heavy fabric, sometimes a useful technique is to zigzag-stitch over a cord. To shirr with elastic, zigzag-stitch over elastic cord and then gather the fabric to the desired width.

When attaching a gathered edge to a straight edge, distribute the fullness evenly. Divide the straight edge into four equal parts. First place the center half of the gathered edge in position, and then line up the two side quarters with the corresponding areas of the straight edge. Pull or release the gathering threads as necessary to match the lengths of the two edges accurately. Adjust the gathers

with your fingers to distribute them evenly within each section.

Place the gathered edge on top when stitching fabrics together. This permits you to stitch accurately, distribute the fullness evenly, and avoid accidentally catching other parts of the garment in the seam.

Pleating

Pleating is another attractive method of handling fullness in fabric. There are many kinds of pleats. They range from knife-sharp accordion pleats to large unpressed box pleats to inverted kick pleats. Each type is unique in purpose and design.

Pleats present no challenge in the cutting process, but their symmetry depends upon precision in marking and fastening. The pattern markings may be transferred to the fabric by any of the methods described in Chapter 12.

Follow carefully the directions of the pattern guide sheet in making pleats of all types. The following suggestions, however, may be helpful for several kinds of pleats.

All-around Pleats

Patterns for all-around-pleated skirts are sized on the basis of hip measurements. The waistline can be adjusted if necessary.

In transferring the pattern markings for all-around pleats to the skirt fabric, exercise particular care and accuracy. If working with a plaid fabric, however, it is better not to use the pattern marking; instead, form pleats according to the design of the plaid. Often a pattern for an all-around-pleated skirt indicates two different sets of lines for marking. One set indicates the underfold line of the pleat, and the other indicates the outer fold line. To eliminate confusion, it is wise to mark each set of lines in a different color. Diagonal or regular basting can be used to hold each pleat in position along the waistline until the skirt is finished.

Pressing with an iron is a quick method of making all-around pleats but one which requires a high degree of accuracy. To employ this method, lay the skirt on the ironing board and form the pleat beginning at the top of the skirt. Make a fold the desired width and use a pin to anchor the fold to the board. Holding the fabric taut, continue the pleat formation to the bottom of the skirt, and pin it to the board at the other end. Measure several times along the length of the pleat to ensure that the pleat width is equal at all points. Then, using a pressing cloth, steam-press the pleat in position. Repeat the procedure for each pleat.

All-around pleats can be stitched down partially or left unstitched. If stitched down, they may be sewn between waist and hip from the inside or they may be topstitched from the right side. In topstitching pleats, stitch from the lower area toward the waistline, using either the inside edges or the outside edge of the presser foot as a stitching guide.

To decrease the size of the waistline of an all-around-pleated skirt, slightly taper all pleats at the waistline. Release each pleat slightly to increase the waistline measurement. When the skirt fits, stitch the pleats flat along the waistline seam to prevent ripples or distortion of the fabric during attachment to the band or bodice.

Kick Pleats

A single inverted pleat which is at least partially hidden within a seam allowance but which opens out at the hemline is called a kick pleat. It is usually located at the center back, the center front, or the side of narrow skirts. Its purpose is to allow freedom of movement in walking.

The kick pleat can be made as a separate inset panel or as a cut-on extension of the skirt. Usually the pattern layout specifies the stitching and fold lines. A pattern is sometimes included for a special inset piece. The pattern may indicate a pleat extending the full length of the skirt or just from the top of the pleat opening down to the hemline. A full-length pleat is generally preferable, as pleats

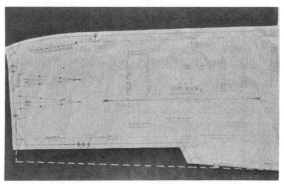

Courtesy McCall Pattern Company

For a strong kick pleat that hangs well, extend the pleat cutting line to the waistline seam.

anchored in the waistline seam are strong and hang more perfectly.

If the pattern does not show a full-length pleat, draw an extension of the cutting line on the edge of the skirt from the top of the pleat to the waistline. Cut on this line. Then transfer to the fabric the line which indicates the seam line of the skirt and the fold line of the pleat.

Stitch kick-pleat seams as follows: Machine-baste the fold line of the pleat from the lower edge of the skirt to the upper end of the pleat opening. Then adjust the stitch-length regulator to resume regular machine stitching. After fastening the thread at the top of the pleat by knotting or backstitching three or four stitches, stitch along the seam line of the pleat all the way to the top. On the seam edge of the pleat, stitch with a regular stitch from the fold line of the hem to the top waist-line edge. Press the seams flat. When the pleat is folded and the skirt is attached to the band or bodice as the guide sheet directs, remove the basting from the pleat section. Hem the skirt, and stitch the pleat seam through the hem. Re-press the kick pleat.

Prepleated Fabrics

Prepleated fabrics can be purchased by the yard. Often such fabrics are designed to co-ordinate with unpleated fabric in making dresses and suits with pleated skirts. Choose prepleated fabric which is hemmed or finished for use without hemming to avoid the problem of permanent creases which fold the wrong way.

Compute the yardage of prepleated fabric you need on the basis of your hip measurement. Add to the amount an extra $2\frac{1}{2}$ inches for ease plus a seam allowance.

Before removing the paper backing from the pleats, baste across the top of the skirt $\frac{5}{8}$ inches from the edge and again along the hipline. With the backing still attached, pin the seam together, leaving a placket opening. There is only one lengthwise seam in this type of skirt.

Try on the skirt. If fitting is necessary, there are two areas in which it can be done: at the waist and at the hips. If the garment is too large around the hips, cut off a number of pleats to make it fit correctly. If the garment fits around the hips but is too large around the waist, insert a row of basting stitches at the waistline. Gently pull the thread to decrease the waistline measurement to fit. After fitting, machine-stitch the seam. Make a suitable placket in the underfold of the pleat which is positioned next to the seam line. Complete the skirt by attaching a band.

How is a square corner stitched?
What is the function of mitering?
Why do curved seams require special treatment?
Why is bias binding particularly useful for finishing curved edges?
How is bias binding made?
How is a gusset inserted?
How are simple pockets made?

Handling Square Corners
Another garment feature requiring special sewing techniques is the square corner. Such corners are commonly encountered in sewing hems and in stitching the seams of rectangular or square pockets, lapels, sailor collars, and faced square necklines. Square corners must be stitched and treated to form a sharp right angle without puckering or bulging at the seam line.

Stitching Square Corners
In stitching a corner, short stitches (about 18-22 stitches per inch) are used both for strength and for elasticity. You may find it easiest to use the short stitch for the full length of the seam involved including the corner. An alternative method is to use a regular stitch up to a point 1 inch from either side of the corner but to stitch the corner itself with short stitches. Sometimes a second line of short reinforcing stitches is overstitched on the seam line for added strength, particularly in necklines made with square corners.

The basic technique required for turning a sharp corner is pivoting. In pivoting, the sewing-machine needle serves as the pivot and holds the precise point of the stitching line while the presser foot is lifted and the fabric turned. The presser foot is then lowered for the continuation of the stitching. (See the illustration on page 294.)

Treating the Seam Allowance in Stitched Corners
A square corner needs to be clipped or trimmed after stitching to ensure smoothness of the seam line. The method of treatment depends on whether the turn forms an inside or outside corner. If it is an inside corner, clip once through the seam allowance at the corner from the fabric edge to the stitching line. Clipping will release the fabric and prevent puckering of the seam.

If it is an outside corner, eliminate excess fabric by diagonally trimming off the seam allowance across the corner, removing the corner triangle. This will prevent bulging of the seam when the corner is turned right side out.

Mitering
Mitering is a method of treating the seam allowance at a square corner by pressing or stitching to remove the excess fabric. It can

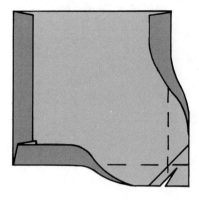

Fold and press along the seam lines. Trim the corners diagonally.

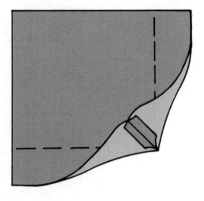

Stitch the diagonal corners and press the seams flat.

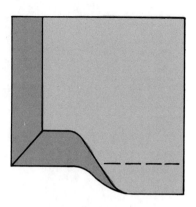

Complete the hemming or decorating process.

be employed at a square corner in most hems and certain seams. It is especially effective on seams made in the application of binding.

The procedure for mitering, which precedes the stitching of the hem or seam, is as follows:

1. Prepare the corner to be mitered by pressing under all seam allowances to the desired finished width.

2. Open the pressed seam allowances. Creases will remain to mark the seam lines.

3. Fold the fabric diagonally across the corner. The fold line should intersect the point at which the seam lines meet, and it should intersect the fabric edges at points equally distant from the fabric corner. Press the fold. Trim this corner diagonally, leaving a seam allowance of about 1/4 inch beyond the diagonal fold line.

4. Next fold the seam allowances back to the original position with the fabric overlap that remains folded towards the inside of the seam.

5. The resulting tapered corner can then be stitched into position. Turn the corner wrong side out and stitch accurately along the diagonal fold line extending from the intersection of the seam lines to the intersection of the

fabric edges. In certain decorative trim, stitching is not necessary.

6. Turn the corner right side out, and complete the hemming or decorating process.

Handling Curved Seams

Curved edges are commonly encountered on pockets, collars, armholes, necklines, waistlines, and cuffs. Joining these edges requires special techniques to produce a seam of sufficient strength, minimum bulk, and professional appearance.

Stitching Curved Seams

Stitch all curved seams with small stitches for maximum strength. Stitches of sizes 18-20 are usually best. The seam guide may be placed on the machine at an angle to ensure an even stitching line.

When joining a curved edge to a straight edge, keep the curved edge on top. This prevents other areas of the garment from catching in the seam line.

Reinforcing Curved Seams

Curved seams require reinforcement after stitching. It may be provided by extra rows of

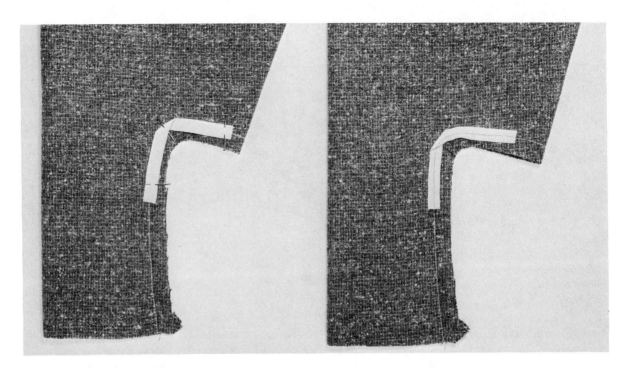

To reinforce a curved seam such as the underarm area, pin preshrunk reinforcement tape along the seam line and overstitch it to the garment directly on the seam line.

permanent stitching or by attaching a strip of tape.

Topstitching is a common type of reinforcement stitching. With a stitch size of 20-22, it is usually applied close to the original seam line, catching one thickness of the outer fabric and both seam allowances at the same time. (For a general discussion of topstitching see pages 388-389.) To reinforce underarm seams, however, reinforcement stitching is usually applied over each side of the seam allowance separately. After the underarm seam has been completed and the seam allowance has been pressed open, topstitching may be applied on both sides of the seam about $\frac{1}{8}$ inch from the original stitching line. Stitch the garment fabric and one layer of the seam allowance. This reinforcement stitching should extend only along the curved area. Confined to this location, it will not show when the garment is worn.

Reinforcement tape may consist of preshrunk seam binding, straight woven cotton tape, or a strip of lightweight selvage cut $\frac{1}{2}$ inch wide and 6 inches long. Place it directly over the seam line, folding it over at the deepest part of the curve to make it lie flat. Pin and sew it to the garment, applying a single row of stitches through the middle of the tape.

Treating Curved Seam Allowances
After a seam has been stitched and trimmed, a curved seam requires special treatment to prevent bulkiness in the seam allowance. The type of treatment depends on whether the seam curves inward or outward.

Inward Curves
Areas in which seams commonly curve inward include necklines, armholes, and waistlines. Because the stitching line on inward, or concave, curves exceeds the length of the seam

allowance, it is necessary to release the seam allowance by clipping it. Clipping consists of slashing the seam allowance at intervals to the line of staystitching with the tips of the shears. This permits the fabric to expand to accommodate the curve without puckering.

When an inward curve is joined to a straight edge, as in the attachment of a straight collar to a round neckline, only the curved edge requires clipping. When two inward curved edges are joined, as in the stitching of sleeve-armhole seams, both edges require clipping. If a seam is to be turned, as in a neck facing, both edges must be clipped for a smooth finish.

Outward Curves

Seams are most likely to curve outward along the outer edges of rounded collars, on rounded pockets, and on circular cuffs. On outward, or convex curves, the stitching line is shorter than the edge of the seam allowance. Thus the extra fabric must be removed to prevent bulges and allow the seam to lie flat. Removal is accomplished by cutting wedges, or notches, from the seam allowance. Make a fold in the seam allowance itself, and cut out a triangle of fabric extending from the staystitching to the outer edge. The more pronounced the curve, the greater the number of wedges removed.

When an outward curved edge is joined to an inward curved edge, as in attaching some collars to neck edges, the inward curved edge must be clipped with slashes and the outward curved edge must be notched.

Bias Bindings

A bias binding is a narrow strip of fabric cut on the diagonal slant of the fabric. It is most frequently used to cover raw edges of garments. It can be used to edge necklines, armholes, pockets, and sleeves. Because of its bias cut, it is somewhat elastic and thus makes an excellent finish for curved edges. Straight seams and hems are usually bound

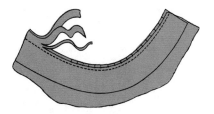

INWARD CURVED SEAM

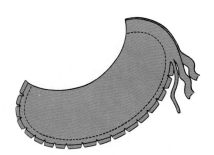

OUTWARD CURVED SEAM

To treat curved seams, grade them carefully. Then clip inward curved seams (top) and cut wedges from outward curved seams (bottom).

with a straight seam binding or hem tape rather than a bias binding.

Bias bindings can serve a decorative as well as a practical function. They may be made of commercially prepared bias tape, of self-fabric, or of contrasting fabric. For a plain-colored dress, bias bindings may be cut from a contrasting plaid or checked fabric.

Bias bindings are cut on the *true bias* of the fabric; that is, the cutting lines make a 45-degree angle with the lengthwise and the crosswise grain. To mark accurate cutting lines, fold the fabric so that the crosswise grain parallels the lengthwise grain. Press the fold line, and then mark other cutting lines parallel to the fold line and an equal distance apart. The width of the binding is determined by the style of the garment, the thickness of the fabric, and the finished effect desired.

After they have been cut from the fabric, the bias strips may be joined into a continu-

STEPS IN MAKING BIAS BINDINGS

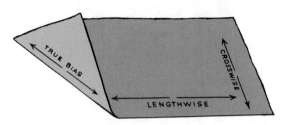

1. Fold the fabric to form a true bias and cut off the corner.

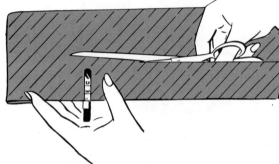

2. Cut bias strips, using a gauge for accuracy or follow crease marks made by pressing.

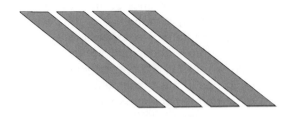

3. Lay strips in rows, right sides up, with ends slanting in a single direction.

4. Join the strips with a regular-width seam, right sides together.

5. Press the seam allowances flat and trim the corners which extend past the edges.

ous binding as follows: Lay the strips that are to be joined side by side and right side up, making sure the ends slant in the same direction. Then place one strip on top of another with their wrong sides out, ends even, and seam lines keyed at the edges of the strips. Pin the seam line, checking that the lengthwise edges form a continuous line. Stitch the seam and press it open.

Bias tape gives three different effects in garments, depending upon the choice of tape and the method of application: bias bindings applied with a machine binding attachment, commercial bias tape applied by machine or a machine and hand combination, and custom-made bias tape which is applied by machine or a machine and hand combination.

Attaching Tape with a Binder Attachment

The machine attachment for applying bias is engineered for effectiveness with precut and pressed commercial bias tape or unpressed bias strips. The machine binder positions the binding over the raw edge of the fabric, with the raw edges turned in, so that both edges of the binding can be attached at the same time. The binder can be used only to bind the edges of a single thickness of fabric or multiple layers of very lightweight fabric. It requires careful adjustment to ensure the flawless attachment of both sides of the binding.

Attaching Commercial Bias Tape

Commercially prepared bias tape may be applied to raw edges with the regular sewing-machine presser foot as follows:

1. Trim the garment seam allowance to a width of ¼ inch.

2. Open the prepared binding along one fold, and place the right side of the tape against the wrong side of garment. Stitch along the crease of the fold.

3. Fold the binding, with the outer edge

404

turned under, over the raw fabric edge to the right side of the garment. Machine-topstitch as close to the outside fold edge as possible or hand-stitch the fold into position.

Attaching Custom-made Bias Binding

Custom-made bias bindings include those made of self-fabric and contrasting fabric. It may be cut in a variety of widths. Such bias binding might be applied to a neckline or other continuous edge as follows:

1. Trim the garment seam allowance to a width of ¼ inch and press a ¼-inch fold on one side of the binding.

2. Selecting a starting point in an inconspicuous area, preferably not at a seam, place the right side of the binding against the right side of the garment with the unpressed edge of the binding even with the edge of the garment. Begin stitching about 2 inches from the starting point and about ¼ inch from the edge of the binding.

3. Stop the stitching 2 inches before completion of the area being bound. Cross the diagonally cut ends of the binding at right angles, and join them. Pin the unstitched edge to the garment to check the accuracy of the length of the binding. Adjust the length if necessary. Stitch it together when it fits accurately. Trim the right-angle seam allowance to ¼ inch and press it flat. Then complete the stitching along the edge of the bound area.

4. Fold the prepressed edge of the binding over the garment edge. Hand-stitch or machine-stitch it to the garment on the inside, being careful to catch the unstitched edge of the binding at all points. If a sewing machine is used, stitch from the *right* side of the garment inside the ridge created by the first binding seam. The stitching will then be invisible from the right side of the fabric.

Gussets

A gusset is a small insert of fabric, usually triangular but sometimes diamond-shaped. It is usually set into a garment to provide extra room for comfort during body motion, but it is also used, to some extent, for design purposes. The gusset is most often located at the underarm seams of kimono or raglan sleeves. Regardless of the location or the method of application, accuracy is important for the successful insertion of a gusset.

If a pattern for a gusset is not included among the pattern pieces, you can cut your own. For each pair of gussets cut a piece of fabric about 5½ inches square. Cut this square diagonally to form two gussets. One gusset is set in the front section of a sleeve area, and a matching one is located in the adjoining back section.

If your pattern guide sheet includes directions for inserting gussets, follow them closely. If directions are not given, you may employ either of the two common methods of insertion here described. The basic principles underlying both these methods include accuracy in marking and pivoting, precision in stitching, and care in following instructions.

Gusset Insertion Method 1

The first method of inserting a gusset may be outlined as follows:

1. Reinforce the garment area in which the gusset will be inserted. To do this, apply short machine stitches on the seam line where the gusset will be inserted. Generally, 18-22 stitches per inch are made. Keep in mind that the seam allowance on a bodice will taper from a width of ⅝ inches at the edge farthest from the gusset point to no allowance at all at the point. Carefully slash right up to the pivot point of the stitches, but not beyond.

2. Match the seam line of the gusset to the seam line of the garment opening. The seam allowance on the gusset will be ⅝ inch along the entire edge.

3. Stitch the gusset to the slash in the bodice, starting at the open end of the slash and continuing right up to the last thread at the slash point in the bodice. Leave the needle in the fabric. Raise the presser foot. Take *one* crosswise stitch to catch the point firmly,

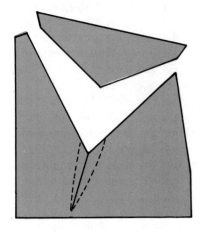 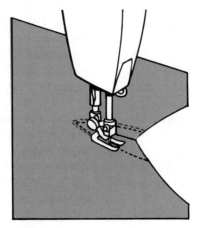 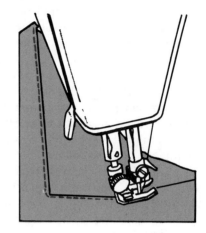

Mark the stitching line and slash line in the body of the garment. If necessary, transfer the marks to the right side of the garment.

Machine-stitch along the outer marking line to reinforce the garment; then slash along the marked slash line of the garment.

Fold the garment on the line of stitching. Pin and topstitch it over the gusset allowing a ⅝-inch seam allowance on the gusset.

turning the balance wheel by hand. Lower the presser foot again, and continue stitching forward down the other side of the gusset. The gusset may be reinforced by another row of stitching on the bodice along the seam line through both seam allowances about ⅛ inch away from the original seam.

Gusset Insertion Method 2

This method of inserting a gusset is similar to the first one. Before attaching the gusset, however, an invisible, lightweight facing is applied to the garment to reinforce the gusset seam area. Then short machine stitches are inserted along the seam line on the garment. Next the garment is slashed. The final step in Method 2 is to lap the folded edge of the faced and stitched garment over the gusset and to topstitch it in place.

Simple Pockets

Pockets come in all sizes and shapes. They can be set into the garment itself, attached to seam allowances, or applied to the outside of the garment. Each type of pocket requires its own unique method of application.

Pockets which are set into the garment itself include bound and welt pockets. Because their application is somewhat complicated and they are primarily used in tailored garments, these pockets are discussed in the section on tailoring (see pages 518-529).

Pockets attached to seam allowances are easier to apply. Pockets applied to the outside of the garment are usually some form of patch pocket. Pocket flaps are sometimes used as mock pockets. Each of these pockets requires accuracy, but the process of application is sufficiently simple for beginning projects.

Pockets Attached to Seam Allowances

Pockets which are set into seams are very popular and useful. Their ease in application lies in their location within a seam, which eliminates the need for topstitching. They are frequently found in the front sections of princess-style dresses and in the side seams of dresses, robes, and slacks. Most patterns give step-by-step details for making such pockets. They usually include the following steps:

1. Cut an under and an upper pocket section, marking each carefully for accurate assembly.

2. Stitch the upper pocket section to the garment front section, right sides together, according to the markings. Do not stitch past the marks at the ends of the pocket opening. Understitch the edge of the opening for a smooth finish.

3. Stitch the lower pocket section to the garment back section, right sides together, according to the markings. Again, do not stitch past the markings.

4. Complete the seam of the garment.

5. Join the shaped parts of the upper and lower pocket sections together with regular machine stitching on the seam line.

6. Press the pocket carefully toward the front of the garment. Clip the garment seam allowance above and below the pocket and press it open.

Patch Pockets

One of the easiest pockets to construct is the patch pocket. It is applied as a separate piece to the right side of the garment. The top edge of the pocket may be finished either with a hem or a facing. The following procedure describes the steps in making a patch pocket.

1. Staystitch curved edges of the pocket to retain its shape.

2. Finish the top edge of the pocket with a hem or a facing.

3. Press the seam allowance under on the sides and bottom of the pocket. If the fabric is crease resistant and resists the press mark, hand-baste around the outer folded edge.

4. If the lower edge is curved, remove the excess fullness in the seam allowance by cutting wedges from the allowance (see page 403). Trim square corners by removing the triangle from the corner of the seam allowance.

STEPS IN MAKING AN INSET POCKET

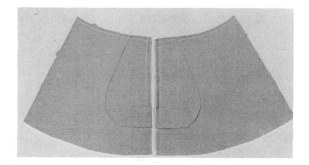

Stitch the pocket pieces to the skirt side seam lines, right sides together, from the termination mark upward to the top of the pocket.

Clip the skirt side seam at the pocket termination point, understitch the seam on the front pocket section, and press the seams toward the pocket sections.

After the side seam is completed, join the pocket sections below the termination point and around the shaped edge of the pocket. Press and fasten the pocket to the front part of the garment.

407

STEPS IN MAKING A PATCH POCKET

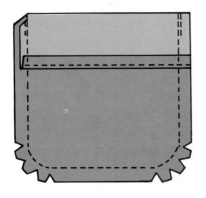

Staystitch the pocket on the
seam line, and hem or face it.

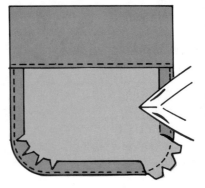

Turn the hem or facing, and press
along the line of staystitching.

Stitch the pocket in position
against the marked garment.

5. On the garment, transfer the markings indicating pocket location from the wrong to the right side of the garment with hand- or machine-basting.

6. Lay the garment on a flat surface and carefully pin the pocket in position.

7. Machine-stitch the pocket to the garment. Stitch close to the outer, folded edges, using the inner edge of the presser foot as a seam guide. Reinforce the top corners of the pocket by back-stitching or by sewing additional stitching lines in the form of a tiny triangle or square. This reinforcement will help to prevent the pocket from pulling away from the garment at the top corners.

Pocket Flaps

The pocket flap is a simple faced piece of fabric which is used to cover the top of a patch or bound pocket. Perhaps even more frequently it is used purely as a decoration. When used in this manner, garments which are very simply made can appear to have intricate pocket detail.

Pocket flaps may have circular or square lower corners. Occasionally they are made with ornate scallops or other individualized shapes.

Make a pocket flap by this step-by-step method:

1. Cut two pieces of the desired shape from the garment fabric.

2. Cut one identically shaped piece from the interfacing fabric, if interfacing is desired.

3. Arrange the two pieces of garment fabric, right sides together, with all corners matching.

4. Lay the interfacing layer on top of the two pieces of the pocket flap, and pin the three layers together.

5. Stitch, leaving a ⅝-inch seam allowance, around three edges of the flap, leaving the top edge of the flap open.

6. Grade and trim the seam allowances on the stitched edges of the pocket flap. Clip wedges from curves.

7. Turn the flap right side out, and press it carefully.

8. Lay the flap in the desired location on the garment with the underside of the flap up and the seam allowance of the flap keyed to the location marking line. The flap will lie above the line.

9. Stitch the flap securely in place.

10. Fold the flap down, and press it in place. The edge of the raw underseam may be turned under and the folded edge stitched to the garment for a completely finished look. This finish is called a *mock flat-fell seam.*

1. Understitching is applied to facings to prevent them from showing on the right side of a garment.

2. In topstitching, permanent machine stitching is applied to show on the right side of the garment.

3. Curved seams may be reinforced by means of short machine stitches.

4. Hand basting is useful for matching intricate designs at seam lines and for working with delicate fabrics.

5. Permanent hand stitches are used for attaching hems or for finishing details to give a garment a custom-tailored look.

6. Darts are made to shape a garment for proper fit.

7. Directional stitching of darts, from the wide end to the point, helps to preserve the design and fit of the garment.

8. Stitching the narrow end of the dart directly on the fold for the last three stitches prevents bulges at the point of the dart.

9. Ending all darts precisely at the termination line at the narrow end ensures that paired darts will be equal in length.

10. Accuracy in marking, pinning, and stitching darts is essential to achieving the desired garment shape.

11. Gathers are made by stitching one or more rows of machine basting and then pulling on the bobbin thread to adjust the fullness.

12. The ends of gathering threads may be temporarily wrapped around a pin to permit easy adjustment of the gathers.

13. In marking an all-around-pleated skirt, one color is used for the outer fold line and a second color is used for the underfold line to avoid confusion.

14. A sharp, right-angle corner can be stitched by pivoting the fabric on the machine needle.

15. In a square corner, excess fabric can be controlled by mitering.

16. A curved seam requires clipping or notching of the seam allowance to prevent bulk.

17. A gusset may be inserted if room for body motion is needed in the sleeve area of a garment.

18. The patch pocket, the pocket flap, or a combination of both can be used to give the appearance of intricate pocket detail on a simply made garment.

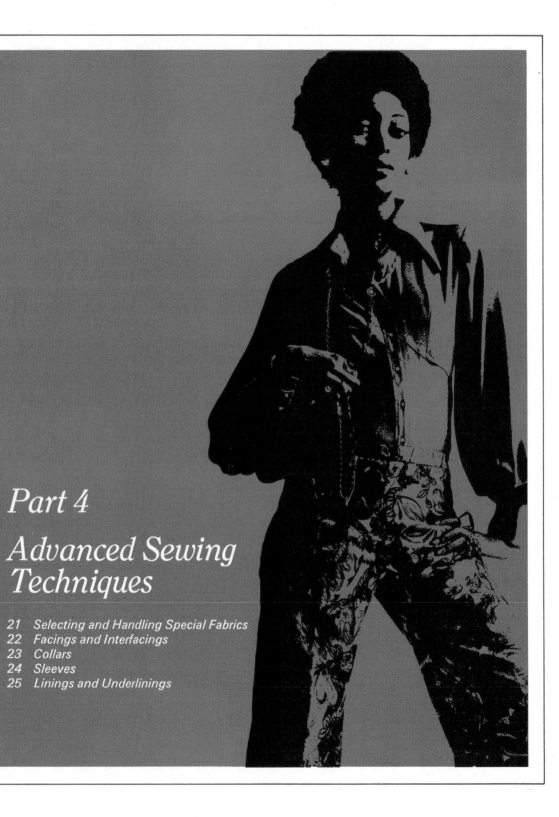

Part 4

Advanced Sewing Techniques

21 Selecting and Handling Special Fabrics

Knits, sheers, laces, stretches, bondeds, naps, piles, and designs are
common among the fashion fabrics available to the modern seamstress.
Understanding the individual characteristics of these special fabrics will
help you choose them effectively and handle them in such a way as to produce
smart-looking garments.

*Why do some fabrics require special care in
    handling?*

*What are the special handling techniques re-
    quired for double knits? Sweater knits?
    Lingerie knits?*

*What special construction techniques are
    necessitated by the transparency of sheers?*

*What are the advantages and disadvantages of
    lace as a garment fabric?*

Decisions About Special Fabrics

Decisions concerning the choice of special
fabrics are many and complex. A person considering one of these fabrics needs to decide
what a garment made from one of them will
do for her wardrobe and her morale. It might
give the necessary boost to both. She must
also decide whether her sewing ability has
advanced to the stage where she can handle
such a fabric effectively. Further, she needs
to determine whether her sewing equipment is
of the type necessary for accurate cutting,
marking, and stitching of the particular fabric
in question. She needs to consider the cost of

purchase, as well as the cost of upkeep, in
relation to value. Finally, as in earlier, simpler
projects, she needs to determine whether she
has the time and energy necessary to complete
a project made from a fabric which offers new
learning opportunities.

In order to feel relatively secure with a
project which is to be made of special fabric,
consider it from the viewpoint of need, sewing
ability, available equipment, cost, time, and
energy. If your decisions through these steps
are generally affirmative, the selection of such
fabric for your project is probably a sound
one.

Knits

Knits are versatile, comfortable to wear, well
suited to travel, and easy to maintain. There
are several kinds of knits, including double
knits, sweater knits, and lingerie knits. While
each type has a few specific requirements, the
basic principles of working with knit fabrics
apply to all.

Cotton and wool knits tend to stretch
more in the crosswise and diagonal directions
than in the lengthwise directions, so it is wise

Courtesy Miss America Division, Brown Shoe Company

Choose patterns for sweater knits (above left and center) which emphasize lengthwise seams to avoid the stretch tendencies of crosswise and diagonal seams.

to avoid patterns with crosswise or bias-cut seams as much as possible when working with these fabrics. Since patterns calling for yokes, raglan sleeves, and flared or circular skirts fit into these categories, avoid them when choosing patterns for cotton and wool knits. Knits of man-made fibers, particularly the polyesters, do not have this tendency to stretch off grain. Consequently, they are good selections for a wide variety of patterns.

Almost all knits will shrink. Each should be washed and dried or shrunk, following the recommended care instructions given on the fabric bolt, before cutting and sewing. Woolens can be preshrunk by a drycleaner, or you can shrink them at home. (See the directions for preshrinking woolen fabrics on pages 266-267.) It is recommended that cotton and polyester knits be washed and dried as a preshrinking process before cutting.

The lengthwise rib of the knit is the equivalent of the lengthwise grain of woven fabrics. Therefore, the rib needs to be checked

to be sure it is not twisted out of line. If the rib is crooked, straighten it by pulling it gently on the bias, and then press. Use the rib as the straight-grain-of-fabric indicator when laying the pattern. If the rib is difficult to see, it can be marked lightly with marking chalk or with a row of basting.

Check the original fold line in the fabric to see whether it can be pressed out before beginning to lay the pattern. Most fold lines can be removed by using a wet pressing cloth and steam iron directly on the flattened fold line. If the fold line cannot be removed, it is best to avoid it and refold the fabric.

Staystitch garment pieces immediately after cutting to reduce the strong tendency of knits to stretch. Staystitching is particularly necessary on neckline, shoulder, and armhole seams. When a knit is a loose construction or is very stretchy, it may be necessary to add preshrunk woven seam tape at waistline, armholes, and shoulder seams and on seam lines in any bias areas.

If it is necessary to use a regular machine needle rather than the recommended ball-point type, a size 9-11 is recommended for most lightweight knits and a size 11-14 for medium or heavier knits. Select a polyester or a cotton-polyester combination thread for stitching on knits so the seam can stretch with the garment. Although a zigzag or elastic stitch is preferred, the effect of a special stretch-stitch attachment can be partially achieved on a conventional straight-stitch sewing machine by stretching the seam slightly while you stitch. Hold the fabric firmly with your left hand behind the presser foot and stretch the fabric very gently as you stitch. This technique will help prevent puckering and later breaking of the seams. A regular machine stitch of about 8-10 stitches per inch will be satisfactory if it is stitched while the fabric is in a stretched position. Check the effect of such stitching on one long garment seam before proceeding to complete the garment.

Darts in heavy knits are best slit and pressed open to avoid bulkiness. In lined sheer knits, darts are made by sewing the two fabrics together as one.

In tailored knits, the following areas need to be interfaced: faced edges; buttonholes, waistbands, collars, and cuffs. In simple dresses, blouses, and skirts, interfacings are seldom necessary except in the buttonhole areas of acetate and other relatively sleazy fabrics made of man-made fibers. When interfacing is desired, select one that is suited to the pliability of the knit. Generally, interfacing should be lighter in weight than the knit on which it is used. Lightweight bonded interfacings are very effective for use in buttonhole areas and in other locations where final detail work must be completed. Usually darts are handled separately in the two fabric layers and the interfacing is attached early in construction.

Nylon or polyester zippers are well suited to knits. Either an invisible or regular coil-type zipper is satisfactory. Avoid stretching the fabric when stitching the zipper. For safety, shrink the zipper tape at the time you shrink the fabric to prevent puckering when the garment is cleaned. Also temporarily fasten it to the garment with an adhesive-type tape which can be removed after the zipper is stitched into the garment.

Because of the elasticity of knit fabrics, it is best to let a garment hang for 24 hours before hemming it. A bias-bound hem or a tailor's hem is appropriate for knits (see pages 379-382).

Double Knits

Double knits are probably the most popular of all knit types, particularly of those knits chosen for outerwear such as dresses, skirts, suits, and coats. Double knits are so named because of the knitting process used in their construction. In the process of double knitting, two sets of needles make separate fabric faces which are attached into a relatively thick, single layer of fabric by the knitting machine. These double knits, first available in quality woolens, are now commonly made of cotton

Courtesy Bobbie Brooks, Inc.

In tailored knit garments, use a pliable, lightweight interfacing for collars, pocket flaps, cuffs, and buttonhole areas.

and polyesters as well as other fashion fibers.

Most double knits, because of their relative sturdiness, are ideal for tailored garments. They can accommodate tailored collars, bound buttonholes, welt pockets, and other marks of high fashion. Their popularity lies in the ease of their care which can be combined with this high-fashion look.

When choosing a pattern for a double-knit fabric, either a regular pattern or one marked *For Knits Only* is suitable. Avoid patterns made for sweater knits. Since double knits have only limited give, a pattern designed for sweater knits would result in a garment too small for satisfactory appearance and comfort.

413

Most double knits, particularly those made of polyester fibers, have a tendency to snag during wear. Many such snags can be effectively corrected by pulling the snagged thread to the underside of the garment with a very small crochet needle. After puckers have been carefully smoothed and pressed from the damaged area, snags so corrected are usually almost invisible in double-knit fabrics.

Sweater Knits
One of the newest additions to knits for home sewing are the sweater knits. They may vary from the clinging, stretchy rib knits to a more stable knit which handles more easily during both construction and care.

The type of sweater knit you have chosen is a key factor in determining the type of pattern you select. Stretchy sweater knits require no darts or ease. For this type of fabric choose a pattern marked *For Stretchy Sweater Knits Only.* Stable sweater knits require a pattern marked *For Knits Only.*

After shrinking sweater knits, allow them to lie flat on a table for several hours so the fabric will relax. If this time is allowed before the pattern is pinned to the fabric, more accurate cutting can be accomplished.

Premade bands and ribs are available for sweater knits. They are dyed to match the fabric. Bands can also be cut from the fabric of the basic garment.

Because of the stretch characteristic of sweater knits, ease is a minor consideration when sleeves are attached to the garment. For a professional effect, before joining the underarm seams pin the sleeve to the armhole with the fabric lying flat. Stitch the seam with the bodice side up, gently stretching the armhole if necessary to fit the sleeve cap. After the sleeve is stitched into the garment, stitch the bodice side seam and the sleeve seam as one continuous seam.

Lingerie Knits
Tricot is the most popular lingerie knit. It is a warp-type knit and most often is made from

Courtesy Eleganza

Double knits, which dominate the fashion field, are also used effectively for occupational uniforms.

414

SELECTING FABRICS FOR SPECIFIC STYLES

Styles with pleats   When pleats are to be pressed, use a fabric which creases sharply and will retain the crease or, if possible, can be durably pleated. Since unpressed pleats fall into soft folds, they require a fabric which is soft rather than stiff.

Styles with intricate details   Construction details, such as darts and tucks, show up best in plain, firm fabrics. A fabric with bold design hides the details, and the details in turn interfere with the effect of the design.

Tailored styles   Plain fabrics or fabrics with a small design made by either the color or the weave are best for tailored styles. The interest in tailored garments is created by the construction lines and the simple detail of the garment style rather than by the fabric design. Heavier fabrics are frequently used for dresses, suits, and coats because they have qualities suitable for tailoring.

Close-fitting styles   Either plain or figured fabrics are appropriate for close-fitting garments. They are flattering to both the small and the large figure, if properly fitted, though the plain fabrics are better for the large figure in this type of garment.

Draped styles   Draping, shirring, and soft details, which are becoming to nearly everyone, are best achieved with soft, dull-surfaced crepes and knitted fabrics.

Styles with borders   Bordered fabrics may be chosen for pattern styles in which it is possible to place the border on a straight structural line of the garment. Trimming may be applied as a border design for such styles. For example, bordered fabrics or border trimming may be used on a skirt which is straight at the lower edge, whether gathered or fitted at the hipline.

Dressy styles   Garments for dress may vary all the way from a style that is pencil-slim to one that is bouffant and small-waisted. Luxury fabrics which are rich in their own texture and color are best for styles which have few seams and little detail or ornamentation. These include satins, brocades, damasks, moirés, and velvets. Styles which include severe darts or tucks and pressed pleats are too severe for the softness of these fabrics.

Bouffant styles lend themselves to the use of crisp fabrics, such as organdy, taffeta, and faille, which usually tend to increase the figure size.

Sheer voiles and chiffons require ample fullness in the style to bring out the full beauty of the fabric.

When sewing lingerie knits, whether in single layers or quilted variations, use a ball-point needle and a sewing-machine throat plate which has a small needle hole to prevent breaking yarns in the fabric and to keep the stitching smooth and even.

man-made fibers such as nylon, rayon, acetate, or triacetate. Depending to an extent on the fiber content, tricot knits have easy-care qualities.

Special patterns are available for sewing all types of lingerie: bras, slips, panties, slippers, nightgowns, and robes. Sizes for lingerie patterns are determined in the same way as those for other garments.

A few manufacturers have designed ready-to-sew lingerie kits. These kits contain all sewing notions and trim needed, and some even include precut fabric.

A large flat surface is needed for pattern layout and cutting of tricots to prevent stretching. Because tricot knits have a tend-

ency to curl along the edge, pins must be placed close together when the pattern is laid for cutting.

If it seems to be effective for your particular fabric, select any one of the marking methods recommended for knits. Avoid wax-based chalks and papers on knits made of man-made fibers, however, as they are almost impossible to remove. If marking appears to be a problem, a unique method of marking is available that is especially suited to lingerie: Pattern markings are transferred to the garment pieces on strips of cellophane tape. The tape is removed after the darts or other sewing details have been stitched.

A ball-point needle is highly recommended for stitching on tricots, since regular needles tend to cut threads, causing holes along seam lines. If ball-point needles are not available, insert a new size 9 needle in the machine before starting a project.

A special throat plate with a small hole for the needle prevents the fabric from becoming caught between the plate and bobbin during the stitching process. When beginning a seam, hold both the upper and lower threads together with the fingers of the left hand behind the presser foot to prevent them from tangling. Using a zigzag stitch or a stretch stitch, guide the fabric through the machine carefully. Avoid stitching over pins, because a pin may pull up the fabric and cause the seam to be uneven. Stretch bias seams slightly to prevent puckering. Proceed with caution, however, as overstretching will cause such seams to ripple. Several rows of stitching placed close together are another method of stitching seams that provides a seam finish at the same time. This seam finish is effective on nylon and rayon but should be avoided on acetates and triacetates. If this method is used, it is particularly important that seams be stretched slightly during stitching. Narrow seam allowances are satisfactory for tricot because it does not ravel. If tricot seams tend to ripple after being stitched, press them with a warm iron.

If the garment is to be decorated with lace trim, it is best, when possible, to add the lace before sewing the garment together so that the garment pieces will still be flat and easy to handle. Special laces are available for use with tricot fabric. Sometimes, however, scraps of regular lace can be used to make decorative appliqués. To use these, cut around the motif just outside of the raised threads. Tape the piece to the garment, and then stitch it by hand or machine. If a sewing machine is used, the outline of the lace motif can be followed with a zigzag stitch. When insetting large areas of lace, the technique for achieving the effect of transparency while providing for wearing comfort is to add a lining of chiffon or sheer tricot behind the lace.

Sheer Fabrics

There is a wide variety of sheer fabrics from which you can make frilly and feminine-looking blouses and party dresses. Examples are organdy, voile, chiffon, dotted Swiss, and embroidered sheers. Special techniques are needed to make attractive garments from these delicate fabrics.

Since sheers have a tendency to be elusive, they are apt to slip around as you work with them. It is best, therefore, to avoid a hard or polished cutting surface, to use shears with serrated cutting edges, and to follow carefully the laying and cutting recommendations given in the chart on pages 430-431. If a cutting board is available, use it when cutting any one of these fabrics, since they can be fastened to the board to prevent slippage.

If a cutting board is not available, it helps to place a sheet of tissue paper between fabric and worktable, or to take other precautions against slippage. In pinning, be sure to use enough pins to hold the pattern pieces firmly against the fabric.

In stitching, it is helpful to lay strips of tissue paper along the seam. After the stitching has been completed, they can be torn away. Gently guide the fabric back of the presser

Courtesy Bridal Originals

Transparency is a factor that must be considered in finishing seams and selecting hems in sheer fabrics. Because of their design, lace fabrics often must be matched at seam lines but can be left unhemmed or hand-trimmed along hemlines.

foot as you stitch sheer fabrics. Line dart areas if possible, and stitch the dart in the outer fabric and lining as one. Avoid tight-fitting darts in sheer fabrics.

The transparency of sheer fabrics demands special precautions in the selection of interfacings and other sewing notions. For interfacings use an equally sheer, carefully matched fabric, or use a layer of self-fabric. Sometimes lightweight net, tulle, or marquisette can serve as interfacing for sheers. Facings of self-fabric may be used, or the edges may be finished with binding, cording, or an embroidery finish.

Filmy sheers require small, delicate buttons and finely made buttonholes. Usually

417

machine-worked buttonholes or fabric loops are best with these fabrics (see Chapter 18).

Laces

The elegance of lace is found in a wide assortment of fibers and fabrics, ranging from delicate silk to easy-care man-made fibers, from fragile and filmy to heavily sculptured textures, and from moderately priced to very expensive fabrics.

Lace fabric usually has a right side, which can be identified by its raised surface and the cord which outlines the design. Lace has no grain. However, the design itself frequently requires matching. Extra yardage is sometimes required for repeat designs or for matching the lace motif. Experiment with pattern placement to get the most pleasing effect. The repeat design of some laces can be hand-cut to give a decorative edge at center front, on the neck edge, at the lower edges of sleeves, or at the lower edge of the skirt.

Lace fabric sometimes has a variable lengthwise effect. In such cases it must be handled like other fabrics with this effect, as described elsewhere in this chapter (see pages 423–426).

Most laces, with the exception of heavy or bonded lace, need the extra strength of a backing or lining. A backing usually is made of sheer fabric such as net, organdy, China silk, or marquisette, and it is sewed as one with the lace. Opaque fabrics such as taffeta can be used as either backing or lining. The same pattern pieces that are used to cut the garment are used to cut the backing. In pinning the pattern pieces, use enough pins to hold the piece firmly against the fabric.

To prevent lace from catching on the feed dog or presser foot during stitching, cover the seam-line area both below and above the fabric with thin tissue paper. Seams on lace are best made as inconspicuous as possible and reinforced with backing, lining, or double stitching. The double-stitched seam is made by first stitching a conventional plain seam and then placing a second row of stitching inside the seam allowance about 1/8 inch from the first row. The seam is trimmed close to the second row of stitching.

Darts are usually stitched with the lace fabric and its backing or lining held together as a single piece of fabric. To make sure that these two fabric layers do not slip out of position, baste through both fabrics down the center line of the dart. Darts in unlined laces are often slashed open *before* sewing to make them easier to stitch.

Hems are unnecessary on laces which have a border design or where the lace motif has been hand-trimmed to create an edge finish.

Hems on unlined lace with raw edges can be made narrow and inconspicuous by staystitching 1/4 inch from the fabric edge, folding under on the line of staystitching, turning the hem up about 3/8 inch, and machine-stitching close to the upper edge of the hem. A very narrow rolled hem is an alternative hem type for full skirts of delicate, sheer unlined lace. Another alternative is to finish lace edges with strips of tulle. The strips are cut about 2 1/2 inches wide, folded in half, and stitched to the hem edge on the right side of the garment. The edge is then treated as a faced hem (see page 382). Narrow horsehair braid, which adds stiffness, can be machine-stitched to the underside of narrow, flared, or full hems before they are attached to the garment.

For a lace skirt that is lined, the lining needs to extend to the lower edge of the lace hem yet not show below it. Hems in lined lace garments can be hand-stitched or machine-stitched. When the lace is bonded or the lining is treated as one with the lace, the hem may be finished in a conventional manner, using an appropriate width, edge finish, and hand-hemming stitch.

Stretch lace is effective for lingerie because it combines the elegance of lace with close-to-the-body fit. The sewing technique it requires combines the techniques used for knits and sheers.

Seams for stretch lace must stretch with the lace to avoid breaking. If a machine that makes a special stretch stitch or a zigzag stitch is not available, a certain degree of elasticity can be achieved with a straight-stitch machine by stretching the seam slightly by hand as you stitch.

Stretch lace can be joined to another edge by zigzagging or by making two rows of straight stitching ⅛ inch apart. Trim away the excess fabric under the lace for a sheer look, or leave it opaque by retaining the fabric underneath. Darts can be stitched twice and then trimmed. See also the discussion of stretch fabrics which follows.

How can certain areas of a garment made of stretch fabric be handled to prevent stretching?

What are the unique techniques applicable when working with leather and suede?

What are the special sewing techniques necessary for successfully completing garments made of vinyls and other coated fabrics?

What are the main considerations in selecting bonded fabrics?

Stretch Fabrics

Stretch fabrics comprise one of the more recent groups of fabrics available to the home seamstress. These fabrics have an elasticity which permits freedom of body movement, improves fit, and makes garments made from them comfortable to wear. Stretch also provides retention of shape and wrinkle resistance. The stretch fabrics include fabrics for swimsuits, ski pants, slacks, and other sportswear, as well as lingerie, blouses, dresses, and suits.

Among stretch fabrics there are three different types of stretch: horizontal stretch, vertical stretch, and two-way stretch. The type to select depends on the purpose for which it will be used.

Courtesy United Airlines

When making garments of stretch fabrics, cut garment pieces to provide stretch in areas of strain. Preferably use polyester thread or stretch stitches to prevent the stitches from breaking when the garment is stretched.

When cutting garments from stretch fabrics, place the pattern on the fabric so that the stretch feature will be in the correct direction. For example, in slacks, shorts, or ski pants, the stretch feature runs from the waistline to the ankle. In dresses and jackets, patterns are placed so that the stretch features run across the garment. Garment pieces, such as the waistband, for which you do not wish to utilize the stretch feature, are cut in the nonstretch direction.

Roll or fold the excess fabric so that all of it can rest on the cutting surface. This will prevent stretching of the fabric during the laying and cutting process.

To stitch stretch fabrics, select a thread such as polyester or a cotton-polyester blend so that the stitching will have sufficient strength and elasticity to stretch with the fabric. Use preferably a ball-point needle (size 11 to 14) and 12 to 14 stitches per inch.

419

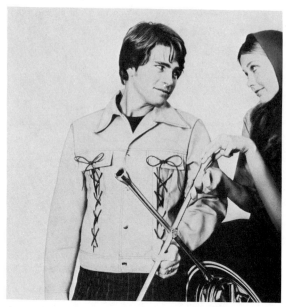

Leathers and simulated leathers can be effectively made into modern clothing. Choose a sewing-machine needle made especially for stitching leather, and stitch only after it is certain the garment fits.

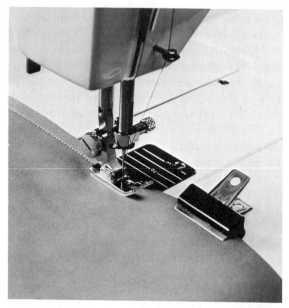

Hold leathers and coated fabrics together with a clip or tape to avoid the holes made by pinning.

Adjust the tension and pressure to suit the specific fabric. Use a roller presser foot to help keep the layers of fabric smooth and even.

Loose hand basting is recommended for stretch fabrics. During machine stitching, keep the fabric under tension by stretching it slightly in front and back of the presser foot. This will ensure adequate elasticity in the seams. Avoid stretching when inserting a zipper in a stretch garment, however, because the zipper itself will not stretch. If you have a zigzag machine or a special stitch adjustment for stretch sewing, utilize this feature for stitching stretch fabrics. Stitch at a slow speed, and backstitch at each end of a seam for reinforcement. In seams where the stretch feature is not desired, sew tape into the seam line. Interfacing is used only where the stretch is not desired.

Leather, Suede, and Simulated Leathers

Leather and suede provide a sporty look that is fashionable for separates and sportswear. Real leather and suede skins are costly and considered luxury items. Simulated-leather and suede fabrics, however, can provide the appearance of leather inexpensively. Simulated leathers may consist of a vinyl surface with or without a backing, cotton canvas covered with resin, or an embossed nylon knit. They are, for the most part, treated like other fabrics of the same fiber content, construction, and texture. The vinyls, for example, may generally be handled as described in the information on vinyl and other coated fabrics given in the next section and in the chart on pages 432-433. The simulated leathers are also included here, however, as their basic characteristics involve some of the same special considerations as leather.

Leather and suede skins require a costly investment and costly upkeep. Considerable care is necessary during construction, as stitching cannot be removed without leaving marks. Before cutting and stitching leather goods, it would be helpful to study the chart on pages 432-433.

You will find leather and suede skins for sale in fabric, hobby, and craft shops. Leather ranges in quality, or grade, according to the amount of usable skin. Scratches, thin areas, and stains lower the grade but may affect only slightly the wearing qualities. The grade, however, relates directly to the price. It may be to your economic advantage to buy skins with imperfections and work around them.

Leather and suede are sold by the individual skin or by the square foot, rather than by the yard. You can convert the footage to equivalent yardage by dividing the number of square feet by 9, since 9 square feet equals 1 square yard.

For simulated-leather fabrics the cost per yard can range from inexpensive to a price comparable to that of real leather skins. When purchasing simulated leather, consider the fiber content, fabric width, general appearance, and ease of care. For example, a vinyl-coated fabric that is inexpensive and authentic looking might be a poor buy if it were neither washable nor drycleanable. A simulation of leather achieved by a resin finish might last for the life of the garment or it might lose its appearance after a few washings. The simulated-leather fabric that appears costly to purchase may be inexpensive in the long run if it is satisfactory in quality and width and is machine-washable. If you feel inadequately informed to buy such fabrics intelligently, ask for the help of the fabric buyer in your local store, keeping in mind the questions listed on pages 78-79.

Examine leather and suede skins carefully for flaws before laying your pattern. Thin spots or irregularities can be reinforced with iron-on tape but should be avoided when cutting major pattern pieces.

Avoid folding leather, suede, and, in some cases, simulated-leather fabric for either storage or cutting, as folding may mar the fabric. Store it, rather, by rolling it. For pattern pieces marked *Place on Fold*, cut a dupli-cate pattern of tissue or wrapping paper. Tape together the edges of the duplicate and the original pattern piece to make a complete pattern for the entire piece. Planning the complete pattern layout in advance is particularly helpful when you have to work around leather skin irregularities.

Allow a little extra length in sleeves or pants of leather because, as it is worn, the fabric creases and shapes to the body contours, becoming slightly shorter.

Because leather skins are irregular in size and length in addition to having skin irregularities, piecing may be necessary in places. Piece only small sections or those that will not show, such as facings, hems, or the underside of sleeves. Avoid piecing at points of strain or near a major seam.

If darts, seams, or hems do not lie flat in leather or suede garments, they may be flattened by pounding with a mallet or you may apply rubber cement to glue them down. Cutting wedges from the inner fold of hems will also help keep hems flat. In some cases rubber cement can be substituted for hem stitching. Zippers may be inserted by hand or by machine, using a zipper adhesive to eliminate pinning or basting. Invisible zippers are sometimes preferred. Facings on leather can be made of a lining fabric or the leather itself, or the edge can be turned and topstitched.

Vinyl and Other Coated Fabrics

Coated fabrics are those that have been given a vinyl finish or similar coating. Because many are also waterproof, they are particularly popular for rainwear.

Crease lines, including hemlines, made in coated fabrics are permanent. Alterations are therefore feasible only before stitching, and can best be made before the garment pieces are cut. Perhaps the best alternative, however, is to construct a trial garment. Stitch the trial garment with basting stitches which can be easily ripped out so that the

Vinyl-coated fabrics can be used for making a wide variety of rainwear.

pieces of the fitted trial garment can be used as a pattern. (See "Making a Trial Garment" and "Adjusting Your Pattern" on pages 249-255.)

Coated fabrics are firm and do not ravel. They generally require little or no interfacing and no seam finishes. Before constructing a garment of coated fabric, study carefully the suggestions given on the chart on pages 432-433.

If you plan to topstitch on a coated fabric, place tissue paper below the area to be stitched so that it will move easily.

Loop closures, hook-and-loop tape, and gripper snappers are suitable fastenings for garments of vinyl and other coated fabrics. Sometimes machine buttonholes and zippers can be applied. Test their effectiveness on a scrap of fabric before inserting them into a coated-fabric garment.

Bonded Fabrics

A bonded fabric consists of two different fabrics that have been joined by means of an adhesive or a fusing process. The permanent backing can provide a built-in lining, give stability to the outer fabric, aid in shape retention, and, in some instances, make the fabric reversible.

Check the appearance and the hand of bonded fabrics before you buy. Be sure that the face fabric is on grain. Bonded fabrics in which the face fabric is off grain are best avoided as they cannot be straightened. The straightness of the backing is less critical. Avoid also bonded fabrics in which the face fabric is pulling away from the backing. Check carefully the fabrics you are considering for weight, bulkiness, stiffness, and pliability, and select the type best suited to your pattern choice.

In making garments of bonded fabrics, darts may be slashed and pressed open to prevent bulk. If the fabric is heavy, facings can be made of lightweight lining fabric, attached to the garment, and understitched for a sharp edge. Interfacings are often omitted.

Fabrics with a Diagonal Effect

A diagonal fabric is one which has a prominent slanting rib. Such fabrics require special techniques in handling because of their weave or because of the variations in shading or color. Examples of diagonal fabrics are twill, covert, and gabardine.

It is important in laying the pattern on fabrics of this type to make sure that the diagonal lines run in the desired direction in each garment piece. Usually a diagonal design that continues unbroken all the way around the garment is particularly satisfactory. If the fabric has no right or wrong side, another possibility is a *chevron* design, in which the design lines create V-formations. To form chevrons, open up the fabric into a single thickness. Cut it to proper width for a given pattern piece along a crosswise fold, and place the right side of one half of the fabric against the wrong side of the other half, matching the design and grain exactly. Then lay the pattern on the double thickness for cutting. A chevron design will result in the completed garment. Slip basting will probably be necessary for perfect matching of a design (see page 391).

You may wish to experiment with the pattern placement for pockets, trimmings, and other details to determine the most interesting employment of the diagonal effect. For example, a collar could be cut on the bias for design contrast.

Why do some fabrics require extra yardage for garment construction?

Why do fabrics with a variable lengthwise or crosswise effect usually require more yardage for a given pattern than fabrics without such an effect?

How can an even or uneven plaid be recognized?

Why does an uneven plaid necessitate more extra yardage for a pattern than an even plaid?

Why is it true that the larger the design, the greater the amount of fabric needed?

Fabrics with a Variable Crosswise Effect

Fabrics with a variable crosswise effect have a definite right and left in their design. For such fabrics the garment must be planned so that the design motifs either all face in the same direction or face each other. Either plan requires care in laying the pattern to ensure that each piece is placed accurately.

Fabrics with a variable crosswise effect may also have a variable lengthwise effect. In such cases the handling techniques required by both types of fabrics are entailed.

Fabrics with a Variable Lengthwise Effect

The variable lengthwise effect in a fabric results from a fabric design with definite up and down directions. Such designs change in ap-

pearance when the position of the fabric is reversed vertically. The effect may be caused by the construction of the fabric or by its applied design. The types of fabrics which have such an effect are (1) fabrics with a one-way design, (2) napped fabrics, (3) pile fabrics, (4) deep-pile or furlike fabrics, (5) fabrics with a satin weave, and (6) iridescent fabrics. All fabrics with a variable lengthwise effect must be cut with special care. When arranging the pattern pieces on the fabric, lay them as for *Fabric with Nap*, that is, in a single direction.

Fabrics with a One-way Design

One-way fabric designs include some large designs, many plaids, and certain horizontal stripes. Because fabrics with these designs often require handling considerations in addition to the variable lengthwise effect, they are discussed separately later in the chapter (see pages 426-429).

Border designs are another type of one-way design. A border design is generally located along one selvage of a fabric. Garment styles in which the border may be placed along a straight structural line are the best choice. When a pattern must be laid on the crosswise grain, the yardage must be figured in relation to the width of the fabric. Wide fabric can be cut to better advantage than can narrow. In order to have the garment retain its shape, choose fabric which is firm and arrange the pattern on the fabric so that there is minimum strain in the portions of the garment cut on the crosswise grain of the fabric. The motif in the border design should be matched on the seam lines.

Napped Fabrics

Napped fabrics are woven from short fibers, the ends of which are brushed up to form the typical soft, fibrous nap surface. Because of the construction, the appearance of the fabric varies with the position of the nap. Napped fabrics include wool napped fabrics such as fleece, wool flannel, and wool broadcloth,

Courtesy Streisand, Zuch & Freedman, Inc.

Garments made from border prints are usually cut on the crosswise grain rather than the lengthwise grain of the fabric. Such an arrangement allows for matching the borders horizontally around the garment.

and cotton napped fabrics such as suede cloth and cotton flannel.

One of the most important techniques in working with these fabrics is to first establish the direction of the nap in the garment. This necessitates determining the direction of the nap before laying the pattern. To do this, hold opposite ends of the fabric to the light, one at a time or beside each other if length permits. Because of the difference in the way they reflect light, one end will look lighter than the other. Because of the position of the nap, one end will also be smoother to the touch than the other. Choose the effect you prefer before arranging the pattern layout on the fabric. The nap must lie in the same direction on all pattern pieces.

Pile Fabrics

Pile fabrics are varied in their fiber content and appearance. They are woven or knitted in such a way that an additional thread forms loops on the surface. The loops in pile fabric may be cut, as in velvet, furlike fabrics, and velveteen, or uncut, as in terry cloth.

The direction of the pile affects the light reflection on the fabric, creating an illusion of changing color. Hold up and observe opposite ends of the fabric, one at a time, or side by side if possible. One end will appear lighter in color than the other. Select the effect that you like best. Generally, most of these fabrics are cut with the pile running *up* for a richer color. Corduroy, however, is frequently cut with the pile running *down* for longer wear.

Deep-pile or Furlike Fabrics

Simulated fur is usually made of man-made fibers with a woven or knit backing. Its depth varies from a fraction of an inch to several inches. The basic principles for handling nap and pile fabrics can also be applied to these fabrics, but, in addition, special techniques are required.

Before buying deep-pile or furlike fabrics, read the labels regarding the fiber content and care requirements. Some are washable but others are drycleanable only. Some even require the same costly cleaning process as real fur.

The wearing quality of a deep-pile fabric can be determined by examining how the fiber is attached to the base. To check for quality, fold over a corner of the fabric and examine the fabric base. If the pile is sparse, the fabric will quickly show signs of wear. Further, if the pile is glued, rather than woven or knitted to the base, it will deteriorate quickly in wear and cleaning.

When purchasing pile fabrics, use the yardage figure on your pattern envelope indicated for *Fabric with Nap.* If this information is not shown, a trial layout of the pattern may be made on paper to determine the extra amount of fabric needed.

Before constructing a garment of deep-pile, or simulated fur, check the pattern for fit and make the necessary alterations in the pattern before pinning it to the fabric. A trial garment made of muslin or an old sheet is helpful in assuring a good fit. Considering the cost of most furlike fabrics, time spent in making such a trial garment is time well spent as it is a safety measure against failure.

In cutting furlike fabrics, follow the layout for *Fabric with Nap.* Be certain that all sections of the garment are cut in the same direction. Because of the thickness of these fabrics, it is usually best to lay all pattern pieces on a single thickness. If a piece is marked *Cut on Fold,* cut a duplicate pattern of tissue or wrapping paper and tape together the edges marked *fold* of the original and the duplicate. This will provide a complete pattern for the entire garment piece. If one pattern piece is used to cut two garment pieces on the single thickness of the fabric, remember to turn the pattern over to cut the second piece. Reduce bulk by eliminating seams whenever possible. For example, if the pattern calls for separate front facings, they can be cut as one with the garment front (see page 442).

When cutting deep-pile fabrics, use sharp or serrated shears or a special single-edge razor. Cut only through the backing to avoid defacing the pile. Before stitching, check the machine stitch on a scrap of the fabric. Usually a loose tension, light pressure, and large stitch are required for stitching on furlike fabrics. Stitch in the direction of the pile, using a needle to push the pile away from the seam line whenever possible. On very deep pile it may be necessary to shear some pile from the seam allowance before stitching. Use a fine-tooth comb to pull the fibers to the surface of the garment after a seam is stitched.

Darts in deep-pile fabrics may be slashed and pressed open to reduce the bulk. If the cut edges do not stay flat, they can be hand-stitched to the fabric backing.

Machine understitching is not possible on bulky pile and fur fabrics. If it is desired, the seam can be rolled slightly and sewn with a hand stitch resembling understitching.

If hand-hemming stitches are used on

Courtesy Butterick Fashion Marketing Company

Give special attention to the placement of patterns on fabrics with variable effects. The garment at the left is made from fabric with a variable crosswise effect. Both the center garment and the one on the right are made from fabrics with variable lengthwise effects. The fabric in the center garment has a one-way design, whereas the one on the right is made of napped fabric which must be cut as a one-way design.

these fabrics, they should catch only the backing of the fabric.

If zippers are needed, it is best to use the invisible type and to apply them by hand. In long-haired furlike fabrics, zippers should be avoided because the fur will catch in the zipper teeth. Avoid making buttonholes of any kind in the fabric itself. Instead, use oversized hooks, snaps, frogs, buckles, hook-and-loop tape, or hidden buttonholes. Hidden buttonholes can be made by attaching to the underside of the garment a strip of a lightweight, firmly woven fabric in which machine-worked buttonholes have been constructed.

Satin-weave Fabrics

Fabrics with a satin weave have a variable lengthwise effect because the long, lustrous floating threads on the surface provide unique reflective characteristics. On satin fabrics, all pattern pieces must be laid in the same direction. Only if the threads lie in the same direction can the light reflect equally on all parts of the garment and the color appear uniform.

Iridescent Fabrics

Iridescent fabrics fall into this category because they are woven of yarns of contrasting colors on the lengthwise and crosswise grains. Usually one set of yarns is darker than the other. The effect of light on the contrasting yarns makes the overall color seem darker when viewed from one direction than when viewed from the opposite direction. Some iridescent fabrics also have a right and wrong side. For color uniformity, therefore, the direction of the fabric weave must be kept the same throughout the garment.

Fabrics with Large Designs

A large design, whether regular or irregular, requires that the outline of the design be matched at the major seam lines to prevent interruption of the flow of the design. Spacing of large designs within a garment piece also requires care to ensure that the designs will be located to best advantage in the garment and will be broken as little as possible by construction lines. The design lines should always match at lengthwise seam lines and, whenever possible, at crosswise seam lines. The design should be balanced right and left, above and below the waistline, and front and back. A satisfactory arrangement usually requires extra yardage. For ease in arranging design placement, it is helpful to lay the pattern on the right side of the fabric.

The larger the design, the greater amount of fabric needed. If you know the exact size of the design in the chosen fabric, the space required by the repeats of the design may be marked off on a sheet of paper, on which the pattern can then be temporarily laid. From this trial layout, the amount of the particular fabric that will be needed can be determined.

Pin basting or hand basting on the seam line ensures matching the lines of the design precisely during stitching.

Plaid Fabrics

Select plaid fabrics carefully because plaids can vary tremendously in the degree of difficulty they present in cutting and sewing. Basically plaids can be classified as even or uneven. An *even* plaid is one in which the design is identical on both sides of the prominent design line in both the lengthwise and crosswise directions. In *uneven* plaids, the designs are dissimilar on either side of the prominent design line in either the lengthwise or the crosswise direction or both.

There is an easy way to determine whether a plaid is even or uneven before you buy. Fold the fabric diagonally through the center of the plaid design. In an even plaid, lines, spaces, and colors in the upper and lower fabric layers match perfectly. In an uneven plaid these lines do not match.

Even plaids (above) are much easier to match than uneven ones. For optimum beauty, plaids require matching at every seam line, particularly at vertical seam lines and at those joining sleeves to the body of the garment.

426

Even plaids are much easier to match at garment seam lines and therefore require less fabric than do uneven plaids. If you are working with an uneven plaid, it is almost necessary to cut each garment piece individually to avoid cutting errors and to ensure matching.

When determining the amount of a given plaid fabric necessary for a garment, consider the size of the plaid you are selecting. Generally small plaids necessitate less extra yardage and can be matched more easily than large plaids. When buying even plaids, usually an extra ¼ to ½ yard of a small plaid is needed for matching purposes. For large plaids, at least an extra ½ to 1 yard is required. Uneven plaids require even more extra yardage. Scrap fabric can often be used, however, to construct hats, purses, or other matching accessories.

Check plaid fabric to determine whether the plaid design is *printed* or *woven.* This is done by examining both sides of the fabric to see whether one side is lighter, or by raveling out a thread or two for examination. If the color is lighter on the wrong side or has failed to penetrate all areas of the thread so that light or white spots are left, the plaid is printed.

A printed plaid must be checked for grain perfection. Determine the grain by straightening the end of the fabric along a crosswise thread. If the crosswise lines of the plaid are parallel with the edge of the fabric, the design is on grain. If they are not, avoid buying the fabric as it would present insurmountable problems in sewing. The plaid would probably always look crooked in a garment.

Off-grain woven plaids can usually be straightened by one of the conventional methods of straightening fabrics (see pages 261-265).

Plaids can have both a variable crosswise effect and a variable lengthwise effect. Plaids of such complexity present challenges in layouts and matching for the most experienced seamstress. They are best avoided by a beginner.

When folding an even plaid fabric for layout, check the design placement on the two thicknesses of the fabric. Be sure that the plaid lines match in both directions. Then pin the layers together at frequent intervals to prevent the design from shifting in position during pattern layout and cutting.

In laying the pattern, follow the layout for fabrics with nap, or lay all the pieces in the same direction.

Matching design lines at the seams can be ensured by placing on the same lines of the plaid the patterns for garment areas to be joined. Lay notches that will be matched on identical lines within the plaid. For example, suppose that notch 2 in a sleeve is to be matched to notch 2 in a bodice. You can make sure that the design lines match at the armhole seam by placing both notches on exactly the same line of the plaid. If notch 2 of the sleeve is on the red line of the plaid, for instance, notch 2 of the bodice must also be

Courtesy R. & M. Kaufman

A garment cut from uneven stripes requires placing of all pattern pieces in a single direction so that widths and colors of stripes will match at the seam lines.

427

A. VARIABLE CROSSWISE EFFECT

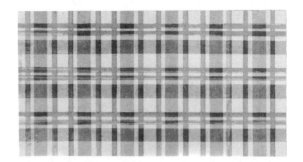

B. VARIABLE LENGTHWISE EFFECT

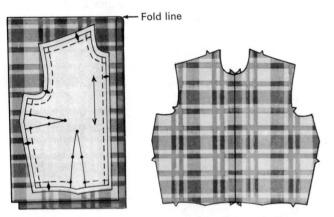

Pattern layout   Resulting balanced effect

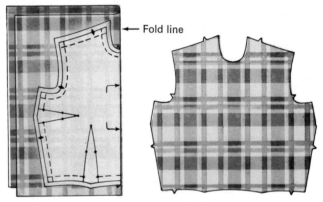

Pattern layout   Resulting balanced effect

located on an identically placed red line. Long seam lines, however, can seldom be matched correctly unless they are cut on an identical slant.

Striped Fabrics

Striped fabrics, unlike plaids, have design lines running in only one direction. Like plaids, however, they can have either an even or an uneven overall design.

Even vertical stripes require only that you place the pattern pieces to be matched on the same type of stripe. *Uneven* vertical stripes require that you lay all pattern pieces in a specific left or right direction to ensure the desired direction of the stripes. They also re-

quire that pattern pieces be placed in a single direction.

Some uneven-striped fabrics may also have a variable lengthwise effect. Since pattern pieces are positioned with all tops headed in the same direction, this lengthwise variable effect will be provided for as the crosswise variable effect is controlled.

When placing the pattern on uneven vertical stripes, you may arrange the pieces so that the design either is balanced on each side of the garment center or is continuous all the way around the garment.

To obtain a balanced effect with fabric that has no right and wrong side, plan a center front and back seam instead of centering the pattern on the fabric center fold. On a single

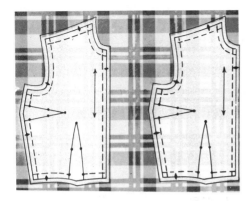

C. VARIABLE CROSSWISE AND LENGTHWISE
EFFECT (NO RIGHT OR WRONG SIDE)

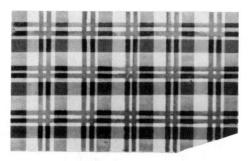

D. VARIABLE CROSSWISE AND LENGTHWISE
EFFECT (WITH RIGHT AND WRONG SIDES)

Resulting balanced effect

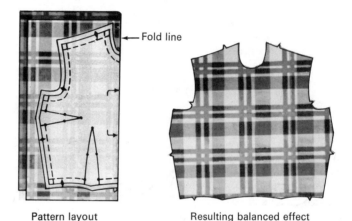

Pattern layout — Fold line

Resulting balanced effect

Courtesy Simplicity Pattern Co., Inc.

thickness of fabric, locate the center front seam along the major line of the stripe. Be sure to consider whether the addition of a ⅝-inch seam allowance is necessary for pieces intended for cutting on the fold.

When planning to make the striped design continuous all the way around the garment, use special care in cutting set-in sleeves. A continuous design requires that the stripes of the sleeve continue the arrangement of the stripes established by the bodice.

Garments with uneven horizontal stripes also require special consideration. It is important in such garments that the sequence of the stripes be retained all the way down the bodice and the skirt. The sleeves must also be included in the design scheme.

Whether the stripes are even or uneven, they are matched at the seam lines, including the center front and back. Stripes can be accurately matched the complete length of a seam only if the degree of slant is the same in all the joined garment pieces. Slip-baste such seams for accuracy in final stitching.

When cutting a yoke of striped fabric, it is often effective to run the stripe horizontally in the yoke but vertically in the bodice and skirt. This element of contrast adds interest to the garment design.

Pockets, collars, and cuffs can be cut on the crosswise or bias grain of striped fabric. Cutting them on the bias gives these pieces diagonal stripes that can be a pleasing variation.

429

Type of Fabric	Suggested Type of Pattern	Special Layout Instructions	Special Pinning Instructions	Recommended Cutting Techniques	Recommended Marking Techniques	Recommended Basting Techniques
Knits		Place grain line of pattern along rib of knit. On striped or patterned knits, lay pieces to match perfectly along length-wise seam lines. Use layout marked *For Fabric with Nap*.	Ball-point pins or very sharp silk pins placed in direction of lengthwise rib.	Use large table to prevent stretching. Make long strokes with sharp shears. When possible, cut direc-tionally with shears which have serrated edges.	Marking chalk. Tailor's tacks. Tracing wheel and tracing paper on fabrics which are not sheer or not easily marked. Avoid using tracing paper on fabrics made of man-made fibers.	Pin basting. Slip basting for matching designs.
Double knits	Basic tailored designs with minimum of seams.					
Sweater knits	Designs made espécially for type of sweater knit used.					
Lingerie knits	Softly draped designs, no creases or pleats.					
Sheer Fabrics Organdy, voile, chiffon, and embroidered sheers	Design with fullness or easy fit, few seams, and few darts.	To avoid slip-page, lay out on cork board or over a bed sheet or tissue paper. If pat-terned, follow instructions for designed fabrics.	Very sharp pins placed on grain. On very delicate fabrics, use needles.	Choose long, thin, sharp shears. Cut with smooth long strokes, keeping nonslip material under fabric on cutting surface.	Tailor's tacks or marking pencil. If fabric holds a crease well, iron in darts, tucks, or pleats.	Pin basting.
Laces Conventional, bonded, and stretch	Simple design with minimum of contruction details.	If one-way design, lay as napped fabric. Match designs along seam lines. Position center of each major pattern piece on center of a lace design.	Very sharp silk pins placed at right angles to edges of pattern. On very fragile lace, use needles.	Choose long, thin, sharp shears. Cut with long, smooth strokes. Some designs can be hand-shaped along garment edges by cutting around edges of the design.	Tailor's tacks.	Hand basting recommended. Slip basting for matching designs.

FOR SPECIAL FABRICS

| Thread Type | Needle Size | Machine-stitching Instructions | | | | | | Recommended Pressing Techniques | Recommended Seam and Hem Finishes |
		Stitch Type	Stitch Length	Tension	Pressure	Technique			
Polyester or cotton-polyester combination.	Ball-point preferred. Sizes 11-14. Sizes 11-14. Sizes 9-11.	Zigzag, stretch, or stitch-and-overcast stitch.	8-10.	Loose, according to fabric.	Light.	Use roller presser foot. Allow knit to flow through machine evenly if using any type of stretch stitch.	Adjust temperature of iron to fiber content of fabric. Press only in length-wise direction. Place paper between seam allowance and garment to avoid seam imprint. Press on wrong side, or use light-weight pressing cloth when pressing on right side.	No finish required. Stitch-and-overcast effective if machine allows. Narrow French seam for sheer fabrics.
Poly-ester-cotton combination. Sizes 60-80.	Sizes 9-11.	Straight stitch.	15-20.	Regular.	Regular.	Use regular presser foot. Choose throat plate with small hole to prevent fabric pulling through to bobbin area. Place strips of tissue paper between seam and throat plate.	Adjust temperature of iron to fiber content of fabric. Press lightly to shape, directionally when possible.	Narrow seams, French, bound, or double-stitched and trimmed very near outside stitching line. Hems either very narrow or very wide, hand-rolled, or bound.
Cotton-polyester combi-nation.	Sizes 9-11.	For stretch lace, a zigzag or stretch stitch preferred.	Medium.	Slightly loose.	Light for bonded or stretch lace.	Slightly loose machine tension. Place tissue paper between fabric and machine to prevent catching lace on machine.	Adjust temperature of iron to fiber content of fabric. Steam-press over wool or terry cloth, using thin pressing cloth.	Inconspicuous seams, such as narrow and double-stitched, stitched as one with lining, or stitched and pinked or over-cast. Hems narrow and in-conspicuous or cut to design of lace.

Type of Fabric	Suggested Type of Pattern	Special Layout Instructions	Special Pinning Instructions	Recommended Cutting Techniques	SPECIAL TECHNIQUES FOR Recommended Marking Techniques	Recommended Basting Techniques
Stretch Fabrics	Patterns of regular size with a minimum of construction details.	Lay each piece according to desired direction of stretch. Major stretch needs are horizontal rather than vertical.	Ball-point or very sharp pins placed at right angles to direction of stretch. Heavy weights may be used instead of pins during cutting.	Avoid stretching fabric during cutting. Hold fabric flat on large table.	Tracing paper on heavy fabrics such as swim-suit fabrics. Tailor's tacks on sheer stretch lingerie fabrics.	Hand basting.
Leather and Suede	Simple lines with minimum of flare. Avoid pleats and gathers.	Use layout marked *For Fabric with Nap.* Lay pattern on single thickness of wrong side of fabric. Lay all pieces in one direction.	Avoid pins if possible. Tape, paperweights, or paper clips preferred. If necessary, silk pins can be placed sparsely in seam allowance.	Cut out pieces from top to bottom with single-edged razor blade. Sharp shears may be used on lightweight leathers.	Pencil, ball-point pen, crayon, or tailor's pencil to mark wrong side of fabric.	Avoid basting. Use paper clips, tape, or rubber cement.
Vinyl and Other Coated Fabrics	Pattern with few pieces, few details, and little or no ease. Kimono or raglan sleeves recommended.	Avoid laying pieces in areas containing deep creases or folds. Follow straight-of-fabric markings on pattern pieces.	Avoid pins if possible. Tape, paperweights, or paper clips preferred. If necessary, use silk pins in seam allowance.	Use long, sharp shears. Cut from wide to narrow section of each piece.	Toothless tracing wheel or tailor's pencil.	Avoid basting. Use paper clips or tape to hold sections together.
Bonded Fabrics	Simple pattern with few seams, few details, and little or no ease. Avoid circular skirts and soft draping.	Face fabric determines layout. Lay pieces on right side of fabric and follow lengthwise grain or rib. Lay on single thickness if possible.	Ball-point or fine, sharp pins placed at right angles to eges of pattern.	Cut directionally with long, sharp shears.	Tailor's tacks or marking pencil. Tracing paper except on fabrics made of man-made fibers.	Slip-baste seams for matching stripes or plaid. Otherwise use pin basting.

SPECIAL FABRICS (continued)

| Thread Type | Needle Size | Machine-stitching Instructions | | | | | | Recommended Pressing Techniques | Recommended Seam and Hem Finishes |
		Stitch Type	Stitch Length	Tension	Pressure	Technique		
Polyester.	Ball-point preferred. Sizes 11-14.	Zigzag or stretch stitch.	12-14.	Regular.	Adjust to fabric.	Use a roller presser foot. Stitch at slow speed. Backstitch at each end for reinforcement.	Use slightly warm iron. Steam-press gently to avoid stretching. Place paper between seam allowance and garment to avoid seam imprint.	Sew tape into seam line where stretch feature not desired. Machine-stitched hems are recommended.
Heavy-duty mercerized cotton or cotton-polyester combination.	Sharp or wedge-shaped, size 11.	Straight stitch.	7-10.	Loose.	Light.	Use roller presser foot. Stitch carefully to avoid imprints. Round corners. Avoid backstitching or overstitching. Place tissue paper between leather and machine to prevent slippage.	Flatten seams by pounding with mallet. Press on wrong side with warm iron. Use brown paper both as pressing cloth and to protect board from suede dyes. No steam.	Stitch preshrunk tape inside seams for reinforcement. Overlapped seams require no finish. Hems less than 2 inches wide and regular seams, reinforced with topstitching, or rubber cement, or both.
Heavy-duty mercerized cotton.	Size 16.	Straight stitch.	8-10.	Regular.	Light.	Place tissue paper between fabric and presser foot. Avoid double-stitching and backstitching.	Cannot be pressed. Flatten seams with fingers, pounding mallet, or wodden clapper.	Flat-fell or lapped seams. No finish needed. Attach hem with slip stitching, top-stitching, or rubber cement.
Polyester or cotton-polyester combination.	Sizes 11-14.	Zigzag or stretch stitch for areas of strain. Otherwise, use straight stitch.	8-12.	Loose.	Light.	Support fabric both in front and in back of pressure foot.	Adjust temperature of iron to fiber content of fabric on side of garment which will be pressed. Press directionally.	No finish needed. To reduce bulk, trim backing from seam allowance. If desired, bind, zigzag, or top-stitch seam or make flat-fell seam. Attach hem to under-layer of fabric only.

Type of Fabric	Suggested Type of Pattern	Special Layout Instructions	Special Pinning Instructions	Recommended Cutting Techniques	Recommended Marking Techniques	Recommended Basting Techniques
Fabrics with a Diagonal Effect	Patterns with basic lines and few major pieces. Slim skirts, straight underarm darts, and set-in sleeves usually best. Avoid bias-cut seams and bands. Avoid patterns marked *Not suitable for diagonal fabrics.*	Plan layout so that all pieces have identical diagonal effect or fit together in chevron designs.	Pins suitable for type of fabric placed in direction of grain.	Cut woven fabrics directionally with long, smooth strokes.	Tracing paper on medium-weight opaque fabrics. Tailor's tacks on sheers.	Slip basting for chevron designs. Pin basting for regular seams.
Fabrics with a Variable Crosswise Effect	Avoid patterns which bring bias edges together. Consider effect of design on pattern yardage requirement.	Lay each piece so that fabric design faces correct direction for desired garment design.	Pins suitable for type of fabric placed at right angles to edges of pattern.	Cut woven fabrics directionally with long, smooth strokes.	Tracing paper on medium-weight opaque fabrics. Tailor's tacks on sheers.	Slip basting for matching designs. Pin basting where matching is unnecessary.
Fabrics with a Variable Lengthwise Effect						
Napped fabrics	Simple pattern with minimum of details and seams. Consider effect of design on pattern yardage requirement.	Follow layout for fabrics with nap, or lay all pieces in one direction.	Pin directionally with pins at right angles to edges of pattern.	Cut directionally with sharp shears and with long, clean strokes.	Marking chalk, tailor's tacks, or tracing paper and wheel.	Hand-baste if necessary. Pin basting often adequate.
Pile fabrics	Pattern with few seams and construction details. Avoid pockets, cuffs, etc. Consider effect of design on pattern yardage requirement.	Follow layout for fabrics with nap, or lay all pieces in one direction.	Long, sharp pins. Pin selvages together before pinning pattern.	Cut directionally with sharp shears and long, clean strokes.	Tailor's tacks or marking chalk. On sturdy fabrics, tracing paper and wheel may be used.	Hand basting sometimes required.

		Machine-stitching Instructions					Recommended Pressing Techniques	Recommended Seam and Hem Finishes
Thread Type	*Needle Size*	*Stitch Type*	*Stitch Length*	*Tension*	*Pressure*	*Technique*		
Fiber compatible with fiber of fabric.	Variable with type of fabric.	Straight stitch on regular weaves. Stretch or zigzag stitch on knits or stretch fabrics.	Variable with type of fabric.	Variable with type of fabric.	Variable with type of fabric.	Use roller presser foot to ensure perfect matching of designs.	Adjust temperature of iron to fiber content of fabric. Press directionally on the wrong side or with a pressing cloth on the right side.	Choose seam finish and hemming method suitable for weave of fabric.
Fiber compatible with fiber of fabric.	Variable with type of fabric.	Straight stitch on regular weaves. Stretch or zigzag stitch on stretch fabrics.	Variable with type of fabric.	Variable with type of fabric.	Variable with type of fabric.	Use roller presser foot to ensure perfect matching of designs.	Adjust temperature of iron to fiber content of fabric.	Choose seam finish and hemming method suitable for weave of fabric.
Polyester or cotton-polyester combination.	Ball-point sizes 9–11.	Straight stitch.	10–12.	Loose.	Light.	Stitch in direction of nap.	Steam-press lightly on wrong side on needle board, or press over terry cloth.	Choose seam finishes and hemming method suitable for specific fabric.
Polyester or cotton-polyester combination.	Sharp, about size 14.	Straight stitch. In areas of strain use zigzag or stretch stitch.	8–12.	Loose.	Light.	Sew in direction of pile.	Steam-press on wrong side on noodle board. Do not touch iron to fabric.	Usually no seam finish required. Bind or face hem edge and attach to backing.

Type of Fabric	Suggested Type of Pattern	Special Layout Instructions	Special Pinning Instructions	Recommended Cutting Techniques	Recommended Marking Techniques	Recommended Basting Techniques
Deep pile or furlike fabrics	Patterns with simple designs and straight lines. Especially for bulkier piles, avoid intricate detail.	Follow layout for fabrics with nap, or lay all pieces in one direction and with pile inclined in downward direction. Lay pieces on wrong side of single thickness of fabric.	Dressmaker's pins placed in seam allowance when possible.	Use sharp shears or single-edged razor blade. Cut directionally through backing only with short strokes. Avoid cutting notches; mark notch locations with marking chalk.	Tracing wheel, tailor's tacks, marking pencil, or chalk. Test to see which shows up best.	Hand-baste.
Fabrics with satin weaves and iridescent finishes	Consider effect of design on pattern yardage requirement.	Lay all pattern pieces in the same direction on fabric.	Very sharp pins for satins. Pin directionally.	Use sharp shears, cutting directionally with long, smooth strokes.	Tailor's tacks for satins. Tracing wheel for sturdy iridescent	Pin basting. Slip basting for intricate designs in satins.
Fabrics with Large Designs	Consider effect of design on pattern yardage requirement.	Lay pieces to match design lines at major seam lines. Work with single layer of fabric, design right-side-up.	Pin directionally with points of pins toward edges of pattern.	Cut directionally. Cut pieces singly for perfect matching of designs.	Choose marking technique suitable for fabric.	Slip basting for matching of designs.
Plaid Fabrics	Simple pattern with minimum of seams. Avoid circular or gored skirts and kimono sleeves.	Lay pattern to match plaid lines at seam lines of major pieces.	Use sufficient pins to prevent slippage.	Cut directionally. If necessary, cut pieces singly for perfect matching of designs.	Mark on wrong side of fabric with tracing wheel and tracing paper, or use marking chalk or tailor's tacks.	Slip basting for matching plaids.
Striped Fabrics	Simple pattern with minimum of seams and construction details.	Pattern layout depends on whether stripes are even or uneven. Uneven stripes may require that opposite sides of garment be cut separately.	Use sufficient pins to prevent slippage.	Cut directionally. If necessary, cut pieces singly for perfect matching of designs.	Same as for *Plaid Fabrics*.	Slip basting for matching stripes.

436

		Machine-stitching Instructions					Recommended Pressing Techniques	Recommended Seam and Hem Finishes
Thread Type	Needle Size	Stitch Type	Stitch Length	Tension	Pressure	Technique		
Polyester.	Size 14.	Straight stitch.	10.	Loose.	Light.	Stitch in direction of pile, using a needle to push pile away from seam line. Use fine comb to extract any fibers caught in seam.	Finger-press or pound. Use heat only with *extreme* care.	Pile may be sheared from seam allowance to reduce bulk. Double-stitch seams, hand-stitch edges of seam allowance to backing, or bias-bind edges. Bind or face hem and attach to backing.
Fiber compatible with fiber of fabric.	Sizes 9-11.	Straight stitch.	10-12.	Regular.	Regular.	Use regular presser foot and regular stitching techniques.	Press with warm iron from wrong side of fabric. Protect fabric with pressing cloth.	Choose finishes suitable for specific fabric and garment design.
Fiber compatible with fiber of fabric.	Variable with type of fabric.	Straight stitch unless knit or stretch fabric.	Variable with type of fabric.	Variable with type of fabric.	Variable with type of fabric.	Use regular stitching techniques unless fabric is knit, stretch, or pile.	Adjust temperature of iron to fiber content of fabric. Press directionally with lightweight pressing cloth.	Choose seam finish and hemming method suitable for weave of fabric.
Fiber compatible with fiber or fabric.	Variable with type of fabric.	Straight stitch.	Variable with type of fabric.	Variable with type of fabric.	Variable with type of fabric.	Use roller presser foot to ensure perfect matching of designs.	Adjust temperature of iron to fiber content of fabric. Press directionally with lightweight pressing cloth.	Choose seam finish and hemming method suitable for weave of fabric.
Fiber compatible with fiber of fabric.	Variable with type of fabric.	Straight stitch unless knit or bonded.	Variable with type of fabric.	Variable with type of fabric.	Variable with type of fabric.	Use roller presser foot to ensure perfect matching of stripes.	Adjust temperature of iron to fiber content of fabric. Press directionally on wrong side or with lightweight pressing cloth on right side.	Choose seam finish and hemming method suitable for weave of fabric.

1. In the positioning of patterns and cutting of garment pieces, the lengthwise rib of a knit is equivalent to the lengthwise grain of woven fabric.

2. For effective stitching of knit fabrics, use a ball-point machine needle, stretch thread such as polyester, and a stretch or zigzag machine-stitch setting.

3. Pattern pieces for stretch garments are laid on the fabric in accordance with the desired direction of the stretch.

4. Tissue paper placed under the fabric during stitching prevents sheer, coated, or other slippery fabrics from slipping out of position.

5. Extra yardage is needed for layout and cutting of special fabrics such as plaids, stripes, napped, pile, and furlike fabrics, as well as those with large or one-way designs.

6. Seams of leather, suede, coated, and deep-pile fabrics can be held together temporarily by using masking tape or paper clips to avoid holes in the fabric made by regular basting methods.

7. An off-grain bonded fabric or a plaid fabric which is printed off grain can never be straightened.

8. A plaid is *even* if the spaces and lines match in both directions when the fabric is folded diagonally.

9. A plaid napped fabric requires following the pattern layout for *Fabric with Nap* as well as matching the plaids.

10. Plaid and striped fabrics require accurate matching of the design lines at the notches and seams.

22 Facings and Interfacings

Facings and interfacings are types of fabric layers attached usually to the inside of a garment. Facings are used mainly to finish edges of a garment, although they also provide reinforcement. Interfacings are inserted between a garment and its facing for additional support. Both facings and interfacings are usually invisible on the outside of the garment.

What are the functions of facings?

How do facings differ from other edge finishes?

What alternatives are available for finishing a garment edge attractively?

How can an edge be faced when no facing pattern has been provided?

What are the steps in applying a shaped facing? An extended facing? A bias facing? A combination facing?

Decisions About Facings and Interfacings

Both facings and interfacings provide a seamstress the opportunity for creative decisions. Facings can be made in a wide variety of shapes, sizes, and colors. They may be small or they may extend the full length of the garment. They may be round, square, V-shaped, or scalloped. They may be of self-fabric or contrasting fabric. They may be purely functional or decorative.

Interfacings vary greatly in both function and fabric and require choices on the part of the seamstress. Knowledge of the alternatives and principles involved in selecting both facings and interfacings will help you make good choices in present and future projects. You will then have at your disposal an effective method of enhancing the comfort, attractiveness, and wearability of your garments.

Types of Facings

There are three basic types of facings: shaped, extended, and bias. The combination facing is actually a variation of the shaped facing. While all facings serve the same general purpose of covering and reinforcing edges, there are some basic differences in the way they are cut and applied. Bias bindings, which are sometimes used instead of facings, are discussed on pages 403-405.

Shaped Facings

A shaped, or fitted, facing is cut on the same grain and in the same shape as the edge it will face. It may be curved, square, round, scalloped, or pointed. Shaped facings are most frequently employed to finish armholes and neckline edges. However, they are sometimes used to extend or finish lower edges of garments, to substitute for a waistband, and to line cuffs, pockets, collars, and other small

*Shaped facings are often used to face the armhole
edges of garments whereas extended, or cut-on, facings
might be cut as a part of a skirt and turned back
to face the slit in the skirt.*

*A bias facing that has been cut from fabric or a ready-
to-sew stretch facing that has been purchased
can be stitched along the edges of seams
to form decorative edging.*

areas. These facings are usually cut from the garment fabric, but they may be made of a lighter-weight cloth if the garment fabric is bulky. Occasionally, they may be cut of a contrasting color or design and applied to the right side of the garment for a decorative effect.

Sometimes, when pattern alterations are made on a garment, a faced area may be involved. In such cases the corresponding facing must be altered identically for proper fit.

Extended Facings

An extended, or cut-on, facing, as its names imply, is cut as an extension of the garment edge to be faced. Extended facings are most likely to be used on straight edges to reinforce button and buttonhole areas of blouses, dresses, jumpers, jackets, or coats. The facing together with the edge of the garment provides a sturdy area on which to locate buttons and buttonholes. Because extended facings are cut as an enlargement of the garment, they eliminate unnecessary seams, require very little stitching to secure them to the garment, and produce a flat edge.

Bias Facings

Bias facings are different from other facings in that they are not cut to shape. They are strips of fabric cut on the true bias and of an equal width for the length of the area to be faced. It is not necessary to cut bias facings to shape because of the *give* characteristics of their bias cut. They do not envelop an edge, as do bindings, but fit flat against either the inside or the outside of a garment.

Combination Facings

Many garments must be faced along both neckline and armhole. Since the inner edges of these facings must be finished to prevent raveling and must be anchored securely, they are often noticeable from the right side of the garment. Sometimes the neck and the armhole facings can be cut together in what is called a combination, or a cut-in-one, facing which may provide a more satisfactory finish and give more adequate support to the two areas than can separate facings.

Cutting Facings

Frequently facing patterns are included as a part of a garment pattern. If so, you need only to cut the pieces and follow the instructions in the pattern guide sheet. However, there are times when facing patterns are not included, or when you want to change a pattern from sleeved to sleeveless, to omit the collar, or to make other modifications in your pattern. In such cases it is helpful to know how to cut your own facings. If you decide to make bias bindings rather than facings, following the directions given on pages 403-405.

Cutting Shaped Facings

When a facing pattern is not included as one of the pattern pieces, use the garment pattern for the area requiring facing. For small

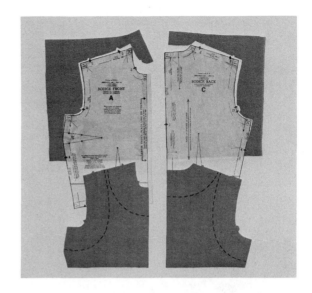

When tissue patterns are not provided for shaped facings, the facings may be made by cutting along the outside edges of the original patterns for the garment areas to be faced. Cutting lines are then marked along inner edges and cut to produce custom-made fitted facings.

areas that are to be completely faced, such as collars and pockets, the whole pattern is required. For areas to be faced only at the edge, such as neckline or armholes, only the edge of the pattern need be laid on the fabric.

Place the pattern on the fabric on the same grain as the garment piece. Whether self-fabric or a contrasting fabric is selected, place the pattern for the garment piece on only enough of the fabric to represent the garment area that requires facing. Pin the pattern to the fabric and cut, following the original cutting edge and carefully observing notches and other markings. Remove the pattern. To complete the facings, use a measuring tape and chalk or pins to mark on the fabric the completion of the facing outline. Draw the marking line parallel to the cut edge and at a distance from it to ensure the desired width of the facing. Simple neck and armhole facings are usually about 2 to 3 inches wide. For front and back openings a wider facing may be desirable. Cut along the

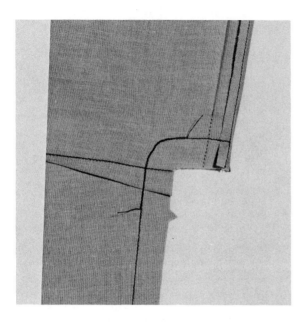

An extended facing for a sleeve or lower edge of a garment can be cut as an elongation of the area to be faced.

marking line. The shaped facing can then be staystitched, finished, and attached to the garment in the manner suitable for the fabric.

Cutting Extended Facings

Patterns for extended facings are generally included as parts of the pattern pieces. When such is not the case, extensions can be constructed. Usually such an extension will involve the hem of a sleeve or the front or back opening of a buttoned garment. To add such an extended facing, follow these steps:

1. On the pattern, press under the seam allowance along the edge to be faced.

2. On a sheet of suitable paper, such as tissue or lightweight wrapping paper, press a lengthwise fold far enough from the edge of the paper to allow ample space between fold and edge for the extended facing.

3. Pin the garment pattern piece onto the paper, carefully fitting the edge of the pattern to the matching folded edge of the paper.

4. Cut out the entire pattern piece from the paper, and mark the fold line. Transfer all other pattern markings to the new pattern.

5. Remove the original pattern and open out the facing extension.

6. With chalk or pencil, shape the facing extension to a width of approximately 3 inches for front or back facings. Most sleeve facings are 1½ to 2½ inches in width.

7. Use the new pattern in place of the original pattern piece when cutting the garment from fabric.

Cutting Bias Facings

The principle for cutting bias facings is the same as that for cutting bias bindings (see page 403). For accurate fit, bias facings are cut on the true bias. They may vary in width and in construction. They may be cut for a single-thickness or a double-thickness application. For a single-thickness application the width of the bias strip is the width of the desired facing plus two seam allowances. For a double-thickness application the width of the bias strip is twice the width of the desired facing plus two seam allowances. For example, for a double-thickness ½-inch-wide bias facing for a collar atttachment, cut a 2¼-inch-wide strip. One inch is needed for the doubled facing, and 1¼ inches are needed for the two ⅝-inch seam allowances.

Cutting Combination Facings

To cut a combination facing, first check the grain line in the garment area to be faced and in the fabric from which the facing will be cut, since they must be identical. Complete the cutting of the combination facing as follows:

1. Position the garment pattern on the facing fabric, making sure that the center back or center front is on grain or on a fold.

2. Pin the pattern to the fabric for approximately 3 inches below any edge to be faced.

3. Cut directionally the neck, shoulder, and armhole edges and along the bodice-underarm edge for about 3 inches.

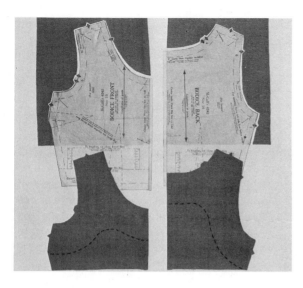

To cut a combination neck and armhole facing, cut around the outside edge of the pattern. Mark a curved line from about 3 inches below the lower armhole edge to about 3 inches below the center neckline. Then complete the cutting of the facing.

4. Remove the pattern, and mark with chalk the shape of the inner edge of the facing. Shape a neck-and-armhole combination facing from 3 inches below the underarm seam to 3 inches below the center of the garment neckline.

5. Cut the facing along the chalk marks.

Applying Facings

Each facing, whether shaped, extended, bias, or a combination, varies slightly in the specific details of its application. General guidelines for the accurate application of each type include the procedures for fitting, pinning, stitching, grading, clipping, understitching, and anchoring.

Applying Shaped Facings

Shaped facings are probably used more than any other type in general clothing construction. They are applied by a four-step process

STANDARDS FOR HIGH-QUALITY FACINGS

1. *Flat and smooth seam lines free of bulges or puckers.*
2. *Close adherence to the body area, except where the facing takes the place of a hem.*
3. *Invisible on right side of garment.*
4. *Effective in retaining original shape of the garment.*
5. *Firm enough to avoid wilting or stretching.*

443

which includes: completion of the facing unit, attachment of the facing to the garment, finishing of the facing seams, and anchoring of the facing to the garment.

Completing the Facing Unit

Staystitch and join the facing pieces. Trim the facing seams to 1/4 inch. Then finish the raw, outer, *unnotched* edge of the facings to prevent raveling or fraying in use. Several alternative methods of finishing are possible. The best alternative depends on the fabric— its weight, its firmness, its weave, and its likelihood of raveling. There is at least one suitable finish for each type of fabric. For example, a pinked edge which is suited to a heavy, firmly woven fabric is a poor choice for a fabric that ravels easily. The raw edges of a lightweight, washable facing might be clean-finished by folding under the staystitched raw edge and stitching close to the fold (see top left illustration page 445). Clean finishing would be inappropriate for a heavy fabric, however, because the folded edge would be too bulky and might also leave an imprint visible on the outside of the garment. If a fabric ravels easily, seam binding, zigzag stitching, and hand overcasting are three possible choices. Try to make the best choice for the given set of circumstances.

Attaching the Facing to the Garment

To attach the facing, place the right side of the facing against the right side of the garment, matching notches and seams. Stitch the edges together, leaving a precise 5/8-inch seam allowance and using a seam guide if necessary. Strive for an even, accurate seam, since irregularity in the stitching line will cause bulges or puckers in the finished edge. Use 18-20 stitches per inch for curved seams.

Finishing the Facing Seams

Because the seam allowance of a facing attachment is enclosed, trimming and grading are required to reduce bulk. When grading the facing seam, first trim any *interfacing*

down to the seam line. Then trim the seam allowance of the *facing* to 1/8 to 1/4 inch and the seam allowance of the *garment* to 1/4 to 3/8 inch. (See the discussion of trimming and grading on page 307.)

Clipping of the seam allowances is necessary if the facing seam is curved. The clipping process is done by cutting slashes into the seam allowances or removing small notches from the seam allowances. If the curve is concave, or inward, as in the case of armholes and necklines, the seam allowances may be slashed to release the fabric. If the curve is convex, or outward, as in certain collars, they may be notched to remove extra fabric and bulk. (See "Treating Curved Seam Allowances," pages 402-403.)

If the seam has one or more square corners, clip once diagonally at each corner (see page 400).

To keep the facings from rolling to the right side of the garment, understitch with a row of machine stitching inserted through the facing and both seam allowances from the right side of the facing (see pages 387-388).

Anchoring the Facing

Anchor the facing by stitching it at intervals to the wrong side of the garment. This process will prevent the facing from flapping over to the right side of the garment during wear. Facings can be anchored either with hand or machine stitches. Hand tacking consists of four or five tiny stitches taken over and over in the same place. Anchoring positions are usually located at seams or darts. Sometimes, on underarm or shoulder seams, machine stitching can be used. To anchor by machine, first pin the facing in correct position. Then stitch the edge of the facing to one seam allowance of each garment seam.

Applying Extended Facings

Extended facings are generally used on the lower edges of sleeves or on center garment openings. When applying sleeve extensions, stitch the seam of the extension as the under-

1. Join the facing sections and finish the inner edges. Clean finishing is a suitable finish for lightweight, washable fabrics.

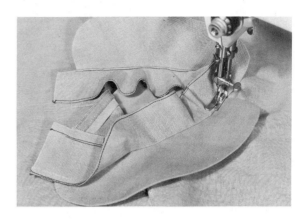

3. After grading and slashing along the seam line, understitch the facing to prevent its rolling to the outside of the garment.

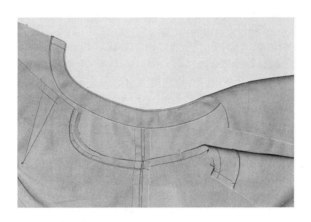

2. Stitch the facings to the garment. Slash and grade the seam allowance.

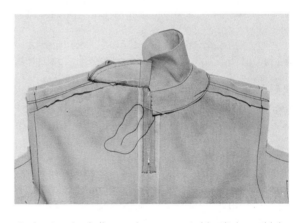

4. Anchor the facing to the garment with stitches which are invisible on the right side of the garment.

arm seam is stitched in the sleeve. Trim the seam allowance of the facing. Press the seam open, and press the extension to the wrong side of the lower sleeve edge. It will fit flat, as it was cut with the same degree of slant as the sleeve. Fasten the facing to the sleeve with a pick stitch or another suitable hand-hemming stitch (see pages 392-395).

Center-front or center-back extended facings are also shaped like the portion of the garment against which they fit. They must be stitched to the garment along the neckline edge and possibly along the lower edge. In combination with this attachment, however, the portion of the garment neckline which has no center opening must be treated either with a bias facing or with a shaped facing. Often a collar has previously been fastened to this neckline. When it is finished with a bias or fitted facing, all raw edges are hidden.

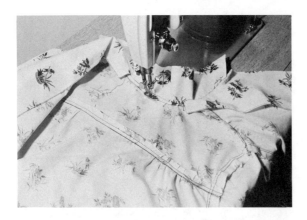

When center-opening extended facings are combined with a bias neck facing, a machine-stitched finish increases the sturdiness of the garment.

To make a shaped facing fit flat against a garment, clip the seam allowances, understitch through the facing and seam allowances, turn and press the facing in place, and anchor it to the garment.

A center-opening extended facing that is combined with a bias facing is attached as follows:

1. Finish the inner and shoulder-line edges of the extended facings with a suitable finish.

2. Fold the extended facings back against the garment neckline, right sides together, and pin each facing to the neckline.

3. Lay and pin a bias facing of the desired width on top of the extension along the unfinished neck edge, right sides together. Check the layers of fabric for puckers, and clip to the stayline where necessary to make a straight line for stitching.

4. Stitch the neck edges of the extended facings, and the bias facing to the neck of the garment from one center garment edge to the other.

5. Grade the seam, understitch it, turn the facings right side out, press the seam, and anchor the facings with a suitable stitch.

A center-opening extended facing that is combined with a shaped facing is attached as follows:

1. Locate the shoulder seam line on the extended facing and the shaped facing section.

2. Pin and stitch this shoulder seam together on each side of the facing, press the seam open, and trim it.

3. Finish the edge of the facing from one lower edge around to the other lower edge with a suitable finish.

4. With right sides together, notches matched, and shoulder seams keyed, pin the unfinished edge of the facing to the neck edge. Clip as necessary to ensure a straight stitching line, and then machine-stitch the neckline from center edge to center edge.

5. Grade and clip the seam, understitch, press carefully, and anchor the facing.

Applying Bias Facings

Bias facings may be applied as a single or a double thickness. Either fits easily around curves and other, similar points of stress.

If a single-layer bias facing is desired, finish the inner edge with an appropriate finish such as clean finishing or a zigzag stitch. Trim away unnecessary bulk from the finished edge. Pin the other edge to the garment edge. Check for puckers and wrinkles before machine-stitching the two edges together. Grade and clip the seam as necessary. Understitch and press the seam. Attach the loose

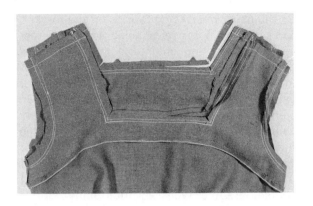

1. *After joining the facings at the underarm seam line, attach them to the garment, leaving the shoulder seams open and using large basting stitches for 3 inches along the upper armhole.*

3. *With right sides together and notches and seam lines keyed, stitch the front and back together across the shoulder line of the garment and facing.*

2. *Remove basting stitches from the armhole area, turn the facing section to the wrong side of the garment, and understitch areas that can be reached by machine.*

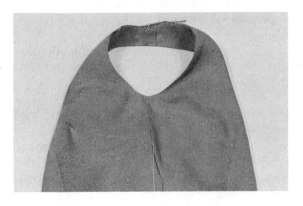

4. *After grading and pressing the shoulder seam line, slip-stitch the upper armhole facing to the upper armhole area.*

edge of the bias facing to the garment with a suitable stitch.

If a double-layer bias facing is desired, fold the bias in half lengthwise, wrong sides together, and press. Pin both edges along the garment edge. Check for puckers and wrinkles before machine-stitching. Grade and clip the seam as necessary. Understitch and press the seam. Attach the folded edge of the facing to the garment with a suitable stitch.

Applying Combination Facings

The combination facing is applied in an intricate series of steps. When the steps have been completed on a neck-and-armhole combination facing, both the armholes and neckline are completed. Apply this type of facing as follows:

1. Staystitch the facing units.

2. Pin the front and back facing units together along the underarm seam lines, stitch

the seams, press them open, and trim them to ¼ inch.

3. Finish the inner edges of the facing with a suitable finish such as clean finishing and pinking and stitching.

4. Place the facing on the bodice with right sides together, notches matched, edges even, and underarm seams keyed. Pin the sections together accurately, with pin heads out for easy removal during stitching. Leave all shoulder edges free.

5. Stitch the facing to the neckline and armhole edges of the garment along the seam line, using a regular stitch in all sections except for the first 3 inches at the upper armhole edges. Here use large machine-basting stitches. Trim and clip the permanently stitched seams.

6. Understitch all possible sections of both the neckline and underarm facing areas. Underpress the basted section of the armhole seam.

7. Remove the armhole basting stitches, turn the facing to the inside of the bodice, and press.

8. Pin the shoulder seam of the bodice and facing, right sides together, turning the armhole seam allowances out.

9. Make the shoulder seam by stitching a continuous line of stitching through the bodice and the facing. Press the seam open, and trim the facing seam.

10. Turning the facing to the wrong side of the bodice, pin the unstitched armhole edges of the bodice and facing together and slip-stitch them in place.

11. Anchor the facing to the garment seams and darts.

What are the functions of interfacings?

Why might one garment require several different types of interfacing?

How do woven, nonwoven, and press-on interfacings differ in appearance and purpose?

In what ways are seams and darts in interfacings stitched differently than seams and darts in the outer garment fabric?

Factors Affecting Choice of Interfacing

Of the many interfacing fabrics on the market, each is chosen for its specific set of characteristics. Selecting an interfacing calls for a decision as to which fabric will do most for the appearance of the finished garment. Your pattern guide sheet may help you, but in some cases the decision may be entirely yours. The choice depends mainly upon the function of the interfacings in the particular project and the fiber and characteristics of the outer garment fabric. Other factors, of course, are the types of interfacing fabrics available and current fashion trends.

Function of Interfacing

Choose interfacings that will effectively fulfill their specific function in the garment. Interfacings can serve many different purposes even within one garment. They can add body, reinforcement, shape retention, design emphasis, or rigidity. For example, a dress of medium-weight fabric may have a crisp, detachable collar, buttons and butttonholes down the back, and a welt pocket, all of which require interfacing. These three garment areas may need three different types and weights of interfacing. A crisp, resilient interfacing could be chosen to add body to the collar. A pliable, lightweight interfacing might be suitable for reinforcing the button and buttonhole area. A featherweight interfacing might add the right degree of shape retention to the welt pocket. Each specific function will affect the choice of interfacing fabric.

Compatibility with Garment Fabric

Choose an interfacing that is compatible with the outer garment fabric in weight, body, and care requirements. Particularly avoid those that are stiffer than the garment fabric. A stiff, heavy interfacing would not be suitable for a soft jersey dress but might prove ideal for the hem of an A-line skirt made of a heavy furlike fabric. A washable easy-care outfit requires a preshrunk, washable interfacing. A

INTERFACING FABRICS

Type	Width	Characteristics	Use	Care Requirements
Woven Canvas, hair-canvas, worsted canvas, and blends	25-45 inches	Crease resistant. Provides body and shape retention. Lightweight to heavy. May ravel. May need preshrinking and straightening. Must be cut with grain. May be crisp.	Tailoring collars, cuffs, and lapels.	Determined by fiber content of garment and interfacing.
Nonwoven Regular nonwoven	25-36 inches	May be cut in any direction. Provides excellent shape retention. Little give. Preshrunk, crease resistant. Will not ravel or discolor. Lightweight to heavy.	Waistbands, pockets, flaps, front panels in buttoned garments. Craft items.	May be washed or drycleaned. Quick drying.
All-bias nonwoven	25-45 inches	Flexible and drapable. Provides give in all directions. Crease and crush resistant.	Cuffs, necklines, hemlines, center fronts, collars and lapels in garments of man-made fibers.	May be washed or drycleaned. Quick drying.
Press-on Woven and nonwoven	18-36 inches	Requires no sewing, easy to apply. May loosen with cleaning on some fabrics.	Reinforcing buttonholes, slashed areas, gussets, and other small areas.	May be washed or drycleaned. Quick drying.

crease-resistant fabric calls for an interfacing that maintains this characteristic. A wool suit might indicate a drycleanable interfacing that is resilient but easy to shape. The fiber content of the garment fabric usually provides essential clues to a good choice.

Because interfacing lies between the garment fabric and the facing, color is also an important consideration. There is usually a choice of white, black, or tan. However, some of the new lightweight fabrics suitable for interfacings are available in a full range of colors. To prevent a shadowing through on the right side of the garment, choose interfacing that is at least as light in color as the garment. Generally it is safest to use white interfacing with light-colored fabrics and black interfacing only with fabrics of the darkest shades.

Types of Interfacing Fabrics

Knowledge of the types of interfacing fabrics available will help you make a good choice for your project. There are three basic types of interfacing: woven, nonwoven, and press-on. Each type, which includes a variety of fabrics, possesses characteristics which make it the best choice for a particular garment. The characteristics are summarized below. More detailed descriptions of the three groups are given in the above chart.

Woven Interfacings

Woven interfacing fabrics have a lengthwise and a crosswise grain. Their weave provides an elasticity that permits them to be manipulated into desired shape. This is an especially important consideration in choosing interfacing for tailored garments. The elasticity of

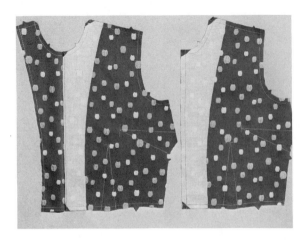

Since crease-resistant interfacing fabrics will not yield easily in handling, remove interfacing corners from areas where sharp corners or creases are desired or where bulk is undesirable.

woven interfacings requires that they be positioned to match the grain line of the garment fabric. Because these fabrics resist creasing, they are best kept free from the stitching at corners and other such areas where a sharp fold is desired.

Canvas Interfacing

Canvas interfacing is a type of woven interfacing designed primarily for use in garments of wool, wool-like fabrics, or blends. Crease-resistant and resilient, canvas comes in various weights and degrees of firmness.

Hair-canvas Interfacing

Hair-canvas interfacing, known to the tailoring profession as Hymo, is a type of canvas to which a percentage of goat's hair has been added. Generally the higher the percentage of hair, the more resilient the interfacing. Hair canvas is used extensively in the tailoring process.

Worsted-canvas Interfacing

Worsted-canvas interfacing is a lightweight canvas interfacing with a high wool content. Its crease resistance and resilience make it popular in tailoring.

Blends for Nontailored Garments

Garments made of cotton, linen, silk, man-made fibers, or blends often require some type of interfacing for reinforcement. Such garments which are designed with a soft look rather than a tailored appearance can usually be interfaced with a fabric consisting of a woven blend of natural and man-made fibers. A blend of this type provides a degree of crispness as well as crease resistance.

When choosing a woven blend for an interfacing fabric, make the selection in relation to the weight of the outer fabric. Check the compatibility of the two fabrics by holding a piece of the outer fabric over the interfacing to determine whether the woven blend will produce the desired appearance and offer the proper degree of crispness to the garment.

Nonwoven Interfacings

Nonwoven interfacings are made by a random intermeshing of fibers as heat and pressure are applied. Because the fibers are not woven, these interfacings have no grain. They can be cut in any direction and thus usually require less yardage than do woven interfacings. Generally their lack of weave results also in less pliability. Their pliability varies somewhat, however, with their weight, lighter ones being more pliable than heavy ones.

Regular Nonwoven Interfacing

Regular nonwoven interfacing, made from a blend of man-made fibers, is used for support in small, flat areas. It is especially useful for interfacing narrow front openings of blouses and dresses and for interfacing sleeve cuffs. Because of its limited elasticity, it is unsatisfactory for use in large areas of the garment, such as the shoulder areas.

All-bias Nonwoven Interfacing

This type of interfacing, made of crimped man-made fibers, has a pliability similar to that of woven fabrics. Its structure and fiber content make it a good interfacing selection for most fabrics made of man-made fibers.

Press-on Interfacings

These interfacings, available in both woven and nonwoven versions, have a special bonding material on one or both sides of the fabric. This coating permits their attachment simply by pressing them onto the garment fabric. However, most bonded interfacings do not adhere as permanently or smoothly to woven fabrics as to knitted ones. Press-on interfacing is designed only to reinforce small areas. It is used mainly for such details as pockets, flaps, narrow facings, and button and buttonhole areas. Its lack of give after application limits its usefulness in large areas.

Cutting Interfacings

If the needed interfacing pattern piece is not included in the pattern envelope, the interfacing can be cut from the pattern for the facing or from the pattern for the garment piece that is to be interfaced. An interfacing for a collar or a cuff, for example, is cut identically to the collar or the cuff itself.

A woven type of interfacing requires that the grain be identical in the corresponding interfacing and garment pieces. Since nonwoven interfacings have no grain, patterns can be placed on them in any direction.

Interfacings consist of a single layer of fabric. Consider this fact when cutting an interfacing from the pattern for the corresponding garment pieces. In some cases the pattern is folded in half so that the resultant interfacing will be half the size of the garment piece. A waistband interfacing, for example, is cut only half the width of the outer fabric waistband, but a ¼-inch extension must be added to this width to permit the fastening of the interfacing to the under portion of the band.

When interfacing the front of a tailored garment, use the pattern for the front facing and cut the front interfacing ½ inch wider than the facing. If cutting the interfacing by the pattern for the garment, cut the front piece in the exact shape of the front along the front

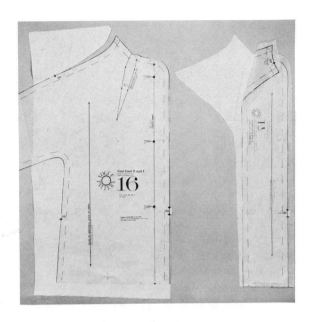

An interfacing may be cut from the garment pattern (left) if darts are needed, or from a facing pattern (right). In either case the interfacing is cut ½ inch wider than the facing pattern.

edge, neck, shoulder, and armhole. Extend the interfacing downward along the side seam to a point 2 inches below the armhole. Remove the pattern, and mark a curved line extending between this point below the armhole and the lower edge of the garment, as shown in the illustration on page 497. Cut on the marked line.

If using a back facing pattern for a tailored garment, cut the interfacing ½ inch wider along the unnotched edge. If the garment back pattern is used for an interfacing pattern, place the center back of the pattern on the folded interfacing fabric. Follow the pattern and cut along the neck, shoulder, and armhole edge and down the side seam line for 2 inches. Remove the pattern, and with chalk or a pencil mark a modified S curve from a point at the center back ½ inch below the lower edge of the facing to a point 2 inches below the garment armhole, as shown in the illustration on page 498. Cut along the curved mark shown in the photograph.

STANDARDS FOR HIGH-QUALITY INTERFACINGS

1. Compatible with garment fabric in weight, body, color, and care requirements.
2. Carefully selected for a specific function, whether for providing body, reinforcement, shape retention, design emphasis, or rigidity.
3. Inconspicuous.
4. Preshrunk.
5. Correctly fitted to garment.
6. Smooth seam lines free of ripples and bulges.

Lengthwise or bias strips of interfacing can be cut to interface various small areas of garment, such as under buttons and buttonholes and inside the hemlines of jackets, sleeves, and skirts. Such strips are used extensively in tailoring. They are usually cut from a lightweight fabric, such as preshrunk muslin, regardless of the type of interfacing used elsewhere in the garment. Their length and width vary according to the requirements of the particular garment area. Bias interfacings may be cut in the same way as bias bindings (see pages 403-405). For treating interfacing edges in fronts of tailored garments, see pages 500-501.

Applying Interfacings

Interfacing is attached to a garment by one of two methods. Most interfacings are applied by stitching. The press-on type, however, is attached by bonding with the heat of the iron.

Stitching Procedure

Interfacing is prepared for atttachment before being stitched to a garment. Preparation in-

cludes trimming the points from interfacing corners just inside the seam line to eliminate interfacing fabric from the corners which must be turned. In some instances it may also include joining pieces of interfacing and making darts.

Joining Interfacings

If two pieces of interfacing are to be joined, the two seam allowances are overlapped and topstitched or zigzag-stitched. The stitches are applied in a rectangular formation close to one edge, and the excess fabric is trimmed off. Such a seam minimizes bulk.

Marking Darts in Interfacing

Darts in lightweight interfacing are made similarly to darts in the outer fabric (see pages 395-397). If a crease-resistant interfacing is used, the darts are slashed and overlapped in the same way as darts in tailored garments (see pages 501-503).

Attaching Interfacing to the Garment

The completed interfacing is usually applied to the wrong side of the garment pieces be-

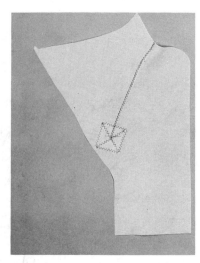

*When making a dart in crease-resistant interfacing, slash, overlap,
and zigzag-stitch the dart along the stitching lines. Reinforce the dart point with an
extra layer of fabric.*

fore the seams are stitched or the facing applied. The interfacing corners are cut off before it is joined to the outer fabric to make for sharp-edged corners. Attach the interfacing to the outer fabric directionally; this requires stitching one half of the seams from the interfacing side and the other half from the outer fabric side.

Complete the seams with a regular stitch length suitable for the outer fabric. Then carefully trim the seam allowances of the interfacing with sharp shears as close to the stitching line as is possible without weakening the seams. For the remainder of the sewing process, the garment and interfacing are treated as one. For edging interfacing and attaching it to garments with extended facing, see page 501.

Bonding Procedure

Press-on interfacing is applied by the process of bonding. A quick method of interfacing application, bonding includes the following steps:

1. Cut the interfacing to the desired shape and size.

2. Mark the ⅝-inch seam lines along the edges of the interfacing pieces, and trim the seam allowances and corners. This eliminates all interfacing material from the seams, leaving a pliable seam allowance.

3. Preheat a *dry* iron to the correct temperature as indicated in the instructions accompanying the interfacing. Because some bonding granules from the outer edges of the interfacing may drop onto the ironing board, it is wise to protect the board with a scrap of waste fabric. Then place the coated side of the interfacing against the wrong side of the garment area to be interfaced. Press the interfacing to the fabric, using an up-and-down motion with the iron. Avoid sliding the iron back and forth.

4. If it is found that the interfacing has been incorrectly placed, simply press the area again to soften the bonding material, reposition the interfacing on the garment, and press again.

1. Facings finish and reinforce garment edges, whereas interfacings provide shape or extra support.

2. If a faced or interfaced garment piece is altered, the corresponding facing or interfacing requires identical alterations for proper fit.

3. The application of a facing includes making the facing seams, finishing the inner edge of the facing, stitching the facing to the garment, grading and understitching the edge seams, and anchoring the facing to the garment.

4. If curved facing seams are stitched with small stitches, 18-20 per inch, the garment edge will have sufficient strength and elasticity.

5. The choice of interfacing fabric best suited for a specific garment area depends on the function of the interfacing and the fabric of the garment.

6. When two interfacings are joined, their seam allowances are overlapped, topstitched or zigzag-stitched, and trimmed to reduce bulk.

7. The seam allowances of the facing and interfacing are trimmed and graded to reduce bulk.

23 Collars

Collar construction constitutes a unique learning experience and is an important aspect of sewing, as it contributes significantly to the total effect of a garment. The manipulation of both inward and outward curved seams must be mastered on some collars, as must the attachment of an outward curve to an inward curve. Further, enclosed seams must be finished carefully in order for a collar to have a smart professional appearance.

What creative decisions are involved in planning and constructing a collar for a garment?

What alternatives do you have in choosing a collar style and fabric?

What are the basic principles for sewing collar edges to achieve a professional look?

How do the applications of rounded and convertible collars differ? Of mandarin and tie collars?

What are the alternatives in finishing a neck edge after the collar has been attached?

Decisions About Collars

Because it frames the face, the importance of the neckline in dress design is paramount, and since a collar affects the appearance of the neckline, it plays a major role in determining the success of a garment. Although collar patterns are included with most patterns for blouses, dresses, coats, and jackets, they may be adapted or exchanged in order to produce a more stylish garment or to emphasize your most attractive facial features. For example, a round collar of self-fabric might be replaced by one of contrasting fabric which would emphasize the color of your hair or eyes. The decision-making process can help you arrive at the best choice for each project, given a particular set of circumstances.

Factors Affecting Choice of Collar

If you are deciding upon a collar for a garment, several factors will influence your choice. These include the shape of your face, the garment design, fabric considerations, and your sewing skill, as well as your available time and energy. Consider carefully each of these factors as you plan the collar.

Face Shape

Each person has a facial shape which is uniquely his own. Face shapes, however, tend to fall into general categories. The oval is the

Courtesy Simplicity Pattern Co., Inc.

STANDARDS FOR COLLARS

1. *Sharp-edged, smooth, and well pressed.*
2. *Follows the natural neckline of the garment without gapping or pulling.*
3. *Garment facing and undercollar invisible on the outside of the garment.*
4. *Accurately and symmetrically curved or pointed.*

ideal face shape. However, most faces tend to be broad, whether round or square, or long, whether oblong or diamond-shaped. Consequently, the goal of each person choosing a collar or other neckline finish is a style which makes the face appear oval.

While persons with oval-shaped faces look well in any type of neckline, others need to choose a design which gives an oval illusion to their face shape. Variations of V-necklines, usually created by the combination of a collar and lapel, can be worn effectively by almost anyone. However, square and round neckline patterns should be carefully fitted, since their depth and width affect the apparent facial contour. All types of collars can be worn by persons with each face shape if the

collar is adapted to the individual for maximum attractiveness.

Garment Design

Choose a neckline that harmonizes with the overall garment design. For example, a large sailor collar covering most of the front and back of a blouse can make a stunning collar for the right type of garment. However, if such a collar were to hide a tucked front highlighting a blouse design, it would be a poor choice. Similarly, an attractively ruffled collar might ruin the effect of an otherwise severely tailored tweed suit. The collar must be considered as an integral part of the total garment design in order to be effective. You will probably also want it to be a style that is currently in fashion.

Fabric Considerations

Different kinds of fabrics best lend themselves to specific neck finishes. While a medium-weight, firmly woven fabric is usually adaptable to almost any collar style, bulky tweeds and furlike fabrics are difficult to use in any type of collar. In garments of such thick, heavy fabrics, it is usually best either to omit the collar or to construct one of another fabric. If a contrasting fabric is chosen, it must blend or contrast with the garment fabric in color if design unity is to be maintained. Polyesters and permanent-press cotton blends are examples of fabrics easy to handle and well suited to a wide range of collar styles. Laces and organdies, while equally easy to sew, have the disadvantage of transparency, which permits the seams to show through. When used, they are usually made into detachable, easily cleanable trimmings.

Your Resources

In deciding upon a collar pattern and fabric, be sure to consider the extent of your sewing experience and the amount of time and energy you can devote to the construction of the collar. Like fabrics, patterns vary in their degree of difficulty.

Peter Pan and mandarin collars, for example, are simple to make. Convertible and tailored collars, on the other hand, are quite complex. It may be that you want to complete the collar quickly for a special occasion. Or perhaps the occasion is so important that the amount of sewing time and effort required is secondary to the results desired. Perhaps, if your sewing experience or time is limited, you will want to consult your clothing teacher or another qualified seamstress before making your decision. Attractiveness is not based entirely on difficulty.

Types of Collars

Collars come in a variety of shapes and styles suited to many purposes. Several of these styles, such as the Peter Pan and the convertible collars, are classic; that is, they are always fashionable and are used extensively. Others, such as the mandarin, tie, and turtleneck collars, vary in popularity according to current style trends. Six of the most widely adopted styles are discussed here. The tailored collar is included in the section on tailoring (see pages 531-538).

Peter Pan Collar

The Peter Pan collar is flat and round. This collar may have the appearance of a single collar extending around the neckline, or it may be made as two separate pieces which meet at the center front and at the center back. The Peter Pan collar is versatile and attractive to most face shapes. It is a popular style for blouses, dresses, children's clothing, and sportswear.

Convertible Collar

The convertible collar is a collar with pointed ends. Like the Peter Pan collar, it usually extends around the neckline, but it can be made in two separate pieces which meet at the center back. In a front opening, it can be worn open in a V-shaped neckline with a lapel, or it can be buttoned high. It is a versatile style which suits almost any type of garment from casual to dressy.

Mandarin Collar

The mandarin, or Chinese, collar is a narrow, standing collar about 1 to $1\frac{1}{2}$ inches in width. It can be cut as a straight strip or with a slight curve. It is most frequently used on pajamas, dresses, blouses, suits, oriental costumes, and robes.

Tie Collar

The tie collar fits closely around the neck area but has long, loose ends which can be tied into a knot or bow. Either wide or narrow, the tie collar can be cut on the lengthwise or bias grain of the fabric. It is appropriate for blouses, dresses, and sports outfits which are made of soft, drapable fabric.

COMMON COLLAR TYPES

PETER PAN COLLAR

Courtesy Simplicity Pattern Co., Inc.

MANDARIN COLLAR

Courtesy Simplicity Pattern Co., Inc.

CONVERTIBLE COLLAR

TIE COLLAR

TURTLENECK COLLAR

SAILOR COLLAR

Turtleneck Collar

The turtleneck, or bias, collar is a wide, bias-cut, standing collar with an upper edge that folds downward. Some turtleneck collars are successfully cut on the straight grain of fabric if the fabric is a sweater knit or other loosely knit fabric. This type of collar gives an outfit a casual or sporty look.

Sailor Collar

The sailor collar is a large square collar somewhat like that of a traditional sailor's uniform. This collar is cut on the lengthwise grain of the fabric. It is frequently trimmed with military braid. Sailor collars look well on sports outfits, children's clothing, and dresses.

Constructing a Collar

There are four major steps in the construction of a collar. They include preparing the garment for the collar, making the collar, attaching the collar, and finishing the neck edge. Successful completion of these steps depends on accurate stitching, careful clipping and trimming, and effective pressing. These basic techniques, once learned, can be applied at any time to construct an attractive collar of professional quality.

Preparing the Garment

Since curved edges tend to stretch out of shape, carefully staystitch the garment neckline. Fasten the seam-stitching threads, and press open the seams which extended into the neckline area of the garment. Check the fit of the neckline. Any alterations which will make the neckline larger or smaller must be made before the collar is attached. Such changes always necessitate similar changes in the collar. Any bodice decoration that ends at the neckline is correctly attached before the collar.

Making the Collar

Certain steps are basic to the construction of most collars, regardless of their shape. These basic steps include applying the interfacing

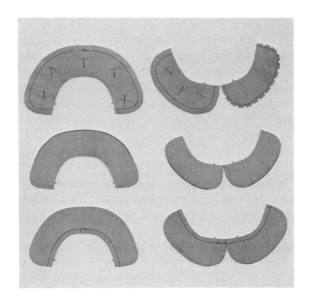

When making a collar, pin and stitch the interfacing to the inside of the undercollar. Then stitch the upper collar and undercollar together and grade and clip along the outer seam (top). Turn the collar right side out and understitch in areas which can be reached by machine (center). Staystitch the inner edge of the turned collar in preparation for its attachment to the neck edge (bottom).

to the undercollar, stitching the undercollar and the upper collar together, trimming and clipping the seam allowances of the enclosed collar edge, and pressing.

The interfacing is a layer of special fabric inserted between the collar and the undercollar to provide firmness and to help the collar retain its shape. The same pattern piece used to cut the undercollar may be used to cut the interfacing. The interfacing is then machine-fastened to the wrong side of the undercollar ½ inch from the outer edge before the upper collar and undercollar are joined.

After the interfacing has been attached, the upper collar and undercollar are assembled with the right sides together. They are pinned along the outer edges and ends with center backs, ends, and notches matching. Sometimes the undercollar must be eased slightly to the upper collar for accurate fit. (See the discus-

sion of ease on page 304.) After stitching, the collar seam is trimmed in layers. Trim the interfacing as closely as possible to the seam line. Trim the seam of the undercollar to within ⅛ to ¼ inch of the line of stitching, depending upon the sturdiness of the fabric. Trim the seam of the upper collar to within ¼ to ⅜ inch of the seam line. Cut off the corners diagonally very near the stitching. Wedges are cut from outward curves so that the seam will lie flat (see page 403).

Special attention is necessary to ensure that the undercollar does not show on the outside of the garment. If the collar design will allow for it, a row of understitching will assure a finished look. On a pointed collar, understitch to within 1 inch from each end. On a round collar, understitch all around the stitched seam. (For a description of understitching, see pages 387-388.) Then turn the collar right side out and carefully press it using a pressing cloth and steam iron.

Pin and stitch together the raw neck edges of the collar. Check the length of the finished collar by folding it in half and matching the notches. The ends of the collar should meet exactly. When a collar meets these specifications, it is completed and ready to attach to the garment.

Attaching the Collar

The basic process for attaching a collar to the neck edge of the garment applies to most simple collars. Usually several variations of the process can be effective. However, the inexperienced seamstress is wise to follow the method suggested on the pattern guide sheet. The precise steps in a particular project depend upon whether the collar is attached with a shaped facing, a bias facing, or no facing as is sometimes done with straight convertible and mandarin collars.

In attaching a collar to a garment, the first step is to find the exact center front or back of the collar, depending upon the style of garment. This is usually indicated by a clip or other mark placed during cutting or mark-

Before attaching a collar, clip the neckline to provide a straight line for stitching and check to see that the collar is perfectly centered at the line of stitching.

To face a neckline which has a regular collar, attach the completed collar to the neckline and pin the completed facing over the collar, wrong side out. Clip the curved seam line and machine-stitch the three sections together.

ing. If such a mark is lacking, the center can be found by folding the completed collar in half so that the exact center point can be located and marked with chalk or a clip. Repeat this process on the neck edge of the garment. Then match the center of the collar to the center of the garment, and pin, placing the pins at right angles to the neck edge.

Next, accurately match the notches of the collar to the notches on the garment neck edge. Pinning at right angles to the neck edge, attach the two edges securely. Carefully check the distance from the end of the collar to the garment edge to be sure it is the same at both ends. If the collar and neck edge do not fit together perfectly, clip the smaller one down to the stayline in several places. Then ease the two edges together, and baste the collar to the neck edge. If the collar is to be attached with a neck facing, whether the facing

is a bias or a shaped one, finish the outer edge of the facing by clean-finishing (see page 445). Lay the facing, wrong side up, on top of the collar, and fit it into place with edges even and notches matched. Pin it in place. The collar will lie between the neckline and the facing. Make sure that all shoulder seams and notches match and that the neck edge is free of wrinkles. Clip the neck edge of the garment or collar to the stayline to give a straight line for stitching. Place a clip on each side of the shoulder area close to the seam. Then stitch the three layers together.

Finishing the Neck Edge
Check the collar for accidental puckers or other stitching errors. Then understitch the facing and inside collar seam together along the neck edge for a smooth finish. (See "Understitching," pages 387-388).

*To finish an unfaced collar, turn under the loose edge of the upper collar
along the seam line and fasten it to the garment with hand or machine stitches.*

If an unfaced neck edge has been chosen, first attach the edge of the undercollar to the neck edge of the garment. Then fold and press under the seam allowance on the upper collar neck edge. Pin it in place, and topstitch through the upper collar, the neck edge, and the undercollar.

Special Techniques for Specific Collar Styles

While the basic collar-attachment procedure just outlined applies directly to the Peter Pan, convertible, mandarin, and sailor collars, other collars require slight variations of the procedure. The specific variations needed for tie and turtleneck collars are described here.

Tie Collar

The tie collar is made as it is attached to the garment. To make this collar, pin one edge of the collar to the garment neckline, right sides together, and machine-stitch it in place. Fold the collar lengthwise, right sides together, and stitch across the ends and along the length of the ties to the point where the undercollar is fastened to the neckline. After the seams of the ties are pressed open and trimmed, turn them right side out, press under the seam allowance of the unfinished collar edge, pin it in place along the neckline, and stitch it to the garment. This stitching can be inserted by machine, as in the case of washable blouses, or by hand in delicate garments.

 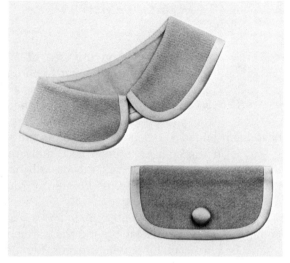

*Creative adaptations of standard collars can be made by adding such features as
machine-made embroidery stitches to give a braid-like trim to standing collars
(left) or bias binding to give a dressy matched effect to the edges
of simple collars and pocket flaps (right).*

Turtleneck Collar

The turtleneck, or bias, collar is folded in half lengthwise, the ends are stitched, and the collar is turned and pressed before it is attached to the garment. The basic procedure for attaching and facing the neck edge may then be followed. Either a bias or a shaped facing is suitable. The unfaced application is generally ineffective except on straight-cut knits because of the stretch of the fabric caused by the bias cut. Hooks and eyes may be used to hold the collar together in the back. Often the ends of a turtleneck collar are fastened together with a zipper in the back neckline seam. In such cases a smooth zipper finish can be obtained by leaving the collar ends open. The zipper is attached to the edges of the back of the garment and the end sections of the undercollar. Then the upper collar is stitched to the back side of the zipper tape for a finish. Often a single hook and thread loop are attached above the zipper.

1. Alterations affecting the size of a garment neckline require corresponding alterations in the collar to permit correct collar fit.

2. Collars are interfaced for firmness and shape retention.

3. Curved seams are clipped or notched to reduce bulk.

4. After the upper collar, the undercollar, and the interfacing have been joined, the seam allowance is graded to remove bulk.

5. If the collar has been accurately made and positioned along the garment neckline, the collar ends will not extend beyond the center front or center back and the pointed or rounded ends will be equally distant from the bodice edge.

6. When a collar and neck facing are stitched to the garment, the collar lies between the facing and the garment.

7. Understitching will prevent the neck facing from showing when a garment is worn.

24 Sleeves

Sleeves, along with the hemline and the waistline, determine the fashion silhouette of a garment. They may provide a bouffant look, a slim look, or by their absence a look of either utility or glamour, depending on the fabric of the garment. The cut and fit of the sleeves can enhance or detract from the total appearance of an outfit.

What creative decisions are involved in planning and constructing sleeves for a garment?

What alternatives do you have in choosing a sleeve style, length, and lower-edge finish?

How do the appearance and application of set-in sleeves and raglan sleeves differ? Of cap sleeves and kimono sleeves?

What are the advantages and disadvantages of setting a sleeve into an armhole before the side seam and underarm sleeve seam are stitched?

How may the armholes of sleeveless garments be finished?

Decisions About Sleeves

In planning the sleeves for a garment, there are many styles from which to choose. Sleeves may be long, short, or in between. They may be full or tightly fitted. They may be simple or ornate, utilitarian or decorative. They may even be omitted altogether. Decisions are necessary in selecting a sleeve style. Entirely

different sets of decisions are required in choosing fabric and a method of construction. Understanding the principles involved in planning and constructing sleeves will help you to make sound choices for every garment you make.

Factors Affecting Choice of Sleeve

If you are deciding upon a sleeve style for a garment, there are several factors to be considered. You will want to select a style that is becoming to you, that fits the overall garment design and function, that suits the garment fabric, and that presents no undue construction difficulties.

Style Becomingness

Consider your figure type, your height, and your arm length and width before making a decision about sleeve style. Most styles are more becoming to some people than to others. For example, a raglan sleeve tends to emphasize the horizontal design lines in a garment. It would thus become a tall, slender person but might make a short person look even shorter. A long, fitted sleeve stresses the vertical design lines. Creating an illusion of height, it might better suit a short person than a tall, slender person. A style that is attractive on the wearer and is currently in fashion is usually a good choice.

Garment Design and Function

Consider the overall garment design and function as you choose or adapt a sleeve pattern. Sleeves play a significant role in garment design. They can complete or destroy the desired illusion, and they can enhance or diminish a garment's usefulness. For example, a long, full, gathered sleeve especially suited for a party dress would look out of place in an otherwise tailored shirtwaist sports outfit. A graceful kimono sleeve, elegant in a hostess gown, would be hazardous in a work garment. A long, fitted sleeve might provide desirable warmth in a winter outfit but prove uncomfortable in a summer dress.

Fabric Considerations

The selection, adaptation, or omission of sleeves is often determined by the fabric chosen for a project. A heavy wool, for example, lends itself best to a tailored set-in sleeve. A soft, sheer fabric has a draping quality which makes it particularly suitable for a long, gathered sleeve. Most fabrics are somewhere between these two extremes.

When a fabric is difficult to handle, it is sometimes best to omit the sleeves. With a furlike fabric, for example, you might enjoy making a vest whereas a jacket might prove to be a difficult project for a person of your sewing experience. If you are converting a pattern with sleeves to a sleeveless version, be sure to check whether the armhole requires adjustment (see page 212). If an armhole facing pattern is lacking, the facing may be cut and applied as described in the chapter on facings (see Chapter 22).

Your Resources

Sleeves range in construction difficulty from the simple to the complex. It is wise to begin with an easy-to-make type such as the cap sleeve before proceeding to those as complicated as the set-in sleeve. Consider the extent of your sewing experience, as you contemplate a sleeve style, to avoid choosing one that presents complexities beyond the range of your skill. Other practical considerations are the amount of time and effort you can devote to sleeve construction.

Types of Sleeves

There are basically two major categories of sleeves: sleeves cut-in-one with the bodice and sleeves cut separately. Each can be easily identified by its unique shape.

Sleeves Cut-in-One with the Bodice

This type of sleeve includes the many variations of cap and kimono sleeves. It is the simplest sleeve to make. Because it is cut as an extension of the bodice, it is generally simpler to complete than are set-in sleeves and thus is a good choice for a beginning seamstress.

Cap Sleeve

The cap sleeve is the most common example of a sleeve cut-in-one with the bodice. It is formed by a short, rather loose extension of the garment shoulder area. Cap sleeves are found in basic blouses, shells, sports tops, and some dresses. Usually the underarm seam has a slight outward curve in the underarm area. The cap sleeve is finished with a hem or a shaped facing at the lower edge.

Kimono Sleeve

The kimono sleeve, like the cap sleeve, is formed by an extension of the shoulder area. It is, however, a longer full sleeve particularly effective in hostess gowns and robes. The kimono sleeve has a shoulder seam and an underarm seam extending its full length. The

COMMON SLEEVE TYPES

Courtesy The Wool Bureau Inc.

CAP SLEEVE

Courtesy Coty Inc., New York

SET-IN SLEEVE

Courtesy Bobbie Brooks, Inc.

RAGLAN SLEEVE

Courtesy Schenley Imports Company

SLEEVELESS ARMHOLE

467

lower edge is typically finished with a hem or facing.

Sleeve Cut Separately

The second type of sleeve comprises those that are cut separately from the bodice and later stitched to it. These include the raglan, epaulet, and set-in sleeves.

Raglan Sleeve

The raglan sleeve is identified by its long, slanting seam lines extending from the underarm to the neckline on both the shoulder front and back. It may be cut in one or two pieces. It is found in coats, dresses, suits, and some sportswear. Raglan sleeves may be short, three-quarter, or full length. Because they taper to a smaller, fitted edge at the lower end, they are frequently finished with a facing.

Epaulet Sleeve

The epaulet sleeve is distinguished by a narrow portion extending from the armhole area to the neckline. The sleeve is shaped much like a raglan sleeve except that the unusual shape of the shoulder area calls attention to this portion of the garment. Sometimes decorative epaulet-like attachments are sewn over the shoulder area of other types of sleeves to give a military look to a garment.

Set-in Sleeve

The set-in sleeve, like the raglan and epaulet sleeve, is cut separately from the garment. It includes two types: the regular set-in sleeve and the shirt sleeve. This sleeve may be cut in one piece or in two pieces and joined by a lengthwise seam. Because a set-in sleeve provides ease in the shoulder area, a garment with set-in sleeves can be made to fit the figure more accurately than can garments made with other types of sleeves.

Constructing Sleeves

While each type of sleeve is made somewhat similarly to the other sleeves in its basic category, the details of the construction procedures are unique for each type. The procedures for the five previously described sleeves are given in this section. Appropriate finishes for the lower edges of sleeves are described and illustrated on pages 471-472.

Cap Sleeve

Cap sleeves are completed in the following five steps. The techniques of understitching, short stitching, topstitching, and clipping curved seams are described on pages 387-390 and 402-403.

1. Staystitch the lower edge of the sleeve ¼ inch from the edge for a hem or ½ inch from the edge for a facing.

2. If a facing is used, join it to the lower edge and understitch.

3. Join the underarm seams. A short stitch is required in the curve of the underarm if the seam line curves sharply.

4. Reinforce the curved underarm area with topstitching or overstitching. Clip the seam allowance on the curve, and press open the underarm seam.

5. Hem or complete the facing on the lower edge of the sleeve.

Kimono Sleeve

A well-made kimono sleeve is smooth and even. It neither ripples along the upper arm seam nor draws in the underarm area. Its method of construction varies according to whether or not a gusset is included. Without a gusset, the kimono sleeve is an easy one to make. With a gusset, it is considerably more complicated and best reserved for the experienced seamstress. For a description of the procedure for inserting gussets, see pages 405-406.

The steps for making a kimono sleeve without a gusset are as follows:

1. Staystitch the upper arm seam for the length of the shoulder and the lower edge for a hem or facing.

2. If a facing is used, join it to the lower edge and understitch.

3. Stitch the elbow darts, if they are included.

4. Join together the extended shoulder seam of the bodice front and back, matching the notches carefully.

5. Stitch the underarm seam. The curved portion is stitched with short stitches, clipped, and reinforced with topstitching or preshrunk seam tape. (For details regarding these techniques see pages 401-403.)

6. Hem or complete the facing or band on the lower sleeve edge.

Raglan Sleeve

The beginning seamstress will find the raglan sleeve relatively easy to make. Accuracy in matching notches and stitching seams is important. The construction steps are as follows:

1. Staystitch the lower edge of the sleeve.

2. Join the facing, if used, to the lower edge and understitch.

3. Stitch the shoulder dart, which in the raglan style is part of the sleeve.

4. Carefully match by both number and position the notches and seams of the sleeve with those of the bodice.

5. Join the sleeve to the garment, easing any fullness. (For a description of the procedure for easing, see pages 472-473.)

6. Join the underarm seams of both the sleeve and garment.

7. Complete the lower sleeve edges by hemming, facing, or finishing with a band or cuff.

Epaulet Sleeve

Like the raglan, the epaulet sleeve is one of the easier types of sleeves that are cut separately, but its construction requires accuracy. The steps for its insertion are as follows:

1. Staystitch both the upper and lower edges of the sleeve.

2. Stitch and press darts located in the upper area of the garment or the sleeve itself.

3. Carefully match by both number and position the notches of the sleeve inset with

Courtesy Simplicity Pattern Co., Inc.

The appearance of a kimono sleeve can be accomplished by making a regular set-in sleeve with a flared shape.

The appearance of an epaulet sleeve can be accomplished by adding trim to the shoulder line of a garment.

469

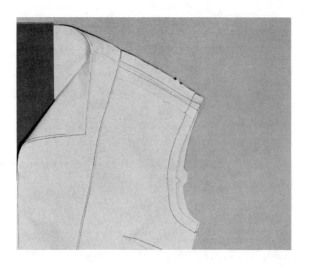

To prepare a garment for attachment of a set-in sleeve, staystitch the armhole edges, join and finish the shoulder seam, complete the neck opening, and join and finish the underarm seam.

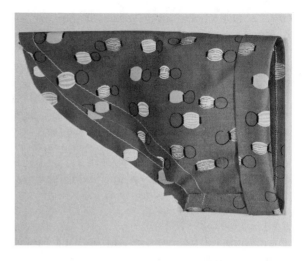

Before attaching a set-in sleeve to a garment, insert a row of staystitch-gathering stitches along the sleeve armhole seam line, join and finish the underarm seam, and finish the lower sleeve edge.

those of the bodice front and back. Stitch this seam from the neck edge to the underarm on both front and back of the sleeve.

4. Join the underarm seam, stitching directionally from the underarm to the sleeve edge. Then, overstitching the underarm area, complete the seam by stitching from the underarm to the bottom of the underarm seam.

5. Finish the lower sleeve edge.

Set-in Sleeve

A well-set sleeve can greatly enhance the appearance of any garment. Conversely, a poorly set sleeve can impair the total effect of a garment. Because the attractiveness of a set-in sleeve depends largely on rather intricate fitting processes, even the simpler form of this sleeve requires skill and effort. The procedure for making a tailored set-in sleeve is included in Chapter 28 (see pages 538-545).

Before the sleeves are begun, the bodice shoulder seam and neckline edge should be completed. The following steps are then completed in order: The armholes are prepared, the sleeves are prepared, the sleeves are

fitted into the armholes, and the sleeves are attached to the garment.

Preparing the Armholes

First staystitch the armhole edges. Then, before setting in the sleeves, it is wise to try on the bodice to check the position of the armhole seam lines on your figure. The placement of these seam lines is an important criterion of a well-made garment. If a sleeve is to fit properly, the armhole seam line should fall precisely at the tip of your shoulder bone and extend downward for a proper fit in the underarm area. In some cases the entire armhole may need to be trimmed out slightly for accurate fit. When trimming, leave sufficient fabric for a $\frac{5}{8}$-inch armhole seam. Excess fabric may be trimmed off. If so, replace the staystitching in the newly shaped armhole.

Preparing the Sleeves

An important step in the sleeve-making process is cutting and preparing sleeves to produce a *pair*; that is, to make a specific sleeve for the right armhole and one for the left armhole. This is automatically guaranteed when sleeves are cut on double fabric and the wrong side of the fabric is carefully marked. However, when sleeves are cut on a single layer of fabric, the pattern must be reversed, or turned over, for the second sleeve.

When making sleeves, first staystitch the armhole edge of the sleeve on the seam line, using a basting stitch over the cap of the sleeve, between the notches. This row of long stitches will later be used to ease the sleeve into the garment. (The procedure for fitting the sleeve is discussed on pages 472-473.) Staystitch the lower edge of the sleeve according to the finish which will be used. If darts or gathers are needed for ease in the elbow area, these are also completed before the underarm seam is stitched.

The next step is usually to stitch the underarm seam. However, if the sleeve is to be hemmed, it is wise to block the sleeve hem before joining the underarm seam (see the illustrations on page 539). As you proceed to the underarm seams, fold the sleeves and pin them in position for stitching the underarm seam with the right side of the fabric on the inside. This will ensure against stitching errors which will result in the construction of two sleeves for a single armhole. It is wise to check at this point that the sleeves are of an appropriate and attractive length for your arm. Alter their length if necessary to suit your personal taste or comfort. If necessary, adjust the underarm for better fit. Then stitch and press the seam.

You are then ready to finish the lower edge of the sleeve. There are several ways of doing so. The lower edge may be hemmed, faced, or finished with a band or cuff.

Hemming the Lower Edge   One of the easiest methods of finishing the lower edge of the sleeve is to hem it. To do so, fold the edge back to form a hem of the desired width and press it. The hem width is usually determined by the pattern unless you have made adjustments. Finish the upper edge of the hem by the method best suited to your fabric, that is, by clean finishing, pinking, edge

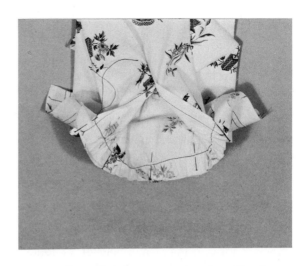

When making cuffed sleeves, complete the cuff and attach it to the lower edge of the sleeve. After the cuff is completed, the sleeve can be attached to the garment.

stitching, or binding (see pages 379-382). Then attach the hem to the sleeve with stitches which do not show on the right side (see pages 392-395).

Facing the Lower Edge   If the lower edge of a sleeve is to be faced rather than hemmed, you may apply either a shaped facing or a bias facing (see Chapter 22).

Attaching a Band or Cuff   Often a sleeve is designed to be finished with some variation of a band or cuff. If so, there are at least two general types that can be used: those in which the ends are joined to form a type of band and those that are finished at both ends to form either a straight cuff or a folded French-type cuff. The application varies with the style of the garment, the weight of the fabric, and the desired finished appearance. Check your guide sheet for the specific plan for the sleeve bands or cuffs on your garment.

As with most other garment features, there is a basic process common to the making and applying of most bands and cuffs. Many of the steps of this process are variations of sewing procedures which you have used in attaching facings and collars. To attach a sleeve band or cuff, complete the following steps:

1. Complete the band or cuff before attaching it to the sleeve unit. Usually cuffs are interfaced similarly to collars (see page 460). The ends of sleeve bands are stitched together and pressed open before they are attached to the sleeve unit, while the ends of cuffs are finished separately: Seam allowances of cuff ends are trimmed to ¼ inch or less and tapered to a point at the cuff corner. Then the finished cuff is carefully pressed.

2. If there is a placket in the sleeve, follow the directions on your pattern guide sheet for making the sleeve placket, or follow the directions for a faced, bound, or hemmed placket on pages 360-361. Upon completion of the placket, key the end seams of the cuff to the edges of the sleeve opening. If it is a sleeve band, key the seam of the band to the underarm seam in the sleeve.

3. Divide the band or cuff in quarters by folding it crosswise, not including the end seam allowances.

4. Match the notched edge of the band or cuff with the notches on the sleeve, right sides together. Pin the band or cuff in place, leaving the underside free for a later attachment.

5. Stitch a ⅝-inch seam to join together the outer edge of the band or cuff and the lower edge of the sleeve. Grade the seam.

6. Press the seam into the band or cuff before turning the undercuff in place.

7. Turn under the seam allowance of the undercuff, and pin the undercuff to the sleeve edge, allowing it to extend ⅛ inch past the stitching line which joins the upper cuff and sleeve if it is to be attached to the sleeve by machine. If it is to be attached by hand, it should extend exactly to the seam line.

8. Fasten the undercuff in place by machine-stitching from the top side of the sleeve, in the ridge formed by the joining of the upper band or cuff and the sleeve itself. If preferred, the underedge of the band or cuff may be hand-stitched to the under sleeve edge.

Fitting the Sleeves

As the circumference of the sleeve cap usually exceeds that of the armhole, a set-in sleeve generally requires easing or gathering to fit the armhole. If the fabric is difficult to ease, as are some with permanent finishes, fullness may be reduced by making tiny pleats in the cap area of the sleeve pattern before cutting out the sleeves.

The difference between easing and gathering is mainly one of degree. Whereas the effect of an ease line is virtually invisible, gathers are a deliberate display of fullness for design purposes. In either case the sleeve cap is machine-basted directly on the seam line along the sleeve cap from notch to notch. The weight of the fabric largely determines the stitch length. If the stitch is too long, the gathers may shift into undesirable pleats or tucks. If it is too short, the thread may break when pulled in gathering the fabric.

Insert additional rows of stitching in the seam allowance if needed. Then temporarily gather and distribute the fullness, and secure the thread ends with pins. (See pages 397-398 for the procedure for gathering and page 304 for easing fullness.)

The accuracy of the sleeve-cap fit may then be checked by pinning the sleeve to the armhole. Place the sleeve in the armhole with the right sides together. Holding the top of the sleeve toward you, adjust the amount of ease or gathering as necessary. Key and pin the top-of-sleeve marking and the shoulder marking or seam, the sleeve and garment underarm seams, and all notches. Most patterns include one notch to indicate sleeve front and two notches to indicate sleeve back, or vice versa. Care in matching garment and sleeve notches in both position and number prevents setting a sleeve in backwards.

When the sleeve cap has been correctly eased to the circumference of the armhole, adjust the gathering threads. Postpone securing them permanently until after the sleeve has been joined to the garment. Distribute the ease or gathering while the sleeve is still

A sleeve is fitted to an armhole by first pinning the two together at the shoulder, underarm, and notches. Then the gathering thread is pulled to reduce the size of the sleeve to fit the armhole.

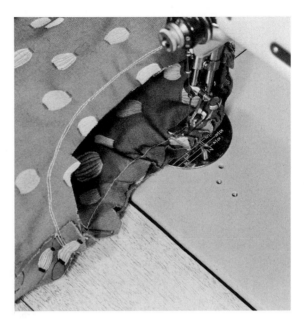

After the sleeve has been removed from the armhole and blocked to shape, it is repinned into the armhole and machine-stitched in place. Overstitching is desirable in the underarm area.

pinned to the armhole. There should be no ease along the underarm seam and none for about 1½ inches across the top of the sleeve where the fabric grain is straight. The easing should be greatest where the sleeve is most off grain.

When the sleeve cap has been accurately fitted, it is ready to be unpinned from the garment and blocked. For a description of the procedure for blocking a sleeve, see pages 317-318.

Setting In the Sleeves

After the blocking has been completed, the sleeve is again keyed to the armhole and repinned at the key points in its former position inside the bodice. Place the pins at the seam line, and perpendicular to it, with heads out. Hold the ease in position with additional pins if more help is needed.

Keeping the sleeve up, machine-baste each sleeve into the armhole, leaving a ⅝-inch seam allowance. Then, once again, try on the garment to check the position of the armhole seams, the distribution of sleeve-cap ease, and the fit of the sleeves. If both sleeves seem to be accurately positioned and fitted, they may then be attached permanently to the garment.

Stitch the armhole seams from the sleeve side. Starting at a notch, stitch toward the underarm seam, around the armhole, and overstitch with a short stitch across the underarm from notch to notch. This overstitching across the underarm serves as reinforcement at a point of strain.

The armhole seam may then be underpressed (see pages 314-315) and finished by pinking or by pinking and stitching (see chart on page 309).

Attaching Shirt Sleeves

The shirt-type sleeve is a variation of a set-in sleeve. This sleeve is loose fitting at the arm-

473

When attaching a shirt-type sleeve, stitch the sleeve to the armhole before the underarm seams of the garment and sleeve have been stitched.

hole and has only a small amount of ease in the cap. Because the shirt sleeve does not need to be blocked, an alternate method from that of the regular set-in sleeve may be preferred. The sleeve may be joined to the garment while both the garment and the sleeve are still flat, before the underarm seams are made.

Attach a shirt sleeve as follows:

1. Prepare the garment by completing the front and back units and joining them at the shoulder. Leave the underarm seams open.

2. Prepare the sleeve by staystitching, using a basting stitch between the notches on the top of the sleeve. Finish the placket at the lower edge if one is included. Attach a facing, or block a hem at the lower edge if either of these is the specified finish.

3. Attach the sleeve to the garment with both the sleeve and the garment opened out flat, making either a plain or a flat-fell seam. For a plain seam, pin the sleeves in the garment with *right* sides together. Stitch the sleeve to the garment, easing in the fullness between the notches. Finish the seam, turn it toward the sleeve or the neckline as preferred,

and press. For a flat-fell seam, pin the sleeve in the garment with *wrong* sides together. Stitch the sleeve to the garment, easing in the fullness. Trim the seam allowances and complete the flat-fell seam. (See page 308.) Press the seam flat.

4. Stitch the underarm seam of the sleeve and the side seam of the garment with a continuous line of stitching. A flat-fell seam can be used if preferred.

5. Finish the lower edge of the sleeve with a hem, facing, band, or cuff.

Finishing Armholes in Sleeveless Garments

There are times in the construction of a garment when neither a cut-in-one nor a set-in sleeve is used; the garment is made sleeveless instead. In this instance, facings or bias bindings are frequently used as a finish. The step-by-step process of preparing and applying facings is described in Chapter 22 (see pages 441-448). Bias binding is discussed on pages 403-405.

STANDARDS FOR A SET-IN SLEEVE

1. Top of the sleeve seam accurately located at the tip of the shoulder of the wearer.
2. Accurate positioning of the sleeve in armhole to ensure a straight fabric grain line in the sleeve.
3. Cap smoothly rounded.
4. Even distribution of ease around the sleeve cap, usually with no visible gathers or puckers in the seam line.
5. An accurate armhole seam line that is smoothly and evenly stitched.

STANDARDS FOR ARMHOLES OF SLEEVELESS GARMENTS

1. Necessary alterations in garment armholes have been made identically in corresponding facings.
2. The curved seams used to join the facing to the garment are stitched with small stitches for strength.
3. Underarm seams are carefully graded and clipped to provide a flat finish without ridges.
4. Armhole seams are understitched to prevent rolling of the facing to the right side of the garment.
5. The facing is anchored to the garment with stitching which does not show on the right side of the garment.

1. Cap and kimono sleeves are cut-in-one with the bodice whereas raglan, epaulet, and set-in sleeves are cut separately and later stitched to the garment.

2. A simple kimono sleeve is made by stitching shoulder and underarm seams, reinforcing the underarm area, and finishing the lower edge.

3. The underarm seam of a cap or kimono sleeve can be reinforced with stitching or tape.

4. When cutting sleeves from a single thickness of fabric, a matching pair can be obtained by turning the pattern over before cutting the second sleeve.

5. A well-set sleeve requires correct placement of the armhole seam, accurate matching of notches, careful easing of the sleeve cap into the armhole, and accurate blocking of the sleeve cap.

6. The ease in a sleeve cap is correctly blocked into the area extending above the sleeve notch to within $\frac{3}{4}$ inch of the shoulder seam line.

7. The lower edges of a set-in sleeve may be hemmed, faced, or finished with a band or cuff.

8. Armholes in sleeveless garments may be finished with a facing or bias binding.

25 Linings and Underlinings

Linings and underlinings each play a major role in enhancing the finished appearance of specific garments, though differing slightly in function.
A lining is a garment within a garment used to conceal the raw edges of seams and tailoring, to enable you to slip a garment on and off easily, and to protect the body from the coarse or textured outer fabric as a garment is worn or removed. An underlining is a layer of backing fabric added to the major garment pieces primarily for support.

What are the purposes of linings?

What types of lining fabrics are available on today's market?

What are the factors to consider when selecting lining fabric?

How do the processes of cutting and sewing a lining differ from the cutting and sewing of an underlining?

Decisions About Linings and Underlinings

There is no one type of lining or underlining fabric best suited to all garment fabrics. Just as garment fabrics come in a variety of weights, textures, and colors, so do the supportive fabrics. Linings and underlinings may be firm or soft, lightweight or heavy, washable or drycleanable, dull or shiny, solid-colored or figured, expensive or inexpensive. Usually a pattern envelope suggests suitable lining fabric. When the alternatives are many, however, a good choice may be made by applying the decision-making process on the basis of the factors which are described in the following pages.

Types of Lining Fabrics

There are a variety of fabrics made specifically for use as linings. These include twills, crepes, taffetas, satins, and metallic-backed fabrics. There are also a wide range of quilted, foam-backed, and pile linings. In addition, there are several crease-resistant apparel and underlining fabrics which can also be used as linings. Each lining fabric has its own unique characteristics. Twills have a slight luster and a diagonal weave that gives them a tailored look. Crepe fabrics have soft, draping qualities. Taffeta has crispness and some luster. The silky, lustrous satins add elegance to a garment. Metallic-backed, quilted, foam-backed, and pile linings provide warmth. The characteristics of the most commonly used lining fabrics are detailed in the chart on pages 484-485.

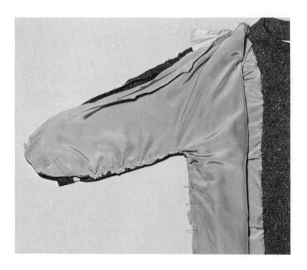

Choose a lining fabric which will wear well, one which will yield to the design of the garment, and one which looks well and can be cleaned in the same manner as the outer fabric.

Considerations in Choosing Linings

Since a lining serves to add support to a garment, to cover unattractive seams, and to improve the appearance and comfort of a garment, a number of factors influence its choice. When selecting lining fabrics, consider the wear requirements, unity of garment design, and compatibility with the outer fabric.

Wear Requirements

An important factor to consider when selecting a lining fabric is durability. A lining should be chosen to last the life of the garment it will line. Lining is subjected to greater stress in some garments than others. A coat, for example, requires a sturdier lining than a dress or skirt, since it undergoes the wear and tear of being frequently put on and removed and may be worn for more years than a dress or skirt. A school coat requires a stronger lining than a dress coat, as it will probably be worn more often.

Lining fabrics vary in durability. Twill, for example, is sturdy in wear, whereas crepe linings, unless backed in a type of double-weave construction, tend to sag or stretch under stress. Satin-weave linings, while luxurious in appearance, have floating yarns which tend to snag or pull during wear. The metallic backing on an insulated lining may rub off under friction or after several cleanings. Consider the differing characteristics of lining fabrics as you make a selection.

When choosing a lining, shape retention, wrinkle resistance, and colorfastness are all qualities to be sought. A lining that is durable will eliminate the time and expense of a later replacement.

Unity of Garment Design

A lining fabric should be chosen to harmonize with the rest of the garment in design, texture, and color. A printed satin lining, for example, might add elegance to a dressy suit but look out of place in a sports jacket. Conversely, a pile lining, well chosen to add warmth to a sports jacket, would seldom be appropriate for a dressy garment.

It is usually best to choose a lining that is as close to the color of the outer fabric as possible unless a contrasting fabric is desired for decorative or novelty effect. Prints, plaids, checks, and contrasting solid colors can be utilized effectively for linings to add flair to a garment.

The attractiveness of a lining fabric, while always a factor to consider, varies in importance with the visibility of the lining. It is of greater significance in a coat or jacket, for example, where the lining is frequently seen, than it is in a dress or skirt, where it is usually hidden.

Compatibility with Outer Fabric

To be satisfactory a lining fabric must be at least as light in weight as the outer fabric of the garment and must be equally pliable. A twill lining, for example, might be ideal for a wool coat but too heavy and stiff for a silk party dress.

It is important, too, that the lining have the same care requirements as the rest of the

Courtesy McCall Pattern Company

garment. If the outer fabric is an easy-care, no-iron variety, for example, the lining must also have these characteristics if the completed garment is to be cared for with the expected ease. To line a washable garment with a nonwashable lining automatically makes the completed outfit drycleanable only.

Lining a Coat or Jacket

Linings are usually cut for all major coat or jacket pieces including the front, back, and sleeves. They generally are not required for collars, facings, and cuffs. These small pieces are sometimes lined, however, if the garment fabric is too heavy to handle in a double thickness.

The preparation of the lining depends upon the fabric selected. Cotton linings are prepared in the same way as any other cotton fabric. If necessary, they are preshrunk and straightened. Most rayon, acetate, and silk fabrics for linings have been preshrunk before purchase. They must be straightened, how-

ever, to hang correctly in a finished garment. (See the sections on straightening fabric grain and preshrinking washable fabrics on pages 261-267.)

Pattern Layout and Cutting

Linings may be cut from pattern pieces designated as lining patterns or from the same pattern pieces as the coat or jacket. If using the original garment pattern, you may in some cases find special lining cutting lines to guide you. In the absence of special cutting lines, several alterations are necessary to adapt the pattern for a lining. An extra inch of fabric is required along the center-back fold line to allow for a ½-inch ease pleat. The width of the front facing is excluded except for a seam width on the front edge. The back neckline is lowered slightly so that the back neckline facing will extend below it, allowing only a seam width for joining the two sections in a smooth and even fit.

If separate pattern pieces for the lining are provided, check them against the corre-

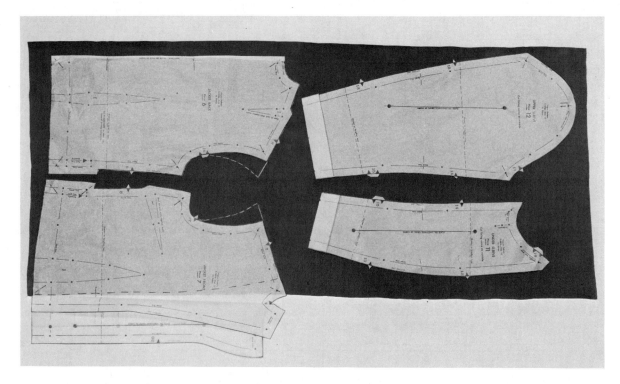

When cutting a garment lining, the garment pattern may be used. Shorten the sleeve to the finished length of the outer sleeve and add space in the shoulder area or center back area to provide roominess for body movement.

sponding pattern pieces for the garment to be sure that they are of the correct length and width. The length of the body lining is the same as that of the garment pattern. The sleeve lining is as long as the *finished* coat or jacket sleeve.

Any alterations made in the garment must also be made in the lining to ensure proper fit.

Linings are cut on the same grain as the outer fabric. If the lining is a slippery type of fabric, it may be helpful to use a cork cutting board or to cover the cutting surface with tissue paper. If tissue paper is used, pin the pattern and fabric to it and cut through all layers to add stability for cutting accuracy. An old sheet pinned tautly over a cutting board will also facilitate the cutting of slippery fabrics. Detailed instructions for working with hard-to-handle fabrics are given in Chapter 21.

Constructing the Lining

A jacket or coat lining can be constructed almost as a duplicate of the garment itself. After the lining is stitched, the seams are finished as necessary and pressed. Finally the lining is inserted into the garment and attached along lengthwise seams, the neckline, and front facings. The sleeves are attached to the garment along the underarm seam, the armhole, and the lower sleeve edges.

Shoulder darts in a jacket or coat lining are left as unstitched pleats or are stitched only partially to allow ease of body movement. If they are stitched, the stitching should extend only 1½ to 2 inches from the top of the shoulder downward along the dart line. All other darts are made as in the garment itself. (For directions on making darts, see pages 395-397.)

To make the extra ease pleat in the center back, press the inch of extra fabric to one side to form a ½-inch pleat. It is necessary to work on a flat surface so that the lining may be accurately shaped. Machine-stitch the top edge of the pleat in place along the neck edge, and then catch-stitch the folded edge for 1½ to 2 inches from the neckline downward. (For a description of catch stitching, see page 393.)

The side and shoulder seams of the lining are then stitched. They must, of course, incorporate any alterations that may have been made in the garment seams. Often the lining seams require a seam finish to prevent fraying. They are then ready for pressing. The lining sleeve seams are made in the same way as the garment sleeve seams except that dart fullness at the elbow is eased in.

Attaching the Lining

A coat or jacket lining may be attached to the garment by one of several methods. Alternatives include attaching it by hand, by machine, and by a combination of the two methods. Generally the lining of a tailored suit or coat is put in by hand to allow for outer garment give and to provide a professionally tailored look. (See "Lining Tailored Garments," pages 508-511, for this method.)

The machine method for attaching linings is suitable for garments which receive considerable wear and tear and need to be sturdy. The machine method can also be used when sewing time is at a premium. Linings in children's clothing, simple sports jackets, and casual clothing can be successfully attached by machine. The lining is generally attached after facings have been anchored to the garment and the lower edge and the sleeves of the outer garment have been finished with hems or facings. If the lining is to be hemmed separately, the lining hem is finished.

To line a garment by the machine method, pin the neck edge of the lining to the inner edge of the garment neck facing, right sides together, matching seams and notches.

Shoulder darts in a lining can be partially stitched along the dart line or left open to provide ease for body movement.

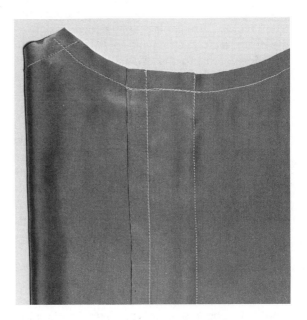

After stitching the back lining pieces together, form an ease pleat by shifting a seam line to one side and forming the edge of the pleat along the center-back marking line. Stitch across the top of the pleat at the neck seam line to hold the pleat in place.

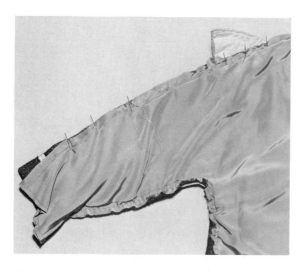

After fastening a cut-in-one sleeve and lining to the garment and lengthwise sleeve seams, pull the lining through so that it lines the sleeve.

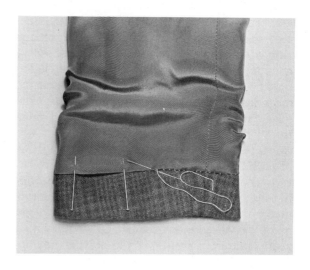

Hand-fasten the lower edge of a sleeve lining to the top edge of the sleeve hem or facing with a suitable hemming stitch.

Pin the lining and outer garment together downward along the inner edge of both side front facings. Beginning at the lower edge of the front facing, stitch up to and around the neckline facing to the opposite lower edge of the garment. Clip any curved areas (see pages 402-403 for the clipping of curved seams). Press the seam allowance toward the lining. If the lining has not been hemmed, fasten the lower edge of the lining to the upper edge of the garment hem with a slip stitch or another suitable hand-hemming stitch. Make a fold of the excess length in the lining, and slip-stitch the lining to the garment facings for the width of the fold. (The slip stitch and other hand-hemming stitches are described on pages 392-395.)

If the sleeve linings have been attached to the garment lining, push them into the sleeve and slip-stitch the lower edge in place along the upper edge of the hems or facings on the lower edges of the sleeves. If the sleeve linings are to be attached separately, hand-stitch them to the garment armhole edges, wrong sides together and notches matched. Turn under the seam allowance of the lining,

and slip-stitch the garment lining to the sleeve lining all around the armhole edge. Then attach the lower edges of the sleeve linings to the upper edges of the sleeve hems or facings. The extra length in the lining provides necessary ease for body movement.

Lining a Skirt or Dress

A separate lining is sometimes used in a skirt or dress. Such a lining, if well made, permits freedom of body movement while helping to retain the garment shape and protect the body from exposure to the outer garment fabric.

The length of the lining is determined by the style of the garment, the outer fabric, and personal preference. It may be finished at any length between the lower hip area and the full length of the skirt.

Pattern Layout and Cutting

Whether lining a skirt or dress, use the major garment pattern pieces to cut the lining. If the lining is full length, place the pattern on the same grain as the outer fabric. If the plan calls for only a partial lining or if the lining fabric is not stretchy, place the pattern on the crosswise grain. Place the lower edge of a partial lining on the selvage to eliminate the need for a hem in the lower edge of the lining.

If a skirt has a kick pleat which is cut on the straight of the fabric, omit the pleat from the lining by planning for the lining to extend only to the top of the pleat opening. Otherwise, cut the lining the same size as the outer fabric. Remember to make the same alterations as were made in the outer fabric and to transfer the markings. If the lining fabric is slippery or otherwise hard to handle, you may wish to use a special cutting surface (see Chapter 21).

Steps in Lining a Dress

When lining a dress which has a waistline, line the bodice and skirt separately before fastening the bodice and skirt together. Fasten the bodice lining to the neckline and armhole edges of the garment before finishing them in a suitable manner. When attaching a dress lining which has no waistline seam, fasten it to the shoulder seams, neck edge, and armhole edges of the garment. If the lining tends to slip about in the garment, hand-tack it to the side seams of the outer garment.

There are several alternatives for attaching the lining at the neck edge. One method eliminates facings by allowing the lining to serve as both a lining and facing. When this method is used, place the right sides of the garment and lining together and stitch a ⅝-inch seam at the neck edge. After clipping, trimming, and understitching the neckline seam, turn the lining to the inside as you would a facing, and press the garment.

An alternative method is to use facings as well as a lining. When using this method, stitch the lining and garment together along the neck edge, with wrong sides together. Complete the neck edge with facings as described on pages 443-444.

Sleeves of most dresses are not lined. If it becomes necessary to line dress sleeves, follow the directions for lining the sleeves of a jacket or coat given on pages 542-545.

After attaching a dress and its lining at the neckline and armhole edges, apply the facings as in an unlined garment.

The lining of a skirt is often cut on the crosswise grain of the fabric so that the selvage can be used for an unhemmed lower edge.

LINING FABRICS

Type	Fiber Content	Characteristics	Use	Care Requirements
Twill	Silk, rayon, polyester, or cotton.	Firm, diagonal weave. Good body. Smooth, some luster. Does not stretch.	Jackets, sportswear, coats, and suits.	Drycleaning preferred for silk and rayon. Washing preferred for polyester and cotton.
Crepe	Blends, acetate, silk, polyester, or rayon.	Pliable, soft, drapable. Durable. Versatile. May stretch or sag.	Dresses, jackets, and skirts.	Drycleanable.
Taffeta	Silk, acetate, polyester, or rayon.	Semicrisp, firmly woven, smooth. Provides body and shape retention. Durable, wrinkle-resistant, static free.	Coats, jackets, sportswear, and formal dresses.	Drycleaning preferred.
Satin	Silk, acetate, or rayon.	Lustrous, luxurious looking. Drapable, smooth, static free. Adds body. May snag or break with friction.	Jackets, coats, suits, and dresses.	Drycleanable only.
Sateen	Cotton.	Same as for satins.	Same as for satins.	Washable.
Crepe-back Satin	Blends, acetate, silk, or rayon.	Lustrous, luxurious looking. Reversible, ravels, has qualities of both crepe and satin.	Suits, coats, and jackets.	Drycleanable only.

484

Type	Fiber Content	Characteristics	Use	Care Requirements
Nap-back Satin	Rayon or acetate with cotton or other backing.	Lining and interlining woven as one. Shiny on lining side, provides some extra warmth in minimum sewing time. Bulky in seams.	Coats, jackets, and sportswear.	Drycleanable only.
Metallic-backed Lining Fabrics	Rayon or acetate with aluminum coating.	Gray metallic look, shiny, adds warmth without weight. Stiff, easily wrinkled.	Coats, jackets, suits, and sportswear.	Drycleanable only.
Quilted and Foam-backed	Man-made fiber face quilted to cotton or polyester wadding or bonded to man-made foam.	Sturdy, warm. Adds body.	Coats and jackets.	Drycleaning preferred for cotton-backed fabrics. Most polyester and foam-backed fabrics may be washed.
Pile	Acrylic or cotton.	Warm, soft. Durable.	Jackets, coats, and sportswear.	Washable or drycleanable, depending on the fabric.

Steps in Lining a Skirt

When lining a skirt, attach the lining to the skirt before the waistband or waistline seam is made. Place the lining in the skirt with the wrong side of the lining toward the wrong side of the skirt. Key the waistline edges at the center fronts, center backs, seam lines, and darts. Baste the lining to the skirt along the waistline edge on the stayline. The lining is fastened to the skirt along the placket edges after the zipper has been applied. Attach it by turning in the seam allowances on both sides of the placket opening and sewing the lining to the zipper tape by hand.

What are the purposes of underlinings?
What factors determine whether a garment should be lined or underlined?
What are the factors to consider when selecting underlining fabric?
How do the cutting and sewing of an underlining differ from the cutting and sewing of a garment? From the cutting and sewing of a lining?

Types of Underlining Fabrics

An underlining is a layer of fabric attached to the outer fabric pieces of a garment and handled in construction as one with the outer fabric. It can be made of any one of a variety of fabrics including acetate and cotton sheath, China silk, and crepe. In addition, there are underlining fabrics sold under a variety of brand names, each with unique characteristics. You can check with your local store for available brands. Be sure to read the labels regarding fiber content, characteristics, and care requirements. Many apparel fabrics and a few lining fabrics can also be used as underlining fabrics. These include crepes, rayon twills, and lightweight taffetas.

Underlining fabrics as such come in widths of 36 to 45 inches. The width often varies with the fiber content. For example, fabrics of cotton are often 36 to 39 inches wide. Those of man-made fibers are usually 39 to 45 inches wide. Prices for underlining fabrics also vary considerably, depending on fiber content, width, and quality. Generally silks are expensive, cottons and blends moderately priced, and acetates least expensive.

UNDERLINING FABRICS

Type	Fiber Content	Characteristics	Use	Care Requirements
Sheath	Polyester, acetate, rayon, or blends.	Lightweight, firmly woven. Retains shape. Wide range of colors. May tear with stress or pull at seams. Ravels.	Skirts, slacks, pants, and dresses.	Drycleanable. Low pressing temperature.
	Cotton or cotton-polyester blends.	Crease resistant. Lightweight, soft, pliable. Colorfast. Wide range of colors.	Skirts, slacks, pants, and dresses.	Requires preshrinking. Machine washable.
China Silk	Silk.	Very lightweight. Soft, pliable, but firm. Slippery. Ravels.	Wool or silk slacks, pants, or skirts.	Drycleanable.
Crepe	Blends, acetate, silk, or rayon.	Soft, pliable, drapable, but strong. May stretch or sag.	Garments designed with softness and drapability.	Drycleanable.

Considerations in Choosing Underlinings

Since underlining fabrics are varied in both type and function, a number of factors influence their selection. The chief considerations are the specific function the underlining will serve in the garment in question, the compatibility of the underlining fabric with the outer fabric, and the desired quality of the underlining fabric.

Specific Function of the Underlining

The purpose for which an underlining is to be used is perhaps the most important factor in determining the choice of the underlining fabric. Underlinings may be used to support a lightweight fabric, add body to a loose novelty weave, stabilize a stretch garment, emphasize the silhouette of an A-line skirt, add warmth to an unlined jacket, or provide opaqueness to an otherwise sheer garment. Each of these functions requires specific underlining characteristics. Choose the underlining fabric which best fits the particular needs.

Compatibility with the Outer Fabric

It is important that an underlining be compatible with the garment outer fabric in weight, pliability, and care requirements. This necessity is even greater for underlinings than for linings since they are treated as one with the garment. An underlining as light in weight as the garment fabric prevents bulkiness. An underlining as pliable as the garment fabric prevents drawing at the seams and wrinkling.

Be sure that a chosen underlining may be cleaned in the same way as the rest of the garment to ensure that the expected care procedure may be carried out. A machine-washable cotton or cotton-polyester dress requires an underlining that is preshrunk and machine washable.

Desired Quality

Appearance is generally less critical in an underlining fabric than in a lining fabric, as an underlining is generally less visible. To prevent disappointment with your finished garment, however, avoid sacrificing quality

STANDARDS FOR HIGH-QUALITY UNDERLININGS

1. *Inconspicuous in color.*
2. *Compatible with garment fabric in weight, pliability, and care qualities.*
3. *Capable of retaining garment's shape.*
4. *Static-free to resist clinging.*
5. *Comfortable and smooth in wearing.*

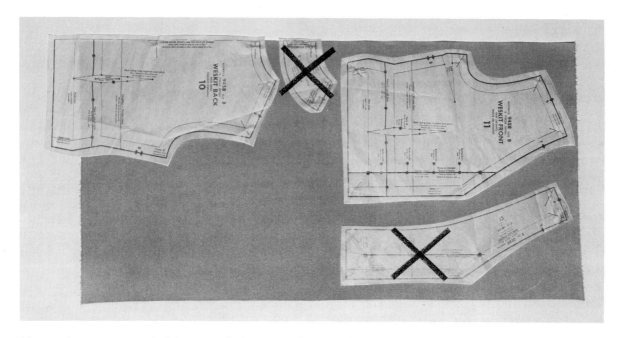

When cutting a garment underlining, use only the patterns for the basic garment pieces. Refold the fabric if necessary to avoid waste.

merely because an underlining is hidden from sight. Since it plays a supportive role in a garment, the underlining should be of a quality comparable to that of the outer fabric. It should be appropriate in color and sufficiently durable, comfortable, and attractive to serve its function well throughout its wear life.

Steps in Underlining a Garment

Since underlinings and linings serve somewhat similar purposes, many of the steps in underlining are similar to those in lining a garment. It is the attachment of the two which differs. The fabrics are prepared and cut in a similar manner. Either underlining or lining may cover only part or all of the inside of a garment. However, while a lining is essentially a separate garment, an underlining is stitched into the garment seams.

Preparing the Underlining Fabric

When preparing underlining for a garment, be sure to preshrink any fabric not marked *Preshrunk, Shrinkage less than 1 percent*, or *Sanforized.* If you are uncertain about its shrinkage properties, it is best to shrink the fabric for safety. (See "Preshrinking Fabrics," pages 265-267.)

Straighten the underlining fabric to make it grain perfect before cutting it. Use the same procedures employed for straightening other fabrics. (See "Straightening Fabric Grain," pages 261-265.)

Pattern Layout and Cutting

A full underlining extends under every major garment piece. Minor pieces are usually not underlined. When separate patterns are not included for underlinings, the major garment pattern pieces may be employed. For example, when underlining slacks, use only the patterns for the front and back sections. When underlining a skirt, cut underlining sections for both the skirt front and the skirt back. Sometimes an underlining is cut for an entire dress except for the sleeves. The decision to underline sleeves varies with the style of the garment.

Accuracy is necessary when cutting an underlining. Lay the pattern on the same grain as for the corresponding garment pieces. Cut the underlining separately but exactly on the cutting lines so that it will fit together precisely with the outer fabric. Any alterations made in the garment must also be incorporated into the underlining.

When an underlining is cut for a skirt in which there is a center pleat, omit the pleat in the underlining. To do this, place the pleat stitching line on the fold of the underlining fabric.

When cutting underlining fabric, use sharp cutting shears and long, firm strokes. If the underlining is extremely lightweight or slippery, place tissue paper or a sheet under the fabric to prevent slippage while cutting. For further details on working with hard-to-handle fabrics see Chapter 21.

Attaching the Underlining

After the underlining is cut, it is treated as one with the corresponding garment piece. However, there are several alternatives for attaching it to the garment. The method selected depends largely on how similar the garment and underlining are in weight and pliability.

Attachment Method 1

When the garment and underlining fabrics are very similar in pliability and weight, they may be handled successfully as one fabric. To underline by this process, follow the procedures listed below.

1. Work on a large, smooth surface and keep the fabrics flat to prevent the two layers from slipping apart. Place the underlining on the outer fabric, wrong sides together. Pin the two pieces together carefully, matching the notches, curved edges, and seams. Key the grain lines at center front and center back.

Courtesy McGraw-Hill Clothing Construction Film Loop Series

Most underlining fabrics can be pinned and stitched to the garment pieces. Afterward the two layers are treated as one.

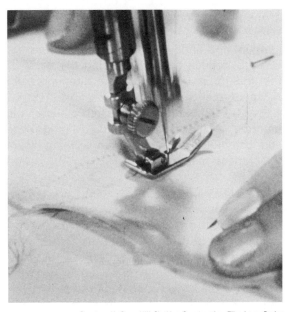

Courtesy McGraw-Hill Clothing Construction Film Loop Series

The outer fabric and underlining are stitched together on dart fold lines to increase construction accuracy.

2. While staystitching each piece of the garment, attach its corresponding underlining piece. Stitch directionally ½ inch from the cut edge. On loosely woven or stretchy fabrics, stitch from the underlining side.

3. Machine-baste through both fabrics at the center of each dart to secure the two fabrics. Then, treating the two fabrics as one, machine-stitch the darts.

4. Machine-stitch the seams. Trim the underlining to within ⅛ inch of the stitching line to reduce unnecessary bulk.

Attachment Method 2

When a garment and its underlining are quite dissimilar in pliability and weight, they are treated as two separate fabrics up to a point. This method may also be effective if the garment fabric is bulky. Complete the underlining of a garment by this method in the following series of steps:

1. If the fabric is bulky or heavy, stitch the darts on the wrong side of the garment fabric and slash them open along the center line. Then stitch the darts on the wrong side of the underlining pieces. Slash or trim.

2. Press and block the darts in both the garment and underlining. If the darts were not slashed, reduce bulk by pressing the darts of the underlining in the opposite direction from those of the garment.

3. While staystitching each piece of the garment, attach its corresponding lining piece and complete the steps of underlining as in attachment method 1.

Partial Underlinings

There are times when only a partial underlining is needed in a garment. A partial underlining might be used in either the front or the back of slacks, shorts, skirts, pants, or dresses. Sometimes underlinings are used in both the front and back sections of garments but extend for only a partial length of the garment. A partial underlining might also be used to make an area of a sheer garment opaque or to retain the shape of a particular garment area.

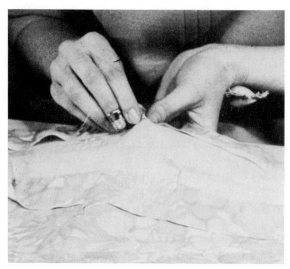

Courtesy McGraw-Hill Clothing Construction Film Loop Series

Hems can be fastened with hand stitching to the underlining fabric to produce an invisible hem.

For example, an underlining might be used only in the bodice of a sheer dress to cover undergarment straps or only in the back of skirts, slacks, pants, or shorts to prevent sagging or wrinkles from sitting.

The procedure for attaching a partial underlining is identical to that for attaching a full underlining. The basic difference is in the length of the underlining and in the sections to be underlined.

If cutting a partial underlining for a skirt, use the skirt pattern. Allow a length that extends at least 10 inches below the hipline, and cut off the extra fabric. If there is a center-back pleat in the garment, omit this pleat when cutting the underlining by placing the pleat *stitching line* on the fabric fold. This will eliminate bulkiness in the pleat.

Finish the lower raw edge of the partial underlining to prevent raveling. If the underlining is firmly woven and raveling is not a problem, a row of stitching and pinking may be sufficient. Edges of fabrics that ravel may be zigzagged or clean-finished. Avoid a method of finishing that adds unsightly bulk.

1. A lining may be considered a garment within a garment, whereas an underlining is treated as one with the garment it underlines.

2. In choosing a lining or underlining fabric, consider its compatibility with the outer fabric in weight, pliability, and care requirements.

3. When sturdiness is desired in a lining fabric, a firmly woven fabric such as a twill fabric might be appropriate.

4. When luxury, luster, smoothness, and body are desired in a lining fabric, possible choices include satin, twill, and taffeta.

5. If no separate pattern is included for a lining or underlining of a skirt or dress, the major garment pattern pieces may be used instead if facings and pleats are omitted.

6. Using a coat or jacket garment pattern for a lining pattern requires four adjustments: omission of the front facings, lowering of the back neckline, the addition of a ½-inch pleat down the center back, and cutting the sleeve lining the finished length of the garment sleeve.

7. Alterations made in the seams or darts of a garment necessitate similar alterations in the lining or underlining.

8. If darts are to be stitched in the garment and underlining as one, a row of basting inserted through the two layers of fabric at the center of the darts will hold them in position during construction.

9. If darts are made separately in garment and underlining, bulk may be reduced by pressing the garment darts in the opposite direction from the underlining darts.

Part 5

Tailoring Techniques

General Tailoring

Tailoring is a process of stitching and shaping flat pieces of fabric until they become smoothly molded to the contour of the body. This process, applied mainly to coats and suits, requires time and sewing skill. However, it is an art which yields practical results. Handsome, stylish, high-quality garments can be made by those who master the art of tailoring.

How does tailoring differ from the construction of untailored clothes?

What special factors should be considered in selecting fabrics for a tailored garment?

In what ways does tailoring affect the procedure for cutting interfacing?

Why are tailor's tacks sometimes the preferred method of marking the outer fabric in tailoring?

Decisions About Tailoring

The decision-making process is vitally essential in the area of tailoring. Foremost is the decision whether or not to tailor. Tailoring is a time-consuming, skill-oriented undertaking. An affirmative decision requires that the necessary time and skills are available. Beginning tailoring projects can seldom be justified purely on the basis of economics. However, the satisfaction of creativity cannot be measured in dollars and cents. Further, a beginning tailoring project, time-consuming though it might be, can open the door to the eventual pleasure of being able to tailor attractive clothes inexpensively for oneself and others.

Once the decision to tailor a garment has been made, other important choices are involved in the selection of fabrics. Will the outer fabric yield to the tailoring processes? Will the lining and interlining fabrics blend in color and hand with the outer fabric? Are the various fabrics effective choices for the garment intended? Wise decisions must be made on all of these considerations for a tailoring project to be a successful one.

Processes Unique to Tailoring

While many of the basic sewing techniques learned in clothing construction will be utilized when tailoring a garment, there are also techniques that are unique to this process. They include the extensive use and complex treatment of inner layers of fabric, special shaping procedures, and special processes involving construction of pockets, buttonholes, collars, and sleeves. Since the tailoring of these four last-mentioned features requires detailed instructions, the specific techniques entailed are discussed separately in later chapters. A general overview of tailoring is presented here.

When choosing outer fabric for a tailoring project, select one which is stable enough to maintain its shape during the construction processes but pliable enough for easy shaping.

Selecting Fabrics for Tailoring

Because tailoring is essentially a process of molding and shaping during construction, the fabrics chosen for a tailoring project must be pliable. Often three or more separate layers of fabric are involved in this process. The outer fabric, the interfacing, the lining, and, if used, the interlining must be considered separately and as a unit. Effectively chosen, they combine into a single attractive garment.

Outer Fabrics

To be suitable for the outer layer of a tailoring project, a fabric must have both adequate pliability for shaping and sufficient body for shape retention. It is important, too, that it withstand the tendency to shine. Generally the pattern guide sheet is your best aid in selecting fabrics.

A smooth-textured, firmly woven fabric is easier to handle than is a bulky, heavily napped, or thick pile fabric. Wool or wool blends are particularly well suited for tailoring. The characteristics of the wool fiber permit these fabrics to be molded by means of heat, moisture, and pressure into such intricate shapes as curved lapels and stand-up collars.

The weight of the fabric selected depends on the purpose of the garment. For example, a fitted suit might require a lightweight fabric, whereas a semifitted coat or jacket might require a medium-weight fabric. A full-length coat usually requires medium-weight to heavy fabric in order to maintain the desired silhouette, regardless of the warmth considerations.

Some fabrics may be sufficiently pliable for the tailoring process but too loosely woven to retain their original shape. If such fabrics are used in a tailoring project, it is necessary to back each garment piece with a lightweight, preshrunk, firmly woven fabric.

Interfacing Fabrics

Since it is used extensively throughout a tailored garment, the interfacing fabric for tailoring must be carefully chosen. It must be pliable enough to give during manipulation in the tailoring process, yet resilient enough to maintain its shape in wear. For these reasons woven interfacing fabrics are more effective than most nonwoven ones for use in tailored garments. (See "Types of Interfacing Fabrics," pages 449-451.)

Muslin is a lightweight, preshrunk cotton suitable for interfacing the back of a coat, for cushioning seams and the edges of hems, and for edging the interfacing. Hair-canvas, a type of canvas to which a percentage of goat's hair has been added, and known to the tailoring profession as Hymo, is used in collars and lapels of most tailored garments.

Interlining Fabrics

Coats are generally warmer than other garments because they include several layers of fabric which retain body heat. For additional warmth, an extra inner layer of fabric, called *interlining*, is provided in many winter coats between the outer garment fabric and the lining. This interlining may be made of woolen flannel or a type of quilted wadding.

Lining Fabrics

Lining fabrics suited for tailoring have many traits in common with those used for lining dresses and other untailored garments. They include twill, satin, lightweight taffeta, and crepe. These fabrics are pliable, smooth, lustrous, and comfortable to wear. For coats which are made for cold weather, consider linings with metallic coatings, those made of pile, or those to which warm layers of fiber have been bonded or quilted. (For details regarding these fabrics, see the lining-fabrics chart on pages 484-485.)

Preparing the Fabrics for Tailoring

All fabrics used in the tailoring process need to be preshrunk. Check the label on each bolt because preshrunk fabrics are clearly marked

Courtesy R & M Kaufman

When choosing an interfacing fabric, select one which will blend with the color of the outer fabric and which will spring back into shape after the strain of wear.

495

by such terms as *Preshrunk, Needle-ready,* and *Sponged.* If there is a question as to the preshrinkage of any layer of fabric to be used in a tailored garment, it is best to err on the side of caution and have it professionally preshrunk or preshrink it yourself (see "Preshrinking Fabrics," pages 265-267). The general exceptions are such fabrics as lining fabrics marked *Dryclean Only.*

Fabrics used in tailoring must also be thread perfect and grain perfect if the completed garment is to hang correctly. If straightening is necessary, it may be accomplished as described in Chapter 11 (see pages 261-265). The fabric may then be pressed and folded for cutting.

Cutting and Marking Tailored-garment Fabrics

If pattern pieces are to be cut on folded fabric, fold each layer of fabric wrong side out to protect the right side while cutting and to have the pieces ready for joining after they are marked. If pattern pieces are to be cut from a single layer of fabric, lay the pattern on the right side. Patterns for facings, interfacings, interlinings, and linings of tailored garments are placed so that the grain of these fabrics is identical with that of the corresponding pieces of the outer fabric. When the pattern is pinned to the fabric, mark wherever an alteration is necessary. Then remember to make an identical alteration in all other layers of fabric which are cut from the same pattern.

Cutting the Outer Fabric

In laying the pattern on the garment fabric, follow as nearly as possible the layout shown on the guide sheet of your pattern (see Chapter 12). If the outer fabric is napped, as are flannel, fleece, and wool broadcloth, or if it has other one-way characteristics, follow the layout designated *For Fabric with Nap.* If there is a plaid design, determine whether it is even or uneven, and proceed with the special lay-

out necessary for matching the plaid design (see "Plaid Fabrics," Chapter 21).

Place the undercollar pattern on the fabric to ensure that the center-back seam will lie on a true bias. Since the grain on the two halves of the undercollar must be identical, the two pieces must be cut separately. To lay the pattern for the undercollar when a one-piece collar pattern is provided, fold the pattern in half at the center back and lay the fold line on a true bias. Mark a reminder so that a seam allowance will be cut on the center back.

Lay the patterns for the facings on the same grain as the patterns for the corresponding garment pieces. If no pattern for the back neck facing is provided, use the pattern for the garment back, and plan for a facing 3 inches wide (see pages 441-442). Strips for the bound buttonholes and bound pockets are cut by measurement as described in Chapter 27 (see pages 515-516 and 519.)

Cutting the Interfacing

Interfacing is used extensively throughout a tailored garment: in the bodice front, across the back shoulder area, in collars, and in shaped hems. There are certain differences between interfacing for the tailoring process and interfacing for regular garments. These differences sometimes affect the cutting process. One difference is that front and back interfacing sections are cut large enough to maintain the shape of the front and the back of the tailored garment. Another difference is that the interfacing for the undercollar is cut on the true bias of the fabric. Still another difference is the treatment of folds and of edges which will be stitched into seams: Where sharply turned edges are desired, the interfacings need to be edged with lightweight stripping and trimmed to reduce the bulk in the turned edge. Otherwise garment edges will look thick and the finish nonprofessional.

If an adequate interfacing pattern is provided, lay it and cut the pieces as the pattern guide sheet directs. A front interfacing pat-

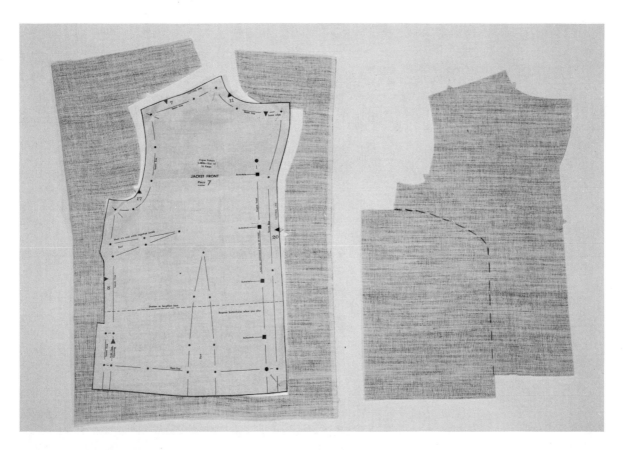

The front interfacing for a tailored jacket or coat, can be cut from the patterns for the garment and facing. Cut around the shoulder, armhole, neck, and front edges of the garment pattern. Mark the interfacing about ½ inch wider than the facing upward to a point 3 to 4 inches below the bust-line. Curve the line below the underarm, and cut on the marked line.

tern sufficient for use in tailoring measures the same length as the front pattern for the garment outer fabric. Both front and back interfacing patterns are shaped exactly like the patterns for the outer fabric along the seam lines of the neck, shoulder, and armhole, and they extend 2 inches below the armhole along the side seam. They should be ½ inch wider than the facings.

If the interfacing pattern provided does not meet tailoring specifications or if no pattern is provided, interfacing pieces can be cut by using the garment and the facing pattern pieces. Cut the interfacing ½ inch wider than

the facing pattern indicates. To cut a front interfacing without a pattern, use the garment pattern to cut the interfacing shape along the armhole, shoulder, neck, and front edges, and for 2 inches below the armhole on the side seam line. Use the facing pattern to determine the correct width of the interfacing. On the inner edge of the front interfacing, locate a point 3 to 4 inches below the armhole and ½ inch wider than the facing. With a curved line connect this point with a point 2 inches below the armhole on the underarm seam line. Extend this line down the full length of the front.

497

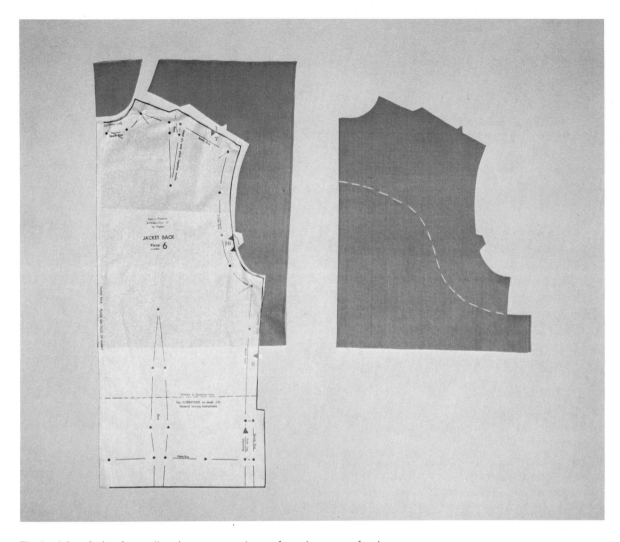

The back interfacing for a tailored garment can be cut from the pattern for the garment back. Cut around the shoulder, neckline, armhole, and 2 inches down the side seam. Remove the pattern. Mark a curved line from a point ½ inch below the width of the back neckline facing to the point 2 inches below the underarm. Cut on the marked line.

Cut the back interfacing on a fold of the interfacing fabric or, if the center back of the outer garment is not cut on the straight of the fabric, cut the interfacing on a grain line identical to that of the outer garment. To cut a back interfacing without a pattern, use the back garment pattern to determine the interfacing shape along the neckline, shoulder, and armhole edges and for 2 inches below the armhole on the side seam line. On the inner edge extend the back interfacing from a point ½ inch below the center back of the neck facing to a point on the side seam line 2 inches below the underarm seam.

Cut interfacings for the undercollar and sleeve facing areas. Since these pieces must be cut on a true bias, lay each pattern on a single layer of fabric. Cut the sleeve interfacing ½ inch wider than the sleeve facing. Cut the collar interfacing the same shape as the undercollar. Relocate the pattern pieces on a second area of interfacing fabric, and cut the second sections identical to the first.

Cutting the Lining and Interlining

In most patterns for tailored garments, separate lining patterns are included. There are usually pattern pieces for lining the garment front, garment back, sleeves, and sometimes pockets and other small areas. In such instances follow the guide sheet for pattern layout and cutting (see Chapter 12). If no pattern for the lining is furnished, use the garment pattern pieces instead as described in Chapter 25 (see pages 479-480). The length of the body lining should be the same as the pattern for the outer fabric. The sleeve lining should be the finished length of the sleeve. If separate interlining is used, it is cut identically to the lining pieces except for the length of the front, back, and sleeves, which should be cut the length of the finished garment and finished sleeves respectively.

Marking the Fabrics

The best way of transferring pattern markings to most fabrics is with tracing paper and tracing wheel. Tailor's tacks are sometimes the preferred method of marking the outer fabric if the fabric is hard to mark. If hand-stitched with embroidery floss, they will usually remain intact throughout the tailoring process and can then be removed with ease.

Center-front, center-back, and buttonhole lines can be marked by tracing or by basting stitches made with thread of a contrasting color. Interfacing, interlining, and lining fabrics can be marked with a tracing wheel or tailor's tacks. Those tracing marks which must be transferred to the right side of the fabric can be machine-basted. (For descriptions of these methods, see "Marking the Fabric," pages 280-284.)

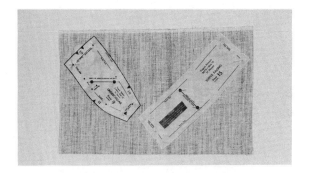

Cut the interfacings for the undercollar and lower sleeve edge a single layer at a time so that both pieces will be on identical grain of the fabric. Cut the inner edge of the sleeve interfacing ½ inch wider than the pattern for the sleeve facing.

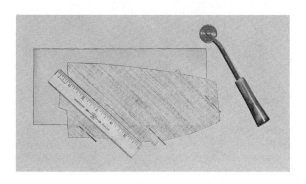

Tracing paper and a tracing wheel are effective for marking most parts of a tailored garment. The marks, obvious on the interfacing and outer fabric, can be transferred with basting stitches from the wrong side to the right side of the garment.

What are the special tailoring techniques that produce finely shaped garments?

How is interfacing treated in tailoring to prevent bulk in the seams? In the outer edges of facings?

What are the unique ways in which shoulder darts are made in the back unit of the interfacing?

What techniques may be employed in hemming tailored garments which will prevent a ridge or other bulkiness from showing on the outside of the garment?

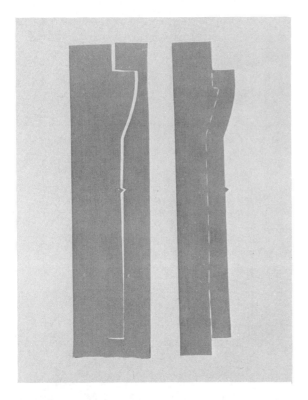
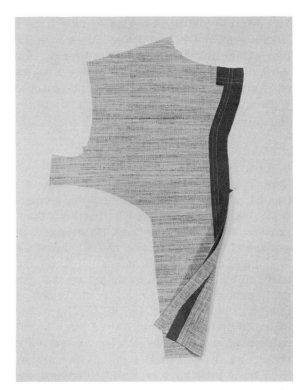

To edge interfacing with muslin, cut a piece of muslin by placing the
pattern over the muslin and cutting the edge to shape (left). Mark the strip
to a width of 1½ inches (second view). After cutting along the marked line,
stitch the muslin to the interfacing with two rows of stitches — one
which is ¾ inch and one which is 1 inch from the edge. Trim away the
edge of the interfacing to prevent its being caught in the seam.

Interfacing the Front
of Tailored Garments

Before the interfacing front unit is attached to
the garment, special preparatory steps are required by the tailoring process: Darts, if
needed, are treated by slashing and overlapping before stitching. The corners of the interfacing are trimmed to reduce bulk in seam
corners. If a crease resistant, stretchy interfacing has been used, an edging is applied to
the outside edges of the interfacing. Then the
seam allowances along the outside edges of
the interfacing are trimmed off to prevent
bulkiness along the garment seam or fold line.
A strip of lightweight cotton muslin or pre-

shrunk seam tape can serve as edging. While
cotton muslin is generally used to reduce the
bulk along the edge of shaped facings, tape
is more often used to edge the interfacing of
extended, or cut-on, facings to prevent their
stretching. The attachment procedures for both
these alternatives are described below. Be
sure to apply the edging so that you have
both a right and left front interfacing unit.

Edging the Interfacing
with Cotton Muslin

If the interfacing is shaped on the front edge,
or, if the interfacing is straight on the front
edge but the garment has an applied fac-

ing, the interfacing should be edged with a strip of lightweight cotton muslin or similar fabric. The muslin edging for the outside edges of the front interfacing are cut and applied as follows:

1. Pin the interfacing pattern to the cotton muslin, and cut along the front and neck edges and for 1½ inches along the lower edge.

2. Remove the pattern, and trim the shaped strip to a width of approximately 1½ inches.

3. Place the strip on the interfacing, aligning the interfacing and strip outer edges. Attach the strip to the interfacing with two rows of stitching. Locate the first row about ¾ inch from the outer edges, and position the second row about ¼ inch inside the first, farther away from the garment edge.

4. Trim the outside edge of the interfacing down to within ⅛ inch of the first stitching line.

Edging the Interfacing with Tape

If the interfacing is straight on the front edge and the garment has an extended facing, the interfacing may be edged with ½-inch-wide straight-woven cotton or linen tape or with preshrunk seam tape. The tape is applied to the outside edges of the front interfacing as follows:

1. Place the tape on the interfacing, aligning the outer edges of the interfacing and the tape.

2. From the interfacing side, stitch the tape to the interfacing with two rows of stitching. Locate the first row ¼ inch from the outer edge and the second row close to the inner edge of the tape, or ¼ inch from the first row. One front unit will be stitched from the neck down, and the other front unit will be stitched from the lower edge up. Be careful to avoid easing or stretching the fabric.

Making Front Shoulder Darts
in Interfacing

Darts in tailored garments require special treatment to prevent bulkiness. In order to

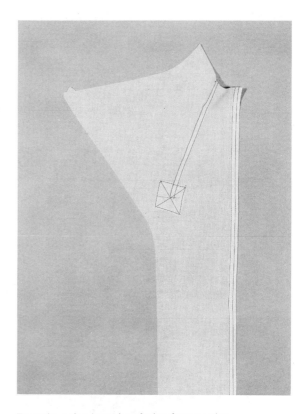

To make a dart in an interfacing front section, slash along one of the stitching lines and slide one side of the dart over the other so that one stitching line is directly over the other. After double-stitching the dart and trimming it, reinforce the point with a small square of muslin.

create a flat, smooth dart in the shoulder area, follow the steps listed below:

1. Slash the dart stitching line that is the more nearly on grain.

2. Lap the cut edge to the marking line on the other side of the dart. Make sure that darts in the right and left sides of the garment are lapped in opposite directions to produce an interfacing for the right and left fronts.

3. Stitch close to the cut edge on the right side of the interfacing, from the shoulder edge to the point of the dart. Then stitch a second time the width of the presser foot away from the first stitching line. If a zigzag ma-

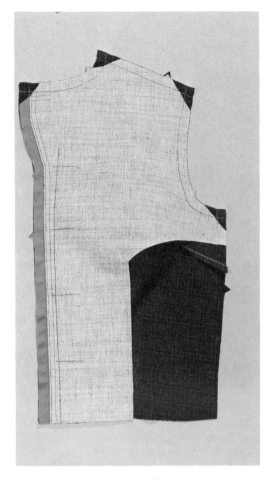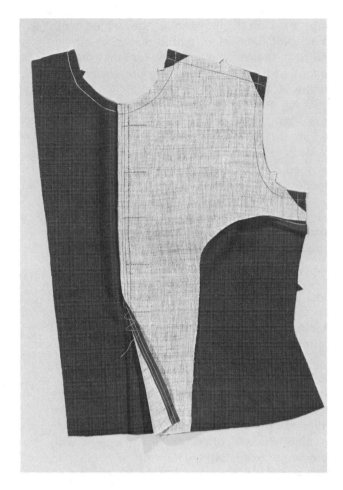

Before attaching interfacing to a garment front, remove its corners. Stitch a muslin-edged interfacing to the garment ½ inch from the edge (left). If the interfacing has been edged with tape, fasten the taped edge to the garment fold line with hand stitches (right).

chine is available, simply zigzag-stitch one layer of fabric over the other from the right side of the interfacing.

    4. Trim away the excess dart fabric from the wrong side, close to the stitching.

    5. Reinforce the point of the dart on the wrong side with a 2-inch square of preshrunk muslin. Press creases in the muslin on the diagonal to mark a stitching line. Stitch diagonally on the crease lines across a square which is perfectly centered at the dart point, and then stitch around the edges of the square.

Attaching the Interfacing to the Garment Front

After the interfacing has been prepared, it is attached to the garment front. The method will depend upon whether the interfacing has been edged with a shaped muslin edging or with tape.

    If the interfacing has been edged with muslin, attach it as follows:

    1. Place the interfacing on the wrong side of the outer fabric with the neck, shoulder, armhole, and front edges even. Pin.

2. Cut off the corners of the interfacing just enough to prevent their being caught in the stitching at the points where seams cross.

3. Machine-stitch the interfacing to the outer fabric: Stitch it directionally $\frac{1}{8}$ inch outside the seam line on the neck, shoulder, armhole, and side seam edges; stitch it exactly on the seam line on the front edge. On the edged portion of the interfacing the stitching will be on the edging.

If the interfacing has been edged with tape, attach it as follows:

1. Place the interfacing on the wrong side of the outer fabric with the neck, shoulder, and armhole edges even.

2. Cut off the corners of the interfacing just inside the seam lines.

3. Machine-stitch the interfacing to the outer fabric directionally, $\frac{1}{8}$ inch outside the seam line, on the neck, shoulder, armhole, and side seam edges.

4. Attach the tape to the outer fabric along the front fold line with hand stitches that are invisible on the right side. Make sure that the stitches catch the tape but not the interfacing fabric.

Interfacing the Back of Tailored Garments

To prepare the back unit of the interfacing for attachment, first stitch the center-back seam if one is planned. This seam is usually stitched identically to the center-back seam in the garment outer fabric but omitting any topstitching. Follow the directions given in your pattern guide sheet.

The next step is to make the shoulder darts. These darts are made differently from those in the back of the outer fabric because they are not stitched. Their construction procedure is as follows:

1. Slash the dart marking line that is the more nearly on grain.

2. Overlap the cut edges, bringing one edge to the other marking line.

3. Anchor the dart in position with a

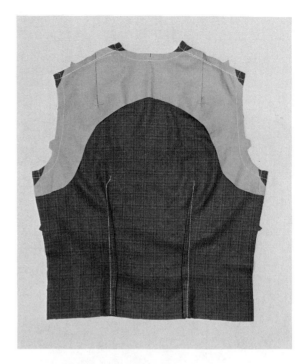

To attach interfacing to the back section of a tailored garment, cut the darts on one of the stitching lines, slide one dart stitching line over the other, and stitch the darts along the upper seam lines. Clip corners from the interfacing and stitch it directionally to the garment piece.

row of machine basting along the shoulder edge on the seam line. Do not stitch the dart itself.

Upon completion of the darts, cut off the corners of the interfacing just inside the seam allowance. Pin the interfacing to the garment back along the neckline, shoulders, armholes, and underarm areas. Machine-stitch the interfacing to the outer fabric directionally, placing the stitching $\frac{1}{8}$ inch outside the seam line.

Special Shaping Procedures

Like all other garments, a tailored garment is made by machine-stitching the seams together. First the pockets and, if used, the bound buttonholes are made. Then the outer garment

Facings are joined to each other and stitched to an interfaced garment. After seams are graded and clipped, the facing is turned to the inside of the garment, pressed, and tacked in a few places.

After the hem is completed in a tailored garment, the edge of the facing is firmly attached to the hem and closed with hand stitching along the lower edge.

is stitched as one section, with its interfacings included. Facings are made and attached. Next the lining is constructed as three separate sections: body section and two sleeve sections. Interlining, if used, is usually stitched as one with the lining. Finally, each section of the lining is attached to the garment, completing an assembled single garment.

In addition to stitching, however, the process of tailoring includes shaping during the construction. The shaping established by tailoring should be accurate and permanent. A person who wishes to tailor effectively must therefore master the basic techniques of shaping. Those most frequently required include pressing and blocking (see Chapter 15) and fitting (see Chapter 17). They also include establishing of the roll line and pad stitching, which are described in Chapter 28.

Facing Tailored Garments

The procedure for preparing and applying the facings for tailored garments is similar to that used in facing other garments as described in Chapter 22 (see pages 441-448). It varies mainly in the amount and placement of tacking after the facings have been attached to the garment and finished along the seams. This tacking is the hand stitching that joins two layers of fabric at intervals. Tailored facings need to be tacked only in a few places because the lining partially holds them in position. The placement of the tacking depends on the location of the facing in the garment and the length and width of the facing. The back neckline facing may be anchored to the garment in one of two ways. Either tack it at the shoulder seams and at any other intersecting seam line, or attach the facing seam allowances to the garment seam allowances with running stitches. On a short lined garment, the front facing is attached to the garment only along that portion of the facing which overlaps the garment hem and along the lower fold of the completed hem. (The hemming of tailored garments is discussed on pages 505-507.) Finish the portion of the front facing edge which overlaps the garment hem in either of the following ways:

1. Stitch two or three closely spaced rows of regular machine stitching, placing the first row a scant ¼ inch from the edge of the end of the hem. Trim the edge of the turned-up portion of the hem close to the line of stitching.

2. The alternative method is to trim the edge of the turned-up portion of the hem to ¼ inch before stitching and then to place zizag stitching over the edge of the facing.

Whip-stitch the finished edge of the front facing to the completed garment hem from the fold to the top edge and back again so as to form cross stitches. Take care not to penetrate the right side of the outer fabric. Then fasten the facing to the interfacing with hand running stitches along the lower fold in the hem. If the garment is full length, attach the full length of the front facing to the interfacing with running stitches. (The whip stitch and running stitch are described on page 395.)

If the garment front contains buttonholes, they are finished after the front facing has been attached. The procedure for tailoring buttonholes is given in Chapter 27. To finish them, follow these directions:

1. Pin the facing to hold it in position against the garment.

2. Mark the center line of the buttonhole on the facing by inserting pins from the right side of the garment at the ends of the buttonholes.

3. Slash the buttonhole opening through the facing between the pins on the grain of the fabric.

4. Turn in the raw edges of the facing, tapering at each end of the buttonhole so that the opening in the facing layer forms an ellipse around the inside of the bound buttonhole.

5. Hand-stitch the folded edge of the facing to the binding all around the buttonhole (see illustration above).

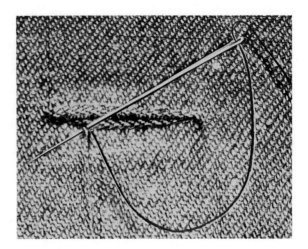

To complete their application, bound buttonholes are cut through the facing and the facing is turned under and hand-stitched to the buttonhole binding.

The completed facing may then be pressed. Underpress it on the facing side, and lightly top-press it on the outside of the garment, using a pressing cloth.

Further information on the attachment of facings to specific areas of tailored garments is given in the discussions of collars and sleeves (see pages 531-532 and 539-540).

Hemming Tailored Garments

Before a tailored garment is hemmed, the buttonholes, pockets, collar, and sleeves are completed and attached to the garment. Because these features vary from garment to garment and involve rather intricate tailoring techniques, they are discussed separately in the following chapters. Hems, however, apply to all garments and are therefore included here with other general tailoring techniques. They differ from regular hems in that they are cushioned to prevent a noticeable ridge on the outside of the finished garment.

Preparing the Hem

After the garment length has been determined and the hem width adjusted (see pages 374-

Before hemming a garment, trim away the interfacing below the hem fold line, trim ½ inch from the lower edge of the facing, and grade the seams in the fold of the hem.

378), the hem area of a tailored garment is trimmed to prevent bulk as follows:

1. Cut off the lower edge of the interfacing at the hem fold line.

2. Trim off ½ inch from the lower edge of the facing.

3. On only the turned-up portion of the hem, trim to ¼ inch the seam allowances of all seams that intersect the hem.

4. On the garment side of the hem, cut off the corners of these seam allowances at the fold line. This will prevent bulging of the hem at vertical seam lines.

Turn and block the hem with the front-edge facings turned out away from the garment and with the front-edge interfacings lying flat on the garment (see "Blocking a Hem," page 318).

Cushioning the Hem

A bias muslin strip is stitched inside the hem of a tailored garment to cushion the upper edge of the hem and prevent it from showing on the outside of the garment. Cut the cushioning strip from preshrunk muslin, or other lightweight but firmly woven fabric. It should be ½ inch wider than the hem and of a length equal to the entire length of the hem.

To prepare the cushioning strip, lay it on top of the hem, lapping one end of it over the side edge of the front interfacing ½ inch. With the strip located on top of the hem, block it to fit the garment hem by steam pressing. Lap the strip over the interfacing ½ inch at the other end of the garment hem, and trim off any excess stripping.

Insert the cushioning strip in the hem while the garment is still on the pressing board. The upper edge should extend ½ inch beyond the cut edge of the hem, and the lower edge should extend exactly to the hem fold but not beyond it. Pin as necessary. From the garment side, attach by hand the ends of the strip to the front interfacings with running stitches. Then machine-stitch the strip to the upper hem edge ¼ inch from the cut edge, easing the garment fabric to the muslin. Re-press the upper edge of the hem.

Finishing the Hem

Finish the hem with the front facings opened out. To do this, pin the hem in position, and attach it to the garment with the pick stitch or another suitable hand-hemming stitch (see pages 392-395). The facings may then be tacked in place (see pages 504-505).

Make a bias cushioning strip which is slightly wider than the finished hem and block it to the exact shape of the lower garment edge.

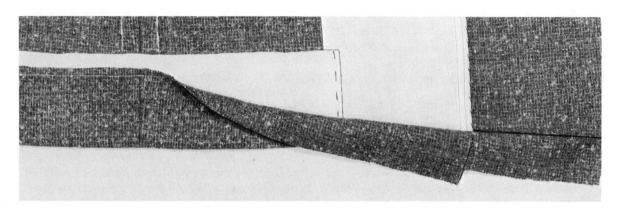

Insert the cushioning strip within the hem, fasten it to the edge of the interfacing, and machine-stitch it to the upper edge of the hem.

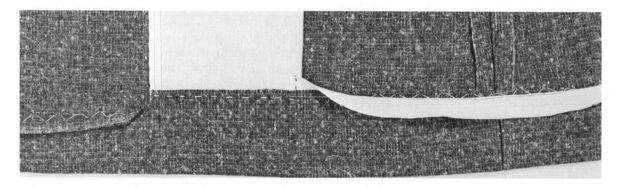

Use a pick stitch to hand-fasten the hem to the garment.

Interlining Tailored Garments

Tailored garments are sometimes interlined for additional warmth. The interlining is cut identically to the garment lining except in the length of the garment body and sleeves.

The most commonly used method of attaching interlining is to stitch the interlining and the lining as one. When this method is used, seams of the interlining can be trimmed away to remove bulkiness before the lining seams are pressed. The outer edges of the two layers of the garment can be stitched together directionally. After the interlining seam allowance has been trimmed away, the two layers of fabric are pressed and attached to the garment as a single unit.

An alternative method of interlining is to stitch the interlining as one with the outer fabric. This method is seldom used, however, because it adds bulk to the outer seams of the garment. It also entails the additional step of fastening the interlining in place around facing edges of the garment.

Lining Tailored Garments

Generally the lining is constructed as described in Chapter 25 (see pages 479-482). In a tailored garment, however, the sleeve linings are usually not attached to the rest of the lining until after they have been stitched into the sleeves, as described in Chapter 28 (see pages 542-545). Although sleeve linings can be attached to the garment lining during their construction, it is difficult to achieve a professional look in a garment lined in this way.

Certain sleeve linings, such as those in kimono sleeves, which are cut in one piece with the garment, are necessarily assembled as one with the garment lining. Linings for other garments which have armhole seams can be lined more effectively if left sleeveless until after the sleeve lining has been attached to the sleeve and the sleeve is set into the garment.

The completed lining is most frequently attached to a tailored garment by hand. Allowance for the pliability of the garment fabric is made by carefully positioning and easing the lining to the faced garment as the two are joined.

Attaching the Lining to the Garment

The attachment procedure is as follows:

1. Place the lining on the left front facing, right sides together, matching edges, notches, and shoulder seams. The lower edge of the lining should extend about ½ inch beyond the fold line of the garment hem. Pin the left edge of the lining in place, with the lining folded back over the left facing, distributing the ease evenly along the entire length. Machine-stitch or hand-sew the lining to the facing along the seam line. Use small, loose running stitches and ease the lining to the garment so that the lining looks full. Begin the stitching at the shoulder seam, and end it about 1½ inches above the top of the hem. Secure it at both ends.

2. The lining seams are attached to the vertical garment seams in the following order: (a) left side seam, (b) center-back seam, and (c) right side seam. Complete the attachment of each seam before proceeding to the next one. It is not necessary to attach side-front or side-back seams. Match the lining seam and the garment seam accurately, easing the lining to the garment and distributing the ease evenly. The lining should extend ½ inch beyond the fold line of the hem at each seam, just as at the left front edge. Hand-sew the lining and garment seam allowances together with ¼ inch, loose running stitches on each seam line. On the side seams, begin the stitching 1½ inches from the underarm seams, and end it 1½ inches above the garment hem. On the center-back seam, begin the stitching at the waistline. Secure each row of hand stitching at both ends.

3. Pin and machine-stitch or hand-sew the right edge of the lining to the inner edge of the right front facing as on the left front

facing. An alternative method is to turn in the seam allowance of the lining and pin it in place against the facing. Then attach the lining to the facing with slip stitching (see pages 392-393).

4. Pin the front lining to the shoulders in one of the following ways: (a) If no shoulder pad is used, key the shoulder seam line of the lining to the shoulder seam line of the coat. (b) If shoulder pads are used, attach them in place by hand stitching them to the back shoulder seam allowance and to the upper armhole seam. Then, along the shoulder seam lines on the right side of the garment, insert pins all the way through the outer fabric and the shoulder pads. On the inside of the garment, key the shoulder seam line of the lining to the line of pins. After the lining is pinned in place, hand-sew the seam allowance of the lining to the pad and in sections where there is no padding fasten the lining seam allowance to the garment shoulder seam allowance. Secure the stitching at both ends.

5. Fasten the lining to the back facing by attaching the neck edge of the lining to the lower edge of the back facing. To do this, turn under the lining at the neck edge along the seam line, clipping the curve up to the staystitching. Lap the lining over the back neck facing for the width of the seam allowance, keying the shoulder seams and the center back of the lining to the center back of the garment. Make sure that the planned 1/2-inch pleat remains intact at the lining center back. Pin the lining in place. Then whip-stitch or slip-stitch the lining to the facing with very small stitches placed close together, holding the lining toward you and working from right to left. Use heavy-duty thread or buttonhole twist if desired.

6. Attach the garment lining to the armholes, first clipping the seam allowance of the lining along the curve as far as the stayline. Turn under the armhole edge of the garment lining along the stayline. Lap the lining over the armhole seam for the width of the seam allowance, matching the notches, and keying

When lining a tailored garment, attach vertical seam allowances of the lining to vertical seam allowances of the garment wherever possible.

the underarm seams of the garment and the lining, and the top of the sleeve marking to the shoulder seam line of the garment. Pin the lining in place. Then whip-stitch the lining to the armhole, covering the armhole seam.

Hemming the Lining
There are two alternatives for finishing the lining hems in tailored garments. By one method, used for loose fitting coats and jackets, the hem of the outer fabric and the hem of the lining are first completed separately and later tacked together. By the alternative method, used for fitted jackets and coats, the lower edge of the lining is hand-stitched to the upper edge of the finished hem on the outer fabric.

509

Attach the curved neck edge of a garment lining by hand-stitching its turned edge to the lower edge of the back facing.

Hemming Method 1

When hemming the lining and the garment separately, select hemming techniques appropriate to each (see Chapter 19; also see "Hemming Tailored Garments," pages 505-507). Attach the lining hem to the lining with a suitable hand-hemming stitch. When both hems are completed, they are French-tacked together at the seams (see the upper illustration on page 511).

Hemming Method 2

Turn the lining under on the line of stay-stitching along the lower edge. Pin the folded edge of the lining along the upper edge of the garment hem. In doing this, the excess length of the lining will result in a fold over-hanging the lining hemline. The purpose of this excess length is to allow room for body movement without causing puckering of the seams. If the lining was cut the same length as the outer fabric and was eased correctly when it was attached, this fold will terminate slightly above the lower edge of the garment and will not show from the outside.

Pin or baste and then hand-stitch the lining in place. The slip stitch is effective because it is invisible on both the lining and garment side. Press the lining to shrink out the fullness and to flatten seam lines. Press the garment hem, and then press the fold in the lining down over the upper edge of the hem. Try on the garment to check that the lining does not extend below the garment.

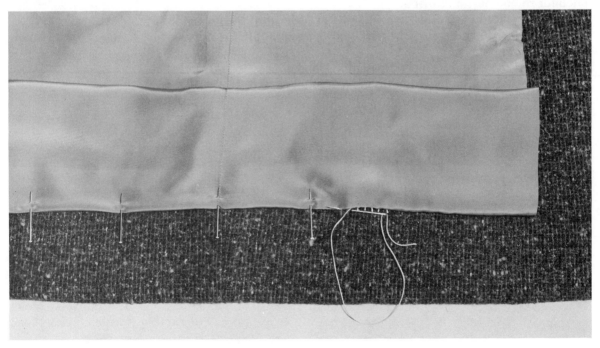

A lining can be hemmed with a separate hem (above) or it may be fastened to the garment hem with hand stitches (below). The separately hemmed lining may be fastened to the garment with French tacks.

1. Effective tailoring allows for flat pieces of pliable fabric to be molded smoothly to the contour of the body.

2. Considerable time and sewing skill are required for making a tailored garment.

3. In order to be suitable for a tailoring project, all layers of fabric must be easily pliable for shaping and must possess sufficient body for shape retention.

4. When outer fabric, interfacings, facings, interlinings, and linings are used in tailoring, companion sections are cut on identical grain lines for proper fit and for an attractive appearance.

5. In tailored garments, interfacing covers a larger section of the garment than in nontailored garments, and its front edges are treated and corners removed to reduce seam-line bulk.

6. Interfacing for the undercollar is cut with the center seam on the true bias to ensure proper shaping of the collar.

7. In tailored garments, facings are generally tacked in fewer places than in nontailored garments, because they are partially held in position by the lining.

8. Hems of tailored garments are specially trimmed and cushioned for smoothness and shape.

9. Linings for tailored garments which have armhole seams are more easily fitted into a garment if left sleeveless until after attachment to the garment.

10. In loose-fitting tailored garments, lining hems are hemmed separately from the garment hem and later French-tacked to the garment hem.

Tailoring Buttonholes and Pockets

Bound buttonholes and tailored pockets are the hallmarks of distinction
for most tailored garments. Well made, they add a look of quality and elegance.
Since they can add so much to a finished garment, the person who successfully
completes the intricate steps of their construction is usually pleased with
the results.

How are bound buttonholes made?

*How can the width of the binding strip for
bound buttonholes be constructed with
precision?*

*What button and buttonhole markings can be
provided which will serve adequately
throughout the tailoring process?*

*How can bound buttonholes be reinforced
when the garment interlining is extremely
heavy or stiff?*

*In what way are bound buttonholes finished
to provide an opening in the garment and
the garment facing?*

Decisions About Tailored
Buttonholes and Pockets

In general, several or many factors affect every
sewing decision. The decisions regarding
tailored buttonholes and pockets, however, are
relatively simple to make. Usually only two
major decisions are involved: Does my tailoring project require buttonholes and pockets?
Am I interested in the learning challenge and
willing to devote the time and effort required
to tailor them? By following through the steps

of the decision-making process, you will be
able to determine whether to tailor these details of the garment or to choose simpler sewing alternatives.

Procedure for Making
Bound Buttonholes

The strategic difference between bound
buttonholes and worked ones is that bound
buttonholes are tailored with a strip of fabric
covering the edges. This binding may be
applied in a flat, doubled strip or with cording enclosed.

If working with solid-colored fabric, plan
for bindings which are cut on the straight of
the grain. If, however, your project is made of
striped or plaid fabric, consider bias bindings.
They often add a dramatic effect to an otherwise simple garment. Whatever your choice,
the binding pieces of both the buttonholes and
pockets on the same garment should be cut on
identical grain.

To achieve a look of quality, accuracy
must be maintained throughout the making of
bound buttonholes. For uniformity in a series

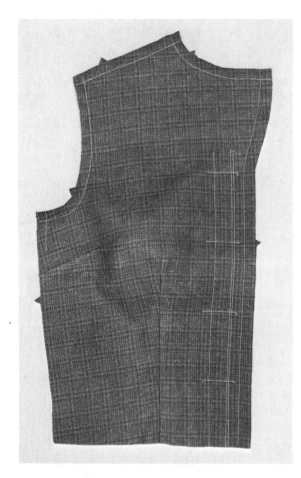

To prepare a garment for buttonholes, machine-baste the markings on the interfacing through to the outer fabric. Stitch accurately the center front or back and the two rows of buttonhole size markings. For the buttonhole location markings, stitch ¼ inch above the actual marks provided.

ing the binding strip, attaching the binding strip to the garment, making the openings for the buttonholes, stitching the ends of the buttonholes, and finishing the buttonholes. Before making buttonholes on a garment, make a test buttonhole on a scrap of the fabric from which the garment is made. As you follow the procedure, refer to the accompanying illustrations on this page through page 518.

Interfacing the Buttonhole Area

The area where bound buttonholes are located must be interfaced. Ordinarily the front edge of a garment is interfaced early in the tailoring process (see pages 500-503). This interfacing is usually adequate to support bound buttonholes. Occasionally the interfacing used in a tailored garment is too firm or bulky to be used in bound buttonhole areas. In this case, mark and trim out a rectangle of the interfacing slightly larger than the size of the buttonhole in each buttonhole area.

In place of the heavy interfacing, substitute in the area around the buttonhole a lighter type of preshrunk fabric such as muslin or organdy, or, where appropriate, a press-on interfacing. If woven interfacing is selected, hand-stitch it in place. If bondable interfacing is used, fit it into the rectangular spaces and bond it to the outer fabric, following the pressing instructions given on the interfacing backing paper. The pattern markings, such as buttonhole locations, contained on the removed interfacing rectangles must then be accurately transferred to the new rectangles by means of a tracing wheel and tracing paper. These procedures require care and accuracy for successful results.

Preparing the Garment for Buttonholes

Prepare the garment for buttonholes by transferring from the interfacing to the right side of the garment the pattern markings which have been traced on the interfacing for the center fronts, buttonholes, and buttons. To transfer these markings, machine-baste over the markings through both the interfacing and

of buttonholes, it is advisable to complete each step on all the buttonholes in the series before proceeding to the next step. It is also a good idea to make all the buttonholes in a garment during a single work period if possible. Make these buttonholes on an individual garment unit before it is attached to another unit.

The procedure for making bound buttonholes includes interfacing the buttonhole area, preparing the garment for buttonholes, prepar-

the outer fabric, using contrasting thread to stitch exactly on the grain of the fabric.

Check the size of the buttonhole marking by the actual button to make sure of the accuracy of the stitching line. The buttonhole length is usually the diameter of the button plus ⅛ inch. The outer end of the buttonhole marking extends ⅛ inch beyond the center-front line toward the edge of the garment. When the garment is closed, there should always be some space between the edge of the button and the edge of the garment to provide a background for the button. It is advisable to use buttons of the size planned by the designer.

Machine-baste the markings as indicated on the interfacing according to the following procedure:

1. Machine-baste the marking for the center front the full length of the garment.

2. Machine-baste the buttonhole size markings onto the buttonhole front of the garment. These are two parallel vertical rows of stitching: One is a continuous line connecting the buttonholes ⅛ inch toward the garment edge beyond the center front. The other connects the inner termination points of the series of buttonholes.

3. Machine-baste the location markings for the buttonholes by stitching horizontal lines ¼ inch *above* the pattern markings indicated on the interfacing. This relocation provides that the actual openings of the buttonholes will coincide with their original position on the pattern.

4. Transfer the location markings for the buttons to the outer fabric by machine-basting the markings shown on the interfacing. Stitch through both layers of fabric.

Preparing the Binding Strip

Prepare a binding strip in one piece for all the buttonholes. Cut the binding strip on the lengthwise grain of the fabric unless the decorative effect of a bias pattern is desired. Complete the binding strip according to the following procedure:

MAKING THE BINDING STRIP

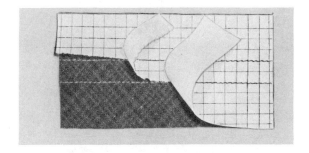

Stitch along marked paper to provide two straight rows of stitching on the binding strip.

Press a fold along each of the two stitching lines.

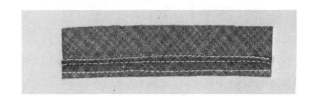

Insert a row of stitching ⅛ inch from each of the folded edges.

1. Cut or tear the binding strip 2½ inches wide, for a ⅛-inch binding, and twice the combined length of all the buttonholes.

2. Cut a 2½-inch-wide strip of paper of the same length as the binding strip. Use lined paper or mark on unlined paper lengthwise lines at ½-inch intervals. Place the paper on top of the binding strip, edges even, and machine-baste with contrasting thread on the two lines nearest the center of the paper for the full length of the strip. Then tear away the

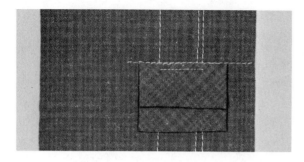

With the edges of the binding strip facing down, and the upper fold located along the buttonhole location mark, stitch it to the garment between the size lines ⅛ inch below the fold.

After turning up the raw edges of the binding strip, stitch ⅛ inch above the lower fold line of the binding strip exactly between the buttonhole size lines.

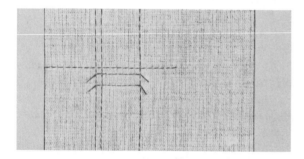

Before cutting the buttonhole, check the accuracy of all stitches and fasten the threads. Imperfect stitching can be removed and redone if necessary before the buttonhole is slashed.

paper. This leaves two stitching lines exactly ½ inch apart.

3. Fold the binding strip along each of the basted guidelines, wrong sides together, and press. Stitch ⅛ inch from each fold through the two layers of binding, letting the cut edges hang free.

Attaching the Binding Strip to the Garment

For each buttonhole, cut a section of stitched binding strip 1 inch longer than the planned buttonhole. This allows each end of the strip to extend ½ inch beyond each end of the buttonhole. If the fabric ravels, make the strip 1½ inches longer than the buttonhole. Attach the binding strip to the garment according to the following procedure:

1. Locate the binding strip on the right side of the garment. Place it *below* the buttonhole location marking. Position it with its shorter side on top, with the fold line exactly on the location marking line, with the cut edges down, and with the second basted fold line concealed. The ends of the section should extend ½ inch beyond each of the buttonhole-size marking lines.

2. Stitch the binding section to the garment between the size lines ⅛ inch below the fold lying along the location line. Use a very short machine stitch (size 30). Stitch exactly from end to end of the planned buttonhole, inserting the stitches through the two layers of binding, the outer layer of garment fabric, and the interfacing. Secure the thread firmly at the beginning and end of the stitching.

3. Turn up the raw edges of the binding strip over the fold that has been stitched. Stitch ⅛ inch from the second fold line between the buttonhole size lines.

4. Check the accuracy of the stitching before proceeding further, and make any corrections that may be needed. In order to check the accuracy to this point, consider the following questions in relation to the quality of the buttonholes:

a. Are the lines of stitching straight and exactly parallel?

b. Is the distance between the two lines of stitching equal to exactly twice the width of the binding strip from the stitched line to the fold?

c. Does the stitching end exactly on the size lines at each end of the buttonholes?

d. Have all threads been secured?

e. Does the binding strip extend ½ inch beyond each end of the buttonhole?

5. Repeat steps 1-4 for each buttonhole in the series.

Making the Openings for the Buttonholes

Make the openings for the buttonholes with extreme care, as inaccurate cutting can ruin a garment. To make each opening, slash the binding strip through the center between the lines of stitching. The strip will then be in two pieces with a ⅛-inch seam allowance on each side of the slash.

From the wrong side of the garment, cut the buttonhole through the interfacing and the outer fabric, using the point of sharp scissors. Clip midway between the parallel lines of stitching to within ⅜ inch of the buttonhole size lines. Then cut diagonally to the corners, leaving a triangle at each end of the buttonhole. Avoid cutting the edges of the binding.

Fold the bindings through the buttonhole to the inside of the garment. Pull the ends of the bindings gently to square the corners. The lines of machine basting should meet exactly in the center of the buttonhole.

The procedure is repeated for each buttonhole in the series.

Stitching the Ends of the Buttonholes

The ends of each bound buttonhole are stitched to hold the binding in place as follows:

1. Press the buttonhole and remove the basting. While pressing, turn back the triangle at each end of the buttonhole, forming a straight fold on the lengthwise grain of the outer fabric.

OPENING A BOUND BUTTONHOLE

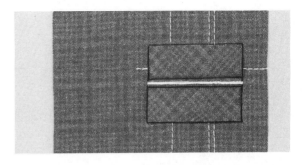

With sharp scissors, cut apart the two sections of the binding strip on the right side of the garment. Exercise care to avoid cutting the fabric of the garment.

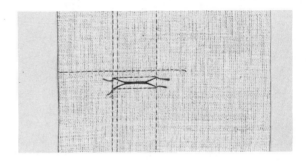

From the wrong side of the garment, cut the buttonhole through the interfacing and outer fabric, forming long triangles by cutting from the center into each corner.

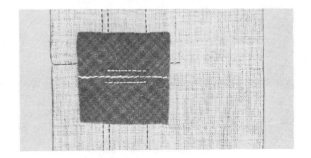

Fold the binding strip through to the wrong side of the garment. Pull the ends of the binding gently to square all corners in preparation for final machine stitching of the buttonhole area.

COMPLETING A BOUND BUTTONHOLE

Stitch each triangular end of the binding fast against the binding strip below it.

Press the buttonhole carefully.

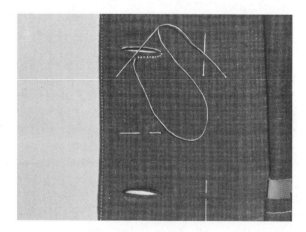

When the garment is completed, hand-finish the slit in the facing fast against the buttonhole.

2. Place the garment front containing the buttonholes on the machine right side up. Fold back the edge of the garment on the grain to reveal the triangle at one end of the binding strip.

3. Stitch the triangle to the strip with a shortened stitch to fasten it securely. Insert the first line of stitching on the straight of the grain precisely across the end of the buttonhole. Other rows can crisscross over the rest of the triangle.

4. Repeat steps 2 and 3 to finish the other end of the buttonhole.

5. Repeat steps 1-4 for each buttonhole in the series. Carefully underpress and toppress the completed buttonhole section.

Finishing the Buttonholes

After the buttonholes have been constructed as described in the preceding sections, the final steps in their completion are postponed until after the front facing has been stitched in place. The final steps, including the slashing of the buttonholes through the facing layer and the attachment of the facing to the binding, are described in Chapter 26 in the discussion of facing tailored garments (see page 505).

How are bound pockets made?

How are bound pockets similar to and different from bound buttonholes?

How can bound-pocket markings be made which last through the tailoring process?

Why is a reinforcing strip used in the tailoring of a bound pocket?

How can the depth of a bound pocket be varied in the tailoring process?

Procedure for Making a Bound Pocket

Bound pockets are an inconspicuous, flat tailored type of pocket especially well suited to jackets, coats, and tailored skirts. A bound pocket has the finished appearance of a large, bound buttonhole. This is not surprising be-

Courtesy Simplicity Pattern Co., Inc.

cause the procedures for making them are quite similar.

As in bound buttonholes, the many steps in making bound pockets require accuracy and precision. Procedures for completing this advanced tailoring technique include cutting the pocket, preparing the garment for the pocket, attaching the pocket to the garment, making the opening for the pocket, binding the pocket opening, topstitching the pocket opening, and finishing the pocket.

Cutting the Pocket

A bound pocket consists of the binding and pocket cut in one piece and a reinforcing strip. The pocket piece is cut from the garment outer fabric and may be cut on a true bias or on the straight of the fabric, but the grain line must be the same as in the binding of the buttonholes. Cut the pocket piece 1 inch wider than the pocket opening and twice the desired depth of the finished pocket. Allow an additional 2 inches in the pocket's length for seam allowances and binding. On heavy fabric allow 3 inches.

Cut the reinforcing strip for the pocket opening of sturdy, preshrunk muslin. To prevent stretching of the pocket opening, cut the reinforcing strip on the lengthwise grain of the fabric 1½ inches wide and 2 inches longer than the planned pocket opening.

Preparing the Garment for the Pocket

Preparation of the garment for the application of the bound pocket includes marking the garment where the bound pocket is to be inserted and reinforcing the pocket opening with the reinforcing strip. To complete the marking, machine-baste from the wrong side of the fabric along tracing marks or between tailor's tacks to transfer the pattern markings to the outside of the fabric. Use thread of contrasting color, and keep the stitching on the grain of the fabric. A horizontal line shows the *location* of the pocket. The *size* of the pocket is indicated by termination lines stitched ver-

PREPARATIONS FOR A BOUND POCKET

Stitch with contrasting thread to transfer location and size marks from the wrong to the right side of the garment.

Press a center lengthwise crease in the reinforcing strip.

Pin the reinforcing strip to the wrong side of the garment. Stitch along the location marking line from the garment right side.

tically across the ends of the intended pocket opening.

Reinforce the pocket opening in the following series of steps:

1. Fold the reinforcing strip in half lengthwise and make a crease along the fold line.

2. Place the strip on the *wrong* side of the garment, positioning it with the crease precisely aligned with the location marking line and with each end extending 1 inch beyond the size marking line.

3. Pin the strip in place and machine-baste it to the garment from the right side along the location marking line.

Attaching the Pocket to the Garment

Attach the pocket to the garment from the right side in the following series of steps:

1. Turn a 1-inch fold to the wrong side of one end of the pocket, and press along the fold line. On heavy fabric make the fold 1½ inches wide.

2. Place the pocket, turned end up, on the *right* side of the garment *below* the location marking line, with the crease precisely aligned with the location line. The side edges of the pocket should extend ½ inch beyond the size lines.

3. Unfold the creased pocket piece, and pin it along the marking line. Insert the pins at least ⅜ inch from the fold line on both sides of it.

4. Stitch the pocket in place from the inside of the garment. Start the machine stitching at the center of the pocket and ⅛ inch above the location marking line. On very thick fabrics a wider binding can be planned. Stitch a continuous line around the location marking, maintaining a distance of ⅛ inch above and below the marking line, and across the ends directly on the size lines, shortening the stitch at the corners for reinforcement. Be sure the corners are exactly square. (For a discussion of stitching corners, see pages 400-401.) Overstitch for about 1 inch beyond the starting point to secure the stitching.

Making the Opening for the Pocket

Cut the pocket opening from the right side of the garment by slashing through the pocket piece, the garment, and the reinforcing strip midway between the long lines of stitching to a point ½ inch from each end. Then cut diagonally to each of the four corners. This will leave a triangle of fabric at each end of the pocket opening. Turn the pocket piece to the

ATTACHING THE POCKET TO THE GARMENT

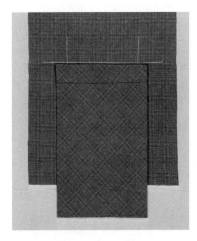

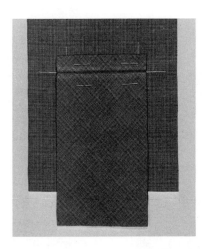

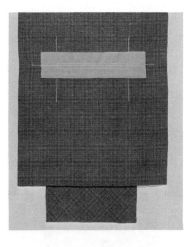

After pressing a 1-inch fold in one end of the pocket, position the folded end of the pocket along the garment location line, right sides together.

Unfold the crease in the pocket section, and with the crease exactly on the pocket location line, pin a safe distance away from the stitching line.

From the inside of the garment, stitch around the pocket opening, making a rectangle ¼ inch wide by stitching ⅛ inch above and below the location line.

OPENING AND BINDING A BOUND POCKET

Cut the pocket opening from the right side of the garment by slashing midway between the lines of stitching and into the corners to produce triangles.

Turn the pocket piece to the inside of the garment through the slashed opening and pull gently at the pocket ends to square the corners.

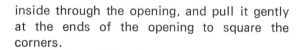

With the pocket opened out flat, stitch along the ridge formed by the seam joining the binding to the lower edge of the pocket. Check the accuracy of the stitching.

After folding the pocket piece in half (above), stitch from the outside upward along one pocket end, then along the seam ridge of the upper pocket binding, and down across the other pocket end.

inside through the opening, and pull it gently at the ends of the opening to square the corners.

Binding the Pocket Opening

Bind the pocket opening by making a fold in the pocket piece on each edge of the pocket opening, turning the pocket back over the seam allowances to form a 1/8-inch-wide binding. This binding width may vary, depending on the distance between the lines of stitching. From the pocket side, press the seams of the opening toward the slash on both edges. The folds meet in the center of the slash and form an unstitched binding of the slash with small

inverted pleats on the inside at the ends of the opening.

Topstitching the Pocket Opening

Topstitch the pocket opening to hold the binding and the pocket in position. Accurate stitching will be inconspicuous on the right side of the pocket. The topstitching procedure is as follows:

1. Topstitch the binding to the garment along the *lower edge* of the opening on the seam line. During this stitching the pocket should be opened out flat and the folds of the binding should meet precisely at the center of the pocket opening.

*Stitch the sides of the pocket section together
from the top of the pocket section to the folded
lower edge.*

*Press the finished pocket (above) first by underpressing
and then by top-pressing, protecting the garment
with a pressing cloth.*

    2. Turn the lower end of the pocket up,
and pin it in position on the inside of the garment, exactly matching it to the upper pocket
edge. The folds that form the binding meet
in the center of the opening. Pin far enough
from the line of stitching to avoid stitching
difficulties.

    3. Topstitch the upper binding to the
garment from the outside along the upper
edge and the ends of the opening. Apply the
stitching in a continuous line along the ridge
of the seam line on the upper binding and
across the ends of the pocket. Stitch through
the garment, the reinforcement strip, and both
layers of the pocket.

Finishing the Pocket

If the garment fabric is medium-weight or
lighter, finish the pocket by stitching the two
side seams of the pocket. Each of these seams
extends from the top of the pocket, where
the edge of the lower section meets the upper one, down to the fold line, where the
pocket ends. Make each side seam ½ inch
wide.

    If the garment fabric is heavy or bulky,
cut off the lower part of the pocket 1½
inches below the pocket opening and replace
it with suitable lining fabric. Join the lining to
the outer fabric with a ½-inch seam, stitched
so that the seam allowances are on the out-

side of the pocket. Press the seam open. Then stitch the two side seams of the pocket for the entire length.

Press the pocket as a final finishing technique. First underpress from the inside of the garment, and remove any remaining basting threads. Then top-press slightly from the outside of the garment, using a pressing cloth.

How are welt pockets made?
What are the similarities and differences between welt and bound pockets?
How can welt-pocket markings be provided which will last through the tailoring process?
How can the seam width of the welt area be predetermined?
How can the length of the upper pocket be determined?
When are the upper and lower sections of a welt pocket joined?

Procedure for Making a Welt Pocket

The major difference between a bound pocket and a welt pocket is that a bound pocket features a binding along the upper and lower pocket edge whereas a welt pocket features a stitched-in extension, or wide binding, usually located at the lower edge of the pocket opening. Welt pockets are frequently featured in designer quality coats and suit jackets and sometimes in skirts and dresses.

A welt pocket includes four parts: two pocket pieces, a reinforcing strip, and the welt, which is the extension piece. The style desired and the outer fabric used for the garment determine what fabrics are best for each part. The perfection of each step depends upon the precision with which all preceding steps have been completed. Properly made welt pockets require precision in all construction techniques. The steps in this tailoring process include cutting and preparing the welt and pocket pieces, attaching the welt and the pocket pieces to the garment, making the pocket opening, and finishing the pocket.

Cutting the Welt and Pocket Pieces

The welt may be cut from the garment fabric or a contrasting fabric. Cut it on the lengthwise grain of the fabric unless the decorative effect of a bias or crosswise cut is desired. The width of the welt may be varied according to individual preference, the garment being made, or the fabric that is used. Regardless of the width selected, cut the piece for the welt 1 inch longer than the pocket opening and twice as wide as the finished welt, allowing also for a seam allowance $\frac{1}{2}$ the width of the welt along each edge of the opening. For a finished welt $\frac{1}{2}$ inch wide, for example, this would mean cutting a strip $1\frac{1}{2}$ inches wide: 1 inch for the folded welt, and $\frac{1}{2}$ inch for the two $\frac{1}{4}$-inch seam allowances.

Both pocket pieces may be cut from the garment fabric, or the lower pocket section may be cut from a lighter-weight fabric. If you wish, you may change the depth and shape of the pocket pieces from the pattern specifications. The width, however, should always exceed the width of the pocket marking by 2 inches. The length of the upper pocket section must be cut longer than the lower pocket section by $1\frac{1}{2}$ times the width of the welt in order for their lower edges to hang evenly. For example, the upper section of a pocket with a $\frac{1}{2}$-inch-wide welt is cut $\frac{3}{4}$ inch longer than is the lower pocket section.

The reinforcing strip for the pocket opening may be cut from preshrunk lightweight muslin or another preshrunk cotton fabric of similar weight. To prevent stretching the pocket opening, cut the strip on the lengthwise grain of the fabric and make it $1\frac{1}{2}$ inches wide and 2 inches longer than the pocket opening.

Preparing the Garment for the Pocket

To prepare the garment for the pocket, first transfer the pattern markings for the pocket from the inside to the outside of the garment.

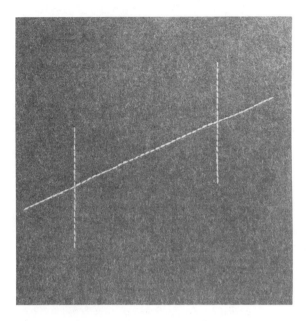

Machine-baste to transfer to the outside of the garment the location markings and the size markings which have been marked on the wrong side of the fabric.

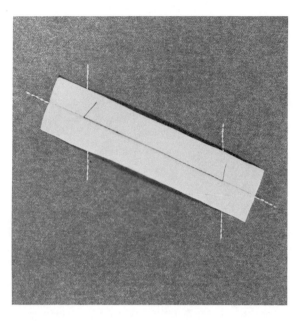

Press the reinforcing strip in half lengthwise, and, using the fold as a mark, machine-baste it to the wrong side of the garment on the location marking line.

To do so, machine-baste through the pocket *location* marking line and *size* marking lines, using thread of contrasting color. Stitch the *size*, or termination lines, on the grain of the fabric. Then reinforce the pocket opening according to the following steps:

1. Fold the reinforcing strip in half lengthwise, and press a crease along the fold.

2. Place the reinforcing strip on the wrong side of the garment, with the crease precisely aligned with the pocket *location* marking line and with each end extending ½ inch beyond each *size* marking line.

3. Machine-baste the reinforcing strip to the garment from the right side along the location marking line.

Preparing the Welt and Pocket Pieces
Fold the welt in half lengthwise, wrong sides together, and press it. If the welt has been

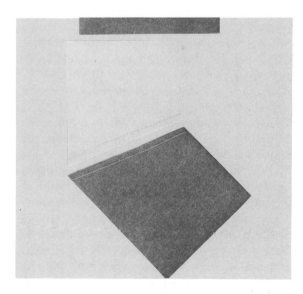

Press the welt in half lengthwise, wrong sides together, and staystitch the slanted top edge of both pocket sections.

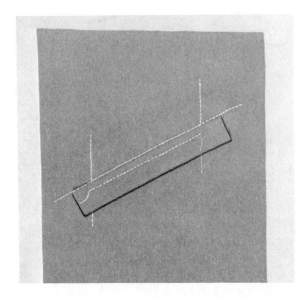

Position the folded welt with raw edges against the location marking line, on the garment outside. Baste it to the garment with a seam one-half the width of the finished welt.

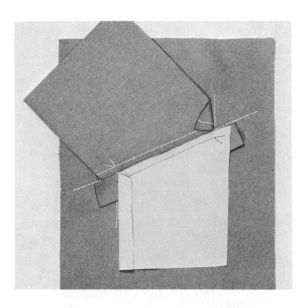

Stitch the small pocket section in place directly over the welt, and stitch the larger section in place directly above the location marking line with a seam allowance identical to that of the first.

cut on the bias, stitch the two sides together a scant ¼ inch from the cut edges. Staystitch the pocket pieces ¼ inch from the edges which will be attached to the opening.

Attaching the Welt and Pocket Pieces to the Garment

Place the welt on the right side of the garment below the location marking line, with its raw edges positioned exactly on the marking line. Pin or machine-baste the welt in place, allowing for a seam one-half the planned width of the finished welt (¼ inch on a ½-inch welt).

Place the pocket pieces on the outside of the garment. The shorter pocket section is placed directly over the welt with the garment and pocket right sides together and with the staystitched edge aligned with the raw edges of the welt along the location marking line. The longer pocket section is placed above the welt, again with the staystitched edge along

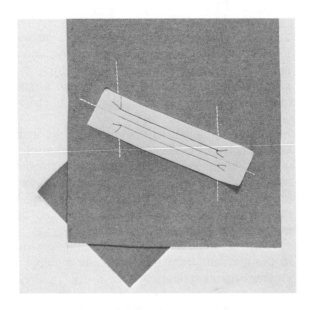

Check for accuracy of stitching on the wrong side of the garment. Fasten the threads when the stitching is acceptable.

Slash the pocket from the wrong side of the garment along the location marking line to about ½ inch from each end of the stitching. Slash diagonally to the end of the stitching to produce triangles.

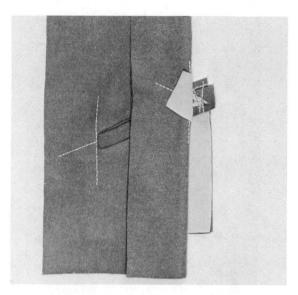

Turn the pocket sections through the garment to the wrong side so that the welt fills the pocket opening. Stitch the triangles against the welt and pocket sections.

the location marking line and with the pocket piece and garment right sides together.

Stitch the welt and the two pocket pieces to the garment with two rows of stitching equidistant from the location marking line and exactly the length of the marking line. Keep each seam perfectly even and one-half the width of the finished welt. If the finished welt is to be ½ inch wide, for example, locate the stitching lines ¼ inch above and ¼ inch below the marking line. Secure the stitching at both ends of each seam. The distance between the two lines of stitching must equal precisely the finished width of the welt.

Check the accuracy of the stitching at this point, while corrections can still be made. It may help to ask yourself the following questions:

1. Are the lines of stitching straight?
2. Does the stitching end exactly on the size line at each end of the pocket?

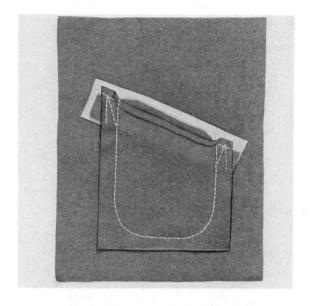

Join the two sections of the pocket together in a pleasing shape, stitching from one upper edge of the pocket area around to the opposite upper edge.

STANDARDS FOR BOUND POCKETS

1. *Placed and stitched accurately so that matching pockets are positioned identically.*
2. *Evenly bound on both edges.*
3. *Constructed with a suitable lining fabric replacing the lower section of the pocket if the garment fabric is heavy or bulky.*

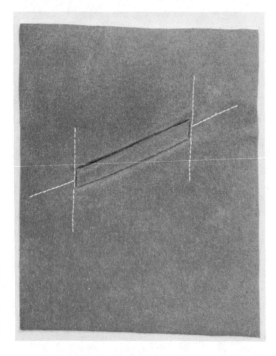

STANDARDS FOR WELT POCKETS

1. *Accurately located and shaped.*
2. *Sturdily reinforced to ensure shape retention.*
3. *Stitched with seams exactly half the width of the welt joining the pocket sections, welt, and garment.*
4. *Sewn with small, accurately positioned stitches.*
5. *Securely machine-stitched at the ends before the pocket sections are joined.*

3. Are the two lines of stitching parallel?

4. Is the distance between the two lines of stitching precisely equal to the width of the finished welt?

5. Are the threads secure at the ends of the lines of stitching?

Making the Pocket Opening

From the wrong side of the garment, cut the pocket opening along the location marking line to a point ½ inch from each end. Then cut diagonally to the ends of the lines of stitching, being careful not to cut the seam allowances of the pocket pieces. A small triangle of fabric will be left at each end of the pocket opening.

Turn the pocket pieces and the ends of the welt through the opening to the wrong side of the garment. The two pocket pieces will lie flat below the opening with right sides together and edges even. The welt will fill the pocket opening exactly. The folded edge of the welt will align with the upper seam line of the pocket.

Press the pocket opening as follows: Underpress the seam at the top of the pocket open. Press the seam at the lower edge of the pocket opening, with the raw edges of the seam allowance turned down and with the welt turned up. Press the small triangles back over the ends of the pocket, positioning the fold lines on the fabric grain line and precisely at the ends of the seam lines.

Finishing the Pocket

The ends of the pocket opening must be stitched to reinforce the opening and hold the pocket in correct position. Complete this technique in the following four steps:

1. Place the garment on the machine right side up.

2. Fold back the garment fabric and the reinforcing strip at one end of the pocket opening, folding on the grain of the fabric.

3. Stitch back and forth with a small stitch through the triangle, welt, and both pocket pieces. The first line of stitching should be exactly on grain and exactly at the end of the pocket opening. Other rows can crisscross over the rest of the triangle. Keep the pocket pieces together, flat, and with edges even during the stitching.

4. Repeat this stitching procedure on the underside of the other end of the pocket.

To complete the welt pocket, stitch the two sections of the pocket together according to the following three-step procedure:

1. Place the garment on the machine with the pocket side down and the rest of the garment folded out of the way.

2. Stitch the pocket edges together, beginning at the upper-right-hand corner and proceeding around the pocket to the upper-left-hand corner. Shape the pocket by stitching along a predetermined stitching pattern.

3. Press the completed pocket when the front unit of the garment is pressed.

1. The tailoring of buttonholes requires the ultimate degree of precision in marking, stitching, and cutting.

2. In transferring the pattern markings for buttonholes from the interfacing to the outer fabric, the location markings are positioned ¼ inch *above* the location marking lines.

3. A buttonhole binding strip is cut on the straight of the fabric unless the special effect of bias-cut plaid or striped binding is desired.

4. In preparing binding strips for bound buttonholes, accuracy is achieved by using grain-perfect fabric, cutting and marking with precision, and stitching through guidelines marked on paper.

5. Tailored buttonholes are reinforced at the corners by stitching the triangle at each end, first on the straight grain of the fabric and then diagonally.

6. The final step in making bound buttonholes consists of slashing the buttonholes through the completed facing and hand-fastening these slits to the buttonhole facing.

7. In a well-tailored garment the grain line of a bound pocket is identical with the grain line of the accompanying bound buttonholes.

8. When a bound pocket is made in a garment of heavy fabric, the lower section of the pocket may be cut off and replaced with a suitable lining fabric to reduce bulk.

9. The welt for a welt pocket is cut on the lengthwise grain unless the decorative effect of a bias or crosswise pattern is preferred.

10. When the welt and the pocket sections are stitched to the garment, accuracy requires that the seam width on both the upper and lower sections be exactly half the width of the finished welt.

11. To provide sturdiness in a welt pocket, the triangles at the ends of the pocket opening are stitched to the ends of the welt before the pocket sections are joined.

28 Tailoring Collars and Sleeves

The tailoring of collars and the tailoring of sleeves are actually two distinct sewing processes. However, since one closely follows the other as tasks to be accomplished in the tailoring process, they are considered together in this chapter for convenience.

In what ways do the procedures for tailoring a collar differ from those for making a regular collar?

What are the alternative methods for pad-stitching a tailored collar?

What are the advantages of machine–pad-stitching a tailored collar? Hand–pad-stitching?

What is the collar stand? The collar fall? The roll line?

Decisions About Tailored Collars and Sleeves

Collars and sleeves involve essentially the same decisions in tailored garments as in basic garments. They may be added to or omitted from a particular garment, they may incorporate creative fabric combinations, they may be varied in style, and they may be attractively correlated with sleeve cuffs matching the collar. Perhaps, however, creative variation is slightly more limited in a tailored garment than in a simple garment. Tailoring is a time-consuming and difficult art. Decisions in the area of collar and sleeve choice must be tempered by your own ability to make successful adaptations of ideas in a difficult project which is apt to be rather expensive.

Tailoring a Collar

Tailoring a collar is different from any other sewing process. This difference lies in the fact that the interfacing is first attached to the undercollar, producing a double under-layer, which is shaped by stitching and blocking before the outer layer, or upper collar, is attached. The interfaced undercollar is attached to the neckline of the outer garment. The upper collar is joined to the garment facings. Then any remaining unfinished edges and the ends of the collar and the upper edges of the lapels are stitched. In such a procedure the back neck facing is usually attached only to the upper collar. It may be hand-stitched to the neckline seam as a final finish to ensure sturdiness.

Applying Interfacing to the Undercollar

The interfacing is applied to the undercollar by machine stitching. Check to see that the grain of the interfacing and the undercollar fabric is identical. Ideally both units are cut with a center-back seam line on the true bias of the fabric. (See "Cutting the Outer Fabric" and "Cutting the Interfacing," pages 496-499.) If the pad stitching is to be done by machine, mark a stitching pattern on the interfacing with continuous lines from one end of the collar to the other, across the center seam line but not beyond the seam lines on the outer edges. Follow both the lengthwise and crosswise grain of the fabric.

Attach the interfacing to the undercollar as follows:

1. Key the interfacing to the undercollar for each half of the collar, with the marked sides out. Trim off the points of the interfacing corners slightly inside the seam line to prevent their being caught in the intersections of the stitching lines.

2. Machine-stitch the interfacing directionally to each half of the undercollar. On the outer edge and on the ends, stitch ⅛ inch wider than the seam allowance, so that the stitching will show on the right side of the undercollar when the collar is finished. On the neck and center-back edges, stitch ⅛ inch *outside* the seam line.

3. If the undercollar is to be pad-stitched with machine stitching, trim the interfacing close to the seam line along the outer edge and the ends. Do not trim along the neck edge or the center-back seam line. If the undercollar is to be hand–pad-stitched, leave the interfacing seams to be trimmed after the pad stitching has been completed.

4. Join the two sections of the undercollar at the center back in the following series of steps:

a. Stitch the seam through the four thicknesses of fabric.

b. Trim the center-back seam allowance of the interfacing close to the seam stitching.

c. Press the seam open.

d. Trim the seam allowance of the outer fabric to ¼ inch at the center-back seam.

5. Topstitch the center-back seam line from the neck edge to the stayline at the outer

edge. Turn and stitch two or three stitches across the center seam line and then back to the neck edge.

Establishing the Roll Line

Another important technique in shaping tailored garments is establishing roll lines. The *roll line* is the line along which an area of a garment folds over. Roll lines are crucial in the backs of tailored collars, in shawl collars, and in lapels.

If the roll line is not marked on your pattern, you will need to establish one for the collar and lapels. It is necessary to do so before pad-stitching the collar and lapel by hand. If the collar is to be machine–pad-stitched, establishment of the roll line is postponed until after the on-grain rows of pad stitching have been inserted (see page 533).

To establish the roll line, pin the interfaced undercollar to the garment, starting at the center back and matching the seam lines. Then try on the garment. Ask another student or your teacher to help you determine where the collar and lapel should roll. Pin the center fronts together at the location for the top buttonhole. The collar and lapel will then fold over, revealing the natural roll line. Your helper can place a row of pins along this roll line. Check to see that the roll line allows the outer edge of the collar to cover the neck seam by at least ½ inch. When you remove the garment, replace the pins with a row of basting stitches.

If tailoring at home at a time when no one is available to help you, you can determine roll lines by alternative methods. A dress form is quite effective for this purpose. If one is not available, a heavy, wooden suit hanger can be substituted. However, neither of these methods is as accurate as having the roll line pinned while you wear the garment.

Pad-stitching the Undercollar

The undercollar is one of the areas in a tailored garment which is shaped by pad stitching. The pad stitches can be applied by machine or by hand. Machine pad stitching forms a continuous pattern over the interfaced undercollar. Hand pad stitching includes two types: Small stitches are inserted in the area called the *collar stand*, between the roll line and the neck seam line. Larger stitches are fanned out in the outer area of the collar, called the *collar fall*.

Pad-stitching by Machine

Machine pad stitching is simpler and quicker than hand pad stitching. Because the sewing machine is a flat surface, the resulting stitches are also flat. The actual shaping must be accomplished by steam blocking more than by stitching. Machine pad stitching appears to be in diagonal rows but is actually inserted on the grain of the fabric. The on-grain rows of stitching extend all the way from the neck seam to the outer seam and may be rather widely spaced. Be certain to mark the seemingly diagonal pattern onto the interfacing so that the rows of pad stitching will be properly positioned on the straight of the fabric. As pad stitching is permanent, machine-stitch with thread of the same color as the outer fabric.

After these rows have been completed, the undercollar is carefully blocked into shape (see "Blocking a Tailored Collar," pages 318-319). After establishing the roll line (see page 532), steam-press it to form a visible crease. Then machine-stitch along the roll line, all the way from one end seam to the other to reinforce the fold line and to help the collar hold its blocked shape.

Pad-stitching by Hand

Hand pad stitching requires holding and shaping the collar in its wear position. It is more difficult and time consuming than machine pad stitching but may be more effective if expertly done. It permits the fabric to be shaped a bit at a time as the stitching is completed. As a result, there is less chance that the shaped section will flatten out when the garment is worn.

STEPS IN MAKING AND MACHINE-PAD-STITCHING AN UNDERCOLLAR

Clip the corners from the marked interfacing pieces, and attach the interfacing directionally to the wrong side of the undercollar sections. Then trim close to the line of stitching on the outer edges and ends of the interfacing.

Join the center-back seam. Trim the interfacing seam allowance away. After pressing the center back seam open, trim the seam allowance of the outer fabric to ¼ inch.

Topstitch the center-back seam of the undercollar from the neck edge almost to the staystitching, across the seam line, and back to the neck edge.

Machine-stitch the padding design which was marked on the interfacing sections.

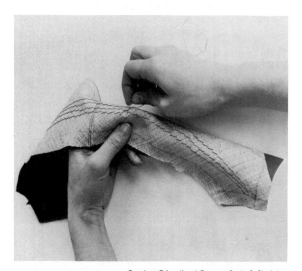

To form the collar stand, make a row of small pad stitches along the roll line from collar end to collar end. Add similar rows of stitches to stiffen and shape the collar stand between the roll and the neckline seam allowance.

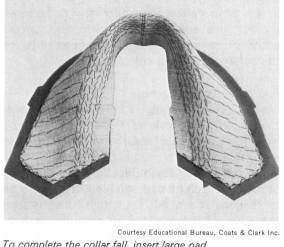

To complete the collar fall, insert large pad stitches almost perpendicular to those in the collar stand. The edges of the interfacing can be hand-fastened to the undercollar to allow for a smooth outer collar edge finish.

The first row of small hand pad stitches is inserted close together on the roll line, parallel to the neck seam line. The stitches are made through the undercollar and the interfacing. This row of pad stitching generally extends from one collar end seam line to the other. Several additional parallel rows are then inserted between the roll line and the neck seam line, completing the pad stitching of the collar stand.

The pad-stitching procedure differs for the collar fall. The stitches are larger and are inserted in more widely spaced rows along the grain of the fabric. Because the collar sections have been cut on the bias, these rows look diagonal. When completed, the entire collar fall as far as the seam lines is covered with rows of pad stitching, which appear to fan out almost perpendicularly to the pad stitching on the collar stand. The undercollar may then be blocked (see "Blocking a Tailored Collar," pages 318-319).

Pad-stitching the Lapel

The lapel is pad-stitched only by hand. Otherwise, the pad stitching is omitted since machine stitching would very likely be visible when the garment was worn. Lapel pad stitching must be inserted after the roll line on the lapel has been marked with basting and before the collar is attached to the garment. Begin these pad stitches at the roll line. Work from the interfacing side, and keep the stitches as nearly invisible as possible on the underside of the lapel. Make the first pad stitches about $\frac{3}{8}$ inch long, and position the rows parallel to the roll line.

To form a smooth lapel roll line, mold the lapel over your fingers as you make the pad stitches. Continue stitching in an up-and-down direction, making additional parallel rows until the lapel has been covered. As the rows of stitches extend toward the edge of the lapel, the stitches should become progressively smaller and closer together. The roll of

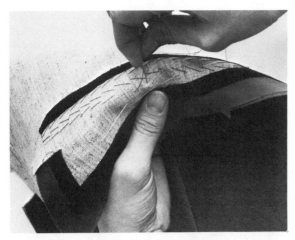

To pad-stitch a lapel, first insert a row of hand stitches along the lapel roll line, followed by other rows of stitches extending to the garment seam line.

the lapel is shaped during this stitching process.

Attaching the Collar

After the undercollar has been interfaced, pad-stitched, and blocked, it is ready to be attached to the upper collar. If the garment has a front facing that has not been attached, it is joined at this time to the outer fabric along the front edge by (1) stitching on the line of staystitching, shortening the stitch for 1 inch below the neck edge for reinforcement, (2) trimming the seam allowance of the interfacing, (3) underpressing the seam open, (4) grading the seams, (5) understitching. Then, in a tailored garment, the undercollar is attached to the garment and the upper collar is attached to the facing along the neck edge.

Join the upper collar to the undercollar only along the outer edge for a collar with straight ends, or all the way around for a collar with rounded ends. Accomplish this procedure in the following series of steps:

1. Stitch the upper collar to the undercollar from the interfacing side, with right sides together, edges even, and center backs keyed. On the straight-end collar, shorten the

stitch for 1 inch at the beginning and the end.

2. Grade the seams by trimming the undercollar seam allowance to $\frac{1}{8}$ inch and the upper-collar seam allowance to $\frac{1}{4}$ inch, slanting toward the seam line at the point.

3. Turn the collar right side out exactly on the line of stitching. Press along the outer edge only.

Attach the undercollar to the garment neckline edge in the following series of steps:

1. Pin the collar to the garment, right sides together, notches matched, edges even, and the center backs and seam lines at the ends of the collar keyed to the markings on the garment.

2. Clip the curved neckline seam allowance of the garment to the staystitching to give a straight line for stitching.

JOINING COLLAR SECTIONS

Block the pad-stitched undercollar.

Join the upper and undercollar sections along the outer edge and grade the seam.

Turn the collar and press the outer edge.

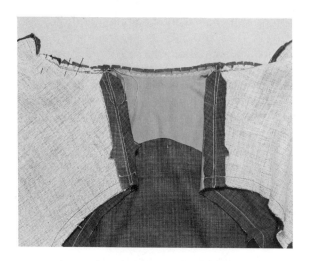

Pin and baste the undercollar to the garment with right sides together. Clip the curves to provide a straight line for stitching.

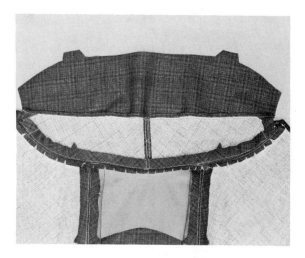

Stitch, trim, and press open the seam which joins the undercollar to the garment neck edge.

3. Stitch the undercollar to the garment from the garment side, starting and ending precisely at the marking which is keyed to the seam line at the end of the collar. Check the placement for accuracy by measuring from the end of the stitching to the edge of the front facing. The distance should be exactly the same on both sides. If it is not, the collar must be readjusted until the distance is identical. This is extremely important. Only if the placement is accurate will the collar and lapels hang evenly when the garment is worn.

4. Clip the seam allowance of the garment precisely at each end of the collar on the grain of the fabric. Clip the seam allowances of the neck edge to the seam line in any area where sharp curves require clipping for smoothness. (See "Treating Curved Seam Allowances," pages 402-403.)

5. Underpress the seam open on a seam board or a tailor's ham, maintaining the shape which has been blocked into the collar.

6. Trim the seam to ¼ or ⅛ inch, depending upon the thickness of the fabric and its tendency to fray.

Attach the upper collar to the facing in the same manner in which the undercollar was

attached to the garment, stitching from the facing side. Trim the neckline seam to ⅜ or ¼ inch. This is equivalent to grading, because it makes the seam of the garment and undercollar slightly narrower than the seam of the upper collar and facing.

If the collar has straight ends, complete the collar by attaching the upper and undercollar along the ends. Pin the ends of the collar sections together, with right sides together, edges even, and ends of the neckline seams keyed exactly. Stitch the ends of the collar from the outer edge to the end of the neckline seam, shortening the stitch for 1 inch at the outer edge to reinforce the corners. Secure the ends of the stitching firmly. Cut off the outer corners of the garment fabric in order to press the seam open easily. Press the seams open, directionally, on a point presser. Then grade the seams, leaving the seam allowance of the upper collar slightly wider than that of the undercollar, and slanting toward the seam line at the point.

Completing the Lapel

Attachment of the top edges of the garment fronts and the facings to finish the lapel is the

Attach the neck edge of the upper collar to the facing as the undercollar was attached to the neck edge.

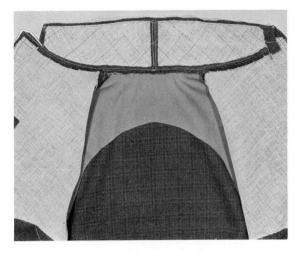

After both neck edges of the collar have been joined to the garment, close the collar ends, tops of the lapels, and any other open edges.

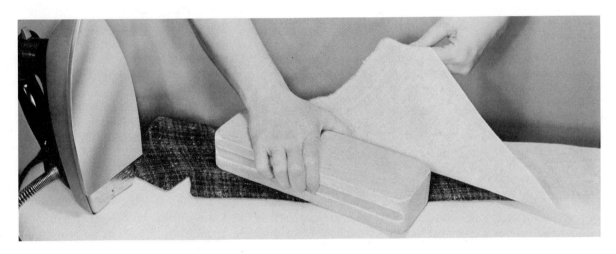

When pressing a completed collar, lapel, or front facing, use a clapper if necessary to pound and flatten its edges to a sharp turn.

final step in tailoring a collar. Complete this procedure in the following series of steps:

1. Pin the facing to the garment with right sides together and edges even, keying the ends of the neckline seams exactly. Stitch the facing to the garment from the front edge to the end of the collar, shortening the stitch to reinforce the corner.

2. Cut off the outer corners of the garment fabric to reduce bulk. Press the seams open on a point presser, or seam board.

3. Grade the seams so that the seam allowances which will extend toward the outside when the garment is worn are slightly wider than the others. Slant the seam allowances toward the seam line at the point.

4. Turn the collar right side out and the facing to the inside of the garment, working each corner of the collar to a sharp point on the interfacing side.

5. Press the lapel and the collar, using a dampened pressing cloth and a clapper to make a sharp, thin edge. Maintain the curved shape that has been blocked into the undercollar.

6. Attach the neckline seams of the facing to the garment by joining the corresponding seam allowances with small hand stitches, keying the lines of seam stitching and the center backs of the collar, garment, and facing.

In what ways do the procedures for tailoring sleeves differ from those for making regular sleeves?

Why are hems in tailored sleeves treated with a cushioning strip?

Why is interfacing used in the lower edges of faced sleeves?

Why is a tailored sleeve often lined before it is attached to the garment?

What is the purpose of a tuck in a sleeve lining?

What types of sleeves must be lined simultaneously with the rest of the garment?

Tailoring Set-in Sleeves

Except for the usual addition of a lining, tailoring a set-in sleeve is quite similar to making set-in sleeves in any other garment (see pages 470-473). It is, however, a far more complex task. Making the sleeve, fitting it perfectly to the arm, setting it so the grain falls accurately, and shaping and lining it for comfort and freedom from unnecessary bulkiness constitute a major tailoring process.

Making and Fitting the Sleeve

Frequently tailored sleeves are made in two parts: an upper sleeve and an undersleeve. Such sleeves are staystitched, elbow fullness is inserted, ease in the cap is adjusted, and the two parts are basted together for fitting before final stitching of the lengthwise seams. When trying a sleeve for fit, check the following points: the lengthwise and crosswise grain, the amount and location of ease at the top of the sleeve, the length of the sleeve, the location of elbow ease or darts, and the tightness or fullness along the entire sleeve length. If necessary, make adjustments. Under ordinary circumstances the sleeve fitting at this point will be merely a routine check since the sleeve has been cut to fit (see pages 249-255). When fit is adequate, permanently stitch the lengthwise seams according to the finish that will be used at the lower edge and press.

Finishing the Lower Sleeve Edge

The lower edge of the tailored sleeve can be finished with either a hem or a facing. The hem is blocked and cushioned or the edge is interfaced and faced before the lengthwise seams are completed.

Hemming the Lower Edge

If finishing the lower sleeve edge with a hem, use the following procedure:

1. If the sleeve is made in two sections, stitch the two together on the top seam line and press the seam open. Leave the underarm seam open at this point.

2. Grade the seam for the width of the hem by trimming the seam allowance of the turned-up portion to 1/4 inch. Cut off the corners of the seam allowance on the sleeve side of the hem at the fold line. Turn up and block the hem in place.

3. Cushion the hem with a bias strip of muslin similar to that used in tailored hems (see page 506). Let one edge of the strip extend 1/2 inch beyond the cut edge of the hem, and let the other edge just reach the fold at the lower sleeve edge. Block the cushioning strip, and insert it in the hem while the sleeve is still on the pressing board. Avoid stretching either the hem or the cushioning strip.

4. Pin the upper edge of the hem to the cushioning strip at the sleeve seam lines. Ease and pin the garment fabric to the strip along

Cushion the hem by cutting, blocking, and inserting a bias strip which is ½ inch wider than the hem.

Machine-stitch the cushioning strip to the edge of the hem. After the underarm seam is finished, fasten the hem to the sleeve with a pick stitch.

the entire edge, keeping the strip and the hem flat with no suggestion of fullness or tightness.

5. Attach the cushioning strip to the hem with machine stitching ¼ inch from the cut edge of the sleeve hem.

6. Make the underarm seam with the hem opened out flat, grade as on the top seam, and press the seam open.

7. Attach the underarm seam allowances of the hem to those of the sleeve with short running stitches.

8. Attach the upper edge of the cushioning strip to the garment with the pick stitch or small running stitches.

Facing the Lower Edge

The procedure for facing the lower edge of the sleeve varies, depending upon whether the facing is continuous or divided. A continuous facing continues the entire length of the lower sleeve edge, whereas a divided facing breaks, providing a slit in the sleeve edge or cuff.

Attaching a Continuous Facing   If finishing the lower edge of the sleeve with a continuous facing, use the following procedure:

1. If the sleeve is made in two sections, stitch the two together on the top seam line

and press the seam open. Leave the underarm seam open at this point.

2. Choose an interfacing fabric with permanent body, and lay the pattern for the interfacing on the true bias. Cut the interfacing the same as the facing but ½ inch wider at the upper edge. Cut off the corners of the interfacing at the lower edge to reduce bulk.

3. Stitch the interfacing to the wrong side of the sleeve along the lower edge and the underarm seam lines, matching notches and edges.

4. Stitch the facing to the sleeve along the lower edge, right sides together. Grade the seam by trimming the interfacing close to the line of stitching, the facing to ⅛ to ¼ inch, and the sleeve fabric to ¼ to ⅜ inch.

5. Understitch the seam, stitching on the facing side if the sleeve is to be worn turned down or on the sleeve side if the facing is to be turned back as a cuff. If the sleeve is to be worn both ways, omit the understitching and press especially well to set a sharp edge on the fold line.

6. Make the underarm seam, with the facing opened out flat, right sides together. Pin, stitch directionally, underpress the seam

STEPS IN ATTACHING A CONTINUOUS FACING

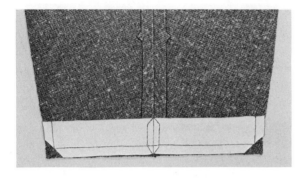

1. Trim the lower corners from the interfacing, and stitch the interfacing to the inside of the lower sleeve edge.

4. If the sleeve has convertible cuffs, press a sharp lower edge. In such an instance omit understitching along the lower edge.

2. If the sleeve is to be worn without cuffs, attach the facing and understitch on the facing side of the attachment.

5. With short running stitches, attach one seam allowance of the facing to the corresponding sleeve seam.

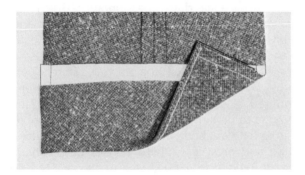

3. If the sleeve is to be worn with a turned back cuff, attach the facing and understitch along the lower sleeve edge.

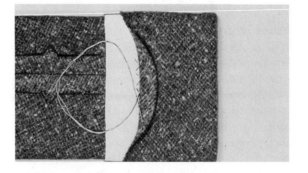

6. Turn the facing back against the garment, and attach the facing to the interfacing with the pick stitch or with running stitches.

open, and re-press the fold line at the lower edge.

7. Grade the underarm seams for the width of the facing as follows: Trim the interfacing close to the stayline. Trim to $\frac{1}{4}$ inch the outer-fabric seam allowance which will be toward the outside when the garment is worn. Then cut off the corners of the seam allowances that were not trimmed at the fold line.

8. Attach the facing to the sleeve, turning the facing to the wrong side of the sleeve. Pin it in position, keying the seam lines of the facing and the sleeve. With short hand running stitches, fasten one seam allowance of the underarm seam of the facing to the corresponding seam allowance of the sleeve. Attach the upper edge of the facing to the interfacing at the top sleeve seam with pick stitches or running stitches.

Attaching a Divided Facing   If finishing the lower edge of the sleeve with a divided facing, use the following procedure:

1. If the sleeve is made in two sections, stitch the two together on the top seam line for about half the length of the sleeve. Stitch the underarm seam with permanent stitching, and press the seams open.

2. Cut the interfacing the same as for a sleeve with a continuous facing.

3. Stitch the interfacing to the wrong side of the sleeve along the lower edge and the top seam lines, matching notches and edges.

4. Stitch the facing to the sleeve along the lower edge, grade and understitch the seam as in steps 4 and 5 of the procedure for a sleeve with a continuous facing.

5. Stitch the seams of the sleeve and facing with the facing opened out flat, right sides together. Stitch the top sleeve seam from the end of the permanent stitching already applied to the marking at the upper end of the sleeve opening. Stitch the end seams of the facing from the end of the opening to the edge of the facing. Secure the stitching firmly.

6. To stitch the facing to the sleeve along the edges of the opening, turn the fac-

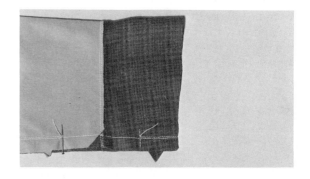

After attaching the interfacing to the wrong side of the sleeve edge, join the underarm seam below and above the planned cuff slit.

Stitch one open part of the facing back against the lower opening of the sleeve. Repeat the process on the other edge of the sleeve slit.

After careful grading and pressing on a point presser, attach the upper edge of the divided facing to the interfacing with hand stitches.

ing back on the sleeve, exactly on the seam line, with the right sides together and the opening edges of the sleeve and facing even. Then stitch from the outer edge to the end of the sleeve seam. Repeat this process at the other edge of the opening.

7. On a point presser, underpress the seams open at the top of the sleeve, the end of the facing, and the edges of the opening.

8. Grade the top sleeve seam and the seams at the edges of the opening so that the wider edge will be toward the outside when the garment is worn. Press the opening edges with the facing turned to the inside of the sleeve.

9. Attach the divided facing to the sleeve in the same way as a continuous facing (see pages 539-541).

Completing the Sleeve Lining

Sleeve linings can be stitched to the garment lining, which is then inserted as a single unit into a garment after all tailoring has been completed and the hems of the garment and sleeves have been finished. In fact, this must be the technique used when a sleeve is cut in one piece with the garment, as are kimono-type sleeves. However, for set-in sleeves, this lining technique is generally less effective than its preferred alternative. In tailoring it is generally best to line the sleeve before it is joined to the rest of the garment. The armhole seam joining the sleeve outer fabric and lining is later covered as the armhole edge of the garment lining is hand-stitched in place over the whole armhole seam.

Making the Sleeve Lining

To make a sleeve lining, cut the lining pieces as the pattern guide sheet directs, making the sleeve lining the finished length of the sleeve. Stitch the top of the sleeve with a continuous staystitch and ease line as on the sleeve of the outer fabric, and staystitch the lower edge. Stitch directionally the lengthwise seams of the lining pieces. If elbow darts are shown in the pattern, replace them with gathering stitches, which can be used to ease a long section and fit it to a shorter section. Ease is necessary in the sleeve lining for comfort in wear. Press the lengthwise seams open, blocking the fullness in the elbow area.

Attaching the Lining to the Sleeve

Attach the completed lining to the sleeve by the following step-by-step procedure:

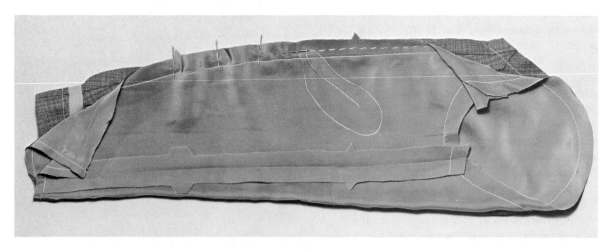

With the finished sleeve and lining wrong side out, fasten the lining to the sleeve with running stitches within the seam allowances.

1. With both the sleeve and lining wrong side out, fasten one lengthwise seam allowance of the sleeve and lining together. Starting 2½ inches below the armhole edge, ease the lining to the outer sleeve and hand-stitch the two seam allowances together to within 2½ inches of the top edge of the sleeve hem or facing.

2. Turn under the lower edge of the lining on the stayline. Pin it to the hem or facing on the outer sleeve approximately 1 inch above the lower edge. Hand-stitch the lining to the sleeve hem.

3. Allow the extra fullness in the sleeve lining to form a tuck at the lower edge of the sleeve. This extra fabric is needed for ease during body movement.

4. Press the lining, and turn the sleeve right side out for attachment to the body of the garment.

Turn under the seam allowance of the sleeve lining lower edge. Pin and hand-fasten the lining to the sleeve hem or facing approximately 1 inch from the lower edge.

Blocking and Setting the Sleeve

After the cap of both the outer fabric and lining have been blocked (see pages 317-318), place the sleeve into the armhole of the garment with the right sides of the sleeve and garment together and with the sleeve keyed to the armhole in the following four places: top of sleeve to shoulder of garment, notches at sleeve front, notches at sleeve back, and underarm seams.

Hand- or machine-baste the sleeve to the armhole with the *sleeve* side up, easing the fullness smoothly. Keep the basting on the seam line, being careful not to stitch beyond the ease line. Try on the garment to recheck the fit of the sleeve (see "Making and Fitting the Sleeve," page 538). If it fits properly, permanently stitch the sleeve into the armhole. A second row of stitching located just outside of the seam line is recommended for reinforcement.

Padding and Rechecking the Sleeve

A well-tailored sleeve has a smooth, rounded curve at the sleeve cap. To maintain this curve, an extra strip of bias fabric is inserted just

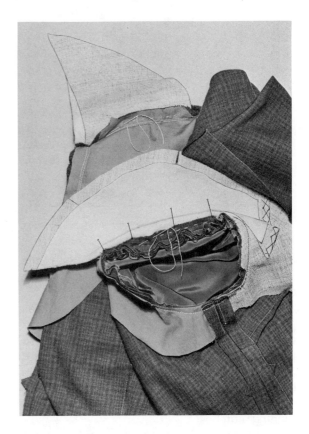

If shaping is required in a garment, attach padding or stripping by hand-fastening it to seam allowances in the armhole or shoulder area.

Courtesy Misty Harbor Division of Jonathan Logan

STANDARDS FOR TAILORED COLLARS

1. *Permanently shaped for a definite collar stand and collar fall.*
2. *Accurately and symmetrically curved or pointed.*
3. *Shaped to merge perfectly into the roll line of the garment lapel.*
4. *All parts of undercollar invisible during wear.*

STANDARDS FOR TAILORED SLEEVES

1. *Adequate fit in both width and length.*
2. *Positioned in armhole with even distribution of ease to ensure proper shape and grain line.*
3. *Accurate stitching with no visible puckers or gathers in armhole seam.*
4. *Adequate ease in sleeve linings for comfort in wear.*

across the sleeve cap. The strip may be made of bias which is cut from either self-fabric or lamb's wool.

If self-fabric is used, cut a strip of bias that is about 6 inches long and 1½ inches wide. Attach the strip to the sleeve cap so that it is centered on the shoulder line and one edge is even with the outer edge of the sleeve seam. Stitch by hand as close to the original stitching line as possible, using loose running stitches.

If lamb's wool is used for padding, cut a strip that is 6 inches long but 3 inches wide. Fold the lamb's wool into thirds lengthwise,

making a 1-inch strip. Catch-stitch or whip-stitch the edges together. Hand-stitch one of the folded edges to the armhole seam line, with the strip centered on the shoulder line. Press the padding to extend it outward into the sleeve cap.

Before giving the sleeve a final pressing, try on the garment for a last sleeve fitting. If shoulder pads of any kind are being used, pin them in place at this time and pin the center fronts of the garment together. Recheck the sleeve for lengthwise and crosswise grain, smoothness of the armhole seam, and sleeve width and length.

Attaching the Sleeve Lining
to the Armhole

When the sleeve has been correctly fitted, attached to the armhole, and padded adequately, it is completed by pulling the lining up into place and attaching it to the armhole. During the construction of the sleeve, the lining was made and an ease line was inserted along the armhole edge. The lining was attached to one of the sleeve seams and to the lower sleeve hem or facing. Then the sleeve cap was blocked. As a final procedure in the sleeve tailoring process, the lining must be attached to the armhole edge. Complete the sleeve lining attachment by following these steps:

1. Pull the lining up through the sleeve so that its armhole seam line exactly matches that of the outer sleeve.

2. Pull the threads of the ease line stitching to concentrate the fullness in the side area above the notches.

3. Ease and pin the lining to the armhole edge at key points including the shoulder line, the front and back notches, and the underarm seam line.

4. With small hand running stitches, fasten the lining to the garment around the entire armhole, just outside the seam line.

5. Trim all four layers of the underarm section of the seam to ¼ inch from notch to notch.

6. Turn the seam toward the sleeve.

After the garment is lined, the armhole edge of the garment lining is turned under and hand-stitched over the upper edges of the sleeve lining. This attachment further secures the sleeve lining in place and covers all unfinished seam edges in the inside of the tailored garment.

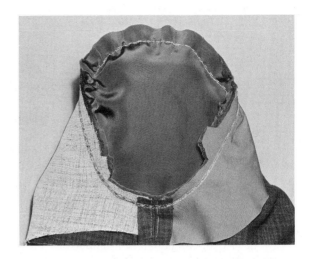

After pulling the thread of the ease-line stitching to distribute ease, fasten the lining to the garment and attached sleeve with small running stitches.

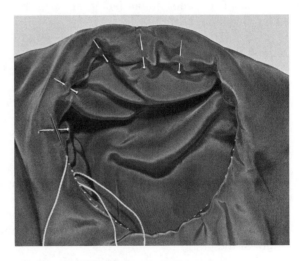

Turn under the seam allowance of the garment armhole lining. Pin it in place over the upper edge of the sleeve lining, and fasten it with invisible hand stitches.

1. A well-tailored collar is interfaced with a permanently stable fabric, such as canvas or hair canvas.

2. The undercollar and the interfacing are cut with a center-back seam line on the true bias.

3. Pad stitching, whether applied by hand or by machine, is inserted on the straight grain of the fabric for effective shape retention.

4. A machine–pad-stitched collar is shaped mainly with steam and heat after the pad stitching is completed.

5. A hand–pad-stitched collar is shaped with the fingers during the stitching process.

6. An *upper* collar is attached to the *garment facing;* an *undercollar* is attached to the *neckline of the garment.*

7. The ends of straight-end collars and the lapels of any tailored garment are stitched after the upper collar and undercollar are attached to the garment neckline.

8. The upper collar facing seam is hand-stitched to the undercollar neckline seam.

9. The outer edges of tailored collars and lapels are flattened with steam, heat, and a clapper.

10. Ease is provided in the elbow area of tailored sleeves by inserting darts or easing in fullness.

11. A cushioning strip is inserted in the hems of tailored sleeves for increased body, proper hang, and improved appearance.

12. Interfacing is applied to the lower edges of faced sleeves to preserve shape and to improve appearance.

13. Before an eased sleeve is attached to the garment, it is blocked carefully to avoid the appearance of gathers or puckers in the armhole seam line.

14. A sleeve is best lined before it is attached to the garment. When lining sleeves, allow for ease in the elbow area and in the total length of the lining.

15. A sleeve cushioning pad is used to give a sleeve cap a rounded, professional look.

16. To improve the appearance of an armhole seam, the seam is pressed into the sleeve.

Bibliography

Books

Archer, Elsie. *Let's Face It: The Guide to Good Grooming for Girls of Color.* J. B. Lippincott Co., Philadelphia, 1968.

Bancroft, Vivian S. *It's So, Sew Easy.* Burgess Publishing Co., Minneapolis, 1970.

Bane, Allyne. *Creative Clothing Construction.* McGraw-Hill Book Co., New York, 1972.

Better Homes and Gardens. *Tailoring Suits and Coats.* Meredith Publishing Co., Des Moines, 1966.

Bishop, Edna Bryte, and Arch, Marjorie Stotler. *Bishop Method of Clothing Construction.* J. B. Lippincott Co., Philadelphia, 1972.

Brockman, Helen L. *Theory of Fashion Design.* John Wiley & Sons, Inc., New York, 1965.

Carson, Byrta. *How You Look and Dress.* Webster Division, McGraw-Hill Book Co., New York, 1969.

Chambers, Helen G., and Moulton, Verna. *Clothing Selection: Fashions, Figures, Fabrics.* J. B. Lippincott Co., Philadelphia, 1969.

Delavan, Betty C., Adams, Aurelia K., and Richards, Louise G. *Clothing Selection: Application of Theory.* Burgess Publishing Co., Minneapolis, 1964.

Dunn, Lucille, and others. *Steps in Clothing Skills.* Chas. A. Bennett Co., Inc., Peoria, 1970.

Erwin, Mabel D., and Kinchen, Lila. *Clothing for Moderns.* Macmillan Co., New York, 1969.

Fashion Group, Inc. *Your Future in Fashion Design.* Arco Publishing Co., Inc., New York, 1966, 1970.

Garrett, Pauline, and Motzon, Edward J. *You Are a Consumer of Clothing.* Ginn & Company, Boston, 1967.

Herington, Viola B. *Begin to Sew.* McKnight & McKnight Publishing Co., New York, 1968.

Hollen, Norma, and Saddler, Jane. *Textiles.* Macmillan Co., New York, 1970.

Iowa Home Economics Assn. *Unit Method of Clothing Construction.* Iowa State University Press, Ames, 1965.

Jarnow, Jeannette A., and Judelle, Beatrice. *Inside the Fashion Business.* John Wiley & Sons, Inc., New York, 1965.

Johnson, Hildegarde, Sheffner, Sarah, and Clawson, Barbara. *Sewing Step-By-Step.* Ginn & Company, Boston, 1969.

Johnson, Mary. *Guide to Altering and Restyling Ready-Made Clothes.* E. P. Dutton and Co., Inc., New York, 1964.

Johnson, Mary. *Sewing the Easy Way.* E. P. Dutton and Co., Inc., New York, 1966.

Jones, Candy. *Finishing Touches.* Harper & Row, Publishers, New York, 1961.

Joseph, Marjory L. *Introductory Textile Science.* Holt, Rinehart & Winston, Inc., New York, 1966.

Labarthe, Jules. *Textiles: Origins to Usage.* Macmillan Co., New York, 1964.

Laver, James. *Costume Through the Ages.* Simon & Schuster, Inc., New York, 1967.

Lester, Katherine Morris, and Kerr, Rose Netzorg. *Historic Costume.* Chas. A. Bennett Co., Inc., Peoria, 1967.

Lewis, Dora S., Bowers, Mable Goode, and Kettunen, Marietta. *Clothing Construction and Wardrobe Planning.* Macmillan Co., New York, 1960.

Logan, William B., and Moon, Helen M. *Facts About Merchandise.* Prentice-Hall, Inc., Englewood Cliffs, New Jersey, 1967.

McDermott, Irene E., and Norris, Jeanne L. *Opportunities in Clothing.* Chas. A. Bennett Co., Inc., Peoria, 1968.

McJimsey, Harriet C. *Art in Clothing Selection.* Harper & Row, Publishers, New York, 1963.

Martensson, Kerstin. *Sew Knit and Stretch Fabric; It's Easy, Here's How.* Sew-Knit-n-Stretch, Inc., Golden Valley, Minn., 1969.

Mauck, Frances F. *Modern Sewing Techniques.* Macmillan Co., New York, 1963.

Morton, Grace Margaret, and others. *The Arts of Costume and Personal Appearance.* John Wiley & Sons, Inc., New York, 1964.

Oerke, Bess, and Gawne, Eleanor J. *Dress.* Chas. A. Bennett Co., Inc., Peoria, 1969.

Payne, Bianca. *History of Costume.* Harper & Row, Publishers, New York, 1965.

Ryan, Mary Shaw. *Clothing: A Study of Human Behavior.* Holt, Rinehart & Winston, Inc., New York, 1966.

Schwebke, Phyllis W., and Krohn, Margaret B. *How to Sew Leather, Suede, Fur.* Bruce Publishing Co., Milwaukee, 1966, 1970.

Schwebke, Phyllis W. *How to Tailor.* Bruce Publishing Co., Milwaukee, 1965.

Singer Educational Department. *Singer Dressmaking Course in Eight Easy Steps.* Grosset and Dunlap, Inc., New York, 1961.

Spears, Charleszine Wood. *How to Wear Colors.* Burgess Publishing Co., Minneapolis, 1965.

Stout, Evelyn E. *Introduction to Textiles.* John Wiley & Sons, Inc., New York, 1970.

Tate, Mildred, T., and Glisson, Oris. *Family Clothing.* John Wiley & Sons, Inc., New York, 1961.

Todd, Elizabeth, and Roberts, Frances. *Clothes for Teens.* D. C. Heath & Company, Boston, 1969.

Troelstrup, A. W., *The Consumer in American Society: Personal and Family Finance.* McGraw-Hill Book Co., New York, 1970.

Vanderhoff, Margil. *Clothes, Part of Your World.* Ginn & Company, Boston, 1970.

Whitcomb, Helen, and Lang, Rosalind. *Charm.* McGraw-Hill Book Co., New York, 1971.

Wilson, W. Harmon, and Eyster, Elvin S. *Consumer Economic Problems.* South-Western Publishing Co., Cincinnati, 1966.

Wingate, Isabel B. *Textile Fibers and Their Selection.* Prentice-Hall, Inc., Englewood Cliffs, New Jersey, 1970.

Booklets and Pamphlets

American Home Economics Assn., Washington, D.C. *Textile Handbook,* 1966.

The Butterick Company, Inc., New York, New York:

Fur and Furlike, 1971

Knits, 1971

Leather and Leatherlike, 1971

New Vogue Sewing Book, 1964

Celanese Fibers Marketing Co., New York, New York, *Textile Topics,* Quarterly.

Co-ed/Forecast Books, Division of Scholastic Magazines, Inc., New York, New York, *Clothing: Better Buymanship,* 1967.

Educational Bureau, Coats & Clark Inc., New York, New York, *Coats & Clark Sewing Book,* 1967.

Household Finance Corporation, Chicago; Money Management Booklet: *Your Shopping Dollar,* 1966.

Money Management Booklet: *Your Clothing Dollar,* 1967.

Institute of Life Insurance, New York, New York, *A Discussion of Family Money — How Budgets Work and What They Do,* 1962.

Man-Made Fiber Producers Assn., Inc., 1000 Connecticut Ave., Washington, D.C., *Man-made Fiber Fact Book,* 1967.

McCall Corporation, New York, New York, *McCall's Step-by-Step Sewing Book,* 1969.

National Education Association, Department of Home Economics, Washington, D.C. *Clothing for Young Men* and *The Clothes We Wear.*

J. C. Penney, Inc., New York, New York, *Job Opportunities in Retailing*

Simplicity Pattern Company, Inc., New York, New York, *Simplicity Sewing Book,* 1970.

U. S. Department of Agriculture, Washington, D. C.:

Bulletin G38 *Buying Your Home Sewing Machine,* 1969.

Bulletin HERR 12, *Clothes for the Physically Handicapped Homemaker,* 1961.

Bulletin G107 *Clothing Repairs,* 1970.

Bulletin 7700-002 *Dangers in Flammable Clothing,* 1968.

Bulletin 0303-0680 *Fiber and Fabrics,* 1970.

Bulletin PA-766, *Fix New Clothes to Make Them Last Longer,* 1966.

Bulletin G68 *How to Prevent and Remove Mildew*, 1964.

Bulletin A 1.68:701 *How to Teach Sewing Machine Use and Care*, 1965.

Bulletin 113 *Protecting Woolens Against Clothes Moths and Carpet Beetles*, 1970.

Bulletin 62 *Removing Stains from Fabrics: Home Methods*, 1968.

Visuals and Kits

American Home Economics Assn., Washington, D.C.

HELP Packages:

1001, *Advertising Appeal*

1003, *Bargain Hunters*

1007, *Clothing Expresses You*

1013, *Money Might*

1016, *The Consumer is King*

1021, *Knit Stitching*

1023, *Advertising and You*

1024, *Today's Washbasket*

1026, *Get Acquainted with Cotton*

1028, *Come Alive with Color*

1030, *Suds for Duds*

Fairchild Visuals, 7 East 12 Street, New York, New York. Film, *Careers in Retailing and Marketing*.

Guidance Association, 41 Washington Avenue, Pleasantville, New York. 2 filmstrips with cassettes, *Exploited Generation*, 1970.

Webster Division, McGraw-Hill Book Company, New York, New York. *Clothing Construction Film Loops*, Grieser, Edwina H., 1969.

Webster Division, McGraw-Hill Book Company, New York, New York. Clothing Transparencies: *Line and Color in Clothes*, Sturm, M., and Grieser, E.

Webster Division, McGraw-Hill Book Company, New York, New York. Clothing Transparencies: *Design in Clothes*, Sturm, M., Grieser, E., and Roberts, J., 1969.

Westinghouse Corporation, New York, New York, Series of 6 filmstrips: *Buyer Beware*, 1971.

Index